THE APOCALYPSE

BIBLIOGRAPHICAL NOTE

ROBERT GOVETT, born 1813. Matriculated at Worcester College, Oxford, 1830. Eaton Scholar 1834; B.A. 1834; Fellow of Worcester 1836; M.A. 1837. Sometime Curate of St. Stephen's, Norwich. Died at Norwich 1901. Author of many books and pamphlets on scriptural and kindred subjects; among the most important are his *Commentary on Isaiah* (1843), *Reward according to Works* (1853–5), *Commentaries on John's Gospel, The Epistle to the Hebrews*, and *The Epistle to the Romans* (1891). His *Apocalypse* was originally issued under the pen-name of "Mathētees."

THE APOCALYPSE

EXPOUNDED BY SCRIPTURE

BY
ROBERT GOVETT M.A.
Late Fellow of Worcester College, Oxford

(Abridged from the Four Volume Edition, 1864)

WIPF & STOCK · Eugene, Oregon

Wipf and Stock Publishers
199 W 8th Ave, Suite 3
Eugene, OR 97401

The Apocalypse
Expounded by Scripture. Abridged from the Four Volume Edition, 1851
By Govett, Robert
ISBN 13: 978-1-62564-937-9
Publication date 5/31/2014
Previously published by Charles J. Thynne, 1920

PREFATORY NOTE

MR. GOVETT'S four volumes on the Revelation, in a complete set, have long been unobtainable. It is inevitable that in this abridged edition, containing less than a fourth of the original, much critical and even essential matter has had to be omitted, together with proofs decisive on many disputed points. So also the cost of printing has made it necessary to omit his penetrating and pulverizing criticisms of all interpretations of the Apocalypse which, by taking it as a huge symbol, reduce it to the unintelligible. Scripture quotations also, most regrettably, have had to be given as references only. Nevertheless, to quote Mr. Spurgeon, " Mr. Govett wrote a hundred years before his time, and the day will come when his works will be treasured as sifted gold " ; and this exposition of the Revelation without a peer was never more vital or more urgent than in the moment when we are manifestly entering the penumbra of the last judgments.

THE
APOCALYPSE EXPOUNDED

CHAPTER I

1. "The Revelation of Jesus Christ, which God gave to him, to show unto his servants what must come to pass shortly; and (*which*) he sent by his angel and represented to his servant John; who testified (with regard to) the word of God and the testimony of Jesus Christ, whatever things he saw."

By a "revelation" is meant the taking off a veil. In Scripture it intends the disclosure of secrets of God incapable of being divined by man. It is also called a "prophecy:" "Blessed is he that readeth and they that hear the words of this *prophecy*."

Jesus, when Israel blasphemed the Holy Spirit, clothed himself with a seven-fold *veil of parable*. Matt. xiii. But the Revelation is *the taking off of that veil*.

But if it be the *taking off a veil* from the future, then it must be written in a way capable of being understood before the things predicted occur. And it is thus probable that it would in the main consist of representations to be taken literally. For these are most easily understood. It is when Jesus would *hide* himself from the comprehension of unbelieving Israel, that He uses parables of emblems. Mark iv. 11, 12.

As one well says, "These words—'which *God* gave unto him'—show how peculiarly this book is to be regarded as coming from God *as God*. It is not the instruction of the *Father* to children in the bosom of the family: but it is God on the throne of government, instructing the servants of Jesus.

From the disclosure being *given by God* it is rendered certain, that *some part* of the book *contains new truth:* though it appears also (as the sequel will show) that a considerable portion of it had more or less been discovered to the prophets and apostles. But even where they were permitted to declare something of the same times, *this prophecy is far more complete.* This is the golden thread, on which may be strung all the pearls of former prophecy.

They are things which must take place "*shortly.*" From this word some have argued that the book must have begun to be accomplished soon after it was written: and hence that it contains a *continuous history of the Christian Church.* But the very same expression is used of an event, which, as all acknowledge, has yet to be accomplished. "The God of peace shall bruise Satan under your feet *shortly*" (Rom. xvi. 20). But this promise is in the very manner of prophecy; the style of Him with whom a thousand years are as one day.

A point of deep importance lies couched in the next words. "Unto His *servants.*" First, this warns us that we are *not* on the ground taken by the Epistles of Paul, where the writer addresses *the saints as the sons of God:* and the Most High is discovered to them as their *Father.*

The angel was sent to "*show*" unto the servants of God the future. The word employed denotes generally the manifesting a thing to the senses. And hence, after the admonitory addresses to the churches are finished, and the future begins to be treated of, the style changes. *Events* are seen to transpire.

I have chosen the word "represented," in preference to "signified." The Greek expression intends that the Revelation is peculiar in its mode of making known the future to us. It was not given in words at first, as in the case of prophecies in general. It was presented before John as a series of moving visions, which he described, pen in hand, as they appeared before him. And we are left from those representations to gather the meaning of God, and the character of the events about to come to pass. The problem of the Revelation then is: Given certain persons, things, and actions, to penetrate from thence into the meaning and plans of men and of God.

From this word many have come to the conclusion that the Apocalypse is a "*book of symbols.*" But this is a hasty inference. Its prophetic part is a series of representations. But representations are of two kinds, direct and indirect.

In the Apocalypse *both styles of representation occur*: and it is from supposing that it contains *only* symbols, that much of the obscurity of the book is owing. *Symbols there are in it; but not a few of them are explained; and they are far far fewer than the direct representations of the future.* There are twice seven symbols which are explained; and *perhaps as many more* that *are not explained.* The explained are as follows:—

1. Lamp-stands = Churches.
2. Stars = Angels of Churches.
3. Torches = Spirits of God.
4. Horns and Eyes = Spirits of God.
5. Odours = Prayers of Saints.
6. Dragon = Satan.
7. Frogs = Spirits.
8. Wild Beast = a King, xvii.
9. Heads of Wild Beast = Mountains.
10. Horns = Subordinate Kings.
11. Waters = Peoples.
12. Woman = A City.
13. Fine Linen = Righteousness.

14. The Bride Wife of the Lamb = City of God, xxi. 9, 10.

The past tense is used,—he "testified,"—because the *first ten verses* of this chapter are a *preface*, added after the writing of the rest.

"The Word of God" in the division of the book stands first; because that is by pre-eminence "the Revelation," or the part *which God gave to Christ*, and which was chiefly a *series of visible signs*.

"The *testimony* of Jesus" *relates to things then present, and is His decision as to the state of the Churches.*

3. "Blessed is he that reads, and they that hear the words of the prophecy, and keep the things written in it; for the season is nigh."

The *blessing is attached specially* to the reader of "the words of the *prophecy*." Many will admit the usefulness of the addresses to the Churches, who treat very lightly the prophetic part: yet the prophetic portion is that specially blessed.

The intention of the book extends much beyond the Church of Christ. The *whole* is profitable to the Churches; even the prophetic part, in which the Church is not directly addressed. The *Seven Epistles* will be *useful to Israel also*.

With such a blessing attached to the study of this portion of God's word, how sad it is to find this book so generally proscribed or neglected! But the Holy Spirit foresaw the undue neglect of it, and therefore determined to compensate for it by the peculiar blessedness attached to it.

It has been well observed by one, that this book is manifestly by these words designed to open our understandings and to act upon our affections, *whilst it still remains prophecy*. It is while the season is yet "near," and not actually arrived, that the book is to be read and pondered. Hereby then is *destroyed the unscriptural idea,* that *prophecy is only intended to benefit us,* by the perception of its fulfilment, *after its prophetic aspect is past.*

What season and time is at hand ? *That of "temptation,"* against which we shall do well to watch and pray ; *that of "harvest,"* in which *the ripe* shall be *taken,* and the *unripe left*; *that of " refreshing,"* in which the long-stored *promises of the prophets* shall be fulfilled ; *that of "judgment,"* when every work shall come into notice, whether it be good or evil ; and *the time of " reward "* to the saints.

The prophecy is not to be put off, as something not demanding our present study, because relating to things immeasurably remote. " The season is *near.*" Long as the time is which has elapsed since that was written, there was then, and is now, *no necessary interval* to arise ere the prophetic part begins to be fulfilled. In this it is *contrasted with Daniel,* who is dismissed from study of his prophecies, because *the book is sealed* up, and a long time must pass ere it be fulfilled.

It is *practical.* Hear that, all you who think that nothing is worthy of study which is not so ! Yes ; the *prophecy is practical* ! " Blessed . . . they who keep the things written in it." In order *rightly to understand it,* we must be *right in our spiritual position* before God ; and of *a single eye,* willing to *follow the truth* wherever it may lead us.

Reader, do you love to set yourself where the God of all pronounces you " blessed " ? Is that a sunshine wherein to bask ? Then are you in it while reading and hearing " the prophecy of this book."

4. " John to the seven churches which are in Asia ; Grace be unto you and peace, from Him who is, and who was, and who is to come, and from the seven Spirits that are before His throne ;

5. and from Jesus Christ, the faithful Witness, the First-born of the dead, and the Prince of the kings of the earth."

At this point begins a special message to *a certain class of God's servants*, then recognized on earth during the dispensation of mercy, under which the Revelation was given. But we soon learn that the distinction of the Church as God's sole *witness is about to cease*, owing to its *unfaithfulness*, when tried by God's just demands upon those so privileged. Hence the Apocalypse does *not* anywhere give the *distinctive glory of the Church*, as the Epistles of Paul do. *The glory of the New Jerusalem is one enjoyed in common by all the servants of God.* Nor was it fitting, that the peculiar glory as a body, of that which fails in its collective capacity, should be presented in this book.

We are apt to speak of the "Church of England," "of Greece," "of Rome." The Scripture, however, uses a different expression. It speaks of "the seven *churches in* Asia." It does not suppose the whole country to constitute one Church. But it recognizes churches subsisting as *assemblies of the saints*, in the midst of the ungodly world around. Each church was an assembly *independent* of the other, having its own angel, and elders, and deacons, and *looking up to no higher corporation than itself.*

But why were the churches *of Asia* addressed ? Probably those of Judæa were broken up by the destruction which had now (A.D. 95 or 96) fallen on Judæa and Jerusalem.

But why were only *seven* churches in Asia addressed ? There were other churches doubtless then in being, as those of Hierapolis, Colossæ, and Tralles. The reason is in keeping with the book. In it numbers are significant. *Seven* is the number of *dispensational fullness*, or *perfection as instituted by God*. *Three* represents the

Divine nature, as Father, Son, and Spirit. *Four* represents the material world, or *the creature*.

Seven, then, or the *addition of four and three*, signifies the *Divine and human brought into contact ;* such a contact as obtains in *dispensations*. But as dispensations are only trials of man under various conditions appointed of God, so the *series of sevens do not abide*.

Twelve, on the other hand, is the number of *eternal perfection*. It is composed (as well as seven) of three and four, only in a far more intimate state of union. Twelve is *three multiplied into four*. Thus it represents *the creature by grace taken into close and intimate connexion with the Deity*. Hence, as we shall afterwards see, *seven does not once occur* in the eternal city of the just ; but *only twelves*.

Only *seven churches* then are taken, because the *Church was set on its trial*, and *could not abide*. So it was with Judaism. The many sevens that appeared in it noted it as a dispensation that was not to continue for ever. Similarly, the *sevens* which prefigure *the millennium*, exhibit *that* as another arrangement of God *which is to be but temporary*.

Another point also is worthy of notice : the manner in which the seven is divided. *Seven is usually divided into four and three, the four preceding*. But in the Epistles to the seven churches, *three precedes the four*. The first three Epistles are separated from the four last by the place given to that exhortation which runs through them all—the call on every hearer to listen. In the three first epistles this *precedes* the promise to the conqueror. In the four last it comes *after*.

Now the meaning of this arrangement I take to be, that the *Church was about to fall from its standing*. The divine glory and grace were to be visible in the *early stages* of the Church, the human and earthly elements, which would cause its rejection, *at the close*.

The *contrary order* to this is observed, where the *transition is from evil to good :* as in the seven parables of Matt. xiii.

There the *four* parables *which precede* speak of the hand of man and *Satan for evil*: the *three which follow* exhibit the *hand of God outstretched for good.*

Where *unmixed evil* is *found in the seven*, the arrangement is different: as in the *seven heads* of Antichrist, where the division is into *five, one, one* (ch. xvii.).

To these seven churches John sends "*Grace and peace.*" This is characteristic of the present dispensation. "Grace" stands opposed to law; "peace" to war. When this dispensation ends, *justice* and *war* are sent on the Gentiles, and on Israel.

But why is the Holy Spirit called "the Seven Spirits"? It seems probable that he is so called, from *his relation* to "the seven churches;" as indicating the fullness of grace and power for all their need. How great *the importance of the throne* in this book is seen herein, that *even the Holy Spirit takes his name from his relation to it.* The Holy Spirit is described as God's *agent for rule,* as executing the counsels of the enthroned One. In the *Acts and Epistles* the Holy Spirit is viewed, not as in heaven, but *as present on earth.*

"The seven Spirits that *are before the throne.*" No wonder, then, that the Churches themselves are referred to it, and that demands of equity from the throne are laid before them.

Here grace and peace flow from the seven Spirits to "*the seven churches of Asia.*" But in the *next dispensation* it is "the seven Spirits of God *sent forth into all the earth.*"

These three titles of Jesus are not His personal position

as the Son; but His *relation to the throne* and to *the churches*.[1]

1. He is "the Faithful Witness." He was faithful unto death in bearing witness for God while on earth. He is therefore fully to be credited, now that, having risen, He proclaims to the churches *their state*, and their *consequent recompenses*.

2. He is also "the First-born of the dead." This relates to Jesus' *present standing*, as *Priest in the temple of God*.

3. He is also "the Prince of the kings of the earth." This refers to Jesus' manifested position, when He comes forth from heaven, to rule over the earth.

These three titles of honour assumed by the Saviour are predicated as given to David's son. Ps. lxxxix. 27, 37. "I will make him my *firstborn, higher than the kings of the earth*." His throne should be " as a *faithful witness in heaven*."

Thus Jesus' three titles answer nearly to His position as Prophet, Priest, and King.

5. "Unto him that loveth us,[2] and washed [3] us from our sins in his own blood, and made us [4] a kingdom (and) priests unto his God and Father; to him be glory and dominion for ever and ever. Amen."

Jesus loves us. 'Tis a *present* love. He washed us. 'Tis a *past* washing. Blessed be God for a *past washing*, and a *present*, ever-during *love!*

After the titles of Jesus presented to the churches, their love appears to break forth in a doxology. This doxology takes its form and burthen from the body of

---

[1] Hence the *church is not the Bride*, as Jesus is *not the Son*, in this book.

[2] Ἀγαπῶντι.

[3] Some very good MSS. have λύσαντι ['redeemed'], which Tregelles reads in his Translation. [And so R.V.]

[4] Ἡμῖν βασιλείαν ἱερεῖς is T.'s second reading.

the book. It is an echo of the elders' words—"Thou art worthy to take the book and to open the seals thereof : for thou *wast slain*, and *redeemed unto God by thy blood* (some) out of every kindred, and tongue, and people, and nation ; and *madest them unto our God kings and priests, and they shall reign over the earth* " (v. 9, 10).

He " washed us in his blood."

Whom do we wash, but the unclean ? And sin is our uncleanness. It is universal, so that the bathing must be universal. " *Our* sins." Sin is almost all that we can call our own. It must be *blotted out, as it is in God's book ; washed out*, as it is *a stain on us.*

Jesus' love unto death is here recorded ; but it abides still.

The *washing in his blood* appears to refer to the rites appointed by God for making Aaron and his sons priests. " Aaron and his sons thou shalt bring unto the door of the tabernacle of the congregation, and shalt *wash them in water* " (Exod. xxix. 4).

Their bathing was in *water*, to fit them for the earthly tabernacle, and they were touched with the blood of a ram on the right ear, the right thumb, the great toe of the right foot, in order to consecrate them (ver. 20). But *our bathing is in blood*, to *consecrate us for the heavenly temple*. There the ransomed are shown to us, after the prophetic action is begun (ch. vii.). The blood fits us also *for the heavenly city*, which is our great temple (ch. xxi.). These words then give token of the better covenant, by the blood of which better priests than those of Aaron's line are prepared ; while as yet, Israel (the people with whom the better covenant is one day to be formally ratified) stands aloof in unbelief.

It was promised too to Israel, as the very condition of the old covenant, " *If ye will obey my voice indeed and keep my covenant* . . . Ye shall be *unto me a king-*

dom of priests" (Exod. xix. 5, 6). But the people broke the covenant in forty days; and their whole after history showed, that no such dignity could ever be attained by man on the *ground of his obedience*. Hence the better covenant bestows *as a gift*, what was in vain *offered as a condition of service*. We are *made* kings and priests *by Christ*.

We are made kings and priests "to *his* God and Father." *Not* to "*our* God and Father," as in the Epistles of Paul. 1 Thess. i. 3; iii. 11, etc. God is not presented to us in this book as *the Father of all who believe*; but only as the *Father of Jesus*, the ruler of all others.

To whom could such a doxology, sanctioned by a solemn "Amen," be given, but to one who is Divine? When John worships the angel, he is twice corrected and reproved. Here he bestows divine honour, and it is ratified by inspiration. The Spirit of God has set His seal to its lawfulness and propriety.

7. "Behold, He cometh with the clouds; and every eye shall see Him, and whosoever pierced Him to death: and all the tribes of the land shall beat (their breasts) at Him. Yea, Amen."

In the 7th verse we have reached a much lower level. *The Jew and the Gentile on earth* are addressed. The risen saints are on high, with Christ in the glory. To us it is given to "walk by faith, not by sight." But *in this verse our dispensation is manifestly ended*: for "every *eye* shall *see* Him." Those who behold Him "coming in the clouds' are the Jew and the Gentile, who belong not to the assembly of the risen. The apostle refers to our Lord's own words directed to His disciples as the Jewish remnant—"Then shall appear the sign of the Son of Man in heaven; and then shall *all the tribes of the earth mourn, and they shall see* the Son of Man coming *on the clouds of heaven* with power and great glory" (Matt. xxiv. 30).

"Yea, Amen," is a *combination* of a Greek and of a Hebrew word, both expressive of the same thing. Similar conjunctions occur more than once in the book. It is *addressed to Jew and Gentile ;* and is certified to each in their own tongues.

8. "*I* am the Alpha and the Omega, saith the Lord God, who is, and who was, and who is to come, the Lord of hosts."

It is Jesus who calls Himself by this name, as the close of Revelation shows. "Behold, I come quickly, and my reward is with me, to give every man according as his work is. *I am the Alpha and Omega, First and Last, the Beginning and the End*" (xxii. 12, 13).

The title which Jesus next assumes is—"*the Lord God*."[1] This is that name which God receives in the account of the creation of man in Eden. Gen. ii., iii. And the book before us describes the accomplishment of the plans of the Most High, at the conclusion of all things ; by the institution of a new Eden, whence man is never to fall. "*Lord God*" *is His name in connexion with the new Eden.* xxii. 5, 6. It combines two names of God ; "Jehovah," which was God's title as the God of the Jew ; and "Elohim," which is His general name, designating His supremacy over all men. This title is very appropriate, as uniting all previous dispensations : the same God is the God of each.

The name denoting His eternity, "Who is, and was, and is to come," is next added. It seems nearly equivalent to Jehovah. The last dignity mentioned is that which I translate by "the Lord of Hosts."[2]

The *three successive views* of Jesus given in the three consecutive verses 6, 7, 8, belong, if I mistake not, to the *three great divisions of mankind.* which God recognizes. Ver. 6 rehearses what *Jesus has done for "us."* Ver. 7 describes the *result of His advent*

---

[1] יהוה אלהים   [2] Ὁ Παντοκράτωρ.

to the twelve *tribes* of those who pierced Him. Ver. 8 gives His titles as the *God of the nations*.

9. "J, John, your brother and co-partner in the tribulation and kingdom, and patient waiting in Jesus, was in the isle that is called Patmos, because of the word of God, and the testimony of Jesus."

This brotherhood and fellowship were "*in Jesus.*" *It is addressed to believers, members of Christ.* As this word of the Apostle is directed to all the churches, it is a proof that the kingdom of which we are more particularly informed in the twentieth chapter, is the *common hope and prize set before Christians.*

He was "in the isle called Patmos." From which we learn, that places are to be taken *literally* in this book, unless there be sufficient reason to the contrary.

"The testimony of Jesus," however, refers to the *doctrine* peculiar to *the New Testament*. John, as a believer in both covenants, testified to them both. And both gave umbrage to the Roman ruler. John believed in "another King, one Jesus: " and looked for an empire greater than the Roman, in which he was himself to rule.

10. "I became in the spirit on the Lord's day, and heard behind me a great voice as of a trumpet, saying"—

The apostle on the first day of the week was rapt in inspiration, and fitted thereby to be the vehicle of the disclosures of God. *The Lord's day*, it is thus shown, was signalized above the other days of the week by the early Christians. On that day the Lord Jesus rose : and it was suited to be the day of communication from Him, one of whose titles, as we have seen, is "the First-born of the dead." It *has taken the place of the Jewish sabbath, or seventh day*. The Jew was to celebrate *creation* completed, and *God's rest in it*. But that *rest is broken*; and Christians ought to celebrate *God's rest in the work of Christ completed in resurrection.* The Lord's supper is fitly associated with the Lord's day.

Some have supposed the meaning of the passage before us to be, that John was in spirit transferred into "the great and terrible Day of the Lord." In that case a different expression in the Greek would have been used for "the Lord's Day." And the *churches* are *no longer recognized,* when that *day of justice is begun.* They are *witnesses of the mercy of God.* Besides, the nineteenth verse of this chapter proves that the churches are spoken of as the things then existing.

11. "What thou seest, write in a book, and send to the seven churches: unto Ephesus, and unto Smyrna, and unto Pergamos, and unto Thyatira, and unto Sardis, and unto Philadelphia, and unto Laodicea."

John was to *write what he saw.* It appears, from hints dropped in the course of the prophecy, that John wrote at once, while the *objects were before him,* and while the words were sounding in his ears. "Out of the throne *are proceeding* lightnings" (iv. 5). "A great hail *is descending* out of heaven on men" (xvi. 21).

God Himself charged that these sights should be described. How important then! *How merciful the transmission by writing!* Had they been handed down by memory how much would have remained now? What God thinks worthy of being written, may we account worthy of all diligent study!

The first chapter (*or at least the first ten verses*) are a sort of introduction and preface, *written after the rest of the book;* and of great importance to all who would understand its bearing.

These *seven churches were not,* I believe, *prophetic of seven successive states of the Church.* They were *specimens* of "*the things that* ARE," *not prophetic of what was to be.* They gave a fair average of the standing of the churches of Christ before the last of the apostles died ; and we see from the Saviour's words, how likely they were to have their candlesticks removed. *Abounding grace still spares the churches*, but they have not continued in God's goodness, and *are soon to be cut off.* Rom. xi.

12. " And I turned to see the voice which was speaking with me. And being turned, I saw seven golden lamp-stands."

He beheld then *seven golden lamps* upon their stands. On this point I must differ from most or all who have preceded me. They speak of the lamps, altars, censers, etc., beheld by John, as mere *images* and allusions to the utensils of the tabernacle. But such a conclusion is not derived from Scripture. Scripture would assure us, that the things which John *beheld were the* REALITIES, of which the Mosaic tabernacle contained only the *copies*. It were strange indeed, if, while the law of Moses gave only the *copies* of the things in heaven, John saw only the *shadowy appearance* of those *shadows !* If Paul may be trusted, *there is really a tabernacle in heaven, in which are the originals* which Moses, and John, were permitted to see. What other conclusion should we gather from such passages as these ?—" A minister of the Holiest, and of the TRUE TABERNACLE, which *the Lord pitched and not man.*" The priests of Aaron's line " serve the *example* and *shadow of the heavenly things ;* as Moses was admonished when he was about to make the tabernacle." For " see (saith He) that thou make all things according to the *pattern showed thee in the mount* " (Heb. viii. 2, 5). If the person of Jesus be a reality, why not the lamps amidst which He moves ?

There are then real vessels in heaven, about which the ministry of Jesus as high priest is at present engaged ; things which were purged with His blood. Heb. ix. 23. Besides their *reality*, they are *significant* of *things below*, and generally of spiritual things, as the lamps in the present instance.

This temple is the temple of the new covenant, as the *earthly* one was of the *old* covenant. *The Jew then is as much interested in it as the Christian.* This is the Priest, by whose blood the *new covenant was ratified :* the Mediator, on whose *suretyship it is to stand.*

Jesus is the priest tending the lamps : it is night then. The lamps were to burn from *evening* to *morning* before the Lord. Exod. xxvii. 21. Aaron was to light the lamps at even. Exod. xxx. 8. 'Tis remarkable, that the lamps are not said by John to be lighted. Nor does he speak of their wanting oil.

13. " And in the midst of the lamp-stands one like a son of man, clothed with a garment down to the foot, and girded around at the breasts with a golden girdle."

Jesus walking in the midst of the lamps is the priest in charge of them. *The throne is not seen.* 'Tis *Jesus and the churches alone with each other.* The priest of old was responsible for the state of the lamps. Here the lamps are moral beings, and *they are responsible to the priest ;* while *the priest* is *responsible to God* for his tending the lamps. Their design is to light the darkness : *they are responsible so to do.* Jesus is turned, *not* towards God in intercession, but towards the churches, as *the priest judging of leprosy in the camp.* He is demanding of the churches His rights.

Our Lord is habited in the *priest's ordinary garment* of service ; not in the High Priest's robes of glory and beauty, with the breast-plate. Lev. vi. 10 ; xvi. 4.

The resemblance of the personage seen here with the Great Agent of Dan vii. and x., and with Ezek. i., seems designed to teach us, that *the same* Mighty One both presides over the churches, and is concerned in the redemption of Israel.

14. "Now his head and his hair were white as white wool, as snow; and his eyes as a flame of fire."

These piercing eyes discover to us Jesus' power to read the secrets of the heart ; as the sword out of His mouth shows His power to destroy those whom His eyes convict. On the human eye shines a point of light, which shifts as the rays fall on it. Here there is light in a stream darted forth from within. Naught shall be concealed at last. Believe it, Christians !

But the priest has no censer : for he is only walking amidst the lamps, not trimming them. The book before us exhibits the *lamps' responsibility to burn,* not Christ's to tend them.

15. "And his feet (were) like fine brass, glowing with fire, as in a furnace ; and his voice as the sound of many waters."

The further description contained in this verse corresponds with that of the angel who appeared to Daniel.

This seems, I think, designed to teach us, that there is a great resemblance also in the *subjects* of Daniel and of Revelation.

16. "And he had in his right hand seven stars ; and out of his mouth proceeded a sharp two-edged sword : and his countenance (was) as the sun shineth in his strength."

This seems quite destructive of the democratic idea of church government : as if all power proceeded from the members of the Church, who are supposed to possess authority to constitute their presiding minister, and to cashier him when they please. The angels are held by Christ, as appointed and sustained by Him. They are dependent on Him, and accountable to Him. The charge concerning the state of each Church is given to them, as though He held them responsible. But His power over them is supreme. He holds them in His hand. As one has well said—" If they be faithful, none can *pluck* them out of His hand : if unfaithful, none can *deliver* them out of it."

They are stars in His *hand ;* they are not on His *head* as His crown, for they are as yet on trial. Only those who are permanently found faithful, shine as the *stars for ever*. Unfaithful teachers are compared to " *wandering stars*, to whom the mist of darkness is reserved for ever."

The sharp sword out of His mouth is a singular, but most significant feature. The sword marks Him out the Avenger appointed by God. The sword is the notification of His readiness to execute judgment on offenders, whether of the churches, or of the world. For *judgment* must *begin at the house of God ;* and the *first three chapters of the Apocalypse are the proof of it.* Be it observed, too, that this appearance of the sword comes immediately after the stars ; as if to teach us that, on those set in so high a station, the demands of justice will be more severe. Nay, and we have the sword taking effect in its full sweep on one of the offending angels of the churches. What says Jesus of the steward who shall beat the man-servants and maidens, and associate with the worldly and the drunken ? "The lord of that servant shall come in a day when he looketh not for him . . . . . . *and shall cut him asunder*" (Matt. xxiv. 50, 51 ; Luke xii. 46). Paul warns offenders of lower degree in like manner. To the Christian guilty of uncleanness he says, "The Lord is the *avenger of all such ;* as we also forewarned you and testified" (1 Thess. iv. 6).

The sword is not to be taken as a symbol of the sharpness of His words, or as equivalent to the Word of God. The Word of God is the *Sword of the Spirit, not of the Son*. The voice of Jesus is described no less than the sword.

The sword is to fight with, and to slay. It has two great relations : as used against offending *subjects*, and as drawn against armed *foes*. In the first of these aspects, it is threatened to some amidst the churches.

ii. 12, 16. In the last, it is employed by Jesus as *King*, when, His priestly duties being ended, He comes forth to war and slay. xix. 15, 21; Luke xix. 27.

But Jesus' direct and most grateful work is upholding the ministers of the churches: the use of the sword is His strange act. The stars are " in His *right hand :* " the sword is only " out of His *mouth*." They are in the place of honour, " His right hand."

17. "And when I saw him I fell at his feet as dead. And he laid his right hand upon me, saying, Fear not, J am the First and the Last."

John's fall was partly *in*voluntary, as we may believe. So great was the glory, that mortal eye and mortal frame could not endure it. If now the mere beholding this Majestic One were so mighty in its effects, on one who had no cause to fear Him, what shall be the result of beholding Him, in the case of those to whom He comes as Avenger ?

His word of compassion—" Fear not ! "

'Tis one of vast moment, in consideration of the awful subjects of which this book treats. It is full of " the great and *terrible* day of the Lord : " that day which is to render to each according to his works : which is " to destroy sinners out of the earth." Yet there are some among men, who need not fear any disclosures concerning that day. Who may thus be at rest in soul, according to our Lord's own words of comfort ? Those who occupy the spiritual position of John. Those who know Jesus as One who loves them, who washed them, and made them priests and kings. Those who now, professing Christ in His Church, are brethren and companions in the tribulation, and kingdom, and patience *in Jesus*.

18. And "I am he that liveth, and I became dead, and behold I am living for ever and ever, and I have the keys of Death and of Hades."

Both are names of places. "Hades" is the general name for the abode of souls departed, awaiting the day of resurrection and of judgment. The spirit does not at once go to heaven or to hell. The word "Hades" is wrongly translated "*Hell.*" *It never signifies the final abode of the lost.* That is described by quite another word—"Gehenna."

"Hades," in this book, is used in a stricter sense than ordinary, to define *that portion of the underground world, where the souls of the righteous are in God's keeping ;* His jewels, soon to be made up in resurrection. *This place is also called "Paradise."* It is the locality in which Jesus promised the dying robber a place, on the day of his departure from earth.

"Death" is also, in this book, the name of a *place*. The death of the body introduces the soul of the wicked to a new region, which is also called "Death." 'Tis the place of the spiritually dead. 'Tis called in the Old Testament, "Abaddon," or Destruction ; " because *the lost suffer there the law's penalty of endless death*, and destruction already begun. "*Hades* is naked before him " (God) says Job, " and *Destruction* hath no covering " (Job xxvi. 6). "*Hades* and *Destruction* are never full," says Solomon (Prov. xxvii. 20), again showing that they are *places*.

This fearful place is called, also, the Abyss, or "Bottomless pit." 'Tis a place of fire ; for when it is opened, smoke, and creatures that torment, come forth. Rev. ix. Into this, as a place of punishment, Satan is cast for the thousand years. In it was the rich man of the parable fixed. *The nearness of "Hades" and of "Death" is clearly implied in that parable :* for Dives and Abraham can converse together across the great gulf.

But *after the world is destroyed*, the first "DEATH," or place of punishment for the souls of the wicked, gives place to Gehenna, or the lake of fire eternal, which is the "SECOND DEATH." The sinner's body and soul have then been re-knit, and the sentence of endless woe has been passed. Jesus has the keys of both Hades and Death, and *summons the departed* thence, at the Great Judgment of the dead (Rev. xx.) after which the old prisons, "Death and Hades," *are broken up.*

19. "Write *therefore* the things which thou sawest, and the things which are, and the things which are about to take place after these things."

We have, in this verse, a key to the true analysis of the book, and a lever to upturn from the foundations several erroneous schemes of interpretation.

The division of the book is *threefold*: answering to the three titles of the Father, and of the Son; and it relates to the Past, the Present, the Future.

1. "THE THINGS WHICH THOU SAWEST." (Past.)
2. "THE THINGS WHICH ARE." (Present.)
3. "THE THINGS WHICH ARE ABOUT TO TAKE PLACE AFTER THESE THINGS." (Future.)

The first division contains the vision which has just been commented upon. To it the Saviour refers in the next verse, in a way that makes His meaning quite clear. "The things *which thou sawest*" ($\grave{a}$ $\varepsilon\tilde{\iota}\delta\varepsilon\varsigma$) is Jesus' description of the first section. And in the next verse, He says, "The mystery of the seven stars *which thou sawest* ($o\hat{v}\varsigma$ $\varepsilon\tilde{\iota}\delta\varepsilon\varsigma$) upon my right hand, and the seven golden lamp-stands."

"*The things that are*" *abide still.* Till the dispensation is changed, the churches are recognized. And it does not appear that the *new dispensation will begin,* till Israel has returned to his own land in unbelief, and *restored the temple with its sacrifices.* God has no memorial of Israel before Him, now that they are rooted up from their land. But when once the temple *and its sacrifices are restored,* Israel comes again under

His eye for judgment, and the long-delayed wrath of the day of the Lord (which is seen beginning in chapter iv. of this book) descends.

Yet I would not lead the believer to suppose that *any series of earthly events* must *precede* the removal of the *Lord's watchful ones* from the earth.

If the Church still be recognized in our day (which few will deny), *then we are not under any of the seals, or trumpets, or vials,* as most affirm. We are yet among "the things that *are*." The dispensation has not yet altered. It is not till it changes, that the prophetic part begins.

3. "And the things which are about to take place after these things." This sufficiently explains itself. *The last division of the book begins on the completion of the two first: and not till then.* The last epistle to the Church of Laodicea declares that Jesus is about to spew her out of His mouth. iii. 16. Herein we have Christ's notification of the rejection of the Church from being His witness. And the preceding epistle to Philadelphia warns us of the "hour of temptation which is about to come upon all the world;" while the word ($\mu\acute{\epsilon}\lambda\lambda\omega$) seven times repeated in the prophetic part of the book, points us to what is meant by "the things which are about ($\mu\acute{\epsilon}\lambda\lambda\epsilon\iota$) to come to pass."

That, in the *prophetic* part of the book, we obtain quite a *new dispensation*, is manifest from *the removal* of the *former vision*. The lamps are no more beheld. *The holiest portion of the temple,* before concealed by a door, *is thrown open,* and the *throne of God's justice appears.* Jesus takes a new attitude altogether. He who was Priest is seen as the Sacrifice, and the Kingly Agent of the throne. He who was all mercy rides forth to take vengeance.

Of deep consequence is it to note the words of the last division. Of itself it overturns the ordinary interpretation, which assumes that the *prophetic part is a history of the Christian Church*. Nay! the prophetic part does not begin till *the churches*, as unfaithful witnesses, *are rejected by God*. A defective translation, by rendering the clause, "the things which shall be *hereafter*," covered up this pit-fall. Taken in so general a sense, it was supposed to mean only the prophetic part of the book. But when the full force is given to the words, and when we compare it with the statements at the opening of the prophetic portion, the *proof against the usual theory is complete*. At the opening of the prophetic vision, notice is given that the third division is commencing, by the *repetition of the words of Jesus*. "*After these things*, I saw, and behold a door opened in heaven, and (there was) the first voice which I heard, as of a trumpet, talking with me; saying, Come up hither, and I will show thee *the things which must take place after these things*."

This bears again upon the half-way view, which would reconcile the opinions of the Futurists and the Preterists. Some assert, that there are two interpretations of the Apocalypse, a longer and a shorter scheme. *But no!* if the third part speaks only of things which are to take effect when the churches have ceased to be recognized of God, then *either* the *churches are not now recognized*, and have not for eighteen hundred years been owned; *or* the *prophetic part is not yet begun*.

As the four Evangelists and the Acts give us the transition from Judaism to Christianity, so does *this* book give the *transition from Christianity to Israel*, the Millennial age, and the eternity beyond it.

20. "(Write) the mystery of the seven stars which thou sawest upon my right hand, and the seven golden lamp-stands. The seven stars are the angels of the seven churches: and the seven lamp-stands are the seven churches."

A portion only of the vision which John first beheld

is explained; because only that portion was symbolic. The lamps were a visible material reality. But their significance was a secret, they were emblematic of a spiritual reality on earth. *They are not called " symbols," but " mystery."* Our Lord's explanation is very important. *Whatever is symbolic is covered with the veil of mystery.* As then the book in general is called by God " the Apocalypse," or " the unveiling," IT IS NOT SYMBOLIC. Symbols there are in it, but many of them are explained. Symbols there are, but *wherever* they are found, *there is a veil over them.* I conclude, then, that the Apocalypse is not " a book of symbols," *but to be taken literally,* wherever absurdity does not result.

These stars are rulers, despised on earth, shining in heaven; rejected by the world's governors, but owned as part of the furniture of God's temple above. They are appointed by Christ, and not by men. They are not created by each Church's vote, retaining their place and power so long only as they please the Church, and by virtue of their so doing. And, as they are not created by the churches, so neither do they cease to exist, if displeasing to them. Christ upholds. His supply of grace and His appointment made them what they are, *and to Him they stand or fall.*

" Angels," be it observed, is their *literal designation.* It is given as the explanation of the *mystic " star."*

These are the messengers of *Christ.* "As my Father *sent me,* even so *send* I *you* " (John xx. 21). They are ministers of the Priest of the heavenly sanctuary.

They are entitled " angels of the churches," as Hengstenberg remarks, because they were sent of God to the churches, to be guardians of them. And he very appropriately compares with the expression before us, the one used by our Lord concerning guardian angels— " In heaven *their angels* [angels of the little ones] do always behold the face of my Father " (Matt. xviii. 10).

As the angel of the little one is he to whom he is committed by God, so is *the angel of the Church* that overseer to whose presidency the Church is, by our Lord, committed. And as those angels have in consequence the high honour of always having an audience of the Father, so these angels are always borne by Christ upon His hand.

Some regard the angels of the churches as *messengers sent by the churches to John*. But we have no account of any such persons being sent to the apostle. The angels were stationary in their especial sphere, and were persons of great influence, as is evident from the fact that *Jesus* in each case *holds them responsible for the state of the Church*.

Some regard them *as angelic beings presiding over churches*, as the angels of Daniel presided over nations. But this cannot be; for the angel of Smyrna is required to be "faithful unto *death* "(ii. 10). And angels do not die.

They are thought by some to be merely *representatives of the churches*. But it is evident, that they are quite distinct from the body of the Church. The lamp represents the body of the Church; and amidst the lamps Jesus walks. The star represents the angel: and the stars are carried by Jesus on His hand. As clearly as possible *he distinguishes the angel from the church*. " The seven *stars* are the *angels* of the seven *churches*, and the seven *lamp-stands* are the seven *churches*."

The only explanation which meets with ease all the conditions of the case, is that which supposes them to be the presidents, superintendents, or chief ministers of the churches. They were bishops, not of a diocese, but of a city-church. The name given to these officers in the Epistles of Paul is of equivalent meaning to that employed here. He styles them "apostles."[1] The angels were local, stationary apostles.

[1] Ἄγγελος and ἀπόστολος, both mean " one sent "; so do the equivalent Hebrew words, מלאך and שלוח.

There was, I believe, a *divinely-appointed form of church government*, the same in all the seven before us. Each Church has its angel : there is but one angel to each Church. *Each angel is independent of the other.* There is no epistle to *the angel of the seven churches.* Each ruled the one Church found in each of the seven cities. He did not preside over the many churches of a country. This order was, I suppose, the complete and divine order. As the number of the churches is the dispensationally-perfect one of seven, so is the organization the perfect one, as designed by Christ.

Why are the angels and churches symbolized ? The principle which, I believe, runs through the symbols of the Apocalypse, is, *that where any thing or person has two places, when it is in its natural place, it is described literally ; but when away from it, it takes another form, and is represented in symbol.* The churches were literally on earth, and hence are literally addressed in the two next chapters. But they are only mystically and spiritually in heaven, and hence they are represented emblematically there.

" And the seven lamp-stands are (the) seven churches." *Each Church was an assembly of believers.* All the believers in every city should be united in one fellowship. There was, in the day of its perfection, but one Church to each city ; and but one government. This is represented by there being but one star, and one lamp to each city. Believers are designed of God to constitute one body. When viewed in relation to heaven, and the temple of the new covenant, they are a lamp-stand. *We are already in heavenly places representatively.* We are soon to be *really*, and in body there. (chap. vii.) We are *mystically*, while on earth, *part of the furniture of the heavenly sanctuary.* We are *soon* to be *priests really there.*

Believers are not presented in this book as *priests*

entering into the Holiest, through the rent veil, as they are in the Hebrews. *There* the throne is "the throne *of grace*" (iv. 16). *Here* it is *another throne:* and all things in this book are adjusted with reference *to that throne.*

While seven churches alone, and those of Asia, are directly addressed, Jesus includes in one of His epistles, "*all* the churches" (ii. 23); and the Spirit speaks to "the churches" generally (ii. 11, etc.).

CHAPTER II

I

EPHESUS

1. "Unto the angel of the church in Ephesus [1] write; These things saith he that holdeth fast the seven stars in his right hand, who walketh in the midst of the seven golden lamp-stands."

"WRITE." John was the secretary of our Lord. He penned these epistles, at the dictation of the great Lord to whom the churches belong.

The description of Jesus in the front of each epistle has a reference to the peculiar state of each Church. Jesus then informs us of his relations, both to the star, and to the lamp. For He addresses the angel directly; but not the angel alone. His words are designed to affect the Church also, and each member of it.

The name of the angel is not given in any case: and vainly should we inquire for it. It is the office that is addressed; and the lessons *belong to the dispensation, through its whole course*. Hearken, oh star! *He* addresses you, from whom you derive all your brightness, all that prevents your fall. He speaks, to whom you will give account.

The danger to the golden vessels of the sanctuary no longer arises from the might of a Babylonian army

---

[1] It has been supposed that the names of the churches carry a secret meaning. In regard to some of these it is, I think, plain. But it is not clear in all. If it be true throughout, then Ephosus signifies "desire" (ἔφεσις), i.e. Love to Christ.

outside, but from the judicial decision of the Lord Himself in the Holy Place.

The *churches here addressed are assemblies of believers;* each was a "congregation of faithful men." It is not said, "the Church of Ephesus;" but "*in Ephesus.*" The faithful were but a portion of the citizens in each of the cities addressed. Ephesus was still heathen; it was a witnessing remnant alone that constituted the Church. And thus it should ever have continued. Its standing was lost, as soon as ever the Church was made co-extensive with the population of the city.

2. "I know thy works, and labour, and thy patience, and that thou canst not bear them which are evil; and thou triedst them which say they are apostles, and are not, and foundest them liars."

"I know thy works." This preface occurs before most of the epistles. He *who would judge aright must previously know.* Jesus does. He is the Faithful Witness; and His testimony arises from perfect acquaintance with the facts.

"And labour." The *person is accepted,* and *then the service.* Jesus begins with praising whatever He can find of good in each Church. The angel was active; probably in doctrine, toward the Church; and in evangelization, toward the world.

"And thy patience."

As patience is twice named, and occurs among points which specially refer to believers, I am apt to suppose that the patience has a double reference. First, toward the *Church.* The body of believers themselves need patience from the chief pastor. There are the ignorant, perverse backsliders, those compassed with each variety of infirmity, and beset with each kind of trial.

"And thou canst not bear those who are evil."

The wicked outside the Church of Christ are not to be judged. But discipline comes in to rebuke or exclude those among the disciples who are guilty of sin. 1 Cor. v. Nor must the ungodly be admitted within the fold. Their persons must be rejected, as well as their works.

" And thou triedst those calling themselves apostles, who are not, and foundest them liars."

From *this it is clear*, that *Apostles* were *reckoned*, both by the churches and by our Lord, to *be a standard office* in the Christian Church. For if it were not so, if it were believed in the churches that but twelve apostles were to arise, these impostors could only have attempted to palm themselves off by assuming the names of some of the twelve. But the original twelve were at this late date all cut off, but John. And John was well known at Ephesus. Under such circumstances, there was room for but one impostor, and for him to assume the name of John. But how durst he attempt it at Ephesus? But here were more claimants of the apostleship than one. Then, too, it would have been a question of physical identity. Jesus, besides, would have worded the charge differently, were but the original twelve to arise.

The tests applied therefore by the angel were those by which Paul proved his apostleship, where it was doubted. The churches he had raised, his beholding the Lord Jesus, his signs, wonders, and mighty deeds, were the proofs of office which he gave to the Corinthians. 1 Cor. ix. 2 ; 2 Cor. xi., xii.

3. " And thou hast patience, and didst bear for my name's sake and hast not been wearied."

The patience commended on this second occasion I suppose to be patience in regard to the taunts and persecutions of the ungodly. The angel bore with these various trials through the love of Christ.

Nor, though the trials from within and without were heavy, was He weary in doing well, or in suffering.

4. "Nevertheless I have this against thee, that thou leftest thy first love."

High is the praise given; but higher yet is the standard maintained by our Lord. He has blame in store for one so commended. His eye is on perfection.

The first love both toward Christ and His Church was slackened. To begin well is not enough: we must go on as we began; yea, and make progress. Christ is jealous of our affections.

Not force from without, making wide breaches in the walls, but the waning brightness of love, gives the first symptom of the passing away of the churches from being the witness for God.

The angel and the Church are thereupon called to *repent*. Remarkable word, as addressed to *believers!* Five churches out of the seven are thus exhorted; Ephesus is called to repent of decaying love; Pergamos, of false doctrine permitted; Thyatira, of evil acts; Sardis, of unwatchfulness, and institutions falling to ruin; while Laodicea is found boasting, at a time when her lukewarmness was rendering her loathsome to Christ.

But the repentance of the *angels*, and of the *churches* under their superintendence, is of course very different from that demanded of the *world*. The Saviour supposes the first parties to be *already renewed by the Spirit, and forgiven by His own blood*. But their life, in some respects, fell short of His commands: and in these things they are enjoined to change their conduct. But what if they should not? The threat held out to Ephesus is not eternal death; but *the removal of the Church from its post of witness for God*.

But in the prophetic part, where the world is in question, God sends visitations of *wrath*, expecting that men should be led by His judgments to repent of "murders, idolatries, fornications, sorceries, thefts."

The first epistle leads us to recognize the general tone of these seven addresses. It is *not the testimony of God's grace*, and His provisions of mercy, for the solace, and enlightening, and standing of the saints, individually, or as a body, before God. The tenor of the seven epistles is that of *demands levied on parties responsible*. The mercies which they had previously received, embracing everything needful, are assumed; and thereupon, answerable conduct is expected. Defection from this high standard is everywhere rebuked. The place of witness given by God is to be sustained in its fullness, both before God and men. The past is noticed, as the subject of praise or blame. Their *future destiny* is spoken of, as *dependent upon their deeds*. The issue of their trial is mentioned, not directly as prophecy, but as made to turn upon their *acquitting themselves answerably* to *their responsibilities or not.* ii. 5, 16, 21, 22 ; iii. 2, 11, 18, 20.

5. " Remember therefore whence thou hast fallen, and repent, and do the first works : or else I am coming to thee [quickly] and I will move thy lamp-stand out of its place, except thou repent. 6. But this thou hast, that thou hatest the deeds of the Nicolaitans, which J also hate."

Here is a fall, not of the star from Christ's right hand : for John saw all seven there : but a *descent* from the *previous high degree of grace*.

" Or else I am coming."[1]

Jesus threatens to remove the lamp. What is intended by that ? It means, not the destruction of Ephesus, though Ephesus has been destroyed. The removal was an invisible one, in the heavenly sanctuary. To worldly eyes all might have been the same after the act, as before it : but its standing as God's accepted witness, would be gone.   So, when Jesus left the temple

[1] The word "[quickly]" is noted by Tregelles as doubtful.

at Jerusalem desolate, as the house of the Jews, not of His Father, the marble and gold shone as ever: only a spiritual eye could note its desolation.

Jesus does not say He would *put out* the lamp. The stand being removed, the lamp would go out. The Church, unsustained of grace, would cease to be. Jesus does not say that He would give the place left vacant by Ephesus to another Church. No! The *dispensation is not to last*. This threat addressed to the *first* Church, and the solemn reproof of the *last*, combine to testify the same truth.

From this we learn, that *no congregation of the faithful upon earth is infallible, or steadfast*. But does not Jesus promise that "the gates of hell shall not prevail against His Church?" (Matt. xvi. 18). No, He does *not!* He promises, "That the gates of HADES shall not prevail against His Church." But *Hades* is a very different place from hell, and the Saviour's promise does not assert that His churches on earth shall never cease to exist, nor be overcome by Satan's deceits, or by force. He declares only, that the gates of the place of *departed spirits shall not detain His chosen in custody*, whenever He shall proclaim the hour of resurrection.

"Except thou repent." This passage is very important, as asserting the *efficacy of believers' repentance*, in turning aside the threatened judgments. *All threats* uttered against them are *conditional*—" To be fulfilled, if not repentant."

Jesus, ever ready to notice points worthy of praise, again commends the rejection of the practices of the Nicolaitans.

Who were they? Probably a branch of the Gnostics.

From the epistles to Timothy, who was left at Ephesus to counteract false doctrine, we infer, that they denied either the deity or the humanity of the Lord Jesus.[1]

[1] "The Church of *God* which He purchased with His own

They held fables, and the endless genealogies of the æons. They were guilty of profane babblings, and blasphemy. They set up contrasts, or "Antitheses," between the Old Testament and the New, rejecting the former. They refused marriage, and certain articles of food: probably wine, and animal food; practising austerities of various kinds. They denied the resurrection, explaining it away.

7. "He that hath an ear, let him hear what the Spirit saith to the churches."

The Lord foresaw, that the churches, as corporate bodies, would not answer to the demands of God. Therefore He *addresses Himself* to *each individual* of them. Where the mass was a ruin, there might be individuals who maintained their Christian position. Hence the Lord, at the close of each admonition to the whole, lifts up His voice to each. The churches, *as bodies, are judged now in this dispensation. The members of them are to give account hereafter.* If impenitent, the lamp was (in this dispensation) to be removed; but the individual was to be requited in resurrection; as the promise proves.

"To him that overcometh I will give to eat of the tree of life, which is in the paradise of God."

No promises are made, throughout these epistles, to *the Church, as a unity.* The churches are *nowhere* in Revelation dealt with *as a unit,* to be rewarded alike. Nor are even the members of *each several Church* set upon the same level of reward. There were "*a few* names in Sardis" that should *receive a prize* at the hand of Christ, when the rest were accounted unworthy of it. The maintenance of our dispensational position of witness, or not, is that whereon the reward to each

blood" (Acts xx.). "*God* was manifest in the *flesh*" (1 Tim. iii. 16). This truth is prominent in both addresses to *Ephesus.*

is made to turn. The responsibility which the Lord lays on each is a partial responsibility. Ephesus is responsible for Ephesus alone : the indifference of Laodicea is not laid to its charge. The *seven churches are not regarded as parts of a greater whole, possessed of a united responsibility.* The *prizes held forth* to view are not to members of each Church, as such, or as simple *believers ; but to them as overcomers.* This is very important. *Believers themselves are divided into victors and vanquished !* How possible it is for believers to sink down in worldliness, and lusts of the flesh of various kinds, experience will amply show. Life is a warfare with Satan, the world, the flesh : and some fall in a struggle against the stern necessities of life ; some are drawn away by the pleasures and lures of the world. The *victory* is *not to every warrior* that enters the battle, *nor will the crown be awarded to each.*

The concluding call and promise are expressed in such general terms, that I suppose we should extend them beyond the members of the Church.

The rewards of the victors are something distinct from *a bare salvation :* they are a *special recompense* attached to some *special excellence of conduct,* under peculiar kinds of trial. To the *detection* and *resistance of the frauds of Satan, a different reward* is promised from that *attached to suffering for Christ unto death.* As in a variety of ways we may be overcome by our enemies' fraud and force, so in a variety of ways may we receive corresponding reward.

II

SMYRNA

8. "And unto the angel of the church in Smyrna write: These things saith the First and the Last, who became dead, and returned to life."

THE first attribute of Christ *imports His Deity*— He is "the First and the Last."

But this Mighty One, who once descended to death, has now risen out of it, and is beyond man's power for ever. What believer then need fear death? The Saviour has passed through its fortress. He is Almighty, and will make a way for His people's rescue. Beyond death lies their reward.

9. "I know thy tribulation and poverty."

The ordinary reading, which inserts "thy works," is rejected by the critical editions. *Internal evidence is against it also.* Jesus is speaking throughout of suffering, and not of action. In times of persecution, the Church can do but little.

Jesus was aware of the "*trouble*" of the saints. He knew it by experience, having Himself passed through the same. Both Jew and Pagan joined to persecute the saints. This word is, in the Apocalypse, only used of the churches; and it hence serves to *identify the Great Multitude* of chap. vii. 14 *with the saved of the churches.*

The angel was poor, and most probably the Church

was so too. The poverty was, as we may gather, the *result of persecution;* for it is spoken of *between* the "tribulation" and the "blasphemy" as the persecutors.

9. "And the blasphemy from those who say that they are Jews, and are not, but are the synagogue of Satan."

The Jews were the great enemies of the Church in Smyrna, and the agents of Satan against the angel.

It was, no doubt, felt to be peculiarly trying to the believers of that day, that the Jews, to whose sacred writings they appealed, made common cause with the heathen against them. It was calculated to suggest the doubt whether they could be right.

The sin thus noticed as beginning under "the things that are," and confined to the Jews, in *the prophetic part*, embraces *the whole world*, and attains its most fearful height. The *seeds* of each future development of iniquity *cluster round the churches*, or are found *within them*.

The blasphemers said they were Jews, but were not. They were *Jews outwardly*, but *not within*. And in this dispensation *only the inward Jew* is recognized of God. Rom. ii. 28.

They are *Jews literally taken*, but had they been in God's sense, *true Jews*, they would have *joined the Church of Christ*.

10. "Fear not [1] the things which thou art about to suffer; [2] behold the devil is about to cast some of you into prison, that ye may be tempted; and ye will have a tribulation of ten days. Become [3] faithful unto death, and I will give thee the crown of life."

The Saviour is fortifying the president of the Church in Smyrna *against troubles to come*. They are beforehand known to Christ. He is our watchman, from His tower above foreseeing, and *forewarning of trials* in the distance.

[1] For $\mu\eta\delta\grave{\epsilon}\nu$ read $\mu\acute{\eta}$.   [2] $M\acute{\epsilon}\lambda\lambda\omega$.   [3] $\Gamma\acute{\iota}\nu o\nu$.

But the affliction was to assail, not only the president but some of the members of the Church. "The devil will cast *some of you* into prison." Here *the angel is distinguished from the believers generally*. Here too is *special membership*. The Church of Smyrna constituted a body, of which those in communion were the special members.

In this is Jesus *the prophet* of His Church : and His far-reaching eye discerns evil to come, not only in its human branches and stems, but in its root in the heavenly places, among *wicked spirits there*. Eph. vi. 12. He points out to us *Satan*, as the *prime agent and mover* in the *afflictions of his churches*.

God was pleased to give Satan permission, for His own glory's sake, and for the vindication of His saints. They were not insincere : and in the fire of persecution their steadfastness would prove them genuine gold.

The duration of the persecution is defined. The Lord on high limits His enemies' rage, and lets us know that the chain is upon the ravening lions and raging bears.

It was to be " a tribulation of ten days."

How strangely has it been asserted as the rule, that in prophecy a day is to be interpreted as signifying a year ! (1) " For yet *seven days*, and I will cause it to rain upon the earth *forty days and forty nights* " (Gen. vii. 4). How was this fulfilled ? After *seven years* did it rain for *forty years* ? " And it came to pass after *seven days*, that the waters of the flood were upon the earth " (10). " And the rain was upon the earth *forty days and forty nights* " (12).

(2) "The three branches are *three days*. Yet within *three days* shall Pharaoh lift up thy head." How fulfilled ? " And it came to pass the *third day*, which was Pharaoh's birthday, that he made a feast unto all his servants " (Gen. xl. 12, 13, 20).

(3) "Behold I will rain bread from heaven for you; and the people shall go out and gather a certain rate *every day*. .... On the *sixth day* they shall prepare that which they bring in" (Exod. xvi.). How fulfilled? In days.

(4) God promises flesh to Israel. "Ye shall not eat one day, nor two days, nor five days, nor ten days, nor twenty days, but even a *whole month*, until it come out at your nostrils." How fulfilled? Was it for thirty years that the quails were given? No! Literally, for thirty days. Num. xi. 19, 20.

(5) "Prepare your victuals," says Joshua, "for within *three days* ye shall pass over this Jordan" (Josh. i. 11). Did they wait three years? or three days only?

(6) The very case on which opposers rest, makes against them. "Your children shall wander in the wilderness *forty years*" (Num. xiv. 33). How fulfilled? Did they wander 144,000 years? Nay, but forty years only. To make the *year-day theory* correct, God should have said, "Ye shall wander in the wilderness forty *days;*" which they should have found by experience to mean forty *years*.

But there is one passage which, more than any other, gives its *full and decisive denial to the scheme*.

(7) "As Jonas was three days and three nights in the whale's belly, so shall the Son of Man be *three days* and three nights in the heart of the earth" (Matt. xii. 40). How was this fulfilled? Was Jesus three *years* in the tomb? No!

Then is the year-day theory false!

The angel is exhorted to be faithful unto death. It is of course supposed that a violent death awaits him. This is the highest and last test of fidelity. Life might be offered to him upon evil conditions; but they were to be refused. The kings of the earth expect allegiance of their subjects, even to the surrender of life. Much more may the Creator and Redeemer ! Jesus does not say, " Till I come." *Nowhere* is the *Saviour's coming* made *equivalent in meaning to death*.

The reward is held up before the warrior. " I will give thee the crown of life." Resurrection, specially as already realized in our Lord's instance, is the *grand antidote to the fear of death*. In that, life lost for Christ is found again. Those who suffer unto death reign with Messiah the thousand years. Rev. xx. 4. But there are also special rewards distributed among those who are privileged to obtain a place in the first resurrection. There are *special crowns for special services*. To the elders who watch over Christ's flock well, " the crown of *glory* " (1 Pet. v. 4). But this is " the crown of *life* " promised also by the apostle Jacob (commonly called James).

1. This crown is the crown of *victory*. As men offered a parsley-wreath to the victors in their games, so does the Lord offer His crown to the wrestlers against Satan and his potentates. 1 Cor. ix. 25 ; 2 Tim. ii. 5 ; Heb. ii. 7, 9. Satan threatened *death*. Christ promised *life*. Satan would cast into *prison*. Christ would lift up to a *crown*.

2. 'Tis also the sign of *royalty*. " If we suffer, we shall also *reign* with him." 2 Tim. ii. 12 ; Rev. xx. 4.

11. " He that hath an ear, let him hear what the Spirit saith unto the churches : he that overcometh shall not be hurt by the Second Death."

The lesson of the Spirit is designed for each who has an ear : not only for those of that day, and of that Church. The Saviour finds no blame with this Church. As it was suffering for Him, He lays on it no unnecessary burthen. He bids it only be steadfast.

Then follows the promise to the victor. These promises divide the believers of each Church *into conquerors and conquered*. And the promises are, I suppose, special: that is, that not every overcomer will enjoy all the promises; but only those who have been tried by the *special form of temptation* will receive the *prize* held out to the *victor in that contest*. For instance, some have to defeat Satan's wiles, and to that a definite reward is held out. Some have to meet his violence, as in this case; and, therefore, I conclude, that the reward now offered belongs to those who face prison and death for Christ's sake.

"The overcomer shall not be hurt by the Second Death."

1. The promise is equivalent to the assurance, that he shall be a *partaker in the first resurrection,* and the bliss of the thousand years. It is a manifest allusion to Rev. xx. 6. *The Second Death* does not mean spiritual death, but (as has been shown above) it denotes the place of eternal torment—" *the lake of fire* " (xx. 14).

The victor then over the fear of death obtains two desirable results: one negative, he escapes *all touch of the wrath of God*: one positive, he is a crowned conqueror and king for a thousand years.

This brings us to the (2) implication.

How strangely these words sound in our ears, if once we listen to their evident meaning! "The *conqueror* is to escape all touch of the lake of fire! Why, I thought—I have always believed—that this is the lowest and surest advantage, common to *all the saved!* Does it not belong to every believer?"

It would seem not. We must make room for scripture truths in our system; not cut and clip scripture to our systems. What is the evident implication of these two agreeing passages? Clearly, that it is *possible* that some *believers*, members of the churches of Christ, may *be hurt by the Second Death.*

"Do you mean, then, that all believers who do not obtain part in the first resurrection will be cast into the lake of fire ? " *Certainly not !* To be liable to a thing, and to experience it, are very different.

But he would steady His people against *the fear of man* by a more *tremendous fear*—even that *of God*.

When the last trial comes, and the persecutor says to the believer, " Abjure your faith, or die ! " there is great glory to God and profit to His churches, when the confessor accepts death, rather than abandon the faith. But what if he succumb before the enemy ? Great is the shame and mischief to God's cause, to himself, and others.

Can a believer, under such trying circumstances, fall ?

Alas ! English ecclesiastical history has furnished sad instances of it.

"Promise to read this paper in public, without omitting or adding a single word " (said Barnes' judges to him). It was then read to him. " I would die first," was his reply. " Will you abjure, or be burnt alive ? " said his judges : " take your choice." The alternative was dreadful. Poor Barnes, a prey to the deepest agony, shrank at the thoughts of the stake : then suddenly his courage revived, and he exclaimed, " I had rather be burnt than abjure." Gardiner and Fox did all they could to persuade him. " They entreated him ; they put forward the most plausible motives : from time to time they uttered the terrible words, *burnt alive !* His blood froze in his veins : he knew not what he said or did . . . they placed a paper before him—they put a pen in his hand—his head was bewildered, he signed his name with a deep sigh. This unhappy man was destined, at a later period, to be a faithful martyr of Jesus Christ ; but he had not yet learned to ' resist even unto blood.' Barnes had fallen." *D'Aubigné*, vol. v. p. 250.

While then there are joyful promises, positive and negative, to him who, at the cost of life, maintains the faith, what shall we say to those who are overcome in the struggle ? The overcomer shall not be hurt by the Second Death, in consequence of his victory. Shall not then, the one so conquered be hurt by it, in consequence of his defeat ?

Do these two texts stand alone ? By no means. "Whosoever shall confess *me* before men, him will I also confess before my Father which is in heaven. But whosoever shall deny me before men, *him will I also deny before my Father who is in heaven*" (Matt. x. 32, 33). The consequence of Jesus' confession of any before His Father, will be their entrance into the millennial kingdom. But what will be the result of denying the Lord Jesus, and of being denied before the Father ? Jesus is speaking to disciples, and He says, "Fear not them who kill the body, but are not able to kill the soul, but *rather fear Him which is able to destroy both body and soul in Gehenna*" (28). Again, Jesus, treating of the very same subject, says, "I say unto you, *my friends*, be not afraid of them that kill the body and after that have no more that they can do. *But I will show* (Greek) *you whom ye shall fear : fear him who, after he hath killed, hath authority* (Greek) *to cast into hell : yea, I say unto you, fear him*" (Luke xii. 4, 5).[1] What is this but to tell the believer, that it is better to suffer at man's hand his worst afflictions, than to suffer from God both before and after death ?

"You do not hold the perseverance of the saints then ? Now this is certainly a scriptural doctrine. 'My sheep shall never perish' (John x. 28)."

The perseverance of the saints is *a true doctrine* : yet there must be room found for *this* also. John's gospel testifies both these at once. But the text just quoted

---

[1] The same idea is given by John xv. 6. But there the offender departs from Christ freely, uncompelled by force.

should be rendered—"I give unto them (my sheep) eternal life, and *they shall not perish for ever.*"[1]

HENGSTENBERG gives nearly the same view of the inference. " He that overcomes, not only obtains a glorious good, but he also *escapes a dreadful evil.* Let him ponder well, when a choice is set before him, between the bodily death, as it is usually called, and the Second Death or eternal damnation [here I agree not] which they have to expect, who are not faithful unto death. Matt. x. 28. ' Fear not those who kill the body,' etc., coincides in thought."

The reader will thank me for supplying him with the following fine passage from ISAAC TAYLOR :—

" We of this age may expound as we think fit these appalling words ; or may extenuate these phrases ; or, if we please, let us cast away the whole doctrine as intolerable and incredible. Let us do so : but it is a *matter of history, out of question,* that the *Apostolic Church,* and the Church of later times *took it, word for word, in the whole of its apparent value.* It is true that several attempts were made to substantiate a mitigated sense : but it is certain, that the language of Christ, in regard to the future life, was constantly on the lips of martyrs throughout the suffering centuries. Often and often was it heard from out of the midst of the fire, and was lisped by the quivering lips of women and children while writhing on the rack."

---

[1] Οὐ μὴ ἀπόλωνται εἰς τὸν αἰῶνα. Read the same in the following texts, John iv. 14 ; viii. 51, 52 ; xi. 26. "Not for ever."

III

PERGAMOS[1]

12. "And to the angel of the church in Pergamos, write—These things saith he who hath the sharp two-edged sword."

JESUS would steady the believers of Pergamos against the fear of the human sword, by the greater fear of the sword proceeding from Himself. If man is dreadful, God is tremendous. But the Saviour also exhibits this weapon as a warning against the false teachers of that place.

13. "I know where thou dwellest, where Satan's throne is; and thou holdest fast my name, and deniedst not my faith, even in the days (in which) ANTIPAS was my witness, my faithful one, who was slain among you, where Satan dwelleth."

The Saviour makes allowance for circumstances. To Him are known the peculiar difficulties of our abode. Where wickedness abounds, and the current of example is almost universal, where the lures of sin are importunate, and force is employed on its behalf, 'tis an arduous task for the Christian to stand his ground.

The angel and the Lord's people at Pergamos were in a situation peculiarly trying. They dwelt beside " Satan's throne."

It was situated at Pergamos. How is this explained ? 'Tis not easy to do so. We know but little of the city in question: not enough to settle the matter to our

---

[1] I am unable to perceive any profound meaning in the word Pergamos : and cannot agree with what has been suggested.

perfect satisfaction. But, I think, a beam of light falls upon the subject, when we know *that the worship of the Roman Emperors*, which was so rampant in John's day, and which is to be the last form of sin bringing Christ down from the sky, especially flourished in PERGAMOS.

Is it not marvellous to find five out of the seven cities mentioned by our Lord, *contending for the privilege of worshipping the emperor* ? and *such* an emperor as TIBERIUS ? But PERGAMOS appears the most prominent of the eleven. " The city of PERGAMOS made a merit of having already built a temple in honour of AUGUSTUS." It now covets the distinction of worshipping a second emperor.

This connects itself very closely with the awful height of wickedness which appears in the xiii. chap., and hints, very significantly, what the " IMAGE of the WILD BEAST " is.

Remember, Christian, that in the very apostolic age, while the churches flourished, and the lamps stood yet unremoved in the sanctuary, and tended by our Lord Jesus, Satan had his throne on earth ! He was able to hold his ground, close beside a Church of the living God. Was the Church to overthrow his throne ? Nay, it had already begun to give way to his deceits. He was more ready to prevail over the Church, than the Church over him. Are God's churches to convert the world ? and to dispossess Satan of his usurped dominion ? Nay ! *Satan holds his throne on earth*, through *all the period* characterised as—" the things that ARE." In " the things that are *after these things*," his throne blazes out into a lustre of dominion which it never yet has attained ; and 'tis only after " the BATTLE of the Great Day of God Almighty," and the devouring of his defying legions by the birds, that his throne is overturned, and his reign for ever at an end.

Jesus glorifies the name of His martyr. "ANTIPAS, *my* witness, *my* faithful one." 'Tis a name not noted elsewhere. But it is the real name of one who suffered unto death for Christ. Unknown to men, 'tis enough that Christ has named him with terms of endearment. "Right dear, in the sight of the Lord, is the death of his saints." He will remember such a one in His kingdom and glory. The life lost shall then be found. Not ANTIPAS alone, but all His martyrs will then shine as the sun.

Again, our Lord notes the peculiarity of the situation of PERGAMOS. There, Satan not only held his throne, but dwelt. We must not marvel to find broken bones, and traces of blood, near the lion's den. Let us praise God, that we are not in a post of such danger! What a difference there is in the moral character and atmosphere of different places on earth! Satan, no doubt, would choose as his habitation one of the worst; and his presence there would make it worse still.

14. "But I have a few things against thee, that thou hast there them that hold fast the doctrine of Balaam, who taught Balak to cast a stumblingblock before the children of Israel, to eat things offered unto idols, and to commit fornication."

The Saviour will not pass by just occasions of reproof, even in those found worthy of praise. There were those in the Church *who ought not to be tolerated there*. They held the doctrine of Balaam. He instructed the king to seduce the tribes to fornication and idolatry by means of the Moabite women.

Satan has two chief plans of mischief against the people of God. He seeks to raise against the Church *the anger of man*. If that avail not, and the Church stand firm, he endeavours to raise against it *the displeasure of God, by alluring it into sin*. 'Tis often a very efficient plan. Smyrna resisted his assault in force. The wall of Pergamos begins to fall by secret mining.

The seductions of Balaam were two : " the eating of *things offered to idols*, and the *committing fornication*." Against their sins, so closely allied in heathen worship, the Holy Spirit by Paul raised a loud testimony. 1 Cor. vi., viii., x. But the corrupt leanings of nature prove too hard for the witness, and the terrors of the Most High.

15. " So hast Thou also, those that hold fast the doctrine of Nicolaitans in like manner."

In the epistle to Ephesus, the " *deeds* " of the Nicolaitans were condemned. In this, their " *doctrine*." Evil deeds never reach their height, never dare stalk abroad unabashed, till evil *practice* is sustained by evil *theory*.

Satan was now trying them, by the same device which he had contrived in the desert. *Nicolaitan doctrine had sprung up within the Church*. Those deceived by it were, *many* of them, *believers in Jesus*. Over such only had the angel of the Church power. For such only was he responsible. 1 Cor. v. 12, 13. They were *members of* the *Church of Christ*, not *mere pretenders*. For the Saviour, throughout the Epistles to the churches, *exposes false pretensions*. He twice discovers the Jews who falsely so called themselves ; He exposes the pretended prophetess of Thyatira, Laodicea's vain boast of riches, and the angel of Sardis' name of life, with sad reality of deadness.

Under the churches, there is the *lure* to eat " *things sacrificed to idols ;* " in the prophetic days, *compulsion* to *naked idolatry*. *The great False Christ is a Cæsar*. Rev. xvii. 9, 11. How appropriately then is the city that first introduced into Asia the worship of the Cæsars made to show the germ of the last outbreak of sin !

16. " Repent therefore ; or else I am coming to thee quickly, and will war against them with the sword of my mouth."

The angel was some one *possessed of the chief authority* in the Church; and by the Lord Jesus, therefore, was held *responsible for the doctrines professed and taught*. He did not hold these evil views himself: but *he did not attempt to put them down*. Evil had entered into the Church more fully than at Ephesus. The angel there was praised, as unable to endure the wicked, and hating the deeds of the Nicolaitans. Here they were *permitted to teach*, and to *practise* their abominations.

He is, therefore, required to repent. *He must use discipline against the offenders.* Discipline, lovingly and firmly applied, would either recover the unsound to the true faith and practice, or exclude them. Left to itself, *false doctrine is leaven*, which is apt to spread, till the whole is leavened.

Be it observed, that the purity which the Lord Jesus sought, and the want of which He reproved, was not the purity of written articles of faith, which might remain unchanged, despite the complete falling away of the living members from the truth; *but a purity of the persons united in fellowship*.

"But to what extent is it lawful to seek to put any out from communion *because of difference of doctrine? Is no difference of opinion to be tolerated?*"

Yes! Differences of view on very many and important points are to be met with forbearance and Christian love. Rom. xiv., xv.

There are but *two exceptions*: (1) one of *doctrine;* (2) one of *practice*.

(1) *That of doctrine* is found where the *parties are* "*Antichrists*," denying *the Trinity*, or the *two natures of Christ*. 2 John 6; 1 John iv.[1]

[1] [Mr. Govett modified this view in later years. In his *Exclusion for Doctrine Unscriptural*, p. 23 (1885), he says: "Even the Antichrists were not, by the authority of God, put out of communion after once being received at the Lord's Table. They went out of themselves: 1 John ii. 18, 19."]

(2) *That of practice*, where *open immorality* is held and *practised*. 1 Cor. v.

If the angel should be remiss after this warning, Jesus would come to him. No threat against himself, individually, is *expressed*; but the removal of the lamp, as at Ephesus, seems to be implied. The Lord's coming may be *either joyous or grievous* to His own people, according as He *finds their work to be*.

Here is "evil unjudged" in a church; yet the Saviour only warns. The *sound portion of the believers did not leave communion*. They are not taught by our Lord to do so; even if, after divine warning, the angel should leave the evil untouched.

But a sterner menace is directed against the criminals. Jesus held not the sword in vain.

How awful a threatening to be uttered against a portion of his servants! "I will war against them with the sword of my mouth."

"He that hath an ear, let him hear what the Spirit saith unto the Churches."

The Holy Ghost again throws wide the lessons of the epistle to every one of spiritually-opened ear. Where the majority fall away from their true standing, individuals may yet retain their integrity, and receive approval from the Lord Jesus. The address to the angel is over; every member of the Church is now appealed to.

17. "To him that overcometh will I give of the hidden manna; and I will give him a white stone, and on the stone a new name written which none knoweth, save he that receiveth it."

What is the *meaning* of the promise? Here interpretations file off in two directions: some regarding it as spiritual; others as literal. Our maxim is, to apply the principle of *literality first*. Is it absurd to take it thus? Some may say, they think it is. How shall we decide it *then?* By scripture instances. *That cannot be absurd, which has already been in fact fulfilled.*

There was a literal eating of manna : why not again ? Christians are perpetually *forgetting the resurrection of* THE BODY. And though it may not, after that great change, need any supply of food, still it may be a pleasure to partake of it. Did not the Lord Jesus eat and drink more than once with His disciples, after He rose from the dead ? *The manna is the food of the tabernacle,* while the Lord's people are still in the *wilderness,* ere yet the new heavens and earth are reached. *The fruit is the food of the city,* after earth is destroyed, and the new earth is tenanted by its nations.

Here then we establish a very important difference between the *Gospel of John,* and his *Apocalypse.* Our Lord while on earth, arguing with the faithless Jews, *presents to them Himself as the spiritual manna.*

In the *Gospel,* Jesus is offering Himself to the *unbeliever,* that he may have *eternal life.* The manna is *spiritually taken.* In the *Revelation,* Jesus is *offering reward* to those who are *believers, already possessed of Himself as their everlasting life.* The promise now is to be fulfilled, not to every believer, and not to be received now by faith, but to *be enjoyed only* by the *conquering* believer, *after resurrection.* We cannot then understand it, in the same sense as in the Gospel.

'Tis *literally* to be taken then ! It stands as the Lord's antagonist promise to the Gnostic enticements to sin. They offered a place at the idol feasts ; both at Ephesus and at Pergamos. To each Church Jesus exhibits the promise of a better food. He promises the hid manna, as the *High Priest,* having the right of entrance into the Holiest, and having power over its ark. What were the idol-banquets in the temples of the heathens to this ?

We arrive at the second promise.

Jesus would give a white stone, on which should be engraven a new name.

What is the allusion here ? Almost all commentators seek the reference in some custom found among the Greeks or Romans. But Jesus is assuming an attitude of opposition to the heathen and their abominations ; is it likely that He would choose His allusion from among the things condemned ?

Both *the manna* and the *white stone* are *taken from the priestly functions of Aaron*.

There is one case, which applies more nearly than any. It is that of Joseph, who is tempted to fornication, as these of Pergamos are. He overcomes, and receives from the hand of king Pharaoh great honours. " Pharaoh took off his *ring* from his hand, and put it upon Joseph's hand." " And Pharaoh *called Joseph's name Zaphnath-paaneah* " (Gen. xli. 42, 45).

But there is one point in all these cases which prevents entire parallelism. *They were all names publicly given, and known to many. This is to be a new name, unknown to any but the receiver.* It marks a secret understanding, and a gracious confidence between the giver and receiver.

Some have inquired—What will the name be ? This it is useless to ask. It will be different in each case. It is of its own nature *a secret*. To attempt to know, what Christ declares none but the receiver shall know, is absurd.

It seems a reward founded upon those words—" Thou holdest fast *my name*." In the day of trial, this bespoke firm love. It will be requited by a new name, in the day of glory, when Jesus Himself takes His " *new name, which none knoweth but himself.*" xix. 12.

Against the Gnostic enticement to the believer—that, " if he joined their party, his eyes should be opened to see secrets and wonders unspeakable "—Jesus offers heavenly secrets, and the confidence of His divine friendship.

IV

THYATIRA

18. "And unto the angel of the church who is in Thyatira write: These things, saith the Son of God, who hath his eyes as a flame of fire, and his feet (are) like to fine brass."

IN the present letter, for the first time, the name of the speaker is given. He who was seen by John as Son of *Man*, proclaims Himself also Son of *God*.

Two attributes of His, derived from the first vision, are given. "His eyes are as a flame of fire," to detect evil, and to terrify transgressors: and His feet as fine brass, to avenge himself upon them.

The Saviour's feet seem to be compared to fine brass (or copper rather), with reference to this: because copper is remarkable for its hardness. "Arise and thresh, O daughter of Zion! for I will make thy horn iron, and *I will make thy hoofs brass: and thou shalt beat in pieces many peoples*" (Mic. iv. 13).

19. "I know thy works, and love, and faith, and service, and thy patience, and thy works, the last more than the first."

The Son of God is looking at the works of *the Church* now. The Lord is not, as yet, imputing to the *world* its trespasses. "Love" is put first, as the chief of all graces: in this the angel was praiseworthy. He held fast, too, the great facts and doctrines revealed by our Lord. He was active in the supply of others' wants, whether temporal or spiritual. He was, it would appear, remarkable for patient endurance; for "thy" is repeated before patience, as if to point it out to especial attention.

Moreover, there was no declension in works, but progress rather. Herein he stands favourably compared with the angel of Ephesus.

> 20. " But I have (this) against thee that thou lettest alone thy wife Jezebel ; who calleth herself a prophetess, and teacheth and seduceth my servants to commit fornication, and to eat things sacrificed unto idols."

In the point in which he is blamed, the angel of Ephesus is his superior. His unbalanced love enervated his resistance to evil. What a story of imperfection is man!

The Saviour now *divides the Church into two parties*, the guilty, and the innocent ; and gives suitable admonitions to each.

A great deal turns upon the reading here. Our translation has " the woman Jezebel : " I prefer, with Griesbach, Scholtz, Lachmann, Tischendorf, Moses Stuart, and Hengstenberg, " thy wife." The latter observes, " That the external reasons in support of the first reading greatly preponderate, is clear alone from its admission into the text of Lachmann. How should anyone have thought of thrusting in this ' thy '—the cross of expositors—into the text, if it had not originally existed ? "

We can thus account for the *severity of our Lord's rebuke*. This offender was *doubly under his control*. (1) As head of the Church, he was bound to take the oversight of the members of it, and *could not be ignorant of his wife's proceedings*. (2) And, as *husband*, he was especially *bound to check conduct so lawless*.

It is not enough for those in authority not to favour what is evil : they *must resist it*, and use discipline against the offenders.

Even if the name were not a real one, but one bestowed by prophecy, she might still be a real person. Jer. xx. 3.

"Who calleth herself a prophetess." Either she had no inspiration at all, or it was that of an evil spirit. She would need some authority to enable her to palm off her awful doctrines upon the Lord's people. Pretending to receive intimations from God, she could speak of them as mysteries reserved for a select and sagacious few. Montanism and its false prophetesses arose afterwards near the same spot.

"She teaches and seduces my servants." Three grounds of blame are stated. (1) She falsely professed herself a prophetess. (2) She taught *men*; which Paul by the Spirit forbid; even when the truth was taught. 1 Tim. ii. 12. (3) She taught abominable doctrine. Saints of God! Be not secure! The strongest may fall! She not only taught fornication as a theory: but she seduced to it in practice. The doctrine must needs lead on to the act.

21. "And I gave her time to repent, and she chooseth not to repent of her fornication."

This is the day of God's mercy, and He is slow to wrath. He is not careless of human sin, though sinners so misinterpret His grace, and treasure up wrath against its coming day. But long-suffering was tried in vain upon her. We are left under the belief that there was no hope of her recovery. Jesus accuses His servants to their face, in order that they may repent and amend. Satan accuses the Lord's servants behind their back, that he may raise God's anger against them: xii. 10.

22. "Behold I cast her into a bed, and those that commit adultery with her into great tribulation, except they repent of their deeds."

Three judgments overhang her: (1) one on herself:

(2) one on her paramours : (3) one on her children.

(1) For the bed of sin, God would send the bed of pain. In her punishment she should read the displeasure of the Most High at her guilt. Hers was a sin unto death, and she should not recover.

(2) Vengeance would next fall on the adulterers. She was, as we again infer, a married woman. Her offence was literal adultery, not spiritual. As truly as the eating things offered in sacrifice was literal, so was the other sin.

Her fellow-sinners were to suffer great tribulation, if impenitent. When ? Must we assume that it would necessarily be in this life ? What says Romans ii. ? "To them that are contentious, and do not obey the truth, but obey unrighteousness, indignation, and wrath, *tribulation* and anguish, upon every soul of man that doeth evil,"..... " *in the day when God shall judge the secrets of men by Jesus Christ according to my gospel* " (8, 9, 16). "Marriage is honourable in all, and the bed undefiled : but *whoremongers and adulterers God will judge* " (Heb. xiii. 4).

The words " great tribulation " expound to us the meaning of " casting into a bed." Severer judgments are threatened, with increasing sin. And these menaces, be it observed, are addressed to *believers*, members of apostolic churches. "Therefore put away from yourselves that *wicked person* " (1 Cor. v. 13). But the same person, having become penitent, was restored to the Church at the next epistle. 2 Cor. ii. 5–10.

An opening for amendment is, in their case, left. They might repent, and the threatening not light on their heads. How gracious is the Saviour, who received repentant Peter !

23. "And I will slay her children with pestilence, and all the churches shall know that J am he who searches reins and hearts; and I will give to each of you according to your works."

(3) Thirdly, her *children* are to be cut off by a special kind of death. That the Greek word signifies "pestilence" is clear, from its frequent use by the Septuagint, as the translation of the Hebrew דבר. "Lest he fall on us with *pestilence* (Gr. $\theta\acute{a}\nu a\tau o\varsigma$) or the sword" (Exod. v. 3). "For now will I stretch out my hand, that I may smite thee and thy people with *pestilence*" ($\theta\acute{a}\nu a\tau o\varsigma$). Exod. ix. 15; Lev. xxvi. 25, etc. The offenders with the *Moabitish women* were cut off by *pestilence*. Num. xxv. 8, 9. We have an instance of God's cutting off by sickness the child of David's adultery. 2 Sam. xii. 15–18. Was not that literal?

The design of the judgments of the Most High is to awake a solemn awe, and to deter others from sin. Thus, after the cutting off of Ananias and Sapphira, "Great fear came on all the Church, and upon as many as heard these things" (Acts v. 11). In the words—"*All* the churches," Jesus recognizes others beside the seven. In the next words, and by the emphatic **J**, Jesus challenges to Himself the possession of that peculiar prerogative of Deity, the reading of the thoughts of all hearts.

But the principle of retribution is not only to be exhibited to us as carried into effect on others, it is to be applied to ourselves in particular. The Lord's knowledge is with a view to this active result: xxii. 12. It is to embrace not the guilty only, but "each." *It is to affect both believers and unbelievers.* "According to works," will be the great rule of the Saviour's millennial judgment. 'Tis often so asserted. Ps. lxii. 12, 13; Matt. xvi. 27; Rom. ii. 6. No one can obtain eternal life by his works. That is the gift of God to faith. *No believer will finally be lost because of his evil works;* for electing love and the righteousness of Christ will prevent that fearful issue. But for *a thousand* years he will *reap the bitter fruits of them.* Gal. v. 19–21; vi. 7, 8; Rev. xx. 4–6.

24. "But unto you I say, the rest that are in Thyatira, as many as hold not this doctrine, who knew not Satan's 'DEPTHS' as they call (them); I cast upon you no other burthen: But what ye hold, hold fast till I arrive."

The sound portion of the Church is now addressed. What was the relative proportion of this remnant we are not informed: but amidst the sin of some, they were guiltless. How full of instruction is this case! *Here was " evil unjudged " by the angel of the Church;* there is no call from Christ, for the *healthy portion to separate itself.* There is no hint given by our Lord, that the churches in general were to excommunicate all at Thyatira for the offences of some. Jesus Himself, after blaming the angel for his negligence, bids them only hold fast to the truth they possessed already.

The whole Church was not defiled. There was a sound remnant, owned by Christ, while they and He still acknowledged the offending angel as head of the local Church. *They were not responsible for the angel's offence.* They are not instructed to depose him. They were not to leave communion, but to hold on as they stood. The Lord added "no other burthen" to them. The Lord can acknowledge the offending angel as not only a believer, but possessed of many graces.

Why were the sound disciples at Thyatira not to leave the Church? Because it was *God's assembly of believers in the name of Jesus.* As Mr. Darby has well said, "The simple answer is, They were God's churches or assemblies in the place mentioned; and they could not be left: *corruptions are no ground for leaving the church of God." Claims of the Church of England,* p. 31. "*I should think it a great sin to leave a church of God because corruptions were found in it.*" 32.

The ground of difference between the sound and the guilty was that the *former held not the false doctrine,* which our Lord is reproving. *We are responsible for the doctrines we hold.* They are the masters of our spirit and conduct, as truly as the compass is the director of the ship's course.

The guiltless ones were ignorant of the awful wickedness of the others. "They knew not the depths of Satan." How wrongly then do Christians argue, that if *there be evil in a church, and false doctrine* allowed there, *all must be regarded as aware of it,* and be dealt with as if they not only knew, *but approved of it !*

The Saviour's words introduce us into the defence set up by the deceiver and the deceived ones. If remonstrated with because of the awful wickedness of their acts, they replied—" That merely superficial Christians might think so ; but that enlightened men were not to be deterred from a right course by hard names. They had been led to *see their freedom from the law,* and would maintain it. Common Christians who halted at the surface might reprove, but it was only because it was a ' *depth* ' beyond them."

Jesus seems to employ the word in the sense of " precept." He would add no new command to those previously given. They were on right ground, and had only to maintain it still. How long ? Till death ? No ! "Till I arrive." The Saviour may come before we die ; He will so come to some. Death is not the Lord's coming to us, but our going to Him—" to *depart,* and to be with Christ."

The return of the Lord is the *object of the believer's hope,* not merely amidst the persecution of the world ; but *amidst the troubles of the Church.* The churches are not to be restored to perfection, but to pass away : a better dispensation is to come in, with Christ's return.

26. " And he that overcometh, and he that keepeth my works unto the end—I will give to him authority over the nations, and he shall tend them with a rod of iron, as the vessels of earthenware are shivered ; as Ʒ also have received from my Father."

The promises to the *conquering* believer *separate every Church that is not perfect into two classes*. While believers are regarded as *accepted* through the perfect work of Christ, *there is unity*. But, as soon as *our own works* are brought into question, as they *are* throughout these seven epistles, then *discrimination, differences, separation come in*. And these differences in present standing before Christ will, in the day of recompense, be *openly manifested by reward, reproof, or punishment*.

To the victorious is to be granted " authority over the nations." This marks the arrival of a new dispensation. *To rule* as a king *now, is exaltation out of due time :* and against it Paul warns the disciple : 1 Cor. iv. 8–14. We are to be subject to the powers above us (Rom. xiii. 1), and *to wait,* till He to whom all authority in heaven and earth is given *shall appoint us to reign*. Luke xix. 17.

The manifest reference of the passage is to Rev. xx. 4. That passage does not stand alone : see 1 Cor. vi. 2, 3. And our Lord's reference in this epistle is peculiarly valuable, as showing, that not the martyrs *only*, but the *keepers of Christ's works to the end* will have *part in the kingdom*, and *be possessed of royal power*.

A staff of *wood* will suffice for sheep, but the nations are not so gentle and useful. The chief shepherd over them and his subordinates must have a staff of iron.[1]

For behold the attitude of the nations when Christ returns ! xix. 15–21. They are assembled in arms against the Son of God ! And, *while the whole population at first will be servants of God,* yet, during the millennial reign, it will be shown again, *that the children of the renewed are not renewed*. Israel is the *only all-righteous nation :* for *to it alone is the promise made :*

---

[1] This expression, resumed xii. 5, enables us to identify the Man-child with saints of the Church.

Isa. lx. 21. The last rebellion of Gog and Magog under Satan's seducing proves that human nature is at its root the same. And the threats of God in Zech. xiv. against the nations that come not up to keep the feast of tabernacles at Jerusalem (17-19) discover to us that *not every heart* of the millennial age *will be holy.*

The meaning of the promise then clearly is, that the Gentiles will be kept in subjection, during the thousand years, not by the silken cords of love, but by the weight of superior force. Might will be on the side of right. Justice will be swift and strong.

The difference of the two natures—that *of the risen saints,* and *that of men in the flesh,* is set forth to us in the two objects compared. Flesh has its strength and its hardness. But 'tis only as the hardness of earthenware: what chance has it to withstand the swing of an iron rod? It will be shivered at the blow. There will be no recovery of delinquents then. Clay may be moulded anew; but hardware, once shattered, is not to be put together again. We are not to be passive assessors with Christ in the judgment of the dead, as some think, *but to rule the living.*

The breaking will be *benevolent.* It will be the power of holiness, destroying those who would overthrow the world's happiness. Our patience is not to be for ever, nor is power for ever to be dissevered from righteousness. When our Lord's attitude changes, so does ours.

28. "And I will give him the morning star."

How strong the seduction to evil at Thyatira, we may gather from the severe threats, and from the twofold promise. Where the enemy puts forth his power, the Lord exerts an answerable antagonist force.

Of all the promises this is, I think, the most difficult to understand.

This is the best interpretation that has been proposed. My only objection is, that it is not said, "I will make *him* a Morning Star," or, "like *the* Morning Star:" but, "I will *give* him *the* Morning Star." In what sense is Christ given to the victor?

29. "He that hath an ear, let him hear what the Spirit saith unto the churches."

The usual exhortation succeeds; but in a different place from that which it holds in the first three epistles. It now comes *after* the promises to the victor; as if the call would be listened to, not by the main body of the churches, but only by the victorious remnant.

V

SARDIS [1]

III. 1. "And unto the angel of the church in Sardis write—These things saith he that hath the seven Spirits of God, and the seven stars; I know thy works, that thou hast a name that thou livest, and art dead!"

IN the spiritual state of Sardis, as represented by its angel, we find not rampant iniquity, but slow and steady decline.

To the angel of this Church Jesus presents Himself as the Possessor of the Spirit without measure. With Him is the fountain for the supply of the thirsty: to Him should those who are sensible of their drought make application.

The angel possessed the name of life. The angel had probably acquired the fame of zeal and vigour for Christ in his early days; his name as an energetic and successful servant of the Lord Jesus had widely spread. But slow and secret decline had set in. His character was still maintained before men; but the reality was continually ebbing, till it could scarcely be said to exist. Jesus, who is full of the Spirit, and hates formalism destitute of spirit, Jesus, who hates hypocrisy and loves the full affection of the soul, is disinclined to acknowledge in him the possession of life.

---

[1] If there be any mystic meaning in the name Sardis, it is derived from שָׂרִיד—"the remnant," which occurs so conspicuously in this Epistle.

"Thou art dead."

Jesus is denying to the angel, not "*life*," but "*liveliness*." This use of the word is common enough among ourselves: as when we say, "The churches of New York are in a very *dead* state."

The expression is also applied in the New Testament, where spiritual life is not supposed to be extinct. Where Paul is speaking of the widows of the Church, he says, "Now she that is a widow indeed and desolate, trusteth in God, and continueth in supplications and prayers night and day; *but she that liveth in pleasure is dead while she liveth*" (1 Tim. v. 5, 6). Thus also our Lord calls Peter "Satan;" and His apostle describes one of the saints as a "wicked person," and the whole assembly of Corinthian believers as "carnal." Our Lord then intends, I suppose, to discover to us an *assembly of believers* with their *chief pastor grown cold and* worldly, drowsy, and *neglectful of spiritual things*.

Their worship before God was heavy, infrequent, and formal; their testimony to the world all but extinct; their graces toward each other almost vanished; their good works it were hard to find. That this is the sense, we shall see to be borne out by the exhortations which follow.

2. "Become watchful, and strengthen the things which remain that were about to die; for I have not found thy works fulfilled before my God."

The *hope* and expectation of the *Saviour's return* had faded away from the eyes of the Sardian believers in general. It ought not so to be; it was not so once. *To this expectation*, and to the attitude appropriate to such a faith, *they were to return*.

But *the call to become watchful*, is not a call to the world; *it supposes life possessed*. Jesus would have the angel to wake up in expectation of His reappearing and to keep wakeful.

"Strengthen the things which remain."

This probably refers to the celebration of ordinances and of worship which was still kept up, though languidly. The preaching was cold: the attendance at the Lord's supper thin: the prayer-meeting lifeless and formal, and few were they who were present.

They "were about to die." So cold were they, that there was talk of giving them up; so few would come, so few would take any part. *That word "about to die" expounds to us the Saviour's previous word, "dead."*

Under these circumstances, what was he to do? To establish and strengthen these things as best he might, by exhortation, and by diligence in his own person and example.

From whom then should the spirit of revival come, but from the Holy Ghost? Yet the angel was also to do his part: and here the Saviour calls for it. Hard was it, no doubt, to do even that, where there was either no answer from the saints, or but the very feeblest. But it was to be done. That he had suffered the fire to fall into the embers, without fresh fuel added, appears to have been his fault.

"For I have not found thy works fulfilled before my God." "I have not found." There was an eye silently examining the proceedings of the Church at Sardis. There was a vine-dresser, looking for fruit from the fig-tree in the garden. Here the Saviour does not complain so much of the positively bad, *as the lack of what is good.* It is not what He *does* find, which He blames, *but what He "has not found."* At length His tongue speaks of the discoveries of His eye.

Again our view of the meaning of the deadness complained of, is confirmed. *How should one wholly dead strengthen what was about to die?* How should any

F

acceptable works have proceeded from the dead ? Here the complaint is of the omission of some services, which surely were not " dead works."

We are warned by these words, that it matters little how our deeds appear to men, or to our brethren in the Church : " The Lord seeth not as man seeth ; for man looketh on the eyes (Heb.) : but the Lord looketh on the heart " (1 Sam. xvi. 7). Do we approve ourselves to Him ? is the question of questions.

3. " Remember therefore how thou hast received, and heardest, and observe, and repent."

Vainly do *we forget*, if *Christ remembers*.

Strictly taken, this appears to refer to the peculiar circumstances attendant on the preaching of the word of God there at first, and to the zeal and fervour of mind with which the truth was received by him who then was the chief pastor.

But he was also to take heed to the doctrines he had listened to. They are apt to slip away from one growing cold.

He was also to " observe." Part of what he had heard was doctrine, part was rite. Both were to be kept, or observed. Again we see, that we have not to do with words addressed to one unconverted.

" And repent ! " This call is put last : not first, as it would have been, had the angel been unconverted. It was a *partial* repentance, such as the Lord Jesus requires of backsliding saints. There was to be a change of conduct, arising from the casting off of the love of pleasure and sloth.

3. " If therefore thou shalt not watch, I will arrive over thee as a thief, and thou shalt not know what hour I arrive over thee."

The Saviour had repeated His command to be vigilant. But what if it should be disobeyed ? He evidently anticipates that it will not be kept ; therefore a threat is added. The ill consequences of such disobedience would be reaped at the Saviour's coming. In each epistle, whether for encouragement or warning, the coming of the Lord (and not death) is presented. As is the position of the disciple, so is the Saviour's return to Him joy, or grief. Do any think or say, that we millennarians " make too much " of the coming of the Lord ? That can hardly be, if we judge by these epistles, dictated by Christ Himself.

The word for " coming " is the definite one, noticed above, which describes our Redeemer as ceasing to move, because the goal at which He aims is won.

The preposition used may signify " at " or " over ; " it refers to the Lord's descent from heaven into air above the earth, and the watchful saint's ascent to Him, while the sleeper is left behind.

" And thou shalt not know what hour I arrive over thee."

The result of the Lord's coming, in proportion to the offence, may be either the being *left upon the earth* to pass through the Day of Great Tribulation, or it may be *positive punishment*.

Be it observed, that this warning found in the body of the book supposes that certain of the Church will be left upon the earth even at the last vial, which consummates the Great Tribulation. *The denial of this has arisen from neglecting that division of the Church into conquerors and conquered*, which has been so often noticed.

Observe again, that *the warning to the Church relates to our Lord's coming :* which is characteristic. The world will be unaware even of " the great and terrible *day* of the Lord," when God will take vengeance on the living sinners of earth. But the *Saviour's coming* is to precede that dread *day*, and forms the great hope of His Church. The terrible "Day" does not begin till after the prophetic portion of the book is begun : vi. 17 ; xvi. 14. This is evident also from Paul's epistles. 1 Thess. iv. describes our *Lord's advent* as the hope of His *Church.* 1 Thess. v. gives the descent of the "Day" upon the *world.* Also in 2 Thess. ii. the "*Presence*" *of Jesus* is offered to the *Church,* as her consolation against the fears of the "*Day :*" ver. 1, 3.

4. " But thou hast a few names in Sardis who defiled not their garments ; and they shall walk with me in white, for they are worthy."

Jesus does not commend anything in Sardis but the few who were unlike the rest. His expression is peculiar—" a few *names.*" This refers to numbering, or to lists. *It supposes a church-book.* "Let not a widow be put on *the list* under three-score years old " (*Greek*). 1 Tim. v. 9 ; see also Acts i. 15.

These names the angel possessed. He was keeper of the church-book ; *he admitted converts to communion, and entered their names.* Jesus, as the chief Shepherd, knows the names of all His sheep. And these simple unofficial Christians He notices with honour. Grace is not according to dignity in the Church.

In the former churches, a few were wrong ; in Sardis but a few are right. This is the only commendation ; but the Saviour can discriminate, and discern the faint sparks of good in the midst of evil. How little ought we to appeal to the doctrines or practices of the early churches, when, even in John's lifetime, there was so much of declension from true doctrine and right practice !

From these words of the Saviour we learn, that in the midst of bad examples, individual Christians may still live so as to glorify God. It will not suffice to excuse us from rebuke, that our superiors and all around us were as cold and dark as ourselves.

It is observed that Jesus does not call on the few whom He can praise, *to withdraw* from the angel, or *from the Church in Sardis. The lesson is important.* The assembly of saints is not to be left because of imperfections. But let us take heed what a Church is. *No national confederacy of congregations is a Church,* in the sense of the New Testament.

The glory of these few worthy ones is, that they " had not defiled their garments." Amidst evil examples, a few maintained pure religion and undefiled before God and the Father, and kept themselves unspotted from the world (Jas. i. 27), refusing to have a " garment spotted by the *flesh* " (Jude 23).

To these the Saviour gives a promise—" They shall walk with me in white." White is the colour of purity, in all nations. A white garment given to any, marks his justification by the giver. vi. 11. White is the colour of the raiment of angels. Matt. xxviii. 3; Mark xvi. 5; John xx. 12; Acts i. 10. White was the colour of our Lord's apparel, when, on the Mount of Transfiguration, He gave a specimen of His kingdom. Mark ix. 3. This was the colour of the robe of the Ancient of Days Himself : Dan. vii. 9.

Nor shall they be thus clothed only : they shall walk with Christ, when thus attired. This speaks their glory— they shall be priests and kings, companions of the King of kings.

These favoured companions of the Lord stand in blest contrast to the unwatchful, who are left naked below, exposed to the scornful eyes and words of the wicked.

" For they are worthy."

Remarkable words ! from which Christians in general seem disposed to shrink. But every word of God is to be received. First, then, they are not worthy *in the Romish sense :* not worthy of *eternal life.* That is the *gift of God :* Rom. vi. 23. It is the worthiness of those *justified by faith*, and set, as needy sinners, *on the ground of grace.* There is *no running for reward*, till we are delivered by another's righteousness from the curse of law : Rom. iv. 13–15.

But, after starting from the point of justification by faith, they *may at the close* be *counted worthy* of the *kingdom of God, or of the first resurrection :* Luke xx. 35 ; xxi. 36 ; 2 Thess. i. 5.

The actions of these were right : God would requite them with answerable honour. As they had kept their spiritual garments unspotted, so, when Christ reigns, they shall, as the sign and recompense of their holiness, walk in robes of white on high.

We may also say that the *worthiness of these favoured ones is, at the root, due to grace.* But when justice is to apportion reward to each according to his works, *worthiness is not traced beyond the acts* of the saint himself.

5. " He that overcometh thus shall be clothed in white raiment ; and I will not blot out his name out of the book of life, and I will confess his name before my Father, and before his angels. 6. He that hath an ear, let him hear what the Spirit saith unto the churches."

If we may regard the promises to the conquerors in each Church as a divine counterpoise to the temptations locally besetting them, then one of the temptations by which the saints of Sardis were overcome, was a love of dress.

" And I will not blot his name out of the Book of Life."

Hence arises a difficulty. It is implied in the promise to the conqueror, that the believer who is conquered shall be blotted out of the book of life. But those not found in the book of life are, at the general judgment, cast into the lake of fire.

How is this difficulty solved ?

I have no better solution to propose, than that there

may be a *temporary* blotting out of the name of the believer from the book of life, *during the period of reward enjoyed by the others ;* and a restoration of the name, ere the final award settles the position of each for ever : xx. 15. It seems certain, (1) that the Book of Life of the Apocalypse is but one. (2) And, that the name be blotted out, *must first be enrolled there,* is also certain. A like difficulty has pressed us in the epistle to Smyrna, and a like solution was offered there. ii. 11. The insertion of the name there, was of God's sovereignty at the first. But may not the unsaintly lives of God's saints make God appear to act unlike Himself ? though at last His gifts and callings be unrepented of.

"And I will confess his name before my Father and His angels."

VI

PHILADELPHIA

7. "And to the angel of the church in Philadelphia write; These things saith He that is holy—He that is true—He that hath the key of David, that openeth, and none will shut : [1] that shutteth, and none openeth."

By "the key of David" is to be understood, as a part of its meaning, the *Saviour's power of raising the dead*. Thus it runs parallel with our Lord's words in the first vision : "I have the *keys of Hades* and of *Death*" (i. 18).

But the opening of Hades is in order to the kingdom of Messiah, as Rev. xx. 4–6 shows. Then will David attain his promises. In coincidence with this, our Lord gave to Peter first, and to the other apostles afterwards, "the keys of the kingdom of heaven." They had power to exclude from millennial glory any offender of the Church; or again, on his repentance, to take off the exclusion : [2] 1 Cor. v.; 2 Cor. ii.

Jesus, then, as possessor of the power of resurrection, holds the key to all the promises made to David, and can admit any to them, or exclude any from them.

"He that openeth, and none will shut."

Jesus, in the vision to the churches is a priest. Now,

---

[1] Κλείσει, Treg.

[2] The Pope, or bishop of Rome, is no apostle, nor has he an apostle's power. *That Peter was ever at Rome has not been proved*. He was apostle "of the *circumcision*" (Gal. ii.), not of the Gentiles.

to open and shut was part of the priest's office. Lev. xiii. 4, 5 ; xiv. 38.

If then the Saviour shall pronounce any clean, He shall be no longer detained in custody. His opening of the door none shall gainsay, or counteract.

But Jesus is also steward of all the palace of David. Under the hand of this Joseph are all the king's prisoners. If He open the prison, none shall detain them. "That thou mayest say to the prisoners, 'Go forth ; ' to them that are in darkness, ' Show yourselves ' " (Isa. xlix. 9, 10). " The gates of Hades shall not prevail."

Jesus opens, too, the *temple above, and the gates* of the *New Jerusalem ;* as he goes on to intimate.

He opens Hades also, and out of the Abyss come forth the tormenting locusts : ix.

" That shuts, and none openeth."

Both powers are necessary, both are possessed in unchallenged dominion, by Jesus. Thus Jesus also shuts up in the abyss or bottomless pit, for a thousand years, Satan the great adversary, that during the millennial bliss he may not deceive the nations. So, at the close, the pit is opened and again he comes forth. While the pit's mouth is shut, there is no escape. When Christ shuts, none can open : Isa. xxiv. 22.

Jesus must open the *temple of heaven to His saints.* The Man-child is caught up to the throne of God. But there their enemies meet them, and seek to enter. Therefore, Jesus, in His character as Michael, shuts His people *in*, and shuts their foes *out*. The *opening* introduces *friends :* the *shutting* keeps out *foes*. See Ps. xci.

8. " I know Thy works : behold I have set ('given,' literally) before thee an open door, which none can shut : for thou hast a little strength, and keptest My word, and deniedst not My name."

" Which none can shut : "—

Though many were attempting it, as the next verse tells us. After Paul had spoken with joy of the " great door and effectual " which God had opened to him, he adds, " and there are many adversaries." "*And* "— we should expect, " *but*." But the Apostle doubtless considered the " many adversaries " as almost the necessary and to be expected consequence of the opened door. Where Christ by His Spirit moves mightily, Satan as powerfully bestirs himself.

This is a gracious word, full of encouragement to servants of Christ, engaged in labour for Him. (1) It seems to say, that opportunities for service are in general *granted in proportion to diligence*. For it is added " for thou hast a little strength." (2) It teaches us also, that let men and devils rage as they may, Christ will not suffer a door to be shut which He has opened to His servant, till his service there is over. *Christ* opens, *Christ* shuts.

Remember, believers, that *our opened door of present privileges is of Christ's bestowal*. He speaks of it as *a great gift on His part*. Let us duly value it, and give thanks because of it ! There are wicked men, who are seeking every opportunity to shut it ; and the marvel is, that, in a world of foes like this, it still stands open.

" For thou hast a little strength."

The angel and the Church under his care were possessed of some power, both of fortitude in bearing for Christ, and of activity in service, toward the Church and the world.

This is the blessed superiority which they possessed above Sardis. There, there was total inactivity : here both life and some degree of spiritual power. It was, however, a *little* measure only : and thus a gentle, tacit reproof is conveyed. We should be like Abraham, " strong in faith, giving glory to God."

" Thou keptest my word."

"If ye love me, keep my commandments." This they did: and the love they felt led to service.

"And deniedst not My name."

'Tis not unlikely that the angel was especially called on to own the name of Christ as connected with "David"—his coming *kingly authority over the earth*. This was the point at which the rulers of the earth felt most sensitively the religion of Jesus. This was the point which the Saviour had to testify, in His "good confession" before Pontius Pilate.

This hints to us, further, the character of the temptation which is about to overtake the world: it will be an attempt to set up another king, as Jesus' superior. Persecution the most fierce will lend its aid to seduction the most bewitching. That saying, "Thou deniedst not *my name*," gives force and vivid meaning to the word which four times occurs in the prophetic part, concerning Antichrist, "That none might buy or sell save he that had the mark, or the NAME of the Wild Beast, or the number of his NAME" (xiii. 17; xiv. 11).

9. "Behold I make (those) of the synagogue of Satan who say they are Jews, and are not, but lie; behold I will make them to come near and worship before thy feet; and know that J loved Thee."

These deniers of Messiah, the Son of David, the hope of the fathers, had lost the spirit of the Jew altogether. God had rent away from them the temple, and cast them out of their land, for their sin. There remained, therefore, only their synagogue worship, devoid of priest or sacrifice. This Jehovah would not own. They were on Satan's side: those who are not friends of Christ are against Him.

The door is shut against Israel throughout this dispensation. "Not my people," is the true word concerning them. Vainly do they boast of the door as open still. "They lie."

The Redeemer then states the issue as regards these enemies. "I will make them to come and worship before thy feet."

The very nation to which promises so lofty are made will have itself to stoop, in the presence of others *as far loftier than themselves* as they are above the Gentiles. "The last shall be first." This promise then will receive its *accomplishment at the first resurrection;* after God's love, which now flows in secret towards His children, shall then display itself openly " at the manifestation of the sons of God."

As of Christ in that day it is said, "To me every knee shall bow, and every tongue shall swear," so shall part of the radiance which falls upon the King of kings be reflected on His subordinates : Ps. lxxii. 9 ; cx. 1 ; Phil. ii. 10.

After having boldly, and with blasphemies, denied Jesus to be Messiah, David's Son, and derided believers in Christ as followers of a deceiver, when at length Jesus sits upon His throne, these Jews shall with awe and dismay confess Him Lord ; and His people the true and worthy rulers of earth.

"And know that **I** loved **Thee**."

The " I " and " Thee " are both emphatic in the original. They will find themselves excluded from the kingdom which they boasted as theirs ; they will perceive a nobler people of God, a more excellent order of priests and kings than those known to Israel, and the better covenant established on better promises. The Lord's promise to these saints is not, however, a word, as it is generally said, " *to all true Christians.*" No ; 'tis the result of a special testimony, not borne by all believers.

10. " Because thou keptest the word of my patience, **I** also will keep **Thee** out of the hour of the temptation that is about to come upon the whole habitable earth, to try the dwellers on the earth."

Christ is patient, "expecting" the Father's hour, "till His enemies be made His footstool." There is then a "word" or doctrine, which takes up and asserts that waiting attitude of the Saviour. The angel of Philadelphia was patiently expecting the coming of the Lord from heaven : 1 Thess. i. 3 ; 2 Thess. iii. 5 ; Rev. i. 9.

"*I* also, will keep thee out of the hour of the temptation."

This is distinct from the promise to the conqueror, given at the close. Herein we find a clear answer to the question sometimes tauntingly put—" What is the use of prophecy ? " We might answer, that it has great present advantages, as enabling us to see our true position and calling, and to keep clear of many mistakes and delusions. But an object of most especial importance is here shown to be attained. The holders of the truth in this matter will be preserved from that day of darkness, trial, and peril which is now nigh at hand.

While those ignorant of it are painting vain pictures of the happiness of earth close at hand, to appear under the ordinary operation of the causes and agencies now at work, the student of prophecy knows that *this expectation will never be realized;* nay, that evil is about to expand itself to prodigious and overwhelming magnitude ; and that it will be *girt with supernatural power.* The Lord, in vengeance for His truth rejected, is about to send on the earth an energy of delusion ; that men should believe a lie, which seals all who receive it to utter damnation. In belief of this, Jesus bids His disciples, " Watch therefore, and pray always, that they may be *accounted worthy to escape all these things that are about to come to pass*" (Luke xxi. 36).

We must either *suffer from the world now*, or *with the world by and by.* But, if faithful testimony brings present trial, it keeps us out of being mixed up with the judgment coming on the world.

Now this is *not true of all Christians:* some then will be left to pass through that hour of temptation, for the *promise does not encompass them.*

"The hour of temptation."

The world, the flesh, and the devil seem to be very potent and tempting now. In what, then, will the superior force of temptation in that day consist?

In the false doctrine then abroad, identified with the person of the false Messiah, who is backed by miraculous powers. In the enthusiasm of all the lost in his behalf : in the rage of Satan, cast out of heaven, and furious, because his time is short. In the persecution which requires worship of the false Messiah, or death. But to worship, is damnation! And God's wrath is then descending on the world, in streams of intense bitterness.

This "hour of temptation" is part of "the Great and Terrible Day of the Lord." It is an "hour," a brief, definite season, of three years and a half, closing with the manifestation of the Lord Jesus in the clouds.

What is its *extent* of power?

"It is about to come upon the whole habitable earth."

Here, many fall off from the breadth of the Redeemer's word. "All the world" may (says one) "either denote the whole world : or the whole Roman Empire, *or a large district of country, or the land of Judea!*"

No! It will embrace *every inhabited country.*

Both Jews and Gentiles will be caught in this grand net of Satan's.

What is the *purpose* of this awful temptation?

"To try the dwellers on the earth."

The design of this hour of temptation, is to try or test the dwellers on the earth. The earth's inhabitants are becoming more and more proud of themselves, and boast more and more of their goodness and progress. The Church itself is become boastful of its deeds. These fair appearances then, these high thoughts shall be tested. The reality of man's heart, both in relation to God and his fellows, shall be shown. Its rottenness, its poison shall be broadly displayed. The world was once tested by the appearance of Jesus, and His manifestation of the truth. And then the fair show of the Jewish religiousness was discovered to be but dust and ashes. And the injustice of the Gentile rulers of the world was fully laid open, by Pilate's condemnation and crucifixion of Christ Jesus. But there is yet to be a testing, both of the Gentile and the Jew, by the appearing of the false Christ, and his deceits.

God means to put all men to the test. Are they such as He represents them, blind, at enmity with Himself, loving darkness rather than light? He will prove His words by a solemn experiment. With *His truth* and *Satan's lie* both before them, men will prefer the devil's deceit, and blaspheme God and His Christ: Luke ii. 34, 35.

The parties tried are "the dwellers upon earth." They are men whose hearts are where their bodies are. Their home is here, here their treasures, their honour, their pleasures.

" But if the trial be coming upon the whole world, how would Philadelphia, situated in so well known a part of the world, escape it ? '

It is not promised that Philadelphia should escape it. It is not said that the *city* should be delivered, but the *Angel only, and those who occupied the same moral position with him.*

Jesus would remove from the earth these watchful saints, either by death, or by rapture without tasting death. As the whole habitable earth shall be caught in the snare, so the deliverance would be effected by the Lord's taking them to another sphere—the heaven, which is then delivered from the foe.

The man-child is caught up to God and His throne.[1]

Sardis and Philadelphia are contrasts. Sardis is the unwatchful saint, on whom the Lord comes as a thief. Philadelphia, the watchful believer taken, like Enoch, to his Lord's presence with joy. And Laodicea represents, I suppose, the state of the Church, *after the salt that kept its taste is removed*.

This promise, then, has yet to be accomplished. But, if so, it follows that churches are still recognized before God, as His witnesses on earth. Till the rapture has borne away the waiting ones of Christ to His presence, Jesus still occupies His post as the Priest of the Sanctuary, overseeing the lamps of heaven.

11. "I am coming quickly: hold fast what thou hast, that none take thy crown."

In those words, " I am coming quickly," is conveyed to us an intimation of the way in which the saint will be taken out of the Great Day of the Lord, and its hour of dread temptation. The apostle Paul sets before the Thessalonian believers the Presence of the Lord Jesus after His descent from heaven, as the point to which they would be lifted, and so be delivered out of the storm below: 2 Thess. ii. 1. The word " Behold " is rightly omitted in this verse, as we gather from internal evidence, as well as external.[2] For the coming spoken of is the thief-like secret one, in which the waiting believer is rapt to his Lord, but no hand is seen.

Jesus encourages His saints to hold out, by a prospect of the brevity of the struggle.

---

[1] There is a lower place of safety on earth for the believing remnant of the Jews. It is " the wilderness," a place not inhabited, Rev. xii. 6. Hence the employment, not of the terms γη, or κοσμος, but οικουμενη, " *habitable* earth."

[2] Ιδου omitted by the critical editions.

"Hold fast that thou hast."

Hold fast the faith, and a good conscience, which some, losing, have made shipwreck. Hold fast patience, hope, right practice. This is the contrary to the Saviour's cry, ' Repent ! ' The one is the red flag, or the signal of danger ; and the call to stop, and to back the engine. The other is the green flag, which bids the engineer proceed with his train fearlessly.

"That none take thy crown."

What crown is intended ? It is not specified, whether it be the crown of "life," of "righteousness," or of "glory." But it was one conditionally destined for the then presiding pastor of Philadelphia. The crown means not a bare salvation : it is not something designed for all believers. Are all believers diligent ? Have all Christians nothing to do, but to hold fast what they possess ? The other epistles utter no uncertain sound on this point.

It might be *lost by remissness*. Let none grow slack, as if he had so long walked in Christ's ways that he could not fall ! Perseverance in service is essential to reward. We may lose by misconduct, a glory we had else won. 2 John 8.

There are *degrees of glory:* some will have one crown, some more than one, and some be without any, having lost it by misconduct. What is lost by one, is handed over to another who is worthy. Thus, the talent taken from the slothful servant is given to the possessor of ten talents.

12. "Him that overcometh will I make a pillar in the temple of my God, and he shall go out no more : and I will write upon him the name of my God, and the name of the city of my God, the new Jerusalem, which is coming down out of the heaven from my God, and (I will write upon him) my new name."

We have now arrived at the promise to the conqueror. On this, Hengstenberg remarks, "It is spoken, not of some peculiarly distinguished Christians, but of Christians generally (for to be a *conqueror and to be a Christian is the same thing*)." In these words behold one of those false assumptions, which have introduced such vagueness into this and other portions of God's word. No! Every Christian must indeed be a conqueror at last, as compared with the *world*. But the conquerors here spoken of are conquerors as compared with some of their *fellow-Christians*. The Saviour in the other views which He gives of His coming, divides His disciples into the watchful and the sleepers : Matt. xxiv. 40–51; Mark xiii. 32–37; Luke xii. 31–48. To each of these He foretells a different recompense.

A pillar is used either to (1) support parts of a building, or (2) for ornament. The promise refers to the latter use of a pillar. Observe first, how the figure of a building runs through the whole. We have *a door, a temple, a pillar, a key, a city*. Amid some ancient ruins in the city of Philadelphia, " one solitary pillar has often been noticed, as reminding beholders of the remarkable words in the Apocalypse—' Him that overcometh will I make a *pillar* in the temple of my God.' " *Kitto's Cycl.*

The manifest reference therefore is to the remarkable pillars of Solomon's temple, which were evidently considered masterpieces of art and of the artist, so special is the account given to us of them. 1 Kings vii. 13–22; 2 Chron. iii. 15–17.

" He shall go out no more."

His reward, once begun, shall receive no after-check, or conclusion. Steadfastness in *duty* shall be recompensed by steadfastness in *glory*.

The names of the two pillars of Solomon were JACHIN —[" He shall *establish* "]—and Boaz—[" In strength "]. This shall be truly fulfilled on high, in resurrection.

" And I will write on him the name of my God."

Jesus came to discover to us the new name of

God, as "*Father, Son, and Holy Spirit:*" Matt. xxviii.

This name Jesus would inscribe on the conqueror. As the high priest carried on his mitre, graven "like the engraving of a signet, HOLINESS TO THE LORD," so should the conqueror wear the name of the God whom he had devotedly served.

"The name of *my* God."

Jesus, though He is addressing His servants, never forgets the subordinate place He now holds, as the servant of the Father. Four times in this verse He speaks of "my God." This is especially beautiful here, as He is speaking in the character of the Son of David to whom the kingdom is promised. Antichrist comes in his own name, and blasphemes the true God. *Jesus reverently confesses the name of His Father as His Commissioner*, and as appointing Him Priest and King.

"And the name of the city of my God."

Why should it not be a literal city? All that Barnes says against it is, "It is a departure from all proper laws of interpretation, to explain this *literally*, as if a city should be actually let down from heaven." What proper law of interpretation this construction violates is left, as well it may be, in silence. The one proper law is, to take each statement literally, which is not absurd, or does not involve a contradiction. Is there anything absurd in the supposition of God's letting down a city from above? Anything more absurd than in the casting down of a mountain, or a star from the sky? "And equally so [improper] to infer from this passage and the others of similar import in this book, that a city will be literally *reared* for the residence of the saints. If the passage proves anything on either of these points, it is that a *great and splendid city*, such as that described in ch. xxi., will *literally come down from heaven*." Just so! "But who can believe that?" *A great many!* Almost as many as believe that God will create new heavens and a new *earth*, and that we shall rise again in our *bodies*.

Ere yet the new city is entered, the conqueror will be distinguished, as one evidently enrolled its citizen.

"The New Jerusalem, which is coming down out of the heaven from my God."

Our city is, like Christ, as yet hid with God; to be brought forth, in all its beauty, in millennial days. *The tense of the participle here bears witness against its being applied to the Church.* The *Church has* come down from God long ago: *it does not habitually come down from Him*; nor has it, at some future day, to descend. Believers will have to ascend to God; but that is another thing.

"And (I will write upon him) my new name."

The columns of victorious cities are oft inscribed with the names of conquerors, or of those to whom they were dedicated. In this case the conqueror should take the name of the God under whose commands he fought; of the city to which he was promoted to become a citizen; and of the Captain under whom he conquered.

So solemnly important to all is this, that every one in possession of an ear is anew invited to attend to this message of Christ and of the Holy Ghost. Let us not receive listlessly these words; they are not the words of men. Has it not been for want of some such pondering, that it is currently supposed, "that the concluding promises generally unfold only what is *common to all Christians—eternal blessedness?*"

VII

LAODICEA

14. "And unto the angel of the church in Laodicea, write; These things saith the Amen, the faithful and true Witness, the beginning of the creation of God."

THE titles by which our Lord introduces Himself to this angel are not those found in the first vision : as if to warn us that He was retreating farther and farther from his original position, as the state of the churches became more and more fallen, and unlike its original standing.

Jesus is "the Faithful and True Witness."

As there were two opposite opinions about the state of the angel and Church : the one, their own, which was very flattering ; the other, that of the Lord ; Jesus first establishes His own character, as the fulcrum to overturn their unfounded opinion of themselves.

"The beginning of the creation of God."

He is "the Beginning of Creation," as its First Cause. This attribute John has more than once assigned to Jesus. John i. 1–3. There is probably a reference to Jesus' previous words—"I am *Alpha and Omega*, saith the Lord, which was, and is, and is to come, the Almighty" (i. 8). And again—"I am Alpha and Omega, the first and the last, *beginning and end*:" xxii. 13. These titles, as we have seen, import Deity. There is probably a further reference to Prov. viii. There Jesus speaks as Wisdom, the Wisdom of God. "Jehovah possessed me THE BEGINNING OF HIS WAY (Heb.)

BEFORE HIS WORKS of OLD. *I was set up from everlasting, from the beginning, or ever the earth was*" (22, 23). Here the Saviour's being the beginning of God's way, is not meant to deny His creative power, for He is declared to be in existence *before* God's works. But the chief passage bearing on the question is the following—" His dear Son—who is the image of the invisible God, *the first-born of every creature.*" Does not that imply, then, that Jesus is a creature, though the first-produced creature ? No ! " *For by Him were all things created,* that are in heaven, and that are in earth, visible and invisible, whether they be thrones or dominions, or principalities or powers : *all things were created by Him, and for Him, and He is* BEFORE ALL THINGS, and by Him all things consist (are upheld). And He is the head of the body the Church : who is *the beginning*, the First-born from the dead : " Col. i. 16–18. This is not only full to the point, but it seems definitely to be pointed at by our Lord, as that is the epistle, the only one in which *Laodicea* is mentioned, and that four times. On the second occasion the Holy Spirit directs that the epistle to the Colossians should be read in Laodicea.

15. " I know thy works, that thou art neither cold nor hot. I would thou wert cold or hot. 16. Thus, because thou art lukewarm, and neither cold nor hot, I am about to [1] vomit thee out of my mouth."

At this point I have to correct an error, which runs through all the commentaries on this epistle which I have seen. Because Jesus expresses so much displeasure against this angel and Church, it is assumed that therefore, he, and those in communion, were *unconverted and hypocrites*.[2] This cannot be. The churches

[1] Μέλλω.

[2] The Copyists, led by examples in common speech, wrote " the church *of the Laodiceans.*" But Christ bid John write to " the church *in Laodicea.*" Not all Laodicea were believers.

addressed by Christ were assemblies of believers : and, therefore, of converted men. There was small temptation in those days to be a hypocritical Christian. The angel must have been one appointed with Christ's sanction ; else he had not been a star on Christ's hand. The disciples in Laodicea must have held the fundamental principle, that the Church is an assembly of the callers on Christ's name, effectually-called saints ; or else Jesus could not have recognized them as lamps in the holy place above. The light is quenched, as soon as a Church is merely nominal—the assembly of those born into fellowship. And, long ere that took place, the lamp would have been removed from the sanctuary, as we see proved by our Lord's words to Ephesus. It throws us, therefore, on a wrong tack, to speak of this and Sardis as " the *professing* Church," or " Christendom."

Jesus knew the works of the angel ; and the works are an infallible index to the state : as surely as the action of any substance upon those with which it is brought into contact, is a sure index to its internal structure.

" Thou art neither cold nor hot."

That which is alive, is more or less warm. That which is dead, is cold.

The angel of Laodicea was in neither state : but in one between both. He was *not cold :* therefore he was not *dead in sins*, one who never had been made alive of God. He was not hot, however. He had greatly left His first love. The world's atmosphere is a wintry one, and they who adventure into it voluntarily are almost sure to grow colder. Then the Christian becomes like a bar of iron, once heated to redness, but withdrawn from the fire, and left on the anvil. Its light and warmth grow less and less continually. It should not be so. The person and glories of Christ, as they were fitted to awaken holy affection at the first, so are they capable of continuing the warmth of love to the end. Are we not, very frequently, deficient in warmth, because our religion is rather a bundle of orthodox *doctrines, than attachment to a person ?*

" I would thou wert cold or hot."

If they were fervent of spirit, the Lord would gladly own them as His friends ; if cold, He should know them as the worldly. But now they occupied an intermediate position. What was to be done with them ? How were they to be classified ? Their coldness prevented their being regarded as true friends ; their warmth forbade their being treated as enemies.

"Thus because thou art lukewarm."

Any trifle will keep away such a one from prayer, the Lord's Supper, the preaching of the Word of God ; there is no zeal for the truth, or for the glory of God ; Christian holiness is too " strait-laced," and self-denial impossible. Such a one is satisfied easily. " If I can but get to heaven, that is enough for me ! " He will, in the meanwhile, grasp as much of the world as he can, without wholly losing caste among his fellow-believers.

This bears a sad testimony to the world ; it tells a tale, which the world understands at once, of the little delight that is found in Christ ; it teaches them to believe that the religion whose claims are so easily set aside cannot be of any great authority or value.

" I am about to vomit thee out of my mouth."

Lukewarm water acts as an emetic. Jesus was disgusted at their state, as a man loathes the taste of water neither hot nor cold. The consequence would be their rejection by Him. This does not suppose that they would be finally lost. It teaches us how displeased was Jesus at the witness they gave of Him since they believed ; and that He would in consequence cast them down from that place of testimony. Here is brought before our eyes, as near to be accomplished, that which the Saviour spoke as a hypothesis, in the Sermon on the Mount. After appointing His disciples to give light to the world, and to check its corruption as salt, He inquires, what would be the result, if the salt should lose its taste ? He decides that in that case it would be by the master cast out of his house, and then be trodden underfoot of men.

The last view of the Church then is not the most glorious. It is not seen as a gallant warrior returned victorious from the fight ; but as a half-hearted friend disowned for ingratitude. Is it any wonder that the Apocalypse never was, nor ever will be popular ? How should it find favour in the eyes of those who, with trumpet-tongue, are proclaiming the greatness and splendid acts of the churches, and foretelling its victories yet close at hand ?

17. "Because thou sayest, ' I am rich, and have grown rich, and have need of nothing,' and knowest not that Thou art the wretched one, and the pitiable one, and poor and blind and naked."

They estimated themselves the most highly of all the seven churches. Boastfulness and lukewarmness are coupled together. High thoughts of itself, with judgment close at hand ? Jesus spares it not ; to humble, if possible, the self-conceit breathed in these words.

The lowly walk humbly and safely : but a haughty spirit is near a fall. There is consolation to many in this view of things : we have not yet arrived at Laodicea's state, if we are not vaingloriously boastful.

" I am rich, and have grown rich."

These are not two expressions signifying exactly the same thing.

The first exhibits only the *fact* of present wealth. " I am rich." The second notices the *mode* of becoming so. A man may become rich by inheritance, or by bequest. The second phrase, I suppose, is designed to inform us that the angel and Church had become rich by their exertions : they sought for wealth, and found it.

But how are we to understand its boast of riches ? Are they to be taken literally or spiritually ? Our maxim is, that the literal is the true sense, if it be not inadmissible. Here it falls in perfectly with all the conditions. That then is the sense.

For thus we have explained to us the secret source of the spiritual coldness of the Church. Jesus had declared that it is impossible to serve both God and mammon. So different are the masters, so opposite the commands, that service to the one is a fraud on the other. The heart cannot be devoted to two of characters so contrasted; the man, at length, struggle as he may, will become the servant of one, or of the other. This truth the angel believed not ; and the fatal consequences to himself and the Church are apparent. His heart was more and more drawn away from Christ. " They that wish to be rich (*Greek*) fall into temptation and a snare, and into many foolish and hurtful lusts, which drown men in destruction and perdition. For the love of money is a root of all evil, which while some coveted they erred from the faith, and pierced themselves through with many sorrows. *But thou, O man of God, flee these things* " (*Greek*) (1 Tim. vi. 9-11). The example of the chief pastor spread far, and with sad weight. It may remind us of what Cyprian says of his times, A.D. 250. " Forgetting what believers did in the times of the apostles, and what they should always be doing, Christians have laboured, with insatiable desire, to increase their earthly possessions. *Many of the bishops, who, by precept and example, should have guided others, have neglected the divine calling to engage in worldly concerns* : " *Neander's Church History*, i. 181.

Riches were the law's promise : but Jesus lifts a woe against them now : Luke vi. 24 ; Matt. xix. 23, 24.

"And have need of nothing."

Higher and higher rises the boast! How great the self-sufficiency, that could say so! How debased the soul, which riches and the earth could fill! "Need of *nothing!*" "Give me but a continuance of my lot on earth, and it suffices me!" "The resurrection of the just," the return of the Lord Jesus, the kingdom of glory were unsought and forgotten!

Is not the world's spirit of boastfulness creeping into the Church in our day? Do we not talk largely and self-complacently of our "unparalleled efforts for translating and diffusing the Scriptures, and extending the knowledge of Christ?" 'Tis a bad sign.

"And knowest not, that **Thou** art the wretched one."

The contrast between their thoughts of themselves, and the Lord's estimate of them, is broadly and sharply brought out. They *fancied*—Christ *knew*.

"Thou art the wretched One."

How direct the assertion enforced on the angel! As Nathan said to David, "Thou art the man."

We usually apply the term "wretched" to one who is in misery, and is conscious of it. Here, of course, the consciousness does not exist. Wherein then did the wretchedness consist? 1. In the *low spiritual state*. 2. In the *future loss of the millennial kingdom*. Then, at all events, he would see his sad state, in his being thrust out among the excluded.

"And the pitiable."

The angel and Church considered their condition as worthy to be *envied*. Jesus tells them it was worthy of *pity*.

"And poor, and blind, and naked."

These express their three great spiritual wants. They made three boasts. Jesus asserts three great defects.

1. They were "poor." Not as regarded this world:

they were rich, as men count riches. But there are riches before God, and here they were poor. Luke xii. 21.

2. " And blind." This must, of course, be understood of spiritual blindness. Natural blindness is no just subject of rebuke. If suffering under this affliction, a heart full of earth would not have said, " I have need of nothing." The wealth of this world dims the spiritual eye.

Therefore, Jesus, after warning disciples against laying up treasure here below, proceeds to tell us that if our eye be single, our whole body shall be full of light.

3. They were " naked."

Pride of dress is a frequent symptom of purse-pride. The wool of Laodicea was in high repute.—Wetstein. But while their robes were costly in texture and splendid in dye, they were naked before God. They spent all upon themselves. They clothed not the poor. Their selfish expenditure was a spiritual nakedness. It would appear at length to their dismay, when they stood before Christ.

18. " I counsel thee to buy of me gold refined out of the fire, that thou mayest be rich : and white raiment, that thou mayest be clothed and that the shame of thy nakedness be not manifested : and eyesalve, to anoint thine eyes, that thou mayest see."

Jesus might *command :* He *counsels* in grace. He addresses the angel with a view of his best interests. His state was not beyond remedy, if he would but listen to his best friend, so much overlooked.

His poverty might be displaced by wealth, if he would but buy gold of Christ.

Buying is the exchange of one commodity for another. He might exchange the false mammon for the true. He might give up his riches before men, to become rich before God. Luke xii. 33.

This last citation is a word, not to the ungodly and unconverted, but to one of Christ's "little flock." Again, then, we learn that Jesus is addressing believers. He directs them away from themselves, and the world's riches: they are to apply to *Himself*.

What is the gold which Christ proposes?

By this is meant faith. "That the trial of your *faith*, being much more precious than of *gold which perisheth yet is tried by fire (Greek)*, might be found unto praise and honour and glory at the revelation of Jesus Christ" (1 Pet. i. 7; James ii. 5).

In speaking of this gold as "refined out of the fire," Jesus seems to observe that faith of the kind He spoke of would be made perfect by suffering, losing its dross in the furnace, and glistening in the day of His appearing.

"And white raiment."

Jesus is here urging on believers the doing of good works. They were already clad with *Christ's righteousness*. But theirs was an inactive faith. Jesus therefore counsels first the procuring of active faith, purged of all dross, and working by love. They were spiritually naked. They were trees without fruit. Jesus therefore urges on them the application to Himself, that by His grace they might do good works, *the fruits of faith in His righteousness*. That this is the meaning, is proved by xix. 8. "To her was granted, that she should be arrayed in fine linen, clean and white: *for the fine linen is the righteous acts of the saints*" (*Greek*).

Their dresses were probably of showy colours, scarlet or purple. But Christ designed that they should hereafter be clad in white.

"That thou mayest be clothed, and that the shame of thy nakedness be not manifested."

From our Lord's words we gather, that those will be ashamed before Him at His appearing, who with abundant means and opportunities to do good, never did it.

"And eyesalve to anoint thine eyes, that thou mayest see."

The application of our Lord's words to those of Laodicea was peculiarly close, as wool formed its staple commodity, and its eyesalve was in special repute. Wetstein has extracted the following words from Galen, the well-known writer on medicine—"The best ointment of nard was formerly prepared in Laodicea alone of all the cities of Asia."

Pride blinded their eyes. Jesus tacitly proposes the Holy Spirit, as the great Enlightener. He who had anointed the blind man's eyes with clay, could by His Spirit confer spiritual vision. They had lost sight of the Saviour's millennial kingdom, or they would not have sought riches : much less would they have boasted of that which is an obstacle to entering the kingdom. They, too, are justly accused of blindness, who had lost sight of that first of all spiritual truths—the creature's dependence for *all* good upon the Great Creator. And if this be true of angels unfallen, how much more of man the sinner! How can such a one ever stand before God, save as the constant receiver and suppliant ?

19. "As many as I love, ✝ rebuke and chasten : be zealous therefore and repent ! "

As Jesus loved the angel and Church, they were neither unconverted nor hypocrites.[1] He addressed them with exhortations, that they might not think their case desperate, and so go on in what was evil, with a more assured step. This admonition, severe as it was, was the effect of love. By sharp words He sought to rouse from their sleep. If words were not enough, Jesus

[1] "But did not Jesus love the rich young man, and was not he lost ?" Mark x. 21. That he will not obtain the *kingdom*, is clear. But Jesus does not shut him out of *eternal life*.

uses deeds. He chastens. Heb. xii. 5, 6 ; 1 Cor. xi. 32 ; 2 Sam. vii. 14.

The " I " is emphatic. It is designed to hint to us, that it is often quite otherwise with mistaken human love. It conceals, denies, pampers the faults of those it loves : till their wickedness attains fearful dimensions. So did David deal with his sons, Absalom and Adonijah ; and both requited him with rebellion. Fathers and mothers ! learn a lesson from Christ ! His love is not blind to what is evil. He seeks in grace to remove it.

Rebuke is not unfrequently the result of enmity, and it outsteps all measure of truth. Not so our Lord's.

" Be zealous therefore : and repent ! "

They were to become fervent in love and zeal ! " But is that in a man's power ? " Not directly. But a consideration of the truths which woke his first love would be the way to effect it. Those were no transient circumstances ; but deep truths fitted to call forth love in its fullness.

They were to repent ! To see and own the wants and defects pointed out, and to seek to remedy them in the manner required by the Lord. The love of the world had driven out the love of Christ. They were to put aside the things which had cooled them, and by prayer, study of God's word, and meditation, to recall those truths, which would make the fire of zeal burn anew. The thorns had choked the good seed. They must pluck up the lusts of other things which had entered in, and give the good seed room.

20. "Behold I stand at the door, and knock : if any hear my voice, and open the door, I will enter in to him, and sup with him, and he shall sup with me."

This is not, as it is usually regarded, the Saviour's call to the unconverted. Jesus displays His grace to His backslidden people. It was their duty to seek and call on Him. But finding them cool, He seeks to arouse them. He represents Himself as one attempting to obtain an entrance at a friend's house. He has knocked once and again, and waits patiently the result of the appeal. He is standing : a position of unrest. He ought to obtain a seat speedily within the house.

He knocks. He will not force an entrance. He appeals to the heart of the owner. Ch. v. 1, 2. Also Luke xii. 35–38.

Jesus now represents Himself as nearer than in any previous epistle. He is not " coming quickly ; " He is already " at the door."

Have we not here a hint of one of the forms of temptation, to which this wealthy angel and Church were captives ? Were they not given to worldly feasting ? Were they not probably givers of expensive suppers ? Were they not faring sumptuously, and collecting at entertainments the great and the rich ? If they would admit Christ to their tables, He would dictate to them a better hospitality. Their own entertainments would receive their return and requital in this life. Jesus would teach them to invite the poor and the outcast, who could not recompense them : that they might be recompensed at the resurrection of the just : Luke xiv. 12–14.

21. " To him that overcometh will I grant to sit with me on my throne, even as $\mathfrak{I}$ also overcame, and sat down with my Father on His Throne. 22. He that hath an ear, let him hear what the Spirit saith unto the churches."

Every Church is called to wrestle with some form of evil. This Church Satan seems content to leave to itself. There was no persecution—no rampant outbreak of false doctrine ; it was already in the net of mammon and worldliness. It was against this that they were called to do battle. Some of this fallen Church might still be roused, and overcome.

The question of victory or defeat, all through these epistles, relates not to eternal life or eternal death :

That, in the case of the believer, is already decided in his favour, by God's electing grace. But the victory refers to his keeping his dispensational standing or not. Has he maintained, by word and deed, the special testimonies given by Christ ? Is he to receive reward or not ?

" Even as *J* also overcame."

The kingdom is adjudged to Jesus by God, *as the result of His perfect obedience.* " A sceptre of righteousness, is the sceptre of Thy kingdom. *Thou lovedst righteousness, and hatedst iniquity :* THEREFORE, O God, thy God anointed Thee with the oil of gladness above thy fellows " (*Greek*) (Heb. i. 8, 9).

Now, if reward according to works be a principle applied to Jesus, it is no marvel if it take its turn on us also. If we are like Christ in duty and in victory, we shall be like Him also in glory and the kingdom.

" And sat with my Father on His throne."

This passage proves a very important point : that there are two thrones. The Father's throne, on which Jesus sat, is unseen by men, in heaven. The future one of the Saviour is to be visible—the throne of David. It is to be at Jerusalem : Ezek. xliii. 7 ; Luke i. 32 ; Ps. cxxii. 5. The conqueror is to share with Christ the latter throne.

In the new earth, after the thousand years, the Son no longer sits on a separate throne. 'Tis thenceforward " the *throne* of *God* and of the *Lamb* " (xxii. 1, 3).

It is not Christ's kingdom as yet. But when Jesus, after His return, sits on His throne of glory, and the twelve apostles sit with Him on their thrones ruling the twelve tribes of Israel, then shall the victors reign with Christ. This is the last hope set before the eye of the churches. Here again, then, is another confirmatory witness of the force of that much-resisted passage in the twentieth chapter. The perception of the millennial reign is necessary to the Church's right conduct. Smyrna, Thyatira, and Laodicea are all three incited to holiness, by belief of Jesus' future personal reign.

There is matter enough in these epistles for thought; enough to sober and humble the proud and self-congratulating. Enough, too, to cheer the downcast and desponding.

He needs no books of evidences, who studies the Word of God! The infidel cannot say, "It is no marvel that the books of Scripture were received by those to whom they were addressed; for they are full of honied words, and ring with the great deeds and praises of the people that received them!" The reverse is the truth, the glaring reverse. Israel holds fast the Old Testament, but it reveals the evil deeds of the great founders of the nation. And of the chosen people it has scarcely anything to record but unbelief, murmurs, rebellions. So also with the New Testament, and especially with its closing book. Must it not have been strong evidence which compelled Sardis and Laodicea to own that such were the words of the Great Master and Faithful Witness to them! But they did! In Asia Minor, the authenticity of the Book was confessed. Here, then, is the wisdom of God: providing proofs of the genuineness of the Apocalypse, level to every capacity.

CHAPTER IV

1. "After these things I saw, and behold a door opened in heaven : and the first voice which I heard as of a trumpet talking with me, saying, ' Come up hither, and I will show thee what must come to pass after these things.' "

WE now enter upon the third and last division of the book. With it a new dispensation opens ; the churches have passed for ever. It will be well to notice some of the prominent features of the new economy.

It is one of JUSTICE. *Grace* is the characteristic principle of the present dispensation. 2 Cor. v. 18, 19.

But, in the succeeding chapters, God appears as the *Just,* calling all to account, and rendering to each according to his works. "*Just* and true are thy ways, thou King of the nations " (xv. 3). " All the nations shall come and worship before thee ; for thy *judgments have been made manifest* " (xv. 4).

Can *we* certainly tell *now,* what acts are God's judgments ? Might we *rejoice* in them, if we did ? *If not, a new dispensation begins here.*

And hence the *power* of God, which slumbers now, begins to be put forth in *war.*

The judgments of God are exhibited. "Fear God and give glory to him, *for the hour of his judgment is come,*" is then the new gospel (xiv. 7).

The great centre of the dispensation, and expression of the change, IS THE THRONE. The scene itself is shifted. It is no longer the sanctuary which is thrown open to us, but the Holy of Holies. *And its centre is the throne.*

The present throne of God is of mercy. Heb. iv. 16.

But the throne revealed in the present chapter is that of *justice*.

As it is a dispensation of justice, WORTHINESS, whether for good or evil, comes into view.

1. First, the worthiness of *God*. iv. 11.
2. Secondly, of his *Viceroy*. v. 2, 4, 9, 12.
3. Of *sinners*. xvi. 6.
4. The worthiness of *saints* under the former dispensation is spoken of as about to be manifested in reward under the coming economy. iii. 4.

THE PLACE OF JESUS IS ALTERED. This is a sufficient proof of the change of dispensation. Here Jesus leaves the sanctuary; and a new prophecy begins. As long as He keeps His attitude, the dispensation abides. So long as He continues with the lamps in the sanctuary, as the priest speaking to His fellow-priests, the church dispensation continues. But when He stands in His new position before the throne, *as the Lamb*, the executor of the mind of the sovereign on both earth and heaven, the new economy is begun.

During the church dispensation, He speaks directly through John to the churches. After that has passed away, he teaches His people through an angel and the elders. In the first three chapters, it is Jesus seen and heard by faith. In the rest of the book it is Christ coming openly to the world.

THE PLACE OF THE JEW IS ALTERED. During the standing of the churches, the Jew, as a Jew, is (as we have seen) only an unbeliever; falsely professing himself an Israelite. ii. 9; iii. 9. So is it in the epistles of Paul. Rom. ii. 28, 29; 1 Thess. ii. 14–16. But in the prophetic part, Jesus is recognized as a Jew by one of the councillors of the throne; and answerably thereto the Jews appear below, and are recognized as "*the servants of God.*" vii.

Also, when He sends forth His *witnesses*, they are of another character altogether from those of gospel times. His witnesses of the gospel go forth to heal disease, harmless as doves. Luke xxiv. 48; Matt. x. 16. Of so meek a character is Antipas, slain at Pergamos. ii. 13. But His witnesses under the new economy slay by fire all who attempt to injure them; and bring plagues on the earth. xi. The Church then has ceased to be God's distinctive witness; for she testifies of mercy.

" After these things," an interval of unknown duration occurs between the end of the appeals to the churches, and the prophecy. These words inform us that the third portion of the book is begun. The churches must have ceased to be recognized ere this part can begin. *This part of the Apocalypse, then, has not yet begun to be fulfilled.*

The phrase " after these things," or something similar, occurs *seven* times in this book, and signifies some considerable interval. iv. 1; vii. 1, 9; xv. 5; xviii. 1; xix. 1; xx. 3. In the last case, a thousand years intervene.

The Saviour silently leaves the tabernacle, and (save to one in the spirit) the first moments of the change of dispensation would be unnoticed.

" A door was opened in heaven." We are *now introduced* into the REALITIES—*the heavenly things* which were revealed to Moses on the Mount; and of which the earthly chambers and the vessels of the Mosaic tabernacle were copies.

With the opened door, John recognized *the voice as that which had first addressed him*, bidding him write what he saw, and send it to the churches. i. 10. The voice was loud, peculiar, metallic, rousing. It was suited to the scenes of justice, of war, of battle, of the throne of a king, and the Saviour's coronation.

2. "Immediately I became in the spirit; and behold a throne was being set in the heaven, and upon the throne One sat. 3. And He who sat was in appearance like a jasper stone and a sardius."

It was no dream that John saw; but at the word of Christ, a new inspiration of the Spirit seized on the apostle. The two first parts were completed under one and the same ecstasy. But with the *new dispensation comes a new inspiration*.

John sees a throne. This is the *centre object of the whole book*, both pictorially and morally. This is the source of all the action on earth and in heaven.

Before it the whole world stands revealed. From it goes forth a challenge to those in heaven, on earth and under the earth. Before it, angels and all creatures bow in worship. *From it go forth the acts of government*; the opening of the seals, the blowing of the trumpets, the outpouring of the bowls of wrath. It takes cognizance of both foes and friends, and dispenses to each his due. Here we may observe a difference from what was foreshadowed under the Old Testament. In the history of Israel, the tabernacle was the place of worship; but only in the wilderness did the decisions of God as the monarch come forth thence. After a human king was chosen to preside over Israel, the king's palace became a separate place from the temple.

We have now before us the *God of the temple*, as before we were introduced to the *priest*. But Jesus' glory cannot decline, though the dispensations, as far as committed to the hand of men, fail. He is here promoted to be the chief councillor and *agent of the throne*, while he is also worshipped both by angels and men.

The throne in Revelation takes the place which was formerly occupied by the ark of the covenant. Instead of the mercy-seat, we have the rainbow. *But the ark appears*, at the close of the trumpet-vision, *on high*.

The apostle beheld the throne *just as it was taking up its rest in the temple*, winged thither by the four *zöa*, or living creatures. This is the force of the tense used. It begins to be set, when the dispensation of mercy in the churches ends.

This is that setting[1] of the thrones which Daniel beheld. Dan. vii. 9–11.

As this throne rules over a guilty earth, its setting becomes at once *a time of visitation*. We have first shown to us the unanimity that reigns among the holy ones on high, with regard to God and His purposes. Then the errands of warning or of wrath go on from this portion of the King's domain, till rebellious earth is subdued; and inferior thrones, in glad subordination and sympathy with the throne in heaven, are raised up to rule over the earth. xx. 4.

The Holy One who sits upon the throne is God the Father. He acts for His Son's establishment, till all is ripe for Christ's acting Himself. "*Jehovah* said unto *my Lord*, Sit thou at my right hand, until I make Thy foes Thy footstool " (Ps. cx. 1). The Son is soon after seen *as the Lamb*; the Holy Ghost as seven torches round about the throne.

The appearance of this august monarch is very distantly described. The spot was holy ground. The light that streamed from Him was not white, but coloured. It was like that of jasper and cornelian. What the character of the first colour was, it is hard to say. Probably the colour of fire is that intended. Ezek. i. 27; Deut. iv. 24. The sardius or cornelian is known to be of a red colour. It denotes the indignation of Him who sits thereon, and is in full harmony with the justice of the throne. " *My fury*," saith God, *speaking of these*

---

[1] It should not be "till the thrones were *cast down*," but " till the thrones were *set*," as all critics allow. Here we see the twenty-four thrones, beside the great central one.

latter times, " shall come up in My face " (Ezek. xxxviii. 18).

From these two stones being mentioned, it is probable that the figure before the apostle presented two colours, one in its upper, one in its lower half, as in Ezek. i. 27.

Around the throne was " a rainbow." This very evidently refers us to the *covenant with Noah*, of which that was the token and seal. A cloud is coming over the earth; yea, it is already beheld. The throne is that cloud, and from it thunders and lightnings dart. But the bow is seen in the cloud; in token, that God, while judging, means not to destroy by a flood. Accordingly, while plague after plague is rained down on men, *no inundation devastates the earth.*

Its colour was the beautiful green of the emerald, that hue which is so refreshing to the eye in the grass covered earth. It is the opposite or complementary colour to red; and hence, *as fitly signifies mercy*, as the fiery or bloody red betokens *justice*. Thus we have an emblematic representation of the word of Habbakuk. " In *wrath* remember *mercy* " (Hab. iii. 3). The promises of grace encompass the throne, so that the floods of wrath shall not wholly destroy the earth, till its last destined day of fire.

4. " And round about the throne (behold) four and twenty thrones; and upon the thrones four and twenty elders sitting, clothed in white garments; and upon their heads golden crowns."

The chief throne was not, it would appear, the segment of a circle, set against a wall, as with men; *but a full circle*, round which the twenty-four thrones were set.

These thrones were occupied by as many " ELDERS." Who are they?

It is commonly said that they represent THE CHURCH. That this is a mistake, take the following proofs:—

1. If the elders had represented the Church, they

would either have been seven in number, or some multiple of it, as coming out of the seven churches.

2. The positions given to them disprove the theory. *They are seen and crowned, before Jesus appears. They are not seen after chap. xix.* ;They do not appear *in* His kingdom (chap. xx.) or *after* it. Thus the facts are just the opposite of what the theory would suppose. *On the contrary, they resign both their kingly and priestly offices to Him and His people.*

3. They distinguish between themselves and those redeemed by Christ. " Thou madest *them* unto *our* God kings and priests, and *they* reign over the earth " (v. 10). " These are *they* who came out of the great tribulation, and washed *their* robes, and made *them* white in the blood of the Lamb " (vii. 14–17). " The time of the dead, that they should be judged, and of giving the reward to *thy servants* the prophets, and to the fearers of thy name, the small and the great, and to destroy the destroyers of earth " (xi. 18). They do *not say,* " *to us thy servants* ; " but speak of the rewarded as bodies distinct from themselves.

" But they *do* say they are redeemed. " Thou hast redeemed *us* by Thy blood out of every kindred.' " *Is that little word genuine ?* Thereupon more will be said by and by.

4. They are not sinners. Their robes are white ; but while one of the elders calls John's attention to the fact that the raiment of the great multitude is white, *because washed in the blood of the Lamb* ; it is never said so of *theirs*. Their song is of the glory of God in *creation*. Ch. iv. 11. Not till the purposes of God undergo a development, and the Lamb appears, do they speak of *redemption*. The hymn about redemption is not their ordinary one ; it is a " *new* song." 'Tis not so to *us*.

5. The Great Multitude is brought before us at the same time with the elders. That the Great Multitude

means the redeemed of the Church is generally, and I think rightly, believed. But how then can the elders be representatives of the Church ? One of the elders asks John concerning the Great Multitude ; and upon his expressing his ignorance, tells him who they are and whence they came. Is it the *Church* enquiring about the *Church*, and giving information concerning it ? John, though of the Church, knows not the Great Multitude. These know of it, and are not of the Church. The book is sent to the churches, because *of their ignorance* of what is known to these heavenly rulers.

6. Again, they offer before the Lamb " golden bowls full of odours, which are *the prayers of the saints* " (v. 8). They are ministering to God the prayers of others. They act as priests for others, before the angel does so (in chap. viii.). The angel then presents " the prayers of *all* the saints." That angel is, I suppose, Christ. Now *he* presents the prayers of the *Church*. We never find the Church called to present the prayers of others, *though it is itself to pray for all men*.

7. It is noticed by Mr. Elliott, that there seems to be no sense of defilement, or of fear, which God's people have ever felt. Nor is there any notice of any change of their dress, when translated from the sorrow of earth to the joys above. Are they priests in the holiest by the force of redemption, and is there no notice of the blood by which they enter ? When the Holy Ghost speaks of the entry of the High Priest into the Holy of Holies, he continually makes mention of the blood by which entrance is obtained. " But into the second went the High Priest alone once every year, *not without blood*, which he offered for himself, and for the errors of the people . . . . . Neither by the blood of goats and calves, but by *His own blood* he entered in once into the holy place, having obtained eternal redemption for us . . . . Nor yet that He should offer Himself often, as the

High Priest entereth into the holy place every year *with blood* of others" (Heb. ix. 7, 12, 25 ; x. 19 ; xiii. 11).

The elders then are both kings and priests, each set over his particular department of creation.

(1) They are *kings*, as seen by their crowns and thrones, and by their sitting thereon ; a posture suited to those to whom judgment belongs.

Yet though these are kings, they are only called " elders." They reign, not by virtue of creation, but by *age* and by the appointment of God. *We* are made *kings* unto God, by our second birth, and washing in the blood of Christ. They are councillors of the throne ; conversant with the purposes of the king, and able to impart intelligence to John, as the servant of God. But though councillors, they are not *consulted*, as in human courts. For who shall impart wisdom to God ?

(2) They are also *priests*. This is betokened by their white raiment, which denotes them pure before God. A linen dress of white was the priest's ordinary attire. Exod. xxviii. 42 ; Lev. vi. 10 ; xvi. 4. They also have harps, and songs, and golden bowls of odours, which they offer before the throne. These were priestly employments.

(3) They are the *heads of the angelic priesthood*. They are the *chief-priests* of the heavenly courses. They are the *chief officers* of the heavenly king, ruling over the angels ; and, through them, over the earth. They are like the elders of the tribes of Israel. It is with the design of enlightening us as to their position, that the name " elder " has been given them. There were " *elders* " both of *the civil rulers and also of the priests*. Isa. xxxvii. 2 ; Jer. xix. 1.

These, then, are the rulers of the angelic sons of God, who kept their government and their abode, when others left it. Jude 6.

They are seen " *sitting*." Inferior angels stand. " I

saw the seven angels who *stand* before God" (viii. 2).

The sphere of the government of these elders is the earth. Hence the close connection between the elders and living creatures. They stand related as rulers and subjects.

Hence " the earth " and its nations occur in all the elders' speeches. v. 9, 10.

"The *nations* were wrath, and Thy wrath is come, and the time of the dead . . . and that thou shouldest destroy them which destroy *the earth*" (xi. 18, 19; xix. 2–4).

For the government of creation these elders have hitherto sufficed. But now the new covenant and the effects of redemption are to come into view. The Redeemer is to be exalted. The government of God at this crisis undergoes a change. Angels have been rulers of the earth during the evil age. Daniel is our witness that during the future age the sovereignty is to be given to *man*, according to the word of God. Also Ps. viii.; Heb. ii. 5. *The Lord Jesus introduces a new body of priests and kings associated with Himself, who take their place*. Accordingly, *the last time* we read *of the thrones of the elders is at the seventh trump*, when the kingdom becomes that of *Jesus*. And the *last time* we *hear of them at all*, is just before *the Saviour comes forth* from the heaven *to take His own kingdom*. They throughout acquiesce in, and assent to, this change. "Thy will be done on earth, as it is in heaven!"

The governments of the churches, of the throne on high, of the millennial kingdom, and of the final state, are all framed on one model.

5. " And out of the throne are proceeding lightnings and voices and thunders."

The present tense here is very observable. It seems clearly to indicate John's writing down at the moment what he saw. This is the way in which one speaks, who describes scenes going on before his eyes.

But these words give us the constant character of the throne. As the place of justice, these indications of God's indignation were continually issuing from it, called forth by the various sins and provocations of men. It was a volcano, sustained in constant activity by the disturbing forces and provocations of earth.

The throne stands not at last. After the judgment is over and sinners are passed away, when only the holy dwell in the new heavens and the new earth, the throne of God appears ; but there are no tokens of wrath in it. " A river of the *water of life* " proceeds from it then ; as now the *fire of death* bursts from it.

5. "And seven torches [1] of fire burning before the throne, which are the seven Spirits of God."

The " lamp " [2] must *always be distinguished* from the " torch." [3] They are always distinguished, both in Latin, Greek, and Hebrew.

The seven *lamps* have been set aside ($\lambda \upsilon \chi \nu \iota \alpha \iota$). The seven *torches* have taken their place ($\lambda \alpha \mu \pi \acute{\alpha} \delta \epsilon \varsigma$).

The *lamp* was for indoor service. Matt. v. 15 ; Luke xv. 8. The *torch* was more fitted for the open air, as being less liable to be extinguished by gusts of wind. Matt. xxv. 1–8 ; John xviii. 3.

The Spirit of God takes a different form with the changing economy, as Christ also had done. The Holy Spirit is the true light of God's throne. *These* torches need no tending ; the lights of the Holiest are superior to those of the sanctuary. There is no danger of their going out. The lamps of the sanctuary derived their oil from the Spirit of God. xxi. 11, 23.

The Holy Spirit is, in regard to the throne, " seven torches *of fire*." As the throne is ready to execute

---

[1] $\Lambda \alpha \mu \pi \acute{\alpha} \delta \epsilon \varsigma$, not $\lambda \upsilon \chi \nu \iota \alpha \iota$ as before.
[2] נֵר. $\Lambda \acute{\upsilon} \chi \nu o \varsigma$.   [3] לְפִיד. $\Lambda \alpha \mu \pi \acute{\alpha} \varsigma$.

wrath on the transgressors, so the Spirit of God is in sympathy therewith. His *light* is not so much in question, as His *anger*. They are "torches *of fire burning*" before the throne; they tell of wrath. When Jesus appeared in the dispensation of mercy, the Holy Spirit descended on Jesus as a *dove*. But now He is the "*Spirit of judgment, the Spirit of burning*" (Isa. iv. 4). These set fire to earth at last.

It is night still. No part of earth now shines on high, since the lamps are removed. The Holiest is only lighted by the light of God.

They are "the Spirits of God." As the elders represent subordinate spirits, these torches do *not*. They symbolize the Holy Spirit. He appears as the Great Physical Actor, as in creation. Gen. i. He gives life physical to the dead. Rev. xi. 11.

6. "And (behold) before the throne as it were a glassy sea, like crystal."

In front of the throne is "a sea." 'Tis a representative sea; as the *zōa* are representative "living creatures."

It is thus put most appropriately in close connection with the living creatures; both as the source whence many took their birth, the field of life for many now, the area on which man and his ships have free course, and the dreadful agent of destruction in the bygone Flood.

That it is *representative of the sea of the earth* seems proved, by its being *no longer found*, after *the old earth and its ocean cease to exist*. In the new earth the throne of God abides still: its great centre there, as here. *But there is no sea in the new earth; nor any representation of it before the throne.*

It was "*as it were* a sea." It was solid apparently, and without any creatures living within it. It was fitted to represent a sea, though not precisely of the same elements as that on earth.

The sea was God's early scourge for the wicked. It was an awful object, as employing the element of *water* to take away animal life. But in *its second and final state*, it becomes the *seat of the element of fire*—" the Second Death." The *sea* becomes the *lake* of fire. We are permitted to see it in its intermediate state in chap. xv., when it is " a *sea* of glass *mingled with fire.*"

"And in the midst of the throne, and round the throne were four living creatures full of eyes, before and behind. 7. And the first living creature was like a lion, and the second like a calf (ox), and the third living creature had a face as a man, and the fourth living creature was like a flying eagle. 8. And the four living creatures have each of them six wings; around and within they are full of eyes: and they have no rest day and night, saying, Holy, Holy, Holy, Lord God of Hosts, who was, and who is, and who is to come."

We have now arrived at the Cherubim.[1]

On the differences between Ezekiel and John, I do not purpose to enter. It is enough, that they intended evidently to represent to us the same beings. Ezekiel afterwards identifies the living creatures which he saw, with the cherubim. " This is *the living creature* which I saw under the God of Israel by the river of Chebar; and *I knew that they were cherubim*" (Ezek. x. 20).[2] Ezekiel uses " the cherubim " and " the living creature " indifferently. Compare i. 22; x. 1. "The *cherubim* were lifted up: this is the *living creature* that I saw by the river of Chebar" (Ezek. x. 15).

They are called " THE CHERUBIM " on the first occasion of their being named. Gen. iii. 24. This probably arose from the fact of their being well known to Moses' readers.

The cherubim are *representatives of the animate creation of the globe.* They are not *symbols*, or emblems; they are *representatives*. The symbols of Rev. iv., v. are

[1] [Space compels the omission of an elaborate and convincing study of the Cherubim].

[2] There is no article in this place before "cherubim"; either in the Hebrew or in the Greek.

expounded to us. The torches, the horns and eyes of the Lamb, and the odours, which the elders present to God and Christ, are explained to us. For they are symbols. iv. 5; v. 6, 8. The elders and zöa are *not* explained: for they are *not symbols*.

Their number is FOUR; for *four is the number of creation*.

And *four* of creation united with the Blessed *Three* of the Ruler of Creation, make up the sacred *seven*. We have them in closest juxtaposition in Rev. iv., v. Beneath the throne the four zöa : upon the throne the Father : in the midst of it the Son, as the Lamb ; around it the Spirit of God.

The four living creatures specified are the heads of their tribes or divisions. (1) The lion is the head of the *wild beasts*, Prov. xxx. 30. (2) The ox is the chief of *cattle*. (3) The eagle is the chief of *birds* : and (4) man, the head of all creation.

Two of these classes are omitted in the cherubim, and very significantly. (1) The *fish* have no representative, for there is no sea in the new earth.

(2) The *reptiles* have no representative : nor is the reason hard to find. It was the SERPENT that introduced sin, and was condemned to take his place among the creeping things.

Accordingly, out of the five animal tribes of earth, God enters into *covenant* with *three* only. Gen. ix. 9, 10. And representatives of these three kinds only appear in the cherubim, in conjunction with man.

When the other creatures are in amity, the Lord's mark of reprobation is still laid on the serpent. " Dust shall be the serpent's meat " (Isa. lxv. 25). The eagle, the serpent's foe, is one of the four. And, in this book, the serpent is Christ's great enemy.

The four zöa have peculiar relations among themselves. Of the four, two are by the law *unclean*—the lion and eagle : two *clean*—the ox and man. But in the cherubic figure, all are cleansed, and able to dwell in the Divine Presence ; a token of the final cleansing of creation. This is the distant announcement, perhaps, of Peter's vision. Acts x. 6.

Two are creatures that prey on others, the lion and eagle : the ox often the victim of the lion, the man sometimes the victim, sometimes the destroyer, of both lion and eagle. But here all are in amity. There is no strife before the Presence of God : token of the final reconciliation of the creation, which Adam's sin had disordered and set at variance. Isa. xi. 6, 7.

As the twenty-four elders are the heads of angels, so are the four cherubs heads of the tribes of earth. Around the throne of the monarch, it is fitting that the nobles of his empire should be gathered. And God is here seated as the Lord of heaven and earth. When these two classes lead, their orders follow, v. 8–13.

Earth comes into the field of view as soon as the zöa call. They herald the outgoings of the Redeemer, of War, Famine, and Pestilence. They note the four natural rods whereby God scourges an evil world. They are *beneath* the throne ; for earth is but God's *footstool.* They celebrate with song the eternity and Godhead of the sitter on the throne ; and this, as Paul informs us, the creatures are designed to manifest. Rom. i. 20. They praise His holiness, and this, most appropriately, in connection with the throne. The mysterious ways of God have brought the animated tribes into suffering for the sin of man ; but they acknowledge His holiness still ; the throne is about to deliver them from the bondage of corruption.

They are the fitting supplement to the RAINBOW and the SEA, which all speak of the covenant with Noah.

While the old earth remains, so do the zöa ; for just so long is the duration of the covenant with Noah.

"*While the earth remaineth*, seedtime and harvest, and cold and heat, and summer and winter, and day and night shall not cease" (viii. 22). But they appear no longer after earth is destroyed. The memorials of the covenant cease, when the covenant itself is at an end.

With this key in our hand, we can unlock the various contexts in the Old Testament which treat of the cherubim.

The redemption of creation, or of the creatures as well as man, is God's declared purpose. Rom. viii. 19-23. This is the key-note of the whole subject: the golden clue to unravel the whole. Creation fell with Adam, not of its own choice. It will rise again, and partake, with the redeemed of men, of their deliverance from the grave, and its iron slavery. It will be made immortal and glorious, when the sons of God in resurrection shine as the sun. "The restitution (or restoration) of all things" is declared by Peter to have been the subject of God's prophets since the world began. Acts iii. 21.

The representation given in the Apocalypse takes up the plan of God where Ezekiel leaves it. Ezekiel discovers to us the throne of God and the living cherubim leaving the earth, and, after an unknown lapse of time, returning to it. But the Apocalypse discloses to us the intermediate events, the millennial joy, and the *final* settlement of creation on the *new* earth. The cherubim are still on high with the throne of God. The God of Revelation carries on the purposes of the God of Genesis. The creatures stand before the God of Noah. They are close to the throne, for they are bound up with all God's actions as the Judge and the Deliverer; and the creatures they represent are to abide for ever. They come into view, now that earth is to be judged.

God, in His full glory of justice, can, and still does, recognise the creation. His Enemy has brought a blight upon it; but it was once good, and it shall be good again. The serpent and his traces shall be erased for ever from creation.

The four creatures call for God's four sore judgments upon the earth, as punishment for bloodshed and violence. They praise God the Father as Creator; they glorify Jesus as the Redeemer. The lion begins the series, the eagle ends it.

The zöa are "full of eyes, before and behind." They are ever wakeful, needing no rest "day or night." They are full of the Spirit of God. This is the meaning given to eyes in the next chapter, v. 6. "Seven horns, and seven *eyes*, which are the seven *Spirits of God*, sent forth into all the earth." The cherubim of Ezekiel were also full of eyes. Ezek. x. 12. The Spirit directs them. "Whither the Spirit was to go they went" (i. 12, 20, 21; x. 12, 17).

They are "*in the midst of* the throne, and *round about* the throne." From this I conclude that there was a central aperture in the throne from which some portions of the zöa might be seen. They stood underneath the throne, as well as around its sides.

8. "And the four living creatures had each of them six wings; around and within they were full of eyes; and they rest not day and night, saying, Holy, holy, holy, Lord God of Hosts, which was, and is, and is to come."

The eyes of the living creatures are again mentioned. They are within as well as without. They are made intelligent of the internal purposes of the throne, as well as of the state of things without.

They are creatures of heavenly powers; for what creature of earth could serve without rest, day and night?

The four animals mention the different names of God, as revealing Himself in successive dispensations,[1] as

[1] That is, if we read "Almighty," instead of "Of hosts."

Darby observes, *except the one of "Father," by which He is made known to the Church*. How then should the animals represent the Church ?

They adore God as holy, in spite of the troubles which, in consequence of sin, affect all creation. They give " glory " to the Creator ; " honour " to the Great Governor ; " thanks " for the benefits of existence as realized by themselves.

The three times repeated " Holy, Holy, Holy " has doubtless a reference to the Three Persons of the Blessed Trinity.

Thus we are brought again to Old Testament ground. " Lord of Hosts," is not a New Testament title of God. It speaks not of mercy, but of justice and judgment nigh at hand. Hence we have one of the proofs, that the book is not to be interpreted on the principles of the church dispensation, but on the literality of the law.

9. " And when the living creatures give glory and honour and thanksgiving unto Him that sitteth upon the throne, who liveth for ever, 10. The four and twenty elders fall down before the Sitter upon the throne, and worship Him who liveth for ever and ever, and cast their crowns before the throne."

The evangelist is describing an action which he saw several times repeated. As often as the zōa glorified God, the *elders* followed in a like strain. But the elders are still their superiors. The zōa have no appearance of authority : they have neither thrones nor crowns. They are under and around the throne as the centre of the covenant. The elders are there, as partakers of the government of God. The zōa " *give glory*," the elders " *worship*." The elders address God directly—" *Thou* art worthy, O *our* Lord and God." The living creatures say only, " Holy, Holy, Holy, is the Lord of Hosts."

The elders confess this great truth of the supremacy and holiness of the Most High, by a suitable attitude.

As liege subjects they bow before the throne. As beings made by Him, they worship the Underived One. And though crowned, they confess themselves dependent kings, unworthy to rule in the presence of the King of kings. In token of it, they " cast their crowns before His throne." They have no claim for continuance in their royal priesthood but God's good pleasure, the duration of which is as yet unknown to them. This is another proof that they are not the Church. God's good pleasure, with regard to that, is known, and it would be unbelief to doubt it. The kings of Rev. xx. and xxii. 5 do not act thus. They are worthy with Christ's worthiness. The Church is not seen as yet : for he who introduces the Church is not yet himself introduced. The Book and its proclamation introduce the Lamb ; and with the Lamb, and on the ground of His redemption, the Church is first spoken of, and then seen. These are not crowned by Christ, as promised. Rev. ii. 10. And they are crowned before the " Presence " of Jesus takes place. 2 Tim. iv. 8 ; 1 Peter v. 4.

11. " Saying, Thou art worthy, O Lord and our God, to receive glory and honour and power : for Thou createdst all things, and by reason of Thy will they were, and were created."

Creation is the especial act of Deity.[1] It cannot be wrought by a creature. It is this attribute which forms the just ground of adoration from every created being. Because none but God can create, none but He should be worshipped. God's will is the reason of the existence of every created thing. He took counsel with none : He was under obligation to none. " THOU createdst." The " thou " is emphatic. " Thou," and Thou *alone*.

---

[1] A remarkable reading is found in verse 11, in some copies. " Because of Thy will they were *not*, and were created." The non-existence of creatures, till the moment of creation, was of God's will.

CHAPTER V

1. "And I saw on the right hand of the Sitter on the throne a book written within, and on the back sealed up with seven seals."

CHAPTER iv. presents God and His officers of the Old Covenant. Chapter v. shows us the change induced by the New Covenant.

This is, I believe, especially THE BOOK OF THE NEW COVENANT. Heb. viii. 8–12.

Many are so accustomed to suppose that the new covenant is *already made* with the *Church*, that they will be startled to find it yet *future*, and to be made with *Israel*. But the passage cited from Jer. xxxi. conclusively proves both points. See also Rom. xi. 27. It is in harmony also with the evidence in Revelation. For Jesus takes the book in virtue of His two Jewish titles, "Lion of the tribe of JUDAH," and "Root of DAVID."

(1) The *blood* of The New Covenant or Testament has been shed: Matt. xxvi. 28; Heb. x. 29.

(2) We are *priests*, or ministers of it. 2 Cor. iii. 6.

(3) The GREAT APOSTLE and HIGH PRIEST of it is come. All its benefits are wrapped up in Christ.

Now the New Covenant is also *the book of the inheritance* embracing the creation, man, Israel, and the Church. The places of all these are provided for in it. The New Covenant and its blood redeem not Israel only, but creation, and the Church of Christ. And Jesus is the Redeemer of the forfeited heritage. It is as the

Goel or Redeemer that He takes the book. He paid the price, and the seals attest it made over to Him.

The covenant offered by Moses was *open*, and was first published to the people of Israel for their acceptance, ere it was written. But this is *sealed*, and in the hand of the sovereign. That covenant was the language of *demand from men :* this rests on the *sovereign purposes of the king.* Thus does the New Covenant differ from the Old. It is *God's* undertaking to fulfil the conditions before required of men. " *I will*—and *they shall* "—is its tenor. Therefore it can never fail.

The covenant, too, is now not *in the ark*, but *on the throne*. That is, power is about to be employed, to carry out all its provisions. It is no longer suspended on the weakness and will of men, but rests on the firm purposes of God, and is to be executed by His full power.

The seven seals sealing *up* the book intimate to us the thick and perfect veil of secrecy enwrapping the purposes of God. And only by degrees does the veil depart : the seals have in them more or less of symbol.

The seven seals are all fastened on the outer rim of the scroll, so that no part of the writing can be read till the last seal is broken. The contrary is generally assumed ; it is generally thought, that, with the breaking of each seal, a leaf of the book was laid open. But this would make it seven books, not one only. The book is not said to be opened, even when the seventh seal is broken.

The three especial uses of the seal, (1) to authenticate a writing, (2) to ratify a deed, and (3) to conceal from undesired eyes, meet in this case.

2. " And I saw a strong angel proclaiming with a great voice— Who is worthy to open the book, and to loose its seals ? ' "

The angel, as the herald of God's will to the various divisions of His empire, is a strong angel. He exhibits his strength by the loudness of his voice. It is to reach through heaven, earth, and the under-world. It is the glory of a herald to possess the power of making his proclamation widely heard. " Then a *herald cried with might* " (*marg.*, Dan. iii. 4). So Homer's heralds have loud voices.

His inquiry is, " Who is *worthy* to open the book ? "

God now asks, who is worthy to stand beside Himself, as chief minister and agent of the throne ?

Who had so glorified God, as to be worthy to be ruler over all things ? Who was so trusty, as to be the fit depository of the secrets of God ? Who was possessed of original intelligence, sufficient to entitle him to enter into the deep designs of God ?

The principle thus enunciated, as the first act of the throne, is carried throughout the book. It is recompense to each according to desert.

3. "And none in the heaven, nor on the earth, nor under the earth, was able to open the book, nor even to behold it."

There was no reply to the herald's challenge. Angels, no less than men, must confess that, in the strictest performance of their duty, there is no real ground of merit. " We are unprofitable servants, we have done that (only) which it was our duty to do."

John was permitted to see the book to which the proclamation related. But they, as set upon their own merits, could not even behold the book, amidst the blaze of light in which the Godhead dwells. The creatures' powerlessness must first be seen, that the glory of the Son of God may be the greater. To them first is given the opportunity to state their claims, if such they had. Angels by nature are no more able to understand God's purposes than we.

4. "And I was weeping much, because none was found worthy to open the book, nor even to behold it."

There was a pause. No claimant appeared. As they could not deserve even to see the book, it was clear that they deserved not to open it.

The second result of the proclamation is, to John, sorrow. The " I " is emphatic. He alone was weeping.

This affection was holy: for " the Spirit searcheth all things, yea, the deep things of God." How carnal then is the temper of Christians in general! They regard not the secrets of prophecy: they are content to be ignorant of things into which angels desire to look. He who would understand this book should feel interest like that of John.

5. "And one of the elders saith unto me, Weep not: behold the Lion who is of the tribe of Judah, the Root of David, prevailed to open the book and its seven seals."

One of the subordinate kings around the throne, intelligent of the issue, and of the rightful claimant, comforts John. The manifested unworthiness of all others was to be the occasion of the greater glory of Him to whom it belonged. The divine secrets should not be lost. God purposed to give a knowledge of them, through Jesus, to His servants.

One was worthy to open the book.

Both these titles present Jesus' connections with the *Jew*. How strange, that so many commentators should labour to exclude them from this prophecy! What can result from such an effort, but darkness and confusion? Israel's blindness was, and is, a mystery: Rom. xi. 25. It is to pass away, when desolations visit the earth: Isa. vi. 11, 12. Israel is brought into view then, when the veil is about to be taken off. Jesus' humiliation is a mystery. The removal of it then is effected by His exaltation, which this chapter discovers.

The translation " *hath* prevailed " darkens the sense. It makes us think that some recent victory is in question, when indeed it refers to Jesus' conquest while on earth. It is a question, whether it were not better to render—" *overcame* to open the book." For this teaches us that Jesus' double victory over Satan (Luke xi. 22) and over the world (John xvi. 33) was won, with design to open this book. And thus it is thrown into closest contact with our Lord's concluding words to the churches —" Even as I also *overcame.*"

6. "And I saw in the midst of the throne and of the four living creatures, and in the midst of the elders, a lamb standing, as if it had been slain, having seven horns and seven eyes, which are the seven Spirits of God sent into all the earth."

Jesus combines seemingly inconsistent perfections. As connected with His previous appearance on earth, He was the Lamb, all innocence, meekness, usefulness, passivity; not breaking the bruised reed, nor quenching the smoking flax. He was the Lamb in His death. He was the Paschal Lamb.

But He is about to be manifested in another and opposite character, as the Lion. His not breaking the bruised reed is His character only for a time. It is only " TILL *he send forth judgment* (that is, *justice*) *unto victory* " (Matt. xii. 20).

As the *Lamb* slain, He associates with Himself the *Church,* which is called to imitate His meekness. As the *lion* of Judah, He will call to battle beside Him the remnant of *Israel :* Zech. ix. 13–15; xii. Hitherto He has been the Lamb before the throne, in all His passive humiliation and loyalty under suffering. He is about to be presented as the Lion, to execute all the throne's indignation. As the Lamb, He put away sin by *suffering ;* as the Lion, He shall put it away by *destruction.*

He is a lamb " as if it had been slain." That is, the marks of sacrificial death were upon it. So Jesus rose with the scars in His hands, feet, and side ; and they identified Him to the disciples. He was not seen in the sanctuary with any mark of His death. But the scars now appear. The throne is about to avenge His death, and the death of His martyrs.

"Seven horns." The work of opening the book demands personal qualifications of the utmost excellence; as, for instance, perfection of *power*.

The strength of the animal lies in its horn: it is its weapon of offence. Power in its fullness is required to put down the force, which wickedness in both heaven and earth musters on its side. Thus Jesus is seen as the great agent about to exercise all the power of the Godhead, with the full concurrence of the throne.

2. He has also " seven eyes." This, as we have seen before, indicates intelligence; and the " *seven* eyes," the full perfection of dispensational intelligence. His seven eyes pierce through the seven seals of the book.

The seven eyes mark Him out as the perfect " *seer*," or prophet; as the seven horns indicate His perfection of *kingly* power. David was a " seer " but the " root of David " has the Spirit without measure. The Spirit *came on* David: the Spirit *dwells in* David's Lord.

The perfection of *intelligence* is needed, as well as the perfection of power, in order to carry out the designs of the throne.

8. "And when He took the book, the four living creatures and the twenty-four elders fell down before the Lamb, having each a harp and golden bowls full of odours, which are the prayers of the saints."

This falling down in worship before the First Begotten indicates, that the time is at hand, when the Father is about to introduce Him a second time into the habitable earth. For of that it is written, "And let all the angels of God worship Him " (Heb. i. 6). The elders and *zöa* are in sympathy throughout, both in the worship of the Father and of the Son.

9. "And they sing a new song, saying, 'Thou art worthy to take the book and to open the seals thereof : for Thou wast slain, and redeemedst to God by Thy blood (some) out of every tribe and tongue, and people, and nation ; and madest them unto our God kings and priests ; and they shall reign [1] over the earth.'"

This new procedure of the throne calls forth a new song. There was no song at the appointment of the Mediator of the Old Covenant. It was only a fresh trial of the fallen nature of man. But here is a surety in whom God, heaven, and earth can rest. If at the creation the angels rejoiced, how much more suitable is joy now!

1. "For Thou wast slain." Here begin the reasons of the homage. Jesus is glorified, not now as the Creator, but as the Redeemer. He who was to be God's king, must pour out His soul unto death.

"Thou wast slain." Here is the sacrifice which fulfils the need of all the previous dispensations.

2. "And redeemedst to God by Thy blood (some) out of every tribe, and tongue, and people, and nation."

It will be observed, that the "*us*," commonly read in ver. 9, is omitted in the present translation. This is done upon the following grounds : external and internal.

1. It is omitted by the Alexandrian Manuscript, and by the Ethiopic Version. It is discarded by Lachmann and Tischendorf, by Ewald and Bleek.

2. Internal evidence is, I submit, decisive in this case. It will be granted me, that at the close of the verse we should read, "Thou madest THEM unto *our* God kings and priests : and *they* reign over the earth." This reading is established on certain authority.

But if so, then the two different relatives cannot subsist in the same sentence. For, as it stands, it makes the

---

[1] Another reading is, "they reign" : supported by very good authority.

elders and zöa distinguish two parties : *one* of whom is redeemed by blood, while *another* is made kings and priests.

1. " Thou redeemedst US to God by Thy blood."
2. " And madest THEM kings and priests to our God."

But this is inadmissible. It is clear on every consideration, that the redeemed and the kings are but one party. The blood is the basis, both of the redemption and of the priestly and kingly authority. This is certain from chap. i. 5, 6.

The washed in blood are those constituted priests and kings. This passage teaches us, too, whence came the " *us,*" whose entrance has proved the cuckoo's egg, dislodging at length the genuine tenants of the nest. No doubt, also, it seemed to some eye, not very critical, that some word was wanting to fill the gap between " by Thy blood " and " out of every nation," while nevertheless this is a common construction, specially with John.

The same conclusion is abundantly confirmed by vii. 9–17. There the redeemed by the Lamb's blood appear, gathered out of every nation, as described. But the elders are not among them. One of the elders asks John concerning them, and informs him of them, as a body quite distinct from the twenty-four elders. " *These* are the comers out of the Great Tribulation : *they* washed *their* robes."[1]

" And they shall reign over the earth." Now a future result is noticed. They were before spoken of as already kings *before God :* here their kingly dignity is to be *over men.*

" But will it not follow from this, that all the redeemed will be partakers of the kingdom ? "

---

[1] Let it be well understood, then, how much of the interpretation of the Revelation hangs on that *doubtful* word " us " : and let each reader remember, that its genuineness has become more and more precarious.

These words do not necessarily affirm such a thing. They view indeed entrance into the kingdom from the side of redemption; or its connection with Jesus' merits. But other passages tell us of a trial which Christ Himself will make of His people's acts, when the question of each individual's entrance or exclusion will be decided: 1 Cor. vi. 8–10.

"But what if the other reading, 'they *reign* over the earth' be the true one?" This would modify the sense but little. It can only be taken as a prophetic present used for the future. The future is confidently anticipated from that act of the Lamb. "It is already certain; for thou dost take the kingdom, and they in thee." It is certain that the Church is not reigning as yet: 1 Cor. iv. 8–14. "They *shall be* priests of God and of Christ, and *shall reign* with him a thousand years" (Rev. xx. 6). And this kingdom of Christ's does not come till the seventh trump has sounded. (Rev. xi. 15.)

"Aye, but are not the departed spirits of the just reigning with Christ?"

Scripture never says so. The answer of Paul to the mistake of the Thessalonian converts sufficiently shows this. They imagined that the departed righteous were excluded from the kingdom; and they mourned for them on this ground. But the apostle, in comforting them, does not tell them that they were reigning already. He only informs them, that at Jesus' descent from heaven they would be raised from the dust, and *together with the living be caught up to meet Christ in the air: after which time they would be ever with the Lord*.

In this scene and song I perceive the elders' resignation of the posts which they hitherto had held. They own the superior worthiness of Jesus, and of those whom He introduces. The elders are kings and priests without redemption: unfallen angels, whom it pleased God in His sovereignty, or for services rendered, to promote to the priesthood and kingly office before Him. But, as they confess the superior worthiness of Jesus, in His becoming incarnate and subjecting Himself to death from loyalty to the throne and from love to men ; so they discern also the superior place taken by those over whom the worthiness of Christ has spread its mantle. His superabounding merits avail to elevate and to clothe others. The elders stand only on their own merits, which avail for themselves, but for none beside. They are already reigning, offering incense, as priests, and seated on thrones, when they anticipate the future kingdom of these, the ransomed of Christ. The rule of men is to begin in the new or millennial age ; and that of angels is to be excluded. Heb. ii. 6. This the elders foreknow, and acquiesce with all readiness, nay, with joy, in the appointment of redeemed men as about to supersede them. There is no jealousy on the part of the elect angels. " Thy will be done on earth, *as it is in heaven !* "

Henceforth the elders do not act : though they display foresight of what is to come.

11. "And I saw, and heard the voice of many angels around the throne, and the living creatures, and the elders : and the number of them was myriads of myriads, and thousands of thousands ; saying with a loud voice—12. 'Worthy is the Lamb that was slain to receive power, and riches, and wisdom, and strength, and honour, and glory, and blessing.' "

The leaders of the angels begin the song ; the rest follow. There is full loyalty to Christ throughout the ranks of the elect of angels.

13. "And every creature which is in the heaven, and on the earth, and underneath the earth, and upon the sea, and all things in them, I heard saying, ' Unto the Sitter upon the throne, and to the Lamb, be blessing, and honour, and glory, and might, for ever and ever !' 14. And the four living creatures said, Amen. And the elders fell down, and worshipped."

The four living creatures in like manner take the

lead in the praise of the Lamb: their constituents follow.

Four regions are specified; *four* ascriptions of praise ascend. It is the whole universe that gives in its homage. From this praise of all in heaven and earth, it would seem that the rebel-angels in heaven, and the ungodly of mankind, whether living or dwelling amidst departed spirits, must be excluded. I am unable therefore fully to comprehend the universality here stated.

When the book is taken, the four living creatures and the elders worship together, as being the leaders of their respective orders.

The zōa worship, for the *earth* is concerned; the redeemed are of earth: the reign is to be on earth. The elders worship: for thus they display their grace in self-surrender.

The *angels* then take up the note of praise, and are followed by the *creatures* in general. The Amen is said by their representatives on high; first the heads of the *creatures* reply, and then the elders of the *angels* conclude. Thus the circuit is completed. The creatures and their heavenly representatives, the angels, their chief priests and elders, are of one mind.

CHAPTER VI

1. "And I saw when the Lamb opened one of the seven seals and I heard one of the four living creatures saying, as with the noise of thunder, 'Go.' 2. And I saw, and behold a white horse: and he that sat upon him had a bow; and a crown was given unto him: and he went forth conquering, and to conquer."

MYSTERY is seen in the book's being fully sealed; the removal of mystery is found in the breaking of the seals. The time for manifesting God and His Son to the world is now to come. The day of the Church, which lasts during the Mystery, is over. Manifestation is the characteristic of Revelation; but its difficulty arises from that manifestation's taking place only by degrees, and out of a previous state of secrecy and mystery. Jesus *speaks* of mysteries in Matthew xiii. Israel was become blind. Here He *breaks* them. Israel's heart is beginning to grow tender.

The Day of the Lord comes on gently, like a thief in the night. Its beginning is only a seal broken on high. The noise is not heard on earth. And, as its consequence, a single horseman only goes forth.

As soon as the seal is broken, one of the living creatures speaks.

His utterance may be rendered either "Come!" or "Go." How shall we decide which of the two translations is preferable? By considering the answer given to the command by each rider.

There is no motion of the rider toward the living creatures.

"And, when he opened the second seal, I heard the second living creature say, *Go!* And there *went out* another horse that was red."

As the call of rightful authority, it is instantly complied with. "Go!" And the horseman, once fully equipped, *goes out*.

The four calls are beautifully illustrated by the words of Elisha to the Shunamite. "Arise, and go thou and thy household, and sojourn wheresoever thou canst sojourn : for *the Lord hath called for a famine :* and *it shall also come* upon the land seven years" (2 Kings viii. 1). And again—"The Lord *shall hiss for the fly* that is in the uttermost part of the rivers of Egypt, and for the bee that is in the land of Assyria. And *they shall come*" (Isa. vii. 18, 19).

But who is the rider ? Most have supposed it to be Christ : and with them I fully agree.

The agreement of His description here with the forty-fifth Psalm, has led many to recognize Him in the present rider. The psalmist delineates "the *king*," and this rider is *crowned*, while none of the other riders are. "In thy majesty ride *prosperously* because of truth, and meekness, and *righteousness;* and thy right hand shall teach thee terrible things." This rider goes forth to conquest, and his horse's colour betokens the righteousness of his warfare. "*Thine arrows are sharp* in the heart of the king's enemies, whereby the peoples fall under thee." The rider here carries a *bow*, and he goes forth "to conquer" enemies. This mark attaches to several of the pictures of Messiah. Of the Lion of Judah it is said, "He shall eat up the nations his enemies, and shall break their bones, and *pierce them through with his arrows*" (Num. xxiv. 8).

That it is Jesus, may be further argued from this, that, whereas to the other riders weapons are given, or directions are communicated teaching them what they are to do, or to leave undone, *no instructions are laid down to this warrior*. He is the trusty secret messenger of the throne, who understands already the designs of the monarch, and is equipped for them.

Thus all the parts of the representation breathe the language of war—the thunder, the horse, the bow, the predicted conquest. And after this follow the trumpets, a still less mistakable sign of war.

"A crown was given unto Him." It has been questioned whether by the Greek word [1] employed in this place, we are to understand a royal crown or merely a chaplet of victory. But it appears that in the Seventy it is used to describe the royal circlet, as witness these passages—" And he took their *king's crown* from off his head, the weight whereof was a talent of gold with the precious stones, and it was set on David's head " (2 Sam. xii. 30 ; 1 Chron. xx. 2). "The *king* shall joy in thy strength, O Lord." "Thou settest a *crown* of pure gold on his head" (Psalm xxi. 3 ; 2 Macc. xiv. 4). And the Saviour's crown of thorns was in mockery of His derided kingly title.

2. But it is also true, that this crown is won by previous services. The rider is the same Lion of Judah that "*conquered*[2] to open the book," and now is crowned, going forth " *conquering* and to conquer." The crown is the gift of the throne : he is now adorned, like the kingly elders who sit around the throne. By it he is distinguished from the other servants of the monarch when he comes forth to reap, xiv.

"And he went out conquering and to conquer." The rider goes forth from the palace, and from heaven towards earth.

[1] Στέφανος. [2] 'Ενίκησεν.

SECOND SEAL.

3. "And when he opened the second seal, I heard the second living creature saying, Go ! And there went out another, a red horse, and to him that sat on him it was given to take peace out of the earth, and that they should slay one another : and a great sword was given to him."

That word "another," preceding "horse," seems designed to sever between the first rider and the three following ones : for the expression is only used on this occasion.

His horse is red. Here also the colour is significant. It is the hue of blood.

To him it is committed to take peace away from the earth. It seems to be implied, then, that previously "the earth sitteth still and is at rest" (Zech. i. 11). "The earth" is now first mentioned as the object against which these warlike preparations are aimed. It is taken, I judge, in its wide sense, as it was before in the proclamation made to heaven and earth.

The object of this horseman is different from that of the first. The war of the first is with the design and certain result of conquest. The object of this rider is to produce internal wars, having no issue but depopulation.

Peace was one of the blessings promised under the law. 2 Sam. xxiv. 13 ; xii. 10.

This removal of peace would be traceable to God, only by the eye of faith. The heavenly warrior is invisible as yet, the heaven is not opened at present. War seems to most the result of the devices of men, and dependent on their will. But the Scriptures teach us, that it arises primarily from the good pleasure of the Most High, and is used by Him as a scourge of the nations : Jer. xxv. 15–29. "I will *call* for a *sword* upon all the inhabitants of the earth, saith the Lord of Hosts." "It was *given Him* to take peace from the earth." This word is one of the key-notes of the Apocalypse. The saint must keep his eye upon the throne as the originator of the various movements on the earth. War rages fiercely on the globe, just before millennial peace broods over the nations. War was the threat of the law against sin. "I will *bring a sword upon you* that shall avenge the quarrel of the covenant" (Lev. xxvi, 25-33 ; Judges vii. 18).

"And that they should slay one another." Human passions rage to bloodshed. This horseman goes to produce war, and especially the worst form of it—civil war—as the words, "that they should kill one another," seem to imply.

The peace of the earth is removed, not simply from different nations in their relation to one another, but one portion of the citizens is set against another. Thus when God smote Midian, He "set *every man's sword against his fellow*, even throughout all the host" (Judges vii. 22). "I set all men *everyone against his neighbour*" (Zech. viii. 10). This is the first of the signs which our Lord gives to Israel of the end of the age. Matt. xxiv. 7.

This agent touches the earth. His is closer warfare than that of the bow.

How all things are preparing for a day of utter discord and bloody feud, it is not difficult to see. But until the seal is opened, the flood, though gathering, does not break forth.

THIRD SEAL.

5. "And when he opened the third seal, I heard the third living creature saying, Go ! And I saw, and behold a black horse, and he that sat upon him had a pair of balances in his hand. And I heard as it were a voice in the midst of the four living creatures saying, A chœnix of wheat for a denarius, and three chœnices of barley for a denarius, and hurt not the oil and the wine."

The agent which succeeds is an angelic messenger producing FAMINE.

The third living creature calls for this minister of God's displeasure. It is the one with face as a man. Accordingly this seal refers to corn, wine, oil, prices and measures, which bring man into especial view.

The horse is "black." This colour is associated in the prophets with famine. "The word of the Lord that came to Jeremiah concerning the *dearth*. Judah mourneth, and the gates thereof languish; they were *black* unto the ground" (Jer. xiv. 1, 2). "Their visage is *blacker than a coal;* they are not known in the streets: their skin cleaveth to their bones; it is withered, it is become like a stick. They that be slain with the *sword are better than they that be slain with hunger;* for these pine away, stricken through for want of the fruits of the field" (Lam. iv. 8, 9). Thus this judgment is worse than the former. Again, "*Our skin was black like an oven because of the terrible famine*" (Lam. v. 10).

The rider has "a pair of balances" in his hand. They are another indication of famine. When corn is plentiful, it is sold by measure, and a few hundred grains either way are not regarded. But when it becomes very precious, every grain is taken into the account.

Also this weighing of food is given as one of the indications of scarcity. "*And when I have broken the staff of your bread*, ten women shall bake your bread in one oven; *and they shall deliver you your bread again by weight; and ye shall eat and not be satisfied*" (Lev. xxvi. 26). This follows after the threat of the *sword* and *pestilence*.

But the voice of God instructs the rider also concerning the extent of the scarcity. It is not to be without parallel, nor the entire want of everything capable of supporting life.

The throne of God appoints the prices of provisions. The weather, the crops, the quantities of money in the country, the extent of speculation in the market, and a multitude of subordinate causes seem to the eye of men to regulate the price. But faith discerns amidst the seeming complexity the One Hand, and hears the voice of God supreme.

But what is the price fixed ? " A chœnix of wheat for a denarius."

On which point take the following statement of Moses Stuart. " The dearness of the price of grain according to this statement is easily seen. A *penny* (denarius) was the usual price of a day's labour : Matt. xx. 2, 9. A chœnix was the 48th part of an Attic medimnus of grain, and the ordinary price of this was *five or six denarii.* Of course, the usual price of a chœnix of wheat was only about the $\frac{1}{8}$th of a denarius ; so that the price becomes advanced in the present case to *eight times the usual cost.* As the statement of the text now is, a man could earn only his own personal subsistence by his labours : and consequently his family are left unprovided for : " p. 542.

While but one chœnix of wheat was to be allowed for a denarius, three chœnices of barley were to be purchased for the same sum. This is not the usual ratio. Barley was about half the price of wheat, not a third, in ordinary cases. 2 Kings vii. 16, 18.

" Barley," says Burckhardt, " is generally not more than half the price of wheat " (*Travels in Syria*, p. 296). From this we may conclude that the barley-crop will be less injured than the wheat : and that the poor will be compelled to live on barley-meal and barley bread. It is only a scarcity that is predicted, not the extreme degree of famine. These are the *beginnings* of sorrows.

" And hurt *not* the oil and the wine." Then he *was* to hurt the wheat and barley, till the market-price should rise to the sum decreed by the throne. But the vineyards and olive-yards were to be uninjured. From this evidence, one conversant with the subject might infer the weather indicated, whether excessive heat or rain, or cold, or mildew.

The famine, then, does not consist in the total destruction of all the necessaries of life; but the Most High, now besieging the earth, is stinting His enemies in their provisions.

FOURTH SEAL.

7. "And when he opened the fourth seal I heard the voice of the fourth living creature, saying, 'Go!' And I saw and behold a green horse, and he that sat on him was named Pestilence,[1] and Hades followed after him. And authority was given to them over the fourth of the earth to kill with sword and with famine and with pestilence, and by the wild beasts of the earth."

A green horse follows the call. The colour of this steed is indeed usually called "pale" But "pale" is, strictly speaking, no colour; it is only a modification of colour.

"Green" is the only meaning of the word in its other occurrences in the New Testament. Mark vi. 39; Rev. viii. 7; ix. 4. This, in a vegetable, is a beautiful colour; but in an animal, it is the livid hue of the plague-stricken and corrupting carcase. It was the colour that in a garment or in a house marked the presence of the plague of leprosy. Lev. xiii. 49.

The rider's name is "Pestilence." It *must* be so taken in the last clause of this verse. His name describes what he effects. So the star. "Wormwood" makes bitter the waters, Rev. viii. 11. The character of the name shows that we have not mistaken the meaning of the previous two horsemen.

---

[1] By the Greek θάνατος here used, the LXX about thirty times translate the Hebrew דבר or pestilence, as in 1 Kings viii. 37; Jer. xxi. 7.

Thus again we see the carrying out of the Saviour's prediction concerning His return. After His prediction of wars and famines, He adds, " and *pestilences* " (Matt. xxiv. 7). Each blow struck by the Most High is heavier than the last.

Pestilence on the horse goes forth first. " Hades followed after him," whether on foot or no, is not said. The place in which departed souls [1] are gathered is personified : so great is to be the deadliness of the plague, that Hades follows as the reaper to gather up the fallen ears. Such a scene Isaiah foretold. Isa. v. 14.

" Authority was given them over the fourth of the earth." The second horseman had power over the earth ; these, over but a fourth part of it. Why, it is not easy to say. But the depopulation here is the more terrible, the fourth portion being assailed by four plagues in united operation.

Mystery is disappearing. The name of the horseman is, in this fourth seal, first given. And now the object of the mission of the previous horsemen is manifestly intimated. The second rider is War, who is to " kill with *sword*." The third is Famine, who is to slay " with *famine*." The fourth is Pestilence, as we have just seen. But there is a further power of death annexed, in " the wild beasts of the earth." God's creatures fight on his side, whether birds or beasts. In former days, God has made use of this or a similar scourge. On the refractory Pharaoh and his servants He sent locusts, and other troublesome animals. Against the murmuring Israelites He commissioned the fiery serpents : Num. xxi. 6. On the Canaanites He sent hornets : Exod. xxiii. 28 ; Josh. xxiv. 12. Lions slew

---

[1] " That ᾅδης [Hades] has reference to *the world of the dead*, lit. *the invisible world, the under-world*, like שְׁאוֹל, there can, of course, be no doubt." Stuart, 544.

the Samaritans : 2 Kings xvii. 25 ; and she-bears the mocking young men : 2 Kings ii. 24.

In the present case there is sin, and this is the secret cause of the peculiar ferocity of the wild beasts at the time predicted. He who holds all creatures in His hand, increases now their numbers, and lets them loose on men, as never was the case before ; because men are more openly his enemies than their fathers were.

They are called " wild beasts *of the earth*," by way of distinction. When these well-known animals of the surface fail to effect their purpose, the Most High brings up creatures *from beneath*. He has many shafts in His quiver :' the lightest are used first. But if they avail not, His judgments deepen in intensity.

It will be understood from the general principles laid down that not one of these seals has been opened : and the various attempts at explaining them have proved unsatisfactory to almost all but the authors. They will not, I suppose, begin to be fulfilled till Israel is restored to his land.

FIFTH SEAL.

9. " And when he opened the fifth seal, I saw underneath the altar the souls of those that had been slain because of the word of God, and because of the testimony which they used to hold : and they cried with a great voice, saying, How long, O Master, the Holy and true, dost thou not judge and avenge our blood upon the dwellers upon the earth ? "

Why so many saints of God have been slain, and He seems not to regard, is a mystery. But His patience is not to last for ever.

The " souls " of the slain were seen by John. At this many stumble : but it is perfectly possible. The soul of Samuel was seen by Saul. The *soul* is a different thing from the *spirit* of man. The soul or ghost appears as a shadowy likeness of a man's self, when the outer framework of the body falls in death. Man had done his worst against them: the soul survived. Have not departed spirits at various times appeared to the living? To deny it on the ground of *a priori* reasonings is unphilosophical; and in marked opposition to credible testimony.

John saw them "under the altar." By this is always meant the altar of burnt offering. There the fire ever burnt, and on it the blood and limbs of the animals slain in sacrifice were consumed while in several cases, it was required that the main portion of the blood should be poured out at the bottom of the altar: Exod. xxix. 12; Lev. iv. 7; v. 9. But the soul is the blood, or in it: Lev. xvii. 11, 14. Their animal souls were the part seen: but the immaterial spirit is most closely connected therewith: Heb. iv. 12. Hence these saints are regarded as sacrifices to God; not of *atonement* either for themselves or others: but sacrifices of *devotion*—" burnt offerings." "But if *I am even poured out as a drink offering* upon the sacrifice and service of your faith, I joy and rejoice with you all" (Phil. ii. 17). "*For I am now ready to be offered*, and the time of my departure is at hand" (2 Tim. iv. 6). They were *under* the altar, whither the blood flowed. There is a real altar on high, that of the new covenant, from which Moses took his copy. Abel's blood had called to God from the ground. The souls of these were on high, and thence put in their plea. The old covenant had its victims of sheep and goats: the new has martyrs for its sacrifices.

In their appearing under the altar, is a reference to the construction of the old brazen altar. "*Hollow* with boards shalt thou make it: as it was shewed thee in the mount, so shall they make it" (Exod xxvii. 8).

They were not, therefore, though martyrs, "reigning

with Christ," as the creed of Pope Pius assumes. Jesus was the Lamb slain, but He had risen, and was now before the throne. These were *disembodied spirits still; and as such, beneath the temple; not admitted to the immediate presence of God, while unclothed.*

Were the gospel-martyrs amidst this company? I think not : (1) from the cry which they raise to God ; (2) from the title by which they address God ; and (3) from the answer which is given to their petition. It is remarkable that it is said indefinitely " for the testimony *which they used to hold*," not, as in other cases, " for the testimony *of Jesus Christ* " (i. 9 ; xx. 4 ; xii. 17).

They ask why vengenace is so long delayed ? The blood of the saints is a reason for God's wrath. " The voice of thy brother's blood *crieth* unto me from the ground." But for thousands of years the murder has been unavenged.

The cry for vengeance then breathes the spirit of the *law :* Ps. lxxix. 10. If the souls of Christian martyrs were there, it could only be because the dispensation had changed, and the Saviour's commands of mercy were repealed.

Their appeal for justice proves that the soul in the intermediate state does not sleep.

The parties against whom they cry are " the dwellers on the earth." The phrase is very simple, yet to define its exact meaning is not easy. Is it a moral or a physical description ? Is every inhabitant of the globe included ? No : for some of the servants of God are found on the earth, as the next chapter proves. I believe, then, that it is a *moral* description of the guilty parties. The men of faith, both before and under the law, confessed themselves to be, not possessors of earth and dwellers on it, but " pilgrims and strangers," looking for a real resting-place, and the country and city which God had provided them : Heb. xi. Those, then, who have the opposite spirit to this—who contend for the sufficiency of things here below, who believe that this world is the only reality, and that God's promises of the future are airy fancies and speculations at the best, are the parties complained of.

11. "And unto each of them was given a white robe; and it was said unto them, that they should rest yet a little time,[1] until both their fellow-servants and their brethren, that were about to be killed as THEY also were, should be fulfilled."

A white robe is given to each. This marks them as *justified*, or accounted righteous. But they are not justified by the merit of their martyrdom. The power of the blood of the Lamb to redeem having been now set forth, they are justified. *But they were not openly justified before.* They belong not to the company of those already declared to be accepted during life, through the knowledge of, and union with, Jesus. Christ had not come, nor his blood been preached when they were slain.

But they are to abide still in the same place for a further period. They are not, I believe, among the Great Multitude. The vengeance promised does not begin till the vials. And then a voice comes from this company under the altar expressive of their sympathy with the justice executing. "*And I heard the altar saying, Yea, Lord God of hosts, true and just are thy judgments*" (xvi. 5–7).

But let us consider the message. They are to "rest *yet* for a little time." This admits, then, that they have already rested for a long time. Their state had been one of peace; and during the whole of the gospel dispensation, or while the throne of grace was set, this cry went not up. It would have been out of season. But it is not even now to be answered in a moment. The fullness of human sin must precede the fullness of the divine judgments.

[1] Χρόνον.

But for what were they to wait? " Until both their fellow-servants and their brethren " should be slain. I am apt to believe, then, that by the first word believers in Jesus, the remnant of the Church, are meant : and that by the other, Jews and disciples of Christ under Antichrist are intended.

For there are two great future persecutions supposed in the body of the book, one by Babylon, before Antichrist has appeared ; or, at least, before he has appeared in his true character as the Blasphemer. xvii. 6. But there is also the war of Antichrist against them (xiii. 7), when whoever will not worship his image is to be killed. 15.

The dwellers on earth must first be proved genuine *children* of the destroyers of God's saints of old, ere the vengeance foretold by the Saviour shall descend. To this seal our Lord's words apply. " *Fill ye up then the measure of your fathers.*" " *That upon you may come all the righteous blood shed upon the earth.* Verily I say unto you, *All these things shall come upon this generation* " (Matt. xxiii. 32, 34–36).

This is the reason of the pause after the seventh seal. Persecution, after the terrors of the sixth seal, is stunned. It is only by degrees, as fears wear away, that men grow bold enough to injure and to slay God's saints. With answering slowness does judgment move.

When men shall slay the servants of God, *on principle*, because they hinder the worldly in careless enjoyment of the things of time, then will the time of recompense be come, because the iniquity of man and his rebellion of spirit against the God of heaven will be matured.

How vainly, then, do those Christians who do not study prophecy expect that the earth is about to submit itself, all but universally, to Christ ! Moreover, this passage gives us to understand that the promised happiness of earth cannot arrive till a period of awful judgment for the sin of putting to death the servants of God, is past.

SIXTH SEAL.

12. "And I saw when he opened the sixth seal, and a great shaking [1] followed; and the sun became black as sack-cloth of hair, and the whole (full) [2] moon became as blood; and the stars of the heaven fell unto the earth, as a fig-tree casteth her untimely figs, when shaken by a great wind. And the heaven departed as a scroll that is being rolled up; and every mountain and island were moved out of their places."

Are the signs in the heaven to be taken literally or figuratively?

Most regard them as figurative.

But we assume as the true principle that each statement is to be taken literally, if it be possible. Is there any absurdity in so explaining the phenomena foretold? There is not, it is granted, in relation to the effects on the sun and moon: but how can the stars fall to earth?

I cannot tell. Yet sure I am that God designed these signs to be taken literally. For difficulties do not lie on the literal side only. Greater besiege the figurative interpretation.

The Saviour is crucified: with what results?

Was the *sun literally stricken with darkness?* Yes. Did the *earth literally quake?* It did, and that as the result of the sin of man in putting the Son of God to death. How clear, then, that the darkening of the sun and the tremulousness of the earth in this seal are literal also!

The earthquake at the crucifixion was not nearly so great. It only rent rocks: it did not hurl islands from their seats. Nor answerably were the effects on men so great. They did not *flee from* their homes, and hide

---

[1] This is more than an earthquake: it is the shaking of heaven as well as earth. The word is applied to a tempest at sea: Matt. viii. 24.

[2] Ὅλη. So Tregelles.

in rocks. They *went to* their homes. But it drew forth the theological views of some of the spectators ; as does the earthquake of the Apocalypse.

The shaking foretold by the prophets is literal. " Thus saith the Lord of Hosts—Yet once, it is a little while, and I will *shake the heavens and the earth, and the sea, and the dry land.* And *I will shake all nations*, and the desire of all nations shall come ; and I will fill this house with glory, saith the Lord of Hosts " (Hag. ii. 6, 7). Here the concussion is spoken of in the most literal terms ; and the shaking of the *nations* is declared to be something distinct from that of the *heavens.* It is to precede the coming of Christ, and the glory of the rebuilt temple. Hag. ii. 21, 22.

It is not denied that the sun, moon, and stars are sometimes taken symbolically : only, in every case, the context must teach us, whether the author meant his words to be taken in the one sense or in the other. Nor can it in most cases take more than a moment to decide.

The tents of the Arabs are often made of black haircloth, to the colour of which the sun's appearance is now compared. The moon, then at the full, becomes ensanguined, or like blood.

Stars fall from their places. They are called " the stars *of the heaven,*" I suppose, in order to distinguish them from the mystic stars which Christ held before in His hand. Not all of them are cast down ; as the comparison appears to prove. For their fall is like that of the untimely figs of a fig-tree, much shaken by a gale. The fruit intended is the winter-fig, that comes out too late in the summer to ripen, and loses its hold of the tree during the inclement skies of the end of the year ; so as to be easily shaken off by any wind which agitates to any considerable extent the branches of the tree. But how can they fall to the earth ? I know not.

This is a physical difficulty, which may be left with God. But I conceive the apostle may be speaking of their all taking a definite direction downwards, as seen from the position occupied by Him in heaven. Can it refer to a copious fall of meteors, commonly called " falling stars " ?

The heavens are rolled up as a scroll. How to render this into modern astronomical language is not easy. But I understand John's meaning to be as follows. The nocturnal heaven decorated with stars is the parchment field unrolled. As manuscript rolls in general were coiled round one stick, and that held in the right hand, the rolling up would commence at the right side, and be continued towards the left, till the scroll was wound up. This would suppose, then, that the stars of the eastern region were first swept from their places, the sky there becoming a blank, and the unpeopling of the sky continuing till it reached the west. This, then, would be another view of the previous statement.

But are we to suppose that the heaven, as the result of the shaking, will be quite unfurnished of stars ? No. For some remain during the fourth trumpet, viii. 12.

But its effects upon the earth are natural enough. It hurls mountains and islands—the mountains of the sea—from their places. Similar effects have occasionally followed such convulsions of nature. In the last great earthquake, the mightiest that ever shall be known, " Every island fled away, and mountains were not found " (xvi. 20).

15. " And the kings of the earth, and the great men (nobles), and the captains of thousands, and the rich men, and the mighty men, and every slave and freeman, hid themselves in the caves, and in the rocks of the mountains."

Kings, nobles, the military officers, and men of

L

courage and daring, slaves and freemen, all are terrified by this awful visitation. But soldiers and strong men are not terrified at revolutions. They are at home in scenes of conflict. Slaves are little troubled at such events, for they have nothing to lose.

All classes of mankind have been guilty of persecuting the saints; and this fearful sight is sent in consequence of it.

Their actions declare their fear. Their houses are no security against the earthquake; but when they flee forth into the open air to escape the falling walls, then the terrible phenomena of the troubled heavens disclose themselves to their terrified gaze. Where now shall they hide? Even kings leave their palaces in haste, and dread both the city and the open field. They flee to the rocks and caves. Revolutions do not make all men alike fearful, nor lead them to desert their homes for the caves of the rocks. Many, aye most, are busily employed then in attack or defence. No, it must mean nothing less than the literal appearance of the sky. There, where all is usually calm and orderly they see tremendous perturbation. How should they not be disturbed? These rare sights of dread, visible to all, strike in a moment profound dread to the heart of savage and of civilized alike.

"There is no event which makes so deep and lasting an impression on the mind as an earthquake, nor does any other phenomenon of nature affect it to an equal degree; hence those who have not experienced an earthquake are unable to judge of the state of mind into which people are thrown by it. Confusion, distraction, and horror carried to the highest pitch, do not convey an adequate idea of what is passing in their hearts. The principal cause of this extraordinary state of mind is doubtless founded in the circumstance that an earthquake unsettles our whole system of thinking and reasoning, by withdrawing the foundation on which it rests. From our earliest years we have been accustomed to consider the soil under our feet as firm and immovable. We have unconsciously connected this idea with all our conceptions, feelings, and actions ; and it thus becomes the basis of all our plans, intentions, and wishes. Our whole life, with all its events and operations, rests on this idea as on an immutable foundation. An earthquake, by turning it into a delusion, overthrows our whole system of thinking and acting. We are no longer able to collect our thoughts so as to form an idea ; we cannot conceive any plan, nor take any resolution. The faculty of thinking is, as it were, paralysed, and our mind thrown into the utmost confusion. The difference between a strong and a weak mind disappears. We are no longer guided by principle or reason ; we follow only the involuntary impulse of instinct, or, in the most favourable circumstances, we are influenced from some feelings arising from some previous idea, which fortunately has been indelibly impressed on our mind."

There are two great occasions on which God will show signs in the sun, moon, and stars, together with signs on earth. One of these occasions is to PRECEDE the Great Day of Trouble : the other is to FOLLOW it.

1. The following passages speak of the great commotions in heaven *at the close* of the Great Day of wrath.

Isaiah xiii. 9–13. Isaiah xxxiv. 1–4. Joel iii. 9–17.

2. The following texts speak of the signs in heaven which *precede* the awful day.

Joel ii. 30, 31.

It is to this passage that Peter refers, when he begins to proclaim the Gospel. These terrible signs would *precede* the terrible day, and give notice that the Gospel was past.

Our Lord speaks of two such occasions.

Luke xxi. 11 gives us the first occasion.

Verses 25–27 present the second and last occasion.

It is from mistaking this point that the men of earth are so terrified. The greatest cause of their consternation is not that which they see. Awful as is the commotion of the sky and earth, there is something more terrible still which they expect. They look for JESUS HIMSELF TO APPEAR IN THE CLOUDS, as He foretold. Matt. xxiv. 29, 30.

This is their greatest terror, which swallows up the exterior sights and sounds of dread.

They do not observe that Jesus is to appear "immediately AFTER the tribulation of those days." But, at this point of time, the Great Tribulation of the earth has not even *begun*. Hence their fears subside, and they grow hard of heart, when Jesus does not show Himself. They laugh at their own apprehensions. "It was a chance that happened unto us."

As expounders of this book have mistaken the *description* given of that hour, as if it foretold the moment of Jesus' visible revelation ; so will the men of earth who behold the *actual sign* be also misled. "As a snare shall that day come upon all the earth."

16. "And they are saying unto the mountains and to the rocks, Fall on us, and hide us from the face of the Sitter upon the throne, and from the wrath of the Lamb. 17. For the great day of His wrath is come, and who is able to stand ?"

Even in their hiding-places, they do not esteem themselves sufficiently hid. Still the earthquake rocks them ; still the sky lowers with ominous frown. Isa. ii. 10, 11, 19–21. The distinctions of rank and degree among men are all over-mastered by irrepressible fear. Kings and subjects, slaves and freemen, all hurry to the same hiding-places. The bold soldier and the timid female are side by side. They all understand it as the act of God above ; and look on it as due to no subordinate and ordinary cause. Here then we have additional proofs that no mere social revolution is in question. There the hardy man of courage, and the military, would not be overpowered with dread, nor rush to hide from God. Nor are the social and physical distinctions here enumerated erased by revolution.

Whenever that day arrives, the literal interpretation will drive out the figurative from men's minds, as with a whirlwind's speed and violence.

Men trace these terrible appearances to the wrath of God and Christ. The former seals were comparatively secret actings of God; and mankind appear to regard them not. But at each opened seal, God more and more manifestly interferes with the present quiet order of things. And men discern it at length. They perceive *design* in these successive judgments, or at least in this last complication of terrors. They understand it to imply His displeasure, and rightly.

The nations at this point of time are nominally Christian. They speak of, and own *God*, and His *Son slain*. They have received this teaching from the Harlot, with whom the kings of the earth commit fornication.

They do not speak of, or rest in, the blood of Jesus, as their confidence. Even this confession is but for a moment. When next mankind are terrified at Jerusalem, Antichrist has risen, and the Son of God is no longer owned: Rev. xi. 13. The Antichrist is to disown both the Father and the Son: 1 John ii. 22. And when men acknowledge *him*, they refuse the true God, and assert the indivisible oneness of the Godhead.

It is instructive to compare this scene with that of the seventh bowl (vial). Rev. xvi. 17–21.

This takes place at the close of the Great Day of wrath. The commotion of the sixth seal is great: this far greater. The effect of the earthquake on the abodes of men, and the consequent terrific slaughter come more into view. There is besides a hail of crashing, crushing weight. But men have fearfully ripened in sin now. They have drunk into the spirit of the False Christ. They are beyond repentance. They are not afraid now, they *blaspheme!* At the sixth seal, they own the Father and the Son. Now they deny both: they blaspheme " God."

CHAPTER VII

THE SEALING OF THE EARTHLY ELECT

1. "After this I saw four angels standing at the four quarters of the earth, holding the four winds of the earth, that wind should not blow on the earth, nor on the sea, nor on any tree."

THE sixth seal having displayed the heart of mankind, and shown how unready and unwilling they are to entertain the reign of Christ, the people of God of two standings, and two destinies, are next set before us.

The four angels spoken of are not those to whom the winds are ordinarily given in charge, as appears by the omission of the article. It is "four angels holding *the* four winds." They are good angels: for the sealing angel addresses them as his fellow-servants. "Hurt not—till *we* have sealed the servants of *our* God." John is so high above the earth that he sees it at once as a ball, and the angels occupying the stations of east, west, north, and south.

The elements of nature keep their quiet course only during the pleasure of the Divine Throne. When let loose, the winds are destructive to the labours and habitations of men on land, and to the ships at sea. Job i. 19; Jonah i. 4, 12. Now no breath of air is to blow—the very leaves of the trees are not to rustle.

2. "And I saw another angel ascending from the rising of the sun, having the seal of the living God: and he cried with a great voice to the four angels, to whom it was given to hurt the earth and the sea, saying, 3. 'Hurt not the earth, nor the sea, nor the trees, until we have sealed the servants of our God upon their foreheads.'"

The expression " another angel " severs this one from the previous four. He is like them ; for he is an angel : he is unlike ; and so is distinguished as " another."

" Another angel " is a title more than once applied to Christ in this book. Thus the descending messenger, who in the tenth chapter claims heaven and earth for God, and who is admitted by most to be Jesus, is called " another angel." So the angel who descends to earth with an intense brilliance that illuminates it (xviii. 1) is called " another angel " ; and is, I suppose, the Son of God. Jesus' horse was " another " than that of the three succeeding horsemen.

But if Jesus appear as an angel, he would be " another angel," one of a superior and commanding description. But if it be Jesus, then we are on *Old Testament ground* : and the book, as far as it is prophetic, is to be explained on Old Testament principles ; that is, literally.

He has " the seal of the living God." This manifests His dignity. He who holds the great seal of the realm is one of its chief officers : greatly trusted by the throne : Gen. xli. 42.

That the mark left by the seal is an object of sight seems proved by these considerations.

1. The locusts, though animals possessed of but small intelligence, are able to see it, and respect it.

2. The sign of the old covenant was a mark visible in the flesh.

3. The sign of God's servants in Egypt was the visible mark of blood on the door.

4. Satan imitates God : and his mark, set on the worshippers of the Wild Beast, is assuredly visible. xiii.

5. The sign set on Cain to preserve him was literal. This mark also is to preserve the receiver. The mark on Cain was to prevent anyone from hurting him, murderer though he was. Much more is this to preserve his true servants. It is a sign to men, and to the

executioners of the judgments of the Lord, not to injure the wearer. Ps. cv. 15.

It is the seal of "*the living God.*" This is the title which God usually takes, as the author of miracles, and as set in opposition to the vain gods of idolaters.

By this mark, then, the faithful remnant is constituted God's witnesses against the idolatry then abroad. ix. 20.

The four angels are those " to whom *it was given* to hurt the earth and sea." That it is by the commission of the throne that all fulfil, either designedly or undesignedly, their parts, is a truth continually enforced upon us in this book. 'Tis God's earth. The power of angels, whether good or bad, is limited by Him.

The interval was to last "till we have sealed the servants of our God on their foreheads." By this sign the Lord distinguishes His people from the terrified and hostile world. "The Lord knoweth them that are His." But that during the churches was a secret thing: now He makes them known to the earth. These are the people whom He would spare, during the judgments abroad on earth. But this marking of the flock by God only points them out to man as those whom He hates and will injure. This is "the flock of the slaughter." These are the elect of earth, for whose sake the days of great woe are to be shortened, as now the coming on of wrath is delayed. Matt. xxiv. 22. They are those who are referred to in the reply to the souls under the altar, as about, in part, to be slain, ere the full woes descend.

These are referred to also by Joel, as those of Israel on whom the Lord would pour out His Spirit : for besides the outpouring upon all flesh, it is to be upon " your sons [O Jews] and your daughters." Presently, too, follow " wonders in heaven and earth, *blood* and *fire*, [first trumpet] and *pillars of smoke* [fifth trumpet]. The *sun shall be turned into darkness, and the moon into blood, before the great and terrible day of the Lord come."* This has already been seen under the sixth seal.

As then the gospel was signalized by the bestowal of miraculous gifts, so will this new dispensation of the crisis just preceding the kingdom be likewise honoured thereby, previously to the breaking forth of supernatural power from Satan on behalf of his delusions.

The origin of the expression, " the servants of God," is to be found in the central object of the book—THE THRONE OF GOD. All throughout is in relation and subjection to that. Now the relation in which all stand to the throne is that of " subject." But the Scripture expression for " subject " is " servant." 1 Sam. viii. 17; 1 Kings x. 5, 8; 1 Sam. xvii. 8.

Now the throne of God abides throughout; and hence this title of " servants " continues to the close. xxii. 3.

4. " And I heard the number of the sealed : a hundred and forty-four thousand were sealed, out of every tribe of the children of Israel. 5. Of the tribe of Judah twelve thousand sealed ; of the tribe of Reuben twelve thousand ; of the tribe of Gad twelve thousand. 6. Of the tribe of Asher twelve thousand ; of the tribe of Nepthalim twelve thousand ; of the tribe of Manasseh twelve thousand. 7. Of the tribe of Simeon twelve thousand ; of the tribe of Levi twelve thousand ; of the tribe of Issachar twelve thousand. 8. Of the tribe of Zebulon twelve thousand ; of the tribe of Joseph twelve thousand ; of the tribe of Benjamin twelve thousand sealed."

They were twelve thousand " out of every tribe of the children of Israel." That the number 144,000 is to be exactly taken is proved, (1) By its standing contrasted with an *indefinite* number, which is given immediately after. (2) The items which go to make up the sum, are given in detail. If this be not to be regarded as exact, what sum may be throughout the Bible ?

Many have stumbled at the exactness of the number of twelve thousand in each case. And if the Lord left the number to *chance*, there would be infinite probabilities against the redeemed out of each tribe being the same number. But if it depends on His decree, where is the difficulty?

They are Jews, or Israelites. This is proved, (1) By the express mention of each tribe. (2) They stand opposed to the multitude out of "*all the Gentiles*," which follows immediately after. (3) Among the churches of Christ, Scripture recognizes no tribeship. "That they all may be *one*." (4) The tribe of Judah has been just taken literally in the title of the Lord Jesus. He is "the lion of *the tribe of Judah*." Is the Church prefigured both by a *stated and limited number of Jews*, and by an *innumerable multitude of Gentiles?* (5) The expression "the children of Israel," has already been employed literally in the Epistles. ii. 14. (6) The Jew is in the latter day to be the test of the Gentile. Matt. xxv. 40, 45. (7) Those who are marked escape the locusts. But it is to *Israel* that God gives directions how to escape the visitation of the locusts. Joel ii. (8) "The kings of the earth" are literally taken in the sixth seal. So then these tribes of one of the nations, which are sometimes put in contrast with them. (9) John, who needed to be instructed concerning the Great Multitude, needed no teaching concerning the twelve tribes. Why? Because they were literally taken.

The last-named of the tribes is Benjamin, of which tribe was Paul, the last of the known apostles. The whole twelve are now acknowledged once more, preparatory to their being made one nation upon the mountains of Israel.

It is very worthy of observation, how very similar are the histories of the apostles, and of the tribes.

But now a word upon the general order of the tribes. The order of the Apocalypse is as follows:—

1. Judah   5. Nepthalim   9. Issachar
2. Reuben   6. Manasseh   10. Zebulon
3. Gad   7. Simeon   11. Joseph
4. Asher   8. Levi   12. Benjamin.

The order of birth is as follows :—
Sons of Leah :—Reuben, Simeon, Levi, Judah.
Of Bilhah :—Dan, Naphtali.
Of Zilpah :—Gad, Asher.
Of Leah (after an interval) :—Issachar, Zebulon.
Of Rachel :—Joseph, Benjamin.

Thus it appears, that the sons of the four mothers are curiously interchanged. Leah's sons precede. In Bilhah's and Zilpah's the natural order is reversed. Arranged with regard to the mothers, the order in the Apocalypse will stand thus :—

1. Of Leah :—Judah, Reuben.
2. Of Zilpah :—Gad, Asher.
3. Of Bilhah :—Naphthali. But Dan, her other son, is omitted; and Manasseh, a son of Joseph, and descendant of Rachel's, takes his place.
1. Leah's earlier sons re-appear; Simeon, Levi.
1. Leah's later sons; Issachar, Zebulon.
4. Rachel's; Joseph, Benjamin.

The covenant of which these are the subjects is of grace. It is not, like the Law, a thing dependent on their previous promises. It is sovereign. The seal is set on those whom the Lord chooses. "*I will* put my law in their hearts.*" "They shall* be my people, *I will* be their God." And the seal is impressed by an angel, though still set on their flesh.

9. "After these things I saw, and behold a great multitude, which none could number, out of every nation and (of all) tribes, and peoples, and tongues, standing before the throne, and before the Lamb; clothed in white robes, and palms in their hands;
10. And they cry with a great voice, ' Our salvation [1] (be ascribed) to our God who sitteth upon the throne, and to the Lamb ! ' "

[1] Force of the article.

"After these things." An interval occurs between this spectacle and the former sealing, during which Jesus, as the sealing angel, has returned on high. The scene now changes from earth back to heaven.

"Behold, a great multitude." Of whom does this great multitude consist ? Are they, as some imagine, men living in the flesh on earth ?

They are, I believe, risen conquerors from the Church of Christ. Are they from the Church alone, or a selection from other dispensations ?

1. First, that some of the Church are amidst the throng, I gather, (1) From their *white robes:* that is a promise made to the conquerors of Sardis. iii. 4, 5. (2) They are caught up, too, before the hour of great temptation comes upon the earth. Hence those are here to whom the Philadelphian promise is made. iii. 10.

2. The souls under the altar form no part of the assembly. For they are told to rest, till another persecution, or persecutions, should complete the number of the martyrs. Now the slain for Christ's sake do not cease till the last vial, or the destruction of Babylon. xv. ; xviii. 24.

3. It seems nearly certain that this is the same body as the Son born to the Woman in heaven. xii. The reasons for so thinking are found in the great resemblance between the two bodies.

(1) These trace their salvation to the Lamb : the elder ascribes their presence before the throne as due to His blood. So of the Man-child we read, "They overcame him *by the blood of the Lamb*" (xii. 11).

(2) "They stand before the throne." So the saints signified by the Woman's Son are "caught up to God, and *to His throne*" (xii. 5).

(3) The Great Multitude ascribe "*salvation*" to God and to the Lamb. When the Man-child ascends, a voice from heaven cries, "Now are come *the salvation,* and

the strength, and the kingdom *of our God and of His Christ*" (xii. 10).

(4) The Woman of chapter xii., crowned with *twelve stars*, seems to answer to the body out of whose *twelve tribes* the 144,000 have just been chosen. The twelve tribes seem to stand somewhat in the place of mother ; the Great Multitude, and the Man-child, in that of son.

(5) The Great Multitude, and the Man-child, both awake the joy of angels on their appearing on high.

(6) The Great Multitude are apparently a part of that company of whom the elders speak in their previous song as about to rule over earth. The Man-child is destined " to rule all nations with a rod of iron " (xii. 5).

(7) Both are risen saints : not disembodied spirits, as is ordinarily assumed. This is proved from their appearing before the throne of God. A disembodied spirit is " unclothed." But it was forbidden to approach the Lord otherwise than as fully clad. Exod. xx. 26 ; xxviii. 42 ; 2 Cor. v. 4. Till the soul and body be reunited, the effects of the curse are not done away, nor are the saints admitted to the heavenly courts. Acts ii. 34.

(8) The same word seems to be used to describe the standing of both. " He that sitteth upon the throne shall *pitch tent* over them " ($\sigma\kappa\eta\nu\omega\sigma\epsilon\iota$). Of the Man-child it is said, " Rejoice, ye heavens, and ye that *pitch tent* in them " (xii. 12).

(9) They seem also to be a party of conquerors in both cases. The two passages quoted above, concerning the white robes, and escaping the scene of temptation below, are promised to conquerors. And of the Man-child it is said, " They *overcame* him by the blood of the Lamb " (xii. 11).

From the above observations it seems to follow, that these two companies are either the same, or very closely related.

It is a multitude "whom none could number." Israel was capable of being numbered, and was actually numbered, even during David's day of prosperity. But this numberless assembly is the fulfilment of the promises. How vast the multitude may be gathered from this, that John gives us numbers in this book amounting to two hundred millions. These then must indefinitely exceed that sum.

"Who can stand before the throne and the Lamb?" say the fugitives of the sixth seal. Here is the answer. *Two great bodies, one on earth, and one on high,* can meet with joy the eye of God.

These are selected out of all tribes and nations: for during the time of the Mystery the moral state of men, not their physical qualities or station, comes into account. *The selection out of every nation is characteristic of the Church.* God visited "the Gentiles (nations) to take *out of them* a people for his name." Acts xv. 14, 19, 23.

Israel is now received once more, as the sealing shows: and the consequence of Israel's reception is resurrection, or "life from the dead" (Rom. xi. 15). This Great Multitude is, I suppose, "*the fullness of the Gentiles*" *come in.*

They have "*palms* in their hands."

This sign denotes their *keeping the feast of tabernacles,* and is a token of their joy. It appears to represent the first day of the feast, as the ninteeenth chapter to exhibit the eighth day, "the great day of the feast," when all the saints of every class are on high.

The feast of Tabernacles took place at the natural period of rest in each year, "when thou hast gathered in thy labours out of the field" (Exod. xxiii. 16). It was to be a season of peculiar joy. Lev. xxiii. 40. Spontaneous joy appears upon the very face of the account. It is heard in their loud shouts of joy, attributing salvation to God.

Salvation is traced by them to the agency of the Father and the Son. This is the spiritual basis of the better covenant. 'Tis the gift of God; not the earning of men. They gladly own that it is not by their works; but by the grace of the Son and the Father. While those below acknowledge the Father and the Son theoretically, these experimentally know them as their Saviour-God.

11. "And all the angels stood round the throne and around the elders and the living creatures, and they fell before the throne upon their faces, and worshipped God, 12. saying, Amen : Blessing and glory, and wisdom, and thanksgiving, and honour, and power, and might, be to our God for ever and ever. Amen."

The angels sympathize, both in the joy of the ransomed and in their praise to God. They add their Amen to the ascription of the saved. But they do not ascribe to God "salvation" as affecting themselves. For they have not fallen, as man has.

Do they rejoice over one sinner who repents ? How much more over the full rescue of the redeemed ? Did they go forth as ministering spirits to aid them in their conflicts ? Much more are they glad, now that those conflicts are ended.

The angels fall down before God : the rescued of men stand. The angels stand *outside* the saved of men : for deliverance from the fall has brought the redeemed nearer to God than unfallen angels. Matt. xviii. 13.

13. "And one of the elders answered, saying to me, 'These, the clothed in the white robes, who are they ? and whence came they ? 14. And I said unto him, 'My lord, thou knowest' "[1]

The question and reply before us bear evidence, *that the elders and John do not represent the Church*. For if so we have three bodies, all supposed to mean the Church. John, *the representative of the Church*, is asked by an elder,

---

[1] See Tregelles for the "my" before Lord.

the representative of the Church, who the Great Multitude —*another figure of the Church*—are.[1] Again, who in the Church should know more than an apostle? But John, by his emphatic "THOU knowest," confesses his ignorance. He *calls the elder, " my lord."* Was any patriarch or apostle the lord of another apostle? The elder does not refuse the title, or correct the mistake. That John might use this title to a ruler of angels, is reasonable enough.

This little dialogue manifests the perfect sincerity of the elders in their congratulations of the Lamb and His flock. Had the scene in chapter five been merely formal, had they been in secret displeased at this elevation of the Saviour and His redeemed above themselves, not one of them had ever voluntarily made renewed mention of the subject to one rejoicing in it.

It was a body but lately arrived in the temple of heaven. It was not seen when the throne was set, nor even when the book was taken.

14. "And he said unto me, 'These are the comers out of the Great Tribulation, and they washed their robes, and made them white in the blood of the Lamb.'"

They have come out of "the Great Tribulation." A question has been raised, whether or not, in translation, the article ought to be inserted before "Great Tribulation." The article is twice repeated in the Greek. But it is urged that the word "tribulation," like the words "blessing," "glory," etc., might take the article as an abstract noun. Possibly it might, if it stood alone; but connected as it is with the adjective "great," this is impossible. An abstract noun with the article intends the object taken universally. But here, an adjective of quantity less than universal comes in to destroy the

---

[1] If the zöa be another symbol of the Church, we have four parties in the same scene with one signification.

abstract sense, and a certain special instance is intended, as here. Where " great tribulation " is meant generally there the article is not used. ii. 22. Acts xiv. 22.

But another question arises. " If it be a special case of trouble, what is that case ? "

1. That to which we should naturally point, would be the Great Time of Trouble foretold, both by Daniel and the Lord. Dan. xii. 1 ; Matt. xxiv. 21.

But several objections present themselves to this view, of weight sufficient to decide against it.

(1) If so, this Great Multitude is out of its place. For the Great Tribulation does not begin till the *woe*-trumpets, and Satan's casting down from on high. viii. 13 ; xii. 12. But these are on high, ere the first trumpet is blown.

(2) Those included in the *promise to Philadelphia are to escape the great temptation, and its tribulation.* iii. 10. Paul holds out the same hope to the *watchful* saint in his second epistle to the Thessalonians. ii. 1, 2. The Great Tribulation, in the Jewish sense, occurs not till the Antichrist be come, and his blasphemy draw down the vengeance. But there is *hope, nay, a promise, that some shall escape* that day of terror.

(3) If it refer to the Jewish tribulation when the temple is taken by the nations, then would it regard exclusively those dying during that period, and so would not include any of the Church of previous ages.

(4) Again, *the Great Tribulation ends not till the last vial ;* and if these come out of it, what time have they to serve day and night in the temple, before entering the city ? For instantly on the last vial, the destruction of Babylon ensues, and then the joy on high is manifested over its fall, and the marriage of the Lamb, or the entrance into the city, takes place.

(5) In Rev. xi. 1, there are worshippers on high who are measured, in order that they may escape the power of

the Gentiles. But none before that date are mentioned as dwelling above, save the Great Multitude. The proof that the worshippers of the inner or altar court are on high will be given by and by. *The Great Tribulation does not begin till the appearing of the two witnesses,* and the plagues brought by them.

The fact is, there are two Great Tribulations ; as surely as Abraham has two seeds ; one like the sand, one like the stars.

1. There is the Great Day of Trouble *to Israel.* Jer. xxx. 7. Of the same day Jesus speaks in Matt. xxiv. 16–22.

2. But *the seed of Abraham by faith* have their Day of Trouble, lasting through the whole length of the dispensation. Israel was in bondage but about 215 years. The Church has had suffering as its foretold portion throughout its existence. In Revelation, " tribulation " is only spoken of in relation to *the churches.* i. 9 ; ii. 9, 10, 13. " *In the world ye shall have tribulation* " (John xvi. 33) is the abiding motto of the saints of the Church ; echoed by Paul's word, " Yea, and *all* that wish to live godly in Christ Jesus, shall suffer persecution " (2 Tim. iii. 12). (Greek.)

It is a sorer temptation and trial than that which Israel endured ; in many cases amounting to martyrdom, and that with torture. Both (1) in *duration,* and (2) in *intensity,* then, it is emphatically " the Great Tribulation."

This assembly, though it have suffered like the souls under the altar, lifts no call for vengeance. Does not that prove it to be of the Church of Christ ?

(6) The *Great Tribulation does not occur till Satan is cast down.* The Man-child is on high ere Satan is cast down. If then the Great Multitude is the same as the Man-child, it is on high ere " the Great Tribulation," in the Jewish sense, has begun. Hence *the expression*

must be taken in *some other than the Jewish sense ;* and that sense doubtless is the one suggested.

It is certain that the " *coming out of* " the Tribulation *implies a previous sojourn in it.* See the passages in which a like expression occurs : Matt. xii. 43 ; Mark ix. 7 ; Luke v. 17 ; xi. 24 ; John iv. 30 ; viii. 59 ; xiii. 3.

We are next enlightened concerning the whiteness of the robes of the saved. It was due to a washing in the Lamb's blood. The doctrine of the imputation of Christ's righteousness to the believer is a blessed truth ; but it is not the one taught here. Christ's robe is one ; here " robes " are spoken of in the plural. These robes were defiled, and needed cleansing. That of Christ does not : much less does it need the saints' cleansing of it. Besides which, the robes are said to be " theirs." " They washed *their* robes." They were guilty of various faults, as Jesus' seven messages to the churches prove. But *they owned them, and removed them by Jesus' blood.* What is intimated, then, in this passage is, that the good deeds of these believers are accepted before God on the ground of the atonement of Christ.

Now they are washed, to be unclean no more ; having put on incorruption, and escaped out of the region of temptation. *Their bodies also are now clean : they have risen from the dead.*

They " made their robes white in the blood of the Lamb." It was not their own blood, shed in martyrdom, that gave them that snowy hue. But " the Fathers," so called, dare to contradict this. Says Aretas, " *We affirm then that the shedding of their blood for Christ's sake delivered them from every stain ! For being baptized in their own blood, they came up white from such a laver* to Christ their king, just like the lambs in Solomon's Song, who come up white from the washing." " Having washed," says Berengaud, " their robes *in baptism,* and also by *repentance and acts of mercy.*" Beware of " the

Fathers!" No! None are there, who whiten their robes with tears, with baptism, and martyrdom.

The washing belongs to the Church of Christ. The same apostle applies it to believers of our dispensation in his Epistle General. "*The blood of Jesus Christ His Son cleanseth us from all sin.*" (1 John i. 7). That present tense "cleanseth" notices the frequency with which believers need to apply. But here the verbs are in the past—"wash*ed*," "ma*de* white." The need is over. Then life is past. They are in heaven.

15. "Therefore are they before the throne of God, and serve Him night and day in His temple : and the Sitter on the throne shall pitch tent over them."

They are taken to the throne of judgment, as the place of refuge from troubles, and they stand there, as at the post of honour. They are kings unto God ; subordinate kings, made so by the blood of the Lamb, and taking the place of the twenty-four elders.

Besides this, they are priests. They are the *new* priests ; admitted to this station, because of their robes cleansed by blood of the Son of God. They are higher than the High Priest of old : they enter the holiest, and abide there. They are possessed of a better nature ; their service is by day and night, endless, and not needing sleep.

"THEREFORE are they before the throne of God." Most important was it, *is* it, for us to know the ground of entry into God's presence. It is through Jesus' blood. It is also in the spirit of holiness : for without it none shall see the Lord. *They were careful to wash in blood, when defiled by sin.*

It is during this period, then, that the promises to the victor of being a pillar in the temple, of eating the hidden manna, and of being priests of God and of *the Christ*, are fulfilled. There is no promise in the closing chapters of a place for the saved in the tabernacle. All their joys are those of the *city* alone. They who are now seen as the *priests of the temple*, become, after the tabernacle is removed, *inhabitants of the city :* while the elect of Israel and of the nations become the inhabitants of the new earth. Thus the distinction between the two flocks here seen is, in principle, eternal.

" They serve day and night." *Here again is a proof that they are above.* What but the risen body could continue serving day and night ? The temple is as real as their bodies.

16. "They shall hunger no more, nor thirst any more : nor shall the sun fall on them, nor any heat. 17. For the Lamb which is in the midst of the throne shall feed them, and lead them to life's fountains of waters : and God shall wipe away every tear out of their eyes."

The hunger and thirst here are literal. Herein this book stands distinguished from John's Gospel, in which Jesus was leading the disciple from the earthly things to learn things spiritual. John iv. 7–15. Now we have come to a dispensation in which " the redemption of *the body* " makes its appearance. Rom. viii. 23.

They are not to abide in the tabernacle for ever. Christ is about to lead them onward to fountains of the waters of life, and to the tree of life. Both these are found in the eternal city.

It is in the time of the Saviour's leading on the saved to the city and the new earth, that the promise to Sardis —" they shall walk with me in white "—is to be fulfilled.

" And God shall wipe away every tear out of their eyes." The Father is here mentioned again, as the author of their comfort. He shall act the part of a parent towards them. This appears to allude to their sufferings from *men*, as the former points referred to the inclemencies of the elements.

CHAPTER VIII

1. "And when he opened the seventh seal, there followed a silence in heaven of about half an hour."

LOOKED at from the throne of God, this silence is a pause of *action* on the part of the Almighty. Immediately upon the former seals, some new voice was heard, and some new agent appeared. But, after this, there was neither voice nor action.

It may be regarded as arising from the inhabitants of heaven. It was only "*in heaven*" that the silence took place. It was the genuine expression of the feelings of those on high. Expectation held them mute.

The Great Multitude and angels pause, therefore, with suspended breath, looking eagerly for some new result of the seal. Surely the final crash will come! For angels are not cognizant fully of the Lord's purposes, or of men's movements; as is manifested by their inability even to see the sealed book. "Of that day and hour knoweth none; no, not *the angels of heaven*." But God is slow to wrath: judgment is His strange act. He will not smite with heaviest indignation till sin is come to the full. But the last seal showed us sin checked and stunned by judgment. Will men repent? Time is given, to show what is in men's hearts. But mercy only ripens iniquity.

The pause, then, of God's mercy after the sixth seal serves to bring out the nature of men's fears. As days wear on, and the expected crash does not come, they recover their courage. Their former dread was but such a pause as might have been enforced on a tiger, if it found itself in a forest on fire. A momentary panic might seize and loosen its limbs, and yet the next day find it quaffing the blood of its prey. Thus men, after assuming that it was "a chance that happened" to them, vent the shame felt at their fancied credulity on the people of God. Persecution manifests the recoil of the heart from its momentary softening.

As men return to their sins, so does God to His judgments.

2. "And I saw the seven angels, who stand before God! and to them were given seven trumpets."

Silently and unknown to the inhabitants of earth, the instruments of war are put into the hands of the servants of the throne. Judgment, it is manifest, must take its course.

The trumpeters are pointed out to us as servants of especial rank. They stand before God, as in perpetual attendance in the presence-chamber of the sovereign of heaven. Their glory is denoted by the article, "*the* seven angels." Of these Gabriel is one, as he himself testifies. Luke i. 19.

Gradations of rank and power, both in heaven and on earth, are part of God's plan. They will take effect, not only in time, but through eternity. Let us gladly acquiesce in this arrangement of God!

To them seven trumpets are given. These spring out of the last seal, and are its real action. Therefore mystery does not cease till they are ended. At the last of them, " the mystery of God is finished ; " but not before. The seven thunders' voices are concealed.

A change of action has set in. A great step of manifestation on God's part is now taken. *The seals were secret judgments. The trumpets are war proclaimed against earth.* His bombardment of earth begins. He looks for the repentance of earth, up to the end of the sixth trumpet; as will by and by appear.

The sound of the trumpet is supposed to be an alarming one. Amos iii. 6. Especially must the trumpets of God be terrible. That at Sinai was so. " There were thunders and lightning, and a thick cloud upon the mount, and the *voice of the trumpet exceeding loud ; so that all the people that was in the camp trembled* " (Exod. xix. 16). The trump of God can give no uncertain, much less an unheard sound. 1 Cor. xiv. 8. How, then, can any, with any degree of plausibility, assert that one of these trumpets has sounded ? Is the seventh trumpet to rouse heaven and earth, and are the previous ones to make no sound ? As the trumpet at Sinai gave notice of God's descent upon the mount, so do these give proclamation of Jesus coming to judge and to reign.

The seals are wrath on undeveloped rebellion: the trumpets are wrath upon those in conscious opposition to God.

3. " And another angel came, and stood at the altar, having a golden censer, and much incense was given to him, that he might put it to the prayers of all the saints upon the golden altar that was before the throne."

As " another angel " superintended the sealing, so does " another angel " now present the prayers of the saints of earth. It is Jesus, I suppose, in both cases. He has finished the sealing, and, having completed it, has returned on high.

" There was given to him much incense." How is this to be reconciled with the angels being Jesus, and the incense His merits ? It is not easy to say. We should have expected, " He *took* much incense."

We learn from this passage, that these prayers of the saints were not sweet odours in themselves, but needed this aromatic addition, to make them acceptable before the throne.

Observe the difference between the *cry* of the *martyred* souls, and the *prayer* of the *living* saints. Dead saints cry to the throne for justice against the wicked; not, as Romanists suppose, for blessings on the righteous. The prayers of the persecuted living saints now join the cry of the departed; and wrath of a severer character comes. Before, heaven asked for vengeance: now, earth also does.

"The prayers of *all* the saints" are presented. From which it would appear that they are of more than one class. The term, "saint" is used of the servants of God both under the Old and New Testament.

What the nature of the prayers is, is evident from the nature of the answer returned. They call forth the trumpets, and the plagues which the trumpets bring. Of the same description is the cry of the dead. The parable of the Unjust Judge is now fulfilling. They cry day and night unto the Lord, as the *Judge of justice:* and He has promised to avenge them speedily. Luke xviii. 1.

4. "And the smoke of the incense went up with the prayers of the saints, out of the hand of the angel, before God."

Prayers for wrath need especially atonement, lest with the same measure they plead for it should be meted out to the petitioners themselves.

The prayers ascended before God in an unbroken stream. Had they been driven downwards, it would have been a sign of their rejection. "As smoke is driven away, so drive them away: as wax melteth before the fire, so let the wicked perish in the presence of God" (Ps. lxviii. 2). The expression is used to signify acceptance. "Thy prayers and thine alms are *come up for a memorial before God.*" "Cornelius, thy prayer is heard, and thine alms are had in remembrance before God" (Acts x. 4, 31). "He *heard my voice* out of His temple, and *my cry came before Him*, even into His ears" (Ps. xviii. 6). Also 2 Chron. xxx. 27. But notice especially Isa. lx. 7 : "All the flocks of Kedar shall be gathered together unto thee, the rams of Nebaioth shall minister unto thee : they shall *come up with acceptance* on mine altar, and I will glorify the house of my glory." The prayers are in sympathy with God's position of Judge, and with the just purposes of His heart.

It is noticed, significantly, that the smoke went up as coming out of the angel's hand. That is, it was owing to *his* presenting the prayers that they were accepted. Exod. xxxii. 4. By themselves, the prayers would not have pleased God. How can this acceptableness be given by any but Christ ?

5. " And the angel took the censer and filled it out of the fire of the altar, and cast (it) into the earth ; and there followed thunders and lightnings, and voices and earthquake."

The angel's intercession is *accepted :* the petitions are *heard.* The wrath descends, *as the result of those supplications.* Without any vocal command, the angel understands the will of God. *The Lamb's sacrifice is the basis of his opening the seals.* The Angel offering incense is the *basis of the trumpet-series.*

The favourable descents of fire from God under the law took effect on the sacrifices. On them they fell, without harming earth. The wrath of God was discharged on the appointed surety. Thus the fire fell in the days of Moses, David, Solomon, and Elijah.

But this falls on "the earth." It is the priest kindling the wood for the sacrifice in which the ungodly are destroyed. It is the accomplishment of that word in Deut. xxxii. "*A fire is kindled in mine anger*, and it shall burn to the lowest Hades, and shall consume the earth with her increase, and set on fire the foundations of the mountains " (22). Its burning down to the bottomless pit is manifested in the fifth trumpet ; its consuming the increase of earth takes place in the first trumpet, where the grass and trees are set on fire.

The priest was to set fire to the wood upon the altar, as preparing for the burnt offering. Lev. i. 7. The wood of earth, accordingly, is burned by the first trumpet. Blood was to be sprinkled upon the altar at the burnt offering. So at the first trumpet, blood is mingled with the fire. The blood of the offering was to be poured out at the bottom of the altar. Lev. v. 9. This is fulfilled in Rev. xiv. 19, 20, where it runs up " to the horse-bridles, by the space of a thousand and six hundred furlongs." Jerusalem is the altar, and the vale of Jehoshaphat at the bottom of it.

Let us observe the result of this fire. Upon its descent followed "thunders and lightnings," as it travelled through the air ; then " voices " of men and angels ; and when it touched earth, "earthquake." The " thunders " and " voices " are the direct contrast to the " silence " that ensued on the seventh seal broken. After that pause in judgment, God's chariot wheels roll on again.

The present scene is predicted in Psalm xviii. 4, 6–9. The next verse, describing the Lord's descent, is not fulfilled till chapter x. 1.

6. "And the seven angels who had the seven trumpets prepared themselves to sound."

The angels preparing themselves to sound, signifies the difference in posture, observable between one carelessly holding a trumpet by his side, and the bending of the arm, the erecting of the figure, the inflating of the lungs, and swelling of the lips and cheeks, as the trumpet is pressed firmly against the mouth. All put the trumpets to their lips together : though they sounded one after another. This preparing themselves together to sound intimates that they would blow the alarm in rapid succession, one after another.

At this point let me offer to the reader a few arguments on behalf of the literality of the plagues inflicted under the trumpets.

1. If the words describing their results be literally taken, then miracles on a stupendous scale are foretold. But as the book before us is the " taking off of a veil," its descriptions, wherever possible, are to be literally taken. Then the plagues are literal and miraculous.

2. The necessity for so taking them is still further apparent, from the circumstances that they are ushered in by trumpets. Who ever announced a *secret* by sound of *trump ?* Then are they not symbols, but open testimonies of what is to be expected by man. If the last trump, as is confessed, is to bring the miracle of the resurrection, why should not the other trumpets bring wonders also ?

3. If taken literally, we are brought into close contact with former acts of God in the Old Testament. Acts of the Most High, of just such a character as these, were once literally wrought in Egypt. Here is another corroboration of our interpretation.

4. But it is also foretold, that the miracles of Egypt are to be, for substance, repeated by God, " *According to the days of thy coming out of the land of Egypt, will I show unto him* MARVELLOUS THINGS " (Mic. vii. 15 ; Isa. xi. 15, 16). Yea, great as those wonders were, the remembrance of them shall be effaced by the greater wonders of the latter day. Jer. xxiii. 7, 8.

5. There is a covenant made by God with Israel which *expressly promises miracles of terror as its basis.* It is remarkable that this should have escaped notice.

"*Behold, I make a covenant: before all thy people I* WILL DO MARVELS *such as have not been done in all the earth, nor in any nation: and all the people among which thou art shall see the work of the Lord: for it is a* TERRIBLE THING *that I will do with thee.*" (Exod. xxxiv. 10). As then these miracles of wrath are to be wrought before Israel, so, before they are sent, the twelve tribes of Israel reappear on the field.

6. The law itself threatens miracles of woe on Israel, if its statutes were broken. "*Then the Lord will* MAKE THY PLAGUES WONDERFUL, *and the plagues of thy seed, even great plagues, and of long continuance, and sore sicknesses, and of long continuance*" (Deut. xxviii. 59). As then the law has in every way been broken, so must these plagues come.

7. The days of Egyptian miracle are, as we have seen, to return. And why? Because the same moral reasons which led God to employ supernatural means in that day, have returned. The great question, "Who is the true God?" is mooted afresh. And as *Jehovah then manifested Himself to be the Creator by His power over the elements,* and over the creatures dwelling in them, so will He again make use of the same most reasonable mode of evidencing His divine attributes. Accordingly, we may observe a particular order in the objects on which the plagues fall, answering to that given in the history of the creation.

But the second great reason for the recurrence of these miraculous plagues is the wickedness of man come to the full. Dan. ix. 23; Ps. ii. The kings and men of earth cast off even nominal subjection to God and His Christ. Why then should the ordinary visitations of wrath smite the earth, when men's wickedness far exceeds that which is found now?

Beside this, Israel will be in danger of being destroyed, under the power of a greater than Pharaoh of old. Ps.

lxxxiii. 4. How shall the Lord deliver them, save by His supernatural power ? Be it remembered, too, that Satan and his agents will work with miraculous might in these times. Rev. xvi. 14. So then must the Holy One of Israel.

8. The latter days are to be like those of Noah and Lot. Luke xvii. But in each of those periods miracles and angels were abroad. If the wickedness be like that day, so will the punishment ; yea, worse ; forasmuch as it is against greater mercies and louder warnings. The same God that worked in the Old Testament on the same material—man—is seen in this book of the Apocalypse. The means used of old are as wise in the last days as in previous ones.

7. " And the first sounded, and there followed hail and fire, mingled with blood, and they were cast unto the earth : and the third part of the earth was burned up, and the third of the trees was burned up, and all green grass was burned up."

May we apply the figurative principle of interpretation to the Old Testament ? Was the Nile turned to blood only Moses' bringing an invading army upon Egypt ? Were the trees there smitten the great men of Egypt, or its ecclesiastical teachers ? Why should the one plague be taken literally ? the other figuratively ? Answer. " To get rid of the awkwardness of MIRACLE being again in operation on our globe : and miraculous *plagues* too ! "

Fire is one of the destructive agents of *war* : sometimes employed by the invader ; sometimes a mode of defence resorted to in order to check the approach of an invading army. It is the Lord smiting man and his wealth through the vegetable creation, which is necessary to his own support and that of his cattle. He deals His blows from a distance first ; afterwards He advances to man's own person, and there strikes with awful force and frequency.

In this and the next three trumpets, a *third* of the elements is smitten. Why is this? First, we may observe, that the span of God's judgments is extending. The fourth seal sent forth agencies that destroyed over a *fourth* only of the earth: now it is a *third*. The judgments deepen too, in intensity and in nearness to the offenders, as they proceed. The first four trumpets affect the natural objects which surround men.

It would seem as if in this third of earth there was a reference to the peopling of earth by Noah's three sons: and that the Asiatic third of earth was intended. At least we see Palestine afflicted by the plague. And not merely is the land of Palestine smitten, but Joel supposes the Jews to be in their land, and the temple to be built. ii. 15-17. Here, then, is another proof that the trumpets have not begun to be sounded.

The plague descends on " the land " generally; as the next trumpet affects " the sea " in general. The issue of the storm is that a " third part of the land is burnt up." The fire is the prevalent and most terrible portion of the plague. It destroys " the land," or " earth: " that is, buildings, flocks, and herds, as distinguished from the crops, and forests, and natural pastures. Such were the effects of the Egyptian plague.

The third of the trees burnt up would refer, I should suppose, to the third of the forests in the portion of the earth which is desolated by the storm.[1] This would account for the next words, " and *all* green grass was burned up." Two-thirds of the stronger trees upon the desolated third of the globe escaped. But all smaller vegetable produce was consumed.

How desolate the aspect of the portion of the globe

---

[1] Hence the importance of the article before "trees," omitted in our translation. " Of *its* trees," that is, of the trees of " the third of the earth," mentioned just before.

visited by this plague! Orchards, forests, cities, meadows burnt: the earth here black and smoking, there blood-red, soon deepening into black, with putrid smell.

8. "And the second angel sounded, and as it were a great mountain burning with fire was cast into the sea : and the third of the sea became blood : 9. and a third of the creatures that were in the sea, that had souls, died ; and the third of the ships was destroyed."

The Psalmist supposes that a mountain may be cast into the sea. Ps. xlvi. 2. Jesus supposes the same. Matt. xx. 21. Not that the mass here hurled into the main is really a mountain torn from the earth and cast into the waters. It is " *as it were* a great mountain." It is a meteoric stone, of the size of Mont Blanc or Ararat, descending from the sky. It is well known that from a clear sky, with intense heat, light, and planetary swiftness, huge metallic bodies have been discharged and struck the earth. This falls into the sea.

The change of the sea, from salt water to blood, poisons the fish. They die and putrefy, and the bloody waves emit a putrid stench.

Partly by the fall of the meteor, partly by the hurricanes let loose, a third of the ships is wrecked.

How appalling the change from the quiet *green* of the ocean, to its opposite colour, a bloody *red !* He will—

> "The multitudinous sea incarnadine,
> Making the green one, red."

Blood, too, is liable to turn putrid, while salt water does not. The river of Egypt " stank," when it was turned to blood. Exod. vii. 18.

"The third of the ships were destroyed." In what way ? It is not said. Many might be sunk by the descent of this fiery mountain on them, and many by the rebound and surges caused by its fall. But probably this is the time when the winds, awhile restrained, are let loose by the four angels. As by the former plague, the agriculturist and grazier were injured; by this, the fisherman, the sailor, and merchant. Each new blow strikes harder than the last. Man's *works* are smitten directly, and of course many men in them; but that is not openly stated.

10. "And the third angel sounded, and there fell out of the heaven a great star burning as a torch, and it fell upon the third of the rivers, and upon the fountains of waters. 11. And the name of the star is called Wormwood: and the third of the waters became wormwood; and many of mankind died from the waters, because they were made bitter."

The mystery of the seven stars existed while the book of seven seals was closed. But those seals are opened now, and mystery is almost gone. Those stars were explained; because they were mystic. This is *not*, for it is literal.

Its appearance, as it falls, is "like a torch." It is on fire at its larger end only; not, like the former missile, blazing all over. It tapers towards the hinder end. The heaven, now, instead of rain to feed the founts and rivers, sends a star to embitter them.

In order to make the expression clear and definite as possible, it is not only said that the star fell on the fountains, but on "the fountains *of waters;*" which is an Old Testament expression. Gen. xxiv. 13, 43; Exod. xv. 27. At Elim were "twelve fountains *of waters*." (Heb.)

This star is called "Wormwood." The name describes its nature. It communicates its bitterness to whatever it touches.

This visitation is foretold by the prophets. Because of sin, "Thus saith the Lord of Hosts, the God of

Israel, Behold, I will *feed them, even this people, with* WORMWOOD, *and give them* WATER OF GALL *to drink*" (Jer. ix. 13–15; Jer. xxiii. 15; Lam. iii. 15).

But it is not only the nauseousness of the taste of that which is ordinarily tasteless, that constitutes this judgment: it produces disease and death. "Many of mankind died of the waters, because they were made bitter." Now, first, the death of men is openly spoken of. Before, his ships were broken: but here man himself is destroyed. The waters of the *sea* would not have injured man, though made more bitter than they are. They, therefore, are turned into *blood*. But the *fresh* waters, made *bitter*, become his bane.

A *star* falling on the waters turns the *sweet* to *bitter*; a *tree cast* into them, in the Exodus, makes the *bitter sweet*. Israel loathed to drink of the bitter beverage, and are indulged with healed waters. But these foes of God must drink of them, such as they are; and they are slain thereby. From Jehovah's calling Himself on the occasion of old, "Jehovah the Healer," it would seem as if the water of Marah had been drunk by some, and had begun to produce disease. Exod. xv. 26. "They could not drink of the waters of Marah [bitter], for they were bitter; *therefore, the name of it was called Marah.*" How closely this corresponds with the plague before us! "*The name of the star is called Wormwood:* and the third of the waters *became wormwood.*"

The great star is a vast aerolite, which traverses in its aerial flight a great portion of the globe. As it travels, it gives off by explosion immense numbers of fragments, which fall on the rivers and into the founts of water, and turn them bitter.

FOURTH TRUMPET.

12. "And the fourth angel sounded the trumpet, and the third of the sun, and the third of the moon, and the third of the stars, were smitten; in order that the third of them might be darkened, and the day not shine for the third of it, and the night likewise."

God remembers mercy still, and His *covenant with Noah*. He promised that as long as earth should remain, "*day* and *night* should not cease" (Gen. viii. 22). Hence day continues still, though its brightness is diminished. God shows His right to call in question man's right to the covenant. He has not kept the terms. Blood for blood is not shed by the nations. By this time the command to put the murderer to death is, through a false philanthropy, refused by the world.

13. "And I saw and heard a single eagle [1] flying in mid-heaven, saying with great voice, Woe, woe, woe to the dwellers upon the earth, from the remaining voices of the trumpet of the three angels who are about to sound!"

The eagle and its cry separates the first four trumpets from the last three. It is not easy to understand why the cry should be by an "eagle," rather than by an "angel." Antichrist rises at the next trump. The eagle appears to be his forerunner. It is a "single eagle." Eagles are often spoken of in the plural. Isa. xl. 31; Jer. iv. 13; 2 Sam. i. 23. Specially when connected with judgment: Matt. xxiv. 28. At the close, in a body, they prey on men. Rev. xix. 17.

But this eagle not only flies, but *speaks*. Is that literal or symbolic? If any think it is not absurd to suppose that an eagle may be made to speak, as

---

[1] "Eagle." This is the reading of the best MSS. and adopted by the critical editions. It is the most *difficult* reading; and internal evidence is thus in its favour.

Balaam's ass was, let him take it literally. If this is beyond his faith, let him take it symbolically. It is, I trust, the only case in which he will find his faith so tried.

CHAPTER IX

1. "And the fifth angel sounded, and I saw a star out of the heaven fallen unto the earth ; and to him was given the key of the well of the bottomless pit."

WITH the woe-trumpets the time of GREAT TRIBULATION on earth begins. Matt. xxiv. 21, 22. It is the time of Satan's ejection out of heaven by the power of Jesus. Rev. xii. 7–12. Of that time it is written, "*Woe* to the earth, and to the sea ! for the devil is come down to you having great wrath, knowing that he hath but a short season."

With this fifth trumpet new personages appear upon the scene, and a new mode of procedure is adopted. The fifth and sixth plagues come, not from heaven, but from the earth, or from beneath it.

What is the star before us ? Not a literal star, but an intelligent being. "But how do you sever between the literality of the stars of the former trumpet, and of this ?" *Because the actions ascribed to this star are impossible to unintelligent matter. A star could neither take a key nor unlock a door.* Judges iii. 25. And this star begins to act after the force of its fall is already spent. But whatever is related of the stars of the former plague is perfectly consistent with the idea of their being literal stars. There the stars are simply smitten ; and the consequence is a natural one, the obscuration of their light.

Who, then, is this star ? Satan. He is come down to deceive the nations, transformed as " an angel of light "

(2 Cor. xi. 14). Angels are described as stars in the Almighty's speech to Job (Job xxxviii. 7). Jesus describes Himself as "the bright and morning star" (Rev. xxii. 16).

Satan reaches earth not voluntarily, but as cast out of heaven: as the twelfth chapter of this book assures us. xii. 8, 9, 12. There he is cast out, as the result of his defeat by Michael. Here, therefore, he is described in reference to that, as already "a star out of the heaven fallen to the earth." So the Saviour prophetically beheld him, "I beheld *Satan* as lightning *fall from heaven*" (Luke x. 18).[1]

The key was given to this fallen star. Our translators have rightly put " to *him* " instead of " to *it*," as seeing that an intelligent being is necessarily supposed. That word " was given " connects this plague with all the main incidents of the Apocalypse. It was by order of the throne. And this key, as we are informed in the first chapter of Revelation, belongs properly to Jesus. i. 18. The key now committed to him is the key of "Death," or of the bottomless pit. xx. 13, 14. As to Jesus is given the key of Hades, and at His opening of it His elect come forth; so to Satan now, at the opening of the Wild Beast's kingdom, the key of the place of the lost is given, and his False Christ, False Prophet, and army come forth. Satan opens the pit: and throughout his time of empire it stands *open*. The angel shuts it while Jesus reigns: it is kept fast *closed* then, and Satan's power is at an end. Men are made fearfully immortal during five months of Satan's reign, as during the Saviour's kingdom the days of man will be as the days of a tree spent in sunshine and in joy. "Hallelujah" is the cry when God reigns: "Woe, woe, woe," when Satan does.

---

[1] Isa. xiv. 12 resembles this, but seems to be spoken of the False Christ.

It is not the door of a house that is opened, but the mouth of a pit. As a good angel shuts it for a good purpose ; so an evil angel opens it for an evil purpose. The good angel that shuts *descends* at his own will from heaven. The evil angel is *cast down* from it against his will.

To the prison below a liberator comes. Now to the interior of a prison none have access but the officers of a prison, or those employed by them. Here Satan enters not as a captive, but, standing without, by authority given, lets loose as many as he is permitted. He does not *break in* by force, but enters by authority bestowed. The exile from heaven *opens*, the dweller in heaven *shuts* the pit, both suitably. Satan is not *in* the pit, as many suppose. He descends *to* it.

But it is not simply " the key of the bottomless pit," as our translators have it, but " the key *of the well* of the bottomless pit." This gives us new information. It supposes a shaft, or well, or mine sunk through the crust of the earth, till we arrive at the entrance to the hollow interior of the globe, which is closed by gates. Of these the Scripture speaks more than once.

The Abyss, or bottomless pit, is a place of departed souls. " Who shall descend into the bottomless pit?[1] (*That is, to bring up Christ again from the dead* ") (Rom. x. 7). It is a dungeon, and a place of punishment, as is manifested by the fear of the demons, lest they should be cast in thither. " And they besought Him that He would not command them to go away into *the bottomless pit* "[2] (Luke viii. 28, 31). This afterwards appears from this very book; for into it Satan is cast, during the thousand years. xx. 3.

The dungeons of olden time were usually pits under ground. Gen. xl. 15 ; xli. 14 ; Jer. xxxviii. 6, 13. God's prison is also situated beneath the earth.

[1] Ἄβυσσον. [2] Εἰς τὴν ἄβυσσον ἀπελθεῖν.

2. "And he opened the well of the bottomless pit, and there came smoke out of the well as the smoke of a great furnace; and the sun and the air were darkened from the smoke of the well."

The first consequence of the opened abyss is the coming forth of smoke. This shows its interior to be the place of fire. It is "as the smoke of a great *furnace*." It tells of a fierce flame, the cause of the thick smoke. xviii. 9, 18; xix. 3. While the opening of the pit is due to supernatural agency, the results of it are natural.

The consequence of the smoke is next described. Smoke always follows the opening of a passage into the deep interior of the earth. From the active volcanoes of the earth smoke is continually proceeding. But this is a sudden eruption, not from any known opening into earth, but from a place till then closed. It is attended with earthquake and flame, and the destruction of herb and tree, of man and beast, in its immediate vicinity.

The predicted eruption appears to have burst forth in Judæa. This is the scene described by Moses and the prophets. "The whole land thereof is *brimstone, and salt, and burning, it is not sown nor beareth, nor any grass groweth therein, like the overthrow of Sodom and Gomorrah, Admah and Zeboim, which the Lord overthrew in His anger and in His wrath*" (Deut. xxix. 23). Jer. iv. 23–28.

So vast is the opening, so dense the smoke, that from earth in general the light of the sun is intercepted. But this is the least portion of the plague.

3. "And out of the smoke came forth locusts into the earth; and to them was given power, as the scorpions of the earth have power."

These are no common locusts: (1) For they eat no vegetable productions. (2) The locusts of earth have no king. Prov. xxx. 27. These have. (3) In the plague of Egypt the inspired recorder had said, "Before them there were no such locusts as they, *neither after them shall be such*" (Exod. x. 14). (4) Yet they are literal creatures, resembling the literal animals named: the *lion*, the horse, the scorpion, the *man*.

Their forms only are described: not any moral character. The grass, herbs, trees, which they are not to injure are literal: so then are they. They are not bad men: for they trouble only the wicked.

The sun is first spoken of as subject to the darkness, for the eruption commences in the day. But the darkening of "air" shuts out all light from the heavenly bodies. If the sun's light be withdrawn by eclipse, the stars shine out, and supply his place. But, on this occasion, as smoke fills the air, neither sun, moon, nor stars can contribute any light.

These locusts usually dwell in the abyss, and amidst its fire and smoke. They are no inhabitants of earth. Creatures in general are stifled by smoke, and certainly consumed by fire.

Earth has its poisonous and noxious creatures, but these have already been used in wrath, and in vain. "The wild beasts *of the earth*" were commissioned under the fourth seal. vi. 8. But though they injured and slew, they availed not to stay the progress of sin. Now the creatures of the infernal regions are let loose. Will men own the hand of God, and repent? Never has such a plague followed on any previous eruption of a volcano and its smoke. Will men confess this the design of God in visitation for sin? Or will they regard it as a natural event?

Here is the proof of the literality of these creatures. (1) Whatever can be taken literally without absurdity, is literal. (2) *Whenever an instrument has actually been used before of God, whether it be the very same, or one resembling it in principle, it cannot be absurd to account it literal when predicted in the future.* But God in former days used noxious insects as a plague. These then are literal creatures. As the smoke is literal, producing its ordinary effects, so are the locusts actual creatures ; and not mere symbols of a heresy, or of an invading army.

But if their chief feature of injury resembles that of the scorpion, why are they directly and prominently called " locusts " ? (1) First, it is evident that they are so denominated, from the locust-plague wherewith Egypt was visited. (2) Next, they are winged creatures, and fly through the air ; not being like scorpions, confined to the ground. They ascend from the bottomless pit, and " the sound of their wings," as we afterwards learn, is terrible. (3) Also their immense numbers are intimated thereby ; and (4) probably in those points of the body which are not specially described, they resemble the locust.

There is force in the seeming insignificant addition, " as the scorpions *of the earth* have power." These are creatures from beneath, never seen before by man. They are compared, therefore, with known animals, whose abode is on earth. From the familiar forms of the surface, the student of the prophetic page is led to comprehend the appearance of creatures hitherto unseen.

How remarkable in this connection are the words of our Lord ! " I beheld *Satan as lightning fall from heaven.* Behold I give unto you power to tread on *serpents,* and *scorpions,* and over all the power of the *enemy,* and *nothing shall by any means hurt you :* notwithstanding in this rejoice not, that the spirits are subject to you ; but rather rejoice, because your names are written in heaven " (Luke x. 18–20). The *scorpions* here, and the *serpents* of the next plague, belong to Satan. But they are forbid to hurt God's own people. The star fallen from heaven is Satan.

4. " And it was said to them, that they should not hurt the grass of the earth, nor any green thing, nor any tree, but only the men who have not the seal of God on their foreheads."

They are under control. Though released, it is not in order to do their own will. " It was said to them ; " where we must fill up the ellipsis with the words, " by God," as in other places.

This command of God supposes the locusts intelligent up to a certain point. Commands are given only to those who can comprehend them. But the degree of intelligence supposed is not greater than that which belongs to a dog. They are free to touch only those who are unsealed by God. A dog can be trained to distinguish game, and to point at it, while he disregards birds which the sportsman cares not for. Or he can be taught to fly at beggars, while he suffers the well-dressed to pass unhurt.

The mark on the chosen of God must be a literal and visible one, to be recognized by these creatures.

From the prohibition against hurting the vegetable creation, we gather, that but for that injunction, these creatures would injure it.

The grass, herbs, and trees, then, are literal here. They had been before injured by the fire and *hail* of the first trumpet. But now they are not to be stricken. *Men* are the prey of these locusts.

That the inhabitants of the earth are to be plagued directly now, is the characteristic of the woe-trumpets ; or, at least, of the two first. Disregarded judgments grow in terrors. The objects of the plague are described as men unsealed by God. This throws us back on the sealing of the seventh chapter. The sealed are abiding on earth still. Therefore I conclude that the plagues succeed one another quickly, and not after intervals of centuries ; else the sealed ones had died off.

From this limitation of the objects of their injury we

may infer, that but for that, they would have attacked the holy ones of God, equally with the wicked, or in preference to them. He who sends them forth forbids them to torment any but His enemies. That their nature and tendencies are to injure is shown by this, that the negative in each case comes first, and the positive point is permissive only, not a command. " It was said to them that they should *not* hurt the grass," " but the men which have *not* the seal of God." " It was given, that they should *not* kill them." So, in the next plague, all that is requisite is to *loose* the fierce angels of evil : no restriction is laid on them, and they slay.

5. " And it was given to them, that they should not kill them, but that they should be tormented five months ; and their torment was as the torment of a scorpion, when it striketh a man."

Ordinarily tormentors dwell in the prison, and the culprits to be tormented are brought to them. Here the tormentors are let loose among the habitations of earth. The globe is one vast prison. It has become like the pit for its wickedness ; it is like it also in punishment.

That the torment is *bodily pain* is proved by this, that it stands opposed to *death*. These locusts torment, without killing. But all prefer death to their tormenting.

But for the limit set by God, they would willingly have slain the objects of their attack. But this plague is torment—insufferable pain of body. God's ordinary plagues are frequently unto death : but here He would show how many and varied are the arrows of His quiver.

In the infernal flames we find the cause of the " smoke " which ascends from beneath ; and from the place of torment ascend the " locusts " that inflict anguish. Earth is a picture of the place of the damned. Darkness and smoke shut out the light of the sun ; and beneath its sulphurous pall the godless are tormented, even as the damned themselves.

The duration of this plague is fixed. It is the first instance of a date given to a plague. "Five months." How dread a lot, insufferable anguish of body five months!

The pain suffered is like that of a scorpion. The scorpion's sting is perhaps the intensest bodily pain that any animal can inflict. "The scorpion is one of the most loathsome objects in nature. It resembles a small lobster; its head appears to be joined and continued to the breast; it has two eyes in the middle of its head, and two towards the extremity, between which come as it were two arms, which are divided into two parts, like the claws of a lobster. It has eight legs proceeding from its breast, every one of which is divided into six parts, covered with hair, and armed with talons or claws. The belly is divided into *seven rings*, from the last of which the tail proceeds, which is divided into *seven little heads* of which the last is furnished with a sting. In some are observed six eyes, and in others eight may be perceived. The tail is long, and formed after the manner of a string of beads, tied end to end, one to another; the last bigger than the others, and somewhat longer; to the end of which are sometimes two strings, which are hollow, and filled with a cold poison, which it injects into the wound it inflicts. It is of a blackish colour, and moves sideways like a crab. Darting with great force at the object of its fury, it fixes violently with its snout, and by its feet, on the persons which it seizes, and cannot be disengaged without difficulty.

"No animal in the creation seems endued with a nature so irascible. When taken, they exert their utmost rage against the glass which contains them; will attempt to sting a stick when put near them; will sting animals confined with them, without provocation; are the cruellest enemies to each other. Maupertuis put a hundred together in the same glass : instantly they vented their rage in mutual destruction, universal carnage ! in a few days only fourteen remained, which had killed and devoured all the others." *Paxton's Illustrations of Scripture*, pp. 123, 125.

The pain is proverbial : far exceeding that of whips made by men. " My father chastised you with *whips*, but I will chastise you with *scorpions* " (2 Chron. x. 11). God has tried whips first, and men have not repented. Now scorpions form his lash of vengeance. Hell-torments are now seen to be no fable. These locusts are witnesses, that there is a worm that can abide the fire.

6. "And in those days shall men seek death, and shall not find it : and they shall desire to die, and death fleeth from them."

It produces not repentance, but desire for death. They seek an escape from anguish, not reconciliation with the offended Majesty of heaven. " The *goodness* of God " was leading men to penitence during the Church dispensation. Now he seeks to produce it by *judgment :* but well-nigh without effect in each case.

" Men shall seek death." The article in the Greek before " men " denotes the universality of the desire. Far as the torment extends, so far does the desire reach.

But men now not only desire death, as a mode of escape from the torment they suffer, but they *seek* it. That is, they use means to effect their purpose. Life is so weak a thread, that it is easily broken. The cord, the knife, the cup, the stream, the pistol, the fumes of deadly ingredients, offer many modes of exit from life. And ordinarily it is as easily found as sought.

But the peculiarity of those woeful five months will be, that they shall not find it. Here is another supernatural feature. How this desire of the tormented shall be defeated, we are not told. Probably the locust-scorpions will prevent it. How terrible the pain, which will make the desire of death universal! How dread the disappointment, that even this disastrous remedy shall not be permitted!

Men are herein still more like lost souls. There is no refuge, no protection from these winged invaders; nor is death itself permitted them.

To impress this dread state of mankind yet more fully on our mind, the statement is repeated under another form. "Death flees from them." Ordinarily he comes undesired, uncalled; every means that skill can suggest is used to keep him at bay. But he breaks through all. Here the earnest wooing of him avails not. Men must live against their wills, and live in anguish. Ordinarily, the attempt at suicide is restrained, wherever expected, by the vigilant eyes of friends, and the police. Here, police and all are alike infected with the desire. But neither singly, nor by joint action, can they effect their purpose. The desire to die occurs only in this case. Under the other plagues, it is no more mentioned.

7. "And the likenesses of the locusts were like unto horses prepared for war; and on their heads were as it were crowns like gold, and their faces were as the faces of men."

The apostle addresses himself now to depict the appearance of these creatures. So important is this point, that four verses are devoted to the purpose. One reason of this, doubtless, is to manifest that these are not ordinary locusts. Common locusts were creatures well known to John and the Asiatics. But who, save one inspired and enlightened of God, could describe to us the shapes of beings of the infernal pit? There is in humanity an awe and terror arising from the first encounter with new and noxious creatures of strange forms. This *is* further heightened in the present case, by their coming from beneath amidst gross darkness. What shrieks of terror, what groans of anguish, what swoons of the fear-stricken and feeble, what curses of impotent fury from the strong, will mount up from earth's cities and vales amidst the sable night that overspreads all and shuts out day!

Their general appearance resembled a horse in armour, and encircled by its war-housings.

They have crowns, or rather something of that shape, on their heads, and it resembles gold in its yellow colour, perhaps in its substance. These armies from beneath answer to the armies of heaven that come down with Christ. The armies of heaven are enthroned and crowned with Christ. The risen with Christ have authority to reign over men a thousand years. These have authority to torment men five months. In Satan's first resurrection, tormentors come up from below. In Christ's, rulers descend from above.

Their faces are like those of human beings. Ordinary locusts have no such appearance: much less have they the hair of women.

But this is what is constantly forgotten in the case of the Apocalypse. The creature there sketched by its resemblances to *men* and lions is supposed to be a *man!*

8. "And they had hair as the hair of women, and their teeth were as the teeth of lions."

This would seem to prove, that they must be very much larger than ordinary locusts.

The common locusts have naught resembling human hair, much less female tresses.

The lion's teeth are peculiar, and characteristic of him. They are of two kinds, the fangs, or front teeth; and the grinders. The fangs have a single sharp point. The grinders have three points, the centre one being the most elevated. Which of these two classes is intended, we are not told; probably both are included. Ordinary

o

locusts have no teeth of bone. They have but four in number, crossing one another like the blades of scissors. To a graminivorous insect, the teeth of a carnivorous quadruped would be highly unsuitable. With these teeth the locusts make their way through every obstruction : perhaps by them they seize their victim.

9. "And they had breastplates, as it were breastplates of iron ; and the sound of their wings was as of chariots of many horses rushing into battle."

It would seem, from the sound of their wings, that they must be creatures of large dimensions : small wings, however numerous, could not create a sound like chariots of many horses at full speed. They are like horses in armour ; and now their breastplates are named. It would seem as though these were their defence against men's attempts to destroy them. For, doubtless, men will use every means to rid themselves of so dire a calamity. Thus Joel says, "*When they fall upon the sword, they shall not be wounded*" (Joel ii. 8). It should here be observed that Joel's description of a locust-army to come runs remarkably parallel with this. Joel ii. He describes the awful darkness, the trembling of men, the fire bursting forth. "*The appearance of them is as the appearance of horses :* and as horsemen so shall they run." Their noise is like chariots on rocks : men are in pain in their presence. They shall keep rank. They are winged creatures : and thus height will be no security against them. "They shall enter in at the windows as a thief." These infernal *cherubim* are like (1) horses, (2) *men*, (3) women, (4) *lions*, (5) birds, and (6) scorpions.

The sound of their wings is warlike, and mighty. Chariots in which many horses are driven abreast and run with speed make a terrible sound. The sound of the wings of the cherubim was like great waters, and like the sound of an army. Ezek. i. 24.

The sound of the advent of the common locusts is not terrible. Their noise when eating is like that of an army foraging in secret, as Volney says.

10. "And they have tails like scorpions, and stings: and in their tails was their power to hurt men five months."

In the serpent, the tail is the weakest part. But in the tail lies the power of the scorpion. As these locusts hurt like scorpions, and the pain produced by their stroke is like the scorpion's, so the instrument by which the blow is inflicted is like the scorpion's. The serpent-tailed horses of the next plague inflict the injuries of serpents.

The apostle now describes that part of the creature which made it terrible to men. For locusts in general are easily slain by men, and are formidable only to the vegetable creation. As they were to hurt men, they have an instrument suited for the purpose, greatly resembling one long dreaded in the east.

11. "They have over them (as) king the angel of the bottomless pit, whose name in the Hebrew tongue is Abaddon, and in the Greek he hath his name Apollyon."

The ordinary locusts have no king, but they go forth in bands. Prov. xxx. 27. But these from beneath have a king set over them, of a different nature from themselves, as appears from the passages in other parts of the book which speak of him. Probably this is the reason why he is not called "king *of* the locusts," but it is said, "They have a king *over* them." This is the preposition used where a foreigner is forbidden as king of Israel.

We can but conclude that this king, "the angel of the bottomless pit," is the False Christ, who is the great antagonist of our Lord. He is first named "the Wild Beast," when he wars with the Witnesses and slays them. There he is described as "the Wild Beast that *cometh up out of the bottomless pit*" (xi. 7). But none of eminence is mentioned as coming up thence, save the King of the Locusts. By this characteristic he is mentioned once more. xvii. 8.

Of our Lord it is said, " Thou shalt call his name Jesus [SAVIOUR] ; for he shall save his people from their sins " (Matt. i. 21). Here, the king of the locusts is named " DESTROYER," for he shall destroy his people in their sins.

Abaddon and Apollyon both signify " destroyer." Abaddon is the name of the bottomless pit in Hebrew. " Hades (Sheol) is naked before him, and Destruction (Abaddon) hath no covering " (Job xxvi. 6). " Hades and Abaddon are before the Lord " (Prov. xv. 11 ; xxvii. 20). Thus the angel of the pit takes the name of the pit. *It* is the *place* of *destruction ; he* is the *Destroyer*.

The Saviour is " *Christ* the Lord " (Luke ii. 11). The Destroyer is Antichrist the False King and Lord. The one descended from heaven : the other ascends from the pit.

By the title of " Destroyer " and equivalent words, the person before us is known to the prophets. Jer. iv. 7; Jer. vi. 26; Isa. xvi. 4; Dan. viii. 24, 25; Dan. ix. 26 ; xi. 44.

THE SIXTH TRUMPET;

OR,

THE EUPHRATEAN HORSEMEN.

13. "And the sixth angel sounded, and I heard a single voice out of the horns of the golden altar which is before God, 14. Saying to the sixth angel, which hath the trumpet, Loose the four angels which have been bound at the great river Euphrates."

WHOSE voice is it ? It is, I suppose, the voice of God. 'Tis a voice of command out of God's altar. As in the order to Famine given out of the midst of the cherubim, the voice was God's, so here also. vi. 6.

Are these four angels the same who stood at the four quarters of the earth, and held the winds ? By no means. Those were good angels: these are evil. Those were free angels. These are bound. They need no command from God to destroy men. Their own nature impels them to slaughter. They only require to be *loosed*. But for their enforced inaction, they had slain men long before.

The place of their restraint is given. "*At* the great river Euphrates." Why this should be the spot, it may be difficult to point out. But this great river has played, and has yet to play, no inconspicuous part in God's plan.

15. "And the four angels were loosed, who had been prepared for the hour, and day, and month, and year, that they might kill the third of men. 16. And the number of the armies of the cavalry was two myriads of myriads. I heard the number of them."

I believe that the divine penman intended to define for us the *duration of the plague*, as in the case of the locusts, the Two Witnesses, and many others. Then we must connect the period named with the loosing, and must regard the " preparing " as subordinate and parenthetic : or else connect it with the slaughter of men.

So accurately is the time determined, that it is bounded by an hour. The former plague was for five months, this is for more than thirteen. Woes deepen in dreadfulness, as men plunge deeper in sin.

They " had been prepared," by their vehement desire, their appropriate elements of destruction, and their proximity to the scene of vengeance.

Their destination is to slay " the third of men." Hence their immense multitudes. Their numbers are two hundred millions. In our day, mankind are supposed to be about eight hundred millions.[1] How terrible, then, the slaughter which is counted by hundreds of millions ! And that, in spite of the terrific devastation of the former plagues !

Before, plagues visited the " third of earth," of the salt and fresh " *waters*," and of the heavenly bodies. But now it is a " third of *men*," who are directly assailed and cut off.

The four angels are identified with the four bodies of cavalry which they lead. When the angels are loosed, so are the horsemen whom they command. It is said "the arm*ies* (not ' arm*y* ') of the cavalry " ; for the four leaders are independent of each other.

The number of the locusts is not given. Who could count their infinitude ? But these might be numbered ; and though John could not reckon them, their sum is named to him.

17. "And thus I saw the horses in the vision, and those that

---

[1] [Now nearer seventeen hundred millions.

sat on them, have breastplates of fire-colour, and hyacinth, and brimstone: and the heads of the horses were as the heads of lions; and out of their mouths proceed fire, and smoke, and brimstone. 18. By these three plagues was the third of men killed, by the fire and the smoke, and the brimstone that proceeded out of their mouths."

The riders and horses have breastplates, not of iron as usual, nor is the material specified; but they are of three colours: fire-coloured, dark blue, and yellow. Out of the horses' mouths issue "fire," answering to the first colour; "smoke," answering to the dark blue or hyacinth colour; and "brimstone," corresponding to the sulphur colour of the breastplates.

The forms of the horses are terrible. Their heads are not the usual horses' heads: they are of the shape of the devouring lion. The horse's mouth has not a wide opening: the lion's is of a mighty span. But these lion-horses seek not to take flesh into their mouths, but breathe fumes of death from them. That is the main instrument of destruction used.

"But who can believe in such creatures? Who ever saw anything resembling them?" True it is, that we have no such monsters on earth, no such spirit-riders. They are "reserved for the day of battle and war." But they who can believe that all things are possible with the Creator, will give Him credit, when He tells us of secret stores and creatures of wrath treasured for more matured and open wickedness than the earth has yet displayed.

The riders are not said to carry any weapons; they have only the defensive armour of breastplates. It is the *horses* that kill; and they slay, not by any of their members, but by their fiery sulphurous breath. They slay, not as the lion, by claws and by fangs; but by stifling and burning their victim: a way unknown to any creature of earth. What creatures of flesh could live, with fire and brimstone abiding in their bodies ?

"Smoke, fire, brimstone," these are foretastes of the penalties of the damned : prelibations on earth of the "*smoke* of torment," and of "the lake which burneth with *fire* and *brimstone*, which is the Second Death" (Rev. xxi. 8). "The inhabitants of the earth are *burned*, and *few men left*" (Isa. xxiv. 6).

19. "For the power of the horses is in their mouths, and in their tails : for their tails were like serpents, having heads, and by them they hurt."

This verse gives us to understand how fully defended against attack or destruction these spirit-horses are. A horse may be struck from behind with little danger. But these horses are armed with offensive weapons in their rear, as well as in their front. The locusts' power lay in their stinging scorpion-tails. But these horses, instead of the usual wisp of horse-hair, which is powerless to injure man, carry a coil of serpents. This cluster of serpents is not a cluster of the tails of serpents, but of the forepart of the snake. By their tails they are fixed to the horses' hinder-quarters : their heads are free to seize any assailants from behind.

This power of the tail seems to affect those who are not slain by the horsemen. Their direct object is "to *slay* the third of men" : say three hundred millions. These they kill outright, by their fiery breath. But the other six hundred millions may be *hurt* by the bite of the serpents' tails. Their power of *death* lies in their mouth : their power to *hurt*, in their tails. Deut. xxviii. 59 ; Exod. xxxiv. 10.

The poets and mythologists have figured Medusa and the Furies as having serpents twining above their brows in place of hair. Bulls breathing fire and burning up the grass are described by Ovid. But now the poets' fancy will be fearfully realized in the infernal monsters seen by John.

This terrible scourge is foretold in several places in the Old Testament. Deut. xxviii. 49–57. The Romans but very partially fulfilled this. See also Jer. v. 15.

Israel in ancient times trusted in Egypt and its horsemen. They are warned that Egyptian riders and horsemen were "flesh and not spirit" (Isa. xxx., xxxi.). See also Ps. lix. 6, 7.

Similar is Jeremiah's testimony. Jer. vi. 22–25; Jer. viii. 13–17. See also Lam. iv. 19.

20. "And the rest of men who were not killed by these plagues, repented not of the works of their hands, that they should not worship demons, and idols of gold and silver and copper and stone and wood, which can neither see, nor hear, nor walk. 21. Neither repented they of their murders, nor of their sorceries, nor of their fornication, nor of their thefts."

At the *sixth* trumpet, as at the *sixth* seal, we get a glimpse of the *wickedness* of man; for six is the number devoted to Antichrist. We see that beneath the strokes of God's hand they have but rushed more deeply into sin. God sums up the state of mankind briefly, to give us the moral key to these His strange acts of wrath. Sin is their cause. The end aimed at by God is the bringing men to repentance by His judgments. But they will not repent.

Though they are but a remnant, vast multitudes having been cut off by war, famine, pestilence, wild beasts, the destruction of the ships, the bitter waters, and now the horsemen of Euphrates, they still go on in sin.

The substance of which these idols are made is mentioned, to prove that literal idols, such as used by the heathen in all ages, are meant.

To worship the work of God's hands, the moon and

the sun of *His* creating, is sin; but it is the greatest folly as well as sin in men to worship what they *themselves* have made, objects which are so inferior to themselves, being brute matter, unpossessed of any of the senses of men, though possessing more or less his shape. As Lactantius observes, if the idol could move, it would rather worship man, as its maker, than receive worship as his superior.

It is not said of idols by John, " which cannot *speak*," for the idol which enraptures men afterwards by its supernatural power does speak.

Men's offences against the second table are next named: these spring greatly from their false worship. God, dishonoured by their idolatry, gives them up to dishonour. Rom. i. Their breaches of the sixth, seventh, and eighth commands are introduced by the repetition of the words "they repented not."

Six sins, then, are specified: two against God, and four against man. It is remarkable that the sin of drunkenness is not among those enumerated.

The world has heard the Gospel, and refused it. Far greater is its responsibility in that day, than in any previous one. Far stouter and more deeply rooted is its attitude of resistance, than at any former time.

Things are advancing with no slack pace towards this dismal consummation. Beneath the thin crust of formal Christianity, the germs of these trespasses here and there peep forth. Idolatry is putting forth its feelers; and the giving heed to seducing spirits is already visible in America. On this basis all the other evils will establish themselves.

Men, and even Christians, who regard not prophecy, are flattering themselves that a day of peace, purity, and knowledge has begun, and is advancing among mankind. God's word frowns out of countenance man's self-sufficiency. Nay! the generation, both Jewish and

Gentile, from which the evil spirit for awhile departed of its own will, will again be possessed by seven others more wicked than the first, its last state being worse than the former.

CHAPTER X

1. "And I saw another mighty angel coming down out of the heaven, clothed with a cloud, and the rainbow was upon his head, and his face was as the sun, and his feet as pillars of fire."

THIS descent of the angel properly comes after Satan's defeat and ejection from on high. He comes in might, the representative of the throne, to claim earth for God, who purposes to subdue it to Himself by *power*. The calls of mercy have been refused: rebellion lifts up its head. God must therefore vindicate His insulted rights by the might of war.

Jesus, then, is the person before us; "the angel of the covenant," the manifester of the designs of the throne. But He has not forgotten His covenant. The rainbow that was about the throne is now encircling His head. The book that was in the hand of the enthroned One, is now held by Him. The thunders of the throne answer Him. This angel is the great antagonist of the Antichrist, who comes as "the angel of the abyss" from below, enveloped in a "cloud" of smoke of the pit.

What are the angel's purposes in thus descending?

1. He comes as a *witness*. He sends forth two other witnesses. Mal. iii. 5.

He comes to notice and report on high the effect of the seals and trumpets. Had men listened to these sounds of awe? Or did each rush on his course, as the horse into the battle?

He comes to investigate the state of the Lord's people. As their intercessor, presenting their prayers on high, he is still interested on their behalf.

2. He comes to *claim earth* for the Most High, who is now about to manifest Himself in the character in which Melchizedec of old bore witness of Him, as " Possessor of heaven and earth."

He descends " clothed with a cloud." This is the great characteristic of the vision.

1. First, then, it signifies *mystery*. When Jesus is visible to all, He comes " *with* the clouds," or " *on* them," but not shrouded by them. He is to come, too, with clouds; not with a single one, as here; and not as angel, but as Son of Man.

2. The cloud was of old the vehicle of the *Divine Presence*. Exod. xiii. 21, 22; Num. x. 34; xiv. 13, 14. The *cloud*, then, is here, and there are " *pillars of fire.*"

3. It descends for *wrath*. Both to Israel and the world, then, the descending cloud is a token of the storm at hand. Luke xii. 54.

In Noah's day, the *bow* was to be in the cloud. In Moses' day, the *Lord* is in it. Now, both the bow and the Lord are in the cloud. Both are parts of the covenant token to Noah. There is iniquity now, and therefore there is the cloud. But earth is not yet to be destroyed, and therefore the bow that was around the throne encircles its angelic agent. When earth is destroyed, there is no bow around the throne. Rev. xx, 11.

Mystery is gradually passing away; the agent of the throne is not now concealed by a door, but only by a cloud, easily dispersed.

"The rainbow is on his head." The rainbow is God's. " *I* do set *my bow* in the cloud " (Gen. ix. 13). But it is given to this messenger. The bow is the merciful token of the covenant-promise to earth. To Jesus the mercy of the throne, as well as its wrath, is entrusted. "He exercises all the power" of the throne "before it." He remembers, too, His covenant with Israel, and the "*mercy*" promised to Abraham and the fathers. Luke i. 54, 72. The rainbow is round the angel's head ; for mercy is his purpose. But his feet are of fire, and they touch earth : for the wrath must come before the mercy. The mercy, too, is as yet in mystery ; the bow is within the cloud.

His face is "as the sun." Thus did our Lord appear, when, at the Transfiguration, He gave a miniature representation of the coming of His millennial kingdom. Matt. xvii. 2 ; Acts xxvi. 13. Thus is He seen in the vision granted to John at the beginning of this book. i. 16. Who can doubt then, with this assemblage of proofs, that the angel is our Lord ? He who appeared before as the Sun of Righteousness by His rising in the east, is now beheld more fully, with His face as the sun.

His feet are "pillars of fire." "Pillars" denote stability. Gal. ii. 9 ; Jer. i. 18. "Fire" denotes vengeance. These, then, are the two pillars of the new kingdom, and of the new temple. They are Jachin and Boaz. "He shall establish by power." The kingdom of Christ shall stand on the footing of justice. Isa. xi. 5. "The *cloud*" is no longer a "pillar." It is not designed to be steadfast ; as it was, so long as the old temple kept its standing. It is now destined soon to be dispersed. But justice will abide, when mystery departs. The establishing and execution of justice will be the passing away of mystery. Man's expectation, that vengeance against an evil work will be speedily executed, will be fully met in the day of the kingdom. Eccles. viii. 11 ; Jer. xxxi. 30. Woe to earth ! The fire of God rests on it. Sinai is re-enacted. "*Mount Sinai was altogether on a smoke, because the Lord descended upon it in fire*" (Exod. xix. 18). "Bow thy heavens, O Lord, and come down : *touch the mountains, and they shall smoke* " (Ps. cxliv. 5).

2. " And he had in his hand a little book opened : and he set his right foot upon the sea, but his left foot upon the earth."

This little book, we suppose, is the one which the Lamb took and opened, and which Jesus in another character now holds and gives to His servant John. It is a "*little* book," because God's " *short* work " is now about to be accomplished upon earth. Rom. ix. 28.

As the eaten book gives the passing away of mystery, and the Lord's people's perception of it, we can account for its being first sweet, and then bitter. It is sweet to know that the character of God shall be displayed in all its fulness, and the glory shall come. But 'tis bitter to think of the destruction which shall befall the enemies of God.

His attitude also is significant. His right foot is set on the sea, and his left on the land. This posture is that of one claiming them both. Deut. xi. 24; Ps. viii. 6. The kings of Persia asserted their claim to a land, by demanding earth and water.

His foot is *on* the sea ; not, as a mortal's would be, *in* it. Thrice is this named. So Jesus walked of old on the sea. Matt. xiv. 25.

This claim is resisted by Satan, his angels, and the non-elect of earth. The cause is tried by battle.

3. " And he cried with a great voice, as a lion roareth ; and when he cried, the seven thunders spake their own voices."

From his actions we are left to gather his feelings. His loud voice, resembling the lion's roar, indicates displeasure, and that the time is near to avenge. The lion roars, just before he springs on his prey. In the address to John, and afterwards to the churches, Jesus' voice was of other characters : first, like a trumpet, then like the sound of many waters. i. 10, 15. His voice alters with the different feelings to which he is to give expression. This roar of His is in character with His place as the lion of Judah, and therefore is foretold by the Jewish prophets, and in connection, too, with the wrath to come. Isa. xxxi. 4, 5; Amos iii. 8; Hos. xi. 10, 11; Joel iii. 16; Jer. xxv. 29–31.

His " cry," then, or " roar " is His own appeal for judgment from God. Before, as the angel with the censer, He offered the prayers of the saints of earth for vengeance. But now, having descended as the witness himself, He adds His own plea beside.

This appeal is immediately answered from on high. " The seven thunders spoke their own voices." What seven thunders ? The use of the article seems to suppose them known; but they are not mentioned before under that distinct title. I suppose them to be the seven thunders of the throne above. The thunders' seven-fold reply proves the entire sympathy with the angel's voice. He calls out the fullness of the divine indignation, expressed by the seven. Here the voices are a part of the thunders. And the expression is peculiar, " they spake their own voices." This seems to imply that they foretold one after another, in unfigurative terms, the judgments of God, which in answer to the angel's roar, should visit earth. Before this time, the " voices " had been separate from the " thunders." iv. 5; viii. 5. But here they were articulate sounds; as well as sounds of so deep intonation, as to be fitly called thunders. The angel's voice was not his usual tone, but like a lion's roar. But these had their usual sound. They only, and always, express wrath. The lion's roar is a sound of earth; the thunder, the voice of heaven.

4. " And when the seven thunders spoke, I was about to write; and I heard a voice out of the heaven, saying, Seal the things which the seven thunders spoke, and write them not."

It would appear that the testimony of each would be too plain for God's purpose in this book, and hence they are sealed up. But how sealed up ? *By their not being written !* That is, if they had but been penned, we should have understood them at once. And, as what is written in this prophecy was *not* to be sealed up, as Jesus says at the close, " *Seal not* the words of the prophecy of this book; for the season is near " (xxii. 10), so the only way to reconcile both parts of God's design was to direct the apostle to leave them out. How different God's idea of this book to that which is generally entertained by Christians ! God thinks that *what is written is* REVEALED : the contrary to what is mysterious and kept back. They think, that *what is written is incomprehensible.* In order to conceal the thunders' voices, God will not have them written.

This proves that mystery is not wholly past, though it is fast removing.

The voices of these thunders are lost for ever, unless God should be pleased specially to reveal them at some future day. John knew their intent : but with him it was to expire. Hence the words " and write them not," are added to the command to seal. It was not thus with the scene at the close of the Saviour's ministry. The words of God were heard by some, and have been recorded by the Holy Ghost. Moreover, the Saviour proceeded to comment on them and expound them. But these were designed of God to be lost, amidst so much that is made known. His will be done ! This is the manner of God. Even where He gives liberally, He reserves something, in token of His right to all. Thus He gave six days, but reserved the seventh ; the whole of the trees of Eden, one excepted ; and all the spoil of the land of Canaan, save that of Jericho. Thus all blasphemy may be forgiven, but that against the Holy Ghost.

5. "And the angel whom I saw standing on the sea and on the earth lifted his right hand unto the heaven, 6. And sware by him that liveth for ever and ever, who created the heaven and the things in it, and the earth and the things in it, and the sea and the things in it, That there shall be no more delay : 7. But in the days of the sound of the seventh angel, when he shall be about to sound, the mystery of God should be finished, as he gave the glad tidings to his own servants the prophets."

"Can it be Christ who swears ? for He does not swear 'by Himself,' as God does." But Jesus appears as the servant of the throne : how should He then take the place of the sovereign ? He appears as the angel : His part it is then to own the name of Him who sends Him. He is the contrast to the Usurper, who owns no equal, much less a superior.

Could any created angel swear by the Creator, that there should be no longer delay ? Would his word be given as the stay of God's distressed servants ? Are angels cognizant of the times and seasons ? Or has not God put these things in His own power ?

The angel *swears*. This marks again the change of dispensation. Under the Law God not unfrequently swears; under the Gospel, *never*.

And therefore under the Law, solemn swearing was allowed or commanded to the Jew: but, under the Gospel, it is forbidden to the disciple of Jesus. Matt. v. 33-37; Jas. v. 12. We have come back again, then, to times of another class. We have here the Lord of the Law again, and His messengers breathe the spirit of the Law. Hence we see why this book has hitherto been so little understood. It turns on the differences of dispensation, and speaks of one yet to come. It never *can* be understood, while supposed to relate to the Church and its economy of mercy.

But what is the tenor of the angel's oath ? "There shall be no more time," but at the seventh trump mystery shall pass away. Of course this first sentiment is equivalent to the announcement, there shall be no more *delay*. Again and again it has seemed as if the purposes of God would come to an end; and as often has the end been deferred.

What, then, is the time fixed ? It is " in the days of the voice of the seventh angel, when he shall be about to sound." The expression is singular, " In the days," not " in the day." And also " when he is about to sound," before he has even begun.[1] True it is, that the proclamation on high is not made till the seventh angel has sounded : but it must be in accord with what is here stated. It would seem as if " the days " of the seventh angel begin to be reckoned as soon as the time specified for the second woe is over.

"The mystery of God shall be finished." The peculiar Hebraistic construction of the original has justly attracted notice. It is literally, " When he shall be about to sound, *and the mystery of God was finished.*" The Jew appears throughout the book. An answer is thus given to the martyr's cry, " How long would God defer His vengeance ? " And also, the angel proceeds to discover to us how man's wickedness shall be filled up, and the long-deferred wrath be drawn down.

But what is " The Mystery of God ? " It is God's great secret : in which are united several smaller ones. It mainly concerns ISRAEL. Israel broke the covenant at Mount Sinai by the molten calf : yet it has never been avenged. How will it be avenged ? and when ? This is one point. But God's secret has another face towards them. Look at the prophecies ; and lofty blessings, spiritual and temporal, are promised to the favoured nation. They are to be God's people, and to know Him from the least to

---

[1] Without warrant our translators have rendered, ὅταν μέλλῃ σαλπίζειν—" when he *shall begin* to sound." Μελλώ never has that meaning : *it always expresses futurity.*

the greatest, to be the first of the nations, rulers of the Gentiles. How is it, then, that they are in a position, both spiritually and temporally, the reverse ? Because God foretold by His servant Isaiah a time, in which Israel would be blind to the clearest work of His hand. Isa. vi. This is the time of "The Mystery." During this period, Israel, after refusing Messiah, are left to their blindness, and He is seated on the right hand of God in heaven, and is invisible. His place of manifestation is predicted by Jewish prophets as the temple at Jerusalem. *Messiah absent in heaven* is a main feature of The Mystery. During this time of His absence, Messiah is *preached to the Gentiles*. This is another lineament of The Mystery, quite alien to the expectations of the Jew, and a point on which the prophets of Israel are silent. Also, the glory destined for those who believe this testimony to Messiah unseen, is another secret. Israel, in the days when the kingdom is come in power, are to be the *subjects of Messiah*. But they who believe now are made *the members of Messiah*, His companions in glory ; permitted, if fellow-sufferers, to reign with him, seated on His throne. But, for the present, mystery rests on the sons of God. They are to be rejected, despised, poor, persecuted. The wisdom which God reveals to them is " wisdom in mystery " (1 Cor. ii. 7). It brings no glory now. It is not coveted by the scientific, or by the kings of earth, as the wisdom of Solomon was. Its view of the Godhead as manifest in the flesh, its name of God as " Father, Son, and Spirit," are both mysteries, secrets unrevealed before. One portion of mystery rests, then, upon the Church. So long as the Church is owned, mercy and mystery are at the height. But the beginning of this book intimates the rejection of the churches, and the coming in of another dispensation, during which mystery rolls away. But it is not removed at once. The Gentiles are the rulers of earth; the city and temple of God are defiled and trodden down; the False Christ arises and blasphemes, works miracles, destroys the saints of God, and prospers. How can this be consistent with the character of Jehovah? This is the trying question. While mercy lasts, the full glory of His perfections cannot be displayed. Hence, just at the very time that patience on God's part is about to be put away, the elements of the mystery are at their fullest development.

8. "And the voice which I heard out of the heaven (I heard) again speaking with me, and saying, Go, take the book which has been opened, (which is) in the hand of the angel who stands on the sea, and on the land. 9. And I went away to the angel, and said unto him, Give me the little book. And he saith unto me, Take it and eat it up; and it shall make thy belly bitter, but in thy mouth it shall be sweet as honey. 10. And I took the little book out of the hand of the angel, and ate it up; and it was in my mouth sweet as honey: and when I had eaten it, my belly was made bitter."

The angel not only accedes to his request, but adds the command to eat it. By the eating of the book is meant faith's reception of its contents. Thus in the parallel case of Ezekiel's roll, God says, "Son of man, all my words that I shall speak unto thee *receive in thine heart*" (iii. 10). Of the New Covenant God says, "*I will put my law in their inward parts, and write it in their hearts*" (Jer. xxxi 33). In the new earth there is no book at all as a rule to men. There is no law without. It is written within.

The opening of the book had been already effected. Thus we still advance. At first the book is beheld by John, but is sealed up with seven seals, and the angels nearest the throne are unable even to behold it. The Mystery of God was at its height. The book is opened in heaven. Mystery is removed by degrees to those on high. But when the book is eaten on earth, The Mystery is understood even by God's earthly servants. But there is yet another step needed. The Mystery is not only to be understood, but to come to an end.

The roar of the angel, the thunders of the throne, are for the ungodly earth ; the oath and the book are for the comfort of the Lord's people, and designed to set their heart on searching and digesting the prophecies.

The book was to produce on John a twofold effect. In his mouth it was to be sweet. This is the effect of a joyful communication. "*Pleasant words are as an honeycomb, sweet to the soul, and health to the bones*" (Prov. xvi. 24). "*How sweet are thy words unto my taste ! yea, sweeter than honey to my mouth !*" (Ps. cxix. 103). But the stomach after the reception of the scroll, was to be made bitter. This is the effect of sorrow. "Call me not Naomi" [PLEASANT], said Naomi, "call me Mara [BITTER], for the Almighty hath dealt very *bitterly* with me" (Ruth i. 20).

Thus the book contained communications first of a pleasant nature, and then of a sorrowful description.

Ezekiel's roll was bitter : for "there were written therein lamentation, and mourning, and woe." After receiving it, "I went," says he, "in *bitterness*, in the heat of my spirit" (Ezek. iii. 3, 14 ; ii. 9, 10).

But it may be said, "How could the reception of the New Covenant of God's grace produce bitterness in the soul ?" We must, I think, suppose that the book contains not only the terms of the new covenant, which are sovereign, but also the sorrowful prophetic circumstances which introduce, and make evidently necessary, the New Covenant. Then the eating of the book and its effects will answer to those words of the angel, in Daniel, concerning the sealed book. "None of the wicked shall understand, but *the righteous shall understand*" (Dan. xii. 10). Intelligence of the Lord's purposes is sweet : but the view of His terrible judgments is sorrowful indeed.

Thus the book and the messenger are in harmony. We first learn of the rainbow around His head, and of His sunlike face, but we end with His feet of fire. His voice is a roar, and the answering thunders accord with the bitterness of the book. He is the messenger of mercy and of justice, and hence a soul in harmony with Him and with God would perceive a sensible difference of taste in His communications. The words of grace and promise are sweet; the threats of offended justice executed must cause sympathetic sorrow. Thus amidst the rejoicing crowd, Jesus wept over Jerusalem. This observation accounts for the strong and frequent connection between the angel and the book.

11. "And they say unto me,[1] Thou must prophesy again against peoples, and nations, and tongues, and many kings."

"Thou must prophesy *again*." The first prophecy begins at the fourth chapter, and ends with the eleventh. The second begins with the twelfth chapter. The prophecy of the Two Witnesses is yet to come. It is of so different a character, as to prove that a new dispensation is begun, as soon as ever it has commenced.

John's second testimony is a prophesying *again*. He goes over the same ground anew in the succeeding chapters. The second prophecy is remarkably dovetailed on to the first. It is predicted, before the first has ceased. It rises out of the eaten book of the first prophecy. There were topics closely connected with those touched on by John in the previous part, on which it was desirable that more detailed information should be given.

He is to prophesy "*against*" nations and kings. This seems to be the force of the preposition. Because of their sins, which are yet more fully manifested

[1] Tregelles.

towards the close, all prophecy *concerning* them is prophecy *against* them.

The word of prediction is against " peoples, and nations, and tongues, and many kings." Accordingly, in the next prophecy, which commences with the woman in heaven, the moral state of the nations and kings of earth is brought out very clearly. Their acceptance of the false Christ, their refusal to acknowledge God in the plagues, their armed organization against the Christ, and their destruction at the entrance and at the close of the millennium, appear in the next series of visions ; and there God's title, " *King of the nations,*" is first asserted.

CHAPTER XI

1. "And there was given me a reed like a rod, saying, 'Rise and measure the temple of God, and the altar, and the worshippers in it.'"

THE instrument offered to John is a measuring-reed It is given on purpose to measure the temple of God. The measuring intends the setting apart a certain space for a special use. Thus God commands the children of Israel concerning the Levites. Num. xxxv. 2, 5; Ezek. xlv. 1, 3.

But still more closely resembling the action enjoined on the evangelist are the passages where the distinction between measuring and not measuring makes the difference between the holy and the profane. Ezek. xlii. 15, 20; Ezek. xlviii. 8, 12, 15.

The part measured, or the temple of God, is the place of safety; as the contrary is seen in the insecurity and fearful danger of the part not measured.

But the instrument of measurement here is of a peculiar character. It was "a reed *like a rod*." Wherefore this? A rod is the instrument of *chastisement*. Ps. lxxxix. 32; Prov. x. 13; 1 Cor. iv. 21.

While, then, the reed is to measure off a part as holy, this is not the only thing intended. Mercy takes the first part, but justice the second. The rod affects the portion given up to the profane; for Jerusalem's day of scourging is come. The temple and city are given up to the Gentiles. The Two Witnesses scourge "the nations" or Gentiles.

What beautifully corroborates this view is, the similar passage in the close of this book. There an angel with a reed measures the New Jerusalem. It is all measured: into it nothing that defiles on man's part is to enter, nor any wrath of God. The peculiarity in the description of the measuring-reed here, is in that passage *omitted*. "He that talked with me had *a golden reed to measure the city*, and the gates thereof, and the walls thereof " (xxi. 15). No part of its circuit is omitted.

The temple-refuge is for those who have eaten the book: which seems designed to teach us that a knowledge of prophecy is the way to escape the coming woe. Thus it answers to Rev. iii. 10. " Because thou hast kept the word of my patience, *I also will keep thee out of the hour of the temptation, which shall come on all the world, to try them that dwell upon the earth.*"

By this command, *the heaven is parted off from the earth*. The limits of the sanctuary of holiness and of refuge are defined. How far shall the proud waves of evil rush ? and where shall they be stayed ? The throne of God shall be a sanctuary for the oppressed " *in the times of trouble* " (Ps. ix. 7, 9).

The temple of this book is not the temple of the old covenant, but of the new. The temple of the new covenant is on high. The proofs that the "temple of God" in the Apocalypse is on high, must have more than once been observed by the reader. This very chapter furnishes an instance. "And the temple of God was opened *in heaven*" (xi. 19). "Another angel came out of the temple *in heaven*" (xiv. 17 ; xvi. 17).

Heaven is the place occupied by the temple during the church dispensation. The Epistle to the Hebrews declares Jesus a priest of the true temple, who entered it in resurrection, while Moses' tabernacle on earth was but a shadow of the true. Heb. ix. 24; iv. 14-16; viii. 1, 2.

The temple of Jerusalem will be yet rebuilt by the Jews in unbelief, and be the scene of wickedness greater than has ever appeared.

This view of the matter, then, explains difficulties otherwise insurmountable. How should the city of Jerusalem and the outer court of its temple be given up, while yet the holy house and its inner court are untrodden by foes? It could only be defended by miracle. But there is no notice of any such defence. Even the Witnesses, who protect themselves by miracle, are slain.

And not only is the *conception* difficult, but it is certain *historically*, or in point of fact, that such a thing has never happened since John wrote. If the outer court of the temple and the city were taken, so was the holy house; and much more its inner court.

The worshippers in question are the great white-robed multitude, who ascribe their accomplished salvation to the Lamb and the enthroned Sovereign of heaven.

2. "And the court that is without the temple cast out and measure it not; for it is given to the nations: and the holy city shall they tread underfoot forty-two months."

The outer court of the earthly temple was the only permitted place of Jewish worshippers. The inner court was for the priests. *The Jewish temple is now the outer court.* In John's day, and at the date here assumed as that of the Apocalypse, the Jewish temple had been destroyed by Rome. But God recognized it as His in a distinct sense, up to the very time of its destruction. This is manifest from the epistle to the Hebrews. There the priesthood and high priesthood are recognized as still continuing; and the Holiest of earth, and the Sanctuary, as the scene of these services, are acknowledged still; though the sacrifice of Jesus had long been offered. On this point the reader should consult chapters viii. 4, 5; ix. 6, 7, 9, 13, 22, 25; x. 1, 11.[1]

Nay more, a *certain actual efficacy* is still attached by the apostle to those ministrations. This is generally overlooked. But what says Hebrews ix. 13? The Holy Ghost admits, that "the blood of bulls and goats, and the ashes of an heifer sprinkling the unclean, SANCTIFY *to the purifying of the flesh.*" On this as a basis Paul infers the greater efficacy of the blood of Christ. The Jewish temple, then, together with its services, was recognized even after Jesus had ascended into the true temple of heaven. It was the temple of earth, in which the *cleansed flesh* of the *Jew* met with God manifested on earth. And hence the Jew, when he became a believer in Jesus, so long as the temple at Jerusalem lasted (or more strictly, perhaps, until the message and apostleship of Paul), was owned of God in worshipping there. "They continuing daily with one accord *in the temple*, and breaking bread in private,[2] did eat their meat with gladness and singleness of heart" (Acts ii. 46). There Peter and John healed the lame man, and thither the angel directed the apostles to go up, when he had delivered them from prison. "Go, stand and speak *in the temple* to the people all the words of this life" (Acts v. 20).

But God at length destroyed the temple by the Roman arms. Then only spiritual worship in the temple on high, worship which can take place by faith alone,

---

[1] The English version is there incorrect; it puts in the past tense actions which in the Greek are spoken of in the present. The priests are spoken of as "stand*ing*," "go*ing*," "offer*ing*," in the apostle's day. [2] Κατ' οἶκον.

was accepted. Then Jesus' words to the woman of Samaria, affirming the rejection of all holy places on earth, were fully in force. John iv. 23, 24.

But the dispensation has now changed. The Church is the witness of the flesh rejected, and of the spirit acknowledged before God. But the churches are no longer regarded as God's sole witness on earth. The Most High has turned again to Israel. The angel of the previous chapter has, as we have seen, claimed earth again for God. The Jew has been acknowledged afresh. But, with the recognition of the earth and the flesh, comes also the recognition of the holy places of earth—Jerusalem and its temple.

While, then, the temple had been destroyed at the date of the writing of the Revelation, it was hereby predicted that it would be rebuilt, and owned of God; while it would only occupy a far inferior position to that which it assumed in a former dispensation. Till the Jew is brought back to his own land, and the temple and its sacrifices are restored, the prophetic part of the Apocalypse does not begin. The new covenant with Judah and Israel owns both the Jewish priesthood and temple; as the close of Ezekiel testifies.

In Matt. xxiv. we learn that "the abomination of desolation" is to stand in the "holy place," as Daniel had foretold: while Luke adds, in the parallel place, that "Jerusalem is to be trodden down by the Gentiles till the times of the Gentiles"—the "forty-two months"—are fulfilled. If Jerusalem be given up to the Gentiles, then the temple must be given up also, unless defended by miracle. But it is not. Then the Jewish temple is the outer court: and its degradation from the height it once held is a measure of the advance of the dispensation.

The court outside the temple, then, is to be "cast out:" a strong expression; much more forcible than the simple omission to measure, which is added immediately after. It is " cast out " as *unclean*. Lev. xiv. 40, 41 ; 2 Chron. xxxiii. 15. This God threatened, while the temple was yet in its first glory. 1 Kings ix. 3, 6–9.

Jesus in His day was filled with a consuming zeal for the glory of His Father's house. At the beginning of His ministry He cleansed it, as John tells us, driving out of the temple those who defiled it. John ii. 13–19. Again, He purged it at His last entry into Jerusalem. Matt. xxi. 12, 13. But it continued unclean. Therefore on it must be fulfilled the word of Ezekiel. "*Because I purged thee, and thou wast not purged, thou shalt not be purged from thy filthiness any more, till I have caused my fury to rest on thee*" (Ezek. xxiv. 13). Now therefore it is given up : the time of fury is come.

Here is another example of that rule of so much interest, that when anything has been done by God *twice*, it is a token of the recurrence of the same thing, in a more marked form, for the third time. The two previous defilements of the temple and the two cleansings predict a future defilement worse than either, and a more terrible cleansing. Once were Jerusalem and its temple destroyed by the *literal Babylon :* once by Rome, or *mystic Babylon :* there remains yet the third and worst destruction, of which many passages of the prophets speak.

Beside casting it out, John is directed not to measure it. It is not only *unclean*, but it is *unsafe*. Had it been holy, it should have been a place of security. But as the place of chief sin, it is the mark for the eagles of judgment. In consequence of its not being measured therefore, " it is given to the nations," or Gentiles. As of yore, the temple for Israel's sin was given up to the Chaldeans, so now it is given up to all nations.

But though the city and temple are given up to the Gentiles, it is not because of the Gentiles' holiness. They are used of God as His scourge of Israel; but it is also with a view to their own scourging, when His purpose in the judgment is fulfilled.

"And the holy city shall they tread underfoot forty and two months." What can "the holy city" be, but Jerusalem? Matt. iv. 5.

There is no other holy city till the New Jerusalem appears. Rev. xxi. 2; xxii. 19. It is holy outwardly, as the place of God's house and choice, though its sin is about to be fully developed. Physical holiness of a place is recognized afresh. The claiming of the earth as belonging to God is a reasserting of His rights to His own land, city, and temple, against the nations or Gentiles.

The Gentiles tread it down. This implies injurious and oppressive treatment. They despise and hate it. The period during which the city is given up to them is "forty-two months," or three years and a half. The period is expressed in months, because that is the scriptural mode of computation when troubles are spoken of. Evil suffered is expressed in months. The time of the flood is computed thus. Gen. vii. 11; viii. 4, 5; 1 Sam. vi. 1. The locusts torment men "five *months*." But this is the time of Jerusalem's sorrow and travail. Luke i. 24, 26, 36, 56. It is the time of iniquity at the full. This is mystically expressed by the number forty-two. For forty-two is composed of the factors six and seven: where six is the number of wickedness, and seven of dispensational perfection. For the same period, expressed by the same mode of computation, the Wild Beast blasphemes. xiii. 5. The number occurs also in significant histories of the Old Testament. Israel's stations in the wilderness were *forty-two*. Num. **xxxiii**. *Forty-two* wicked youths were slain by the she-bears which Elisha sent. 2 Kings ii. 24. The present number is peculiarly significant, when set beside the previous captivity of the ark among the Philistines. That was for a period of *seven months ;* this for a period just *six times as long.*

" Months " is the regulating basis of the Jewish festivals ; the Jew is in the field again. A woman after bearing a male child was to be unclean *forty-two days.* Seven days she was to be separated, the eighth the child was to be circumcised : then was she to continue separated thirty-three days more. This makes forty-one days : to which add the day of birth, and *forty-two is complete.* Lev. xii. 1–5. But that which in the ordinary state is reckoned by days, is here changed into *months.* The city is now the woman. This is connected very closely with the next chapter : but it helps to show the strong bonds which unite the two chapters together.

3. " And I will grant to my Two Witnesses that they shall prophesy a thousand two hundred and sixty days, clothed in sackcloth."

To be a test of the correctness of interpretations, no part of the Revelation is so well adapted as the history of the Two Witnesses.

They are one of the most startling features of the book. They come upon us suddenly, like Elijah. They are persons previously existing ; not like Moses or Samuel, whose history from the commencement is revealed to us.

They are witnesses to Christ ; and persons, as the apostles were. Acts i. 8. They are also witnesses in the sense of *martyrs.* They suffer unto death for the word of their testimony. This proves them to be persons. Thou " hast not denied my faith, even in those days wherein Antipas was my faithful *martyr* [witness], who was slain among you " (ii. 13). They are called by the personal term, " prophets," in verse 10.

They are "*two*" witnesses.[1] "Two or three witnesses" is the number required, by both the law and the gospel, in order to substantiate a truth. Deut. xvii. 6; xix. 15; Matt. xviii. 16.

Who are they? They are ENOCH and ELIJAH :[2] as will be set forth more particularly presently.

They are a new order of witness, quite unlike the Church, both in position and character. John was in Patmos in patience and suffering. These are to face their enemies on the very ground of their power, and to slay them. John is informed of the place they were occupying during his day. They were then already "standing before the Lord of earth." John was to be on high in the refuge of the heaven: these, in the focus of judgment. John was the prophet of the temple:

---

[1] Alford says well, "The article (τοις) seems as if the Two Witnesses were well known, and distinct in their individuality. The (δυσιν) 'two' is essential to the prophecy, and is not to be explained away. No interpretation can be right, which does not, either in individuals, or in characteristic lines of testimony, retain and bring out this dualism."

[2] That this was the early tradition can be shown, by the Apocryphal writings which have come down to us. In the Arabic history of "Joseph the Carpenter" occurs the following passage. "And I say unto you, O my brethren, that it is necessary that these very persons [Enoch and Elijah, above mentioned] should at the end of the times return to the world, and die; in the day, that is, of commotion, terror, anguish, and affliction. For the false Christ will slay their bodies, and pour out their blood like water, because of the reproach to which they will expose him, and the ignominy which while alive they will inflict on him, by detecting his impiety."—*Thilo's God. Apoc.* p. 60.

In the Gospel of Nicodemus is the following passage. "I am Enoch who pleased God, and was translated by him. And this is Elijah the Tishbite. We are also to live to the end of the age: but then we are about to be sent by God to resist Antichrist, and be slain by him, and to rise after three days, and to be caught up in the clouds to meet the Lord."—*Ibid.*, p. 758. See also the Apocryphal Apocalypse of John mentioned by Moses Stuart in his comment on the Revelation, p. 95.

these, of the outer court. John sees within the cloud the Mighty One, the source of their mission : they are outside it.

"They *shall* prophesy." The time of their appearing was to follow on the giving up of the temple, and the city. Lest it should seem to be owing to God's inability to defend His own property against the armed sons of earth, these are sent, who are able, though unarmed, to defy the stoutest mail-clad warriors of the Gentiles.

The duration of their prophecy is given : it shall be for 1,260 days. It is the first half of the last seven years of the Time of the End. It immediately precedes the reign of the False Christ. As, for three years and a half Jesus the first Witness and Martyr of the New Covenant was rejected by Israel ; so, for the same space, will these two testify to both Jew and Gentile, and be rejected also. The fact that their testimony is not to begin till after the trumpets have commenced ; and the additional fact that it is to last for three years and a half, are further proofs that it is not of the Church. The Church is to look for the return of Jesus, without any events interposed : while signs of various kinds must precede the manifestation of the Son of Man to the *Jew* and to the *nations*.

The time of their testimony is expressed in "days," not in "months." I believe this is because their mission carries mercy to the people of God, and even to the Gentiles. This is, I suppose, the "little help" wherewith the Lord's servants in Judæa are hepled. Dan. xi. 34. So the time of feeding the woman in the desert is expressed, as an act of mercy, in "days" also. "That they should feed her there a thousand two hundred and three score *days*" (xii. 6).

They are to prophesy, "clothed in sackcloth."[1]

---

[1] Alford says well, "Certainly this portion of the prophetic

This is the very dress which the Lord commands those who fear Him at Jerusalem to use during its day of tribulation. Isa. xxii. 12; Joel i. 13. The very reason for this clothing may exist at the time supposed. The Gentiles hold the temple: perhaps they forbid the daily sacrifice.

But while this kind of dress is often referred to in the Old Testament, it is never recommended to the servants of God in the New, or used by them. Behold, then, another proof of the change of dispensation! God recognizes this covering only where it is here supposed to be found, and only in connection with *Israel's* and the temple's suffering and desolation.

4. "These are the two olive trees, and the two lampstands that are standing before the Lord [1] of the earth."

They are olive trees and lamps as regards the throne above. Fire proceeds from them in their character as lamps. They are not only *shining* lamps, as the churches were: but *burning* lamps, destroying their foes. They are lamps of judgment, as the Church was of mercy.

This incidental notice is intended to lead us to Old Testament prophets; and to Jerusalem, of which Zechariah prophesies. In Zechariah iv. the prophet has a vision of a lampstand holding seven lamps, and supplied by seven pipes, while on its right and left stood two olive trees. The prophet inquires what the two olive trees mean. The angel replies, "*These are the*

description strongly favours the individual interpretation. For first, it is hard to conceive how whole bodies of men and churches could be thus described: and secondly, the principal symbolical interpreters have left out, or passed very slightly, this important particular. One does not see how bodies of men who lived like other men [their being the victims of persecution is another matter] can be said to have prophesied, *clothed in sackcloth.*"

[1] This is the true reading. So the critical editions.

two anointed ones [' Sons of oil,' *marg.*] *that stand by the Lord of the whole earth.*"

The reference to the Old Testament prophecy, then, is plain. But who are the two ? They are very remarkable persons ; for they are called (if we adopt the rendering of our English version) " anointed ones." They are akin to the Messiah, " the Anointed One." These two lamps of the outer court do not, however, supersede the seven torches of the Holy of Holies. As Jesus was the light of the world, they are " lamps." As He proclaimed Himself " the true vine," so are they olive trees. He stood before the Father the Great Husbandman : these stand before " the Lord of earth."

They were alive in Zechariah's day—" standing before " God. So were Enoch and Elijah. The angel's word to Zechariah, " Knowest thou not what these be ? " imports that it was possible he might have known who they were. And he might, if they were men who had lived before ; men so honoured before God as to have escaped death up to his day ; the only two that had. " Standing " is the position of *life* : in sickness the body reclines ; at death it falls and lies motionless, as the history of these witnesses shows. The expression " standing *before* " implies favourable reception in the presence of majesty, as has been before observed. Gen. xviii. 22–27 ; 1 Sam. xvi. 22, 23 ; Deut. x. 8. They are olive trees bearing fruit accepted before God, amidst the dead and evil trees around. They are lightbearers amidst the darkness encircling the world. It is a word which Elijah twice applies to himself. 1 Kings xvii. 1. To Obadiah he says, " As the Lord of Hosts liveth, *before whom I stand*, I will surely show myself to him to-day " (xviii. 15).

But they were still alive and accepted before God in John's day. They were still standing in the presence of the Lord of Hosts. This, then, absolutely identifies them, as Enoch and Elijah. Who of all that were alive in the days of Zechariah and John, is alive now? As they were alive in John's day, and in God's presence, they must be alive still. There is no death in the heavenly courts, and this chapter shows that they have yet to die.

That one of them is Elijah, is also proved by the promise of Malachi. Mal. iv. 5, 6. These are the last words of the Old Testament. It ends with a conditional curse upon its lips, and the Apocalypse manifests the condition to be fulfilled, and the curse not without cause to come. If the angel of Rev. x. be "the angel of the covenant," one of the witnesses must be Elijah, according to the promise in Mal. iii., iv.

But some smile at the idea of Elijah's return. Was not the very idea rebuked by our Lord? Did not He say, "If ye will receive it, this is Elias which *was* for to come?" (Matt. xi. 14). Our translators being not millennarians, have here overstepped the exact translation. It is, "He is Elias, *who is about to come*."[1] "But does not the Gospel say, that the disciples on one occasion understood Jesus to be speaking of John the Baptist as Elijah?" It does: in a passage most worthy to be noted. The three favoured apostles had beheld Elijah on the Mount of Transfiguration; and as they descended they inquired, "How it could be true, as the scribes affirmed, that Elijah was to precede the coming of Messiah, when Jesus, whom they owned as Messiah, had appeared so long before?" What is our Lord's reply? "*Elias is indeed coming first,*[2] *and shall restore*[3] *all things:* but I say unto you, that "Elias is come already, and they knew him not, but have done unto him whatsoever they listed: likewise shall also the Son of Man suffer of them. Then the disciples understood

[1] Ὁ μέλλων ἔρχεσθαι. [2] Ἔρχεται. [3] Ἀποκαταστήσει.

that he spake unto them of John the Baptist " (Matt. xvii. 11–13). This passage is in no respect hostile to our views. Jesus distinguishes.[1] In one view Elias *had come already:* in another, *he was yet to come.* The point which the apostles needed to have supplied in order to quiet their minds, was the coming of Elijah which was *already past.* For they were fully persuaded of the future and literal coming of Elijah: they knew nothing of the past and figurative one. The latter, after the Saviour's words, they understood to be fulfilled in John. Rightly enough did they so think. In our day, the reverse is the case, and men make the past and figurative coming of Elias to swallow up the future and literal coming of the prophet. Believe *both*, and all difficulty disappears. Jesus does not destroy the opinion of the scribes, that Elijah had yet to come. He confirms the belief by the pointed words—" Elias *is indeed coming first*, and *shall* restore all things." This could not mean John, who was already dead. And these words of confirmation he puts *first*.

We dare not make the words of our Lord and His forerunner oppose one another in point-blank contradiction; as we must do, if we affirm that John the Baptist was Elijah the prophet, in such a sense that no other is to come in order to fulfil that prophecy. For what said John to those who came to inquire of him what position he occupied? " Art thou Elias? " said they. " And he saith, I AM NOT " (John i. 21). The angel said of him only, " He shall go before him *in the spirit and power of Elias* " (Luke i. 17). And our Lord calls him " Elijah " with a certain mark of discrimination, "*If ye will receive it*," while He reaffirms the expectation of the advent of the Tishbite, by the words He adds, "This is Elijah, *who is about to come*."

[1] This is seen more clearly in the Greek, where $\mu\acute{\epsilon}\nu$ and $\delta\acute{\epsilon}$ offer to our notice the opposed clauses.

The expectation, then, of the literal Elijah agrees with both parts of Scripture affirmation. For there were to be two advents of Messiah : one in the days of His lowliness, and before Him there went one in the spirit of Elijah. But there was to be another advent of Messiah in power. And before that the true Elijah was to appear. He was to come, " before the *great* and *terrible* day of the Lord." But our Lord's first coming was neither great nor terrible. That day has therefore yet to come.

They are " lamps." They are " sons of oil." As olive trees they possess oil ; but they also communicate it. They are " sons of oil." Elijah is to " restore all things." He must therefore restore to Israel the spirit of prophecy. As " lamps " they give light amidst the deep darkness. This is a tacit setting aside of the churches from their former position of testimony. The former seven lamps have been removed from on high. Their place is now filled by two, which are set no longer in the sanctuary, but in the outer court. They are not *stars* of *heaven*, as the angels of the churches were; but *olive trees* of *earth*. The symbols or " mysteries " of the churches and their pastors were seen by John, and explained to him. But these are neither shown nor explained. The lamps of the first vision stood before Christ as " the Son of Man," the Priest of heaven, and the stars were in His hand. But these stand before " *the Lord of earth*." During the church dispensation, bodies of men constituted the lamps : now it is individuals. Thus John the Baptist is by our Lord called " the burning and shining *lamp* " (John v. 35). (Greek.)

They have both literal and symbolic titles ; because they have two places. In heaven, and in relation to the temple and throne, they are " lamps " and " olive trees : " on earth they are literal men, " witnesses " and "prophets." That which is literal prayer on earth becomes "odours" in heaven.

They stand before God in His character of "Lord of the earth." This is not God's title while Israel is cast off. In Daniel, after the temple is taken and the city destroyed, the Most High takes the title of "the God *of heaven.*" (Dan. ii. 18, 28, 37, 44, etc.). Nor is this the title which God takes during the church dispensation. Then His characteristic name is, "the Father of our Lord Jesus Christ" (Rom. xv. 6; 2 Cor. i. 3; Eph. i. 3, etc.). But, as the Most High in Daniel's day retired to the heaven, giving up earth to the Gentiles, and leaving Israel beneath their power; so now He is returning to His former position as the manifested Owner of the earth. "Lord of earth" is the title taken by the Most High when He brought Israel by miracle into the land.

5. "And if any wishes to hurt them, fire proceedeth out of their mouth and devoureth their enemies; and if any wishes to hurt them, thus must he be killed."[1]

This marks the abiding enmity of man against God and His people. The Gentiles have possession of the city in armed might: what, then, can withstand their power, or resist their enmity? God has messengers adapted to every emergency. Those of Gospel times could not witness for 1,260 days in such a scene. God then steps back to former dispensations, and brings into the field

---

[1] Alford's candid admission here is worthy of notice. "This whole description is most difficult to apply on the allegorical interpretation, as is that which follows. And as might be expected, the allegorists halt and are perplexed exceedingly. The double announcement here seems to stamp the literal sense, and the (εἴ τις) 'If any one,' and (δεῖ αὐτὸν ἀποκτανθῆναι) 'he must be killed' are decisive against any mere *national* application of the words. [See Elliott.] *Individuality* could not have been more strongly indicated."

one from the times before the law, and one from the legal dispensation. They witness to God as the God of life and of *mercy*, and prove it by their being sustained alive for thousands of years. They prove Him also to be the Inflicter of death, and the God of *justice*, by the powers which they exercise, as deputed by Him.

It is evident that their power and spirit savour not of the Gospel.

The messengers of the Gospel were possessed of miracle, but never used it for destruction of men, or in self-defence.

Fire " proceed*eth* " and " devour*eth*." The present tense denotes the frequency and habitual character of the manifestation. It is not till open attack has been found fatal, that secret is tried. It is not till secret plans have been often attempted and the conspirators destroyed, that men unwillingly perceive that no such guilty secret can be concealed from these messenger-prophets; and they abandon the design in despair. Twice it is said, " if any wishes to hurt." Both Jew and Gentile will desire it. For alas! among the Jews of that hour will be many apostates. There are those that " forsake the holy covenant " (Dan. xi. 30, 32 ; Isa. lxv. 11). These, as apostates, would be the more bitter and zealous against the unpleasing light exhibited on behalf of the truth, and more desirous to extinguish it. These two are alone in the possession of this power. The godly Jews are not defended by miracle, but are required to be patient, and submit.

He who would hurt " must " in this manner be killed. So has God decreed. Thus only could the lives of these His mortal servants be preserved.

The repetition of the same sentiment nearly in the same words is very observable. It expresses a great feature of their future history. " Thus," not by sword, not by poison, not by a king's sentence ; but, as becomes an outraged prophet, by fire from their mouth. God approves the deed.

6. " These have the power to shut the heaven, that rain fall not during the days of their prophecy : and they have power over the waters to turn them into blood, and to smite the earth with every plague, as often as they may wish."

They have power, and, as the word imports, a licensed, lawful power, over the great objects of creation.

They "shut the heaven." It is evident that "heaven" is taken in its physical or Old Testament sense ; not in its spiritual or New Testament import. It is not, the heaven shut, that the Holy Spirit may not descend : but that "*rain* may not fall." They are witnesses to God as the *Creator* of the heaven and earth.

It is in this sense that " the heaven " is taken under the Law. If they served other gods, then would "the Lord's wrath be kindled against you, and HE SHUT UP THE HEAVEN, THAT THERE BE NO RAIN, and that the land yield not her fruit : and ye perish quickly from off the good land which the Lord giveth you" (Deut. xi. 14, 17). So Lev. xxvi; Deut. xxviii. 12. This last passage is peculiarly appropriate, showing very clearly the sense of opening the heaven, and, by consequence, of shutting it.

This plague is foretold by the prophets of Israel. "Son of man, say unto her, thou art the land that is not cleansed, *nor rained upon, in the day of indignation*" (Ezek. xxii. 24 ; Isa. v. 6).

The Witnesses have power, too, over all "waters, to turn them into blood." That great natural element is under the Witnesses' control. Thus did Moses in Egypt smite the Nile, and turn it into blood. No reason, then, can be alleged why this should not be again. The Witnesses have power over both the fresh water and the salt. Moses and the Two Witnesses, acting on the principle of justice, turn waters to *blood*. Jesus, coming in the spirit of grace, turns water into *wine*. John ii. Their shutting the heaven is God's witness against *idolatry*. Thus He shows the powerlessness of other gods. Their turning waters to blood is a testimony against the *murders* of earth (ix. 20).

But these are only specimens of their power to injure. All other plagues are submitted to their discretion.

" Every plague " is in their hand. Under that name are included diseases, as leprosy (Lev. xiii. 2); emerods (1 Sam. vi. 4); and calamities inflicted through the elements, as hail and pestilence. Exod. ix. 14; 2 Sam. xxiv. 15. This infliction of unknown chastisements was threatened in the law. Deut. xxviii. 59, 61; xxix. 20-23; Lev. xxvi. 21. The Apocalypse is the book of the plagues of the Lord, launched against the earth in the season of His war against it. ix. 20; xv. 1; xxii. 18.

These are *trusted* servants of the throne. They are empowered to deal the blows of supernatural vengeance, "*as often as they may wish*." Their wills, by long sojourn in the sanctuary with God, and as filled with His Spirit, are so conformed to His, that they can be trusted with power so tremendous as this. They in this also resemble our Lord. "I do always those things which please him" (John viii. 29). It is designed that there should be an immediate and sensible connection between their threats and the plague sent. Mystery is nearly gone.

The miracles of the Gospel were of a different kind. These law-witnesses smite "with all plagues." But of Jesus it is said, "He *healed* many; insomuch that they pressed upon Him to touch Him, *as many as had plagues*" (Mark iii. 10).

7. "And when they shall have finished their testimony, the Wild Beast, that ascendeth out of the bottomless pit, shall make war with them, and overcome them, and kill them."

As Jesus prophesied His death and resurrection, so it is very probable that they will foretell theirs. That will account for a part of their treatment afterwards.

They are slain by the Wild Beast, when their testimony is ended. Now their witnessing lasts for three years and a half, and the Wild Beast's reign lasts for three years and a half also. Are they then cotemporaneous ? running parallel from the commencement to the close ? I believe not. It would rather appear that the time of his undisputed authority begins only with the day of their slaying. It is their being put to death by him which procures him the wonder of the world. It is that, I suppose, which draws forth from men the admiring cry—" Who is like unto the Wild Beast ? *Who is able to make war with him ?* " (xiii. 4). " He has conquered those against whom human power availed not. He has rid us of those that vexed and smote us. His is supernatural power indeed ! "

But if the end of their testimony and their resurrection occur before the close of the sixth trumpet, then they must begin to testify before the fifth. For the duration of the fifth and sixth trumpets is but a year, six months, a day, and hour. Hence they are on earth two years previously. The Wild Beast ascends, as we have seen, at the fifth trump. But he does not take the undisputed power of earth till some time after his ascent; and, as I gather, not till he has removed out of the way the obstacle to his full reception, interposed by the presence and power of these two martyr-prophets.

Hence the Witnesses' testimony is out of place as regards its beginning, while it is correctly placed in regard of its ending. From this, it is probable that the difference of tenses used in the angel's narrative of their history takes its rise. At verse 3 of this chapter we have the future; in verses 4, 5, 6, the present; in verse 7, the future; in verses 9 and 10, the present again; at the close of verse 10 we have the future; and the rest of their history is told in the past tense.

This verse introduces to us "the Wild Beast"[1] for the first time under that title. He is the great antagonist of the Lord Jesus, attempting to usurp His kingdom and Godhead. He is called, then, the "*Wild Beast,*" as the direct moral contrast to "*the Lamb.*" As "the Lamb" marks Jesus' character of mercy, patient endurance, and submission to the throne of God, so does the title "the Wild Beast" indicate this man's fierceness of passion, violent wilfulness, and insubjection. Nothing is sacred with him. His passions are his only law. He rebels against the God of heaven, and blasphemes Him. As carrying out the significance of numbers in the book, it is remarkable that the Lamb is named twenty-eight times, which is equivalent to four multiplied by seven; while the Wild Beast is mentioned thirty-six times, or *six* times *six*.

He makes "war" on the witnesses. From this it appears that there is resistance on their part. It would seem as if the power and glory of the Witnesses is like that of Moses, subject to a gradual leakage and decay. Their glory would seem to arise from their long sojourn on high. Moses, by his stay of forty days in the presence of the Lord on Sinai, was sustained without food, and the skin of his face gradually acquired brightness, till at length at his descent it positively shone. But that brightness, as the apostle observes, passed away. A mortal body might not hold it long. And thus, it would appear, these supernatural powers

---

[1] Our translators, by calling him "the Beast," have led English readers to imagine that he is of the same character and described by the same word as the four "living creatures" of heaven, which they also call "beasts." But they are two very different words. The one is $\zeta\hat{\omega}ov$, the other $\tau\grave{o}\ \theta\eta\rho\acute{\iota}ov$.

abide not in the mortal bodies of Enoch and Elijah longer than three years and a half. Yet it must be noticed, that even when they are conquered and slain at last, it is by no mortal man, but by an immortal one; by one who, after suffering death, comes up clad with immortality. That adversary, as having died once, cannot be slain again. Hence, while the Witnesses resemble Jesus destroying His foes by flaming fire, yet there is one whom they cannot consume. He is left, therefore, for Jesus' coming. He is to reign, till the Lord shall destroy him "*with the breath of his mouth.*" The resurrection sets the Two Witnesses out of his reach. The force communicated in resurrection as giving wisdom and strength to rule over men, is seen in the case of the two Wild Beasts. Rev. xiii.

The immortal nature of the Wild Beast is the reason, apparently, why he is spoken of with the adjunct of his ascent from the bottomless pit. It is added to enable us to understand how *he* is able to overcome them. This characteristic is very important; as is shown by its being repeated thrice. That he is the same with the king over the locusts is apparent; for none but he is mentioned as coming up out of the bottomless pit (ix. 2, 11). The names of the two agree also. The locust-king is named Abaddon and Apollyon —"DESTROYER." And what is so characteristic of a "wild beast" as its destroying? And if the wild beasts of the *earth* be so savage and destructive, what shall be the rage and the power of the Wild Beast of the *bottomless pit?*

As in their tempers, so in their history, are the Lamb and the Wild Beast opposed to each other; yet with considerable degree of resemblance on many points. Jesus, in order to reign, descends from heaven. The Wild Beast ascends from the bottomless pit. Jesus descends with the armies of heaven; Antichrist ascends with the locust-army of the pit. Jesus, rejected by man, and put to death by him, returned to heaven. Antichrist, after committing suicide, went to the place of the lost below, and shall return to perdition, as soon as his brief reign is over. As it is said of Jesus (Eph. iv. 9) that His predicted ascent to heaven implied a previous descent to earth and to its lower regions; so Antichrist's ascent to earth implies a previous descent from it. The False Christ was a man, and he *ascends* from the abyss of the lost. Then he previously *descended* thither.[1]

He overcomes them and kills them. From these words being used to describe the result, it would appear to be an event requiring some little time. It is by the exertion of a power superior to theirs that he prevails. It is designed of God, and therefore foretold, that His people's faith may not fail. It is purposed of God, that His foe's time of power shall occur at the Witnesses' time of weakness. He designs to give His enemies an apparent victory, to bring out their heart of enmity visibly to light. "The foolishness of God is wiser than man; the weakness of God is stronger than man." They are indulged with a seeming triumph, that the repressing influence of fear being taken off, their emotions of bitter hatred to God in the persons of His ministering prophets may be made manifest. And their refusal of the Witnesses' testimony ripens them for the full energy of the Wild Beast's delusion. There is also a third reason. The Witnesses' death brings in God as the God of resurrection. It identifies the God of the Old Testament with the God of the New. The miracles of judgment under Moses and Elijah, and

---

[1] The height of the ascent is the earth. Therefore previously he was below it. But he ascends out of the abyss. Therefore the bottomless pit is below the earth.

those of mercy by Jesus, both take their rise from one God. These die, because God is the God who sentenced Adam and his race in Eden. They rise, because "as in Adam all die, so in Christ shall all be made alive." Resurrection, the peculiar glory of the New Covenant, is now attached to these worthies of the Old.

The Witnesses are "overcome." But how? Not morally; for they continue their testimony faithfully to the close; and are confessed of God as His, by their ascent to heaven. Had they denied Christ, they had been overcome in another and a moral sense. But the vanquishing here is to be taken *physically*, as the rest is.

The Witnesses' testimony, as is natural, ends with their death. As they die, they are men : as they die for the testimony of God, they are martyrs : as they foretell the designs of God, they are martyr-prophets. A violent death is the usual end of the prophets of God. "Lord, *they have killed thy prophets*, and digged down thine altars, and I am left alone, *and they seek my life*," said Elijah. Rom. xi. 3; Luke xi. 47. "Wherefore, behold, I send unto you *prophets*, and wise men, and scribes, and some of them ye shall *kill*" (Matt. xxiii. 34).

8. "And their dead body (shall lie) upon the broad-place of the great city, which spiritually is being called Sodom and Egypt, where their Lord also was crucified."

That they are men, and not a symbol, is shown by their leaving behind "dead bodies."

These heavenly messengers are not exempt from death, for they are men. But their corpses are treated with the utmost indignity. They lie in the street of the city. So abhorrent a spectacle would immediately be noticed, and removed from a *city*. That they lie in the most public place of a populous city, is not, then, because they are not seen. It is given as a specimen of barbarity, and as a proof of outrageous wickedness.

But still that is not the point on which the Holy Ghost dwells. It is the *place* where this event occurs. It is in "the great city," which is defined by three characteristics. All three criteria assure us that it is JERUSALEM. Before, it was called "the *holy* city," as the place of God's temple. But, now that its sin is being brought to light, its greatness is the only point named. Greatness now is not holiness: it is only in the future kingdom that holiness shall bring greatness.

The great city, which is the scene of the present momentous events, "is spiritually called Sodom and Egypt." The use of the present tense in the verb "to call" manifests that it was already known by those names in John's day amongst the spiritual.

The city was called so "spiritually." That is put in opposition to "carnally," or naturally. It had a literal name, well known to fleshly or natural men, who regard merely the exterior. But among inspired men, or among the regenerate, who look at the moral character of things, it had, besides its literal name, names descriptive of its state before God, and already depicted in the book of God. Whether by "the spiritual," we are to understand one or both of these senses of the word, is not clear. The word signifies sometimes (1) those born of the Spirit, sometimes those (2) inspired of the Spirit.

In both Sodom and Egypt the hearts of the inhabitants were tested and displayed, as they are here also. But sin has advanced since those earlier days. God has come nearer to man in grace, and in discovery of Himself. There is the temple in this city, and the Lord of the Witnesses was once there. The increase of sin is manifested mournfully in this portion of the prophecy.

R

But a third description of the city is given. "Where their Lord also was crucified." This is not a name of the city; nor is it to be spiritually taken, as the two names were. It is a designation of the city by a past fact that occurred in it. The Lord of the Witnesses was crucified there. What city can be meant but Jerusalem? It retains its old character, murderess of the prophets, as our Lord foretold.

The place given to the word " also " in the translation produces two somewhat different senses. If it qualifies " where," it only intends that this is another criterion by which to discover the city. But if it be taken, as it should be, to qualify " their Lord," it gives us by implication the further intelligence, *that the martyr-prophets shall die by crucifixion, as did their Lord*. And if the Two Witnesses be Enoch and Elias, then the patriarchal and legal dispensations are recognized as being alike under the rule of Jesus, as " their Lord." Here is another important point in the remarkable parallel between their history and that of Jesus. Moreover, this very mode of death is foretold by the Saviour, as that which should be inflicted on some prophets whom He would send. Matt. xxiii. 34, 35. When " the *holy* city " has become *Sodom*, it is time that vengeance should descend.

9. "And (some) of [1] the peoples, and tribes, and tongues, and nations, look on their dead bodies three days and a half, and suffer not their dead bodies to be put into a sepulchre."

Representatives of all the Gentiles are encamped around Jerusalem. Joel iii. 1, 2; Zech. xii. 3; xiv. 2. All of this vast multitude wish to see this great sight. But the street is far too narrow for them all to behold it. Discipline, too, must be kept up in armies. But, as the death of the Witnesses is a question of such importance,

[1] For examples of this Hebrew idiom see 1 Kings iv. 34; Num. xxi. 1; Matt. xxiii. 34.

a proof of the supposed supremacy of the Great False Christ, some of all nations shall be indulged with an ocular demonstration of the reality of the ground of their joy—the death of the two prophets. They had signalized themselves greatly in life: and we know how great is the hurry and crowding to see anyone that has made himself famous. But their death is a subject of rejoicing. They are regarded as enemies of mankind, the great obstacle in the way of kings and nations casting off the enforced and hated worship of Jehovah and His Christ. They had long defied the powers of man to put them to death. "*Can it really be a fact, that they are slain ?*" Was it not "too good news to be true ?" But truth fears no defeat. The reality of their death is so evident, that the corpses are exposed to the insatiate gaze of the warriors of the whole earth. "Yes! those are the features of the men that brought plague after plague on mankind. Those the lips whence came forth the bursts of fire that consumed every adversary! How chill and white they are now!" It would seem, then, from the mode of expression, as though certain persons of every nation were deputed to enter the city, and permitted to behold these slain witnesses, that they may testify the truth of the great fact, either to their own camp, or to their nation. The word[1] denotes not merely the nations seeing them, but their directing their eyes to this great sight, and gazing upon them.

The time of the triumph of death over the Witnesses, and of their enemies' survey of their humiliation, is but "three days and a half." How should they be exposed three *years* and a half ? The reference to Jesus' case is express. He predicted "days" as the time of His sojourn in the tomb; and in "days" (not "years") was it fulfilled. And while some would confine the year-

[1] Βλέπω.

for-a-day system to cases of figurative prophecy, Jesus, in a figurative prediction, spoke of His subjection to death as lasting so many days : and in days it was fulfilled. "*Destroy this temple*, and in *three days* I will raise it up" (John ii. 19). Jesus' testimony lasted for *three and a half years*, His sojourn in the tomb for *three days*. These witness *three and a half years*, and are then humbled beneath the power of death *three and a half days*.

The addition to their period of subjection to death of half a day beyond that endured by their Lord, is very important. Jesus rose after three days ; for God's Holy One was not to see corruption. But these are to experience "the bondage of corruption." And to this their exposure to the fierce eastern sun in the open street will greatly contribute. Of the corruption of the body on the fourth day we have a testimony in the case of Lazarus. John xi. 7, 30.

The resurrection following thereon was, of course, so much the more glorious, as it is also here.

The conduct of men upon this occasion discloses most clearly the feelings of their heart.

They suffer not the corpses to be buried. "These enemies of God and man shall not obtain the common decent lot of the departed. Every indignity shall be showed to these causers of trouble. Let the birds and beasts feed on them!" While, then, it would seem that some would be glad to bury them (some saints of God probably roused to faith, or sustained in it, by their testimony), the current of feeling runs vehemently against such an attempt. It is strictly forbidden. Thus we trace the advance of wickedness to this its highest wave.

In the mind of the excited nations, the most excruciating death is a poor revenge on these foes of mankind. They will inflict vengeance on the senseless corpse. They will glut their eyes with its livid paleness. Such have often been the feelings of men in their most savage mood, when wrought on by religious enmity.

But there is another and a very powerful reason of policy tending to produce the refusal of burial. By their remarkable history, the witnesses bring again before the thoughts of men the history of Jesus. They are prophets who prophesy as long as He did, and in the land where He ministered. They are crucified. They probably predict, as he did, their resurrection. In the prohibition here foretold, we see the plan of mankind designed to meet and confute the prediction. The rulers of Israel formerly took another course. They allowed the body of Jesus to be buried, and only watched the sepulchre in order to prevent any attempt of the apostles to carry off the body. But at this time the False Messiah and his counsellors will argue as follows : " The Christian religion was based upon a trick of former times ; the disciples stole away the corpse. But we have the game now in our own hands : and we will be wiser. None saw or pretended to see Jesus rise ; nor after His resurrection did any but *disciples* behold Him. We will destroy any such scheme now. The corpses shall not be removed out of our sight. They shall be before the eyes of all ; and if they can rise, it shall be visible to all ; no hole-and-corner affair ! Men of all nations shall mount guard over them night and day ; and we will see what will become of their dreams ! " But the Lord " taketh the wise in their own craftiness."

10. " And the dwellers upon the earth rejoice over them, and make merry ; and shall send gifts one to another ; because these two prophets tormented the dwellers upon the earth."

The " dwellers on earth " are a wider and more locally-scattered party than those who gaze on the dead bodies.

But few comparatively can see the corpses : only those in the neighbourhood of Jerusalem. But the world at large may hear of the death of the martyr-prophets, and rejoice. The " dwellers on earth " would be especially ready for joy. Their Sadducean denial of *resurrection*, embodied in the creed of Jerusalem in that day, " Let us eat and drink, for to-morrow we die," finds its sharpest rebuke in the supernatural testimony and miracles of these witnesses. Thus the Sadducees were the strongest and most violent persecutors of the apostles, when they rose to testify the resurrection of Jesus, both by word of mouth and by miracle. Acts iv. 1, 2 ; v. 17, 18, 30–3 ; xxiii. 6–10.

It is thus also in the instance before us. Those who would make the earth man's only sphere, and sense the only interpreter of his duty, are met with stern rebuke by this startling testimony and miracle. They refuse to yield to the demand on their faith, made by God's witnesses, and they will not repent. Hence they rejoice when this testimony is silenced, apparently for ever. The tormenting proofs of the contradiction to their vain theories are seemingly swept away. Now they may rejoice. They can go on unchecked in the indulgence of the lusts of fallen nature.

They make it an occasion of joy in every way in which ungodly man can testify it. They " make merry " in feasts. It is a subject of rejoicing at feasts, and over the convivial bowl. Luke xv. 23, 24, 29, 32 ; xii. 19.

They " send presents to each other,"—another token of joy. Thus when Haman, the enemy of Israel, was slain, and the decree against the Jews obtained by him was virtually reversed, " The city of Shushan rejoiced and was glad " (Esther viii. 15, 17 ; Esther ix. 19, 22).

" But how," it is asked, " is it conceivable that men all over the earth should be rejoicing at the news, when only three days and a half intervene between their death and resurrection ? " Allowing the statement that men over all the earth will rejoice, is it not perfectly conceivable, if the electric telegraph shall then have extended itself at the rate it has done of late years ?

Thus God holds all mankind guilty of their death. True, the Wild Beast alone, possessed of supernatural power, is able to put them to death. But their sympathies prove, beyond a doubt, how gladly they would have effected it, if they could. God judges them on the ground of their sympathies.

11. "And after the three days and a half the Spirit of life from God entered into them, and they stood upon their feet ; and great fear fell upon those that beheld them."

"Seven torches of fire" were standing before the throne of God, " which are *the seven Spirits of God* " ; and the Lamb had "seven horns and seven eyes, which are *the seven Spirits of God sent forth into all the earth.*" This is the Holy Ghost, as the great Agent of the purposes of God. One of these Spirits (that of life physical), in carrying out of the purposes of the throne here, undoes the scheme of man, and proves the powerlessness of his utmost efforts. Men have inflicted death by God's permission : but the God of life by His invisible power bestows life renewed for ever. It enters into the slain corpses, and they live. The Holy Ghost is the author of spiritual life. Rom. viii. 2, 10, 11. But here it is the communication of natural life to those long ago alive to God, and only deprived of life physical by ungodly men.

Jesus was the Son of God, having life in Himself ; and of the mode of His resurrection nothing is said. But these rise by the entrance of the Spirit of God into them. The Holy Spirit appears as lord of the physical, as well as of the moral.

The present expression is used to describe the miraculous return of a dead body to life. 2 Kings xiii. 21.

There are spectators of this miracle. Never, during the days of their exposure, are the bodies without anxious gazers. Especially, if they predict their resurrection the fourth day, will the crowd be great to see the completion or refutation of their word.

Their word is fulfilled, to the terror of the beholders, who are their enemies. Joy at their death may be going on in parts around Jerusalem ; but joy at their death is scattered in the immediate circle about their corpses, the moment they arise.

Their fear is "great." They have ventured, as desperate gamesters, their all upon this stake ; and it has, to their intense dismay, gone against them. Their joy is succeeded by terror the most fearful. Here is that resurrection which they denied, and derided as absurd and impossible. Then the story of Jesus' resurrection is true also. They are made to bear reluctant testimony against themselves. The actual first movements of resurrection are disclosed before their eyes, only to their discomfiture. Resurrection is to them not a thing of joy, but of dismay. They have denied the God of resurrection. Its reality comes upon them as a thunderclap, as the steel gauntlet of an armed enemy. Infidels have raised cavils on the possibility that Jesus' resurrection was only the returned consciousness of one who swooned. "We have no proof (say they) of His being really dead. Who accurately examined the matter ? " Here there will be no room for such question. Eyes innumerable, hands unnumbered, will scrutinize the death of these slain. The stronger, then, and the more certain the proof of death, the more powerful the conviction of the reality of resurrection. The fear felt, then, is the proof of the miraculous nature of the thing beheld, and therefore of the literality of the resurrection foretold.

12. "And they heard a great voice out of the heaven saying to them, Ascend hither. 13. And they ascended into the heaven in the cloud, and their enemies beheld them."

The word is with power : at once they ascend. They have hitherto been placed in the outer unmeasured court, which was consequently insecure. They are taken to the secure temple above. They are delivered from the enmity of earth in a moment. For had they been left below, they had been assailed again by their inveterate foes. So Lazarus after his resurrection was exposed to the plots of the chief priests. By this act connected with the voice, it is manifested that God owns them. They have confessed Him by suffering unto death, as Abel; He confesses them by calling them to ascend, as did Enoch before. They are depressed, as God's witnesses, below Moses and Caleb : but it is only that they may be exalted higher. When the congregation of Israel rises against Moses, and against the two faithful spies, God interposes to save them from death. He does not so in this instance ; but it is only that He may give them eternal life in resurrection.

They ascend in "the cloud." Doubtless this refers us back to the cloud which mantled the angel in his descent to earth. x. 1. Jesus after His resurrection ascended thus. "A cloud received Him out of their sight" (Acts i. 9). If the life, miracles, death, resurrection, and ascent of the Two Witnesses is not to be literally taken, neither is that of our Lord, with which theirs is paralleled. If the first resurrection of chapter xx. is to be literally taken, much more is this clear and circumstantial prophecy. I address this argument to those who admit the pre-millennial view. Those who admit *that* as literal, and deny *this*, may be driven off the field by the artillery derived from the death and resurrection of the Saviour, and the ascent of Enoch, Elijah, and our Lord.

It has been objected against Jesus' resurrection and ascension, that neither took place in public ; and that His mounting into the sky was beheld by friends only. But now God will grant, that, as the resurrection has been public, so shall the ascent be. Enemies gaze into heaven now, as the prophets go up. The foundation-stone of the kingdom of God, which is laid in resurrection, is now openly manifested before men. The kingdom itself in power is about speedily to follow. But there is no preaching of mercy now. Testimony, and its day of goodness to the godless, are past.

13. " And in that hour [1] followed a great earthquake, and the tenth of the city fell, and seven thousand names of men were killed in the earthquake ; and the rest became affrighted, and gave glory to the God of the heaven."

An earthquake attended on both the death and the resurrection of Jesus. " Behold, there was *a great earthquake :* for the angel of the Lord descended from heaven " (Matt. xxviii. 2). This continued resemblance to the Saviour, both in their sufferings and in the agency of God on their behalf, gives force to our Lord's words, " Everyone that is perfect shall be as his Master " (Luke vi. 40).

Four earthquakes are mentioned in this book. (1) The one at the sixth seal ; (2) one at the casting down of fire from heaven ; (3) the third occurs on this occasion ; and (4) the last after the seventh trumpet, xi. 19 ; which is the same, apparently, with that of the seventh vial. xvi. 18.

The consequence of the earthquake is a natural one. " The tenth of the city fell."

The natural further consequence is, that men were

---

[1] Some good MSS. read "day."

killed by the falling houses, or by being swallowed up by the opening earth. In Elijah's day, seven thousand men were reserved of God. Here the same number is cut off.

The results here are terrific. "Seven thousand names of men are slain."

By the expression "names of men," is denoted "persons of distinction," or "celebrated men." "Men" simply have been spoken of before. viii. 11; ix. 4, 6, 10, 15, 18, 20. Exactly this phrase nowhere occurs in Scripture, that I am aware of. But the expression "men of name" is found both in Hebrew and in English. "The same became mighty men which were of old:" "*men of name*"—or, as the English version has it, "men of renown" (Gen. vi. 4; 1 Chron. v. 24; xii. 30; Job xxx. 8).

This, then, foretells the slaughter of seven thousand men of distinction. If now the celebrated men of the nations are slain in proportion to the unnoticed and unknown, and if the celebrated man be as one in a thousand, then *seven millions* are slain by the earthquake: and *ten times as many*, if the men of distinction be regarded as one in ten thousand.

For each of these reckonings we should have warrant of Scripture. Deut. i. 15; Num. i. 16; Exod. xviii. 21. Chiliarchs, or "captains of a thousand," are found to represent the military leaders inferior to kings, in the sixth seal. vi. 15; Job xxxiii. 23. "*One man among a thousand* have I found: but a woman among all those have I not found" (Eccles. vii. 28).

The higher calculation also is found. 2 Sam. xviii. 3; Cant. v. 10. At these respective rates of warlike prowess were Saul and David reckoned. "Saul hath slain his *thousands*, and David his *ten thousands*" (1 Sam. xviii. 7).

This is the firstfruit of God's just vengeance. For His two chiefs slain He cuts off seven thousand of the world's chieftains. They refuse to the dead " the house appointed for all living," and God casts down a tenth of the houses of the living. But Jerusalem is not destroyed, as Babylon is. That is swallowed up, houses and inhabitants both. Are these seven thousand slain at Jerusalem only ? or are they slain in other cities also to which the shock of the earthquake extends ? It is not said.

The consequence of their terror is, that they " give glory " to the God of heaven. "Does not this import that they were converted by these evident miracles, and gave up as unavailing and as wicked, all resistance to the Holy One ? " By no means. The expression means no more than that they did not ascribe these events to chance, but owned them as effects produced by the God of heaven. This is proved by the cases in which the same phrase is employed. 1 Sam. vi. 5. Josh. vii. 19, 20. The confession of the Egyptian magicians, " This is the finger of God," was giving glory to Jehovah. Exod. viii. 18, 19.

The glory given is only the effect of fright. It abides not. They perceive that an intelligent being of immense power is against them; and they tremble. But presently, their fright is exchanged for anger. xi. 18. And afterwards, they refuse to give glory, and blaspheme. xvi. 9. A similar slight and transitory effect was manifested by the multitudes who beheld the signs at Jesus' death. Matt. xxvii. 51–54; Luke xxiii. 47, 48.

This confession of men is not a saving one. It has less of the character of faith than the cry wrung from the terror-stricken multitude at the sixth seal. They own there the Father and Son. But here they confess the great Agent of these things as " the God of the heaven only." By this expression much light is thrown on the state of the question, and of their minds.

A new dispensation has opened since the prophetic portion of this book began. God is proclaiming Himself by His angel as the "Lord of heaven and of earth." But this full title, which would have expressed faith, men will not give. They have fallen back to polytheism together with idolatry; and deny the existence of One Supreme God. With them every region and nation has its own God. They have already one whom they worship as the God of *earth*. Therefore they dispute the full title of the Most High. Satan, as the next chapter shows us, has lost all power in heaven after being cast down to earth; and therefore man, when hardly pressed, owns a God on high. There is the refuge of the Witnesses, and of the Great Multitude. "But who," say they, "can resist the Mighty One *on earth*?" They overlook the Witnesses' power over both earth and heaven; and God's interfering to pluck His martyrs away from the very presence and hold of the Usurper of earth.

Is not this a mighty war? where the question lies concerning absolute Godhead, between Satan and his False Christ owned by men on the one hand, and the Father and the Son worshipped by the angels on the other?

Gnosticism has yet to appear in our day. In early Christian times, Gentile philosophers speculated about the place held by Jesus and His Father. They severed between the Creator, the God of the Jews, on the one hand, and the Father of Jesus on the other. Between the Creator and the creature man they interposed a variety of subordinate emanations or gods, whom they called Œons. This doctrine will invade the Christianity of later times and will pave the way with its "fables" and "endless genealogies," for the adoption of the old heathenism, which is here revived.

14. "The second woe is past : behold, the third woe cometh quickly."

But what is the third woe ? For we have no great calamity occurring at the sounding of the seventh trump. The seven bowls (vials) constitute, I doubt not, the third woe. Hence they are called rather the third " woe " than " the seventh trumpet."

The False Christ has now arisen ; and the bowls are God's scourge upon the Great Usurper and his worshippers. The place of the third woe is here left vacant. It is filled up in chapter xvi. In the account given us of the seventh trump, we have only the results *in heaven* stated. But the plagues fall *on earth*. There seems, however, a place left for them in the notice of the consequences of the seventh trumpet given by the elders. "The nations were angry, and *thy wrath came :* " and after that, the judgment of the *dead*.

But why are they not shown at once ? Why are chapters xii., xiii., xiv. interposed ? (1) In order to display man's wickedness at the full ; (2) to give comfort to both classes of God's saints named in the book ; and (3) to discover to us more fully the Usurper.

The iniquity of men against the Two Prophets draws down the final thunderbolt. They have got rid of these two warning voices by daring impiety. But the result resembles that when Hananiah broke the yoke from off Jeremiah's neck. "Go and tell Hananiah saying, thou hast broken the *yokes of wood ;* but thou shalt make for them *yokes of iron*" (Jer. xxviii. 13). No longer do *men* capable of death discharge the wrath of God upon earth ; but angels, whom they cannot touch, pour out from on high the bowls of wrath ! The power of the King of Heaven has not ceased with the destruction of His prophets. He is but stirred up to avenge them : He lets loose the fury of His indignation upon the rebels who refuse to return.

15. "And the seventh angel sounded; and great voices in heaven followed, saying, 'The kingdom of the world [1] is become (the kingdom) of our Lord and of His Christ ; and He shall reign for ever and ever.'"

At the opening of the last *seal* there followed a great silence : after this last *trump* come loud voices. Then there was suspense : now heaven knows and understands the issue. The voices are apparently those of angels and of the Great Multitude.

The fullness of the time, then, for proclaiming the kingdom of God is come. That kingdom comes from heaven, both in its proclamation and in its power. It is the kingdom of heaven set up over unwilling earth by celestial might. This Jesus foretold to Pilate. John xviii. 36.

At this period, as the angel had foretold, mystery passes away. And it passes away by God's taking the kingdom, and rendering, by means of His servant— the Messiah—to each according to his works. The specific results of the trumpet are more fully opened, in the words of the elders which follow.

The former trumpets detail the actions or plagues which ensue, as seen by an observer on the earth. But this trumpet is spoken of only as viewed by heaven. Its period is too long, and its results too many, to be briefly dismissed. Its consequences end not, till the millennial reign is over, and the earth burnt up ; all enemies being perfectly subjugated by the Son to the Father, " that God may be all in all."

It is " the kingdom of the world." In this place we observe a distinction in the use of the word from that

---

[1] So Tregelles.

which it obtains in the Gospel of John. There it means the world *morally* considered; the men who lie within the light and sound of the Gospel, but reject it. It is there the opposite of the elect or the disciples. But now, owing to the different dispensation which John has to announce, "the world" is taken *physically*.

The kingdom at present belongs openly to the Gentiles, and secretly to Satan. The Adversary exhibited them and their glory to Jesus on the mountain, and declared them to be his. Matt. iv. 8, 9. He is called by the Saviour, "the Prince of this world." If there be dissension in Satan's camp, "how then," says our Lord, "shall his kingdom stand?" (Matt. xii. 26). In this book the kingdom is shown to be Satan's, as the next chapter will manifest. The seven heads and ten horns belong to the Dragon. He gives the throne to his servant, the False Christ. Rev. xiii. 2.

In chapters v. and vii. the sentiment was—" Glory to the enthroned One, and to *the Lamb*." But now that the kingdom extends over the earth and heaven, Jesus takes as His title, " the Christ."

" And *He* shall reign for ever and ever." Why not " And *they* shall reign for ever and ever "? Probably to intimate to us that truth which John in his Gospel propounds in our Lord's words—" I and the Father [1] are *one* " (John x. 30). This same idea afterwards appears in a similar mode of expression at the conclusion of the book. xxii. 3, 4.

The millennial reign is not the conclusion of the reign of the Father and the Son: it extends to eternity.

16. "And the twenty-four elders, who sit before God on their thrones, fell upon their faces, and worshipped God. 17. Saying, 'We give thee thanks, O Lord God of hosts, who art and who wast; because thou tookest thy great power and reignedst.' 18. And the nations were wroth, and thy wrath came, and the season

[1] Ὁ Πάτηρ.

of the dead to be judged, and to give the reward to thy servants the prophets, and to the saints, and to them that fear thy name, the small and the great, and to destroy those who destroy (or ' corrupt ') the earth."

This is the epoch of God's *resuming* His power. He had entrusted it, on high, to angelic beings enthroned ; on earth, to Gentiles. This former constitution of things is now changed. The change takes effect both in heaven and in earth. The elders no longer are spoken of as seated on their thrones. *They are never beheld during the millennium, nor after it*. And the Most High now fulfils Mary's song of praise. Luke i. 51, 52. Christ is now the subordinate to the Lord of Hosts, and this change thrusts out the elders from their position. " For not to *angels* put he in subjection the future habitable earth, of which we are speaking ; but one in a certain place testified, saying, " What is *man*, that thou art mindful of him ? " (*Greek*) (Heb. ii. 5, 6). The crisis which the elders foresaw at chapter vi. 9, 10, has now taken effect. Power is transferred to Jesus the Christ, and to His chosen ones.

It is God's reign " *for ever* " which is named here. The millennial reign comes first : but the eternal one follows. There is no real break between the two. It is the reign of Jehovah and His Christ. The form of government somewhat alters in the eternal city : there is one throne, " the throne of God and the Lamb." Jesus is never there called " the Christ." Nor is the kingdom here described as " the reign of Christ and His saints," which would especially describe the millennial reign.

At the sixth seal the nations are affrighted : so are they, for a moment, at the earthquake ensuing on the Witnesses' resurrection. But at length they are angry. When they feared God, there was a pause in God's judgments. But now that they are angry, God's anger comes.

His wrath is more terrible, because of His long previous patience.

The nations in our day are in general quite indifferent about God, and His Gospel. But at the close, hatred to Him and His Christ will burst forth. In the new earth, the nations are all holy. It is because of the sin of the nations, that the opening of the kingdom, and the manifestation of the covenant, take place in wrath.

"And the season of the dead to be judged." This is put in close connection with the coming of God's wrath, and the time of His reign. It must include, then, the general judgment of the dead after the millennium.

By a "season" is meant a brief period which does not return again. The nations are never thus angry again; the reward of the saints is but once; after the judgment of the dead there is no more death; the eternal state of all is fixed. As the season of harvest occurs but once in the year, so this takes place only once in God's great year. There are those who are already risen from the dead and in heaven (chap. vii.). Those are already judged by Christ, and their places decided. They are not reckoned among the dead yet to be judged.

2. "And of giving the reward to thy servants the prophets." When Christ takes the kingdom, the saints are to take it too. John was waiting in patience for it; till then affliction was to be the lot of the Christian. i. 9. Many of his servants have risen ere the seventh trumpet sounds; but the kingdom is still to be waited for by them.

The words are very important. It is not merely the giving of "reward," but of "*the*" well-known and long-promised "reward." And what is this, but the kingdom? That is the subject of the heavenly voices, and of the elders' joy. The "reward" and the "kingdom" are nearly equivalent expressions. It is so seen in the

Sermon on the Mount. " Blessed are the poor in spirit and the persecuted; *for* theirs is the *kingdom* of heaven." " When men persecute you rejoice ; *for* great is your *reward* " (Matt. v. 3, 10–12). This is its positive aspect. It is so also in the negative. " Ye shall in *no* case enter the *kingdom* " (v. 20). " Ye have *no reward* of your Father in heaven " (vi. 1, 2, 5, 16). So Luke vi. 20, compared with 23, 35. So Matthew x. 7, compared with 41, 42. Thus also is it in the First Epistle to the Corinthians. " If any man's work abide, he shall receive *reward* " (iii. 14). " If I do this willingly, I have a *reward* " (ix. 17). Here is the positive side. Then for the negative we have, " Unrighteous ones shall *not* inherit the *kingdom of God* " (vi. 9).

ETERNAL LIFE *is the gift of God to each believer* (Rom. vi. 23); the KINGDOM is a *reward to those accounted worthy.* Luke xx. 35 ; 2 Thess. i. 5. Hence Paul's fear lest he should be rejected at last. 1 Cor. ix. 27.

The kingdom is to be enjoyed as the time of consolation for all the prophets. Luke xiii. 28. The season of reward, then, is the millennial day.

Three classes of the men of God are specified. " Thy servants the prophets." " Reward to thy servants— the prophets, and the saints." But the word " servants " is connected with " prophets " alone, both in this book and in the Old Testament. " The mystery of God should be finished, as He declared to *His servants the prophets* " (x. 7).

The prophets were especially servants of God : full of His Spirit and word, instructing the holy, and peculiarly hated by the ungodly. Thus they are noticed pre-eminently in the New Testament as destined to partake of the reward of the kingdom. " Ye shall see ALL THE PROPHETS IN THE KINGDOM OF GOD " (Luke xiii. 28).

After the prophets come "the saints." This is a general term, embracing God's servants of every dispensation,[1] and here, I suppose, denoting the risen from the dead. The millennial kingdom is thrown open to all: but there are different ranks in it. Matt. x. 41, 42.

Observe again, the elders do not say, "That thou shouldst give reward to *us*." Yet it would naturally be so, if they represented, as is supposed, the saints of the Old and New Testaments. On the contrary, they distinguish between themselves and those about to be rewarded.

But there is a third set of inheritors of the kingdom, "the fearers of God's name, both small and great." It was Israel's characteristic to fear the *Lord* his God. Josh. xxiv. 14; 1 Sam. xii. 24; Ps. xxxiv. 9. But there were Gentiles, who owned the true God amidst the heathen. These are called "the fearers of *God*." This is said of Job, and of the Egyptian midwives. Job i. 1, 8; Exod. i. 17, 21; Ps. lxi. 5; lxvi. 16.

These fearers of God appear to be, in part, those awakened by the angel's preaching; for his cry demands that fear of God which these Gentiles render. xiv. 6, 7.

If I mistake not, this class includes all who dwell on the earth in the flesh, whether Jew or Gentile. For the *fear* of God was the great lesson which the law designed to teach. Exod. xx. 20; Lev. xix. 14, 32; xxv. 17, etc. It is very remarkable, that *Israel* is not distinctly named on this occasion, though the ark of the covenant appears.

The last trumpet is also the season "for destroying the destroyers of the earth." *It is not the earth*

---

[1] The term is applied to men of the law in Ex. xxii. 31; Ps. cxvi. 16. To those of the gospel, Rom. i. 7, etc. In this book it embraces, I think, both, viii. 3, 4; xiii. 7, 10.

itself that is destroyed at the commencement of this trump, but only those who "corrupt," or "destroy" earth. The Greek word used has both meanings, and while it were the most satisfactory to take both words in the same sense, it is not easy to do so in this case, but both seem to be included. Why are they distinguished from the angry "nations"? I suppose it is because they are religious bodies, which may be composed of individuals of any nations whatsoever.

It would seem as if there were three great classes designed by this expression.

(1) First, it relates manifestly to the partisans of Great Babylon. For of her this expression is used. "He hath judged the Great Whore, which did *corrupt* (or destroy [1]) *the earth* with her fornication, and hath avenged the blood of His servants at her hand" (xix. 2). But Babylon, after her destruction in her first form, takes another, and in that second form is totally consumed of God.

(2) It would seem, too, to embrace those who destroy the earth under Antichrist, as being the second great company of rebels.

Their leader is Apollyon or Abaddon, the Great *Destroyer.* Babylon and the False Christ are closely conjoined in action and destiny in the closing days of this dispensation. Reference is here made, as Hengstenberg has observed, to the times of the Flood. "*The earth* also *was corrupt*[2] before God, and the earth was filled with violence. And God looked upon *the earth, and behold, it was corrupt,*[2] for all flesh had *corrupted*[2] *its way upon the earth.* And God said into Noah, The end of all flesh is come before me; for the earth is filled with violence through them; and behold I will *destroy* (*corrupt*[2]) *them with the earth*" (Gen. vi. 11–13).

[1] Φθείρω. In Rev. xi. the word διαφθείρω is used.
[2] In Hebrew שחת, in the Greek φθείρω or καταφθείρω.

(3) And lastly, it would include, apparently, the armies of earth, which go up at the end of the millennium under the leadership of Satan. These are in the strongest sense "the destroyers of the earth." It is for their heinous sin that the earth itself is at last burnt up.

When these three purposes of God are accomplished, mystery and sin will be for ever past, and the new heavens and earth will be come. This war of God's justice, unlike the wars of men, will destroy only the guilty, and cut off the incurable from the earth. The previous judgments aimed at the reformation of the living; but this speaks of the utter destruction of those who refuse to repent. The whole race of men, then, both the living and the dead, are judged under this trumpet; unless we except the saints whose place has been adjudged before.

The destruction of the godless living is here foretold in words; at the end of the fourteenth chapter it is presented in emblem, as the treading of the vintage; at the end of the nineteenth chapter it is described literally as it will appear to a spectator.

19. "And the temple of God in the heaven was opened, and the ark of His covenant was seen in His temple; and lightnings, and voices, and thunders, and earthquake, and great hail followed."

The manifestation of God goes on. The Temple is opened now: by and by heaven itself is opened. xix. 11. It would seem that this opening of heaven is with reference to those on earth. The results of the opened temple and ark displayed, as seen in the hail, thunder, and lightnings, are certainly directed towards those on the earth. If so, this is the time of the fulfilment of our Lord's words to the Sanhedrim. Matt. xxvi. 64. This opening of heaven appears to be the same with that mentioned in chapter xv. 5, as the prelude to the vials (bowls). If so, this would be another argument that the vials constitute the third woe.

The Jews imagine that when Jerusalem was taken by the Chaldeans, Jeremiah concealed the ark from them, and that it is to be brought forth again in the day of Israel's blessing. It is certainly remarkable, that amidst the account given of the Chaldeans' taking the vessels of the temple, the ark is not named. 2 Kings xxv. 13–17. But God has a better ark and a better covenant in store for His people Israel.

After the burning of the temple, the ark was seen no more. Thus, too, after the burning of the old earth, neither the temple nor the ark appear.

As soon as it is seen, " there followed lightnings, and voices, and thunders, and earthquake, and great hail." The consequences of the new covenant are here displayed. God by covenant is to cut off the foes of Israel.

Hence a burst of judgment follows in order to clear the land and earth of the foes of God ; and then comes the day of promised blessing to all nations (Acts iii. 25), when Israel's sins are all forgiven. Rom. xi. 27. The appearing of the ark then, and the outbreak of judgment, are connected as cause and effect. The elders speak of wrath twice in their address. Justice on the foes of God is the paving of the way for mercy to the friends of God. The scattering of the foes by wrath is in order to the gathering of Israel and the remnant of the Gentiles.

CHAPTER XII

THE DRAGON AND THE WOMAN

1. "And a great sign was seen in the heaven, a woman clothed with the sun, and the moon underneath her feet, and on her head a crown of twelve stars : 2. and she being with child is crying out, travailing, and agonizing herself (with a view) to bring forth."

THIS is not properly a " wonder," but a " sign." It is a sign of future events; as the cloud out of the west is a sign of rain at hand. Matt. xvi. 3. It is the sign of Satan's head about to be bruised, of Israel's deliverance, and of the kingdom at hand. It is a " sign," as offering truth symbolically. As the parable of the fig tree, in the xxivth of Matthew, shows Israel in a figurative point of view, nigh to the " summer " of the kingdom, so does it answer to the woman's pregnancy here. Symbol runs through this series of related chapters (xii.–xiv.).

" Why are we to take this woman as symbolic, and not literal ? " Because of her place in heaven, her clothing, and Child. None of these can be literal. She is presented symbolically, because she has two places ; a literal one on earth, and another on high. Since she is now away from her place, she, that is a city literally, appears as a woman.

Who is this Woman ?

1. Some say, It is THE CHURCH. But no : this cannot be. The Church is a " chaste virgin " (2 Cor. xi. 2).

This is a mother, possessed of other sons, besides the one whose birth is here celebrated. The Church ended ere the prophecy began.

2. Nor is it MARY the mother of our Lord. Jesus was the first-born of Mary. This woman has other sons ; she is a symbolic woman, arrayed in clothing never used on earth.

3. It is JERUSALEM. The *harlot* is a city. Rev. xvii. 18. The *Bride* is a city. xxi. 9. So, then, is the *wife*. This vision is a repetition, under another aspect, of things which have preceded. "Thou must prophesy *again*." It was before the "holy city," the place of the temple ; and "the *great* city," place of the gathering of the nations, and of the earthquake. Isa. xxix. 1-9.

Michael stands up on her behalf, and fights for her and for her son. What, then, can the woman be but Jerusalem ? Dan. xii. 1.

This woman possesses all three classes of heavenly glory.

The glories of the sun, moon, and stars are the three heavenly glories. 1 Cor. xv. 41. But these are all connected with the posterity of Abraham, as the persons, and with Jerusalem, as the place, of manifestation.

Jerusalem is the city that is to be in travail in the great day of the Lord. Isa. xxvi. 17, 18 ; Mic. iv. 8-10 ; v. 1-3 ; Jer. vi. 22-25 ; xiii. 19-21 ; Jer. xxx. 6, 7.

But an objection may occur to some. "How can Jerusalem be represented as the mother of the Gospel-seed, when Paul describes her as 'in bondage with her children ? ' " (Gal. iv. 25).

The apostle says that of the Jerusalem of his day, the "Jerusalem that *now is :* " such as she is represented in ch. xi. But she "abides not in unbelief ; " and is graffed in again. Paul regarded the Jew in an unbelief, which lasts through this dispensation ; but when the

Gentile branches are broken off for want of faith, the natural branches are restored.

This is more fully set forth in the words that follow. "A woman *clothed with the sun*." The three celestial glories of the Woman answer to three covenants, which form three dispensations.

By "the sun" is meant the Lord Jesus. He is "the Sun of Righteousness" (Mal. iv. 2). He is represented in this book as having His face like the sun; both in the opening vision, and when appearing as the angel of chap. x.

The woman's being *clothed* with the sun, then, represents her being *justified* by the Lord, her righteousness. Isa. lxi. 10. She is clothed upon with Christ. She is a transgressor, as Eve was: but is now justified by faith. As a transgressor, she is in trouble: but as justified, she is delivered. As she is clothed of God, so her children of faith are sealed of God. Chap. vii.

The evil side of Jerusalem had been displayed from three points of view. It was (1) "Sodom," and (2) "Egypt" spiritually; and the (3) city that crucified the Lord. Here she has three answering aspects of glory, one under each of the dispensations implied in the word just cited. (1) In the dispensations of Sodom or that of Abraham—father of the twelve patriarchs—she has the glory of the twelve stars. (2) In the dispensation of "*Egypt*," or that of the law, she has the moon. (3) In the dispensation of the Gospel, under which she "crucified the Lord," she has the glory of the sun. So the three witnesses of chapters x. and xi. belong in turn to one of these three dispensations. Enoch, to the patriarchal; Elijah, to that of the law; Jesus—the angel—to that of the Gospel. The celebrated prophecy attributed to Elijah—"Two thousand years, a void; two thousand, the law; two thousand, the Messiah; and the seventh thousand, rest"—lends aid to this view.

The *stars* belong to the evening of the void; the *moon* rules the night; the *sun*, the day.

2. The Woman in heaven has " the moon underneath her feet."

This her position is the consequence of her being clothed with the sun. The moon is the Law. It has no glory, by reason of the excelling glory of the Gospel. The moon shines with light borrowed from the sun. The law carried the representations of Messiah and his grace. It had the shadows of " the good things to come." As far, then, as the light was of God, it is owned still. But it is no longer trusted in, as the ground of justification. The woman of faith will not attempt to clothe herself with it: it is under her feet. The moon occupies the lowest point of all. She is not said to stand on it. It is " under her feet."

3. " And on her head a crown of twelve stars." The twelve stars are the twelve patriarchs, the glory of the twelve tribes. Gen. xxxvii. 9, 10. Joseph makes the twelfth star.

Jerusalem wears them all around her head: for she was the appointed centre to which the tribes were to gather, when they presented themselves before the Lord. 1 Kings xviii. 31.

The new Jerusalem also has these twelve stars around her head. Only, as the new Jerusalem is a literal city (chap. xxi.), the " stars " become twelve " gates," and on the gates are the names of the twelve tribes of Israel.

Jerusalem, then, in the above symbolic representation is discovered as the great centre of the dispensations which have come from God. (1) In the patriarchal dispensation, Melchizedec appeared as the king of *Salem*, and priest of the Most High God (Gen. xiv. 18), typing Jesus' day of the kingdom: as Paul notices. Heb. vii. (2) Under the Law, Jerusalem was the place of the temple, and of the glory of Solomon's reign. 1 Kings

viii. (3) Under the Gospel, it was the place where the Holy Spirit descended at Pentecost (Acts ii.), and from which the good news went forth to Jew and Gentile. Thus around Jerusalem cluster the glories of all God's dispensations.

The woman is with child : she is the one, then, that "has an husband." She therefore is the earthly and lower Jerusalem. Gal.iv. The barren woman, who is to rejoice in the far greater multitude of her children, is the "Jerusalem which is above." Her being with child signifies the hope of the Jewish remnant arising from the many promises made to Jerusalem. But before those promises are fulfilled, the threatenings must first take effect. She must receive of the Lord's hand recompense for her previous sins. She must be humbled and purged, by the cutting off of her own perverse sons. There is intestine strife in Israel then. Some are mockers, some the faithful. And without, the enemy assaults.

Hence she "cries." Her loud prayers are prompted both by fear and by faith. Fear urges her ; for the enemies are mighty : faith, because God has given His word for her ultimate deliverance.

Of this period our Lord speaks in His prophecy on the Mount of Olives. "All these things are the beginning of *birth-pangs.*" But after those fainter woes comes the time of Great Tribulation. And in that Jesus bids His Jewish disciples especially to cry to God. "*Pray ye* that your flight be not in the winter, nor on the sabbath day" (Matt. xxiv. 8, 20).

3. "And another sign was seen in the heaven ; and behold a great red dragon, having seven heads and ten horns, and on his heads seven diadems. 4. And his tail draweth the third of the stars of the heaven, and cast them to the earth."

The object beheld is a "great red Dragon." That is,

beyond all doubt, Satan. He is so called afterwards, in the ninth verse. He is described as "great." That is, he is possessed of immense power: the vastness of his body seen was the indication of the extent of his dominion.

Such is his greatness, that he has willing agents and subjects both in heaven and earth. His heads and horns are of earth; his tail is in the heaven. The Woman appears in heaven and in earth: so, too, does the Dragon, her enemy. The temple of God, too, is partly in heaven, partly on earth. And of a like character is the kingdom itself, when fully come. God is to be manifestly "the Most High God, *possessor of heaven and earth*," according to the title given Him by Melchizedec. The intent of these two signs, then, is to enable us to see the extent of the struggle between Satan and the Son of God. The Dragon's effort against the Woman's son takes place in heaven: His effort against the Woman herself and her seed lies in the earth.

His colour is "red." That is the colour of blood, as we have seen before. vi. 4; Kings iii. 22. As applied to an intelligent being, it denotes him cruel, bloodthirsty. Rev. xvii. 3. Thus Satan is discovered to us as "the *murderer* from the beginning," in which character he is noticed by the Gospel and Epistle of *John* only. John viii. 44; 1 John iii. 12. He is manifested by his succeeding actions to be of this disposition. The conquerors who ascend the sky were put to death by his wiles and influence over men. He is the instigator of the slaughter of the saints which ensues on the raising his king to the throne. He pursues the Woman in her flight, with design to destroy her. But for supernatural interference, he would succeed in his murderous project.

Hence this book shows the fulfilment of God's covenant made with Noah. God would take vengeance on human blood shed, both at the hand of man, and " at the hand of every *wild beast* " (Gen. ix. 5). Hence the throne is set to judge this murderous wild beast.

He is described as " the Dragon." By this title we are to think of him as the Old Enemy in possession of power. In the Garden he was the *serpent,* using deceit alone. But now he uses force. Under the present name he seems to be hinted at in the Old Testament. " The young lion and *the dragon* shalt thou trample under feet " (Ps. xci. 13). In the day of His power Christ shall slay the dragon in the sea. Isa. xxvii. 1 ; li. 9.

The Great Agent of Evil, who gives it unity both in heaven and in earth, is now upon the scene. He had appeared before for a moment as the star that had fallen from heaven. But then he was manifested only as the subordinate of God, fulfilling his purposes in the plagues sent on man. In chapter xi. his coadjutor, the Wild Beast, was for a moment exhibited as the destroyer of the Witnesses. But now the union of these two monsters of evil is to be shown ; and the superiority of Satan, from whom the power flows, by which the Wild Beast is elevated to the throne, is discovered. Thus Satan is found in this vision imitating, as best he may, the scene of the first *prophetic* vision of the book. He gives power to his king above all others : only his throne is not, as in God's case, in heaven : it is on earth. But Satan acts for the False Christ, and prepares the way for his sovereignty, as the Father does for the Son. The Devil does not appear as the serpent, till the Woman is beheld. Thus we are designedly led back to the history of Eden. But there he tempted, and gained over the woman to his side. Now he persecutes the Woman, as one who is on the side of the Most High.

This Dragon had " seven heads and ten horns." The seven heads are doubtless the same that we meet with afterwards in the thirteenth and seventeenth chapters.

In the latter place, we are told that they are "seven kings," who precede the final appearance of the Great False Christ.

He has also "ten horns." The horns are also defined by the interpreting angel to be ten kings. xvii. 12. But wherein do they differ, then, from the heads ? The heads are superior and successive : the horns are cotemporaneous and subordinate kings, who give all their power to the last head or emperor, while they receive it for the first time in his day. As the head in cattle and among wild beasts uses the horn, so does the emperor use these his subject kings.

This emblematic representation is designed to exhibit to us the truth that Satan at the close will wield the fullness of Gentile dominion. He will so animate its rulers with his spirit, that all Gentile power is regarded on high as consolidated with Satan's own body. It is afterwards expressed by the sacred writer's saying, that "Satan *deceiveth the whole habitable earth*" (ver. 9). The kings of the earth universally take Satan's side against the Lord Jesus : and that posture the Enemy holds, till the power of the new dispensation overwhelms him and them.

"And his tail draweth the third of the stars of the heaven." A serpent's power lies greatly in his tail. Thus it is here also. Emblematically Satan's power among the angels is described. The extent of his influence as to numbers is also given. The *third* of the angels has followed his rebel standard. They are "the stars of the heaven." While, then, it is said here that " he *cast* (the stars) to the earth : " in the seventh and following verses we read, that " Michael and his angels fought, and *the devil fought, and his angels*, and prevailed not, *neither was their place found any more in the heaven. And the Great Dragon was cast out, that Old Serpent, called the Devil and Satan, which deceiveth* the whole habitable earth : he was cast out into the earth, and *his angels were cast out with him*."

" But is there not a flaw here ? The twelve patriarchs are supposed to be signified by the ' twelve stars ' around the woman's head. *Now*, angels are supposed to be symbolized by stars." But observe, the evangelist interposes a note of difference, which adds confirmation to the preceding view. The stars around the woman's head are called " stars " absolutely. These stars of the dragon's tail are named " stars *of the heaven*." The patriarchs are stars of earth about to be promoted to the heaven : these rebel-angels are stars of the heaven, about to be cast into earth.

In the first chapter Jesus holds in His hand " seven stars," which are the " seven *angels* " of the churches. Jesus raises His stars from earth to heaven : Satan casts down his stars from heaven to earth. The stars of Christ are designed to supply the places of those lost by the rebellion and ejection of Satan and his angels.

Satan's power on earth is universal and unbroken ; in heaven it is only partial, and of that he is speedily dispossessed.

" He draw*eth* the third of the stars." This denotes his habitual control of them. " He *cast* them to earth." Here the Aorist denotes that that was an act which he accomplished once for all. It is the result of his leading them to battle, and their being worsted in fight.

The Dragon resembles the Wild Beast of the next chapter, save that that has not Satan's tail. The False Christ has not, like Satan, power over the angels of the heaven. Heaven is then closed against the power of evil for ever.

" And the dragon stood before the Woman that was about to bring forth, that when she should have brought forth, he might devour her child."

This attitude of Satan discovers his knowledge, and his expectation of the fulfilment of the purposes of God. He is aware of the destiny of both the Mother and the Child. His horned heads are on the watch against the Mother below: and his tail above resists the Child's entrance to heaven.

Satan's wisdom is seen. He is at the post where most danger threatens his realm; to oppose and avert it, if possible.

His *design* in taking this attitude is evident. He vainly hopes to overcome the risen from the dead. He hates alike the Mother and the Child. The Child is the object of his first enmity, because it has already conquered him; and is ready to ascend to heaven, to thrust him out from his forfeited possession there. The Child is also to rule over the nations below: and thus also to eject him from his kingdom of earth, in which he deceives the nations. He has especially bruised the heel of this Child: and this Child in return is especially to bruise his head. v. 5. Indeed this seems to be the bond which unites the many persons into one mystic Child, that they have obtained *victory unto death over Satan on high*. There is another struggle presently after against *Satan on earth, and victory unto death* in that conflict. But that is another dispensation.

Satan's *enmity* and daring are at their height: as those passions are in his seed also. Chap. xi. In the day of the churches he sought to overcome by subtlety, and attempted to deceive by his power from on high, influencing in secret false apostles. (Ep. to Ephesus.) But now he uses, not craft, but power against these conquerors.

Thus the same body of conquerors destined to reign with Christ is the test alike of the holy angels and of the fallen ones. The holy angels and their twenty-four princes welcome Jesus and His ransomed brethren to their places in the temple, and to their thrones of dominion. But the evil angels, and Satan at their head, resist alike Jesus and His subject-kings, and set up another High Priest and another King.

This throws a full light upon the subject of Satan's fall. Let it only be supposed that, when God made man, He informed the angels who rejoiced over the new creation that that being, made lower than themselves, would one day rule them and all things ; and the matter is explained. That would provoke Satan's pride, by which we know that he fell. 1 Tim. iii. 6. "Shall an inferior rule us ? Shall a junior be put over our heads ?" He whispers his dislike, and others assent. He will go then, and secretly derange the purpose of God, by setting the newly-formed creature against its Creator, and laying him under the penalty of God's wrath. He masks himself under the form of one of the animals of earth, as though he could thereby escape God's eye. God seemingly takes no notice of the fallen angel within, who had become thus the liar and murderer : but He sentences the serpent, and that sentence on the serpent clings with links of adamant to the deceiving angel.

But the purpose of God, far from being disconcerted by this division introduced between His creature and Himself, then begins to unfold ; and Satan hears that the exaltation of man shall be the day of his terrible and eternal downfall. Henceforth he and his party stand committed against God, and against the Christ of God, into whose hand the empire of all things is to be given. His enmity at length produces the matured plan of the next chapter.

5. "And she brought forth a male son who is about to rule all the nations with rod of iron."

Of what kind is this birth ?

(1) It is *not literal* birth. For the woman is not a literal woman, but a city. (2) It is *not spiritual* birth, or regeneration; for the persons constituting the child are already born of the Spirit. (3) It is *symbolic* birth, or *resurrection*. "They loved not their lives unto *death*." Hence this is a birth *out of* death; that is, it is resurrection. Christ, the possessor of the key of Hades, opens for them the door, and none can shut it. In this manner Paul expounds the second psalm. "God fulfilled the same (promise) .... in that he *raised up Jesus again*, as it is also written in the second psalm, Thou art my son; this day have I *begotten thee*" (Acts xiii. 33). With resurrection ascension also is connected, as in Jesus' case. And of both regeneration and of resurrection, baptism is the type. It discovers to us death and burial in the *im*mersion, and both spiritual and bodily resurrection, in the *e*mersion of the believer.

"A male son." Who is it?

1. It is *not* ISRAEL; though in the expression "man-child" there is a reference to Israel's history in Egypt; since it was against the male children especially that Pharaoh's persecution raged, and in that point Israel's trouble was especially felt. 'Tis not Israel, for though they overcome the nations of Canaan, they overcame not Satan; nor could it be said of them, that "they loved not their lives unto death."

2. Nor is it CHRIST. The child is a unit composed of many. Christ was His mother's *first-born*. The mother here has other sons. Satan goes forth against "the remnant of her seed." As the mother is symbolic, so must the child be. The mother is Jerusalem, and Jesus was not born there.

3. Nor is it THE CHURCH, simply and singly considered.

(1) For this child is caught up, not into *air* (1 Thess. iv. 16), but to God's *throne*, ere Christ has descended

from heaven. (2) Nor is the Church to rise and ascend at a time so clearly specified as is here foretold. For if so, we can name a period before which the rapture of the Church cannot take place. The rapture of the Child and the flight of the Mother are simultaneous. Then, till the flight of the Jewish disciples, the rapture of the Church is not to take place. Nor is it to take effect till the dragon has seven heads, and the diadems are set upon the heads. But the Church is not to know the day of resurrection.

4. Nor is it the company of those prefigured by the Harvest. xiv. 14–16. For (1) the Harvest occurs after Satan's ejection from heaven. This, before it.

(2) The Harvest is reaped by Christ descended from the throne to the cloud of the air. The Child is caught up to Him, ere He has left heaven.

5. The Child is the same body as the GREAT MULTITUDE of chapter vii. And this new view of them is given to discover to us how they reached heaven. It is not the ascent of holy spirits at death, but of men risen from the dead.

The following points will, I think, satisfy the reader as to the identity of the two bodies.

(1) At the sixth seal the kings of earth are exhibited to us. Here we have Satan as lord of earth's empires, possessor of heads and horns. We have next 144,000 out of all the tribes of Israel. This answers to the Woman here. Her twelve stars answer to the twelve tribes there. Then comes the Great Multitude on high, gathered out of all lands, just as the Man-child follows on the Woman here. After the Great Multitude come the prayers of the remnant. viii. After the Child is caught up, Satan persecutes the remnant of the Woman's seed. The fallen star (ix. 1) answers to Satan's casting out from heaven here.

(2) The Great Multitude stand "before *the throne*." These are caught up to it.

(3) There is joy in heaven over each. vii. 11, 12; xii. 10–12.

(4) The Great Multitude worship in the temple, and God "tabernacles" over them. When the Man-child has ascended, the "tabernaclers" in the heaven are bid to rejoice.

(5) Both parties are conquerors. The Great Multitude are "in white," carry palms, and are led by Christ. These "overcame by the blood of the Lamb," and are victors through death.

(6) In the joyous state of the Great Multitude, as never more to hunger, thirst, or suffer heat, there is perhaps an implied reference to the Woman here. For she in her flight through the wilderness will have to endure hunger, thirst, and heat. So differently situated are the mother and her son. The Mother signifies saints in the flesh, kept during the great day of wrath on the earth. But these are fed and led by Christ above. The Mother is fed by angels below. Both parties are on their way to their promised land and city. But the land and city of the one party are earthly; those of the other, heavenly. Probably also the references to their joys in chapter vii. are taken up here in their "not loving their lives (souls) unto death." Ere they surrendered life they had to endure the lighter trials of hunger and thirst. They had the bruised heel, ere they bruised the serpent's head.

(7) The Man-child is the same party as the worshippers in the temple, who are measured off for preservation. xi. 1. Thus also they are identified with the Great Multitude, who serve God day and night in His tabernacle. That is their priestly aspect. But now their relation to the *kingdom*, or their kingly

standing, is shown to us. Rule over the nations, supplanting Satan's, is theirs.

(8) Lastly, as that Great Multitude was exhibited in close juxtaposition with *Israel* (chapter vii.), so is the Child now represented as being born of *Jerusalem*.

The company consists of :—

1. Martyrs. That many, if not most of them, were slain, seems evident, from their "not loving their soul unto *death*." These reappear, I suppose, as the first of the two martyr companies, in Rev. xx. 4 ; " the souls of the beheaded for the witness of Jesus, and for the word of God."

2. Victors. They belong to the Woman only when she is pregnant, they are no more mentioned when she is on earth. That some of the Church are here, is provable from the rapture promised to the faithful watchers of Philadelphia. As they testify their faith in Christ's coming and reign, they are to escape the hour of great tribulation and temptation coming on earth. Thus are they connected with Jerusalem. For all prophecy is closely connected with Jerusalem and the Jew. There was in Smyrna faithfulness unto death, as here. To the conquerors of Thyatira dominion over the nations is promised : that is the portion also of the Man-child. This body consists strictly of *conquerors :* it is a rapture of especial privilege. May it embrace some of other dispensations ? It is not of the dead alone, but of living victors as well. Since the ascent just precedes Jerusalem's flight, it is closely connected with the taking and leaving of Matt. xxiv. 40, 41. The taking there is that of Enoch ; the leaving, like that of Elisha when Elijah went up.

"Who is about to rule all the nations with iron rod." The Child's reign does not begin at the moment of his rapture. There is a period on earth, during which the plot of Satan prospers, and the saints are given into his hand.

It is this foreknown destiny of the Child which brings on the crisis in heaven. Satan perceives that this is the body who will wrest from him his usurped power over the nations; and accordingly he resists their entrance into heaven. Against them individually he raged while they were on earth; but, now that their time of power is close at hand, his envy and jealousy are fully roused.

The principle of the Child's rule is a stern one. "With iron rod." From which it appears that it will be one of strict justice: offences will be visited with righteous destruction, crushing all resistance. It proves, too, that the spirit of the nations in general is not that of universal love to Christ. Israel, by promise, shall be a nation wholly righteous. But of the Gentiles this is not said. The millennial reign is that of Christ as son of *David*. To David the nations rendered not obedience, till after being overcome in war.

"And her child was caught up to God, and to His throne."

They are taken thither as victors. "They *overcame*." They are brought " to the *throne*." " Even as I also *overcame*, and am set down with my Father on His *throne*."

6. "And the Woman fled into the wilderness, where she hath a place prepared[1] of God, that they should feed her there a thousand two hundred and sixty days."

There are two refuges prepared of God during Satan's time of power: one in heaven, one in earth. The heavenly one is safe for ever. The earthly is provided only for a time; it is not in the *habitable earth;* but

---

[1] Ἐτοιμάζω occurs *seven* times in the Apocalypse.

in the desert, in which any can dwell only by miraculous supply.

The Woman's is the lower *active* escape; the rapture to heaven is the superior escape, whither the saint is *passively* conveyed by others. Her flight must be exceedingly rapid, without once looking back, lest she become as Lot's wife. Luke xvii.

Her spirit is that of faith. She flees because commanded, both by the Old Testament and the New. Jesus bids her to flee, for Jerusalem is compassed with armies, and the idol of the False Christ is lifted up. Matt. xxiv.; Luke xxi. Not till the 1,260 days are over is she delivered from the power of her foes.

It is beautiful to observe, in connection with the three heavenly symbols which encircle the Woman, that there have been *three* RAPTURES, and *three* FLIGHTS INTO THE WILDERNESS : one in each of the three dispensations signified by the heavenly bodies.

1. In the *patriarchal dispensation*, there was a rapture. "And Enoch walked with ('pleased') God; and he *was not; for God took him*" (Gen. v. 24).

2. Under *the Law* there was a rapture. "Elijah went up by a whirlwind into heaven" (2 Kings ii. 11).

3. Under *the Gospel* there has been one. "While they beheld he (Jesus) was taken up: and a cloud received him out of their sight" (Acts i. 9).

There have been also three flights into the desert.

1. That of Hagar, in the days of Abraham. Gen. xvi. 7, 8.

2. The well-known one of Elijah under the Law. 1 Kings xix.

3. That of our Lord, when His forerunner had been slain. Matt. xiv. 13.

She flees into "*the* wilderness," the well-known one, described by that title in the books of Moses. Herein she is distinguished from the Harlot. The Great

Harlot of xvii. is seen by John in "*a* wilderness," or "a wilderness *in spirit*," as we should most probably connect the words.

This woman has a "place prepared her of God." If it be hard that she has to fly, it is mercy that she has an asylum. Her sins drive her out: the promise supports her.

The place is doubtless Mount Sinai. Thither it was that God brought her of old. Exod. iii. 12; Gal. iv. 24, 25.

"That they should feed her there a thousand and two hundred and sixty days." Moses and Jesus were supernaturally sustained in the wilderness for forty days. Elijah was twice fed, and in the strength of that food he went forty days to the Mount of God, where he pleaded against Israel, as violator of the covenant made at Horeb. Jesus, after His forty days' fast and victory over the Wicked One, was ministered to by angels. They are probably the agents understood here. It would seem as if Jesus' conquest of Satan in the wilderness had redeemed that spot from his dominion, to be an asylum for Israel.

The expression, "that they should feed her," denotes her passiveness.

The feeding is not said of her son: food is not *necessary* for him, for he is risen from the dead.

"Twelve hundred and sixty days." For so long a time her enemies prevail, and the full tide of vengeance lords it over the earth. For 1,290 days sacrifice is removed from the temple, and the image of the Wild Beast set up. Dan. xii. 11.

The number 1,260 is compounded of three-and-a-half multiplied by 12, and the product further multiplied by 30. Now these three numbers are all intimated in the three heavenly glories of sun, moon, and stars, which encircle the Woman. *Twelve* are the *stars* around her head: *thirty* indicates the *moon*, or month of thirty days beneath her feet: *three-and-a-half* the years measured by the *sun*, with which she is clothed.

The observance of "days, months, and years," is characteristic of Judaism (Gal. iv. 10), and is another proof that the woman is Jerusalem.

For the same *length* of time, probably also for the same time, the Gentiles tread down the city. But that is reckoned in chapter xi. by forty-two *months*, for it is there represented as the time of oppression and evil. Here it is reckoned by *days*; for her benefit is spoken of.

7. "And there followed war in the heaven; Michael and his angels warred[1] with the Dragon; and the dragon warred and his angels."

Desiring to bar the Child's entrance on his heritage, Satan rushes on his angelic defenders. Previously to this, he plied *accusations* only against the ascending *prayers* of the saints. But when they ascend in person, after his accusations have been proved false, he uses force.

Who is Michael?

It is Jesus' title as the Lord of angels in the battle of angels. Jesus is "the Lamb," as He stands opposed to "the Wild Beast." He is Michael ["He who is as God"] as opposed to the Dragon. Jesus is the stronger than the strong man armed, who is to spoil his goods. Luke xi. 22. Angels Jesus meets as "the angel of the Lord." Men He meets as a man.

1. Jesus is the archangel, or lord of the angels: for the angels are His. Matt. xvi. 27.[2] He is the High Priest of the temple above, till His kingdom; and, apparently in virtue of this, He cleanses the heavenly courts

---

[1] Literally, "to war with," a Hebraism.

[2] Though we often hear of "angels and archangels," yet there is but *one* archangel spoken of in Scripture.

from the presence of Satan and his host. The cleansed sanctuary prepares for the kingdom. Thus our Lord is represented in Dan. viii. 11 as "Prince of the Host."

2. The angels belong to *Michael*. "Michael and *His* angels." The angels belong to *Christ*, as just shown. Matt. xxiv. 31. Therefore Michael is Christ.

3. The seed of the woman is to bruise the serpent's head. This is the first stunning blow. He who delivers it, then, is the Christ.

4. Jesus appears as the angel-helper of Israel, as Daniel foretells. Dan. xii. 1. Angels stand in especial connection with Israel. The very first mention of one occurs in the history of Hagar, who represents Jerusalem. Gen. xvi.

5. Angelic voices celebrate the victory resulting from this war as "the authority of God's *Christ*" (ver. 10). But no power has as yet been put forth against Satan, save by Michael. Therefore again Michael is Christ.

6. To Jesus, by the decree of God, and the joyous assent of the angels, all glory has been decreed. But He would lose much of glory, if this defeat of His Great Antagonist were not due to Him.

Again, therefore, I draw the same conclusion.

7. In Jude 9, *Michael the archangel* says to Satan, "The Lord rebuke thee!" when the subject is Moses' body. In Zech. iii. 2, "*The Lord* said unto Satan, 'The Lord rebuke thee, O Satan!'" where the subject is the High Priest of Israel resisted by the devil. The inference, therefore, is natural, that the archangel Michael is also the Lord, who concerns himself in Israel's welfare. But none can be Jehovah as well as archangel, save Jesus.

The Child's presentation at the throne, then, is entrusted to Michael. He is interrupted on His way, and hence the battle arises. The chief object of Satan's enmity is the Child. But as the Child cannot defend itself, its heavenly patrons step forward, and the war of Satan bursts out against the *angels*. There was always secret enmity of the evil angels against the holy angels : now it bursts forth into the open employment of force on each side. War is the end of Satan's career in heaven. War is also his last game on earth, twice attempted.

The devil wars as the Great Dragon. He delivers battle, as his last desperate resource, now that his accusations are proved untrue, and the time of his deceit on high is over. The serpent of Genesis who deceived Eve is seen to be a heavenly being, lord of hosts of angels, and drawing together the stars of heaven to combat against God's throne.

8. " And he prevailed not, nor was their place found any more in heaven."

It is evident from the statement of the text that the war is yet future. It occurs when there are only 1,260 days to the coming of Jesus visibly to earth : and after the time of patience commanded to the Church, and testified by it, is over.

The result of the victory of the angels is not Satan's casting into *hell*, but his ejection from heaven into earth, as is presently afterwards mentioned. It is the confounding what is spoken of the imprisonment of angels who fell in Noah's day from the *love* of *women*, with the host of Satan who fell from *envy* and *hatred of man*, that Milton has erred, and led so many others astray. Gen. vi, 1–4 ; 2 Pet. ii. 4 ; 1 Cor. xi. 10.

Many are surprised to hear that Satan is on high, because Milton has described him as cast into the bottomless pit. But Scripture never so speaks of him. It always supposes him to be either in heaven or in earth ; as we see by the histories of Job, of Saul, of

David, of Michaiah. Job i., ii.; 1 Chron. xxi.; 1 Kings xxii.

There are two places of security, and two of insecurity. The temple and altar court, which are in heaven, are safe. The outer court and holy city are insecure. The Child taken to the throne is but another view of the worshippers in the inner court. Satan tries to force this stronghold, and hence his defeat.

Is not a dragon a *winged* serpent? If so, he is able to use his wings no more. He is confined to earth thenceforth, unable to mount to his former abode in heaven. On his belly he shall creep.

9. "And the great dragon was cast (down), the Old Serpent, who is called the Devil, and Satan, who deceiveth the whole world: he was cast into the earth, and his angels were cast with him."

"He was cast into the earth." The issue of this war is not slaughter, as in the battles of mortals, and as we find it in chapter xix. 21; it is ejection by force from a certain territory. This casting down was foretold by our Lord. "I beheld Satan as lightning fall from heaven" (Luke x. 18).

10. "And I heard a great voice in the heaven, saying, Now has come the salvation, and the strength, and the kingdom of our God, and the authority of His Christ; for the accuser of our brethren is cast (down), who used to accuse them before our God day and night."

This is the *first* act of power exerted to put down evil. Jesus by His death has purchased the *right* to put down wickedness, whether in heaven or in earth. That right and power slumber during the time of patience. But when Satan abandons his craft for force, the blow of justice falls on him. And that blow is the final deliverance of heaven from the power of evil.

"The kingdom of God" has *then* begun. It has not

therefore begun yet, even in heaven. How much less on earth! We have yet to pray, "The kingdom come!" But in that day it is come. As one has well observed, Satan's ejectment cannot have come to pass yet; or the attitude of the Church of Christ, as wrestling with principalities and powers in the heavenlies, would be lost. Eph. vi. 12. But the kingdom then comes only on high: for that part of God's dominion only is as yet rescued from the presence and power of Satan. The casting out of demons by the Spirit of God was, in principle, the coming of the kingdom of God, as Jesus said. Matt. xii. 28. But now it is the ejection, not of one demon out of a single individual of earth, but of Satan and all his host out of heaven.

"Who used to accuse them before our God day and night."

Satan has his place in the king's court, as a witness. The king's ear must be open to all complaints, whether true or false. Satan's great malignity, and unceasing power as a spirit, are shown in his accusing them "day and night." After accusation, then comes investigation, and the witness is proved true or false. Satan at length is proved, not only the false accuser, but the open rebel.

It appears as if this were Satan's constant post: his angels being employed in bringing him intelligence. Yet he never appears in this book as standing before the throne. It is the throne of *justice*, and before that he cannot appear voluntarily.

11. "And THEY overcame him because of the blood of the Lamb, and because of the word of their testimony, and they loved not their soul unto death."

The stress laid in the original upon the word "they" seems due to the fact that there are *two* victories. One has just taken place in heaven, won by force.

One was effected previously on earth, by patience. We have had the first described. This introduces the features of the second.

This Child existed on earth, ere it was born in resurrection. There it lived, and was slain. To the Church it is given to wrestle spiritually even now with principalities and powers in heaven. Eph. vi. 12. This is the consummation of that contest, decided on their behalf.

Among the overcomers here must be found the conquerors of the Church of Christ. iii. 10. It is the blessed result of the prayer to be "accounted worthy to escape the things that are coming to pass" (Luke xxi. 36; 2 Thess. ii. 1, 2).

In the grounds of their victory we see the points against which the pleas of the Accuser were directed.

(1) Their offences against God were specified by Satan. Against those is set "the blood of the Lamb." They rest on the atonement provided, and by that they are able to worship and to serve God actively, as those cleansed from dead works. They are not perfect, though they overcome. Since many of these are martyrs, it was quite requisite to show that their victory was not meritoriously due to their own work or blood. How soon did this truth fall in the early days of Christianity!

(2) Satan again accuses the saints, too, as not believing the word of God, and as flinching from the assertion of unpopular doctrine. His affirmations are proved untrue, for they credit and uphold in public the truths committed to them. Not only have they secret faith, but open profession. The keepers of Christ's word of patience are delivered out of the hour of temptation, as He promised. The abiding in the word of God is also the overcoming of the Wicked One. 1 John ii. 14.

The Greeks and the Sacred Scriptures use one word

for "life," and another to describe the animal "soul" of man. Man can take away life. But he cannot kill the animal soul. Matt. x. 28. ($\psi v \chi \dot{\eta}$). "He that loseth his *soul* for my sake shall find it" (Matt. xvi. 25). These hated their *souls* in this *life*, to keep them unto life eternal. John xii. 25; Luke xiv. 26; Acts xx. 24. Our translation varies the rendering, and creates confusion by giving the word two senses.

(3) They are accused also as time-servers, who only hold their post for present advantage, as the devil said of Job. That is proved false by the contrary conduct, as in Job's case. They discover to us that life hated and lost for Christ's sake is found in the resurrection; and enjoyed in the glory of the kingdom.

12. "Wherefore rejoice, ye heavens, and ye tabernaclers in them."

It were indeed a subject of rejoicing, nevermore to be tempted; never to be troubled by the Wicked One or his angels; to have the "great gulf" of heaven set between them and us, never more to be crossed by the foe. Well may the angels and the ascended saints be called on to rejoice!

"And ye tabernaclers in them." Who are they? At a further stage of the unfolding of God's plan, we find "saints, apostles, and prophets" (xviii. 20).

They have crossed the Red Sea of death, and are now pitching tents on intermediate ground; ere they come to the new earth and city. The *tents* here are not the promised "mansions." It is the camp of the saints ere they go forth to battle.

"Woe to the earth, and to the sea, for the devil came down to you, having great wrath, knowing that he hath but a short season."

Satan has lost for ever the upper regions. But still

it is permitted him to exert his power on earth and sea, to prove what he is, and what man is. When Jesus descended the song was, "Peace on earth, goodwill to men!" (Luke i. 68). But now there is woe to earth, for the Destroyer has descended in wrath.

His defeat has not dispirited him, much less led him to obey God. It has only exasperated him. He is enraged because his last plan has failed, and his inferior foe, man, has been exalted above him. Some of the hated sons of men have ascended to his place; and songs of victory are being sung over his defeat. Hence his fury rises against all men, whether godless or godly: but especially against the holy. The godless he leads into battle against Christ: the saints he cuts off.

Messiah, Satan knows, is soon to put down his dominion; hence He will make the most of His time. He is acquainted with prophecy, and understands that but three years and a half are before him, ere Jesus will descend to take away his rule.

13. "And when the dragon saw that he was cast into the earth, he pursued the woman who brought forth the male."

He seems to pause a moment, as stunned by his fall. Then, seeing his former position to be incapable of recovery, he rises and pursues.

"The woman which brought forth the male."

This is a new designation. She is no longer seen as the Woman in heaven, after her Son is rapt thither. The Mother is described by her relation to her Son, as He is the superior. She is really on earth, not cast out of heaven as Satan is. But she has both a heavenly and an earthly aspect, as her enemy also has. Both the Woman and the Dragon are shown in heaven and on earth, that the unity of purpose, on God's part and on Satan's, may be perceived throughout the two scenes.

14. "And to the woman were given the two wings of the great eagle, that she might fly into the wilderness, into her place ,(where she is fed for a season, and seasons, and half a season), from the face of the serpent."

The eagle is of all the birds the best able to pursue a long and rapid flight. Her dwelling is in the wilderness and on its *mountains*. The great eagle's flight is the most rapid of all the eagles. And the Jewish disciples will have to flee 200 miles to reach Sinai.

The wings of the chief of the eagles are bestowed on her. Of course these are not literal, for the Woman is symbolic. It signifies that supernatural strength and swiftness for escape will be given to the remnant who flee. Of their deliverance from Egypt of old, God speaks in similar terms. Exod. xix. 4. "Ye have seen how *I bare you on eagle's wings,* and brought you unto Myself" at Sinai. Deut. xxxii. 11, 12.

A specimen of this power of God to aid His people we behold in Elijah, running from Carmel to Jezreel, before Ahab's hasting chariot. 1 Kings xviii. 46.

Her flight is not, like the eagle's, into air; for then the river which the Dragon pours forth could not harm her. Her flight is like that of the ostrich, along the surface of the ground : but it is like that of the largest of the eagles for rapidity.

Her flight is into the wilderness, whither God directed her of old. It is the same flight with that commanded of the Saviour. Matt. xxiv. 16. There the word is, "Flee to the *mountains*." Those are to be the first object of their flight. But they will hasten on yet further into the wilderness.

In the fact that this woman has a "place," and a refuge on the earth from the power of Satan, we may see a proof that she is not the Church. That is not called to flee from Satan to any spot of our globe. It is in heaven that she is called to conflict with him, and she has no "place" on earth : she is but a stranger and pilgrim passing through it to the "place" which Jesus has gone to prepare for her on high. Moreover, the earth does not help, but hinders her.

But though the wilderness be the place of security, where Israelites obtain escape from their foes, yet it is the place of safety only because of its desolation, its destitution of the bread and water necessary for human support. The eagle loves the loftiest and most solitary mountain, and to the Mount of God these eagle wings bear her. Here, therefore, it is necessary that supernatural support should be supplied. Accordingly it is bestowed.

"She is fed." This denotes her passiveness. She cannot sustain herself by her own efforts.

15. "And the serpent cast out of his mouth after the woman, water like a river, that he might cause her to be carried away by the river." [1]

"Water like a river." It did not expand itself gently on all sides, forming a quiet lake; but rushed onward impetuously in the direction of the woman's flight, that it might overthrow her steps and bring her to the ground. To this answers the hot pursuit of an army, not intending to do battle with warriors, but to overtake and destroy fugitives by superior speed. In the following texts armies are compared to rivers :—

Jer. xlvi. 7, 8.   Jer. xlvii. 2, 3.

We can see why Satan is so bent on destroying the faithful of Jerusalem. If he can cut off God's earthly

[1] Literally, "that he might make her river-borne."

people, the word of God has failed. He stabs therefore where the blow will be deadliest. But this brings him into direct collision with God, and then the Most High steps forth with miracle to protect.

The help rendered to the Woman requires a change of plan on his part, that he may overtake her. She is escaping from his pursuit. He adopts a new expedient. He casts a river out of his mouth. This is, of course, symbolic; for the Dragon is so, and so are the stars which his tail casts down.

Its meaning is, I suppose, as follows. Ezek. xxxviii. describes the invasion of the land of Israel from the north by many nations, who come upon them unexpectedly in a time of peace. With great celerity the leader pushes on for Jerusalem, and the believers in Jesus there, warned by the signs given, flee first to the mountains, then to the wilderness. The main body of the army, fatigued with its long and rapid marches, is unable to overtake the flying ones. A special body of cavalry then is selected to pursue with the greater speed of the horse.

He wields a river ($\pi o \tau a \mu o s$) not a flood ($\kappa a \tau a \kappa \lambda v \sigma \mu o s$.) The enemy comes in "like a *river*." Isa. lix. 19. The river comes from the north: the woman flees into the wilderness or south. If I mistake not, this invasion is the act of the seventh head or the Assyrian, out of whom comes a worse king, the eighth head. Isa. xiv. 28, 29.

Symbolic waters are declared to be "nations, peoples, and languages."

16. "And the earth helped the woman, and the earth opened her mouth, and swallowed down the river which the dragon cast out of his mouth."

In what way the earth helps the woman as distinct from its subsequent act, is not said: but the verse seems to assert that some other aid is given.[1] The main deliverance, however, is effected by its swallowing up the detachment of foes in pursuit. (1) So were Pharaoh and his host swallowed up. " Thou stretchedst out thy right hand : *the earth swallowed them* " (Exod. xv. 12). (2) So was the host of Dathan and Abiram engulfed in the wilderness. Num. xvi. (3) The earth opened her mouth to receive Abel's blood at the hand of Cain. Gen. iv. 11. But it did not open it to swallow *him* up. Now, however, it opens to engulf these murderers.

This sudden opening of the earth—the result probably of the great earthquake that is to attend Gog's invasion (Ezek. xxxviii. 19, 20)—cuts off the party of horsemen sent in pursuit. But for this, they would have proved successful. Here is the baffling of the new wile. The swallowing up is literal : for the earth is not a symbol, but a reality. It is also certified by former like cases.

17. " And the dragon was wrath with the woman, and went away to make war with the remains of her seed, who keep the commands of God, and hold the testimony of Jesus."

Though baffled here also, he repents not. His plans turn to dust in his mouth : yet he is only angry, not penitent. He sees this scheme defeated beyond redress, and leaves it, and confesses tacitly that the Woman is beyond his power.

He turns away to another enterprise, to vex and destroy the parties who fled not. Against them he uses mingled force and fraud.

The Woman has two seeds, the earthly and the heavenly. Of each of these there are remainders left behind, which have not been withdrawn from his grasp

[1] Waters may suddenly burst up in the desert for the fugitives. It is so promised. Isa. xliii. 20. Perhaps the earth may suddenly yield fruits also.

by either the earthly or the heavenly escape. There are some of Israel still in the land; there are also some of the Church, not accounted worthy to escape these things, and left when the others are taken. Luke xxi. 36. We were introduced to these two seeds in chapter vii. The 144,000 of the twelve tribes are of the one party; the numberless assembly on high are of the other. They appear to be described in the next chapters by the common term of "saints," a title used by both the Old Testament and the New. xiii. 7, 10; xiv. 12. John Baptist, at the opening of the Gospel, speaks of two classes as tried by the day of the Lord, the trees, and Messiah's floor. Matt. iii. Thus also Abraham's seed was twofold: the earthly, like the sand of the shore; and the heavenly, like the stars of the sky.

"The commands of God," appear to refer to God's older revelation by Moses. "The testimony of Jesus" is His last and nobler revelation. "The testimony of Jesus" may mean either (1) that *concerning* Jesus; or (2) the testimony *which Jesus rendered*. The saints here described hold both. Not improbably there is a reference to the Apocalypse itself, which is described as "the testimony of Jesus Christ" (Rev. i. 2).

CHAPTER XIII

THE ANTICHRIST AND THE FALSE PROPHET

1. "And he stood upon the sand of the sea. And I saw a wild beast coming up out of the sea, having ten horns and seven heads, and on his horns ten diadems, and on his heads names of blasphemy."

IF we read, "He stood," the connection of this chapter with the former is more closely given. Satan after his defeat, in his progress from Jerusalem southward, moves away to the west, till he is stopped by the great sea, or Mediterranean. He looks towards Rome, and the result of his machinations is this coming up of the two Wild Beasts.

The rise of both the Wild Beasts, that out of the sea and that out of the land, is thus accounted for, as the result of Satan's call for them both. The God of this world now resembles the Creator, who called up birds out of the sea, and wild beasts out of the land. Gen. i. 20, 24.

Satan raises his potentate from the dead by God's permission, in imitation of the Father's raising of Jesus.

A Wild Beast came up. The Wild Beast here has two significations. It means first, an *Empire* : secondly, a *person*.

1. It is an *Empire*, as in the visions of Daniel. It is the fourth or Roman Empire, in its last state. Thus

it stands connected with the seven heads and ten horns of the Dragon, which have preceded. John sees the power of the earth, in its unity of rebellion as leagued against God. 2. But it is also an *individual*, who wields the latter-day power of the fourth Empire, and *so* is identified with it. This is proved (1) from the fact, that the Roman empire did not begin to arise when Satan was cast down. (2) Individuals are represented in Scripture by wild beasts. An eagle represents the king of Babylon : another eagle, the king of Egypt. Ezek. xvii. 3, 7, 12, 15. A lion represents the king of Judah. Ezek. xix. 1-3, 6. The king of Egypt, again, is spoken of as a dragon (Ezek. xxix.) ; and Herod as a fox. Luke xiii. 31, 32.

This first Wild Beast is subordinate to the Dragon, as the second Wild Beast is subordinate to the first. He is the same as the Abaddon of chap. ix. ; for he is indebted to Satan for his escape out of the pit.

One wild beast—the serpent—brought on man's first crisis of woe : three wild beasts—one from *heaven*, one from *earth*, and one from the *sea*—bring on the second great crisis. The twelfth chapter showed us the enmity between the Serpent and the Woman ; this discovers to us the enmity between the *seed* of the serpent, and the *seed* of the Woman. The Wild Beasts of earth have been used in vain to bring men to repentance. Wild Beasts of the bottomless pit are now sent to deceive and destroy, in God's righteous judgment for truth refused.

The Wild Beast comes up " out of the sea." When the Wild Beast means an empire, the sea symbolizes the multitude of mankind. But when the Wild Beast intends a literal individual, the sea is literal also.[1] The

---

[1] Thus the heads of the Wild Beasts take two meanings, xvii. 9, 10. They are both territorial heads, or mountains ; and heads of men, or kings.

sea is literally taken when Satan is described as standing on "the sand of the sea."[1]

The Wild Beast comes up out of it. He really "ascends" out of the bottomless pit. xvii. 8. He is the same Wild Beast that destroyed the Two Witnesses, in chap. xi.; and who is hereafter described as a king of Rome in chap. xvii. But he who comes up from earth's centre must ascend to earth, either from the surface of the land, or of the sea. The first Wild Beast ascends through the sea; the second, through the land. "Coming up," is spoken of a soul's arising from the place of the dead, in Samuel's case. "An old man *cometh up*" (1 Sam. xxviii. 13, 14).

"Having ten horns and seven heads."

The heads are the supreme kings, or Emperors. The horns are subordinate, or subject-kings. The head is the ruling and chief power of every creature: the horns are subordinate to the head, and are used in executing its desires.

The heads exist but one at a time, and intend seven *successive* emperors of Rome. Jesus as the Lamb has but one head; for as king He has neither predecessor nor successor. But the horns represent ten kings *cotemporaneously* subject to one of the heads; as is proved by chap. xvii. 12. "The ten horns which thou sawest are ten kings, which have received no kingdom as yet, but receive power as kings *one hour with the Wild Beast*." The Wild Beast, as now seen, answers to the seventh head, ruling the whole Roman empire.

But while in Rev. xii. 3 diadems are upon the *heads* of the Wild Beast, here they are set upon the *horns*. The time, then, which seems to be supposed, is just before the ten kings voluntarily surrender their power

---

[1] It is observable, that the Emperor's substitute who condemned our Lord was named Πόντιος, which signifies "One of the Sea"—both in Greek and Latin.

to the last individual Wild Beast. Now that Antichrist is to appear, the ten kings his coadjutors have arisen also.

Jesus had seven horns, but they were "the seven Spirits of God." Here are ten horns, an imperfect number, and the one which the French Revolution set up against the original seven. It changed the seven days of the week into decades, or periods of ten days.

These ten kings are, I believe, the ten toes of Daniel's image, on which the great stone smites. This would suppose that the empire is parted into the two great divisions of East and West; five kings of the East, and five of the West, answering to the toes of each foot.

" And upon his heads names of blasphemy."[1]

The emperors or supreme kings all are *rivals of God*. They steal His *titles*. This is a mark of all the seven. His attributes they do not possess; but His *names* they can and do arrogate to themselves.

Blasphemy is of two kinds.

1. It is the equalling one's self to God; or *self-elevating* blasphemy. Of this our Lord was accused. Matt. ix. 3; xxvi. 65; John v. 18; x. 33.

2. There is also *God-depressing* blasphemy, when men slander the true God, but do not esteem themselves His equals in nature. Thus the Pharisees blasphemed the Holy Spirit. Mark iii. 28, 29; Rev. xvi. 9, 11, 21.

Antichrist offends in both kinds. "He *exalts himself* above every God." He "blasphemes his name." The former Heads had titles and "names of blasphemy:" but he has a "*mouth*" of it. And his mouth is the utterance of his heart.

The horns have not "names of blasphemy." They content themselves with being kings, and subordinate to Him who is, in their view, both king and God. The superior kings, or "heads," contend with God, and

---

[1] This is the true reading.—Tregelles.

elevate themselves to Godhead. But both heads and horns are alike actuated with enmity against the true God. Jesus lost all of earth by truly professing Himself God. The false Messiah gains everything from man and Satan by falsely asserting himself to be God.

The seven heads of *Satan* as the dragon (chap. xii.) are the same as the seven heads of the *Wild Beast* here.

It is well known that many of the emperors took the titles and homage of Deity. (1) To Julius Cæsar was raised a temple (Dio. 47, 18, p. 337). (2) Augustus permitted temples to Rome and his father at Ephesus and Nice ; and in other parts of Asia, temples where worship was rendered were erected to himself. (Dio. 450, 600 ; Virg. Ecl. i. 6–8 ; Hor. Ep. II. 1, 16 ; Ovid Fast., i. 13). (3) Caligula (Dio. 643 ; Joseph. Ant. 18, 8, 89 ; 191, 1), and (4) Nero (Dio. p. 724) followed in the same sin. (5) Domitian, the emperor reigning in John's day, required men to address him as " Our Lord and God."

At Angora there are the remains of a temple erected to Augustus. On it is inscribed

"TO THE GOD AUGUSTUS,
AND
TO THE GODDESS ROME."

At the same place were found also these awful words, most interesting as illustrative of the chapter before us.

"TO THE
EMPEROR CÆSAR MARCUS AURELIUS ANTONINUS,
Unconquered, August, Pious, Successful.
ÆLIUS LYCINUS,
one most devoted to his godhead,
erects this."

Fellowes, p. 248.

At Nysa is a notice of the consecration of a statue to Nero Claudius Augustus. "This is the emperor known to us by the name of Nero, who, like many others, was in his lifetime styled God by Grecian flattery." Dio. p. 22. Lamps are still in existence inscribed—"Flavians of *our God and Lord*"—which may refer either to Vespasian or Titus, while other lamps are inscribed—"The Domitians of our *God and Lord*, showing that they allude to the emperor Domitian." Birch's Ancient Pottery, ii. 295.

2. "And the Wild Beast which I saw was like a panther, and its feet like those of a bear, and its mouth as the mouth of a lion; and the Dragon gave him his might, and his throne, and great authority."

The Wild Beast resembled in general the panther. This is a more fierce and dangerous animal than the leopard. It is full of spots : and spots are the types of sin. Jer. xiii. 23. The *Lamb* his antagonist is " without blemish and without *spot*" (1 Peter i. 19). The prophets speak of the panther as a cunning, cruel, watchful, and swift animal, used by God for vengeance. Jer. v. 6; Hos. xiii. 7 ; Hab. i. 8.

The panther in Daniel typifies the Grecian Empire. Dan. vii. 6. It will probably be prominent in that day. The order given to the Wild Beasts in Dan. vii. is here reversed, and the worst features of each are combined.

It has "feet like a bear."

The Medo-Persian empire is by Daniel compared to a bear. Dan. vii. 5. The empire in its last form will territorially consist of Persia, as well as Greece. Its strength to destroy will also be derived thence.

It has also "the mouth of a lion."

The Babylonish empire in Daniel's vision resembles a "lion." Dan. vii. 4. This region will also contribute its territory to form the dominion of the False Christ.

But where is the Roman empire? That is seen in the "seven heads and ten horns." The fourth empire includes the domains of the former three. This is the fourth empire in its last state.

Morally, too, such as its mouth is, such is its heart. The mouth of a lion is its deadly part. The conquerors of faith "stopped the mouths of lions" (Heb. xi. 33). Paul, when called to stand before Nero, speaks of his trial thus: "At my first answer none stood with me, but all forsook me: may it not be laid to their charge. Notwithstanding the Lord stood by me, and strengthened me, that by me the proclamation might be completed, and all the Gentiles hear; and I was delivered *out of the mouth of the lion*" (2 Tim. iv. 17).

God threatens to be to Israel in time of vengeance like these three wild creatures. Hos. xiii. 6–8. This passage occurs just before the ever-memorable promise of resurrection—"O death, where is thy sting?" (v. 14).

The Wild Beast before us, then, may be regarded (1) territorially, (2) morally, and (3) personally.

(1) *Territorially*, it will consist of the domains of the former empires.

(2) *Morally* taken, it will combine the splendour, warlike prowess, intellect, and irresistibility of the four great empires, and their sinfulness towards God.

(3) *Personally*, the glory before men, and the sin before God will be concentred in the person of one man. It is this individual aspect which is the chief one throughout, as we shall find in the next words.

Satan "gave him his might and his throne, and great authority." Satan, in John's Gospel only, is spoken of by our Lord as "prince of the world" (John xii. 31; xiv. 30). He has been so represented here, in his character of the dragon with seven heads and ten horns. In this verse he transfers that power to the False Christ, one wholly in his interest. Herein he follows the example and plan of God, who makes over to the true Christ his kingdom and power. Matt. xxviii. 18.

God's king is to be a man. Therefore Satan raises, as his ruler over men, one who has been a man. Only thus, it would seem, could the devil's scheme prosper. Antichrist is one whom he has already proved faithful unto death, just as Jesus is one whom the Father has proved in like sort faithful. Satan attempted to seduce the true Christ (Matt. iv.), by offer of the world's glory, but failed.

The dragon gives him his " might," or power. It seems to refer chiefly to power of miracle, as distinguished from " authority " which follows—Mark ix. 39 ; Luke vi. 19 ; xxiv. 29. This identifies him as " the Man of Sin," of 2 Thess. ii. 9, to whom " all *powers, signs,* and *wonders* of falsehood " are given.

He gives him also " his throne."

Civil power is represented by the throne. Satan has a kingdom, and a kingdom supposes a throne as its centre. His throne is on earth, as Jesus has already told us. ii. 13 ; xvi. 10. God's throne we have seen to be in heaven : but the devil has been ejected thence. This is " the throne *of iniquity,*" of which the Psalmist speaks. Ps. xciv. 20. As Satan transfers his throne of earth to the False Christ, so God promises to the true, " the throne of his father David " on earth. Luke i. 32.

" The *Synagogue* of Satan " is among the *Jews* (ii. 9 ; iii. 9). His *throne* is among the *Gentiles.* The Jew acts with Satan against the *doctrines* of God. The Gentile, as possessor of the kingdom, uses *civil power* against the saints.

" And great authority."

The former word shows us that the devil's king will have the outward splendours of regal power. This adds, that he will possess the reality signified by it.

This word tells us, too, that he will be so introduced as to possess, by virtue of the world's laws, its legal power. "Authority" means legal power. Matt. viii. 9; Luke xx. 20; John xix. 10 (*see Greek*).

Satan takes his king from the fourth empire, and selects him from one of the previous kings of that empire. xvii.

The Pope is the union of king and priest; the *king* being, however, quite a secondary part of the character. He imitates Christ as the priest-king, copying also the Jewish ritual and splendour. This is a *king* with throne and power. He is not a *priest* at all. He refuses mediation; or at least the mediation of priesthood and atonement. His great coadjutor is a prophet. The Popes have civil power, but not miracle. *He* has miracle, as well as authority over men. Miracle departed from the Church when bishops set up their civil courts and thrones. The "miracles" which followed were juggles on behalf of idolatry. The combination of *miracle* and *civil power* before the appearing of Jesus is a moral proof of the corruptness of the source. These two powers are now severed by God. Apostles had miracle, but not civil power. It was arrayed against them everywhere. The possessors of human authority had no right of miracle. Miracle of truth springs from the Spirit of God. But the world rejects the Spirit of God. John xiv. 16; 1 Cor. ii. 12; 1 John iv. 1, 5, 6. Civil power was more than a match for miraculous power, in keeping men steady to itself. That is seen strikingly in Elijah's flight after his exhibition of miracle at Carmel; an exhibition which for the moment carried all before it. But Jezebel yields not, and the seeming national reformation is nipped in the bud. What, then, will be the result when power natural, and power supernatural, are both arrayed on the side of Satan's king?

3. "And (I saw) one of his heads as it had been slain unto death: and the wound of his death was healed, and the whole earth wondered after the Wild Beast."

The Wild Beast under his seventh head is first shown. At length *he* comes, who had not yet appeared when John wrote. "The one *is*." That was true, in John's day. "The other (the 7th) is not yet come" (xvii. 10).

This king, after appearing awhile, is assassinated. He is slain with the sword. v. 14. The reasons of his assassination may easily be guessed. (1) He is cruel and tyrannous. (2) 'Tis a lawless time, and 'tis accounted a "sacred duty to slay tyrants." By violent deaths were many emperors cut off. (3) *He professes himself to be God.*

Where proud men have pronounced themselves gods, the Most High has often caused them to be cut off by assassination, as in the instances of Antiochus, Caligula, Claudius, Caracalla, Domitian, Hakem. Alexander's life was in peril from this cause. Quintus Curtius, ii. 131. Capt. Cook, after allowing himself to be deified by the South-Sea Islanders, was slain by them. "*Wilt thou yet say before him that slayeth thee, I am God? But thou shalt be a man, and no God, in the hand of him that slayeth thee*" (Ezek. xxviii. 9). These words give us the principle of God's government in this respect.

Self-deification, beginning conspicuously with Alexander the Great, was imitated by the descendants of his generals who became kings. This awful crime was rife amongst the Antiochi, Antigoni, Demetrii, and especially among the Ptolemies. A remarkable relic of antiquity, called the Rosetta stone, greatly illustrates the chapter before us. It contains the decree of some Egyptian priests to offer divine worship to Ptolemy Epiphanes. Its date is about 197 B.C. The following is an extract.

"Ptolemy the descendant of the *gods Philopaters*. . .

the 9th year under Ætus the *priest of Alexander* and the *gods Saviours*, and the *gods Fraternal*, and the *gods Benefactors*, and the *gods Father-loving*, and the *god Epiphanes*, the munificent." . . .

"This decree the chief priests and the *prophets*, and they who enter into the shrine to robe the gods, and the wing-bearers, and the sacred scribes, and all the other priests who met the king," make—

In consequence of many benefits received from the king, which are duly enumerated :—

"That the priests tend the *images* thrice a day, and clothe them with the sacred robes, and perform for them the other rites customary for the rest of the gods, at the feasts and assemblies : and that there be erected to king *Ptolemy the god* Epiphanes (Illustrious) munificent, sprung from king Ptolemy and Queen Arsinoe, *the gods Father-loving, a statue* and temple of gold."

"And that they hold a feast and general assembly to the king eternal and beloved by Phthah *Ptolemy the God* illustrious and munificent, yearly"

What light this throws upon the whole scene of chap. xiii !

John beholds the last head " as *slain* unto *death*"—a very strong expression, assuring us of the reality of the death. He saw the mark of the wound of death : the appearance was not deceptive, but real. This is evident, from its parallelism with what is said of the *Wild Beast's* great antagonist—the *Lamb*. John saw before, "a Lamb *as it had been slain* " (v. 6). Both carry the abiding scars of the wounds of death. The death of both is real and literal. In this latter case the expression is stronger than in our Lord's. "A Lamb as it had been slain." "As it had been slain *unto death*."

"And the wound of his death was healed."

The words import a *violent* death. 1. The expression

" slain " implies it. It is the word used of victims employed as sacrifices. By it John describes the violent death which Abel suffered. " Not as Cain, who was of the Wicked One, and *slew* his brother" (1 John iii. 12). By it in the Apocalypse is expressed violent death. The rider on the red horse has a sword given him, " that they should *slay* one another " (vi. 4). And the souls of the martyrs are described as the souls of " those *slain* for the word of God " (9).

2. The expression " the wound *of his death* " proves it. It asserts that the stroke of the sword produced death as its consequence. " If the ministration (ministry) *of death* was glorious " (2 Cor. iii. 7). The ministry of the law produced death as its result. Where a simply dangerous sickness is the result, the expression is different. " Indeed he was sick, *nigh unto death* " (Phil. ii. 27).

3. We have other proofs in this case. (1) The eighth head is one who "*was* and is not " (xvii. 8). The seventh head must be slain, in order to allow the eighth to take the other's place. The eighth head is at present a spirit in the bottomless pit, and comes up out of the place of perdition, to return thither. xvii. 8. (2) Life and death are strictly and literally taken, in the prophecy of this book. This is shown in the case of the Witnesses. xi. 7-11. (3) Thus the False Christ resembles the true. The true Messiah and the false, of opposite characters, are placed in similar situations ; and the results are as fearfully opposed. The Destroyer resembles the Saviour. Of the Destroyer, then, that is true which Jesus spoke generally, though with especial reference to Himself. " Except a corn of wheat fall into the ground *and die*, it abideth alone : *but if it die, it bringeth forth much fruit*." " I, if I be lifted up, will draw all men unto Me. This said He, signifying by what death He should die " (John xii. 24, 32, 33). This

man is slain with the sword. But his death, instead of destroying the delusion, cements it in resurrection. " He shows himself alive after his passion (as did Jesus), by many infallible proofs " (Acts i. 3).

For the stroke that carried death " is healed." Matt. viii. 6, 7, 8, 13.

" And the whole earth wondered after the Wild Beast." Observe first, that while it is said in the first clause of the verse, " I saw one of the *heads* slain," it is said at the close, that the world wondered " after the *Wild Beast*." The whole Wild Beast, then, is identified with the last head. It is an individual who wields the entire force of the empire. And this sense it takes to the close.

That the Wild Beast is an individual man, may be proved thus. (1) His end is perdition, as Satan's is. (xx. 10). This proves him a person. An empire is not adjudged to damnation.

(2) If the Lamb be an individual, so are both the Wild Beasts.

(3) The healing of the wound moves universal wonder. But the restoration of an empire would not do so, however low its degradation. It might surprise the thoughtful, but it would not affect the thoughtless majority. If the barbarian Maltese esteemed Paul a god, because after the bite of the adder he died not—how much more if he had died and risen! But the rising again to life of one who had been violently slain would affect all alike with astonishment. Resurrection was so wonderful a thought, that the apostles would not believe at first, even on evidence given; and they were terrified when Jesus appeared. Luke xxiv. 11, 12, 36–41. It is resurrection, then, which is predicted here. Wonder and terror are the result of the Two Witnesses' return to life. Terror is added there, because a sense of sin accompanies their rising. But the

earth in general has no hand in slaying the Wild Beast, and so the effect is simply wonder.

"The whole earth wonders." It is the "hour of the temptation which is to come upon *the whole habitable earth, to try the dwellers on the earth*" (iii. 10). Satan's throne exists during the Church dispensation, but it does not attract all the earth; nor does the devil's king appear, till the Man-child, the true king, is removed. To Satan is given the power to deceive, by his great masterpiece, the whole world.

All earth hears of, and admits, on undeniable grounds, the story of Antichrist's death. It is known to all, friends and foes; and brings forth joy and grief, according to their respective leanings. Then comes the proof of his rising again, and all wonder. But their belief in, and wonder at, the resurrection of the False Christ, bespeaks also their unbelief in the resurrection of the True Christ. Else they would have foreknown this, as a deceit of the Enemy. And thus it is put by the Holy Ghost. "The Wild Beast which thou sawest was, and is not, and shall ascend out of the bottomless pit, and go into perdition: and *all that dwell on the earth shall wonder, whose names were not written in the book of life from the foundation of the world*, when they behold the Wild Beast, because he was, and is not, and shall be present" (xvii. 8).

The First Wild Beast is the predominant one. As soon as the Second is named, it is distinguished from the First, twice (in ver. 12). Thenceforward the Second is not named "Wild Beast:" but "*the* Wild Beast" intends always the first and kingly one. The "image," "name," and "number" belong to the First Wild Beast alone. He is so pre-eminent, because Satan imitates God's plan; and the kingdom which is to come is that of the *Son*. They wonder "*after* Him."

It concerns them deeply, and they follow him

everywhere. They are continually attracted to gaze and admire. In somewhat of this manner was Jesus followed when Lazarus had been raised. John xii. 9–11, 17, 18.

It is painfully interesting to observe how widely spread is the expectation of the coming of some great man to earth, whose presence is to bring happy times. Thus is the Spirit of Antichrist preparing the way for his advent.

The Hindoos expect the tenth Avatar (*Pye Smith's Testimony to Messiah*, i. 163). The Buddhists look for the *next* Buddh, or deity (*Christian Treasury*, for 1850, p. 5). The Indians of Mexico watch beside a holy fire for the return of Quetzalcoat (*Ruxton's Adventures in Mexico*, p. 192). The Mohammedan Shiites look for the coming of Mouhdi (*Young's Notes of a Wayfarer*, p. 138). The Druses look for the return of Hakem (*Fisk's Pastor's Memorial*, p. 386). The Samaritans expect a prophet called Hathal (*Conder's All Religions*, p. 605). The Chasidim look for one to come (*ibid.*).

The Welsh expect the coming of St. David. "The peasants in Brittany believe that Napoleon the First is not dead; the Prussians expect Frederic the Second; the Swiss, William Tell; the older English, King Arthur; and certain modern fanatics look forward to the appearance of Joanna Southcote" (*Burton's Pilgrimage*, p. 108). They expect the son of Joanna also, and their Prophet exhibits signs and wonders (*Begg's Letters*, p. 204).

4. "And they worshipped the Dragon, because he gave the authority to the Wild Beast; and they worshipped the Wild Beast, saying, 'Who is like the Wild Beast?' And 'Who is able to war with him?'"

Wonder passes into worship; for worship is unlimited and transcendent wonder.

But the worship is first rendered to Satan himself, as the giver of authority to the Wild Beast. As he who honours the Son honours the Father who sent Him ; so he who honours the wearer of the devil's power, honours also the giver of it. Satan is evidently regarded as the author of the healing.

Evil progresses. Rome, holding the shadow of Christianity, worships the *Woman*. The next fearful step is worship of the *Serpent*. The true worship is that of the *Woman's Seed*.

In Eden the serpent was believed, but not worshipped. Now, the cursed Wild Beast of the field receives the homage due to God. Then God's word was disbelieved. Now He is openly blasphemed by men. Faith in God leads to worship. So does faith in Satan lead to adore the Deceiver. Satan covets worship, as we see in his temptation of our Lord.

Mr. Ives, in his travels through Persia, gives the following curious account of devil-worship. "These people [the Sanjacks, a nation inhabiting the country about Mosul—the ancient Nineveh] once professed Christianity, then Mohammedanism, and last of all *devilism*." They expect that Satan will be restored to God's favour. "The person of the *devil* they look on as sacred, and when they affirm anything solemnly, *they do it by his name*. All disrespectful expressions of him they would punish with death, did not the Turkish power prevent them. Whenever they speak of him, it is with the utmost respect : and they always put before his name a certain title corresponding to that of *Highness, or Lord*" (*Burder's Oriental Customs*, i. 395).

The Law ended in idolatry and Baal-worship. The Gospel ends in worship of the devil. Demons were worshipped at an earlier stage (ix. 20); now, Beelzebub, their chief, is adored. Dan. xi. 36–38.

"And they worshipped the Wild Beast."

Israel at Sinai worshipped a *calf*, the work of their own hands. Now they, and Gentiles with them, adore a *Wild Beast*. One is sent them in displeasure by God.

Resurrection is the basis of the worship rendered to the False Christ. He professed himself to be God before he was slain. His living anew, with strong assurance, confirms the doctrine to the eye of men.

They speak his praises. " Who is like the Wild Beast ? "

This is a strong way of asserting that he has no equal. Something very extraordinary must be his. It cannot be simply a rise after great depression. Resurrection calls forth this loud acclaim. True it is, that Jesus also rose. But *His* resurrection is not believed by men. The Saviour's rising again is susceptible of very disadvantageous comparison with that of Antichrist. " Jesus showed not Himself to the world after His resurrection, as His own followers confess. But this Anointed one fearlessly offers himself to every eye."

He possesses supernatural power. That was of old conceived to belong to one risen from the dead. Herod believed Jesus to be John Baptist risen, " and *therefore* the Powers work in Him " (Matt. xiv. 1, 2). See *Greek*. Also Matt. xvi. 14.

The question asked by Antichrist's admirers exalts Him above every being. Thus does the Man of Sin exalt himself above every *object of worship*. 2 Thess. ii. We are, then, to take the words in their full force, as they are used concerning God Himself. After Pharaoh's swallowing up in the sea, Moses sings—" *Who is like unto thee,* O Lord, among the gods ? " (Exod. xv. 11). " O God, *who is like unto thee ?* " sings the Psalmist (Ps. lxxi. 19 ; cxiii. 5).

" Who is able to war with him ? "

Who can slay him, who has the power of resurrection ? " Neither can they die any more." He was once put to death ; but the sword is powerless against him now.

It seems probable also, that this cry is raised after his slaughter of the two miracle-girt prophets. Who can war with him, who has overcome the Two Witnesses ? All others they slew by fire, when injury was designed them ! But he warred against them, overcame, and slew them !

An army is given him, beside his own personal might. Dan. viii. 12. Is not this the host of the horsemen ?

He is a warrior, and the irresistibility of the conqueror has ever been an object of human admiration. By that Napoleon riveted all eyes, and enchained multitudes in his day. Here is a greater than Napoleon. Under his shadow unbelievers repose. He gives men confidence even to appear in arms against Christ at last.

The universal homage and worship which the Antichrist receives, at length elevate his pride beyond all previous bounds of wickedness.

5. " And there was given to him a mouth speaking great things, and blasphemies ; and there was given to him authority to act for forty and two months."

A mouth " is given him." Great is the influence of the tongue to sway men, and he has it in perfection. He is greatest of orators. By it the Wicked One blindly accomplishes Jehovah's purposes.

He uses his mouth to speak (1) " great things." He boasts what happiness he will bring, as a patron of man, and benefactor of the human race. He boasts, also, what he will do as the foe of God and of His Christ.

He speaks also (2) " blasphemies." This is the fullest development of man's iniquity, and is the great characteristic of the Wild Beast. Dan. vii. 8, 11, 20 ; xi. 36 ; Ps. lii. ; 2 Thess. ii. He both exalts himself to superiority above every god, and he utters insults and calumnies against the true God. Other kings have had "*names* of blasphemy," titles given by others, or taken by themselves. But he has the heart and tongue of blasphemy. His title of " God " is no idle affair, worn as the kings of England bore the title of " King of *France*." As God he requires the homage of all. This Wild Beast—" the Little Horn " of Daniel, and the " Man of Sin " of Paul—will exceed all former boasters and blasphemers.

Men think too loftily of him. But he thinks far more loftily of himself, and swells against Jehovah with vain pride and bitter enmity. He is wonderful in his power, but wonderful in his *unholiness* also. Thence comes the title he bears in God's book. He is "*the Man of Sin*." He is such a one as man is, and as man loves. Satan moulds his king to suit human sympathies of wickedness.

At first the Antichrist is revealed, as (1) *passive*. He is the Slain and Risen One, and the receiver of power. Then (2) he *speaks*, and (3) lastly he *acts*. And in both these phases of his character the *wild beast* is seen. By his *speech* he strikes at God, and by his *acts* he strikes at men, who belong to God.

" Who can make war with him ? " He makes war on the saints, and prevails ; because " *it was given him*." How little need we fear the most terrible enemy ! This, the most fierce of all, can do no more than he is permitted. John xix. 11. Six times the expression—" it was given him "—occurs in this chapter ; four times as referring to the chief Wild Beast ; twice to the inferior.

God again is not only the grantor of his licence to act, but the setter of the limits to it. It is for three and a half years. But it is expressed in months, because it is evil. It is 6×7 months, or the height of wickedness and sorrow. It is that time during which the Woman has a place of safety given her in the wilderness. There was a *day* of temptation in the wilderness for *forty years;* there is an " *hour* of temptation " over all the earth for *forty-two months.*

Three years and a half is a period of persecution which has often been noticed before. Such was the duration of the persecution of Antiochus Epiphanes. Such was the duration also of that by Nero. It began in the middle of November, 64, and ended at Nero's death, June 9th, A.D. 68 (M. Stuart).

6. " And he opened his mouth for blasphemy against God, to blaspheme His name, and His tabernacle, those that tabernacle in the heaven."

The expression before us is a very strong one. " He opened his mouth for blasphemy." We sometimes say of the thoroughly profane—' He never opens his lips without an oath." But in such cases the offender probably does it from habit, and without thought. Here it is of set purpose, the result of enmity. He cannot smite God, but he can speak against Him; and that he does with all his heart, and at all times. The Dragon hates Michael his conqueror, and the hatred he feels expresses itself freely through the Dragon's son, who is of his father's spirit.

Men will be prepared for blasphemy against God in the latter day. It will spring out of a false and impious theory concerning the origin of evil. It will be held and taught, that evil arises not from defect of the creature, but of the Creator. That *matter* is the cause of sin; and that evil is defilement from without, not wickedness from within. The works of creation, it will be believed, contain more or less of evil. " The taking away of animal life is sinful. But God has so constituted the world, that without designing so to offend, man must slay." The blame, then, must fall on the Creator.

The special objects at which the Antichrist's enmity strikes, are specified. 1. God's name.

By it is intended,

i. God's *essence* as revealed in Scripture.

The Most High reveals Himself now as Father, Son, and Spirit; or as the Trinity in Unity. Against this the Antichrist is to rise in unmitigable hostility. " Who is the Liar, but he that denieth that Jesus is the Christ ? *He is the Antichrist that denieth the Father and the Son* " (1 John ii. 22-24 ; iv. 3). He blasphemes the Holy Spirit also, and that is the unpardonable sin.

ii. He blasphemes the *character* of God, as both merciful and just, and consequently requiring a Mediator and atonement by blood. Against this many have begun to speak. He will do so with force and vehemence far beyond them.

The essence of God as Father, Son and Spirit, had not been known, save as the result of His display of justice and mercy in Christ. The two senses are therefore closely connected.

iii. He will insult the *authority* and titles of God. Before God's name is "hallowed," it is awfully profaned. Before " His will is done on earth as it is in heaven," His authority is reviled and defied, as by the lost in hell.

" The tabernaclers in the heaven." These, according to the true reading, constitute the mystic tabernacle. They are the Man-child, or the Great Multitude ; who, as we have seen, are dwellers in tents till they reach the land and the city.

The Feast of Tabernacles of the New Covenant is being kept, during its foreknown period, on high. It is a solemn convocation. Lev. xxiii.

This phase of the tabernacle lasts only during the transitional dispensation of the millennium.

Why are these especially singled out as objects of the Antichrist's blasphemy ? They are the ransomed ones, to eject whom the devil ventured on battle, and was defeated. Sorely does their victory, and their entrance on his lost heritage, wound Satan. And Satan's spirit speaks in Antichrist. They are men fully redeemed *in resurrection*, and are monuments of the truth which he has so long instigated the godless to deny. They are out of his reach—pledges of his further and complete overthrow. They are Christ's army, sojourning in tents, because the campaign is not over. They come with Christ as the armies of heaven. xix. Of the two divisions of God's people, then, who are placed in security —(1) the fugitives of earth fed in the wilderness ; and (2) the rescued of heaven—these are the most obnoxious to his hate.

7. " And it was given them to make war on the saints, and to overcome them ; and authority was given him over every tribe and people, and tongue and nation."

The saints cannot league themselves with the Destroyer. They are not to resist him by the sword : though some, no doubt, will ; and as surely as they do, they will be defeated.

Who are the saints against whom the war is waged ? They are " the remnant " of the Woman's seed, whether (1) Jewish, or (2) of the Church. Some of those left on earth know Jesus, and are " in the Lord " (xiv. 12, 13). It is remarkable that the expression " saints," is not throughout the seven epistles to the churches used of believers in Jesus.

Antichrist carries out the plans of his father. Satan wars with the Woman and her Child. Baffled in both attempts, he gives the conduct of further hostilities into the hand of his king. xii. 17. That king is allowed to succeed against the remnant who have not found a refuge, either in earth or in heaven.

He " overcomes " them.

The Two Witnesses resist awhile, are vanquished and slain. But they defend *themselves alone*. He who overcame the Witnesses and their supernatural powers, finds small difficulty with these. He overcomes them *physically*. Their persons are subservient to his will and power. But they overcome him *morally*, as we are taught by and by. xv. 2. He uses compulsory force, imprisonment, torture, death. xvi. 6. Also Dan. vii. 21, 25 ; viii. 24 ; xi. 28, 30, 32, 33 ; xii. 7. But they resist him, and keep the faith. He is the great bruiser of the heel of the Woman's seed, just ere that seed is victorious.

"And there was given him authority over every tribe." Before, *Satan* was represented as bestowing on the False Christ his authority, ver. 2, 4. But here *Jehovah* bestows it on His foe. 5, 7. Both communications of this power are noticed. God gives him the power of the sword, and thus his followers have some ground for their celebration of his praise as the warrior. By God's decree, none, in his brief day of sovereignty, shall successfully resist him.

His extent of domain is like that of Jesus. To the Son of Man it is given, "that all *peoples, nations,* and *languages* should serve him " (vii. 14).

Although all these are given into his hand, it perhaps does not follow that they all worship. That is said universally of the next class, but not of this. A warning, however, is issued to every people to worship the true God alone. And an angelic courier foretells the dreadful wrath which will engulf every worshipper of the Wild Beast. xiv. 6–11.

8. " And all the dwellers on the earth shall worship him, whose

name[1] has not been written in the book of life of the Lamb slain from the foundation of the world. 9. If any have an ear, let him hear."

Who are these "dwellers upon the earth"? The same party we have had oft to consider. They are a distinct party from the tribes and tongues before named. They are *secularists*, who are satisfied with the earth as their portion, and refuse the stranger-and-pilgrim attitude of the Christian.

The infidelity of our day is more and more taking up an attitude of opposition to Christianity on the ground of its unworldliness. As witness the following passages:—

"The Christian, like yourself, looks upon everything with a jaundiced or distorted eye, and is apt to *underrate the claims and pleasures of this present scene of our existence*. I can truly say, that I now enter into them much more keenly than I could when I was an orthodox Christian. *I can say, with Mr. Newman, I now with deliberate approval 'love the world and the things of the world.'*" *Eclipse of Faith*, p. 57.

Christians "*say this world is* NOT *to be the great object for which we are to live, and in which we are to find our happiness; we say, it is: they say it is* NOT *our country or our home: we say* IT IS; *they say that we are to live supremely for the future, and* IN *it: we say* FOR *and* IN *the present; that if there be a future world (of which many doubt, and, I for one have not been able to make up my mind), we are to hope to be happy there, but that the main business of our life is to secure our happiness here, to embellish, adorn, and enjoy this our only certain dwelling place: and in fact to live supremely for the* PRESENT. *Such is the constitution of human nature*" (*Ibid.*, p. 60).

Such is the very spirit of those who apostatize from

[1] Ὄνομα. Tregelles.

Christ. The dwellers on earth, then, are the dark shadow which now girds round Christianity. At length they openly renounce Christ for Antichrist. Luke xvii. 25. They appear no more after Babylon is destroyed, and after the time of waiting for Jesus is over. Satan, in his last war, leads only "the nations" against Jerusalem.

They are the tares of our Lord's parable arrived at their ripeness. Love of the world and preparation for Antichrist go together. John puts the two in immediate connection. 1 John ii. 15–25. Antichrist would glorify the world as it is. On that ground they can meet him. Christ must alter its whole course and tenor. He must subdue it to God.

They worship "*him.*" A person is in question.

"They all worship."

This imports religious adoration. Civil reverence, even to this awful sinner, were right. For "the powers that be, are ordained of God," and of him it is especially asserted that his authority is from God. God's claims and Cæsar's are quite distinct.

But Cæsar demands divine worship. He obtains it too. First comes the burst of astonishment consequent on his resurrection. Multitudes bow, in voluntary, inward veneration of soul, to him as their god. Then follow his acts and deeds of power : and that which was voluntary at first, and which constitutes his followers a party among the religious of the earth, is at length enacted by law, and made compulsory on all. In him unite abilities—riches—power—civil, miraculous, and martial, and a religion which allows them to live as they list.

This new form of religion entraps *all* but the elect. Yes, *all.* The same assertion is made concerning the deadly effects of the appearing of the Man of Sin. "God shall send them an energy of delusion, that they should believe the lie, that *all* may be damned who believed not the truth, but had pleasure in unrighteousness " (2 Thess. ii. 11, 12 ; Matt. xxiv. 24).

This awful scheme is so successful, humanly speaking, because it meets craftily the leanings of fallen man. It offers to superstition, idolatry and miracle ; to the infidel, a religion whose proofs are open to the senses ; to the lawless, permission to live as they list, and to curse the God they have so long feared, if they will but adore this deceiver. To the philanthropist and the politician is held out the prospect of a union of all mankind in one faith, and beneath one dominion. The man of imagination will be captivated by all its aspects

This religion in its main features is heathenism. It resembles Judaism in its miracles, in its King and High Priest, and in its religious mark. It borrows from Christianity its resurrection, and its Trinity in Unity. Not that the Infernal Trinity is put forth as a doctrine : but it is felt as a power, a threefold cord not soon broken.

All worship " Whose name was not written from the foundation of the world, in the book of life of the Lamb that was slain."

Herein behold individual election. Such fearful combination of power will entrap all but those chosen of God from the foundation of the earth.[1] Only those so upheld by supernatural might will stand this hour of temptation. But God's foreknowledge is complete, His power almighty, His purpose unchangeable. Against circumstances the most fearful He will maintain His own, as Jesus also assures us in His sketch of those days of darkness. Matt. xxiv. 24. But three out of many nations, peoples, and tongues, stood the similar but far inferior trial in the plains of Dura. Dan. iii.

[1] This is the true connection of the words, and not that given by our translators. Conf. xvii. 8.

But the current sweeps far more strongly now. So great is the enthusiasm on behalf of this false god, that he who slays the servants of Christ is counted as " doing God service."

Antichrist, therefore, has never yet appeared. For no form of worship has ever caught all but the elect in its meshes.

But even when licence so terrible is given to evil, the Most High has His servants; just as the 7,000 in Ahab's day stood firm.

Even during the time of the Wild Beast's fullest authority his power is limited by the Lamb of God. Whom he may devour, and whom he may not, are questions settled by " the Lamb."

Next follows a word of admonition, calling attention to the importance of the truths announced. It is a solemn call, much needed because of the powerful adverse stream. Men's salvation depends on it. The prophecy is *practical;* let men despise it as they will!

The adherents of the Lamb slain are saved : the worshippers of the slain Wild Beast are all lost.

The difference between this call and the like previous calls is worthy of notice. Before, it was said again and again—" He that *hath* an ear, let him hear what *the Spirit* saith unto the *churches.*" The believer in Jesus has an ear, and is to use it. The churches existed then; but at this period they have ceased. Now the Spirit says, " *If any* have an ear." Few, few indeed will they be. The warning will fall almost unheeded (18).

10. " If any gathereth [into] captivity,[1] he goeth into captivity. If any slayeth with the sword, he must with the sword be slain. Here is the patience and the faith of the saints."

---

[1] Here I differ from Tregelles : and read, as in the received text with the Vulgate, Griesbach, and Scholtz. The next clause proves that we should so read.

To take up arms against oppressive power seems to men always lawful. To the Jew it was permitted, and it often prospered. Abraham by war rescued Lot. The Israelites, under the Judges raised up by God, often by battle recovered their freedom, when oppressed for their sins. The Jews under the Maccabees successfully resisted the attempts of Gentile kings to introduce heathen worship, and to put down the service of Jehovah. Even believers in Jesus have fought for civil and religious liberty, and have prevailed.

Shall it not, then, be lawful to fight against one so wicked? against one in league with Satan himself? Did not Jehovah give Israel promise of victory in battle, if they went out in His name with His priests and trumpets?

But now a warning is uttered against this course. It shall not prosper. This mighty potentate has authority from God; and power is to be owned, even while held by his defiled hands. So long as the "days of vengeance" last, this Destroyer is invincible. Resistance shall only bring woe on the head of the rebel. If he collect a troop and carry off any as prisoners of war, he, too, shall be carried off a prisoner. If he take the sword and smite, he will himself be so smitten. Many, after the Wild Beast's cruelty and tyranny are felt, will rise and resist; but in vain. The saints are to be silent. The sentiment is like that of Jer. xxvii. 7–10. The nations that should refuse the yoke of the king of Babylon should be smitten of God. "Put up thy sword into its place: for all they that take the sword shall perish with the sword."

Jesus makes war at length, and overcomes. But, till He appears, the saints are to be patient. Iniquity is come to the full, and even the Jew in those days of woe is required to suffer and submit, like the members of the Church of Christ. But that submission and patience of faith are rewarded by a place in the millennial glory and reign. xx. 4.

Flight is the only permitted mode of escaping this day of temptation. And only the flight into the wilderness is successful.

The Two Witnesses resisted by miracle, and slew others; but were slain themselves. But here God calls off all from employing force. Patience and faith are the only true armour. If any would preserve their lives, they must be patient. This is, I believe, the meaning of Luke xxi. 19, " By your patience obtain ye your lives." The same is the sentiment of Matt. xxiv. 13, " He that shall endure to the end, the same shall be saved." Patience ! Let the forty-two months roll by, and the Destroyer shall be no more !

God's name is blasphemed, the saints are slain, infernal powers rule, false worship is compelled under pain of death. " Why not stand in self-defence ? why not (the flesh will say) appeal to the God of Armies ? " Because it is forbidden, because it will be unsuccessful, and will draw down the avenging bolt of judgment on the warrior who girds on his sword. The king of whom Samuel warned Israel is come. They cry to God against him, and *He " will not hear in that day "* (1 Sam. viii. 18).

There are only three lawful attitudes. (1) The resistance by *miracle*, found in the Two Witnesses alone, and related in a previous series. (2) *Flight*, chap. xii. (3) *Patience*, as here required. But so difficult is the lesson that it has to be enforced again, in the next chapter. xiv. 9-12.

Antichrist is smitten with the sword, but overcomes it in resurrection. By the sword of mortals he is not to be overcome again. It is victorious on his side. In one respect he resembles Mohammed, for he uses the sword against refusers of his worship. But Mohammed professed to be only a prophet of God. This One proclaims himself THE ONLY TRUE GOD. Mohammed wrought no miracle, Antichrist works many. Mohammed recognized Abraham's God, and compelled the seal of circumcision. Antichrist blasphemes the true God, and sets up a new mark to distinguish his own worshippers. Mohammed allowed recusants to live under tribute : not so the false Christ.

11. " And I saw another Wild Beast coming up out of the earth, and he had two horns like a lamb, and he was speaking like a dragon."

This second Wild Beast is a person, as well as the first. 1. This is the more easily proved, because he is thrice called " the False Prophet " (xvi. 13 ; xix. 20 ; xx. 10). (1) In the first case, a spirit proceeding from him collects earth to battle against God and Christ. (2) In the second, he is spoken of as the great coadjutor of the False Christ, aiding him by his miracles to deceive mankind. Thus is he identified with the Wild Beast before us, as we shall see. (3) Lastly, he is seen partaking of the awful fate of the Dragon and False Christ for ever. 2. Our Lord assigns to FALSE PROPHETS a contiguous place to FALSE CHRISTS. "For there shall arise *false Christs and false prophets*, and shall show *great signs and wonders*, insomuch that (if it were possible) they should deceive the *very elect*" (Matt. xxiv. 24 ; Mark xiii. 22. Also Matt. xxiv. 5, 11). Now here is "*the* false prophet." The Wild Beast, then, with whom he stands so closely connected, is "the false Christ." He works, as is foretold, great signs and wonders, and the elect alone escape his net. 3. As Satan or the Dragon is a person, so are the two others. 4. The Divine nature is a Trinity ; and Satan's wisdom is always to copy the divine plan, as far as is possible.

He occupies much of the position taken by the heathen priesthood ; yet he is never called a priest.

The reason of this is, that the false Christ acknowledges neither sacrifice nor atonement. The False Prophet aims, like the High Priest of the heathen, to exalt his god. He brings back idolatry. He is inferior to the first Wild Beast, in that he is not slain: hence wonder and worship do not pursue him.

The true prophet spoke in the name and by the inspiration of the true God. He bore His commands to men: he sought to exalt the name of the true God. But the False Prophet would say, "Let us go after *other gods*" (Deut. xiii. 2; xviii. 20).

The proper title, then, of the second Wild Beast is "the False Prophet." As regards the first Wild Beast he is his counsellor, trusted in all things. To sustain a kingdom, especially one of world-wide extent as this is, counsel and power are both needed: eyes to see, horns to execute. They are united by God in His kingdom. Jesus is first seen as the *Priest* amid the lamps, then as the *Prophet* opening the book, and finally as the *King* coming forth from the sky. The King, the Priest, and the Prophet, in the Hebrew state were all subject to God. In Satan's arrangement, the Prophet succeeds the King; the Priest is rejected, and with Him the true God.

He comes up out of the *earth,* or out of the *land;* in opposition to the first Wild Beast, who ascends out of the *sea.* If the sea be figuratively taken, it means the Gentiles; if the land be symbolic, it intends the Jews. If the sea mean, as in Hebrew, the west: the land intends the east. But I prefer to take it literally. The Antichrist will rise, like Jonah, out of the sea. The false prophet rises out of the earth, as Samuel. Is not this "*the man from the earth,*" the oppressor of Ps. x. 18?

What mean the "two horns like a lamb"?

1. They are not great horns of fury and strength,

like those of the warrior-beast. They are only two in number, not ten as he has: though together they make up twelve, the number of constancy. I suppose then, that as they are not horns of a Wild Beast, but horns of a lamb, that they are not *kings*, as in the other cases.

2. But there is another sense of the emblem. Jesus' *seven horns* are *seven spirits*. I understand, then, by the two horns here two spirits. One spirit the False Prophet puts within the image. The other spirit is sent by him to gather the nations to battle. He has the power of inspiration and miracle, like our Lord. But he has no eyes in his horns, and thus he works blindly the purposes of God. As the seven Spirits of God are sent forth into all the world (ver. 6) so is the False Prophet's second spirit. xvi. 13, 14.

"He was speaking as a dragon."

What is the sense of this?

1. Does it indicate *guile?* He *deceives men* by his miracles. 2 Cor. xi. 3; xix. 20. 2. Does it indicate fierceness, and bold outspoken reproach? I think it does. Satan, as he is the dragon, is the beast of power.

The union of the Lamb and Dragon indicates his hypocrisy. "The voice is Jacob's voice, the hands are Esau's;" there is entire inconsistency.

This is accordant with what Jesus says of false prophets. They have the sheep's skin, the wolf's heart. The first Wild Beast has the dragon's *throne*, the second his *speech*. Both are remarkable for their tongues. The first blasphemes God: the second threatens and reproaches men.

12 "And he exerciseth all the authority of the first Wild Beast in his presence, and causeth the earth and the dwellers in it to worship the first Wild Beast, whose wound of death was healed."

The second Wild Beast stands distinguished from the

first in this, that authority is not said to be given directly to the False Prophet. He only *exercises* the authority which is *given* to the first Wild Beast. He is so identified with the first Wild Beast, that the two may be regarded as one.

The characteristic word concerning the second Wild Beast is "he causes." It is eight times used of him.

The characteristic word concerning the first Wild Beast is—"It was given."

What means the False Prophet's exercising the authority of the False Christ before him?

It intends that he acts with the other's full knowledge and consent. His position is subordinate, and he willingly takes it. The first Wild Beast sees what he does, and so allows and approves it.

He acts in the name of the false Christ, and is fully trusted. He is worthily trusted by the first Wild Beast. Their evil union is wonderful! How unlike the spirit of our day, and of that also!

Now, each seeks to be independent and to own no superior. Not so the False Prophet. He works with heart and soul to advance his patron and leader. As the Holy Spirit is "before the throne" (i. 4; iv. 5), and fully trusted by the Father, so Satan entirely reposes on the two Wild Beasts, and the false Christ confidently rests on the devotion of his chief Minister.

It is a union, moreover, of Jew and Gentile. The king is a *Gentile*, an emperor of Rome: for to the Gentiles has God given the dominion. The False Prophet is a *Jew;* for the temple of God and the priesthood were not, together with the sovereign power, made over to the Gentiles.

"He causeth the earth to worship."

The worship of the Wild Beast, which was at first a spontaneous thing, is now reduced to system and enactment. This is the *ecclesiastical* Wild Beast, as the other is the *royal* one. The first *wars:* this employs law and force to establish *worship.*

When Mohammed was ruling at Medina, another prophet arose, by name Moseilma. He wrote to Mohammed thus : " From Moseilma the prophet of Allah to Mohammed the prophet of Allah. Come now, and let us make a partition of the world, and let half be thine, and half be mine."

How did Mohammed receive the appeal ?

" From Mohammed *the prophet* of *God* to *Moseilma* THE LIAR" (Washington Irving's *Life of Mohammed,* p. 313).

When Napoleon was at his height of power he sought to draw over to himself the Papal authority. He intended to have bestowed on it great splendour, but to have made it wholly subordinate to himself.

" Napoleon was not actuated merely by the spirit of oppression, or jealousy of a rival, and inflexible authority ; he had great views, which were well matured, on the subject of the Holy See—its more intimate connection with French government—the influence which he might acquire over its members, and the more extended base on which, by such means, he might establish his own power. He not only had no jealousy of, but he cordially approved of every institution which tended to bring the minds of men into a state of due subjection to constituted authority ; all he required was that all these institutions should be placed under his immediate influence and control. With this view he meditated the translation of the papal government to Paris ; the extinction of its temporal dominion, its entire dependence on the French empire for revenue, and the consequent subjection of its chief to his own control; but having effected this, he had no wish to impair its spiritual authority ; on the contrary, he was rather desirous to extend it. Like the Roman emperor, he was anxious to found his own authority not merely on temporal power, but religious influences ; to adorn his brows, not only with the diadem of the conqueror, but the tiara of the pontiff ; and as the forms of the Church prevented the actual union of both offices in his own person, he conceived that the next best system would be to have the Pope so situated that he should be irrevocably subjected to his control" (Alison's *Europe*, ix. 73). How like the last scheme of Satan !

What was the issue of that attempt ?

Napoleon was excommunicated by the Pope. With all his power and threatenings, the Pope could not be made to co-operate with his plans.

Who is the False Prophet ?

He is, I doubt not, one of Christ's original apostles—the traitor JUDAS ISCARIOT.

1. In proof I would observe first, that *his characteristics as here offered to our notice, were typed in his former life.*

(1) Does he here exercise all the power of the first or kingly Wild Beast ? In his betrayal of Jesus he appears as leader of the band that took Jesus. He acts out the plans of the false Jews. They hated Christ, and He sold himself to them. (2) Is the False Prophet partly like the lamb, and partly like the dragon ? Judas meets Jesus with a *kiss*, and the salutation, "Hail, teacher "—while to His enemies he says, "Hold him fast."

(2) The False Prophet presides over the worship of the devil's empire. Judas was sent forth by Christ to spread the true faith : he was selected from the disciples in general to be an apostle. He falls : and Satan now uses him to spread the false faith. God builds His kingdom of righteousness on *one rejected by men, but overcoming Satan*. Satan builds his kingdom of iniquity on two *rejected by God, and overcome by himself*. Both

take their places of power in resurrection. Judas was employed three and a half years by the true Christ: here he labours the same space of time for the false Messiah.

(3) Does the False Prophet do great wonders? Judas was gifted with miracle by our Lord: the Saviour gave him power over evil spirits: but, at his fall, *Satan entered into him*, and energized him. What person so fit for Satan's ulterior designs? Jesus sets Judas at the head of unbelievers and apostates. "But there are some of *you that believe not*. For Jesus knew from the beginning who they were *that believed not, and who should betray him*." Many disciples fall away. Jesus inquires of the twelve—Would they also do so? Peter answers with holy zeal. Our Lord replies, "Have I not chosen you twelve, and one of you is a *devil?* He *spake of Judas Iscariot* the Son of Simon: for he it was that was about to betray him, being one of the twelve" (John vi. 64, 70, 71).

(4) The False Prophet is the great patron of *idolatry*. How can that accord with the character of Judas? He as a Jew was averse to idolatry. He refused its heathen form, it is true: and yet he was blindly and devotedly covetous: and every " covetous man is an *idolater* " (Eph. v. 5).

(5) He, like the false Christ, was also a suicide. When his guilty testimony against himself was rejected with cold contempt by the chief priests—like Ahithophel, he " went and hanged himself."

But let us consider next the direct Scripture *proofs* that he is the party described in this passage.

The Scripture must be fulfilled: no jot or tittle can pass away, till all be accomplished. Now parts of two verses of Psalm cix. are by inspiration applied to Judas. After Peter had spoken of Judas' treachery, and of his violent death, he exhorts his fellow-apostles to choose by lot his successor. "For it is written in the Psalms, 'Let his habitation be desolate, and let no man dwell therein, and his bishopric (*marg.* "*office*") let another take'" (Acts i. 20). "His days were few." They were cut off by his own hand. 8. Of Judas, then, the sixth verse of the Psalm also is written. "*Set thou a wicked man over him, and let Satan stand at his right hand*" (6) Now, during his life, Jesus the Holy One was set over him. And Satan entered into Judas, but we do not read of Satan standing at his right hand. But if Judas be the False Prophet, the Man of Sin would be his superior, and Satan also. As these words have never been fulfilled in Judas, they have yet to be accomplished in him. And his being the False Prophet would fulfil it. HE therefore IS the False Prophet. Like the Two Witnesses, he is reserved for a future time. He went, it would seem, to some especial place among the lost (Acts i. 25), but is destined yet further to display his fearful enmity against God and His Christ. This gives peculiar solemnity and significance to our Lord's words concerning him. "Woe unto that man by whom the Son of Man is betrayed, *it had been good for that man, if he had not been born*" (Matt. xxvi. 24). He is the "Son of Perdition," as being born again (or rising) out of the place of doom of the lost, as well as in being finally cast into the lake of fire with the devil and the False Christ. Rev. xx. 10.

13. "And he doeth great signs, so that he maketh even fire to descend out of the heaven into the earth in the presence of men."

The signs spoken of are real wonders or miracles, as is evident from our Lord's words already quoted. False Christs were to work "*great* signs and wonders, so as to deceive, if possible, even the elect." The False Christ, the "Man of Sin" of Paul, is to make his appearance "with all power, and with signs and wonders of falsehood " (2 Thess. ii. 9). Now, as all jugglery supposes the *absence* of power, he who possesses "all power" will not rest his pretensions on mere deceits. The addition—" of falsehood "—teaches us the character of the system on behalf of which the wonders are adduced. But the same diabolic power which belongs to the Antichrist is possessed also by the False Prophet. Hence, while the prophecy of 2 Thess. ii. relates primarily to the False Christ, it bears secondarily on the False Prophet.

Scripture certainly supposes the possibility of real supernatural evidence being adduced on behalf of wickedness. He who can resist the evidence which appears at the very first glance in the history of Moses' contest with the Egyptian magicians, is impregnable to argument. He can in no way overthrow the truth, but by denying the words of Holy Writ. "Aaron cast down his rod before Pharaoh and before his servants, *and it became a serpent. Then Pharaoh also called the wise men and the sorcerers: now the magicians of Egypt they also did in like manner with their enchantments. For they cast down every man his rod,* AND THEY BECAME SERPENTS : but Aaron's rod swallowed up their rods" (Exod. vii. 10-12, 22 ; viii. 7, 18, 19).

The possibility that supernatural proofs may sustain a false religion is supposed in Deut. xiii. 1-5.

The miracles of the two true prophets come first. Those are rejected, and their persons slain : then permission is given to iniquity to step in and deceive.

One of the False Prophet's wonders is specified : either as being the most popular and convincing, or as the most frequently exhibited. It is the calling down of fire from heaven.

By this we may see, that miracle by itself is not a sufficient proof of the doctrine affirmed. God has now declared that He will allow the wicked to do miracles on behalf of falsehood.

This fire descends from heaven " in the sight of men." The expression imports the opposite to secrecy. 2 Sam. xii. 12.

These words are added, then, to show the readiness of Satan's agent to meet men's jealousy and suspicions of imposture. Few now are willing to believe miracles. Wonderful things can, to all appearance, be performed by science and collusion. Hence they call for an open field as the scene of the wonder : there must be no room for electric wires, and the feats of legerdemain. This Deceiver meets the suspicions readily, confident in his powers. Out of the open sky above him, and with plenty of witnesses around, he calls for fire ; and it descends into the earth.

Its effect is to seal up the godless for destruction. Elijah's miracle of fire turned not Israel to Jehovah. But this will turn mankind to full and entire confidence in the False Christ and his coadjutor.

14. "And he deceiveth the dwellers on the earth by means of the signs which it was given him to do before the Wild Beast; saying to the dwellers upon the earth, that they should make an image to the Wild Beast, who hath the wound of the sword and recovered."

Miracles are very powerful in producing faith in an object of worship. It is true, that where they have to encounter the natural enmity of the human mind against the true God, they are insufficient to overcome it by themselves. But, in the present case, that enmity exists not, and their native energy alone appears.

These miracles are only of God's granting. He could stay them, if He would. He permits them, He gives efficacy to the attempt to work them. He gives warning beforehand, that all who have ears may hear ;

while the unbelieving will be caught in their wicked enmity.

A beautiful confirmation of the moral meaning of "the dwellers on the earth" occurs in the Saviour's address to the Philadelphian Church. "Because thou keptest the word of my patience, I also will keep thee out of the hour of the temptation that is about to come on the whole habitable earth, to try *the dwellers on the earth*." Here they stand in contrast with believers in Jesus who expect His return, and in consequence keep themselves in the position of strangers on it.

The False Prophet's secondary and subordinate position is ever kept before us. He does the miracles "in the Wild Beast's presence," and to his glory; with design to make his worship universal. So completely subordinate is he, that although he is at first represented as a Wild Beast, yet the other is called "*the* Wild Beast."

He bids the dwellers on earth make an "IMAGE." What is meant by that?

The Greek word means a "likeness." It supposes a prototype, or a something which it is made to resemble. It agrees well with the supposition that it is a material likeness, or a statue. It accords with the belief that the Wild Beast is a man; not an empire, nor any creature of the mind.

The spirit of this false worship was in the world long before. God's previous plagues availed not to prevent men from the "worship of devils, and *idols* of gold, and silver, and copper, and stone, and wood, which neither can see, nor hear, nor walk" (ix. 20). It is remarkable that the writer does not say, "which cannot *speak*." Those are called "idols," because their figures were given by fancy. But this is an "image," because it is the likeness of a man, living and acting before them.

John, who in his first Epistle warns us of the

Antichrist and of False Prophets, adds also, "Little children, keep yourselves from *idols*"—his last words in the first Epistle general to the Church. v. 21.

Though Jesus was a man, who died and rose again, the Holy Spirit never moved any to make an image of Him. Rome, indeed, makes images of Jesus and uses them.

What light is cast upon this passage by the following words of the Creed of Pope Pius! "I most firmly assert, that the IMAGES OF CHRIST, *of the Mother of God, ever virgin*, and also of other saints may be had and retained, and that due honour and *veneration* is to be given them" (8th Article). Thus Rome paves the way for the worship of the image of the False Christ.

By the emperor's images, all of ancient days understood the statues of the imperial head of Rome. On this point Chrysostom says, "When the stamps and *images of the emperor* are sent down, and brought into a city, its rulers and multitude go out to meet them with carefulness and reverence, not honouring the tablet or the representation moulded in wax, but the standing of the emperor" (p. 384).

On the close connection between the image and the man, Basil observes, "For the *image of the emperor* is also called emperor, and not two emperors . . . because honour paid to the image passes on to the original." And again, "So he also that honours not *the image*, honours not the *person represented*" (p. 364). Athanasius of Alexandria observes, "To him, who after seeing *the image*, should wish to see the emperor also, the image might say, 'I and the emperor are one, what thou beholdest in that, thou seest in myself;' for he *who worshippeth the image, in it worshippeth the emperor : for their image is his form and likeness.*" And Anastasius of Antioch says, "When the emperor is absent, his *image is worshipped*" (p. 386). See also Sozomen, viii. 20.

This, then, is idolatry in its most revolting form. It is the offence which stands at the head of the curses of the law.

" Cursed is the man that *maketh* any graven or molten *image* " (Deut. xxvii. 15). Yet it is foretold of Israel, that in her, at God's last purging, shall be found images. Micah v. 12, 13.

The height of this idolatry was reached in the reign of Marcus Antoninus ; and of this time Julius Capitolinus says, " *It was not acccounted enough, that every stage of life, both men and women, every rank and condition, rendered the emperor divine honours ;* he was accounted profane who was not possessed of *his image in his house*, when his fortune permitted the purchase of it. Hence it happens, that even at the present day, the statues of Marcus Antoninus stand in many houses among the gods . . . nor were persons wanting who joined to affirm that he had predicted many things that actually occurred, in visions of the night. *Hence also a temple was erected to him, and priests called Antinonian, and associates, and high priests, with all those other institutes which antiquity has decreed to be due to objects of worship.*"[1]

Now it is evident that no Christian could render such worship to the emperors. This, therefore, was one of the great occasions and pretexts of persecuting the followers of Christ. " One might say that this worship, however sacrilegious and ridiculous it may appear, was regarded as a kind of imperial prerogative, inseparable from the sovereign dignity. Even to hesitate at it was a sacrilege, to refuse it a revolt, and it was one of the principal causes of the frightful persecutions of the Christians."[2]

Pliny, as has often been narrated, wrote to the emperor

---

[1] Jul. Capitol. p. 30. Hist. August. Script. Lutet. 1620 fol.
[2] Abbé G., p. 212.

Trajan, requesting to know how the Christians of Bithynia were to be treated. He then describes his conduct towards them. "An anonymous libel was exhibited with a catalogue of names of persons, who yet declared that they were not Christians then, nor ever had been; and they repeated after me an invocation of the gods, and of YOUR IMAGE (Trajan's) *which for the purpose I had ordered to be brought with the statues of the deities. They performed sacred rites with wine and frankincense, and cursed Christ;* none of which things, I am told, a real Christian can ever be compelled to do. On this account I dismissed them. Others named by an informer, first affirmed, and then denied the charge of Christianity; declaring that they had been Christians, but had ceased to be so, some three years ago, others still longer, some even twenty years ago. ALL OF THEM WORSHIPPED YOUR IMAGE, *and the statues of the gods, and also cursed Christ.*"

The compulsory worship of the Roman emperor, which stood in the earliest ages as the great obstacle to Christianity, at length reappears. It is not local, but like the Roman empire, wide as the habitable earth. The features of the last great rebellion have all appeared already, they are all connected with the brilliant period of Roman history. The worship of the emperor, the adoration of his statue and the mark, were all well known in John's day.

And lest it should appear that madness so great can never return, I give an instance close on our own times:—

"Already it (the French philosophy) was drawing people back to the most degrading superstitions; to the ceremonies of paganism. *Idols* had been forged called "Liberty," and "Equality;" France offered incense to them, and bent the knee before *idols of stone and wood*. The trunk of a tree represented *the god Mirabeau*. This trunk had been cut into the form of a statue [as ugly as the god], and had been placed on its pedestal in a square at Brest. The inauguration of it occasioned a civic feast. The National Guard arrives in great pomp; the citizens resort thither in crowds: the incense smokes, and the Marseillaise hymn is chanted. At the time fixed *for the adoration,* a voice is heard which *orders all to fall on their knees before the god* of deformity and rebellion. While the municipal officers, the justices of the peace, the tribunal, the National Guards were lying prostrate, one might have taken them for the slaves of Nebuchadnezzar, who had fallen down before his idol. . . . *In the midst of the* [*pagan*] *crowd, one man alone remains standing; he looks round, feels his indignation arise at what he sees, and cries out,* ' *Wretches, you are guilty of idolatry.*' His voice was heard notwithstanding the noise of the drums and trumpets; the [vile] adorers of the idol grew furious, and cry out, ' *Kneel down, or you must die.*' He answers, ' I will rather die; I know but one God of heaven and earth: I will not bend the knee before the idol.' " Abbé Barruel's *History of the Clergy during the French Revolution,* part ii., p. 47.

But what is the object designed by the formation of this image? It is designed to glorify Antichrist in his character as the conqueror of death. This is seen in the words which follow. It is an image " to the Wild Beast *who has the wound by the sword, and recovered.*"

How grand an affair the creation of the statue will be! What enthusiasm it will excite! The nations engage to make this wondrous work of art to glorify the Risen Benefactor of mankind! Isaiah foretells it. Isa. xli. 5–8. Men are called to frame the image, that all suspicion of collusion on the part of the False Prophet in the wonder which follows, may be excluded. It shall be no hollow statue, into which a confederate may creep, and apparently make the image to speak, while it is really dumb.

The Wild Beast is again celebrated by that which raised the original wonder and worship.

The scar of the wound still abides after its healing, a permanent proof of the reality of the death which resulted. Now not every scar would be a proof of death. But if the head were cut off, and the scar all round the neck remained, it would indeed be a proof of resurrection, when coupled with the testimony that the head had been seen severed from the body.

The False prophet *works* miracles. But the False Christ *is* the standing miracle. The resurrection of the true Christ is the test of the generation of unbelief. They refuse God's testimony, and honour not the Son of God in resurrection. But they own at once the Devil's Son as the truly risen.

15. "And it was given him to give breath to the image of the Wild Beast, in order that the image of the Wild Beast should both speak, and should cause that as many as would not worship the image of the Wild Beast should be slain."

There are two ways of translating the first clause, almost equally good. "It was given him to *give breath to the image.*" Or "*to put a spirit into the image.*"

The two are nearly related. It is the entrance of a living spirit into the image that gives it breath. It is on the permanence of the evil spirit within that the miraculous nature of the image depends.

This is the wonder. Images in general are dumb and breathless. On that the sacred writers several times insist. "The idols of the heathen are silver and gold, the work of men's hands. *They have mouths, but they speak not:* eyes have they, but they see not" (Ps. cxxxv. 15, 16). "Every founder is confounded by his graven image; for his molten image is falsehood, and there is *no breath in them*" (Jer. x. 14; li. 17).

Herein is the wonder of this image, that it has breath given to it by the False Prophet, with God's permission. Thus does Judas imitate the Creator. Gen. ii. 7; Isa. xlii. 5.

The giving breath (or spirit), then, to this mass of gold or stone is equivalent to giving it life; at least in regard of one class of vital actions, speech. Thus as the man himself is a wonder in resurrection, his image is another wonder; for it speaks.

The criticism of Bp. Middleton on the passage is very acute. "In Matthew xxvii. 50, it is said of Jesus that He dismissed *his* spirit; where the article is used before 'spirit.' The spirit which is usual for man to possess, Jesus also had. But here there is no article before 'spirit.' For it would be inconsistent with the sense; for that which was possessed already, could not now be given" (*On Greek Art*, p. 166).

Giving it breath is the miraculous *consecration* of the idol. The worshippers of idols have long been accustomed to prepare their gods for the worshippers' adoration, by peculiar rites. Of which take the following as specimens:—

The Abbé Guasco *On Statues* observes, "That the statues were prepared for worship by consecration. It was supposed that by certain rites the spirit of the god took up his abode in the image" (p. 223). A certain form was used.

"Neither do they (the Hindoos) regard the image of those gods merely in the light of instruments for elevating the mind to the conception of those supposed beings; they are simply in themselves made objects of worship. For whatever Hindoo purchases an idol in the market, or constructs one with his own hands, or has one made up under his own superintendence, it is his invariable practice to perform certain ceremonies called Pran Prátisht'ha, or *the endowment of animation*, by which he believes that its nature is changed from that of the mere materials of which it is formed, and that it *acquires not only life, but supernatural powers*" (Conder, p. 655).

The pagans of ancient date narrate certain instances in which their idols spoke. The Romish writers affirm the same of some of their images. This will be a real and undoubted instance of what they less credibly pretend to.

But its speech is not its only marvel. It causes all refusers of worship to be put to death. What is meant by causing them to be slain is not very apparent. It may signify one of two things. Either—

1. That it passes sentence on them, and bids its executioners carry the sentence into effect.

2. Or itself effects their death, by a sword in its hand, or by treading them underfoot. Thus, in the Inquisition at Madrid, there was an image of the Virgin, which, on the touching of a spring, opened its arms and cut to pieces with a thousand knives the unfortunate being whom it embraced.

There will be some, then, who will worship neither the Wild Beast nor his living statue. The elect of God will stand firm against the terrors presented, and be slain. In the dread alternative, "Adore or die!" they will choose the latter. Men before this prodigy worshipped idols: how surely, then, will they bow before this strong delusion!

16. "And he causeth all, the small and the great, and the rich and the poor, and the free and the slave, that they should give themselves a mark upon their right hand, or upon their forehead."

With idolatry has constantly been connected some mark on the person. It will be so in this day when idolatry is come to the full. It is made imperative on all. No exception is allowed : the small and the great are alike beneath it.

Is the mark literal ? 1. Yes, if it will make good sense in the connection. It does. 2. It is a mark which men give themselves. It is imprinted on the *body*. How can it be any other than a literal mark ? 3. It is something which is to be shown in the market, among the poorest and most uneducated. They can understand an object appealing to the sight. But how should all be able to discover an intellectual mark ?

Under the Old Testament God required His people Israel to mark themselves on the body with the mark of circumcision. He forbade any other.

Under the New Testament His mark was a spiritual one ; the seal of the Holy Ghost, or the supernatural gifts of the Spirit.

The High Priest bore on his forehead the name of Jehovah inscribed in gold. The priests when consecrated were touched with blood, on the right ear and right thumb. Exod. xxix. 20. And in this book of the Apocalypse we have three similar examples, all teaching the spiritual significance of the act. The elect of the twelve tribes receive a mark on their foreheads. vii. 1. The elect 144,000, gathered from the nations of earth into the heavenlies, are marked on the forehead likewise. xiv. 1. The general body of the risen inhabitants of the New Jerusalem wear the name of God on their foreheads for ever. xxii. 4. These three examples show that the mark discovers at once to every eye whose servant the person is. This Satan imitates. The marked forehead tells to heaven and earth—" That is a worshipper of the False Christ."

The Greek word used means a literal and physical mark, a permanent sign made generally by pressure.

This was the old adjunct of *idolatry*, forbidden by the law, no less than the manufacture of idols. Amidst like prohibitions occur the words, " Ye shall not make any *cutting in your flesh for the dead*, NOR PRINT ANY MARKS UPON YOU : I am the Lord " (Lev. xix. 28). With idolatry restored come the old appendages of its worship.

Jehovah ordained to Abraham and his seed a visible mark in the flesh, as the sign that he was *their God*. Gen. xvii. 11, 13. This is the sacrament of the False God. With new doctrines come new rites. The new wine needs new skins to hold it.

Men are to give themselves the mark. Each is to get it done for himself, in his own way. It may be produced as the sailors produce their marks, by the puncture of needles ; or by the pressure of a stamp, as a seal. Men give it themselves ; the False Prophet could not with his own hand mark many millions. He does not desire to do it ; the act shall be their own.

(1) The reasons of this enactment are obvious. *Both soul and body are to be devoted to the False Christ :* the soul, by worship ; the body, by the mark. An angel seals God's people : these seal themselves. This imprint protects men from Antichrist's wrath : the other, from God's.

(2) The visible mark *excludes all concealment*. There can be none who inwardly dissent and disapprove, while they say nothing. In Ahab's day seven thousand were concealed. Now all shall wear their religious badge on the surface. The simple act of worship of the False Christ, or of his statue, leaves no mark behind it. Some might untruly assert that they had worshipped ; and present false certificates of such an assertion. But here is a further test. Have they the mark ? Will they give themselves this imprint in the flesh ?

The mark is probably a representation, more or less perfect, *of the scar of the wound of death left on the False*

Christ.[1] Thus they identify themselves with the resurrection of the Usurper. Thus, too, the Image and the Mark stand easily connected. The image, we may be sure, will wear the *mark* or scar of the wound. On the resurrection turns the worship, and thus the mark is connected with the worship. So there have been Romish " saints " (so called) who have gloried in inflicting on themselves, or in *miraculously* possessing, the five *wounds of Christ*: two of which would, of course, be in the *hands*. And as Jesus' rites of baptism and the Supper are connected with His death and resurrection, so this " sacrament " of the False Christ stands associated with his death and resurrection.

Hindooism is the system which comes the nearest to the misbelief of Antichristianity—in its idolatry, its abstinence from flesh-meat, and its marks on the skin.

The places on which are to be set these marks are next defined for us. This proves them to be literal. The stamp is to be either on the " right hand," or on " the forehead."

Both these parts of the body are generally uncovered and exposed to view: and thus they are the fittest to give testimony to all. God demands confession with the mouth, after faith with the heart. The confession of Antichrist will be a visible one.

Maundrell observes, p. 75 :—

"The next morning nothing extraordinary passed: which gave many of the pilgrims leisure to have their *arms marked with the usual ensigns of Jerusalem*. The

---

[1] Of this idea a remarkable confirmation is given by Herodotus. "When the king of the Scythians dies, they make a procession. On this procession every tribe, when it receives the corpse, imitates the example which is first set by the royal Scythians: every man chops off a piece of his ear, crops his hair close, *makes a cut all round his arm,* lacerates his forehead and his nose, and thrusts an arrow through his left hand." Herod. iv. 71.

artists who undertake the operation do it in this manner. They have stamps of wood of any figure that you desire; which they first print off upon your arm, with powder of charcoal. Then taking two very fine needles tied closely together, and dipping them often like to a pen in a certain ink, compounded as I was informed of gunpowder and ox-gall, they make with them small punctures all along the lines of the figures which they have printed; and then, washing the part in wine, conclude the work."

This gives us a good idea of the future process foretold in the text.

When the mighty enthusiasm of the Crusades seized on the nations of Europe, the soldiers of the expedition signalized themselves by an outward mark.

" His (Christ's) *cross* is the symbol of your salvation; wear it a red, a bloody cross, as an *external mark* on your *breasts* or shoulders, as a *pledge of your sacred and irrevocable engagement* " (Gibbon, vol. vi. 8, *First Crusade*).

"The *cross*, which was commonly sewed on the garment, in cloth or silk, was *by some zealots inscribed on their skins; a hot iron or indelible liquor was applied to perpetuate the mark ;* and a crafty monk, who showed the miraculous impression of his *breast*, was repaid with the popular veneration and the richest benefices of Palestine " (Gibbon, vi. 17).

The practice of wearing indelible figures on the body has always been an institute of idolatry. Philo Judæus says, "Now some devote themselves to the service of idols, confessing it by letters; not letters written on paper, as is customary on slaves, but imprinting the marks on their bodies with a red-hot iron, *for an indelible memorial* " (Op. ii. 220). Cited by Greswell.

Herodotus, speaking of the temple of Hercules in Egypt, observes :—

"If a slave runs away from his master, and taking sanctuary at this shrine *gives himself up to the god*, and receives certain *sacred marks upon his person*, whoever his master may be, he cannot lay hand on him" (Rawlinson's *Herod.*, ii. 113).

And Grotius observes that, in the reign of Trajan, the magicians suggested to that emperor that he should forbid all clubs or colleges, except those which met under the patronage of some one of the pagan divinities. And as it is natural to men to love societies, the consequence of this edict was that there was scarcely one in the Roman empire who had not his name enrolled in some society, dedicated to one or other of the gods. Moreover, those who were enrolled in these companies, at the time of enrolment, received some mark upon their persons; that is, either the emblem of some god, or the name, either expressed in letters, or concealed under some number expressive of it. Those who belonged to none of these companies or clubs were, for that very reason, suspected of being Christians.

The same practice obtains at the present day among the Hindoos, and most fully illustrates the text.

"After performing their religious ablutions, the Hindoos *receive on their forehead the mark* either of Vishnoo or Sivà; this mark, affixed by a Brahmin, varies in form and colour, according to the sect they profess: the one being horizontal, the other perpendicular; it is made from a composition of sandal-wood, turmeric, and cow-dung: the latter is deemed peculiarly sacred" (Forbes's *Oriental Memoirs*, vol. i., p. 286).

In the third book of Maccabees an account is given of the impious attempt of Ptolemy Philopater to enter the Holy of Holies at Jerusalem. He was smitten by God, and prevented from fulfilling his design. But on his return to Egypt, his hatred against the Jews and Jehovah displayed itself.

He commanded that the Jews of Alexandria should be deprived of their ancient privileges of citizenship, and enrolled in the inferior class ; and that when they came to be enrolled, AN IVY-LEAF, EMBLEM OF THE GOD BACCHUS, SHOULD BE IMPRINTED ON THEIR BODIES WITH A HOT IRON ; *and that if any obstinately resisted he should be put to death.* This edict caused some hundreds of Jews to apostatize.

In Mussulman countries similar laws have been enacted against Christians. " Abdallah commanded the Christians to shave their faces, and caused both Jews and Christians to be marked in the hand " (Picart's *Ceremonies,* i. 177).

17. " And that none might be able to buy or sell, except he hath the mark, the name of the Wild Beast, or the number of his name."

See in this verse the proof that the mark is literal and abiding, or at least continually renewed. Ere the bargain is struck in the market—" Show me your hand ! " or, " Uncover your forehead ! " and the transaction stands good, if the mark appear. Each is made a spy on the other. The dealings of commerce are made illegal without this.

How strongly, then, is this misbelief fastened on the world's neck ! All need to buy, if not to sell. The mark is the licence required in order to buy or sell. Thus religion is brought into the common concerns of life. 'Tis planned with devilish wisdom, and fearfully will it succeed. It is designed, that none may be *able* to buy or sell, save the devotees of the False Christ.

The former verse spoke of the *member* whereon the sign was to be impressed. Two were allowed : the forehead or right hand. The forehead, as the most conspicuous, would be used by the enthusiastic : the hand by females, as less detrimental to beauty.

There is a further choice, as regards the *imprint*

itself. It may be either a (1) *mark*, the meaning of which has been considered. It may be also a (2) *name*, or a (3) *number*.

These are all really equivalent, real surrenders of the point at issue. Each says—" Antichrist is *God*, and he is *my* God."

All that is said of the False Christ is easily explainable from its counterpart in the system of the true Christ. The true Christ is a person: and His name is Jesus. The False Christ is a person, and his name is Nero Cæsar. The number contains the name of "a man," not of a series of men. So, in the next chapter, the 144,000 bear the names of the Father, and of the Son, on their foreheads. xiv. 1.

" The number of his name " is the third alternative. Anciently, each letter had a corresponding number. The A was equivalent to one, the B to two, and so on. Take, then, any name, and set against each letter of it its corresponding number. Then reckon up the whole amount, and you have the number of the name. The sum total of the figures is, as it were, an epitome of the name.

Jesus has a *mark* or *marks*, in the wounds of His crucifixion; or in the cross as the implement of His death. He has a *name* given by the angel—" Jesus, for He shall save His people from their sins." He has a *number* to His name, and very peculiar it is; for while His rival's is 666, His is 888.

$$\begin{array}{rl} I & ..\ 10 \\ H & ..\ 8 \\ \Sigma & ..\ 200 \\ O & ..\ 70 \\ \Upsilon & ..\ 400 \\ \Sigma & ..\ 200 \\ \hline \text{Jesus} = & 888 \end{array}$$

18. "Here is wisdom. He that hath understanding let him count the number of the Wild Beast; for it is the number of a man, and his number is six hundred sixty and six."

"Here is wisdom." That is, the problem is a difficult one. It is this—" Given the sum of the figures which are the equivalents of the letters, to find the name." As if God had said by Isaiah—" The number of the name of Messiah is 888. Find out the name from this datum."

Many words possessing significance may be found out answering to this number. But few fulfil the conditions. Few, if any, are *proper names of men*. "Apostatees," "Romiith," "Titan," and so on, are not names of men. "Evanthes," "Kosroes," "Latinus," are names of men. But none of this name was ever *King of Rome*.

Wisdom, then, and the knowledge of God's purposes will be shown, by the discovery of the true name. Some indeed have despised this key, as unworthy. But it is wisdom with God; whatever the worldly wise, whose wisdom is contemptible with God, may say. The astronomer who computes from a portion of its orbit the whole circuit and distance of a comet, is justly reckoned a man of understanding. But no comet ever so powerfully affected our system of worlds, as this dread Deceiver will affect mankind. The *perdition of souls unnumbered is bound up with him*.

1. "It is the number of a man."[1]

[1] One has observed, that the words τὸ μέγα θηρίον [The Great Wild Beast] contain the number 666.

T	300	M	40	Θ	9
O	70	E	5	H	8
		Γ	3	P	100
		A	1	I	10
				O	70
				N	50

666

1. It is not the number of a people, or of a state of men, as "the Latin kingdom" (*Greek*). It is no title of honour, but the name of an individual.

2. "His number is 666."

This is the second point, the sum total of the letters. It is one number *thrice* repeated, and so the more easily retained in the memory. It is remarkable, that it should be so uniform in its modern dress, or in our adopted *Arabic* numerals; as they were not the mode of numeration anciently adopted. In Latin numerals the number is no less singular. It is DCLXVI, or six letters, one of each of the numeral letters. Some have remarked, also, on the peculiarity of the three Greek letters which signify the number : χ represents the cross, ξ the crooked serpent, $\chi\tau$ is a contraction for Christ. The serpent has entered the Christ, and the False Christ is before us.

On the commerce of Israel under Solomon the number 666 is impressed. Just so many were the talents of gold which accrued to the king in a year. 1 Kings x. 14. The same number touches commerce in Revelation. None may buy or sell, without that number, or its equivalent.

What name, then, of a Roman emperor is it, which will fulfil the conditions given ?

NERO ! In the later Syriac, John is said to have been banished to Patmos by "Nero Cæsar." That is a mistake; but it shows us that the two names were usually coupled together, when designating that cruel monarch.

A few cases may be presented here in proof that not the word "Nero" alone, but "Nero Cæsar" was his proper and formal designation.

We may observe, first, that Cæsar is added in the New Testament to the name of Claudius, the emperor who preceded Nero. Agabus foretold the "great dearth throughout all the world, which came to pass in the days of *Claudius Cæsar*" (Acts xi. 28). Again, "There went out a decree from *Cæsar Augustus*, that all the world should be taxed" (Luke ii. 1). "Now in the fifteenth year of the reign of *Tiberius Cæsar*" (Luke iii. 1). These are the only three names of individual emperors given in the New Testament.

(1) Nero visited Greece, and obtained crowns there. When crowned, he made this proclamation by his own lips—"*Nero Cæsar* is victor in such a combat." Crevier's *Roman Emperors*, iv. p. 304.

(2) In the Apocryphal Acts of Peter and Paul, Simon the magician is introduced. "Simon said, Hear, *Cæsar Nero*, that thou mayest know that these are false men, and that I am sent from heaven" (v. 70, 71).

(3) On the temple of Doosh is an inscription: "To the fortune of the Lord Emperor *Cæsar Nero*."

(4) "The 19th year of the emperor *Cæsar Nero*." Hoskin's *Visit to the Great Oasis of the Lybian Desert*, pp. 321, 338.

(5) Professor Benary remarks, "that in the Talmud and other Rabbinical writings the name of Nero, in the form נרון קסר [Nero Cæsar] often occurs" (M. Stuart on *The Apoc.*, p. 788.

This name in Hebrew makes, by computation, 666.

Ne	.. ב	.. 50	Kai	.. ק	.. 100
R	.. ר	.. 200	Sa	.. ס	.. 60
O	.. ו	.. 6	R	.. ר	.. 200
N	.. נ	.. 50			

$N\epsilon\rho\omega\nu = 306$ $K\alpha\iota\sigma\alpha\rho = 360 = 666$

In this there are several further points worthy of notice. The sum is made up of *seven* letters, the significant number of the Apocalypse; and those seven are again divided into *four* and *three*. Two letters are repeated, ב and ר:

and make four of the same name. Three are not repeated. The first word begins and ends with the same letter. Also the four last according to the Hebrew system of numeration, and in the order of the Hebrew alphabet, are alternately consecutive, thus:—

נ = 50. ס = 60. N and S are consecutive, both in numeral and alphabetic order.

ק = 100. ר = 200. K and R are so also.

This name accounts also for another remarkable circumstance. Ignatius tells us that some read 616 as the true number; instead of 666. Now if the Roman Christians believed Nero to be the person indicated, they were very likely to read the name in Roman style without the final N—Nero—which the Greeks used in expressing that emperor's name. But if they so read it, then the omission of the second N would cause the subtraction of the number 50: and the total would be, 666 minus 50, or 616.

This discovery was made by Prof. Benary, a German, of Berlin, as M. Stuart observes; and has been adopted by Moses Stuart as the true answer, though on such grounds as entirely to destroy its value. If Nero be the person designated, he must arise from the dead to fulfil the prophecy. That Stuart rejects as incredible and absurd; and, of course, the plenary inspiration of the passage and of the book is destroyed.

Nero *is* the person, and he will rise to fulfil the word. What fitter person for the task could Satan select? But we shall notice some further confirmatory proofs, when we come to chapter xvii.

Most remarkable were many of the occurrences of his reign. His personal sins were portentous: probably beyond all former example.

In his government, he was the first to persecute the Christians, and he burnt them to death to illuminate his gardens at night. Before him were brought, it is supposed, two of God's especial witnesses in that day—Peter and Paul: and by him they were slain, as the two coming witnesses will be.

By him was the armament sent, which resulted in the desolation of Palestine, and the conflagration and spoiling of the temple of God.

The expectations of the heathen concerning him were very remarkable.

"Some of the astrologers promised him, *after his forlorn condition, the government of the East, and some expressly the kingdom of Jerusalem.* But the greater part flattered him *with assurances of being restored to his former fortune*" (Suetonius, Nero, chap. xl.).

The expectations of the Christians of that day were very similar. Of these Moses Stuart has given the following interesting account:—

"The expectation of Nero's reviviscence was cherished by some, and feared by others, even some centuries after his assassination.

"The expectation that Nero was to reappear and renew his former fortune, was plainly cherished by this most distant and barbarous people.

"Tacitus has given us several hints respecting the same phenomena to which Suetonius has adverted. Thus (*Hist.* ii. 8) he says:—'About the same time, [A.U.C. 823, A.D. 71], Achaia and Asia were terrified without any good reason (false), as if Nero were coming; reports being various respecting his death, and many on this account imagining and believing that he was still alive.' It should be observed here, that the very region in which John lived (Asia) is here designated by Tacitus as one that was filled with alarm at the apprehended reappearance of Nero. This was three years after his death; and it therefore shows how strongly the fear, that what the soothsayers had predicted respecting Nero would come to pass, had taken

A A

hold of the public mind, and how extensively rumours of such a nature concerning him had been spread and believed.

"We have already seen, as related by Suetonius, that some ten years later than this, another Pseudo-Nero appeared among the Parthians. Within this small number of years, then, we have two phenomena of this kind in Parthia, and two in Asia Minor; the latter two in A.D. 71 and 79. These, in addition to the like phenomena at Rome, show that a deep persuasion in respect to Nero's reappearance must have existed in the minds of the community at large, in order that it could be possible for impostors to play such a part with so much success.

"Thus much for the general opinion and feelings of the *heathen* world respecting Nero. It lies upon the face of the matter, that there was a widespread and a kind of undefined hope or fear (according to the political feelings of individuals), that Nero, after his reported and apparent death, would reappear to the terror and confusion of his enemies.

"Nor was this feeling confined to the heathen subjects of the empire. *Christians* far and near participated in it more or less. The evidences of this are ample.

"In *Lib.* viii. p. 714, seq., is another passage representing Nero as coming from Asia with the indignation of a destroyer. Black blood follows the steps of the great monster. 'The dog has produced a lion which will devour the flock.' (Nero's assassins have turned him from a dog into a lion, i.e., they have infuriated him by reason of their assault.) 'But his sceptre shall be taken away, and he shall go down to Hades' (comp. Rev. xvii. 8, 11). The vaticination above quoted was probably written in the time of Aurelius, about A.D. 170–180, and it follows in the track of all the preceding passages which assume the return of Nero from the East, and his devastations of Rome in conjunction with allied kings. Other passages of the like tenor the reader may find in *Lib.* viii. p. 688, seq.; and again in *Lib.* viii. p. 693, seq.; *Ibid.* p. 715, seq. I have indeed quoted but a small part of what is said of Nero. The perusal of the whole must be left to the reader, and it will overwhelm him with conviction that there was spread far and wide abroad for a long time after Nero's death, but specially for the first fifteen or twenty years, an anxious fear and even trembling expectation of Nero's reappearance, who would then pervade his former dominions like an incarnate demon, and from motives of revenge lay them waste with fire and sword.

"How widely diffused and deeply rooted in the minds of the great community such a fear or expectation respecting Nero was, is manifest enough from its permanence among the *churches*, even centuries after the death of Nero. Thus in the brief commentary of Victorinus Patavionensis (§ 303) he expressly names *Nero* as the beast who received the deadly wound, and was to be raised up again to be the scourge of the Jews; in *Biblioth. Max.* iii. p. 420, D.

"Down to so late a period as the close of the third century, we find clear traces of the opinion still widely diffused in the Church, that Nero was yet to return. Thus Sulpicius Severus, the ecclesiastical historian of that period, *Hist. Sac.* ii. 28: 'Nero . . . the basest of all men and even of monsters, was well worthy of being the first persecutor. I know not whether he may be the last, since it is the current opinion of many that he is yet to come as Antichrist.' Again in ii. 29: 'It is uncertain whether he (Nero) destroyed himself. Whence it is believed that although he may have pierced himself with a sword, yet he was saved by the cure of his wound; in accordance with that which is written,

Rev. xiii. 3. "And his deadly wound was healed." At the close of the age (Gospel age) he is to be sent again, that he may exercise the mystery of iniquity.' In *Dial.* ii. c. 14, where the same writer celebrates the virtues of Martimus as a most eminent saint, Sulpicius states that he inquired of him respecting the *end of the world*. Martimus replied that 'Nero and Antichrist must first come ; and that Nero would reign in the West over ten subjugated kings, and that persecution would be carried on by him in order that the idols of the heathen might be worshipped.'

"Finally, in his work *De Civit, Dei,* xx. 19, Augustine says : 'What means the declaration that the mystery of iniquity already works ? Some suppose this to be spoken of the Roman emperor, and therefore Paul did not speak in plain words, because he would not incur the charge of calumny for having spoken evil of the Roman emperor ; although he always expected that what he had said would be understood as applying to Nero, whose doings already appeared like to those of Antichrist. Hence it was that some suspected *that he would rise from the dead as Antichrist*. Others supposed he was not actually slain, but had only withdrawn himself that he might seem to be dead, and that he was concealed, while living in the vigour of his age, and when he was supposed to be extinct, until in his time he would be revealed (2 Thess. ii. 6), and restored to his kingdom.'

"Past all doubt, then, many of the early churches, far and near, believed or feared a reappearance of Nero in the same character which he exhibited in early life. Whence did they derive this belief or fear ? Either from the vaticination of the astrologers, as recorded by Suetonius, and repeated by others, or else through the medium of the text before us " (pp. 769–774, Stuart's *Commentary on the Apocalypse*).

Victorinus, on the *Apocalypse*, says: "Now one of the heads was slain to death, and the wound of his death was healed." He means Nero. For it is well known, "that while cavalry sent by the senate was in pursuit of him, he cut his own throat. *Him therefore raised from the dead God will send as king, a king worthy of the Jews, and such a Messiah as they deserve*" (Lardner, *Works*, 1788, iii. 291).

"Whence many of our party think, that Nero will be Antichrist, because of his excessive fierceness, and baseness" (Jerom., on Dan. xi. 27).

To this may be added an extract from Commodianus given by Bunsen, on *Hippolytus*, iv. 519. Of this Bunsen says, "Commodianus gives a general outline of his views as to the destruction of Pagan Rome. *Nero is to conquer it, coming from the great river Euphrates, according to the popular belief of the time,* known to us, by the Sibylline verses of the latter part of the first century." The following is a translation of the close of the extract.

"Out of the infernal regions he returns, who was once plucked out of his kingdom, and after having been long preserved, he is known by his former body. Now we learn that he is Nero the ancient, who formerly put to death Peter and Paul in the city (of Rome). He returns again at the very close of the age out of his place of concealment, who was reserved for this end. Men wonder that this man known to them should be hated. When he appears, they esteem him to be like a God."

Against this view Hengstenberg objects—"That Nero slew himself, but the False Christ is to receive a mortal blow from another, as the true Christ did." This objection is easily solved. The one who has yet to be assassinated is the seventh head; and Nero's soul revives the slain body of the seventh forerunner of Antichrist.

In conclusion, Satan and the two Wild Beasts form what has been well called "THE INFERNAL TRINITY." Satan takes the place of the Father, bestowing his kingdom.

(1) The Dragon with seven heads and ten horns resembles God on his throne, girt with the seven torches of fire and the twenty-four thrones of the elders.

(2) The one called by pre-eminence—"*the* Wild Beast"—occupies the place of the Son, in death and resurrection as Jesus. As possessed of the seven heads and ten horns he resembles the Lamb with seven horns and seven eyes. As the earth and the angels worship Christ, so do the nations and dwellers on the earth adore him. As Jesus wars against the world in arms and overcomes; so does he war against the saints, and prevails.

(3) This last Wild Beast witnesses to the former one, as the Holy Spirit testifies to the Son. As the angel with the seal of God marks the 144,000 of Israel, so does he demand a mark of his own.

Jesus is both the *Lion* and the *Lamb*. These diverse aspects of the Son of God Satan divides between his two Wild Beasts. The Antichrist has the *mouth* of the *lion*: the false prophet the *horns* of the *lamb*. But the Wild Beast, possessed of but two horns without eyes, cannot withstand the Lamb with *seven* horns and *seven eyes*.

Six creatures are combined in the three. The first is the Dragon. The second unites the panther, the bear, and the lion. The last possesses resemblance to both the lamb and the dragon.

The first Wild Beast cannot stand alone. The False Prophet is called forth as Satan's *one witness* against God's *two true prophets and witnesses*.

The Holy Spirit has two aspects: as related to the *throne*, He is seven lighted torches: as related to the *Lamb*, he is seven horns, and seven eyes. Thus the second monster, as related to the other two, is one of the three wild beasts. In reference to the first Wild Beast he is his adviser and counsellor. The Holy Spirit, after Jesus' resurrection, descends from above: this Wild Beast, the opposite to the Dove, comes up from the earth. The Holy Spirit was to predict the future. John xvi. 13. This deceiver is a prophet. The Holy Spirit brought *words of inspiration*, and *works of miracle*. This false prophet has two horns like a lamb. The Holy Spirit gives life to the Two Witnesses: this, his imitator, gives life to an idol.

CHAPTER XIV

1. "And I saw and behold the Lamb standing on the Mount Zion, and with him an hundred and forty-four thousand, having his name and his Father's name written on their foreheads."

HE stands "on the Mount Zion." What are we to understand by this?

1. Not the earthly Zion. For, as chapter xi. has shown us, the Holy City of earth is given up to Gentile foes. When Jesus is first seen by Israel and the Gentiles, He is in the air, not upon the earth. Matt. xxiv. 23-27. A battle must be fought, ere earthly Zion yields.

2. As the temple of the Old Covenant was situated close to Mount Zion below, so the temple of the New Covenant is seated close to the corresponding heavenly Mount. Jerusalem in the Apocalypse never is the old Jerusalem: nor is the Zion the earthly one. iii. 12; xxi. 2, 10.

3. The 144,000 are "redeemed *from* the earth," therefore they are not then on it.

4. The first-fruits were to be brought into the Lord's house. Exod. xxiii. 19; xxxiv. 26. But that is now on high: the temple below is only the outer court.

5. The Redeemer, when He afterwards reaps the earth, comes from heaven in a cloud, and the harvest of the earth is lifted from earth to Him.

6. The Great Multitude, it is allowed, are in heaven; when there they are "before the throne." So are these.

7. The possession of heaven has been contested with Satan, and he has been defeated. Jesus keeps the heaven as the basis of His operations, till He goes forth to battle.

The 144,000 are some of those who kept the word of the Saviour's patience, and so are preserved from the hour of temptation on earth, according to the promise. iii. 10. They are never said to have come into contact or collision with the Wild Beast. They are beyond the enemy's reach, standing in resurrection, where Christ Himself does.

They are but a small body in comparison with the saved : those are a multitude whom none can number. The ears of a wheat-sheaf may be numbered, but who could count those of a harvest ?

" And with Him an hundred and forty-four thousand." The word "*with*" is emphatic: these are Jesus' special companions. Of the Great Multitude it is said only, that they stood " *before* the Lamb." These are bridesmen. "They that were ready went in *with* Him to the marriage " (Matt. xxv. 10).

Are they the same body as the 144,000 of chapter vii. ?

No ! (1) The remnant of Israel stands connected with Jesus there, as the " angel " only.

(2) These are the heavenly elect. As, in the final city, twelve names appear from Israel's worthies ; and twelve appear also from the Gospel ; so are there two kinds of first-fruits ; one of the earthlies, one of the heavenlies. The sheaf of each is of the same number. But the earthly elect are redeemed from *the twelve tribes of Israel :* the heavenly first-fruits are redeemed " from *the earth,*" " from *among men.*" [1] These are

---

[1] Have the two words ' πανήγυρις and ἐκκλησία of the first-born ' (Hebrews xii.) any reference to such a distinction ?

first-born of the heavens. The first-born of the Old Covenant were peculiarly redeemed ; and then all Israel was brought out into freedom. These are no longer tenants of earth, but risen from the dead : they are a part of the symbolic or mystic Man-child, who has been caught up to the throne of God.

(3) There is no article prefixed to the number ; as would naturally have been the case, if they were the same body as those made known to us in chapter vii. The 144,000 of that chapter have to pass through earth's trials : these are conquerors.

(4) The elect of Israel are *sealed* with the "seal of *the living God*" only. They are only "servants" "of God." These are companions of "the Lamb"; they have *written* on their foreheads, the name of the Son and of the Father. They know God in His New Testament character then, and are therefore His sons ; for as many as so receive Christ and His testimony, are sons. John i. 12.

(5) The song these sing is "new." It is not, then, one of the style of Israel : for to Israel belong the old things. Here the last are first.

(6) The life of the 144,000 was spent upon a principle unknown to the Law, and contrary to its blessing. "There shall nothing cast their young, nor be barren in thy land" (Exod. xxiii. 26 ; Deut. vii. 14 ; 1 Sam. ii. 5 ; Ps. cxiii. 9).

(7) Jesus speaks of His "Father," to the churches only. i. 6 ; ii. 27 ; iii. 5, 21. As, then, this title of God is used, some of the Church are intended.

Those names of God confessed on earth are now their glory on high. The false Trinity of the Dragon, the Wild Beast, and the False Prophet have been displayed in the previous chapter : the True Trinity appears in this antagonistic chapter. Here we have the names of the Father and the Son : the Holy Spirit speaks in ver.

13. The mark set on these advances them to glory; the mark of the Wild Beast stamps for damnation.

> 2. "And I heard a voice out of the heaven as the voice of many waters, and as the voice of great thunder; and the voice which I heard was as of harp-singers harping with their harps."

The sound heard is evidently that of the 144,000. Their voices produce the sound like many waters; their harps, the sound like loud thunder. Antichrist is to be smitten amidst the joy of harps. Isa. xxx. 32.

> 3. "And they are singing, as it were, a new song before the throne, and before the four living creatures, and the elders; and none could learn the song except the hundred and forty-four thousand who had been redeemed from the earth."

These sing "before the elders." The new Levites have supplanted the old; we hear no more of the elders' harps; yet the elders are not jealous. The elders sang in worship *to* the Lamb; these are joined *with* him.

"None could learn the song."

'Tis unlike that of Moses then. Moses was to write and *teach* his, as a witness *against* Israel. Deut. xxxi. 19, 22. This song is a peculiar glory to those who use it. As there is a new name of reward to be known by none but the receiver; so is there a song to be sung and to be known only by a special company.

"The hundred and forty-four thousand had been redeemed from the earth."

All the saved are redeemed; but these are the firstborn, peculiarly ransomed. The Lamb of the Passover and the first-born of the Church are set close together. The Paschal Lamb of the New Covenant lives after his sacrifice. Under the Old Testament the *forehead* of the *house* was marked with blood: here the forehead of the *person* of the first-born is inscribed.

4 "These are they who were not defiled with women: for they are virgins."

How are these words to be understood?

They are commonly explained as *figurative*. "They were untainted by the corrupt influences of that evil day, and especially are they free from the *idolatries*, that will be one of its most grievous marks. I do not mean idolatry in a vague or virtual sense, as we are warned against covetousness, which is such morally; but *positive, literal idolatry*" (Kelly).

(1) Do "women," then, ever mean idols? Why must "women" here be taken in a bad sense? Why should we not translate it—" Were not defiled with *wives*"? No scholar will deny that this is a very common sense. "They all brought us on our way with *wives* (women) and children" (Acts xxi. 5; i. 14). Where the law speaks of defilement, does it take women in a bad sense? Lev. xv.

"This passage," says Barnes, "cannot be adduced in favour of celibacy . . . for the thing that is specified is, that they were not '*defiled* with women,' and a lawful connection of the sexes, such as marriage, is *not* defilement." Certainly not, morally. Heb. xiii. 4, which he cites, proves that clearly: but he rests on but *half* the inspired statement here made.

If we read in any book—" These were never defiled with *wine* or *strong drink*"—the words might be susceptible of two senses; according as we supposed them to be written by a Christian in general, or by a teetotaller. In the one case we should understand that they had never been intoxicated; in the other, that the persons named had never tasted either wine or spirits. But all our doubt would be in an instant put to flight, if following on the words above given, we read—" For they are total abstainers." This would limit the words to the teetotal sense. Thus in the sacred text before us, there is added—"For they are virgins." This excludes the chastity of the married.

The word "women" does not mean something evil. 'Tis women literally taken; not the One Emblematic Woman of chapter xvii. That is a mystery, and it is explained: these are literally taken, and not explained. Nay, the description we are considering is given in the *explanation*.

(2) The excellence supposed is too wide to be the reason of the place given to this special body. What! Are none but these 144,000 guiltless of idolatry? Have not countless thousands, both of Jews and Gentiles, been free from idolatry? Is it not stated as the reason for the descent of God's plagues on the earth, that the inhabitants repented not of their idolatrous worship? ix. 20. But there the accusation is given in literal words. "They repented not of the works of their hands, that they should not worship devils, and *idols of gold*." Must not all the saved be free from idolatry? "*Idolaters* and all liars shall have their part in the lake which burneth with fire and brimstone, which is the second death" (xxi. 8; xxii. 15).

Why, then, should not the description be taken *literally?*

1. We assume as our first principle that the literal is the true meaning of any text, if, when it is so taken, it yields a good sense. Here it fits admirably, both with the Apocalypse and with other portions of Scripture, as we shall see.

2. The four sentences which follow upon ver. 3, give us the *explanation* of the vision which John saw. He first describes the special body he beheld, and then tells us the grounds on which they attained to their post of glory. The words, therefore, are to be taken *literally*. Three explanatory statements are given concerning them, each beginning with, "These are they."

The first description of this body is fundamental, or characteristic: the 144,000 are unlike the earth. Its course is, at the *worst*, fornication (ix. 21), at the *best*, "marrying and giving in marriage" (Matt. xxiv. 38). Antichrist refuses marriage, and so do his crew. Dan. xi. 37; 1 Tim. iv. 3. Jesus sanctions it, as lawful. John ii.

But He has also a company, who, in hope of especial glory in the kingdom, abstain from it. Matt. xix. 11, 12. Similarly, 1 Cor. vii. 1, 6–8, 25–28, 32–35.

Fornication is a crime which may be committed by members of the *Church*, to be visited with especial wrath. Rev. ii. 14, 15, 20–22. But these not merely abstain from what is evil; they refrain from what is lawful. 'Tis a life-long abstinence, and this accounts for the small number of them: it accounts, too, for the exactness of the number. None receive the saying, save "they to whom *it is given.*" It is given only to 144,000, even of the Church, or disciples of Christ.

They "were not defiled." The past tense looks back on their life on earth as now completed. The next words in the present, define their abiding state. "For they *are* virgins."

Again, I say, these words must exclude the married: the married may have chastity, but not virginity. It is remarkable that the word "virgins" is made to describe males: the pronoun is in the masculine, in all three cases.

This body is not Jewish.

"Thou (Israel) shalt be blessed above all people: there shall not be *male or female barren among you,* or among your cattle" (Deut. vii. 14). Virginity was a calamity, then. Judges xi. 37.

Jesus annulled the law's teaching concerning marriage and divorce, and set up His own law instead: withal assuring His disciples, that there was a special height to be attained by some favoured ones. A holiness of the flesh, as well as of the *spirit* (1 Cor. vii. 34), is recognized even under the gospel.

It is the peculiarity of the standing of these that gives occasion to their peculiar song : in their virginity they resemble Christ Himself, who was never wed. They are most truly pilgrims, and most resemble the angels. Luke xx. 35, 36. The Old Covenant had its Nazarites, who abstained from wine, and for a limited interval ; here is a greater abstinence, and for the whole of life. A special command was given to Israel, when the nation was to draw nigh to God for a day at the holy Mount of Sinai. Exod. xx. 15. These are set for a permanency, on the better mount of the New Covenant, on a similar, but stronger basis.

" These are they who follow the Lamb whithersoever he goeth."

Jesus is about to move to and fro through His vast domain, as the Ruler of Creation. Heaven and earth are both His : and as He passes from spot to spot, these are His companions. The celestial and the terrestrial together make up His kingdom. 1 Cor. xv. 40, 41. While, then, some of those who enjoy the first resurrection will be confined to the heaven, or to the earth, or be sent on errands away from Christ, these will be His perpetual attendants.

Their self-denial was separateness to God : it was matter of intention on their part. It was not, however, as Rome would make it, a *vow*. That is quite unsuited to a dispensation which, unlike the Law, declares the powerlessness of the flesh. It gives them a blessed place in the millennial kingdom, but not a *right to eternal life :* in not seeing this distinction lay the error of " the Fathers."

" These were redeemed from men, as first-fruits to God and to the Lamb. 5. And in their mouth was found no lie; they are blameless."

They are not taken from the twelve tribes of Israel, but from men in general : therefore they are not the same body as the first 144,000. While the whole of Israel was redeemed out of Egypt, there were some peculiarly ransomed. " Israel is my son, *my first-born*," said Jehovah to Pharaoh. Exod. iv. 22. Yet there were first-born of the first-born.

These are " first-fruits to God and to the Lamb."
All believers in Jesus are " a kind of first-fruits of God's creatures " (James i. 18). But these are first-fruits of those first-fruits. Paul makes mention of " Epenetus, *the first-fruits of Achaia unto Christ* " (Rom. xvi. 5). And again, " Ye know the house of Stephanas, that it is *the first-fruits of Achaia* " (1 Cor. xvi. 15). These are not first-fruits of any special country, but " of the earth," and of mankind at large.

Jesus is " the first-fruits " in resurrection. 1 Cor. xv. So are these also first-fruits to Him as risen. This risen body are first-fruits of the first resurrection, in which they " marry not, nor are given in marriage." That they do not represent all the saved, or all the Church, is clear from the figure made use of. The *first-fruits* is not the *harvest*. The harvest is cut, when dead to the earth : the virginity of these showed their earlier deadness to earth. That is the scope of Paul's words, when commending the state to believers. 1 Cor. vii. 32.

These are especial witnesses of the Church's calling, as not of the earth, but *out* of it into heaven. They are of Christ's spirit, and so are fitly made His companions. The present revelation is also appropriately made to John—the unmarried apostle.

" But your view condemns marriage." By no means : that is lawful and good, this is better. But not all are called to it. " Each hath his proper gift of God, one after this manner, and another after that " (1 Cor. vii. 7).

"But so saying, you exclude Peter and the married apostles from the kingdom." By no means. They are excluded only from this special song, and from moving about with our Lord in the kingdom; but not from the kingdom altogether.

The 144,000 are truthful, and in this respect like Christ. Isa. liii. 9. " He did no violence, *neither was any deceit in His mouth.*" " Who did no sin, *neither was guile found in His mouth* " (1 Peter ii. 22).

The word spoken of them is employed to describe Christ Himself. Christ as " a Lamb *without blemish* and without spot " (1 Peter i. 19). Thus the outward and inward purity meet: they are undefiled in spirit, as in body. The previously named virginity, then, is not spiritual; for that is asserted afterwards. It is, as we again conclude, to be taken literally.

First Angelic Message.

6. "And I saw another angel flying in the mid-heaven, having the everlasting Gospel to proclaim over those seated on the earth, and over every nation, and tribe, and tongue, and people. 7. Saying, with a great voice, 'Fear God, and give Him glory, for the hour of His judgment is come: and worship Him that made the heaven, and the earth, and sea, and fountains of waters.'"

An angel is now the preacher. This takes us back to the days of the Judges, or of Genesis, or of Exodus. "The word spoken by *angels* was steadfast " (Heb. ii. 2).

Here is a change in God's plans, necessitated by the wickedness of man, and the power of Satan. Even inspired men, possessed of supernatural powers of miracle in order to defend themselves, have been slain by the energy of Satan. xi. An angel, therefore, who cannot be slain, is sent. He does not tarry on his errand : he does not settle on the earth : he speeds through the air on his errand, within sight and hearing of men. It is a brief proclamation which can be delivered while he is on the wing. He has his proclamation to deliver "*over*" those who are settled on the earth. This is a peculiar preposition never used with the word to "preach," or "herald," save on this occasion. It points to the peculiarity of the times just mentioned. It notices that the herald occupies a place never before held : he is suspended over the heads of those whom he addresses.

His message is the "everlasting Gospel." The word "Gospel" is used in Scripture in a far wider sense than we employ it now. The Gospel here mentioned is not our Gospel. Is it "the Gospel *of the kingdom*," preached by our Lord ? Matt. iv. 23 ; ix. 35. The Gospel proclaimed to us is "the Gospel *of the Grace of God*" (Acts xx. 24).

That God is the Creator was true in the past, and will be for ever in the future. It is true, too, that from man the Creator justly calls for fear and worship. But neither of these truths is strictly "good news." Much less is the tidings of judgment at hand : that troubled very greatly the Thessalonian Christians. There seems, then, to be an implied reference to the millennial kingdom, as coming after the judgments. And accordingly, Jesus opens the kingdom to the sheep, as blessed of His Father. Those enjoy, not the thousand years alone, but "go away into life everlasting."

"The earth also is defiled under the inhabitants thereof ; because they have transgressed the laws, changed the ordinance, broken the *everlasting covenant*" (Isa. xxiv. 5).

The classes addressed by the angel are two ; divided by the insertion of the preposition before each. The first is "those settled on the earth." If I mistake not, this means those inhabitants of Christendom who are merely nominal Christians : they are secularists, seeking their portion here. This living for earth, and being all alive to its good things, is becoming more and more the characteristic of the unconverted, and is even taught by ministers of the Gospel.

But the message extends beyond them. It reaches every aggregate of mankind beyond the bounds of Christendom.

It is designed as a warning against the Wild Beast, and his blasphemous pretensions. We read of the Wild Beast, that " authority was given him over every *tribe, and people, and tongue, and nation,*" and that "*all that dwell on the earth* shall worship him " (xiii. 7, 8). Here the same two classes reappear ; and, as they both are in danger, both are warned of his usurpation.

Of the heathen nations, many credit the witness of the angel, and are saved by a simple faith in the *Creator*, producing the good works approved by our Lord in His parable of the Sheep and Goats. Matt. xxv. Such are spared at Jesus' return, and become the nations of the millennial earth.

The angel cries, as he flies, " with loud voice," that all may hear.

But what is the tenor of his heralding ?

It is a call to the worship of God as Creator, on the ground of fear : for He is about to smite His foes.

This is not *our* Gospel, or anything like it. Strange, that any should imagine the words fulfilled in any missionary enterprises of our day ! No wonder that the Apocalypse is not understood, when differences, so great as those that part our Gospel from this, are not noticed.

" But does not Paul pronounce even an angel from heaven accursed, if he preach any other Gospel than that which the Apostle proclaims in the Galatians ? "

That is true, as long as the dispensation lasts : as long as the churches are recognized, as long as the lamps are tended by the Priest in the heavenly sanctuary. " If any preach any other gospel *unto you*, than that ye received, let him be accursed " (Gal. i. 8).

" For the hour of his judgment is come."

This is not true, while the Gospel of the grace of God goes forth with His sanction. " Now is the *accepted time, now* is the *day of salvation.*" Jesus at Nazareth tells us that He came to herald " the *acceptable year* of the Lord." Isa. lxi. 1 ; Luke iv. 17–19.

But that is now past : and next comes, both in the prophet's words, and answerably in fact, " THE DAY OF VENGEANCE OF OUR GOD " (Isa. lxi. 2).

It was the proclamation of this word, while the Gospel lasted, which produced such dismay at Thessalonica among the saints who feared God. A forged letter had taught them, that " the Day of the Lord "—the great and *very terrible*—" had set in " (*Greek*). Some one had by his calculations arrived at the same idea (λόγου). It had been further backed by the utterance of a false spirit. 2 Thess. ii. 2. Believers were troubled. Paul comforts them, by telling them that it was not true. The hope of the watchful saint is, that he shall be taken to the presence of Jesus, ere that awful day set in. At length it has begun. And now fear is the appropriate temper of men ; as before peace, love, and joy were the suited answer to the grace of the Gospel.

We may gather from the angel's calls that men in general believe either that there is no God or that He does not concern Himself with the deeds of men. The angel, therefore, declares that earth has a Creator, an intelligent and holy ruler, who is about to smite sin with destruction.

"The *hour* of his judgment is come."

This is more than "the *day* of his judgment." It bespeaks a brief, definite time of wrath, close at hand. It refers to the Bowls (vials) and the Vintage. It is about to descend on those who worship any other God than the Creator. The appeal bears alike against atheism and polytheism: "There *is* a God, the Creator: there is but *one* God."

"Worship him that made the heaven."

What a state must earth be in, when this primary truth needs to be asserted! The Jew worships a God of miracle: the Christian worships God as redeeming, Father, Son, and Spirit. In that day, the first elements of truth are called in question, and denied; yet the wicked prosper.

Those who acknowledge and obey this message become "the sheep" of Matt. xxv., "the fearers of God," of Rev. xi. 18.

It would seem that this message of the angel must precede the Wild Beast's claims. It would come in vain after any have rendered him worship.

From this appeal of the angel we learn, that the sense of "heaven, earth, and sea, and fountains," is literal. God claims worship as Creator of these things: therefore the literal objects of nature are intended. These four last great features of creation appear in the plagues which follow, and in the order here named. There, too, therefore, they are literal. God shows Himself the God of heaven, by making the sun to scorch. He proves Himself God of the earth, by the earthquake: God of the sea and fountains, by turning them into blood (chap. xvi.).

Second Angelic Message.

8. " And another angel followed, saying, ' Fallen is Babylon the Great ; who hath made all the nations drink of the wine of the wrath of her fornication.' "

This is the true reading of the verse, as may be seen by consulting Tregelles' text. Some authorities would add " a second," before " angel."

This is the first mention of Babylon, which occupies so conspicuous a place toward the close of the book. She is characterized by greatness : her greatness is the result of her fornication. For the Babylon now spoken of is the mystic Babylon of chapter xvii. This is clear if we look at xvii. 1, 2.

This angelic message, then, will be greatly needed, to damp the triumphant feelings, and still the 'words of Antichrist and his party over her fall. Rome is by them identified with Christ ; and her destruction with the ruin of His cause, and the proof of His powerlessness.

Beside the false view of the reason of Rome's final burning, therefore, God sets the true. This guilty city's fall is owing, not to the almightiness of the False Christ, nor is it effected despite God's power to hinder ; *but by God's counsel, and as the result of her sin.* She is the firstfruits of the Vintage, as the 144,000 are of the Harvest. She is smitten as the consequence of God's wrath against idolatry ; judgment begins on that which bears God's name.

No angelic warning is sent to her. She has already had many from Christ, and has refused them.

The two great evils of the last days are :

1. Infidelity, amounting oft to atheism.
2. Idolatry, either Christianized, or openly pagan.

Rome falls ; Satan and his vicegerent, with his associate kings, burn her. She is no longer adapted to his altered position. While he was on high working secretly, she was adapted to carry out his plans of deceiving the nations. But now that he is cast out of heaven, and openly working to compel men to damnable sin, she stands in his way, and is destroyed. She is "*Satan's masterpiece*," during *the time of Mystery* only. He has a more awful one yet.

Her greatness arises from leaving Christ's principles and commands, and substituting worldly ones for them. She is a Church after the world's heart, and the world gladly gives her greatness. He who will follow Christ will be mean, insignificant, small, in the world's eye.

His disciples, who would be great in the coming kingdom, are directed to abase themselves, to become fools in the world's eye, to be least of all, servants of all, and to be like the little child. Matt. xx. 25, 26 ; Phil. ii. 5–10.

She is the strongest exhibition of the Saviour's parable of the Mustard Seed—forbidden and worldly greatness, springing out of His unworldly and self-denying commands. The calling her "Babylon THE GREAT," is therefore one of the counts of her indictment : she has wedded the world, and receives of the greatness of its kings.

"Who hath made all the nations drink of the wine of the wrath of her fornication."

This is the second great charge against her. It contains the reason of her destruction. She has acted as Satan's agent in deceiving the nations, instead of Christ's servant in enlightening and purifying them.

The expression, "the wine of wrath of her fornication," is a difficult one.

I suppose, then, that we should understand it thus.

1. Her "*fornication*" is her worldliness. She mixes together earthly and heavenly principles : the Law and the Gospel, the Church and the world. When the

Church coveted the glory and riches of the world, it allowed the unconverted to enter its pale; then it cried up the sacraments, and made them necessary to the salvation of infants: then Christianity became a religion of rites and ceremonies. The true priesthood, which consists of all believers (Rev. i. 6), was set aside for a sacrificing and atoning priesthood of man's introduction. Then came the worship of the martyrs and idolatry. Rome set herself as the patron of idolatry, against the Iconoclast emperors of the East.

2. "The *wine* of her fornication" is the doctrine arising out of, or procured by, her worldliness. Her false doctrine exhilarates and intoxicates nations, wherever it is imbibed. It allows a man to enjoy the world, while unconverted and unforgiven, and yet it assures him of salvation at last.

But "the wine of fornication" is also "the wine of wrath;" it is not "the cup of salvation," but it exposes her to the wrath of God. The fallen churches of Asia have in general lost even the semblance of a Church: but Rome boasts to be "the mother and mistress of all churches." She is not only evil in herself, but by example and authority the cause of evil in others: hence her doom, at the hands of justice. Her wine of fornication becomes wine of wrath to herself, and to the nations.

From these words I conclude that a strong enthusiasm in favour of Romanism will prevail before the great crisis comes. Vain are all hopes of triumph over Rome, through the nations receiving the pure Gospel of Jesus. While some out of every nation will be gathered by the Gospel, yet the nations in general will prefer the sweet and deadly wine of Rome. 2 Tim. iv. 3, 4.

Wine influences the imagination. Vain visions of joy, and peace, and happiness, will flit before the eyes of the nations, to be dissipated by the sad realities of priestly intolerance, rapacity, and bloodshed. After the world's fit of drunkenness is over, Satan's last snare is spread. Rome paves the way for infidelity by her superstitions—her immorality, doctrinal and practical—and her persecution. But if Rome's idolatry be so awful, and so visited by God, how much more that of the Wild Beast ? Rome's sin is the worship of others beside God and Christ : Antichrist denies and blasphemes the true God. The Great Harlot corrupts what is good : Antichrist denies it.

Third Angelic Message.

9. "And another angel (the third) followed them, saying with great voice :—

"If any worshippeth the Wild Beast and his image, and takes (his) mark on his forehead or on his hand, 10, he shall both drink of the wine of the wrath of God, the mixed unmixed in the cup of his indignation ; and he shall be tormented in fire and brimstone in the presence of holy angels, and in the presence of the Lamb ; 11, and the smoke of their torment goeth up for ever and ever, and they have no rest day or night who worship the Wild Beast and his image, and whoever takes the mark of his name.

12. "Here is the patience of the saints, who keep the commands of God, and the faith of Jesus."

The three angels flying in mid-heaven, each with a distinct message to men on earth, present words of most momentous practical import for those of that day. This angel's soul is aroused to give his warning with the utmost energy ; hence he speaks "with loud voice." That is not said of the tidings concerning Babylon : for that was merely explanatory of the cause of her fall, lest any should be stumbled at it. But on obedience to this cry hangs eternal life, or everlasting damnation.

After Babylon is destroyed the Wild Beast rises into his full powers ; and God's energetic warning against him, as then at his height of dominion, goes forth.

The idolatry of the nominal Christian Church is paving the way for the idolatry of Antichrist. Imagine a council of Christian bishops expressing themselves thus concerning images! "We who believe in the one God in three Persons, embrace images with veneration. Be those who do otherwise accursed! Be those who refuse this, expelled the Church! . . . We take under our care, and venerate images. We smite with a curse those who will not. Whoever shall adduce passages of Scripture concerning 'idols' as if applying to images worthy to be adored, let them be accursed! Accursed be they who call images—the fit objects of our worship—'idols.' Accursed be they who say that Christians worship images as their gods! Accursed be they who knowingly commune at the Lord's Supper with the enemies of images worthy to be adored, or who deface or dishonour images!" Yet thus spake the second Council of Nice. *Ancient Christianity*, ii. 219. Of this decree Rome has ever stood as the defender.

The Wild Beast's power and blasphemous claims do not arrive at their fullness till after the last traces of even corrupted Christianity are swept away. Hence Rev. xvii. 6 is fulfilled, ere this angel is sent.

No doubt a perception of the true meaning of the Wild Beast and his image made the worship of the emperors a thing so awful and horrible to the Christians. It was something which in their day had not arrived at its dreadful association with Satan's bodily presence and miracle, as it will hereafter; but they saw by this means how abhorred such adoration was by the true God. Indeed, the believers in Jesus arose just in time to prevent the Roman empire from becoming that putrid corpse, on which the judgments of God in destruction should be poured.

We have seen the *crime :* next follows the *punishment* decreed of God.

This is twofold : (1) present, and (2) future. Even in this life the criminal will experience the wrath of the offended God of heaven. The bowls of wrath are the expressions of the Divine displeasure against the Wild Beast and his votaries. Earth is plagued because of them, and they suffer, both directly and indirectly. This is described here figuratively : it is drinking of God's wine of wrath. 'Tis undiluted, 'tis mixed of many potent ingredients. They *must* drink it. This is wine of woe, untempered with consolation. But though not mixed with water, powerful drugs are added to increase its potency. Prov. xxiii. 30 ; Isa. v. 22 ; Ps. lxxiv. 8.

God is a jealous God. The glory which is His due cannot with impunity be given by any man to another : that is high treason indeed. Hence the plagues which follow are not the chastisements of a father, not punishments seeking the amendment of the ungodly, but the destroying justice of an offended God.

The experience of the vengeance of the Most High in this life is but the beginning of sorrows : the gloomy portal to everlasting woe. The first death introduces to the second.

Of the woe of the lost the doom of Sodom and Gomorrah was a type. Four things are here taught us concerning it. (1) Its character. (2) Its instruments. (3) Its duration. (4) Its executioners.

(1) In its character, it is "torment;" exquisite bodily pain, designedly inflicted.

(2) Its instruments are "fire," which causes grievous anguish to the limbs ; and "sulphur," which produces so oppressive and stifling a sensation, when but a very small proportion of its fumes is mingled with the air.

(3) The duration of the torment is "day and night," "for ever and ever." Not "for the age" of the millennium only, but for ages without end. They are ever

burning sacrifices on the altar of vengeance. Fumes go up from these sufferers of fire, as of old from the sin-offering, and from the guilty cities of Sodom and Gomorrah. Gen. xix. 28. They continue to ascend as long as justice continues to be an attribute of the Lord.

After the resurrection, sleep belongs neither to the lost nor to the saved. The saved will not need it ; for the body of weakness, the animal body, is shaken off. The lost may not enjoy it. How strange the sinner's infatuation, that after all this solemn warning of the eternity of hell-torments he will still go on coolly provoking God to cut him down, and cast him into the fire !

In these verses the eternity of future punishment is clearly asserted. This is one of the passages which will ever resist the critical rack of those who teach annihilation of the wicked, or the cessation of their woe. For while the penalty is connected with a special class of guilt, belonging to one period of earth's history alone, it yet applies in its principles to all the lost. One spot, " the lake of fire and brimstone," is destined for all. xix. 20 ; xx. 10, 14, 15.

Their torment is inflicted " in the presence of holy angels." Evil angels are cast into the lake, and suffer with the lost. Matt. xxv. 31.

(4) But probably there is a stronger meaning here. It may intend, that the angels will act as *executioners* of the wrath of the true Christ whom these denied and blasphemed.

Their torment goes on " in the presence of the Lamb." His mercy is past. The False God and his worshippers are punished in the presence of the Son of God. " The Lamb " is Jesus' *eternal* title : it is therefore no mere millennial punishment. Luke xix. 27.

Many expect the world's conversion at the fall of Babylon But the third angel shows us that evil then rears its head, in a degree of daring impiety never realized before.

"Here is the patience of the saints."

These words, repeated from xiii. 10, are designed to refer us back to that point. There, resistance to this dread potentate by force of arms is forbid : God has given this Terrible One authority over all the earth in this hour of darkness. Iniquity is to prosper, to try the hearts of men. Then rise "the days of vengeance," patient endurance alone is left then to the saints. Luke xxi. 19. They must "resist unto blood, striving against sin." "Worship, or be slain!" is the cry. They may not fight : they are patient sheep, ready for the slaughter. But they know the limit of these awful days : they have but to wait 1,260 days, and "this tyranny will be overpast."

They stand between two fires. "Of two evils, choose the least." Which is the most to be feared ? the Wild Beast or Jehovah ? The horrors of the damned are sketched, to make men feel how beyond all measure dreadful are the threats of the Great I Am. Luke xii. 4, 5.

Whoever stands out against this blaspheming usurper is a saint : as whosoever receives him is a sinner of deepest dye. Saints are of two classes.

Some keep "the commands of God." When the commands of Satan and of Antichrist are in full force, they refuse to obey. This class will include the Jews who hold to the Law and the Prophets, and the Gentiles who obey the proclamation of the first angel.

But some keep "the faith of Jesus." This may mean either their belief in Jesus, or the articles of faith delivered by Jesus. Either way it seems to prove, that there are those once members of the Church of Christ still on the earth ; as well as Jewish believers in Jesus, occupying the position taken by the twelve apostles, ere the Holy Ghost descended at Pentecost.

THE DEAD IN CHRIST.

13. "And I heard a voice out of the heaven saying, 'Write, blessed are the dead who die in the Lord from henceforth.' 'Yea,' said the Spirit, 'that they may rest from their labours, for their works follow with them.'"

"Blessed are the dead who die in the Lord from henceforth." So consolatory are these words, that there is a natural tendency to apply them to the saints of Christ who have fallen asleep in Him, ever since these words were penned. But that is not legitimate. The saying comes in chronologically: it follows the third angel's message. It applies to the times when the Wild Beast is raging and destroying Christ's people.

The expression "from henceforth," is to be construed with "The dead who die in the Lord."[1] Blessed are those who die in the Lord, after the persecution of Antichrist has begun. The dead are blessed in that day as conquerers of the Wild Beast.

The blessed ones here spoken of seem to be the company for whose death the martyred ones of former ages were directed to wait. vi. 11. Then the full vengeance for blood shed was to descend. Accordingly it is now poured out in the seven bowls (vials).

What is the standing of those here described ? It is not Jewish. They are "in the Lord," as opposed to "in Adam," or "in the flesh." Phil. 16.

---

[1] Ἀπάρτι qualifies the word which it adjoins. Matt. xxvi. 29, 64; John i. 52. So in a similar case. If a verb with νῦν follows, νῦν, and not μακάριος, qualifies the verb. Luke vi. 21, 25; xvi. 15. The contrary is seen Luke i. 48. The ἀπάρτι qualifying μακάριος were out of place. Luke ii. 29; v. 10; xii. 52; 2 Cor. v. 16.

They have "the faith of Jesus." They are "*in* the Lord," and so are His *members*. Eph. v. 30. This is spoken of none but those of the Church, as I suppose. "Those also which *sleep in Jesus* (or are put to sleep by Jesus) will God bring with him." "The *dead in Christ* shall first rise" (1 Thess. iv. 14, 16). So also, "They which are fallen asleep *in Christ* are perished" (1 Cor. xv. 18). There is no doubt that these last are words used to describe those of the Church. Why should we doubt it of those in the Apocalypse?

The peculiar blessedness of these peculiarly-tried saints seems to be that their resurrection follows almost instantly on their departure. The Harvest is the next scene of God's acting, and it embraces them.

Generally the life of a Christian should be one of service, as a labourer in his Father's vineyard. But in those days, service for Christ is peculiarly hazardous and oppressive. They wrestle with "*wild beasts*" in a more fearful sense than Paul at Ephesus. 1 Cor. xv. In the mention of their labours, their sufferings, of course, must be taken into the account. Earth is full of agitation and suffering; they by death enter rest.

The mention of "the Spirit" here (not "the seven Spirits of God," as in chapters iv. and v.) seems to me to confirm strongly the reference to those of the Church. Thus is the Holy Ghost spoken of in the seven epistles.

"He that hath an ear, let him hear what *the Spirit* saith unto the churches" (ii. 7). So also Rev. xxii. 16, 17. "I Jesus have sent mine angel to testify unto you these things in the churches. I am the root and the offspring of David, and the bright and morning star. And *the Spirit* and the bride say, 'Come.'"

Their services and sufferings have not been unnoticed, and will not be forgot. Reward is, of course, implied: they are seeds sown, and will be sheaves borne in their joyful bosoms at last.

These deeds of grace go not *before* them, to procure their acceptance with God; but *follow after*, as the result of their reception on the ground of Another's righteousness.

The Harvest.

14. "And I saw, and behold a white cloud, and on the cloud one like a Son of Man, having on his head a golden crown, and in his hand a sharp sickle. And another angel came out of the temple shouting with great voice to him that sat upon the cloud, 15. 'Send thy sickle and reap; for the hour to reap is come, for the harvest of the earth is dried up.' 16. And the sitter on the cloud cast his sickle on the earth, and the earth was reaped."

Antichrist is the mighty sun of persecution (Matt. xiii. 6) which develops alike the produce of field and of vineyard. The good seed and the tares both run quickly to ripeness.

The Saviour appears on a "cloud."

This is "the Presence" of Christ [1] so often mentioned. It is first seen (in chapter x.) in connection with *Israel*, then in connection with the rapture of the saints as in Matt. xxiv. 30, 31, 37–41.

The cloud is the Saviour's heavenly car: the Harvest is gathered to the heavenly garner where the Son of Man is. 'Tis no common reaping or reaper. The reapers of earth are seldom either rich, or conquerors, or crowned with any crown; much less with a crown of gold.

The cloud portends wrath to earth: but Jesus is the bow in the cloud, and portends blessing. Instead of a bow He bears the curved sickle.

While Jesus is the Lamb in reference to the First-fruits, He is "the Son of Man" in reference to the Harvest. We see that His action is taking out of the earth those who have been abiding on it during the day of Tribulation. But the First-fruits are on high already.

The sitter on the cloud is "like a Son of Man."

[1] Παρουσία. Wrongly translated "coming."

It is in this aspect that Jesus presented Himself at first to the churches. i. 13. He was then in the sanctuary: they were lamps recognized there. But they kept not their standing: the extinguished lights are removed. The watchful saints have been caught up ere this: but disciples of Jesus, remnants of the churches, remain, and disciples have been raised from amidst Israel.

Jesus began to act as the sower as soon as Israel's unbelief rose to blasphemy against the Holy Ghost. He *sowed* in His character of Son of Man.

He *reaps also* as the Son of Man. Matt. xiii. 39. Who so worthy to reap as He who sowed? 'Tis just that He should. He reaps, too, *what* He sowed; not tares, but the good seed, the children of the kingdom.

He is on the cloud, invisible as yet to the earth: for the rapture of His saints is a secret thing to the world.

He has in His hand a "sharp sickle."

Swift is to be the reaping; and in order to its speed, the sickle is sharp. The cutting of the wheat is not in wrath, but in joy. It is observable in this connection, that the angel in speaking to the reaper says only, "Send thy sickle"; while to the grape-gatherer he says, "Send thy *sharp* sickle."

The sickle is a mystery, or a symbol. It means angels; as the Saviour has said, and as we shall see.

The command to the Crowned Reaper to begin His work comes from the temple. An angel brings the message; evidently from the throne of the God of the temple. Jesus is the Father's servant: God has constituted Himself judge of the seasons. Acts i. 7. The Son Himself is excluded from this knowledge: He waits the word, that tells of the complete ripeness of the saints. As Son of Man He calls not *Himself*, but His *Father*, "Lord of the harvest" (Matt. ix. 38). He now receives orders to complete, as the Reaper, the work which He began as the Sower.

What is the HARVEST?

Some would make it an act of wrath on the wicked: as Hengstenberg, Darby, etc. But no!

1. Harvest is a good thing, the subject of the first promise on the renewed earth. Gen. viii. 22.

2. Wheat or corn, the result of harvest, is good. Its colour is good: the fields " are white already to harvest " (John iv. 35).

3. This harvest includes the remnants of the churches, and Jewish disciples. The previous verse spoke of the slain for Christ; but there are those not slain. Their case is now considered, and their destiny fulfilled. Harvest is the result of seed sown. Now the seed sown by the Great Sower is the Word of God. The result is " children of the kingdom."

The Gospels give one testimony concerning the meaning of harvest; showing that it relates to the saving effects of the Gospel on the elect.

(1) Matt. iii. 12.

(2) " The harvest (as a period) is *the end of the age* " ($αἰών$). "*The reapers are angels.*" "*The Son of Man shall send His angels.*" "Then the righteous shall shine forth as the sun in the kingdom of their Father " (Matt. xiii. 37-43).

(3) He teaches us that the crop as a whole would go through several stages. " But when the fruit is brought forth, *immediately He sendeth the sickle, because the harvest is come* " (Mark iv. 26-29). (*Greek.*)

" But," it may be said, " you have omitted to notice the ' chaff ' and the ' tares,' which form no inconspicuous portion of some of the passages quoted."

The answer is obvious. The case of the tares is considered, and met in THE VINTAGE. The evil ones of the latter day are no longer nominal Christians, but blaspheming antichrists.

The Woman's seed furnishes the *Harvest*. The Dragon's seed furnishes the *Vintage*. The Harvest is the judicial disposal of the remnant of the churches of Christ, or of Christ's words sown to them: as the Harlot's judgment is the judicial result to the centre of the false Church.

4. But even if these proofs failed, we have a very near and clear proof of the meaning of the Harvest in its relation to the First-fruits. Such as the Firstfruits are, such is the harvest. Rom. xi. 16; Lev. xxiii. 10. The First-fruits are holy: so is the harvest. The First-fruits are garnered by mercy in heaven, after being taken out of the earth: so is it with the harvest. The First-fruits are of one kind only: so is the harvest. The First-fruits are of no Jewish standing: neither, then, is the Harvest.

"*Send* thy sickle and reap," are the words of the angel. This is the literal rendering of the Greek, and the word used is designed to lead our thoughts to such passages as—" The Son of Man shall *send His angels*, and they shall gather out of His kingdom all stumblingblocks." σκάνδαλα. Matt. xiii. 41. " Immediately He *sendeth* the sickle, because the harvest is come " (Mark iv. 29). "The reapers are angels."

The seeming inappropriateness of the word "send" arises out of its real adaptation to the antitype, or the angels sent.

As the Son of Man is here the reaper, angels are the mystic sickle; a great unity, instrumental to the Harvest's ingathering.

" For the harvest of the earth is dried up."

The word denoting the ripeness of the wheat is peculiar, and ought to be retained. The season of harvest is usually the hottest of the year. Answerably 'tis now a time of the fiercest persecution. The heat dries up the juices of the wheat-stalk, and then it is perfectly fit for the sickle.

"Drying up" is usually a word indicative of something evil; for it is ordinarily applied to succulent and perennial plants and trees. "Let no fruit," says Jesus to the barren fig-tree, "grow on thee henceforward for ever. And presently the fig tree *dried up*" [ἐξηράνθη, as here]. Matt. xxi. 19. The fig-tree represents Israel, long to abide on the earth, and to draw its nutriment from it. But wheat is only an annual herb, and answers to Christians who are strangers and sojourners on earth. The dryness of the wheat is its perfection, and marks its time of *removal* near. Thus the Christian's *deadness to the earth* is indicative of his removal to the prepared mansions. How different the hold of earth which is taken by the roots of the wheat, and by the fig-tree respectively. But this deadness to earth is as yet far from being characteristic of Jesus' disciples: it will require severe persecution to effect it. It was thus with Israel. Lest they should become Egyptianized, persecution was sent: and that was hottest, just as their removal drew on.

At this point a difficulty will arise in the minds of some. "The Harvest occurs here as part of a chronological series. In the order of nature the harvest precedes the vintage. And the Harvest itself only comes after the persecutions of the Wild Beast, and just ere his reign comes to an end. How, then (it may be said), can you speak of the rapture of the saints as a something which may take place at any moment, and which requires not the previous completion of any series of events?" The force of this is so strongly felt, that Darby and others refuse to own the Harvest to be an act of blessing to the holy. But the proofs before given show that this does refer to disciples of Jesus, though they do not now occupy a complete church-standing, as in the opening of the book. The true answer to the difficulty is, that there is more than one rapture. One has already preceded in this series : the Man-child was caught up ere the Great Tribulation for the earth had begun. But, at the first rapture, some disciples were unready. They were left behind to pass through the Great Tribulation. They were not accounted worthy to escape that scene of sin and trouble. But they have now withstood the seductions and compulsion of wickedness, and their trial is over. The heat of persecution has been blessed to wean them from the love of this present evil world.

" And the sitter on the cloud cast his sickle on the earth, and the earth was reaped."

" The earth was reaped."

The suddenness and ease of the work are denoted by the brevity of the description. This reaper *sits*, and the work is done by a cast of the sickle. The saints are passive in this divine harvesting.

Many are the reapers ; and their powers are far beyond those of men.

The Vintage.

17. " And another angel came out of the temple that is in heaven, he also having a sharp sickle. 18. And another angel came out from the altar, who hath authority over its fire, and he called with great voice to him that had the sharp sickle, saying— ' Send thy sharp sickle, and gather the clusters of the vine of the earth, for her grapes are fully ripe.' 19. And the angel cast his sickle into the earth, and gathered the vine of the earth, and cast (the grapes) into the great winepress of the wrath of God. 20. And the winepress was trodden outside the city, and blood came out of the winepress up to the horse's bridles, for one thousand six hundred furlongs."

Earth at length presents the spectacle of the ripeness of both friends and foes ; the one for glory, the other for destruction. Orders regarding both these come forth from the palace of the Great King, the temple of the Most High God.

This angel has a sickle, a sharp sickle, to finish his work of judgment quickly.

But an objection may occur to some. " You say, that the grapes of the Vintage are the tares of the Saviour's parable. Matt. xiii. But if these be the tares, they ought to be bound before the wheat is gathered in. ' Gather ye together *first the tares.*' " (30). The difficulty arises from a mistranslation.[1] It should be " *First* gather the tares, *then* bind them." The words respect the order of the reapers' actions with regard to the tares : not the order of collection, as between the tares and wheat. It is so also in 1 Thess. iv. 16, 17. " The dead in Christ shall *first* rise, *then* we who are alive shall be caught up." It is not designed to teach us that the dead in Christ shall rise before those who have died out of Christ, as it is generally taken : true though that be. But it defines the order of events in reference to the dead in Christ and the living in Christ respectively.

" Gather the clusters of the vine of the earth."

What is " the vine of the earth " ?

We can arrive at our conclusion best by considering what is " the vine of the heaven." Jesus speaks of Himself and His people as constituting the true vine, just when His hour of tribulation and Satan's hour of power was come. Here the vine of the earth is spoken of just after the False Christ has been shown, and when, at the close of his three years and a half of power, he is about to be cut down.

---

[1] The difference of rendering turns on the distinction between $\pi\rho\hat{\omega}\tau o\nu$ and $\pi\rho\hat{\omega}\tau o\varsigma$. $\Pi\rho\hat{\omega}\tau o\nu$ relates to the order of *actions*, and is followed by $\epsilon\hat{\iota}\tau a$ or $\kappa a\hat{\iota}$. $\Pi\rho\hat{\omega}\tau o\varsigma$ refers to the order of *persons*, and is followed by $\delta\epsilon\hat{\upsilon}\tau\epsilon\rho o\varsigma$.

Nominal, worldly Christianity is by this time destroyed. True Christians are reaped; borne away from earth. There remain then only the False Christ and his host of adherents. This explanation suits admirably all the conditions of the case.

As the True Christ and the believers in Him constitute the true vine of a heavenly spirit, speedily to enter on their heritage of heaven; so the False Christ and his adherents form one body. It consists of apostates from the religions of Moses and of Jesus. The Father is the husbandman of the true vine; the lord of the false vine, dooming it to destruction. The Father and the Holy Spirit together cause the true vine to bear fruit to perfection. Thus Satan and the False Prophet bring the false vine to its ripeness. When iniquity is come to the full, it gathers to itself all, both Jew and Gentile, who disbelieve. Antichrist, as its stem, gives it unity. As the *true* vine was made up of Jew and Gentile, one in faith, so is the *false* vine composed of Jew and Gentile, one in unbelief. The false vine meets the wrath of God in the winepress. 19. But the followers of the Wild Beast and False Prophet are trodden in the winepress, in xix. 15. This fully identifies them.

As it is a vine of the earth, the bunches are the natural clusters of nations.

" Her grapes are fully ripe."

The reason for the Vintage is the same as that given for the Harvest. "The crop is ripe." Of the natural ripeness of field and vineyard, man is a judge. But, of the gathering seasons of the better covenant, God is alone the fit judge. Iniquity is come to the full. "The press is full, the vats overflow, *for their wickedness is great*" (Joel iii. 13; Isa. lxiii. 1–6).

The children of the Wicked One are now fully developed: they can no more be confounded with Christians. God's wrath of terrible heat, and the awful sap of the

False Prophet, "the Spirit of Antichrist," ripen them fast. The Bowls (vials) draw out man's heart of enmity against God into bitter blasphemies. Never, not even among the magicians of Egypt, was such wickedness before : sin has passed beyond pardon now. Blasphemy, which at first appears as the characteristic of the Wild Beast, at length penetrates all his branches and bears fruit in them. xvi.

How beautifully the two gatherings are suited to express the moral truths designed ! Harvest comes before the Vintage : the saints are gathered, ere destruction comes on the workers of iniquity. How strongly contrasted is the ripeness of the wheat and that of the grape ! The one is dryness and deadness to earth, the other is the fullness of its juices. To the saints, earth is a wilderness : to the Antichristian dweller on the earth, earth is Paradise. The wheat is lifted up and borne away from its field : the grape is removed, but trodden down upon it.

In both the Harvest and Vintage the command is— "Send the sickle." In both the act of obedience is— "he *cast*." Only, the reaper casts his sickle "*on*" the earth ; the grape-gatherer casts it "*into*" the earth. This difference is in evident accordance with the meaning given. The one agrees best with the removal of the saint from the earth ; the other, with destruction in it.

"And blood came out of the winepress."

'Tis no common press ; 'tis a mystic one, of God's own digging. Not "the blood of the grape," but the blood of men flows from it. Isa. xxxiv. 1-8 describes the awful sight.

The extent of the slaughter is terribly portrayed by a single line. A river of blood four feet deep, by 160 miles in length, will proceed from this destruction !

So awful a sight as this was never beheld before ;

but glimpses of this judgment have been given in some of the previous great slaughters among men. When Jerusalem was taken by Titus, Josephus says that the Roman soldiers slew all they met with, "and obstructed the very lanes with their dead bodies; and made the whole city run down with blood, to such a degree indeed that the fire of many of the houses was quenched with these men's blood" (*Wars*, vi., viii. 5).

Who treads the gathered grapes? This is not mentioned in the present place. "The winepress was trodden"—is all that is said on that point. But in chapter xix. 15, this omission is supplied. Jesus as the Man of War, and King of kings, treads it; and His armies follow in His train. So Jer. xxv. 33. Under this figure the ease with which the Lord overcomes His embattled enemies is set forth. The weight of a man is vastly more than sufficient to break the skin of the grape, and to shed its juices. It is done as it were with indignity, not by the hands but by the feet. These armed enemies will perish by a violent death beneath the Lord's feet, with as little power to resist as grapes beneath the feet of the vintager.

But why is the depth defined by the expression "up to the horse-bridles"? Because the reference is to the heavenly army mounted on horses, the treaders of the winepress, who follow Christ through this Aceldama. xix. 19.

The lake of blood extends for 1,600 furlongs.

Where shall we fix its two limits? One is evidently Megiddo, as xvi. 16 discovers. The other is Bozrah, in the land of Edom, as Isa. lxiii. 1, and xxxiv. 6, will prove. Now between these two points is just the interval of 160 miles, on Hughes' Map (*Bible Maps*, No. 6). Jesus moves from Bozrah towards Jerusalem, and then apparently towards Jezreel (or Megiddo).

What countless multitudes must be slain to produce

such a sanguine flood! All nations must indeed be gathered, after the fearful desolations of the previous plagues, to furnish such a crimson tide. This is the end of the world's martial glory! Thus is fulfilled the Saviour's word. Luke xxiii. 31.

A winepress with its load of blushing purple clusters is a beautiful sight. But how soon its glory is destroyed! It is placed in the press with design to be so destroyed. Thus great will be the martial bravery and glory of the armies of the earth, and haughty their self-confidence, just ere they are crushed for ever. How awful for the creature to contend with God! Yet so he will: and here is his doom. The foretelling of this awful wickedness will not prevent any from taking that stand, but those who are elect of God.

After the Harvest and the Vintage comes the joyful Feast of Tabernacles: which answers to millennial bliss. 'Tis a feast of booths: 'tis not eternal. Here is another proof of the futurity and reality of the millennium, which its opponents would do well to notice.

CHAPTER XV

THE VIALS OR BOWLS

1. "And I saw another sign in the heaven, great and wonderful; seven angels, having the seven last plagues, for in them was finished the wrath of God."

THIS sign is "great and wonderful." It is "great" in its extent. Before, only the third or fourth of earth were smitten; now the whole earth is stricken. It is "wonderful," and therefore the plagues are literal and supernatural. It is not the ordinary course of wars and famines, etc. It is the completion of "the covenant of marvels."

John sees "seven angels having the seven last plagues."

The seven angels are the priests of heaven, pouring out the drink-offerings of wine over the sacrifice, ere it is slain.

These plagues follow, apparently, the sounding of the seventh trump. The six first trumps bring plagues: this inflicts sevenfold wrath. It is the third woe, poured out as the result of the testimony of the Two ascended Witnesses against the iniquity of the earth.

"For in them was finished the wrath of God." This gives us the title of the present series. Wrath has been tarrying and accumulating till now: till these are poured out, the glory cannot come. His wrath is completed, and in it the mystery of God. The plagues become more evidently supernatural, and openly from

God Himself. Men at length cannot hide from themselves the conviction that God is really fighting against them; that a personal, intelligent, Almighty Deity knows their deeds and words, and smites them. Till this wrath is accomplished, Antichrist prospers. Dan. xi. 36.

2. " And I saw as it were a glassy sea mingled with fire, and the overcomers of the Wild Beast, and of his image, and of the number of his name, standing on the glassy sea, having the harps of God."

It is " a glassy sea ; " as if molten by heat, not cool and liquid as its natural counterpart.

It is "mingled with fire." This section exhibits wrath at its height : the present feature accordingly was not named at its first appearance ; nor did it exist. There is now sin, not merely against natural light ; but against the redemption by Jesus. Antichrist by his False Prophet uses fire to seduce men. xiii. 13. Probably he burns some of God's saints in it : but it turns against the Usurper and his flock at last. As the sea was used in God's former judgments, so was fire employed against Sodom. By fire is the world at last to be destroyed. This glassy *sea* emitting *flame* combines those two instruments of God's indignation. It typifies that which is established at the close—" the *lake* (or pool) of *fire* and brimstone."

The first martyrs were shown in chapters vi. and xii. The new series arising from the persecution of the False Christ has now exhibited itself.

In one view, the martyrs are conquer*ed*. To the eye of sense they are fools, who warred in vain against the King of kings, and were defeated. xiii. 7. But their defeat is apparent only ; they lost life for Christ's sake, and now they find it. Theirs was the victory of courage, and of patience unto death : they are conquerors in resurrection. For the Wild Beast inflicts death.

And not until body and soul are reunited, and the traces of the curse done away, can any stand before the throne of God. Nor is death swallowed up in *victory*, till the mortal is clothed with immortality. Shall we not say, that they probably rise with the Two Witnesses, Enoch and Elijah, as the great company of those already risen awoke when Jesus rose from the dead ? Matt. xxvii. 52, 53.

Their numbers are not stated, nor their country. They are one, in regard of the ordeal they have passed and of the place to which they have escaped. They are, I suppose, a remnant from the Church, from Israel, and from the Gentiles. "They sing the song of *Moses* and the *Lamb*." Jesus appears among the 144,000 ; He does not stand among these. The 144,000 precede the advent of these on high. This company cannot ascend before the third warning angel of chapter xiv. 9. But the 144,000 are complete, ere the first of those angels goes forth. They are the remnant of the woman's seed, against whom Satan went to war. xii. 17. The Great Multitude are on high before the Wild Beast arises. These are some of the blessed dead who die in the Lord, and at once are raised up.

They are "conquerors of the Wild Beast." They are brought face to face with him, or his agents, and must worship or die. They refuse, and are slain : he kills the body, and after that can do no more.

They are "overcomers of his image." For the image speaks, demands worship, and wrestles, as if it were a person. But these refuse to be idolaters, though refusal is on pain of death, and though so miraculous is the image.

They have the "harps of God." Harps were not used in God's service of old, *till the kingdom came*. This is one of the signs of the kingdom near. These are real instruments, belonging to the temple-service of the New

Covenant; only they are of God's making, as are the temple and the city.

3. "And they are singing the song of Moses the servant of God, and the song of the Lamb, saying, 'Great and wonderful are thy works, Lord God of Hosts, just and true are thy ways, thou king of the nations.'"

There are two songs of Moses, Exod. xv. and Deut. xxxii.: which is intended here? The song at the Red Sea, evidently.

"And the song of the Lamb." This book is destructive of the Gnostic doctrine of the contrariety of the Author of the Old Testament to the Author of the New. The Most High owns the great teacher of the Law; He confesses, too, and teaches His servants to recognize, the Great Agent of the Gospel. The elect martyrs of that day of tribulation meet before His throne in risen bodies, and join in one song of praise.

Jesus is the Lamb of whom Moses wrote. He is the Passover Lamb; and the passover is now to be fulfilled in the Kingdom of God.

The mixed character of the assembly is shown in the mixed origin of the song. That day of evil is the time in which faith, both in the Old and New Testaments, appears conspicuously. Antichrist denies both Testaments: the saved from his falsehood confess both.

"Great and marvellous are thy works, O Lord God of Hosts."

The first part of this song runs most according to the tenor of the song of Moses: the latter part may perhaps be "the song of the Lamb." For it certainly anticipates the gathering of all nations to God: the song of Moses does not. But to Jesus shall the gathering of the nations be. Gen. xlix. 10. "I, if I be lifted up, will draw all men unto me." His ignominious lifting up, under the curse, has long been fulfilled; the glory of the cross is now at hand.

"Just and true are thy ways, thou king of the nations."

Those who have surrendered life at God's call justify Him: He had a right to demand it: He had nobly requited it in resurrection.

The reading "King of saints," is unanimously exploded as not genuine. God's title, "King of the nations," leads back the thoughts to Jer. x. 7.

Power was granted in Nebuchadnezzar's day to the Gentiles: here it is resumed by God. All kings have arisen against Him; but His kingly authority will be abundantly displayed. Those risen from the dead own the Lord as king, ere they are established as subordinate kings, during the millennial day.

How different the tenor of these titles of God from that given at the opening of chapter xiv.! There God is known as Father and Son. Here, by names known to Moses and the prophets.

4. "Who shall not fear, O Lord, and glorify thy name? For thou only art holy; for all the nations shall arrive, and worship before thee; for thy righteous acts were made manifest."

Here is a great advance on the ode of Moses. Moses, as the result of the judgment at the Red Sea, expects only that fear will trouble the neighbouring nations. These foretell the pilgrimage and worship of all nations.

Acts of open punishment make all aware that God is a righteous governor, and not to be resisted. Not mercy, but justice reforms the world. Isa. lix. 18, 19.

5. "And after these things I saw, and the temple of the tabernacle of testimony in heaven was opened. 6. And the seven angels who have the seven plagues came out of the temple, clothed in linen pure and bright, and girt about the breasts with golden girdles."

It is but a "tabernacle," not the abiding "temple." As the tent of the desert disappeared in the temple of the city, so does this tabernacle vanish in the temple of "the city of God." Its contents pass away with the passing of the millennial dispensation. The tabernacle (which has been previously called "the temple") lasts during the millennium. But as, after David's day, the tent became the temple; so, when the peaceful reign of God is fully established, the tent ceases.

"The *temple* of the tabernacle of testimony was opened." Perhaps it would be better to translate this—"the Holiest." The tabernacle of earth had its Holy of Holies; this has its counterpart in the heavenlies of the New Covenant. Under the law of Moses, the Holiest was concealed from the eyes of the priests themselves. Mystery brooded over God's purposes, even to those who were owned to be His servants. But now "the mystery of God is finished." His Holiest is thrown open. The door through which John was permitted to enter alone (iv. 1) now stands open, and its priests go forth. But smoke for a brief period prevents both sight and ingress.

The opening of the Holiest here is the same apparently as that at the close of chapter xi. 19. In both cases that chamber is thrown open to give exit to the final wrath.

7. "And one of the four living creatures gave to the seven angels seven golden bowls, full of the wrath of God that liveth for ever and ever."

Our translation "vials," entirely misleads the English reader. The vessels intended were broad and flat like a saucer to which a handle was attached, able to contain liquids, and designed to pour them out at once. They are called "basins" or "bowls" in the Old Testament. They belonged to the altar; and all vessels belonging to the copper altar were of copper. Exod. xxvii. 3; Num. iv. 14; Zech. xiv. 20. These are of gold. Out of the bowls oil was poured over the accepted meat-offering, wine over the victim slain. Lev. xxiii. 13.

This is the sevenfold cup of God's fury, given to the living offenders to drink, a *measured* vengeance.

8. "And the temple was filled with smoke from the glory of God and from His power: and none could enter into the temple till the seven plagues of the seven angels were finished."

This is the hour of vengeance: no intercession shall go on. God will listen to naught now but to the demands of His righteous indignation. The Mount is fenced about, till the burst of displeasure is over. The glory is like devouring fire; but it visits not those on high, but the unclean below. The sin of earth is beyond endurance; the unpardonable sin is abroad.

This is the time foretold by Jeremiah, "Thou hast covered thyself with a cloud, that our prayer should not pass through" (Lam. iii. 44).

CHAPTER XVI

THE BOWLS

1. "And I heard a great voice out of the temple saying to the seven angels, 'Go, and pour out the seven bowls of the wrath of God into the earth.'"

SEVEN seals have unfolded the mystery of God. Seven trumpets have opened the war of Satan and of his Christ against the Most High. Now seven bowls from the temple prepare the sacrifice for slaughter.

How different from the Gospel times, when the blood of the Son of God was shed on earth for the forgiveness of sins, and on Jew and Gentile who believed "was poured out the gift of the Holy Ghost!"

2. "And the first went away, and poured out his bowl into the earth (land), and it became a noisome and grievous ulcer upon the men that have the mark of the Wild Beast, and those that worship his image."

"It became a noisome and malignant ulcer."

This is to be taken literally.

That was the complaint of which Lazarus in the parable died. "The dogs licked his *sores*" ($\ἕλκη$: the word used here). Luke xvi. 21. The leprosy took the form of a boil in some cases. Lev. xiii.

Boils have been a plague literally inflicted of God.

(1) They were one of the plagues on Egypt. Exod. ix. 8–12.

(2) Job was supernaturally stricken with this disorder. Job ii. 7, 8.

(3) Hezekiah's malady preternaturally sent, and miraculously healed, was an abscess or boil. Isa. xxxviii. 21.

(4) The emerods sent on the Philistines were probably something of the kind. 1 Sam. v., vi.

(5) On Miriam God sent the leprosy as a punishment for speaking against Moses. Num. xii. 10. Here there is blasphemy against God.

Boils were one of the plagues threatened to Israel by the Law, if they broke Jehovah's covenant. Deut. xxviii. 15, 27, 35; Lev. xxvi. 16. This has never yet been fulfilled; and as the whole law to its least tittle must be accomplished, this plague must be inflicted.

The ulcer or boil is "noisome," or "bad." This epithet probably refers to its pain. Its being "malignant" affirms, no doubt, the difficulty or impossibility of healing it. It continues, I suppose, through all the other plagues.

The mark of the Wild Beast is a literal mark on the body, attesting every one who receives it to be a worshipper of the False Christ. Each impresses it on himself. God owns this mark of Satan in wrath. An intelligent offended God spares His people who are marked on the forehead with the seal of God. But every worshipper of God's enemy receives a foul and painful mark in the flesh which is dedicated to the Wild Beast, in token of the displeasure of Jehovah. Their god can neither defend them from it, nor heal them under it. Not a few worship the False Christ to escape death. But though they are permitted by him to live, God makes their life painful, ere they sink into the second death.

By the true Messiah diseases were healed. Under the False Messiah miraculous disease assails his followers, which he can neither prevent nor cure. He is proved thus, to the discomfiture of his worshippers, not to be Lord of heaven and earth.

3. "And the second poured out his bowl into the sea; and it became blood as of a dead man; and every living soul that was in the sea, died."

The second trump affected the sea, and turned it into blood. But that plague was less severe (1) in extent: but a third of the sea was changed. (2) The sea was converted into blood, but not blood of the dead.

What is the peculiar change here contemplated, I do not feel quite certain of. It no doubt supposes that the waters will be thick, semi-solid. I imagine, also, that they will turn to a lurid reddish black.

This must affect greatly the sailing of ships. It must breed, too, pestilential vapours; specially under the scorching sun which follows.

The change in its waters naturally enough kills the fish. No living creature could inhale its half-solid waters. This is described as one of the acts of God's sovereignty. Ps. cv. 30; Isa. l. 2.

This plague, then, affects greatly the commerce of the world, and destroys the livelihood of fishermen and sailors.

4. "And the third poured out his bowl into the rivers and the fountains of waters; and they became blood. 5. And I heard the angel of the waters say, 'Righteous art thou who art, and who wast holy, because thou judgest thus. 6. For they shed the blood of saints and prophets, and blood gavest thou them to drink; they are worthy.' 7. And I heard thy altar, saying, 'Even so, Lord God of Hosts, true and great are thy judgments.'"

The third bowl affects the same great department of creation as the third trump. On the former occasion, only a third of the rivers and founts was attacked.

Then they were made bitter: now they are turned into blood. They are still capable of supporting life, only they produce horror and disgust. There have been in past times numerous testimonies of waters turned into blood.

Now science may say that this was merely some red animalculæ which fell into the waters and coloured them; or some red dust which gave them the appearance of blood. In the past cases it may be so: in this it will be real blood. The justice of punishment which the angel of the waters alleges, proves this. They shed blood; they drink blood as their recompense.

"Cyrus, thy thirst was blood, now drink thy fill," said Thomyris, queen of the Scythians, when Cyrus' head was brought to her, and was immersed in a bowl of blood.

The expression "the angel of the waters" is remarkable. It proves that angels are not idle: God has given them some office and occupation. This angel is in charge of the waters of earth. Perhaps it is the same who was directed to trouble the waters of Bethesda, in order to heal some favoured ones of Israel. John v. 4. Now they are troubled in order to produce horror and sickness among men. Men must slake their thirst, or die of its pains. They loathe the sight and taste of this their judicial beverage. Athens gave its condemned criminals hemlock to drink: God gives blood to His earth's crew of murderers.

The justice of God and the sin of man are the corresponding reasons of these inflictions. The angel then mentions the sin of which this is the righteous requital, They are not merely murderers, but slayers of the *holy* murderers of those *inspired* by God's Spirit. This is both the greatest crime against man, and manifests enmity against God and His Spirit. "They shed the blood of saints and prophets." This includes all God's martyrs from before the Law till the latest under Antichrist. The generation is the same throughout, perverse, malicious : seed of the serpent, slaying the seed of the woman. The Saviour refers to this time in Matt. xxiii. 34, 35; Luke xi. 47-51.

Times of open persecution of God's saints unto death will come, to prove man unchanged, and to fulfil God's threatenings. The spirit of prophecy will be restored again, and will be peculiarly obnoxious to men's feelings and plans. Elijah must " restore all things," and therefore he will bring back prophecy.

It is remarkable that it is not said, " They *thirsted* for the blood of prophets," because that thirst would be figurative. But it is " they *shed* the blood," and that is literal. Blood, then, must they drink : they shall not find water. An instance of the drinking of blood occurred in the French Revolution. In the massacres of September, in Paris, it was proposed to a young French lady to drink a cup of blood, that her parent might escape assassination. With filial devotion she drank it, and her father's life was spared.

"They are worthy." The throne of justice is now rendering to each according to his works. Past acts of trespass of ages long gone by, and seemingly forgotten of God, are now remembered and avenged. The cry of the souls under the altar is remembered, and close is the requital.

8. " And the fourth poured out his bowl on the sun ; and it was given to it to scorch men with fire. 9. And men were scorched with great burning, and blasphemed the name of the God that hath the power over these plagues : and repented not to give him glory."

The fourth trump also affected the heavenly bodies : but then it diminished the light of sun, moon, and stars. This is an increase of the sun's heat, which is far worse. It is probably summer-time : many are cut off by sunstrokes. And those whose lives are spared feel the heat more acutely, because of the boils which trouble them.

This is one of the predicted " signs in the sun " (Luke xxi. 25 ; Gen. i. 14). The Great Multitude on high escape this stroke of divine wrath. " The *sun* shall not light on them, nor any *heat* " (vii. 16). This is a promise also to those who are under the protection of the God of Israel.

" *The sun shall not smite thee by day,* nor the moon by night " (Ps. cxxi. 6).

To this time Isaiah appears to allude. " The inhabitants of the earth are *burned,* and few men left " (Isa. xxiv. 6 ; xlii. 25).

To this Moses seems to refer. " They shall be burnt with hunger, and *devoured with burning heat* " (Deut. xxxii. 24). " For behold the day cometh that *shall burn as an oven ;* and the proud, yea, and all that do wickedly, shall be as stubble " (Mal. iv. 1).

They have fearfully ripened in sin since the earlier days of the seals. Men, instead of confessing themselves justly punished, cry out against God. Though they are experiencing His wrath, they only curse Him. How little, then, will the punishment of hell convert men, and bring them to love God !

There are two moral results of intense bodily pain. The one is (1) that the desire for death springs up : the other, (2) that men, if wicked, curse God. When stung by the locusts, men desire death : but now they blaspheme the Most High. Whence we may conclude, that the pain described on both these occasions is really bodily pain.

Men blaspheme " the *name* of God." They are bitterly opposed to His character. They see Him determined to execute wrath against the evil-doer, and they hate Him for it. They are in sympathy with Antichrist the False God ; necessarily, therefore, they hate the True God. Men do not then, as at the sixth seal, own one God only. They see intelligence in these plagues, but among the many gods, known or unknown, they do not feel sure which it is that is thus smiting them. They see there is war between their god and the author of these plagues. But they make certain of blaspheming the True God by characterizing Him as the author of their woes.

"They repented not to give Him glory."

"Give glory to God because the hour of His vengeance is come," was the demand of the first angel in chapter xiv. These refuse. They confess the finger of some God, but they will not submit to the heavy lessons He would teach of their wickedness, and need of repentance. Their woe increases, but their sin increases too. They have sealed themselves men of Antichrist, and his spirit dwells within them. They will not cry for quarter, nor will it be given. Their will is fixed for evil, accompanied with a sense of the powerlessness of themselves and their god.

They ought, if they cursed, to curse themselves and their Great Deceiver. They curse the Holy One instead, and so are doomed to His severest wrath. Punishment does not necessarily amend : it does not always even outwardly reform.

10. "And the fifth poured out his bowl on the throne of the Wild Beast ; and his kingdom became darkened, and they bit their tongues from pain. 11. And blasphemed the God of the heaven because of their pains and because of their ulcers, and repented not of their deeds."

The worshippers of Antichrist are in sore pain of body, which exhibits itself in biting the tongue. To the darkness is added agony of body. Earth is become like hell, for darkness and woe. The ulcer of the first bowl remains ; and beside that are the pains which follow on the sun's scorching. These together make them intensely miserable; but they relieve themselves by expressing the bitter hatred of their heart against God. Their words are awfully wicked : but their deeds are as bad as ever. Their tongues offend : they are themselves compelled to punish them. Zech. xiv. 12 ; Ps. lxiv. 3–8. They blaspheme "the God of the heaven." They return to that title, now that it is clear that He controls the heavenly bodies, making His sun either to pour down intolerable heat, or sealing up His light.

12. " And the sixth angel poured out his bowl on the great river Euphrates : and the water thereof was dried up, that the way of the kings from the rising of the sun might be prepared. 13. And I saw out of the mouth of the Dragon, and out of the mouth of the Wild Beast, and out of the mouth of the False Prophet, three unclean spirits, as it were frogs (come forth). 14. For they are the spirits of demons, working miracles, which go forth to the kings of the whole habitable earth, to gather them together to the war of that great day of the God of Hosts. 15. Behold, I come as a thief. Blessed is he that watcheth, and keepeth his garments, lest he walk naked, and they see his shame. 16. And they gathered them [1] together into the place which is called in Hebrew Armageddon."

The kings from the West and those from the East make up the kings of the whole habitable earth : whom the Lord designs to collect in Judea to their destruction. Now against any one travelling from the East to Palestine, the Euphrates interposes its broad barrier, difficult to be surmounted even by individuals ; and much more by kings and their armies. The force of this obstacle, which constituted the barrier and bound even of the Roman empire, can well be estimated by military men. Hence it is called " the *Great* River Euphrates," its breadth and unfordable depths opposing difficulties of no ordinary kind. That barrier is by the sixth bowl withdrawn. This looks more like a blessing than a plague ; and so will it, no doubt, be regarded by

[1] The neuter plural δαιμόνια taking a verb singular.

men. But it is like the opening of the sea to the host of Pharaoh, which encloses them at length to submerge them.

But in vain were the river dried up, did not evil spirits urge men to make use of the opportunity which it produces. Three demons, then, severally proceeding from each person of the Infernal Trinity, go forth on this errand.

The evil spirits appeared to John's eye " like frogs," on purpose to connect them with the corresponding plague of Egypt. The frogs of old were brought up by the *magicians out of the river*. Here, at the smiting of the river, they come forth from the three great magicians. We have been introduced, in chapters xii. and xiii. to this awful trio. They are of one purpose, bent to hurl man into collision against his Maker.

They are master-magicians; out of their mouths proceed spirits who work miracles. Miracles have hitherto been almost uniformly on the side of truth; but, at the close, God sends them to cause an energy of delusion in the rejecters of the truth.

The Holy Spirit, the Sacred Dove, came down from heaven to proclaim peace with God, and goodwill to men. But these go forth to stir up men to fight against God and His Christ. The time is suitable; all are enraged against God and His Christ. Anything is acceptable that will give them an opportunity of displaying their hatred against the Most High. They assemble there avowedly against God and Christ. Awful is the battle: it is described in the conclusion of chapter xix.

In the earlier portion of the book the seven spirits of God and of Christ went forth into all the earth; not for evil, but for good. They were symbolized by horns of the Lamb, or torches before the throne: as these are by frogs.

The frogs of Egypt went even into the kings' chambers. Ps. cv. 30. The magicians of Egypt were silenced at the close of the struggle with Moses. These have fresh licence, and power is given to deceive and destroy. Earth loves to have it so.

The kings of the earth appear at the sixth Seal: but then they are terrified, and own the Father and the Son. Now, others beside the ten of Antichrist appear on His side. Indeed all the crowned heads of earth follow in His train. The kings of the " habitable earth " are here said to be collected: in xix. the kings of " the earth " are gathered against Christ. What a picture for the imagination of a poet is here! How great the effects wrought, how intense the enthusiasm excited, by Peter the Hermit! The Gentile nations of the West were then roused to go to Jerusalem, nominally to fight *for* Christ. These go to fight *against* Him. But how like the scene! *That* Peter believed himself instructed by Christ in a vision, to stir up the nations against the Saracens. " Miracles " were wrought in support of the cause. The pilgrims distinguished themselves by a *mark*, not on their flesh, but on their clothes: *a red cross* on the right shoulder made known their vow.

At Babel, man lifted himself up against God; but the Lord interfered, and wickedness was forbidden to develop itself in that day. Here the natural barriers against conspiracy are removed; and new, and subtle, and most mighty agents kindle all in one common sympathy against God.

The Egyptians at the Red Sea turned to flee: here, men assemble to fight. " Why sit we here groaning and moping in our pains? Let us arise, and avenge ourselves! Let us cut off Israel, and the prophecies of Him who professes Himself the true God are shattered!"

At this point a very singular notice and warning breaks in. Jesus addresses Himself to some servants of

His yet on earth, calling them to watch. *What* servants are they ?

" Behold, I am come as a thief. Blessed is he that watcheth, and keepeth his garments, lest he walk naked, and they see his shame."

If I mistake not, they are some remnants of the churches ; and some Jewish disciples, occupying the moral position which the apostles did in our Lord's lifetime. To these classes Jesus revealed His thief-like coming.

"*If therefore thou shalt not watch, I will come on thee as a thief*, and thou shalt not know what hour I will come upon thee " (iii. 3).

Jesus, then, is here speaking of the sudden separation which He will, by invisible agency, effect between His watchful and unwatchful servants : in a moment raising to His presence the one, and leaving the other on the earth in its darkest days. This is parallel, I believe, with the harvest of chapter xiv., which so immediately precedes the Vintage—or the Great Battle of xix.

In 1 Thess. v. the *day* is said to come as a thief on the world. Here Jesus' *self* comes ; and, as we are warned, may find His people unprepared.

The " garments " here spoken of are evidently not literal : the wicked can keep those. In short, here is another proof that we have now stepped back to the phraseology of the Gospel dispensation, as shown in the Epistles to the churches. Blessed is he who, in those times of unbelief and universal laxity, preserves his faith and the corresponding practice undefiled.

" Pure religion and undefiled before God and the Father is this, to visit the fatherless and widows in their affliction, and to keep himself unspotted from the world " (James i. 27).

The evil steward, who eats and drinks with the

drunken, and puts off his coming, is an example of the contrast. Matt. xxiv. 48-51.

The nakedness of the disciple is not simply the *being* so, but the *appearing* so publicly against his will. The nakedness here is not his *guilt* (as in iii. 18), but his commencing *punishment*.

Who are they that behold his shame ?

1. The unbelievers of earth are one party, as we suppose.

2. But it refers probably, also, to those above who are with Christ, whether they be angels or the risen.

How sudden is this interpolated warning! So sudden, so swift in its results will be the Saviour's secret coming!

"But have not other bodies of saints been caught up to God's presence long ere this ? " Yes! It is clear, therefore, that there must be more than one rapture.

"Blessed is he that watcheth." The world is sunk in unbelief, and ridicules the Saviour's promised return. But that hope and that faith are to be cherished still by every disciple. The call to " watch " is one continually given to the Church of Christ.

"Therefore let us not sleep, as do others ; but let us *watch* and be sober " (1 Thess. v. 6).

"Be sober, be *vigilant :* because your adversary the devil, as a roaring lion, walketh about, seeking whom he may devour " (1 Peter v. 8).

The watchful saint escapes trouble on the earth, and receives reward from his Lord. "He is to keep his garments." The allusion is to one sleeping, to whom a thief draws near, and secretly draws away the dress. Jesus has proclaimed His secret coming as the thief. The saint who is left behind is like the sleeper who arises ashamed ; his hope, which warmed and covered him, is rent away. His brother has been caught away to glory and happiness : he remains dishonoured below.

The wicked see it, and taunt him, as the graceless boys of Bethel taunted Elisha, after the ascent of his Master —" Ascend, baldhead ! " [1]

After this parenthesis the history proceeds as before. It is designed to intimate to us that the miraculous rapture of God's servants to Him will no more interrupt the world's sinful ways than the strokes of judgment already delivered. The embassy of the three spirits effects its purpose. From east and from west, kings, nations, armies assemble. The very spot is indicated. " It is called in Hebrew, Armageddon."

The word signifies " Mountain of Megiddo." [2] This points to the broad valley of Jezreel in the Holy Land, a spot in which so many battles have been fought in days past. There Barak fought against Sisera and Jabin.

17. " And the seventh poured out his bowl on the air ; and a great voice went forth out of the temple of the heaven, saying, ' It is done.' "

The consequences of this bowl, then, appear, first in heaven, then in air, then on earth. First, the voice from the throne ; then, angelic voices ; then in the air, thunders and lightnings ; then the rocking of earth, and its consequences to the abodes of men.

The temple appears at the close of each series of judg-

---

[1] Then the reproach was the nakedness of the head ; at this time the nakedness is general, but figurative. To Elisha, too, was given another cloak.

[2] That Armageddon should be translated " the *mountain* of Megiddo," will appear satisfactorily to any one who will investigate the way in which the LXX represent the Hebrew characters in Greek. Thus " Haran " with the Hebrew " He " (Gen. xi. 26) is by them given as $A\rho\rho\alpha\nu$ (Arran). " Hara " (1 Chron. v. 26) with the Hebrew " He " is rendered in Greek characters by $A\rho\rho\alpha$ (Arral in the Aldine and Complutensian editions).

Had the word begun instead with the Hebrew Heth, they would have represented it thus : $X\alpha\rho\rho\alpha\nu$ (Gen. xi. 31) (Charran). $X\omega\rho\eta\beta$ is the Heb. חרב Exod. iii. 1.

ments, whether the Seals, Trumpets, or Bowls. This is the last occasion on which it is named. John tells us that in the new earth and its new metropolis there is no temple. The temple is, however, opened to us at the commencement of the xixth chapter : and is supposed to exist during the millennium : the blessed partakers of the first resurrection ministering therein as priests of God.

"It is enough," says God. The action of the *throne* of God ceases : that of *Christ* begins. This is the last stroke, ere the Saviour descends to the battle, xix. 11. The smoke now clears away from the temple, and leaves the priests at liberty to enter it. Hence we next see the great company of the victors and the saved, before the throne of the beginning of chapter xix.

18. " And there followed lightnings, and voices, and thunders, and earthquake followed, so great as never occurred since man existed upon the earth, earthquake of such a description, so great."

This, the greatest of all earthquakes, is foretold by the Jewish prophets. Ezek. xxxviii. 20.

19. " And the great city became (divided) into three parts, and the cities of the Gentiles fell : and Babylon the Great was remembered before God, to give her the cup of the wine of the indignation of His wrath."

What is this great city ? Doubtless, Jerusalem. It is distinguished from its rival, Babylon, in this very series of consequences.

But "the cities of *the Gentiles*" are thrown down universally. This expression leads us to infer that the previous great city is the metropolis of the Jews, the other great division of mankind.

"Great Babylon is remembered before God." After the cities of the Gentiles have been spoken of in general, their chief city's fate is declared : and then a long digression gives details concerning it, and tells us of its two falls.

This earthquake is here the blow of utter extermination : its consequences are more fully drawn out in the xviiith chapter. When all earth is at rest under God's smile, she will present the spectacle of His wrath. Isa. xiii. 19–22 ; xiv. 22, 23 ; Jer. l. 38.

20. "And every island fled, and mountains were not found."

The wrath of God grows heavier. At the earthquake of the sixth seal, every *mountain* and *island* were *moved out of their places.* vi. 14. Here they "flee." By that is meant, I suppose, that rapid motion is communicated to them. They are thrown swiftly and far off from their present localities. It does not imply their destruction : then it would have been added, "and no place was found for them." But they are supposed to exist during the millennium. "The Lord reigneth ; let the earth rejoice ; let the multitude of *isles* be glad " (Ps. xcvii. 1).

By the words "mountains were not found," are we to understand that thenceforth the earth becomes a plain ? By no means. The article is not used before mountains : so that all we need supply is "*certain* mountains were not found." What becomes of them ? They are carried into the heart of the sea. Ps. xlvi. 2. The removal of mountains is spoken of as a work of God in His anger. "Then the earth shook and trembled : the foundations also of the *mountains moved* and were shaken, *because He was wroth*" (Ps. xviii. 7). "I beheld the *mountains*, and lo ! they trembled, and *all the hills moved lightly* . . . all the cities thereof were broken down at the presence of the Lord, and *by His fierce anger*" (Jer. iv. 24, 26).

Mountains exist during the millennium. The Lord brings out of Judah an inheritor of His mountains. Isa.

lxv. 9. The mountains are called to rejoice before the Lord when He comes to judge the earth. Ps. xcviii. 8, 9. [See also Ps. lxxii. 3, 16; cxlviii. 9; Isa. ii. 2; xliv. 23; Ezek. xxxvi. 8.

21. "And great hail, as it were of a talent weight, is descending out of the heaven upon men; and men blasphemed God because of the plague of the hail; for the plague thereof is exceeding great."

The hail of the first trumpet, mixed with fire and blood, smote only *grass* and *trees,* and only the third of those. viii. 7. But this strikes *men.*

It is more dreadful than the plague on Egypt: for then the Egyptians removed both themselves and cattle under shelter of their houses: and the hail struck only such as abode in the field. Exod. ix. 18–21. But now God has deprived men of that shelter. The earthquake has laid men's abodes in ruins: the moving mountains have driven men in terror to the open plains. There is no shelter there, as at the sixth seal. And now, when the haggard, troubled multitudes are left all exposed to the artillery of heaven, this awful hail-shower falls to kill and maim.

The size of the hailstones is prodigious: they are huge rugged masses of ice, concreted in the troubled atmosphere above. A talent in Greece was about 56 pounds: a Jewish talent 114 pounds troy. This was the weight of the stones thrown by the Roman catapults against Jerusalem, as Josephus tells us. "Stones of the weight of a talent were thrown by the engines that were prepared for the purpose" (*Wars,* iii. vii. 9).

There is intelligence in the arrangement of these plagues. If the hail had come before the earthquake, the houses would have afforded protection, to some extent at least. But now the earthquake has buried thousands in the ruins of their houses, and the survivors are driven out into the open fields. Then comes the hail on those unsheltered. In the Egyptian plague the houses were spared, and there they were safe. But now God's arm finds out His foes; and they are aware that the Wise One is aiming His strokes against them, and they curse Him. At the sixth-seal earthquake, men hide in the rocks and caves of mountains: here the mountains themselves are places of danger. But to what a pitch of sin have men now arrived!

How prodigious must be the effect of such masses of ice falling with great velocity! How can human bones withstand? Multitudes both of men and beasts must be slain outright, as was the case in Joshua's battle.

But what is the answer to this terrific scourge? Do men bend, and own their sins, and seek pardon? No! None sealed with Antichrist's mark ever repents: he is given up to judicial hardness. They blaspheme! They see God's hand of wisdom and of power laying them bare of all shelter from His dread inflictions: but they curse *Him,* not *themselves.* Here is sin at its most revolting height. It was not so in the world's younger days. Pharaoh confesses his sin, when stricken by the hailstorm; and asks Moses' intercession with God, promising to deliver Israel to freedom. But these are ripe for hell: Antichrist has taught all his followers to curse God and die.

CHAPTER XVII

THE GREAT HARLOT

1. "And there came one of the seven angels who have the seven bowls, and spake with me, saying, 'Come hither, I will show thee the judgment of the Great Harlot that sitteth on many waters: with whom the kings of the earth fornicated, and the dwellers on the earth were made drunk with the wine of her fornication.'"

It will perhaps be the simplest way of leading the reader to the main features of this scene of the prophecy to sketch the chief positions of Babylon.

1. Babylon is literal. The Babylon of Euphrates is well known by us, from its notices in the Old Testament. It was the first great city of man. There flourished the first great rebel monarch, Nimrod. There men were centred in unbelief, and thence were they scattered. But after the flow of ages, and the wrath of God against the kingdom of Judah, Babylon became the great metropolis of the first Gentile kingdom, and Nebuchadnezzar was its head. It was the mighty opposer of Israel, the instrument of God's vengeance in destroying the city and temple of God, and in carrying captive His people. After this Babylon herself was gradually made desolate, and has for ages lain so. Did Babylon cease then to exist? If not, what became of Babylon during that time? For here it is supposed not only to be in existence, but to be known as the sovereign city, having supremacy over the kings of the earth.

2. The answer is that ROME PAGAN succeeded to the place of the ancient Babylon as the capital of the fourth Gentile empire, after the sovereignty was removed from Babylon. She took the place of Babylon in her idolatry, and in the proud elevation of her emperors to equality with Godhead. *She occupies also the same place as it regards Israel.* She was the instrument, in God's righteous hand, of carrying captive the Jew, of desolating the sanctuary and city of the Most High. That Rome is meant, is confessed by most. Her place on seven hills is proof positive. Also the point of time at which John regards her is clear, from the series of the emperors which is given. "One is." This is its point of contact with John's day.

3. But Christianity was now abroad, and had been for years presented to Rome, when John wrote. *It is very remarkable that Jesus, when addressing His seven churches, sets them all in Asia, and does not then own specifically any church of His at Rome; though Paul by the Spirit had done so forty years before.* This seems to hint that the candlestick had already been removed thence.

The entrance of the Gospel, and the destruction of Jerusalem and her temple, brought on the position of things here supposed. Christianity, after long persecution, was nominally received by Rome. It became the religion of the empire. Rome was *nationally* Christian. Instead of being a *Church*, or an assembly of the called out from the evil *world* around, she was in profession wholly Christ's, His chief city and Church.

Coincidently with this, the temporal government was removed from Rome to Constantinople; and by frequent incursions of the barbarians, Rome was brought to the lowest stage of depression. The Grecian emperors retained the rule over it, with greater or less power, till the year A.D. 726.

The occasion of the rupture with Constantinople is

most significant, as regarded in the light of this chapter. The Grecian emperor Leo, the Isaurian, collecting a Council at Constantinople, proclaimed the worship of images unlawful and heretical. But his decree against it was resisted most fiercely by superstitious Rome and its pontiffs. *In defence of images, Rome revolted from the emperor, and set the Bishop of Rome at its head.*

Thenceforth the progress of Rome into darkness and corruption was steady: yet her influence, instead of diminishing, increased. Her sway during the dark middle ages was almost undisputed. *Rome, pagan, ruled by the sword :* ROME, PAPAL, *ruled by false doctrine.* This is the time which the angel supposes to be past, when he unfolds to John the scene of her judgment. She had been long seated on many waters, the harlot lover of many kings, and the deceiver of many nations.

In John's day Rome was simply a pagan city, ruling the world. But the entrance of Christianity, and her profession of it while she is immersed in worldliness, and sunk in idolatry, renders her a *harlot*. It is in this character that she fills up the time of "the Mystery."

Her pagan attitude, as presented in this chapter, breaks off at the sixth emperor. He was ruling. Another of like spirit was yet to come. He has not yet appeared. Whenever he does, the next phase of the prophecy occurs.

4. At the close of the period of God's patience, she occupies the place described by John. She is covered with worldly glory, and surrounded by admiring nations. She is drunken with blood of God's saints. She is then in league with the last great forerunner of Antichrist, or the seventh head of the Wild Beast. Her bloodshed in the days of the pagan emperors is not noticed. It is as the *harlot*, fully decked and wildly applauded, that she drinks, and is intoxicated with blood. This is yet future. Rome is not off her guard

now, nor is she openly drinking blood. At this period arise ten infidel kings, who hate the revolting aspect of religion exhibited by her, and are at enmity with even those portions of Christian truth which she retains. The kingdom reverts to an emperor of the old pagan stamp. He and his ten kings are in full moral harmony, and agree to destroy the city. It is done : and with this ends chapter xvii.

5. The few and scattered relics of old Rome flee to the literal Babylon on Euphrates. And this—as the great commercial city of the world, in contact, not with Christ's new people of the Gospel (as in the former chapter), but with God's literal ancient people Israel— is destroyed of God.

Thus our path lies, through Rome pagan and Rome papal, to the era of Antichrist, and Rome's destruction : after which literal Babylon again appears on the stage, and is finally consumed.

The two chapters before us, then, are retrogressive. They expand to us the position occupied by Babylon at each of her two catastrophes. For, as we have seen, Babylon falls twice. The first time, xiv. 8 ; the second time, xvi. 19.

The xviith chapter then extends our view of the *first* overthrow : the xviiith, our view of the *second*.

The *judgment* of the Great Harlot is to be shown to John ; this is the great object of the vision. Her *history* comes in only as ministering a reason for the stroke of divine justice.

Babylon takes two different aspects. One as the *Harlot*, in which she is first presented. "Fallen is Babylon the Great, who hath made all the nations drink of the wine of the wrath of her *fornication*" (xiv. 8). This is her phase throughout chapter xvii. It is almost wholly mystic : we have " Wild Beast," " horns " and " heads," " woman " and " cup," and " waters."

She is the harlot, as professing to be Christ's great Church and witness. Instead of keeping her character as a chaste virgin, standing aloof from the world's pleasures, honours, and gains, she has wholly plunged into them, and in order to obtain them has sacrificed her allegiance and loyalty to Christ.

She is the "*Great* Harlot." Her greatness arises out of this infidelity to Christ. Greatness means political magnitude, or dimensions in the world's eye. Had she kept to Christ's laws, she would ever have been small, insignificant, despised, a poor band of believers witnessing for Christ's coming and sovereignty against an unbelieving rebellious world. But she at once ran the race for the world's good things, and by obtaining a large share of them, became great. She is the most eminent exemplification of the fulfilment of the parable of the Mustard-seed; in which Jesus predicted that out of His doctrine, so adverse to all worldly greatness, a system directly the opposite in spirit and in practice would arise. And as this greatness can only be obtained by desertion of Christ's principles, so it can only be maintained by the sword of *justice*, while the Church ought to be witness of *mercy*, exhibiting it in her dealings with the world.

She is next represented as "seated on many waters." John does not mention that he saw these waters: but the angel tells us that they were seen by him. Ver. 15. "The waters *which thou sawest*, where the Harlot sitteth, are peoples, and multitudes, and nations, and tongues." Literal Babylon was built on the Euphrates, a "great river." Rome's river, the Tiber, was not great. But her resemblance to ancient Babylon, as seated on great waters, was mystic: she sat on many waters, considered as the ruler of many nations.

"The kings of the earth," who are always spoken of indefinitely, making up no one constant number, are carefully to be distinguished from the *ten* kings of Antichrist. The kings of the earth existed even in John's day, and they were then ruled by the woman with force of arms. xvii. 18.

But between that day of John and her doom, which is here shown, there was to subsist a period intermediate, passed by her in the sins specially described in this verse.

1. *She fornicates with kings of earth.*

Christians are to (1) *obey* kings in things civil. Rom. xiii; 1 Pet. ii. 13-17. Or (2) to *suffer*, if what is evil is enforced on them.

The second Psalm beseeches kings to offer full devotion to Jehovah and His Christ; but only a seeming regard is paid to it, which ends in open opposition. When they are first called for by God at the sixth Seal, they hide with a bad conscience, like Adam and his wife (vi. 15); and at length are found with arms in their hands gathered against Jesus.

Prayer for kings is commanded; *not, that they may be converted and obedient to the faith*, but that God's people under them may enjoy quietness. 1 Tim. ii. 2.

But if kings will not join themselves to Christ, putting off their royalty as incompatible with the Sermon on the Mount, the false Church will debase itself to them.

Rome has taken strangers instead of her husband. She has sought to please earthly kings, and has given her affections and obedience to them. She has prostituted Christ's rites and promises to the worldly: she has surrendered Christ's principles for money and honour, just as the maid sells her virtue.

Kings can understand a State religion with its pomp and forms; and can patronize Rome as the centre of Christianity, great in antiquity, fame, and worldly pretensions. Kings have virtually said, " Accredit us and our people as Christians, and we will accredit you as Christ's Church."

The *Church* is regarded as coextensive with the *nation* : and the ruler of the one is lord of the other. The much-admired " UNION OF CHURCH AND STATE " is therefore described here. The union of Church and State is the union of the *Church* and the *world ;* and the power conceded to the governors of the world in regulating the affairs of Christ's people is the fornication here supposed. No Church of Christ can throw down its hedges, admitting the ungodly to its fellowship and rites ; and allowing kings to be accounted, in virtue of their office, its rulers, in return for royal patronage, wealth, and honours ; without committing the sin here supposed.

Rome was the first guilty of this fault ; and, from her practice and example, this offence has flowed into other nations. Rome has introduced its corrupt Christianity into nations, through the power of princes : so it was that Romanism entered England, under the monk Augustine. Nominal and national religion is the result.

This state of things ends with Satan's casting out of heaven into earth. Then his plans change, and become open and hurried, because of the brevity of time. Coincidently, the ten kings of the False Christ arise, and destroy the Babylon of the west.

Her place is then transferred to the east. A remnant escapes from mystic Babylon to literal Babylon. Then the literal Babylon is cast down by the tremendous final earthquake. She has in that day put off all mask of belonging to Christ, and falls as the world's great city, mourned by all the worldly. This is a brief sketch of what will be more fully developed.

She is called only a harlot, not an adulteress ; because, though professedly affianced to Christ, Christ has never received her.

At the time when John beholds the Harlot's doom, this period of fornication with kings is past. During the middle ages, and just before the close, Rome, which has lost her military greatness, rules by unlawful influence, such as the harlot exercises over her paramours. It seems probable that this influence will reach its height just before the destroying stroke overtakes her.

But her sin has another aspect.

"*The dwellers on the earth were made drunk with the wine of her fornication.*"

To kings she is the harlot: to her subjects she is the dispenser of wine. As kings own her, their subjects receive her doctrine. To those who make the earth their resting-place, she is a centre of influence: she does not rule them by warlike power, but by force of doctrine. As the love of the world increases, Rome's power will increase over the worldly-minded.

Her doctrine is strong as wine; and man is as disposed to partake of it as he is to drink wine. Mankind must have a religion of some kind: and the religion of Rome is suited to his fallen taste. Rome's influence over kings is a sort of *personal* influence, such as that of a harlot: her power over the nations is more distant, like that of wine.

When once Rome's doctrine is received, it exercises a mighty influence, whether over the individual or the community. It intoxicates: it produces false views, and feelings, and conduct.

Her doctrine is "wine of *fornication.*" Christianity is too holy, strict, self-denying, humbling, for men by nature. Rome discovers to the nations a way of enjoying the world to the full, yet with the flattering belief that they are the servants of Christ. Her wine is that of fornication: for her doctrine arises out of her worldliness; and earthly greatness, splendour, physical religion, and the doctrine of sacramental efficacy, are the results. Men are to be justified by their works, and human priests come between God and the sinner.

She occupies prematurely, and therefore on false principles, the place hereafter given to the earthly Jerusalem during the millennium, and to the heavenly Jerusalem after that blessed period. And as she unlawfully takes that position, so she is a contrast to the holy Jerusalem. That *enlightens*, and *heals* the nations. xxi. 24; xxii. 2. She darkens their eyes, and infects them with leprosy.

It appears to me that this feature of Rome's history is not yet fulfilled. That it predicts a period of noisy, tumultuous, universal enthusiasm throughout the nations of Europe on behalf of the doctrines of Rome. They will drink copiously of her cup of falsehood, and shout her praises. No such state of things as that supposed in these words has, I suppose, yet occurred. The nations nominally Christian will turn away their ears from the truth, and be turned to fables. Romish legends, then, are just the preparative for the final rejection of Christ, which is here displayed in the rise of the Antichrist. Already the symptoms of this are visible. Religion is asking the embellishments of art. The spiritual truths of Christ are falling more and more coldly on many ears. But Rome's principles and practices will cause false visions of joy, and peace, and unity, to dance before men's eyes. The drunken man is slow to reason, and the history of the past will not unseal men's eyes to the true principles of Rome, and their dismal effects. A reaction strong and fearful follows.

3. "And he carried me away into a wilderness in spirit: and I saw a woman sitting on a scarlet wild beast, full of the names of blasphemy, having seven heads and ten horns."

1. It needs no proof that Rome dwells in a *spiritual wilderness*. Her worldliness and idolatry have produced that.

2. But it is also very worthy of observation, that Rome sits amid a *literal wilderness*: and thus the outward and visible is the counterpart to the spiritual. The surrounding country, called the Campagna of Rome, has been happily designated a "marble wilderness."

This desolation of the adjacent country began about the time when the Popes rose to especial power. In John's day it was a flourishing region.

Around Rome lies both a moral and natural wilderness. How is that word fulfilled—He turneth " a fruitful land into barrenness, for the wickedness of them that dwell therein " (Ps. cvii. 34).

John sees " a woman." This is afterwards declared to mean a " city." v. 18. She sits or rests upon " a scarlet wild beast."

The time at which she is so beheld, is after the prophetic period of this book has begun, and the throne of Rev. iv. is set up. Jerusalem is in her old place, and God is judging the earth.

The Wild Beast has two forms.

1. The *Territorial*—or the "*Holy* Roman empire" as it is called under the Papacy. The Woman rides the empire as a territory, while the personal heads of the empire, or the pagan emperors of Rome, are in abeyance. This phase of the Wild Beast is supposed in the twofold meaning of the heads; as we shall see presently.

2. But the main aspect of the Wild Beast is the *personal*. The Wild Beast, as explained by the angel, is a series of the supreme rulers of the territory or empire.

It is evident, at a glance, that every trustworthy interpretation must make broad severance between the

Woman and the Wild Beast. The Woman is destroyed by the Wild Beast. The Wild Beast abides and is destroyed, after the rejoicings in heaven over the destroyed city are past. xix. 3, 19.

The Wild Beast presented at the close is the personal Antichrist, either under his seventh or his eighth head, or under both: which last is probably the true view. The seventh head (or immediate predecessor of Antichrist) rises into greatness by upholding the Woman at first. The seventh head is cut off by assassination, and the eighth head, or the False Christ, then takes his place, and in conjunction with the ten kings destroys her.

The Woman rides the Wild Beast. The temporal and ecclesiastical powers co-operate at the close, just before the ecclesiastical is overthrown. The ecclesiastical power appears as a woman: she retains some traces of order and of a Church. *He* is a monster, *without law*, even as to his form. Though a woman, however, she fears not the monster, nor does she abhor it. She endures its lawlessness and impiety against God.

4. "And the woman was clothed in purple and scarlet, and gilded with gold, and precious stones, and pearls, having a golden cup in her hand full of abominations, and the filthiness of her fornication."

"Purple" was the colour of *Roman* authority. Hence the broad stripe of it on the breast was the mark of a Roman senator: the narrow stripe, of the knight. The emperor's robes were of purple, and the taking of the empire is called, "assuming the purple." For a man to wear this colour was regarded as equivalent to aspiring to the sovereignty.

Purple, physically considered, is a *mixed* colour: it is compounded of blue and red. In its spiritual significance it represents the mixture or confusion of the *heavenly* blue with the *earthly* red of Edom. And at this time Rome unites the earthly and the heavenly. An emperor presides over the city, the centre of earth. The "Holy Roman Empire" is restored under its imperial head. And a Pope ruling there also, makes it the professed heavenly centre of earth.

"Scarlet" is the colour of Popes and Cardinals. "I caused (says Barnes) this inquiry to be made of an intelligent gentleman who had passed much time in Rome, without his knowing my design. 'What would strike a stranger on visiting Rome, or what would be likely particularly to arrest his attention as remarkable there?' and he unhesitatingly replied, '*The scarlet colour.*' This is the colour of the dress of the *cardinals—their hats, and cloaks, and stockings being always of this colour*. It is the colour of the carriages of the cardinals, the entire body of the carriage being scarlet, and the trappings of the horses the same. On occasion of public festivals and processions, scarlet is suspended from the windows of the houses along which processions pass. The *inner colour of the cloak of the Pope is scarlet; his carriage is scarlet, the carpet on which he treads is scarlet. A large part of the dress of the bodyguard of the Pope is scarlet*, and no one can take up a picture of Rome without seeing, that this colour is predominant. I looked through a volume of engravings representing the principal officers and public persons of Rome. There were few in which the scarlet colour was not found, as constituting some part of their apparel: in not a few the scarlet colour prevailed almost entirely."

She is "gilded with gold." This denotes its profusion, and its externality. She is not gold within, but only covered lightly with it. She is not incorruptible and eternal, but her destruction is nigh. The Pharisees were whited sepulchres, having one aspect outwardly, another within. Her "gold, precious stones, and pearls" display her incurable worldliness : these ornaments are out of season in this present evil age. 1 Pet. iii. 3; 1 Tim. ii. 9. Then is this evil woman the direct contrast of the picture drawn of a Christian.

This passage is remarkably illustrated by what occurs at the consecration of the Roman pontiff, as described by the official book. " The pontiff-elect is conducted to the sacrarium, and is divested of his ordinary attire, and clad in the papal robes." " The colour of these," says Wordsworth, " is there minutely described ; suffice it to say, that five different articles in which he is then arrayed are *scarlet*. Another vest is specified, and this is covered with *pearls*. His mitre is then mentioned, and this is adorned with *gold* and *precious stones*."

" Having a golden cup in her hand, full of abominations, and the filthinesses of her fornication."

She does not wear a crown, or wield a sceptre : her power is of influence alone. This cup is not a literal one. Rome is a mystic person : so is her cup. She carries no literal cup : nor would a literal cup spiritually intoxicate the nations. Besides, its contents are discovered to us, and they are spiritual.

" The abominations and filthinesses are the shameful transactions of that artful policy by which Rome reduced the nations to a state of utter impotence."—*Hengstenberg*.

It is very remarkable that the Pope has struck a medal, in which Rome is represented as a *woman* holding forth A CUP, with the motto, " She sits upon the universe."

Elliott has given the plate of this. She holds the cup of *seduction*, God will give her the cup of *wrath*.

Of ancient Babylon the Lord says :—

" *Babylon hath been a golden cup in the Lord's hand, that made all the earth drunken : the nations have drunken of her wine ; therefore the nations are mad* " (Jer. li. 7).

This is true still more of modern Babylon. She has taken away Christ's cup from "the laity," to give them one of her own.

It is observable that the Harlot and the Wild Beast are several times spoken of in connection : but she is never mentioned together with the False Prophet. Is it not because the False Prophet, who ascends out of earth later than the Wild Beast, does not arise till she has been swept away from Italy ?

5. "And upon her forehead (she hath) a name written, a mystery—BABYLON THE GREAT, THE MOTHER OF THE HARLOTS AND OF THE ABOMINATIONS OF THE EARTH."

The name here written gives us the city's *spiritual* name, just as " Sodom and Egypt " are the spiritual names of Jerusalem. It is her name as she is seen by God. Rome professes herself to be Christ's chief Church : but Jesus regards her as the hateful city of the Old Testament, destined to be destroyed.

It is a mystery, or secret. The Holy Spirit thought not good to say openly, it is ROME. Neither does He give to Jerusalem its direct and usual name among men. He gives, then, to Rome a mystic name. As in chapter one, the stars were a mystery, but literally signified the angels of the seven churches : so here, Babylon, as away from her literal place, is presented in mystic fashion. By this title, Rome is thrown into its true spiritual connection with the Old Testament. It is in spirit " Babylon the Great."

The Lamb and his Bride is the answering mystery.

Rome now is professedly no longer what she was under the emperors. She is as self-described the centre of Christ's people, as before she was their great persecutor. But she is in spirit still only what she was. It is now the time of " the Mystery of the Christ " (Eph. iii. 3, 4). And during this period, the iniquity of the world is concealed behind a Christian mask. We hear of "*Christian nations:*" millions believe themselves to be Christ's, because they were sprinkled in infancy; while their hearts are at enmity with God, and they are lovers of the world. The so-called Christian nations appear before God not as His children, but (as He described them to Daniel) as ravenous, bloodthirsty *wild beasts*.

Rome is Babylon.

As Babylon smote the Holy Land, and its inhabitants, and burnt the Holy House, carrying away the sacred vessels to its idol temples; so did Rome. Two of its generals entered the Holy of Holies: (1) Pompey, and (2) Titus. Caligula attempted it, but the time for the third and last invasion of it had not yet come. It was attempted also by some of the Grecian kings. From these two sources, the two last wicked ones proceed.

The Harlot is "*New* Babylon," as the bride is "New Jerusalem." But the New Babylon returns to its old place. As during the time of the Mystery the Lord has removed His temple and city, so has Satan removed his.

The Harlot is "BABYLON," which signifies "CONFUSION" (Gen. xi. 7–9). She has confounded whatever she ought to have kept separate and distinct. She has confounded the Church and the world, the Law and the Gospel, the word of man and the Word of God, heaven and earth, mercy and justice, the dispensation of our rejection and the millennial joy, the elders of the Church with the priests of old, and the promises to the Jew with the blessings of the Church.

Rome had a secret name, known only to her pontiffs and great men, and studiously kept concealed. Her name Roma, if transferred into Hebrew, signifies, "*the lifted up*." Now, on "every one that is lifted up," the Day of Wrath is to fall. Isa. ii. 12.

She is a slumbering volcano of paganism, about to burst forth anew, when Romanism has attained her final gleam of triumph.

At Babel of old was men's sinful point of union. Gen. xi. So is Rome the centre of unity to corrupted Christianity. Ancient Babylon had many idols : so had Rome pagan : so has Rome papal. Babylon, as Wordsworth observes, was surrounded by morasses and swamps, which create a dreary and unwholesome neighbourhood. 'Tis thus also with Rome.

She is " Babylon THE GREAT."

Jesus taught His disciples to be little in their own eyes, and instructed them in doctrines the very opposite to worldly greatness.

Rome, as the centre of *empire*, is " Great Babylon : " as the professed centre of the *Church* of Christ, she is the great Harlot. The blending of Christianity with worldly empire is spiritual whoredom in Christ's sight. All the evils of her doctrine have sprung from this root. Romanism is the doctrine of Jesus, leavened with the flesh and the world. She has taken to herself Jerusalem's millennial place : she is the rival of Jerusalem under Solomon. Hence, when Christ's kingdom comes, she is destroyed as the city of His enemy.

God owned Jerusalem of old, as the centre, both of kingly government, and of divine worship. But, in this dispensation, to attempt to unite the two is confusion. Rome's making herself the Holy City, the place of the High Priest and the king ; the centre of pilgrimages and jubilees ; is the wearing of rags stripped from the mantle of Jerusalem. The Most High never owns Rome, save as the centre of Gentile empire. This book, when representing to us Christianity, most significantly *never mentions Rome*. It speaks not even of any Churches of Europe, but of seven favoured ones of *Asia*.

"The Mother of the Harlots of the earth."

It is very observable that *the Pope* does not once make his appearance in all John's description. The wickedness is of a feminine, not of a masculine description. The Holy Spirit's great charge is of false doctrine. The Pope and Romanism are the development of (1) Justification by works. As the result of that, (2) the priesthood of a class of Christians comes in, in order to satisfy divine wrath.

She is not only a harlot herself, she is "the mother of the harlots of the earth." She has set the example of uniting the Church and the world: and other national establishments have followed in her train. Jesus recognizes *churches of believers separated from the world, as lights*. But national assemblies, taking it for granted that all the nation are elect and holy, are a stain upon the truth ; a shame to the name of Christ. Rome calls herself, in the Creed of Pope Pius, "*mother* and mistress *of all churches*." She is indeed mother of many assemblies calling themselves churches, but they are not owned of Christ as chaste virgins. They are "of the earth," and are "harlots."

How shall we know who are her daughters ? They have Rome for their mother. Every church that acknowledges Rome for her mother is a harlot. Those churches which have been set up by missions from Rome, are her daughters.

Morally, that so-called Church is a harlot, which, loving the world more than Jesus, consents to take the civil magistrate as its ruler, throwing open its communion to the worldly, and calling them Christians. The civil ruler, in return for Christian rites, and the name of Christ, gives to the ministers rank and wealth. Then the Church's witness to the world of its iniquity and its danger from Christ's appearing ceases, and the salt has lost its savour.

"And of the abominations of the earth."

"Abominations" signify, in Old Testament language, idols.

Rome, then, is described as the *patroness of idolatry*. And most interesting is it to notice somewhat in detail the confirmation given to this by history. Several of the Greek emperors of Constantinople set themselves to oppose the idolatry which was coming in as a flood, into that which called itself the Christian Church. That was the source of Rome's modern independence and power. "In the eighth century of the Christian era, a religious quarrel, *the worship of images*, provoked the Romans to assert their independence: their bishop became the temporal as well as the spiritual father of a free people."—*Gibbon*, vi. 519.

6. "And I saw the woman drunken with the blood of the saints, and with the blood of the martyrs of Jesus: and I wondered as I saw her, with great wonder."

She "is drunken with the blood of the saints." As loving the world, she hates the renewed in spirit. 'Tis no slight draught of blood that intoxicates her: it is long and deep. Her bloodthirstiness is not occasional, and soon satiated. For many years the Most High has restrained Rome's persecutions: only in secret has she been able to slay. But this predicts a time when those who refuse her superstitions will be cut off in numbers. Rome has slept off her former potations of blood, and is cool and wary. This predicts a day when she will have power to destroy all who will not bow to Trent, and to the Jesuit. Then she will imagine that all is secure. Nothing can withstand her: caution will be cast to the winds. Her open murderousness will disgust her friends: her manifest unbelief will multiply infidels. Then her hour of doom has struck.

When Jerusalem goes off the stage as the shedder of innocent blood, Rome comes on it. Papal Rome indeed nominally refuses to shed blood. She does not kill heretics *herself*: she only intimates her pleasure, *that kings and emperors should be her executioners*. But God despises the flimsy pretext, and lays at her door the guilt of the blood shed. *Jezebel* put Naboth to death, though the letter ran in Ahab's name.

It is instructive in this point of view to notice that she is not said to *shed* blood, but to *drink* it. It is shed by her authority, and she rejoices in it. When the massacre of St. Bartholomew took place, and Protestants throughout France were butchered, Rome appointed religious services of thanksgiving, and struck medals in commemoration of the joyful event.

Rome has been the source of two persecutions.
1. Pagan, or imperial.
2. Papal. It is of the last that the Holy Spirit is speaking. The emperors are in abeyance for the long interval between the sixth and seventh head of the Wild Beast. During this time the Woman coquets with the kings of the earth. After a merciful cessation, continued to our day, papal persecutions revive; and continue till the imperial head is restored and destroys the woman. Then paganism re-assumes its religious hold on men, and its power is put forth to persecute and cut off the servants of the Most High.

In the last verse of the *next* chapter, Babylon is declared guilty of the blood of "*prophets*:" here, of the blood of *saints* only. Hence it appears that prophecy is restored to earth between this point of time and the close. A prophet is more than a saint.

By "the saints," as distinguished from "the martyrs *of Jesus*," I suppose we must understand God's Jewish servants, which were presented early to our notice. (vii.)

How is it that the Church which (as Romanists assert) is to be the guide of all Christians, is never named as a Church in all that prophetic book, which is to enlighten Christ's people till His return ? How is it, on Rome's theory, that the apostle John alone appears, and "St. Peter" is never named, nor the Popes as his successors in the apostleship ?

John, as he gazed, grew amazed. So completely was probability overturned, so utterly had the Harlot outraged all the Saviour's commands, that he marvelled, and was horrorstruck at the wickedness and the impudence of her professed subjection to Christ.

How extraordinary, that out of the meek, lowly body of Christ's persecuted few in Rome should rise a man professing to have authority over the *Holy Roman Empire*, and to possess the right to rule even the Emperor ! How marvellous, that while asserting herself to be Christ's Church, she should persecute to death believers in Jesus more fiercely than the pagan emperors ! How strange, that a professed follower of the *Lamb* should tolerate the *Wild Beast's* blasphemies, and ride his back ! How awful, that out of the Church in Rome, once owned of God, should spring such utter devotion to the world ! that poverty and lowliness should be exchanged for riches and power, ruling for suffering, the diffusion of darkness and superstition in place of light and simplicity, idolatry in place of the worship of faith, and that in place of giving up life for Christ, there should be shedding the blood of those beloved by Jesus ! A rich, ruling, bloodthirsty, drunken harlot, allied to the False Christ, usurps the place of the faithful and patient virgin expectant of her lord ! That as Church of Christ, set to bear witness to the world of its sin and its doom, should be so utterly lost as to stoop to its worst evils, was deserving of wonder indeed ! Babylon in her first aspect (chapter xvii.) is the attempted union of Christianity with "dwelling on the earth" in the Apocalyptic sense. But in chapter xviii. we have the dwellers on earth fully developed; and Christianity, even in its outward form, is gone. John might mourn over the failings of the Churches of his day, and Jesus might send sharp messages to them, but they were not beyond hope : she is.

7. "And the angel said unto me, Wherefore didst thou wonder ? I will tell thee the mystery of the Woman, and of the Wild Beast that is carrying her, that hath the seven heads and the ten horns."

The angel would explain what was symbolic. His explanation, then, is to be taken literally.

Babylon in chapter xvii. is Babylon mystical, or Rome. In the next chapter it is Babylon literal. The angel's explanation ceases with chapter xvii. The passing away of mystery is characteristic of Revelation. There is mystery, while the Church lasts : when the Jew returns to his place, literality returns again.

The Woman is an impersonation of the *spiritual* power centred at Rome, and displaying itself chiefly in the dark ages. The Wild Beast is an impersonation of the *temporal* power centred at Rome. This is the reason why the two are brought into such close contact. The seven heads are common to both; to the city in one sense ; to the Antichrist in another.

In this chapter the previous life of the False Christ is opened to us. In chapters xi. and xiii. his history commences with his rise from the abyss. This tells us of his predecessors, and of his former life.

8. "The Wild Beast which thou sawest was and is not, and is about to ascend out of the bottomless pit, and to go into perdition : and the dwellers on the earth shall wonder, whose names were not written in the book of life from the foundation of the world, when they behold the Wild Beast, because it was, and is not, and shall be present."

There are two senses given to the Wild Beast, (1) a general, (2) a special one. (1) In the general sense, the Wild Beast means the Roman empire. (2) In the special, it signifies a particular emperor of Rome, wielding all the power of the empire. It is to the Wild Beast in the special sense that the angel's explanations apply.

He "was." He once existed as a man on earth. He died, and as dead is found no longer on the earth. His threefold titles are in designed comparison with the threefold title of God. "He who *was*, and *is*, and *is to come*."

"And is not."

This gives his relation to the present, or the time at which the angel was speaking. It is the natural consequence of the former word—"He was." His day is over : he is no more found among men.

"Joseph *is not*, and Simeon *is not*, and ye will take Benjamin away" (Gen. xlii. 36–38).

"He is about to ascend out of the bottomless pit." These words instruct us where he is now to be found. He is a disembodied spirit, and as he was a wicked man on earth, he is among the damned souls in Hades, in the part specially assigned to the lost. But he, unlike the rest of men, is about to appear on earth once more. "He is about to ascend out of the abyss"—or the great central cave of the earth. His ascent brings him again to earth. This shows us that a *person, not* an *empire*, is here spoken of. He returns to Rome, where he dwelt of old.

"And to go into perdition." He does not, as the consequence of his escape from the place of the dead, live for ever. That is true of the saints, but not of him. Nor is he cast again into the pit which he left. Having been anew clothed with a body, he is cast into the eternal "lake of fire." xix. 20 ; xx. 10. Thus he stands in close contact with "the man of sin," who is also "the son of Perdition" (2 Thess. ii. 3).

9. "Here is (seen) the mind that hath wisdom. The seven heads are seven mountains, on which the woman sitteth."

A similar expression occurred in the close of chapter xiii. "Here is wisdom." There it related to the Wild Beast's number: here, to his heads. What is meant by them?

They have two significations; (1) territorial, and (2) personal. For an empire consists jointly of territory and of men.

(1) The Wild Beast, in its general sense as the Roman empire, has territory which always abides. The heads of earth are mountains: the heads of an empire considered as territory, are the mountains of its metropolis.

In this sense the word "head" is used in the Old Testament. Num. xxi. 20; Jer. xxii. 6; Amos i. 2; ix. 2. Thus we speak of Flamborough *Head*, Beachy *Head*, Lizard *Head*.

The heads are seven mountains, on which the woman sits. The heads then are first noticed as they stand related to the *Woman*. They clearly point her out to be Rome. The names of the seven hills are—

Aventine, Cœlian, Esquiline, Janiculan, Palatine, Quirinal, Viminal.

The number seven is peculiarly in keeping with our book. The New Jerusalem has but one mountain (xxi. 10), as the Lamb has but one head.

Rome was, as Dr. Wordsworth says, in John's age " usually called *the seven-hilled city*."

"Virgil, Horace, Tibullus, Propertius, Ovid, Silius Italicus, Statius, Martial, Claudian, Prudentius—in short, the unanimous voice of the Roman poetry during more than five hundred years, beginning with the age of St. John, proclaimed Rome as *the seven-hilled city*."

"On the imperial medals of that age which are still preserved, we see Rome figured as a woman on seven hills, precisely as she is represented in the Apocalypse."

The coin of Vespasian, described by Capt. Smyth (Roman Coins, p 310), represented "Rome seated on seven hills; at the base Romulus and Remus suckled by the wolf: in front, the Tiber personified:" pp. 279, 280.

Horace says, "The gods, who look with favour on *the seven hills*."

Tibullus—"Ye bulls, feed on herbage of *the seven hills*."

Propertius—"The lofty *city on seven peaks*, which rules the whole world."

Ovid—"But Rome looks round on the whole globe from *her seven mountains*, the seat of empire and abode of the gods."

These will suffice as heathen testimonies.

The Fathers regarded Rome as Babylon. "When I dwelt *in Babylon*," Jerome says, "and resided within the walls of the *scarlet adulteress*, and had the freedom of *Rome*, I undertook a work concerning the Holy Spirit, which I proposed to inscribe to the Bishop of that city."

"*Babylon*," Augustine says, "*is a former Rome, and Rome a later Babylon*."

The earliest commentaries on the Apocalypse consider Rome to be Babylon.

Many Romish writers of the first eminence admit the same interpretation; as Bellarmine, Baronius, Bossuet, Hug.

Bellarmine says, "Moreover *John in the Apocalypse everywhere calls Rome Babylon*, as Tertullian noticed, (against Marcion, book 3), and as is *clearly to be inferred from the* xvii*th chapter of the Apocalypse,* where Babylon is said to be seated on seven mounts, and to be possessed of authority over the kings of the earth. *For neither was there any city beside Rome which in John's day professed authority over the kings of the earth, and it is notorious that Rome was built on seven hills." De Rom. Pont.* ii. 2. *Cited by Wordsworth.*

But how, then, do Romanists evade a truth so destructive to the claims of their Church?

1. By affirming that the reference is to Rome *pagan,* not to Rome papal. Rome papal is the infallible holy mother of all Churches. Whereupon Dr. Wordsworth asks very pertinently, If so, how is it that John, while writing of Rome, does not distinguish between Rome as heathen, and Rome as the seat of the universal See? How is it, that while painting in dark colours the iniquity of heathen Rome, he did not drop a word to the Churches to be guided by Rome and her infallible bishop? 2. These Romish writers suppose that the prophecy of Rome's destruction (chapter xvii.) was fulfilled about 300 years after the Apocalypse. If so, then we say, Rome has fallen only to " become *the habitation of demons, and the hold of every unclean spirit* " (xviii.).

The woman sits on these hills. It is primarily a *city* then, not a *system.* It was a city ages ere it was connected with Romanism; and its history is here indicated, before it accepted Christianity. Hence it is said, " On which the *Woman* sitteth : " not yet the *Whore.* She is the Harlot, only as professedly Christian. She is called " the Woman " again in the last verse of this chapter, where the reference is again made to pre-Christian times.

10. " And they are seven kings : the five fell ; the one is ; the other is not yet come, and when he shall have come, he must continue a short (space)."

(2) We are now introduced to the other signification of the seven heads. As the Roman empire consists of *men*, the heads are heads of men, or kings. The heads as they are related to the city are mountains, which are *cotemporaneous* and *abiding*. The heads as they are related to men, are *successive* and abide *not*.

Both senses occur together in one passage.

"The *head* of Syria [a territory] is Damascus [its capital], and the *head* of Damascus [its ruler] is Rezin."

"The *head* of Ephraim is Samaria, and the *head* of Samaria is Remaliah's son" (Isa. vii. 8, 9).

Of the double significance of a symbol or type we have another instance in Gal. iv. 24, 25. The woman Hagar is both a mountain and a covenant.

The heads of Rome, then, are seven "Kings," or emperors. They are currently interpreted to mean "forms of government." This is clearly wrong.

1. The word "king" is never so used, either in the Old Testament or the New, or in classical authors. 2. The seven forms of government specified were not regularly successive, as these kings are. The dictator appears at irregular periods of the history. 3. If the heads are forms of government, so are the horns; for they, too, are "kings" (v. 12). 4. It were strange indeed, if "kings" first signified a "form of government" in general, and then were to be reckoned in their real sense of "kings" as one of those forms of government. 5. As the seven hills are of one kind, so are the seven kings. 6. The leopard of Daniel has four heads. Dan. vii. 6. They are not four forms of government, but four kings. 7. Some would reckon the *Christian* emperors as one of the seven forms. This cannot be: for the whole seven belong to *Satan*, xii. 3; xiii. 1, 2. The seven emperors were all on Satan's side. For the same reason the seven heads cannot be *Christian* kingdoms; for they belong to Satan.

How were there names of blasphemy on the earlier forms of government? "But there were more than seven emperors: why are but seven selected?" There were more churches then seven: why were but seven selected?

Out of the many emperors of Rome, how are we to select the seven? The task is a difficult one. But little is said of the "five who had fallen," and it is with regard to these that the difficulty mainly lies. But there are, I believe, two principles to guide us.

1. They must be kings who assumed the "names of blasphemy," or were worshipped as gods. xiii. 1.

2. They were also, if I mistake not, and as a moral consequence, cut off by a violent death. This is asserted of five of them. "The five are fallen." The sixth, if he were Domitian, was also slain. The seventh, yet to come, is (as we know by xiii. 3, 14) to be cut off by violence.

That the word "fallen" applies most forcibly to a violent death will be proved by the following instances: Judges iii. 25, 27; 2 Sam. i. 19, 25, 27, etc. So also Rev. xviii. 2.

The five first, then, would be—

1. Julius Cæsar, assassinated. He was worshipped as a god. He is reckoned the first emperor by Suetonius, Dio Cassius, and Josephus.

2. Tiberius.[1]

3. Caligula, assassinated.

4. Claudius, poisoned.

5. Nero, committed suicide.

[1] "Some are of opinion that a slow-consuming poison was given him by Caius. Others say that during the intermission of a fever, with which he happened to be seized, food was denied him. Others report, that he was stifled by a pillow thrown upon him:" *Suetonius*, § 73. If these reports be not considered tenable, then Romulus would be the first. He was both assassinated and worshipped.

It may be added, that of the two next emperors, Galba was slain, and Otho slew himself.

"The one is."

These words refer to the time when the angel was explaining the vision. John wrote when the sixth of the emperors according to the conditions supposed by the angel, was alive. That head was Domitian. Domitian was the last of the twelve Cæsars, as John was the last of the twelve "apostles of the Lamb."

Domitian was fearfully extravagant in his blasphemous usurpation of the divine titles; he also was cut off by the hand of the assassin.

"The other is not yet come."

How long a space was to intervene ere this fullness of evil should appear, is not said. *The seventh head has not yet appeared.* He can appear only a short space of time before the true Antichrist. He prepares the way for the Great Usurper. He restores the lost succession of the Emperors of Rome. He comes only when the apostasy from Christianity is taking place, or has been complete.

The Wild Beast was ruling in his sixth head—six being the number of wickedness. Then comes a gap, and the Woman takes the place of the heads, and rules by influence. The power of the sword is taken away. The *Woman* becomes the Great *Harlot* in the interval between the sixth and seventh kings. While the wickedness of the nominally Christian Church is coming to the full, the pagan Emperors of Rome are in abeyance. Indeed, it is most remarkable that the first emperor who professed Christianity left Rome, or the Woman, transferring his seat of government elsewhere. The six emperors embodied the spirit of the *unholy* Roman empire. It was once heathen; it has become professedly Christian: it will become heathen again.

The Book of Revelation does not give us, as is

generally assumed, a history of the Roman empire. On the contrary, there is a huge blank after the sixth emperor; and the history of the empire becomes merged in the few traits told us of the Harlot. As, after Zedekiah, there occurred, and still continues, a large gap in the kings of the line of David, whence the Christ has sprung; so is it also with kings of Rome, whence is to spring the False Christ. While Jerusalem lies desolate, and her kings have ceased, the kings of Rome have ceased also. Restore Jerusalem, when "the Mystery" is past, and the antagonist power rises also.

"And when he cometh he must continue a short space."

When the time is come, a Roman emperor, at first seemingly acquiescent in Romanism, will arise, whose heathen leanings, however, will become more and more apparent, till at length he professes himself to be the One True God. He is a mighty and victorious king. But this impious pretension raises enemies. He "falls," like the preceding six. He is assassinated with the sword. xiii. 3, 14. But his dead body comes to life again. The true Antichrist is then on the stage.

This account of the matter explains how such prodigious results can be effected in so short a space as three years and a half. They are not times of preparation. Antichrist shows himself at once on a fully prepared theatre. The line has long been laid down; the electric wires are in their places; every touch thrills the world.

11. "And the Wild Beast that was, and is not, both himself is the eighth, and is (one) of the seven, and is going into perdition."

1. At times the Wild Beast signifies, *generally, the Roman empire.* xiii. 1. As such it possesses *seven heads*, and ten horns. The Woman sits upon it as such: as " a scarlet-coloured wild beast, full of names of blas-

phemy, *having seven heads,* and ten horns " (xvii. 3, 7).

2. But it signifies also the last or eighth head; that is, the individual emperor who is the Antichrist. The head of the empire is identified with the empire. He wields all its power, and expresses its spirit.

The former view (ver. 8) of the Special or Individual Wild Beast gave his *personal* aspect; this discovers to us his *regal.* It teaches us the place he occupies among the Kings of Rome.

"Himself is the eighth." It is a person who is spoken of, not a thing.

The seventh head is not the Antichrist proper. He immediately precedes, and makes way for him, as John Baptist did for Jesus. He is the crowned head of chapter xiii., that is wounded to death.

The Antichrist is the eighth head. Eight is the number of resurrection. On the eighth day Jesus rose.

The eighth note in music is a resurrection or recurrence of the key-note. The eighth day is a recurrence of the previous first. 'Tis a new person that arises, as compared with the previous one. In the previous cases of resurrection, the same person who was slain has arisen. This were necessary to a perfect resurrection. But 'tis not so in Satan's resurrection. God allows no nearer approximation than this.

There are only seven kings, but behold an eighth, who is one of the seven. Here is an enigma of God's making, a mystery. The seventh head of the Wild Beast will arise, reign a short time, and be cut off with the sword. But he will be reanimated, arise from the dead, and so become the eighth head. It is not strictly speaking a *new* head, for it is *one of the seven heads :* but it is a *new life ;* and as death is reckoned the end of all, this reappearance of the seventh is regarded as the eighth. It is not, however, strictly the reappearance of the seventh head. For though the body of the seventh King of Rome be reanimated, the soul that will restore animation to the corpse is not the soul of the seventh king, but the soul of one of the first five kings who had already died in John's day.

There are seven *bodies*, and seven *souls*, but there are *eight lives*: and the corpse that is restored to life is animated by another soul than that by which it was originally tenanted. For if it were the seventh king's own soul which returned to its own body, it could not accomplish God's mysterious words. For the last king, the Antichrist, is "the Wild Beast that *was* and *is not*." "*Is*" is the contrary to "is not." "Is" signifies *is living*; as is admitted by all; "the one is." "Is not," then, will signify "has lived, and *is dead*." Now it cannot be true of the seventh king, that "he *was*, and *is not*." No, of the seventh king it is written, "He is *not yet come*, and *when he cometh* he must continue a short space." He cannot then be the Wild Beast who *had* come, and had left his place on earth.

Perhaps this is the meaning of that mysterious prophecy: Isa. xiv. 29. The seventh king is the one who smites Israel. His sceptre is broken by assassination. But rejoice not, for out of him springs a worse, even the eighth king. He will be to Israel a more dreadful scourge than the seventh king. He will be the fiery flying serpent to the adder that preceded him.

The eighth is "one of the seven."

He does not on rising occupy his old body. That is corrupted. He enters into the body of the lately slain, scarcely cold, seventh head. A new soul reanimates the former body. But the eighth head is of the same spirit and tendencies as the seventh, and pushes with resistless and supernatural energy the schemes of his impious predecessor. Just as the two Witnesses—

Enoch and Elijah—carry out plans begun during their former life on earth, so does Nero appear like himself.

It seems probable, that while the seventh head is at peace externally at first with the Harlot, that the eighth head never is so : but that as soon as it rises, and among its first acts, it destroys the Woman.

Again, as Jesus' claim to be the Son of God, asserted before those who condemned Him as guilty of blasphemy, was proved true by His rising again from the dead ; so the claims to Godhead made by the seventh head appear to be proved by the Wild Beast's resurrection. This idea fulfils every condition of the sacred enigma. It gives one an awful idea of the great delusion, which will engulf so many thousands in perdition. It approaches so near to the genuine credentials of Jesus, the true Messiah, that, as men's *hearts* are in his favour, it cannot fail.

Jesus and Cæsar alike *living* are presented to the Jews. They prefer Cæsar. "Put Jesus to death." It is done. Jesus and Cæsar *in resurrection* are both set before the Jews again. Cæsar is once more accepted by all but the elect of them.

"And goeth into perdition."

This awful feature is twice repeated. He is "the Man of Sin," the worst of men. Lest his greatness should dazzle us, his fearful doom is left upon our mind.

It is a person ; not an empire, not a city. Persons only are to be damned. Babylon is cast into the abyss ; but Babylon is never said to " go into perdition."

12. "And the ten horns which thou sawest are ten kings, who have not yet received a kingdom ; but they receive authority as kings one hour with the Wild Beast."

The heads are the world-wide emperors, of whom

there can be but one at a time. The horns are many: they may be as numerous as the emperor shall please.

"The seven heads are seven *kings*."

"The ten horns are ten *kings*."

They are both kings in the same sense; they differ relatively, as principal and subordinate.

The ten kings are distinguished from the seven, as being (1) cotemporaneous, (2) subordinate, and (3) military. They probably profess no settled territory, and do not reside and rule.

As the horn of an animal is inferior to the head of which it is a powerful appendage, so are these ten kings inferior to the seven which preceded them. Hence they are set in a class apart.

The seven heads are kings of kings. Rome allowed some subject kings to retain their diadems in subserviency to itself.

These are not kings *of Rome*, as were the seven preceding. And from the expression "they receive *authority* as kings," it would seem that they are not actually possessed of territory, and a metropolis at which they reside. They are, I imagine, kings of *war*: a point illustrated by the history of Napoleon, whose generals through war rose to be kings. That emperor had in his camp, says Croly, "Five *kings*, four princes, twenty-one dukes:" *On the Apocalypse*, p. 116.

They are "ten kings." The Current Interpretation has changed this into "ten king*doms*." This cannot be allowed. Moreover it cannot tell which are the ten kingdoms. *Sixty* different lists of them have been given.

(1) The angel's observation is made in explanation of a secret, and is to be taken strictly.

(2) The substitution of "kingdoms" produces absurdity. "They are ten *kingdoms*, which have

received no *kingdom* as yet, but receive authority as *kingdoms*." "For God hath put it in their *hearts* (persons) to fulfil His will, and to agree and give their *kingdom* to the Wild Beast" (17). The distinction between "king" and "kingdom" is everywhere kept up in this book.

(3) They only come into being as kings in company with the last head. What darkness has been poured around this book, by changing the concrete into the abstract ; by putting " systems " for persons ! If we would gain clearness, we must make what is definite in the prophecy as definite in the exposition. As Jesus and His twelve apostles were persons—as Napoleon and his twelve marshals were persons—so will the Wild Beast and his ten kings be persons.

It is only by substitution of "kingdoms" for "kings," that the current idea of the Apocalypse being a *history of the Church*, or of Christendom, can at all be defended. Once perceive that the Holy Spirit is speaking only of a set of *cotemporaneous kings* ruling at the same time with the brief dominion of the Antichrist, and the fundamental mistake is discovered.

These ten kings are not the same with "the kings *of the earth*." Those were in being long ere the Apocalypse was written.

The ten are cotemporaneous : as the words of this verse indicate. The seven heads are successive : and the steps of the succession are pointed out to us. But these rise to royal authority when the eighth head does. They probably become kings at the assassination of the seventh head : just as at Alexander's death his generals became kings. As the twelve apostles and the unnumbered kings of the millennium become not kings of men till Jesus appears : so with these satellites of the False Christ.

"The kings of earth " are found throughout the

book. Jesus takes one of His titles from them. He is "the prince of the *kings of the earth*" (i. 5). The ten kings are found in this chapter alone. The "ten kings" are never found with the adjunct "of the earth" attached to them. "The kings of the earth" are never found with the definite numeral "ten" prefixed. As commentators have toiled in vain to compress the kings of the Roman empire into the number ten, they should have perceived, in the shifting of boundaries and numbers of the monarchs of Europe, that they had fallen rather among the indefinite "kings of the earth" than among the abiding definite ten.

In this chapter, two great parties are discovered to us, which are not interchanged.

(1) The "*Whore*" and the "kings *of the earth*."

(2) "*The Wild Beast*" and the "*ten kings*." "The kings *of the earth*" are never found with the *Wild Beast*, till the Woman is destroyed, and the three demons working miracles have persuaded them to fight against God, and His Christ. The kings of the earth are nominally Christian kings, loving the Harlot, and imagining her to be the bride of Christ. The ten kings blaspheme Christ from the first, and hate the Harlot, because they mistake her for His bride. The ten kings are never said to fornicate with the Woman. The kings of earth are never said to hate her.

"Which have received no kingdom as yet."

I collect, then, that these ten are all, or most of them, generals of the seventh king, who assume sovereign power when he is assassinated. The resurrection which ensues binds them devotedly to the eighth king.

"But they receive authority as kings."

That is, they possess the kingly office not in its entirety, but with a qualification. Kings are lords of territory, rulers of persons. These have power over persons, but no settled territory and metropolis.

They are only a mutilated copy of the twenty-four elders, and the kings of Jesus' making. For they are not " priests " as well. The Wild Beast has no priest. His second in authority is a prophet. Priesthood, or the necessity of a mediator, because of the fall, is denied by Antichrist.

" One hour with the Wild Beast."

They reign " one hour "—a brief time—the three and a half years of the Wild Beast. Thus the time of the Antichrist and of his ten kings is only, at the utmost, the time of an individual's life : that is, the year-day theory, with its series of kings and many centuries, is false. The Wild Beast's " hour " is 1,260 days.

13. " These have one mind, and give their power and authority to the Wild Beast."

Such a scene as this has never yet been beheld. The kings of Europe, even granting them to be ten, have never been of one mind with the reigning Popes.

Never were there ten kings unanimous with the reigning emperor of pagan Rome.

This concord, so wonderful in the eyes of the world, arises out of two causes, (1) an external one ; and (2) an internal.

(1) The external cause is the resurrection of the eighth head. He whom they serve is no mere mortal, like the world's princes in general. He is proved " Divine," to their eyes, by His rising from the dead. Kings though they be, they, like their subjects, worship and obey. One whom they once regarded as the great king and successful general only, is now invested with the blaze of godhead.

(2) The internal cause is the power of Satan by his evil spirits exerted over their hearts. As the Holy

Spirit is the author of true unity, such as subsisted in the Church when He came down in power at Pentecost, so is Satan the author, when permitted, of that false but mighty enthusiasm on behalf of what is evil, which from time to time has swayed multitudes. Such was the unanimity of the first followers of Mahomet.

From this unanimity springs much of the terribleness of those times. The Antichrist's decrees are not obeyed with exactness in his immediate neighbourhood, becoming less and less enforced as they travel into regions distant from his presence. No : these ten lieutenants carry out his will at the farthest corners of his empire.

They are the military leaders of Antichrist's kingdom ; as the False Prophet is the minister of public worship, the ecclesiastical head.

Their unity of feeling toward the Wild Beast, and their hatred of the Harlot and of Christ, spring out of one and the same state of mind. They hate the Lamb supremely, because He is the great enemy of the False Christ. They hate the Harlot, because she is a witness on earth in some dim measure to the True Christ.

This giving their power to the Wild Beast is the result of a full confidence in him and affection toward him. They next destroy the Harlot, and then fight against Christ.

14. " These shall war with the Lamb, and the Lamb shall overcome them, for He is Lord of lords, and King of kings ; and they that are with Him are called, and chosen, and faithful."

The open war with Christ is the last act of the ten kings. They war first with the Harlot, and prevail against her. This flushes them with vain thoughts of their power, and they are encouraged to attack Christ Himself. They attack the Harlot through hatred to Christ, and expect Him to defend her. Hence their victory intoxicates them, as if it were a victory over the Son of God Himself.

The Lamb "overcomes." He wins the victory by Himself. The armies of heaven follow Him, but the sword of His mouth is that which hews down the nations, and His feet tread the winepress of divine wrath.

"And they that are with Him are called, and chosen, and faithful." If they be the armies of xix., as I suppose, they are all risen from the dead. If I mistake not, the three words are designed to tell us that elect ones out of the three preceding dispensations—the Patriarchal, the Mosaic, the Christian—compose the legions of Christ. Antichrist unites the reprobate of these three dispensations: the Christ, I believe, combines the elect of the same. Not all the saved compose the army: it is an election from the elect of all dispensations.

They are "called," designated by name: "chosen," out of many others: "faithful," as manifested by their life now past. They come with Christ out of heaven, in resurrection-bodies. They form "the armies in heaven" (xix. 14).

15. "And he saith to me, The waters which thou sawest where the Harlot sitteth, are peoples, and multitudes, and nations, and tongues."

The Harlot sits on the waters. But the Harlot is a mystic being: so are the waters therefore. Babylon the Great of this chapter is "Babylon a Mystery." So, then, are the waters mystic waters: hence their meaning is expounded for us. "They are peoples and multitudes."

As literal Babylon derived her splendour and greatness from her natural waters, so does Rome obtain hers from the people and nations she has subjected to her spiritual sway. Thus God says of the Assyrian, represented mystically as a cedar—" The *waters* made him *great*" (Ezek. xxxi. 4).

This tells us the secret of Babylon's greatness and her fornication. Had she been content to gather only Christ's elect, she had never been either a " harlot " or " great."

The Harlot sits on the waters. Three forms of her sitting are mentioned.

1. She sits on the Wild Beast: on him she politically rests.

2. She sits on his seven heads, which are seven mountains, on which the city naturally reposes. xvii. 9.

3. She sits on mystic waters, while she is also situated in a " wilderness." The waters are her *ecclesiastical* point of repose. Observe the difference between the first and last of the three notices of this part. " The waters which thou sawest, where THE HARLOT sitteth." " THE WOMAN which thou sawest is the great city." She sits on the waters at the close, as the Harlot, by virtue of her power derived from corrupted Christianity. She ruled the kings of earth of old as the military pagan city simply.

How remarkably confirmatory of this passage is that coin, already noticed, struck by Rome, in which, representing herself as a woman holding out a cup, the motto is, " *She sits upon the universe.*"

She " sitteth on many waters." The present tense notes her attitude at the moment of judgment.

16. " And the ten horns which thou sawest and¹ the Wild Beast these shall hate the Harlot, and shall make her desolate and naked, and shall eat her flesh, and burn her with fire. 17. For God put into their hearts to perform His mind, and to make one

---

¹ Καὶ. A, B, also the Sinaitic MS., 33 cursive MSS., the Vulgate in MS., and five other versions: Griesbach, Lachmann, Scholtz, Tischendorf, and Tregelles. [Also R.V.]

mind, and to give their kingdom to the Wild Beast until the words of God shall be fulfilled."

Very important is the reading, "AND the Wild Beast." It stands on sure grounds, both external and internal.

1. It is the more difficult reading : the received one has evidently sprung out of the difficulty of comprehending it.

2. It rests on the authority of the best MSS. and the decision of critical editors.

The Wild Beast is distinct from the ten kings. The Wild Beast here is not, as generally taken, the Roman empire divided into ten kingdoms. The Wild Beast differs from the Woman.

The Wild Beast is the special, individual emperor. The Woman is the Harlot, or the city's last development. While the emperor and his city were both pagan, there was harmony between both, as in John's day. But the Woman has become nominally Christian, since John wrote of the reigning heathen emperor, "The one is."

In this change, then, lies the root of the enmity of the Wild Beast or eighth head. He was pagan when he lived on earth : he returns to earth with the same religious predilections. Is it Nero ? Imagine with what disgust and enmity he would learn that *Rome* had become *Christian!* That *his* Rome had imbibed that magical and execrable superstition, which it was his delight to persecute to death !

With the False Christ arise new kings. They are the result of the infidelity engendered by Romish superstitions : the reaction of the intelligence of the last age against anile doctrines and fables. They regard Romanism as Christianity, and reject it. They are military adventurers, and their acts are wars.

"THESE," then, "hate the Harlot."

The word "these" is emphatic. It embraces both the emperor and his subject kings. They hate from the first. Their enmity is not the result of other's persuasion; they never felt any other sentiment. The ten princes hate the Harlot (1) because she is really hateful. Her teaching and practice are shocking, even to unenlightened natural conscience. Her doctrines disgust natural reason. Transubstantiation makes infidels of all who will use their understanding. Her shutting up of the Scriptures because they witness against her, in spite of the many proofs that they were designed to be read by all Christians, is another scandal.

Her doctrines, specially the latter or Jesuit ones now in force,[1] are awful and horrible. Her blood-thirstiness, venality, deceit, tyranny, covetousness, will revolt even the carnal mind. Her acts, specially in the latter days, when thrown off her guard by momentary success, will raise her up enemies, fierce and strong. The ten kings who rise after the first intoxication of men by her doctrines, will find that friends have become foes, and that she may be swept away from earth with the applause of most.

(2) They hate her, then, for what is evil in her: but they hate her also, for what of *truth* yet remains in her. She still testifies to the Trinity in Unity, to Jesus as the Son of God, to His incarnation, death, and resurrection; and to the Holy Spirit's descent. These cardinal truths stand opposed to the Wild Beast's pretensions. *He* is the one true God; he denies both the Father and the Son. These points the Pope cannot surrender and still be Pope: he is committed to them, and must stand or fall with them. The horizon, then, must be swept clear of the last traces of Christianity, ere the deadly lie of Satan can have free play. The hatred, therefore, of the emperor and his ten kings speedily destroys her.

---

[1] See Liguori's Theologia Moralis, and Pascal the Younger.

The kings *of the earth* are lukewarm friends of the Harlot, and do not interpose to defend her from Antichrist's hot enmity.

The seventh emperor may temporize with the Harlot while she rides the Wild Beast : but the eighth has no need for concealment ; he blasphemes and acts out his hatred at once. The imperial and previously ruling pagan power of Rome destroys the subsequent ecclesiastical power, and its abode.

"They make her desolate."

She dwells in the wilderness. The Campagna of Rome is already a dreary desert girdling in the city. They destroy life and its abodes, in the one habitable spot of the Campagna ; and the whole becomes, then, one uniform desolation.

They make her "naked."

She appears, before her judgment, magnificently arrayed. This apparel is stripped off : her wealth is seized on. Her secret iniquities, her crimes on principle, are laid bare. The doings of her convents and inquisitions are discovered. The "secret instructions" of her agents and their results come to light.

They "shall eat her flesh." This refers, I suppose, to the destroying of her inhabitants, and of her great men in particular.

"And burn her with fire." We read not of any defence made by her : she is a woman. Rome has several times been scourged with fire and sword. This is the last time. It is universal : it never rears its head again. Rome was partially burnt by one of the five first kings.

Of Nero, Suetonius writes thus :—

"He spared, however, neither the people nor the city itself. Somebody in conversation saying, 'When I am dead let fire devour the world ;' 'Nay,' said he, 'let it be whilst I am living.' And he acted accordingly: for pretending to take offence at the ugliness of the old buildings, with the narrowness and winding of the streets, he set the city on fire so openly that many men of Consular rank catched those of his bedchamber with tow, and torches for lighting in their houses, but durst not meddle with them. There being near his Golden House some granaries, the groundplot of which he was extremely desirous to come at, they were battered with rams, because the walls were all of stone; and then set on fire, with the view of spreading the flames. During six days and seven nights this terrible devastation continued, the people being obliged to fly to the tombs and monuments for lodging and shelter. Upon this occasion, a prodigious number of stately buildings, the houses of generals celebrated in former times, and even then still beautified with the spoils of war, were all laid in ashes; as also the temples of the gods, which had been vowed and dedicated by the kings of Rome, and afterwards in the wars with the Carthaginians and Gauls; in short, everything of antiquity that was remarkable and was worthy to be seen. This fire he beheld from a tower in the top of Mecænas's house, and 'being prodigiously diverted,' as he said, 'with the beauty of the flame,' he sang the ditty of the destruction of Troy, in the dress used by him upon the stage." *Life of Nero Claudius Cæsar*, § xxxviii.

Did Nero burn Rome, when he was emperor in his days of flesh? How surely would he burn her with these strong reasons prompting him, should he rise from the dead! Out of his first burning of Rome sprang his persecution of the Christians whom he burnt alive in his gardens. He would be but carrying out his former actions, if he burnt nominally Christian Rome.

After these three blows, on her wealth, on her inhabitants, and on their habitations, their work is fully done. As Rome has burnt full many a saint, so shall she be burned! As by kings she became great, by kings shall she be cut down. As by kings she slew Christ's people, by them shall she be destroyed. "With the same measure that ye measure, it shall be measured to you."

17. "For God put (literally 'gave') into their hearts to do His mind, and to make one mind, and to give their kingdom to the Wild Beast, till the Words of God shall be fulfilled."

The horns of the Wild Beast are not, like those of the Lamb, possessed of *eyes*. They blindly fulfil the purpose of God. Bent on their own sinful aims, full of hatred to the true God and His Son, they yet, of their own will, zealously carry out His purposes.

They "*give*" their kingdom to the Wild Beast. They are independent of him, but voluntarily make over all their authority to him. Though they are kings, their whole regal power is devoted to bring others into subjection to him. It is impossible to be even a nominal Christian, and at the same time a follower of the False Christ. Therefore, the very name of Christianity, and its stronghold, shall be swept away.

They give their "kingdom," not their "kingdom*s*." They transfer to Antichrist no territory, but their royal power. They consider that Antichrist's kingdom is only fully come, after the Harlot is destroyed. Hence the zeal of all the eleven. Her destruction is a means to the Wild Beast's reign.

This unity of will and of power in the ten kings subsists only "till the words of God are fulfilled." There may be, there *is*, unity in error and sin. This is a strange thing, 'tis presented to our eyes as a moral marvel. Error and sin are selfish, disuniting, explosive, disruptive in their essential nature. But then they have power to freeze the lost together in one compact body, while this long arctic night of three and a half years lasts.

18. "And the woman whom thou sawest is the great city, which possesses the kingdom over the kings of the earth."

While the angel is depicting her as the pagan city, he calls her " the woman." " The seven heads are seven mountains on which the *woman* sitteth, and they are seven kings." This is her relation to the heathen emperors known to John. But after she professes to be Christ's, abusing her influence thence derived, she is " the Harlot." " The waters where *the Harlot* sitteth." " These shall hate *the Harlot*." When the dispensation changes, and her " judgment " is shown, she is " *the Harlot*."

Her *local* designation closes the explanation: it seals up its sum. This is another and irrefragable proof that Rome is meant. None but Rome was in John's day mistress of the world. While some have objected that Constantinople, as well as Rome, is built on seven hills; this mark suffices to discriminate:—Constantinople was not then in existence: much less was it ruling the world.

Observe, that it is the *city*, not the *emperor*, which is said to be ruling the world; because the city was the unit which was to abide from John's day to the Day of the Lord; while its rulers were to change. It is very remarkable, too, that while the emperors are described as its rulers, the Popes are *not*. There is no designation of the *priest*-king, who sways the crozier and sceptre during the times of the " Mystery."

Observe again, the city is said to be reigning over " the kings *of the earth*." Immediately before, our eye had been fixed on the *ten* kings. Now we return to the indefinite description, which marks another class of kings. The ten had not then risen : the kings of earth had. She never rules the ten; they possess authority over her. Without resistance, apparently, she, when the time is ripe, becomes their prey. The kings of the earth are successive, and over an unnumbered series she reigns by power.

That Rome was ruling the kings of the earth in John's day, is clear from all evidence. Eusebius, in his flattering discourse of the days of Constantine, gives us a view both of the commencing harlotry with kings, and of the point now before us.

" The supreme sovereigns, sensible of the honour conferred upon them by him, now spit upon the faces of the idols." " They also confess Christ the Son of God as the universal king of all, and proclaim him the Saviour in their edicts, inscribing his righteous deeds and his victories over the impious, with royal characters on indelible records and in the midst of *that city which holds the sway over the earth* " (Book x. 4).

That Rome ruled at our Lord's birth, that word makes known, " There went out a decree from Cæsar Augustus that all the world should be taxed " (Luke ii. 1). " The Jews therefore said to him [Pilate, the emperor's lieutenant], It is not lawful for us to put any man to death " (John xviii. 31). At Ephesus, John's usual abode, it ruled. " We are in danger to be called in question for this day's uproar, there being no cause whereby we may give account of this concourse" (Acts xix. 40). King Agrippa and Bernice appear subordinate to Festus. " Then Agrippa said unto Festus, I would also hear the man myself." " Tomorrow, said he, thou shalt hear him " (Acts xxv. 22).

How remarkable, that Rome should hold in her hand and bear testimony to this prophetic book, which describes her, condemns her, and celebrates her doom.

Is it any wonder that she attempts to lock up the book which so discovers and denounces her sin?

CHAPTER XVIII

BABYLON'S SECOND OVERTHROW

THERE ARE TWO DESTRUCTIONS OF BABYLON: one of *Babylon mystic*, which has subsisted during the time of "the Mystery:" and one of *Babylon literal*, which is to survive Babylon mystic, and to be destroyed after her.

Answering to these two different positions is the different style of the prophecy in chapter xvii. from that found in this chapter. The former dealt chiefly with symbols: a harlot, and wild beast, heads, horns, waters, a cup, and so on. To these the angel adds explanations, that we might know they were not to be literally taken.

But in this chapter the horns and heads, and the Wild Beast, do not appear. No explanation is given. Why is this? Because there is no mystery to be explained: that is, it is literal. Mystery rests on chapter xvii., for it describes the city of man during God's time of mystery. But it does not rest on chapter xviii.: for by that time, mystery has fled. Babylon the *Harlot* is past: but Babylon the *city* of old time reappears.

As God is retiring from the Church back to Israel, so Satan retires from the mystic Babylon to the literal one, and destroys her, because she is in the way of his kingdom's appearing.

The reconciling link between the two conflicting

views is found in the vision of the ephah. Zech. v. 5-11. That appears to describe the remnant of Rome as flying from Europe to Babylon, welcomed and flourishing there.

1. " And after these things I saw another angel coming down out of the heaven, having great authority; and the earth was lightened by his glory."

Is earth to shine with the glory of a created angel? Surely not.

This is the angel of chapter x., whose face shone as the sun. Then he was clothed with a cloud. Now that covering has rolled away. The destruction of the Harlot shows the true Bride's advent as near at hand.

2. " And he shouted with strong voice, saying, "Fell, fell Babylon the Great; and became the abode of demons, and the prison of every unclean spirit, and the prison of every unclean and hated bird.' For all nations have drunk of the wine of the wrath of her fornication, and the kings of the earth have committed fornication with her, and the merchants of the earth are waxed rich through the abundance of her delicacies."

An angel speaks with power, that the nations may hear. He expounds the reasons of Babylon's two falls.

Nothing but the twofoldness of Babylon, and a double fall, will explain these chapters.

1. The necessity of two Babylons with a fall to each appears on the face of this prophecy. For after the ten kings have burnt the Harlot utterly, the people of God are told to come out of her, and to avenge themselves of her. After Babylon's destruction by the ten kings she sits a queen still, in the mart of commerce, and promises herself that she shall see no sorrow.

2. As there are two Jerusalems, the Old and the New, in this book; so are there two Babylons, the Old and the New.

3. There are two notices of Babylon's fall, beside

those found in chapters xvii. and xviii. The first is given almost as soon as the False Christ appears, and ere the last bowls begin. xiv. 8. The last is noticed at the last bowl, just before Jesus appears in the clouds, to cut off the Antichrist and his crew. xvi. 10.

4. One of the first acts of the Wild Beast, as we have seen, is to destroy the Harlot as opposed to his empire. Then his worship is set up. The Harlot's doom, therefore, occurs three years and more ere the literal Babylon is cut off. The Harlot is destroyed, before the vials of woe descend on the worshippers of the False Christ. This, with all her sins, is no part of her guilt.

5. As the thrice repeated " Woe, woe, woe," of the eagle announced the three trumpets that were to follow, so the " Fell, fell," point to two falls of Babylon.

By the burning of the kings God delivered Rome over to be a desert. Man, living man, should nevermore dwell there. As it is a wilderness, demons take possession of it. They love solitude and desolation. Matt. xii. 43. The demoniacs of Gadara abode not " in any house, but in the tombs " (Luke viii. 27).

Isaiah, describing Babylon, says, " Satyrs shall dance there " (xiii. 21). The LXX translate this, " *Demons* shall dance there."

Rome is become also " the prison of every unclean spirit." But are not " demons " " unclean spirits " ? They are. They are expressions which are continually used as nearly equivalent. Matt. xii. 28, 43 ; Mark i. 27, 34, 39 ; Matt. ix. 33, 34 ; x. 18. Yet it would appear from this passage, that there are unclean spirits which are not strictly " demons." Demons strictly taken are spirits which never were embodied. But there are spirits of the dead ; or human spirits who in their lifetime were wicked men. It is these, I suppose, which are here distinguished from demons. This throws light upon that prophecy of the great future apostasy, that some shall abandon the faith, giving heed to "*seducing spirits*, and teachings of *demons* who speak lies in hypocrisy" (1 Tim. iv. 1, 2).

Babylon becomes a "prison" for such beings. They are shut up within its precincts, it would appear, by God. These ruined ones are imprisoned amidst ruins. These spirits of the dead are confined to the city of the dead.

As the heavenly city is the free abode of angels, and of the holy risen of men; so is this unholy city the gloomy jail for the lost.

Bossuet, in order to get rid of the terrible woes which here encircle Rome, endeavoured to prove that the description refers not to Rome papal, but to Rome pagan: and that the destruction of Rome took place at the commencement of the dark ages. But the net of God still entangles his feet. If so, from that day forward Rome has become the habitation, not of saints and angels, but of *demons* and of *every unclean spirit !*

"And the prison of every unclean and hated bird." How can we call it "the prison" of every bird? Must we not alter the sense of the word here? Our translators thought so; and accordingly rendered the same Greek word first "hold," and then "cage." But 'prison' is the one sense of it in the New Testament. And here it applies also, though less strictly; God will confine them to the desolations of Rome and its Campagna. They love and choose ruins, and beyond them they will not venture; specially when millennial life and joy fills all other parts of the earth.

This is foretold by the Old Testament prophets also. Isa. xiii. 21, 22; Isa. xxxiv. 13, 17. See also Jer. l. 39.

The kings of the earth fornicated with her. Pagan Rome toyed not with kings. It ruled them sternly by the sword. Rome papal, then, is here.

"And the merchants of the earth grew rich through the power of her luxury."

This charge appears now for the first time. It appears in conjunction with the description of a great commercial and wealthy city. From this I gather that the description is intended to apply not to Rome, but to the literal Babylon. It describes her standing just before the Saviour's manifestation.

How differently does the sacred writer regard commerce and its widely extended operations from the view taken by statesmen! They foster it, boast of it, regard it as the glory of a nation, the source of its greatness and power. It is not indeed evil in itself to barter one thing for another: but as pursued in its higher walks, it can scarcely be followed without the soul being devoted to the world.

This was a city of excessive luxury: and commerce was at work in all its avenues, to supply that luxury. This, then, discovers to us the selfishness and covetousness of it. It spent needlessly, on its pleasures, what would have relieved the pains of sickness, and the hunger and nakedness of poverty. The hearts of the inhabitants were fixed on earth, and the enjoyments of a sentenced life; not on heaven and the resurrection. How little is excessive luxury regarded as a provocation of God! The warning of the parable of the rich man and Lazarus falls on unwilling ears.

4. "And I heard another voice out of the heaven, saying, 'Come out of her, my people, that ye have no fellowship with her sins, and that ye receive not of her plagues. 5. For her sins reached to heaven, and God remembered her iniquities.'"

"Come out of her, my people."
Of what people is this said?
1. Not of the Church. That is no longer recognized, and its better part has long been on high. This people

of God is to avenge itself on Babylon: but the Church is not so to do. The risen are in heaven, and are called to rejoice over God's vengeance taken on Babylon without their aid. Ver. 20.

2. Israel is the people intended. They are often addressed of God in those words: specially in connection with Babylon. Jer. l. 4, 6. To *them* the call is given—"*Remove out of the midst of Babylon, and go forth out of the land of the Chaldeans, and be as the he goats before the flocks*" (l. 8). And again, in the next chapter—"*Flee out of the midst of Babylon, and deliver every man his soul: be not cut off in her iniquity: for this is the time of the Lord's vengeance*" (li. 6). And again—"*My people, go ye out of the midst of her, and deliver ye every man his soul from the fierce anger of the Lord*" (li. 45).

The sentence of Lo Ammi, "Not my people," is now reversed: for Israel now repents.

The command, therefore, to "come out of her" is literal. It is not the spiritual desertion of a body falsely calling itself a Church of Christ. It is the local journey from a literal city: like Lot's out of Sodom, and Rahab's out of Jericho. There is no word of any of Christ's people being in Rome, save as slaughtered there.

But how should this command be obeyed, if there were but one Babylon, and that were a solitude? How could any be in danger of those judgments, if they had already fallen? How could God's people avenge themselves, if there were only ruins without inhabitants? How would there be any need to call on them to come out, if the city were already in flames? This tells them of the *secret* judgments of God close at hand. The city is to be swallowed up. A sign is given to tell the Jew when to leave. Jer. li. 45, 46.

"That ye have no fellowship with her sins."

With thousands around indulging themselves in sin through careless unbelief, how easy is it to fall in with the current! How hard to escape contamination! "Evil communications corrupt good manners."

"For her sins reached unto the heaven."

The expression is a very singular one. It seems to give the idea of each sin being a snowflake that adhered to its fellows, till it made a pile whose top reached the sky, and drew down the lightning.

"And God remembered her iniquities."

So long is the interval between Babylon's first sin at Babel and this point, that it would seem as if God had forgotten her misdeeds. But it was not so. He took notice, though He smote not at once. Thus Israel's sin of the calf is not yet avenged. Exod. xxxii. 34.

That word, "God remembered her iniquities," is a golden hook to connect this with xvi. 19. "*Great Babylon came in remembrance before God* to give unto her the cup of the wine of the fierceness of His wrath." This scene, then, occurs immediately before, and at, the last bowl.

6. "Render to her as she also rendered: and double the double to her according to her works: in the cup which she mingled, mingle to her double."

This is the call of God: but to whom can it be given?

Certainly not to the Church; for that is expressly taught, as its law, not to render to a man according to his ill deserts. The very word here used is employed in Rom. xii. 17, with the negative affixed to it. "Recompense *to no man* evil for evil." "*See that none render evil for evil unto any*" (1 Thess. v. 15). "*Not rendering evil for evil*, or railing for railing, but contrariwise blessing" (1 Pet. iii. 9). These are but apostolic echoes of the Great Master in the Sermon on the Mount. The return of *good* for *evil* is *our* command.

How then are we to understand this? Does God contradict Himself? By no means. He has two peoples; an earthly, and a heavenly. The one are witnesses and agents of His *justice;* the other, of His *mercy.* The time of mercy and the people of mercy are past. The heavenly people are removed to heaven. It is the literal, fleshly people of God who are now addressed. They are ministers of justice. "Eye for eye" is their motto. They stand abreast of the Two Witnesses, and are possessed of the same spirit of righteousness. The passage before us is in the clearest connection and agreement with Ps. cxxxvii. The captive prophet speaks of his people's sorrows in the land of Babylon. Then follows the appeal. "O daughter of Babylon, the destroyed![1] *happy shall he be that rewardeth thee as thou hast served us.* Happy shall he be that taketh and dasheth thy little ones against the rock" (*marg.*) (8, 9). In this sentiment, so contrary to Christian feeling and practice, the intelligent believer may see how wrong it is to make the Psalms the standard of Christian worship.

Not that vengeance on the evil-doer is evil. Far from it. God Himself has sanctioned it: it is evil only to the believer in Christ, and during the present dispensation. It will be the abiding rule of the "Day of Justice," and the millennial dispensation. Be it observed, that no such word as this is found throughout the xviith chapter, which discovers to us, as we suppose, the state of things during the church dispensation.

The people addressed are to "double to her double." Does that mean that they are to give her twice as much punishment as she deserves? By no means. It

[1] Our translators render, "who *art to be* destroyed": but the Hebrew is not so. The very strangeness of the expression throws it into the most entire accordance with the previous desolation of the city here taught.

is to be not beyond her desert, but " according to her works." Her evil works, then, are double, as her destruction is also to be. That is, Babylon has two forms—(1) the LITERAL BABYLON, (2) the mystic or ROME. Both have destroyed the temple at Jerusalem; both have oppressed and slain both Israel and the Church of God. The remnant that escapes the burning of Rome flees to the literal Babylon, as the vision of the ephah (Zech. v.) discovers. Hence the two are both morally, and, to a certain extent, politically, identified.

As then Babylon's crimes are twofold, twofold is the stroke of God and man. The first blow came from the ten confederate kings of Antichrist. The second is given by Israel just before her swallowing up by God. The ten kings destroy her first form in hatred to Christ. Israel smites in obedience to God. The ten kings take vengeance for her western sins; Israel, for her transgressions in the east especially. The day is now come in which God renders to each " according to his works " (Matt. xvi. 27 ; Rom. ii. 6).

" In the cup which she mingled, mingle for her double." This is a reference back to xvii. 4. Babylon has a golden cup in her hand full of abominations, and filthiness of her fornication. This she gave the nations to drink. She is now to drink herself. The word " mingle " refers to the cupbearer's province in ancient times. They drank wine diluted with water. The servants of the master prepared it.

7. "As much as she glorified herself and lived in luxury, so much give her of torment and mourning : for in her heart she saith, 'I sit a queen, and am no widow, and mourning shall I not see.'"

Bellarmine makes "temporal felicity" one of the marks of God's true Church.

Though Rome has so lately been made desolate by God : though Babylon, smitten of the Most High, lay in ruins for centuries ; she is confident of never seeing woe. Though full of her sins, set face to face with a just God in His hour of wrath, she is at rest in false security. Though the prophets of God have foretold her doom, she will not believe. The Church and Jerusalem below have their sorrows now. John xvi. 20–22. Their glory is to come. The saints of the first resurrection and their heavenly city will take, with God's full sanction, in the millennial day the place of glory, and power, and security ; a place which she usurps " out of due time."

8. " Therefore in one day shall her plagues arrive : pestilence, and mourning, and famine ; and in fire shall she be burned up ; for strong is the Lord God who judged her."

The passage of the Old Testament which this brings vividly before us is Isa. xlvii. 8, 9.

It is hard to understand how no note of her connection with the Wild Beast is struck.

There may be remnants of the magnificence of Rome when destroyed by the ten kings : but it will be an utter burning when God's fire is kindled on Babylon. Rome and Babylon both burned both the city and temple of Jerusalem. With fire are they, too, burned up.

This second desolation is directly and peculiarly God's. Man hurled the brand before : but now 'tis God's destruction. He takes one of His Old Testament names here.

It is remarkable that the participle is in the past tense, " the Lord God who judg*ed* her." This confirms the twofoldness of Babylon. She has been already smitten ; the ten kings ignorantly wrought God's mind. God's strength is about to be put forth in the blow to be delivered now. If the human wrath were so desolating, what shall the divine be ?

9. "And over her shall weep and lament the kings of the earth who committed fornication with her and lived in luxury, when they see the smoke of her burning. 10. Standing far off, because of the fear of her torment, saying, 'Alas, alas, O great city Babylon, the strong city, for in one hour thy judgment came.'"

In these words concerning the kings of the earth we have a connection between this and the previous chapter. "The kings of the earth," so conspicuous in the xviith chapter, reappear in this. But the intoxicated nations of the earth are confined to that chapter: and the sailors and merchants are peculiar to Babylon's last phase. Another form of the same connection occurs in ver. 3. (1) "All the *nations* have drunk of the wine of the wrath of her fornication, and (2) the *kings of the earth* committed fornication with her, and (3) the *merchants* of the earth waxed rich through the excess of her luxury." Here the first is peculiar to chapter xvii., the last to chapter xviii., the middle or connecting link, is common to both chapters.

They weep and lament (or "beat their breasts") over her. 'Tis *passive* grief. And yet they are kings. Why do they not put forth *active* powers to aid her? Thousands await their commands; why do they not give orders to quench her burning? I suppose it is because it is divine devastation; 'tis a conflagration beyond human energies to stay.

Babylon's destruction precedes that of Antichrist. She is destroyed finally at the seventh vial. After *that*, the kings go up to battle. Perhaps their sorrow at her destruction turns into rage against God, her Destroyer. It may be that this is one of the motives alleged by evil spirits for the war of earth against the Lord of Hosts.

Their words express their feelings. They grieve over the lost city. Its sins they do not see: they regard only its worldly greatness and strength. It has left a gap not to be filled up. It has been cut off so suddenly, that the wheels of commerce through all the world stand still. It seemed so steadfast, so rich. What is secure, after Babylon has fallen ?

The kings of the earth do not repent of having set her on fire, or their words would have let us know it. Had they repented, they would have attempted to save what remained. So vast a city they could not in "one hour" utterly consume. Nor do the merchants or sailors blame any human hand; as they would have done, had a greatness so necessary to their gains been wrested from them by mortal power.

Thrice is the suddenness of its overthrow bewailed. This is the especial truth which so amazes and saddens the minds of beholders. No human hand did the work. 'Twas instant destruction. It was the effect of the great earthquake of the last bowl. It is from that point (the close of chapter xvi.) that the two views of Babylon take their rise. Of the sudden swallowing up of a city by an earthquake, an example is furnished in the case of Callao in South America.

11. "And the merchants of the earth weep and mourn over her; for their lading none buyeth any more : 12. The lading of gold, and of silver, and of precious stones, and of pearl, and of fine linen, and of purple, and of silk, and of scarlet : and all citron-wood, and all vessels of ivory, and all vessels (formed) out of most precious wood, and copper, and iron, and marble. 13. And cinnamon, and amomum, and odours, and ointments, and incense, and wine, and oil, and fine flour, and wheat, and cattle, and sheep, and of horses, and of chariots, and of bodies and souls of men."

The opposition to the spirit of commerce which this book of God incidentally shows, is very remarkable; especially as running in direct contrast to the avowed plans of rulers and people of our day. "Cherish commerce" is one of the great admitted ends of statesmanship now. But its effects upon the mind are generally the production of covetousness. Commerce flourished in Solomon's day : but it was not approved of God, and it tended to idolatry. There is no commerce in the new earth, so far as we can judge.

This is a very conclusive proof that Babylon in her last phase is not Rome. Rome pagan was not a great commercial city : much less is Rome papal. Hence the merchants of the earth do not appear in the xviith chapter, or while Babylon is mystic.

Rome has no good port, nor is she fitted to become the great commercial city of the world.

Still further, the city before us is not great in her exchanges, produce against produce ; but in her imports. She is great in purchases : the commerce of earth waits upon her luxuriousness.

Her imports are of seven classes : 1. Precious metals, etc., for personal display. 2. Articles of clothing. 3. Furniture. 4. Aromatics. 5. Eatables. 6. Conveyances. 7. Slaves.

Among the articles of furniture we do not read of " vessels of *earth*," both because of their liability to be broken on a long voyage, and also because of their cheapness. The list exhibits articles of *luxury*.

14. " And the fruits that thy soul lusted after departed from thee, and all things that are dainty and splendid perished from thee, and men shall find them no more at all."

Babylon is situated on soil of great fertility, as all travellers testify. The climate is suitable to rear almost all fruits. These will be produced in great abundance, of great excellence, and be largely sought after.

But when God deals His final stroke, all will depart : the arid desert will resume its reign.

15. "The merchants of these things who grew rich by her, shall stand afar off because of the fear of her torment. 16. Say-

ing, 'Alas, alas, for the great city, that was clothed with fine linen and purple, and scarlet, and was gilded with gold and precious stones, and pearls. 17. For in one hour wealth so great was laid desolate."

To give us a high idea of the importance of her commerce, the merchants of the earth appear in two of the sections.

The speakers see not God's hand in the blow. They do not say, "Thy will be done." They are astonished and sorrowful at the sudden wreck of the city and of their own hopes.

"And every captain, and every passenger,[1] and sailors, and as many as plough the sea, stood afar off. 18. And shouted when they saw the smoke of her burning, 'What city is like the Great City!' 19. And they cast dust on their heads, and shouted, weeping and mourning, saying, 'Alas, alas, for the Great City in which grew rich all that had ships in the sea, because of her costly expenditure : for in one hour was she laid desolate!'"

As Babylon is a place of such splendour, passengers from other lands resort to it, to behold its grandeur. These, too, mourn over its fall : the object of their voyage is destroyed. This enumeration of passengers among the company of the sea-borne, leads one to believe that the great capabilities of the Euphrates as a river, navigable for ships for 400 or 500 miles from its mouth, will be fully developed.

20. "Rejoice over her, thou heaven, and ye saints, and ye apostles, and ye prophets ; for God avenged you on her."

"Heaven" now includes three classes : "saints, apostles, prophets." All such are risen from the dead. Heaven and earth are in awful contrast. Earth rejoices over God's slain prophets : heaven rejoices over God's destruction of their murderers. Violence and iniquity cannot be tolerated for ever.

[1] Πᾶς ὁ ἐπὶ τόπον πλέων. Tregelles.

Paul was sent to mystic Babylon, or Rome : Peter writes from literal Babylon. The two great witnesses of that day were thus stationed of God : and not improbably were slain in those cities respectively. If no apostles have been slain either in the mystic or the literal Babylon, this refers to apostles yet to be raised up by God. The " apostle " seems to differ from the " angel." The angel was a stationary apostle of one Church and its adjacent sisters : the apostle was a missionary angel.

She has slain " prophets " also, both of the Old Testament and of the New. But the word probably refers to prophets yet to be raised up by God, and to be slain both by mystic and by literal Babylon.

Thus at length the cry of the slain under the altar is answered. God has avenged. The city of persecution is cut off for ever.

21. " And a single mighty angel took up a stone like a great mill-stone, and cast (it) into the sea, saying, ' Thus with a rush shall be cast down Babylon the Great City, and shall be found no more at all. 22. And voices of harp-singers and musicians, and flute-players, and trumpeters, shall not be heard in thee any more. And no mechanic of any art shall be found in thee any more. And the sound of mill-stone shall not be heard in thee any more. 23. And light of lamp shall not shine in thee any more. And voice of bridegroom and bride shall not be heard in thee any more. Because thy merchants were the great men of the earth, because by thy sorceries were all the nations deceived. 24. And in her was found blood of prophets and of saints, and of all the slain on the earth."

In the emblem of Babylon's doom there seems to be a reference to our Lord's words. Matt. xviii. 6. Babylon, as the mystic city, is an awful stumbler of the little ones of Christ. " Turn, or burn ! " is the alternative she proposed to those wishing to obey the Lord. The literal Babylon preceded her on this path, as the history of Daniel and his comrades shows. Here, then, comes her doom.

The great stone represents the great city. It takes a strong angel to lift it. As that stone with continual acceleration descended into the sea-depths, which presented no obstacle to its complete engulfing, but closed over it, and hid all trace of it from view; so with the effects of the last great earthquake. The city will descend with still increasing speed towards the bowels of earth molten by the internal fires. The earthquake gives the shock that dislodges it from its foundations. The opening earth no more stays its descent than the waves of the sea prevent the stone's submerging. It is for ever withdrawn from sight, as truly as Dathan and Abiram with their tabernacle, their tents, and their goods.

1. Babylon shall be *found no more*.
2. *Sound* of musicians shall be *heard* no more.
3. No artist shall be *found* there any more.
4. *Sound* of mill-stone *heard* no more.
5. Light of lamp shall shine no more.
6. *Sound* of bridegroom *heard* no more.
7. Because her merchants were princes, etc.

Musicians are part of the natural features of a gay luxurious city. That they shall never be heard there, is a proof of endless desolation. This doom embraces both Rome and Babylon.

Babylon shall have no remnant, no rebuilding: no workman shall lift a tool to reconstruct it. Mechanics and artists of various kinds were carried captive from Jerusalem in the day when its sins were come to the full. 2 Kings xxiv. 14, 16.

The mills used in eastern countries are handmills; the women by them grind the corn for daily use. The Holy Spirit gives first the day-sounds, which will be lost to the city of guilt. That sound Jehovah threatened to take away from Judea and the neighbouring lands by means of Nebuchadnezzar. Jer. xxv. 9–11.

When earth is all light and joy, stirring and vocal, Babylon is to be still by day, and dark by night. At night the weddings of the east are celebrated, and the shouts of joy from the bridal procession go up. But this shall never more be heard in Babylon.

The reasons of this sentence of God are next given. They are three.

The first sounds strangely in the ears of a commercial nation like England. The first offence is the immense reach and sweep of her luxurious commerce. "Thy merchants were the great men of the earth." So vast were the transactions of business, as to enrich with princely fortunes those who dwelt in her. "What was there," we are ready to say, "amiss in that?" God looks at it not as man does. Earth is under the curse. Jesus is calling disciples to be little and lowly. Matt. xx. 25-28; xiii. 31, 32. To become great, then, is to contravene His precepts. To become great on earth discloses secret unbelief of the glories of *heaven*, which are set before the Christian's eyes. It manifests unbelief, too, in the prophetic testimony of God, that all greatness on earth is about to be overturned by "the Great and Terrible Day of the Lord" (Isa. ii. 10-17).

The second charge aganst Babylon is witchcraft or sorcery. With many, all belief in this has died out; they ridicule the idea. The intercourse with spirits, however, which has become so common, will speedily reinstate the belief: and not the belief only, but the practice. Babylon will be its great centre. There and in Egypt are its traditional poles. Magicians constituted an integral part of the State officials there in Daniel's day. Dan. i. 20; ii. 2, 27, etc.; Isa. xlvii. By means of these Babylon prevails to become the metropolis of the nations again. Harlotry and false doctrine prevail in the first aspect of Babylon: sorcery in the second. It does not appear that Rome was ever pre-eminent in this particular crime.

She is slayer of "prophets." This seems, with several other Scriptures, to foretell the restoration of the spirit of prophecy. And if prophets be raised anew, once more will men's hands, whether in Rome or Babylon, be lifted to slay.

Lastly, the blood of all the slain on the earth is laid to her door. "The earth," would seem here to be limited to the Roman earth. These words seem to be the echo of Jer. li. 47–49.

CHAPTER XIX

THE MARRIAGE SUPPER, AND THE BATTLE OF GOD

1. " After these things, I heard as it were, a great voice of a numerous multitude in the heaven, saying, ' Alleluia ! Salvation and glory, and might, belong to our God. 2. For true and righteous are His judgments : for He judged the Great Harlot who used to corrupt the earth with her fornication ; and avenged the blood of His servants at her hand ! ' 3. And the second time they said, ' Alleluia ! ' And her smoke goeth up for ever and ever. 4. And the twenty-four elders, and the four living creatures, fell down and worshipped God that sitteth on the throne, saying, ' Amen, Alleluia.' "

THE mighty multitude before us consists not of members of the Church only : it embraces the saved and risen of all dispensations. The Great Multitude in white (chap. vii.) form a part of this assembly.

" Hallelujah " is the key-note of their praise. 'Tis a Hebrew word, " Praise ye Jehovah ! " and occurs only here in the New Testament.

In this context it is to be found four times ; the number of universality. God's people of the Old Testament herein lift up their praise. It is a word borrowed from the Psalms ; and occurring there frequently. It is peculiarly in the spirit of Psalm civ. 35. " Let the sinners be consumed out of the earth, and let the wicked be no more ! Bless thou the Lord, oh my soul ! *Praise ye the Lord !* "

At length " salvation " is come from God : His

people are blest in resurrection. With resurrection comes "glory;" and both "glory" and "salvation" are the forth-putting of God's "might." These things are therefore ascribed joyfully to God.

"Vengeance is *mine*," says God. The Most High avenges His risen saints : His earthly people may be called on to avenge themselves : but for these God works. Long have they waited, and God has had patience. But, as Luther said, "Blood succeeds blood; but this noble blood which Rome is pleased to shed will at length suffocate the Pope with all his kingdoms and his kings."

"Her smoke goeth up for ever and ever." The use of the present is very observable. It was then mounting up to the eye prophetic ; it would do so for ever. Her doom is that of the lost, eternal. As the men of Sodom "suffer the vengeance of eternal fire," so shall the men of Babylon.

The smoke of the ten kings' kindling would not last for ever. But that which arises from the earthquake and its subterranean fires would endure.

The elders and zöa now join in. They are not the Church nor representatives of it : they are *not* of *men*. This is the last time of their appearing. They come in together with the throne : they cease with it. This is the last glimpse of the heavenly arrangements ere the millennium. Another throne closes the earth's history. xx. 11. The elders and animals refer to the old earth, and to one aspect of it—that is—the one which lasts during the evil age, and "man's day." They are no more seen when the kingdom is fully come. Why ? Because "not to angels hath he put in subjection the future habitable earth" (Heb. ii. 5), but to man. And as these are not men, they disappear ; and *men*, with the Son of Man at their head, take their place. xx. 4–6.

The next verse (5) gives us the last view of the throne of God in the *temple*. When the elders and zöa cease their praises, Jesus takes them up. They quit their thrones : He and His saints take theirs. The throne of God henceforward ceases to act for Christ : Christ acts in person.

A white throne of judgment occupies the intermediate position, during the transfer of the saved from the old earth to the new. Then the throne of God and the Lamb is set in the *city*.

The throne has accomplished the purpose for which it was set. It has avenged the breaches of Noah's covenant, and especially the shedding of blood. It has appointed the viceroy of earth, and has defined the time during which the earth itself is to last.

5. " And a voice from the throne came forth, saying, ' Praise our God, all ye His servants, and ye that fear Him, the small and the great.' 6. And I heard as it were the voice of a great multitude, and as it were the voice of many waters, and as it were the voice of mighty thunders, saying, ' Alleluia ; for the Lord our God (Lord) of hosts reigneth. 7. Let us be glad and rejoice, and give glory to Him ; for the marriage of the Lamb is come, and His wife hath made herself ready.' 8. And to her it was granted, that she should be clothed with fine linen bright and clean ; for the fine linen is the righteous acts of the saints. 9. And He saith to me, ' Write, Blessed are the invited unto the marriage-supper of the Lamb.' "

The voice from the throne is no doubt that of our Lord. He is " in the *midst* of the throne " (vii. 17), and therefore far nearer than the elders *round about it*. Jesus owns the Father as His God ; though He is on the throne. He owns also the saved as His associates. " Praise *our* God." " My Father, and your Father, my God, and your God."

The class " ye that fear Him," seems to mark out the men of Israel, and the devout of the Gentiles.

What shall we say to the past tense used in describing the reign of God ? Shall we assert that it is a Hebrew idiom, and is to be taken as a present ? Or shall we affirm that it is to be taken strictly, and that it denotes the giving up of the kingdom by the Father, and the Son's taking it ? The same tense is used in the previous announcement by the elders at the seventh trump. "We give thee thanks, O Lord God of Hosts, who art and who wast, because thou tookest thy great power and reignedst." Here we have, not the surrender of power, but its resumption. And thus it must be here also. In English we should express this by the present tense. "The Lord of Hosts reign*ed*," would to us indicate the cessation of His power at some previous date. The kingdom of God has begun from this point. The judgment of Babylon and the reign of God introduce the rewarding of all God's holy ones.

Now is fulfilled the Lord's word on the Mount. "Blessed are those who have been persecuted for righteousness' sake : for theirs is *the kingdom of heaven.*" "*Rejoice and be exceeding glad ;* for great is your reward in heaven" (Matt. v. 10, 12).

The Bride here is not the Church, as in the Epistles of Paul. Neither the standing of the Church, nor its relations to God and to Christ, are the same as in Paul's Epistles. The Bride there is the body of those saved by faith in Jesus ascended, beginning from the time of the Spirit's descent on the day of Pentecost, to the day of the saints' gathering together to Jesus in the air. It is the great unity of those regenerate by the Holy Spirit's operation during this dispensation of the Mystery of God. But in the Apocalypse the Church is never presented as a unit, not even in the part of the book specially allotted to it.

It is a series of seven parts; rejected, or partially accepted, according to their works. Hence they stand in a position evidently contrasted with the sovereign purpose of the Father in grace, ere time was. Eph. i. They are regarded in the seven epistles as Christ's servants individually. They are never spoken of as His Bride; but each Church is divided into conquerors or conquered. It is a natural consequence of this difference of position occupied by the saints of the Church, that the Bride of the Apocalypse is not the Bride of the Pauline Epistles. In the Apocalypse she is unfaithful, and waning to her extinction. The Apocalypse is designed to lead us to behold a new dispensation; and to unite the previous economies of God. God's redeemed under the Old Testament, the New, and the Day of the Lord, are to be presented in their oneness, as called by the same God; and as dwelling at length in the same earth and city.

The Harlot is a city; so is the Bride. Thus it is also in Matt. xxv. In the parable of the Ten Virgins the Saviour discloses the judgment of that portion of His Church which will be found asleep in death. Hence the Bride there cannot be the Church: it is the city of God, as it is here. The saints at the period of the Apocalypse to which we have now arrived, are in the *temple*. The *city* has not yet arrived: the Bride is yet in her father's house. She descends, when the kingdom comes. The city during the millennium overhangs the old earth. These words introduce the city into the scene, in order to millennial blessing. It settles on the new earth only, when sin can nevermore enter. Our position during the millennium is transitional: or midway between the TEMPLE and the CITY. The *temple* abides during the millennium: for those who reign then are "priests." There is sin still, and the need of atonement. But on the new earth the temple appears no more, nor any of its parts.

Only some select believers are present at the marriage-supper. As this is a privilege, some, doubtless, of the Church are present. But if so, then the whole Church do not constitute the Bride : or all believers in Jesus risen would be there.

All the servants of God, of course including the Church, describe the Bride as something distinct from themselves. How, then, should the Bride be a portion of the servants of God ?

What is the Bride's " making herself ready ? " It appears to refer to her clothing, or bridal attire. The announcement which follows is designed to instruct us concerning it.

It is granted her to appear in white. The city is the result of the Saviour's priesthood, and of His righteousness. The Great Multitude confess their redemption due to the Lamb and His blood. Their robes were dirty of themselves, but were cleansed by His blood. It is granted, then, as a matter of favour that the city which the saints are to inhabit shall be decked out in their good works. They are the Bride's marriage-robes : her fine linen of white. They are " shining," because they are good works accepted of God ; and lustrous, by comparison with the evil deeds, the scarlet garments of the Harlot. xvii. 4 ; xviii. 12, 16. They are " clean," as the result of the washing in the Lamb's blood. vii. 14.

" For the fine linen is the righteous acts of the saints." The translators by reading " the righteousness of the saints " seem to have designed us to understand the righteousness of our Lord alone. But the plural shows that the saints' individual and separate acts of obedience and grace are meant. That word " All our righteous-*nesses* are as filthy rags " (Isa. lxiv. 6), tells us what place the best deeds of unjustified men must take. But here they are the works of those accepted by faith in Christ. They are required by Him, as white raiment. iii. 18. The scarlet attire of the Harlot is, in contrast, the evil deeds of the wicked of the falsely professing Church. As the Bride is not the Church, the "righteous acts" here are not Christ's imputed righteousness.

It would appear from this, that Jesus now takes notice of the holy acts of His saints, in order to their rewarding; or as if there were some abiding record of their deeds connected with the city. The benefactions to the poor written on the walls of the sacred buildings called churches may serve to illustrate the idea.

What is this Wedding Supper?

Many seem to regard it as another name for the millennial joy. But that, I am persuaded, is a mistake. This is a secret scene, taking place in the heaven, ere Jesus and His risen ones are manifested to earth. Heaven is not opened till it is over. ver. 11. It is a very brief period, preceding the thousand years, and the Saviour's advent in glory.

If I mistake not, it is the opening of the city of God to the footsteps of the redeemed. It is the antitype of the opening and dedication of the tabernacle by Moses, and of the temple by Solomon. It answers to the removal of the ark, in David's day, out of the tabernacle into the city. So now, the *throne* moves, I suppose, into the *city*.

Many seem to imagine, that all the saved will partake in this glory. Such an idea is not suggested by the words of the angel. The very contrary would seem to be intended: it is a peculiar glory for certain specially invited ones. And this is suggested by the analogies of like events on earth. Not all the people of Israel were present at the dedication of the temple by Solomon. Not all her Majesty's subjects, not all even of her nobles, were present at Queen Victoria's wedding-breakfast. 'Twas an honour of which only certain invited ones partook. The opening of any great building is its most honourable hour. It was a great honour to have seen the dedication of Solomon's temple : how much greater this ? Blessed is he who attains to this honour ! It is said afterwards, " Blessed and holy is he that hath part in the first resurrection " (xx. 4). But this is a glory preceding that. They who attain to a place at this wedding-feast obtain, I suppose, assuredly a place in the kingdom, as the greater includes the less. But not all, I believe, who reign as kings during the millennium are adjudged worthy to be present here.

There appears to be a reference in this to the promise made to the last of the churches. " I will come in to him, and sup with him, *and he shall sup with me* " (iii. 20).

9. " And he saith to me, These are the true sayings of God.
10. " And I fell before his feet to worship him : and he saith unto me, ' See thou do it not : I am a fellow-servant of thee and of thy brethren that have the witness of Jesus : worship God : for the witness of Jesus is the spirit of prophecy.' "

To what extent shall we apply the words, " These are the true sayings of God ? " Does it refer only to the last announcement of the Lamb's marriage-supper, or to the view of Babylon's overthrow ? I think that it refers to the supper, and is designed to stir up our hearts to desire and seek a place at it. What is requisite in order to obtain a place at that solemnity, is not named here. But the parable of the Ten Virgins shows.

Thrice is especial attention attracted to parts of this revelation by words of the same import : where the final blessedness of the inhabitants of the new world is celebrated (xxi. 5), and where the glorious lot of the denizens of the heavenly city is described. xxii. 6. These other examples, then, may enable us to see that the design of this intimation is to lead us to pay particular attention to the words which immediately precede.

Because *some* believers only will be partakers in this glory, it becomes us to give the more heed to it, that we may be of the happy number.

False worship is one of the great subjects of the Apocalypse. The harlotry of Babylon is the worship of other beings in addition to God. This instance, then, of John's error is given on purpose to correct the worship of angels.

The reason of his offering this religious homage is no doubt to be found in the greatness of the revelation communicated by the angel to him.

The offered worship is forbidden. A holy angel could not receive this honour due to the Most High alone. Only a fallen angel, such as Satan, could desire it. Matt. iv.

It was desirable that the worship of angels should be noticed with disapproval. For under the Law and before it, there was one angel, who is also called "the Lord," to whom adoration was offered by holy men of old; and was not refused. No doubt this angel was Jesus. But He is not any more to appear and to receive worship as the angel during the thousand years. Hence the companions of the Bride are warned not to transgress in this matter, as the Harlot did.

The reason for not offering such worship is then stated. John entertained too high ideas of the standing and knowledge of angels: too lowly views of his own position as a prophet of God. Worship belongs only to the Supreme Master: all others are servants. Angels and saved men are "fellow-servants;" and one servant is not to worship his fellow.

This passage has been misunderstood by the Spiritualists. Wm. Howitt says that "St. John, in the

Apocalypse, informs us that a spirit of the dead was one of the angels who appeared to him then " (Rev. xix. 10).

It is evident that they suppose the angel to assert himself to be one of John's brethren; and therefore, that he was once a man like John. But that arises from not knowing the Greek. A glance at that shows, as Hengstenberg and Alford observe, that the word "fellow-servant," is that which governs both "thee" and "thy brethren," "The angel describes himself as the fellow-servant of John and of his brethren who have the testimony of Jesus."

John is viewed by the angel as a prophet, as the closing words of his speech prove. The angel and he were both servants of the servants of Jesus.

"For the testimony of Jesus is the spirit of prophecy."

How are we to understand this sentence?

Two meanings are possible, according as we take "the testimony of Jesus" subjectively or objectively.

1. "The testimony which Jesus delivers." As in i. 1. Subjective.

2. "The testimony concerning Jesus." Objective.

1. If we take the phrase in the first sense, it will signify, "Thou and I, and the prophets, are witnesses sent by Jesus. The substance of this testimony is the spirit of prophecy, communicated to us all. 'Tis given to me to enlighten thee: to thee to enlighten others. Hence we occupy the same footing in reference to the Giver of prophecy: and so are fellow-servants."

2. If we take it objectively, the sense will be as follows:—

"We all bear witness to Jesus: I, as the unfolder of this communication: your brethren too the prophets of earth testify concerning His glories; and so do you in handing on to the churches this record of His future reign."

Prophecy greatly relates to the future actings and positions of the Lord Jesus : this is its great theme.

The difference between the subjective and the objective views is, in this case, of little moment.

The great discoveries then made by the angel, which led John to worship him, arose only from a greater degree of the spirit of prophecy, common to John and the other prophets. It was a difference of extent and degree, not of principle. Neither party possessed the fount of prophecy : that was in God. They were both but subordinate rills from that fountain. They were both servants of God to minister light to others ; and the inspiring Spirit was the Holy Ghost.

11. " And I saw the heaven opened, and behold a white horse, and he that sat on him was called Faithful and True, and in righteousness doth he judge and war. 12. Now his eyes were as a flame of fire, and on his head were many diadems : having a name written which none knew but himself. 13. And he was clothed in a garment dipped in blood; and his name is called, ' The Word of God.' 14. And the armies which were in the heaven were following him on white horses, clothed in fine linen white and clean."

When first seen as the rider on the white horse, he has one crown : now he appears with many diadems. He is not warrior only, but King of kings.[1] All earth's thrones belong to Him. Satan as the dragon has *seven* diadems on his seven heads. xii. 3. The Wild Beast has *ten* diadems on his ten horns. xiii. 1. Jesus has more.

He had, besides, an unrevealed name, known to Himself alone. How absurd for any to try and discover what God means to conceal ! Not all is to be made known to us. There was a reference to this in Jesus' promise to Philadelphia. " I will write on him my

---

[1] The papal tiara is a *crown* composed of three *diadems.*— *Wordsworth.* A diadem is a bandeau of gold worn round the head as a token of sovereignty.

new name" (iii. 12). To the victor of Pergamos He promised a stone with a new name written on it, of which all but the receiver should be ignorant. ii. 17 This would seem, then, to be one of the results of Jesus victory received from the Father, as rewards of His overcoming.

"He was clothed in a garment dipped in blood."

Here is a difficulty. Is not the blood the result of the winepress trodden ? How then is it named before the act which tinges it with blood ? I cannot say. It would seem to be anticipative. The reference is to the well-known passage, Isa. lxiii. 1-6.

It is strange that any should interpret this of Jesus' sufferings on the cross. It is not *His own* blood that is shed in *weakness* and in *meekness*, but the blood of *foes* trampled in *wrath*. "Those mine enemies, who would not that I should reign over them, bring them hither and slay them before me." He is on His way to battle. And " every battle of the warrior is with confused noise and *garments rolled in blood* " (Isa. ix. 5).

" His name is called ' The Word of God.' "

This is a title of Jesus given only by John ; and so an intimation of that apostle's authorship of the Apocalypse.

"The armies of heaven were following on white horses."

The victory is won by the leader who precedes : these only follow in His train. The "Seed of the Woman" now bruises the serpent's head. He is "Jehovah of hosts : " the armies of the sky are His. His armies from above are all cavalry. The horses and horsemen from beneath prevailed not (ix.), but the cavalry of heaven bring in the kingdom.

Are any of these warriors members of the Church ? I suppose there are many of that body, though not of that exclusively. These are the "called, chosen, and faithful," who were to attend the King of kings in His conquest of the ten kings of Antichrist. xvii. 14. As Jesus who was meek and merciful during the time of grace, wars and judges, now so do they. "*The righteous* shall rejoice, when he seeth the vengeance : he shall wash his feet in the blood of the wicked. So that a man shall say, Verily, there is a reward for *the righteous :* verily he is a God that judgeth in the earth " (Ps. lviii. 10, 11). Now those who partake the kingdom enter as "the righteous" (Matt. x. 41 ; xiii. 43, 49 ; xxv. 37–46 ; Luke xiv. 14). And it is "the righteous" who is to wash his feet in the blood of the wicked. Jesus reigns after the battle : so do they. They partake, then, in the battle which precedes.

"They are clothed in fine linen, white and clean."

They wear no armour : for immortals need fear no wound. Their dress is white, too conspicuous for mortal warriors on the field of battle : but suited to the righteous and risen.

The dress of Jesus on the Mount of Transfiguration was white and glistening : such is their clothing now.

The clothing of the Bride was fine linen : but it was emblematic only : and therefore the explanation of the emblem is given. Here the clothing is literal ; and so no explanation is added.

15. "And out of his mouth goeth a sharp sword, that with it he may smite the nations ; and he ruleth them with rod of iron : and he treadeth the winepress of the fierceness of the wrath of the God of Hosts. 16. And he hath on his raiment and on his thigh a name written, KING OF KINGS, AND LORD OF LORDS."

"He rules them with rod of iron."

This is the persistent character of His rule throughout the millennium. 'Tis strict justice, at once discharging on the offender the wrath which is his due. It is not patience and grace, as now ; but destructive punishment, breaking in pieces the transgressor. This shows that the nations as a whole keep their unrenewed attitude. They fear the King of kings, and so render Him, in the main, obedience : but it is for wrath's sake, not for conscience' sake, that they are obedient. The millennial reign of Jesus and of His saints is conducted on the same principle. Rev. ii. 27 ; xii. 5. And this tells us what is in general the state of the Gentiles. With the Jews it is not so. "Thy people shall be all righteous."

How sadly altered is the position of the Gentiles from that which they occupied at our Lord's first appearing ! John iv. Then they were as a field *white* to *harvest*, expecting and receiving Messiah, while Israel was unbelieving. Now Israel has returned to faith, and they are *red* unto the Vintage !

The smiting of the Gentiles in the crisis of battle with the sword, and the ruling them afterwards by the sceptre of iron, are both parts of one whole. First the sword against open foemen ; then the rod against rebellious single subjects.

And this serves to prove that saints of the Church take part in the battle which precedes the kingdom. The two functions are parts of the same circle. He could not reign with Christ, who should not also destroy transgressors. On single offenders, or unarmed conspirators, judicial vengeance takes effect. But when subjects levy war, military execution is done. This is the fulfilment of that word of our Lord concerning Himself as the stone. "On whomsoever it shall fall, it will grind him to powder " (Matt. xxi. 44). The stone is no longer passive as now, but is descending from the heavens with tremendous momentum.

17. "And I saw a single angel standing in the sun ; and he shouted with great voice, saying to all the birds that fly in midheaven, ' Come, gather yourselves together unto the Great Supper

of God[1]: 18. that ye may eat the flesh of kings and the flesh of chief captains, and the flesh of mighty men, and the flesh of horses, and of them that ride on them, and the flesh of all, both freemen and slaves, both small and great.'"

There is a passage in Ezekiel which greatly resembles this. Ezek. xxxix. 17-22.

There the same scene is presented as it affects Israel. There the Antichrist is prince of Ross [Russia]; Meshech [Moscow]; and Tubal [Tobolsk]. He comes with an immense army, invading the land of Palestine. On Israel's mountains is he smitten • and then the kingdom comes, and Israel never falls away from God again, nor is smitten any more.

The birds that fly " in mid-heaven " are called. It is that portion of the heaven which lies between the earth and the true or more distant heaven. Eagles and vultures soar high above the plains of earth, and far above the smaller birds. At vast distances they discern their prey, and swoop on it. Distance from the spot is a matter of small importance to those possessed of such rapid and powerful pinions. The hateful birds of night dwell in fallen Babylon: the active carnivorous birds descend on the armies of the False Christ. In so vast a feast there shall be enough for all the birds of prey of all the earth. And no doubt answering thereto there shall be a supernatural assembly of these birds scenting the prey from afar.

Why does the angel-herald in this case " stand in the sun ? " I cannot tell. His voice is a shout, and of mighty force, that it may reach through the vast distance.

" Come, be gathered."

Evil angels gather the kings to fight. A good angel gathers the birds to prey on them. All creatures belong to God: His call they obey. They now show

---

[1] So Tregelles.

their sympathy against God's enemies. Men are at this time defying their Creator, and therefore the inferior animals are made to triumph over them.

The issues of the battle are known certainly long ere the armies are gathered. Here are none of "the *chances* of war." Here are not vessels of earth contending against vessels of earth, and all speculation at fault as to which shall prove victorious in the evenly-balanced encounter. The issue is certain and entire destruction to God's foes. Before the battle the leader does not encourage his forces to fight and bid them put out their best energies. The executioners are collected to prey on the carcases of the slain, ere yet the battle is fought. So the deserter has his grave dug and coffin made, and is marched past it, ere the shots are fired, that are to lay his blindfolded head and fettered hands in the dust.

The marriage-supper of the *Lamb* takes place above. 'Tis for His friends. The Great Supper of the *Lion* of Judah is given below. 'Tis the inaugural feast to the lower creation; a proof of the ending of the evil age, by the cutting off of the "perverse generation." The supper of peace and that of war are both real equally.

19. "And I saw the Wild Beast, and the kings of the earth and his armies, gathered together to make war on him that sat on the horse, and on his army. 20. And the Wild Beast was seized, and with him the False Prophet who did the signs in his presence, whereby he deceived those that received the mark of the Wild Beast, and the worshippers of his image. The two were cast alive into the lake of fire that burneth with brimstone. 21. And the rest were slain with the sword of the Sitter on the horse, which (sword) proceeded out of his mouth; and all the birds were filled with their flesh."

How vast the array! All earth defies Christ; all own one leader; before the pretensions of the Great False Christ risen from the dead, all other claims grow pale. The armies of earth are his, under his guidance, fighting in his cause, and each soldier sealed with his mark. The nations are angry, and God's wrath is come. War is the open expression of anger. Each carries deadly weapons; and within, hatred is ready to employ them.

They are at length assembled, and with the express and well-known intention of fighting against Christ. The fears of kings and subjects, so strongly expressed at the sixth seal, are passed away. Men were nominally servants of God and of His Christ then. They are now professedly and really the worshippers of the False Christ, beyond repentance on their part, and beyond forgiveness on God's. The wrath of God is at its height, because the wickedness of man is come to the full. Devils have mustered the host to its destruction.

Some deem it inconceivable, that men will be found daring enough to confront the Son of God from heaven. That is only because they overlook the causes then in operation. Satan's full power is then in play: miracle is on the side of the False Christ: and God has sent an energy of delusion, that they who hated the truth of salvation may love the lie, and be destroyed. How almost incredible it seems, that the next day after the opened earth had swallowed up Dathan and Abiram, and fire from God had burnt up the presumptuous Levites, that the whole congregation should murmur against Moses and Aaron! Num. xvi. Yet so it was.

Men are assembled against Christ's army, as well as against Himself. They expect the saints to come with Christ. The False Christ blasphemes them, while hidden in heaven. xiii. He and his men fight against them, now that they appear in the sky. The apostle speaks of Antichrist's "hosts" in the plural. Many nations, separately arrayed, constitute his forces. But the Holy Ghost speaks of the army of Christ in the singular. It is one : all are alike risen from the dead, immortal in resurrection bodies.

The issue is now told us. The two human leaders are first dealt with. They give confidence to the vast assembly. " Who is like the Wild Beast ? Who is able to make war with him ? " is the cry of his adherents. Here then, he is shown to be quite powerless. He is dragged away from the head of his troops. He cannot protect them, nor they him : he is seized alive, a prisoner of war. He is no system, but a person ; as truly as Christ is. He is distinct from his army, as Christ is.

" And with him the False Prophet."

This expounds to us in clear terms what is meant by the second Wild Beast of chapter xiii. It is no system, no abstraction, no body of men. He is a man, as truly as Mahomet was. It does not appear that he is naturally warlike, but he attends the host to the battle. When Jesus was taken prisoner, JUDAS headed the force. It is now his turn to be arrested : he is seized, and a like punishment with that which overtakes the Wild Beast is inflicted on him. This man upholds by supernatural works the godhead of the Usurper. He is in perfect sympathy with him, and is content to devote all his energies to him : his miracles are in presence of the False Christ. He reigns in the supremacy of the False Christ. He seeks not to make any separate party for himself : the Infernal Trinity uphold each other.

The effect of the miracles, of which we have received notice in the xiiith chapter, is now stated. They deceived men. They were real miracles : but led them to believe a lie. They deceived them to damnation : they led them to be confident in their attitude of open defiance toward God and Christ.

The False Prophet deceives his followers so that they believe the False Christ to be the True God. The False Prophet knows full well who the Wild Beast is: they two were for ages fellows in the pit of perdition. But it serves his purpose to bear false witness, and to ruin men. But for this supernatural deceit, they had hardly embarked on so desperate an enterprise.

There were two especially holy in Old Testament times, Enoch and Elijah; and God gave them peculiar honour, in preserving them from death, and lifting them to heaven. There are also two especially wicked among men; and these are permitted to come forth from the place of punishment to discover afresh their enormous wickedness, and in consequence to endure for a thousand years especial torment. With men there is nothing beyond a brief death for every offence. But God knows how to apportion punishment to sin.

The mark and the worship of the image are both accordant characteristics of the same religion of Satan. The same parties perform both acts. Why, then, are there two articles? one before the giving of the mark? one before the worship of the image? I cannot answer it satisfactorily to myself; though it be true that the acts are quite physically independent one of the other. But it may be because the least devoted worshippers of the Wild Beast may content themselves with the mark alone. That is all that is absolutely required by the False Prophet in order to buying and selling, and that may suffice them.

These are cast "*alive*" into the lake of fire. Great stress is laid on this in the Greek. It is a point worthy of especial notice. Their armies are slain. Why are not they? Because they *cannot* be slain. They have risen from the dead: they can die no more.

Hence we see that neither of the two can be an empire, or a system, or a corporate body. Neither of the two is a demon incarnate. They at once enter on "the Gehenna of fire." In their risen bodies they suffer at once, and for the thousand years, the full penalty of the damned. For their enormous sin they endure especial vengeance. As some for the thousand years are accounted worthy of especial glory and reward, so are these accounted worthy of pre-eminent wrath. They are the firstfruits of the lost.

The lake of fire and brimstone is their place. It begins to exist, therefore, before the millennium. It appears to be transferred to the new earth, when the old ceases to exist.

None but immortal beings could remain alive in that suffocating, consuming region of flames and sulphur, an hour. But these are found there at the close of the millennium. xx. 10. They came up out of Hades, the place of the spirits of the departed: they are cast into Gehenna, the eternal abode of the risen lost.

CHAPTER XX

THE BINDING OF SATAN

1-3. "And I saw an angel coming down out of the heaven, having the key of the bottomless pit, and a great chain on his hand. And he laid hold on the dragon, the old serpent who is the devil and Satan, and bound him for a thousand years, and cast him into the bottomless pit, and locked and sealed (it) over him, that he should not deceive the nations any more, until the thousand years were fulfilled : after that he must be loosed a little while."

THE victory over men is not sufficient. The Evil Spirit, by whose instigation the troops were collected and the battle joined, needs to be arrested. For want of this, former successes have been turned into defeats, sooner or later. New plots have been framed by the great Deceiver ; and new tools found to carry them into effect. Justice then proceeds to seize the chief culprit.

The key that was lent him awhile was taken away to heaven. It is brought again to earth only to be used against him.

He is dealt with by himself : he is not a man, but a spirit. He is not found, like the others, with arms in his hands. Hence his treatment is different : an angel seizes him. He is beyond man's power to retain. In chapter xii. Michael the archangel and his angels cast him down after a battle. Now there is no fight : but a single angel arrests him.

By the act of angels Satan was defeated on high. By an angel he is arrested on earth. This is the last act of an angel in open interference on the earth. The millennium is the time, not of angels' rule, but of men's.

He has "a great chain *on* his hand." The key is *in* the angel's hand; the chain is coiled up *around* it. The chain is long and heavy: for it is to bind the great and strong dragon. His jailor is duly furnished for his office.

He seizes the fallen spirit. If I mistake not, Satan when cast down to earth will appear visible: as visibly as he did to Eve. The world will not receive the Holy Spirit, "*because it seeth him not.*" It will receive the great Adversary: will it not be, because it seeth him? To show that the same fallen being who tempted Eve in the garden is now removed from the scene of his wickedness, both the angel and the Tempter will, I suppose, be seen. Good angels made themselves visible: so may evil angels. Angels ate with Abraham: why may not angels be bound? Another example of this binding of angels has previously arisen. ix. 14, 15. And in Peter and Jude like assertions are made. 2 Pet. ii.; Jude 6. Those angels who fell long after Satan, and received Jesus' preaching, when as a spirit He entered the place of spirits, now come forth from their darkness and chains to be judged, and to be released. It is "the judgment of the great day." Satan, after long liberty, is cast into the close durance from which they have just been delivered.

He is cast into "the bottomless pit."

It is very remarkable how different a style of punishment overtakes Satan, from that which arrests his two coadjutors. They are cast into the lake of fire: he, into the bottomless pit. But the reason of this difference is, that his two assistants were already in the bottomless pit, ere he released them. They go, therefore, into hell proper, or the Gehenna of fire. Satan himself has not yet suffered more than ejection from heaven: imprisonment in the bottomless pit is therefore his sentence.

The angel further locks and seals the pit-door. The open pit was the signal for God's terrible judgments on men. 'Twas the time of woe to earth: locusts tormented, and the False Christ deceived. It remained open all the time of Satan's power. The angel has not to open the pit, in order to cast Satan into it.

Now the pit is shut and locked again. Its sulphurous flames and terrible executioners shall no more be free to come forth.

What is the intent of all these actions? That Satan's deception of the nations of the earth may no longer be carried on. Deception is his constant trade. His angels may deceive individuals: he deceives nations. The truth is against him, he is therefore driven to use falsehood. He excites false hopes. He makes promises of success in sin, which are sure to end in the destruction of his dupes. He knows from the first the wrath which will descend on himself and them: but still he goes on. His deceits prevail: the old serpent rules the old man.

But Satan must be loosed again after the thousand years are over. Why?

It were not necessary that we should be able to see the reasons of this "must" on God's part. But I think several very substantial and satisfactory ones may be assigned.

1. The great aim of God in this and in all other things is not to glorify man, but *Himself*. His design is to display the gulf which severs the Creator unchangeable in holiness, from the creature perpetually changing to evil, whenever he is tried, and not upheld by sovereign grace. It will probably be fancied, as it is imagined by some now, that if Jesus is to appear in person, to raise the dead, to rule the earth, to give

authority to His saints, to cut off His foes, and to display them burning in the fiery lake, that none will be found hardy enough to attempt to resist Him. God means, on the other hand, to discover to us, that man, placed under the most favourable circumstances, will yet fall if left to his own choice under temptation. Yes, even against Christ in person he can rebel!

2. This displays the *foreknowledge of God*. Ages ere they take place, God has foretold the things that shall be. The choice of men, and of Satan himself, is discerned by Him from afar. Much as Satan must desire to dishonour God, and to prove His words false, still his hatred of God will prevail, and thus will he act. God knows, too, what man is, and how he will choose. Man is unchanged in nature, wherever grace has not stepped in to heal.

3. This discovers to us *Satan's incurable wickedness*, and the enduring character of sin in *general*. Though he foresees the coming wrath of God, he is not even restrained for awhile from open acts of rebellion against God. Sin overleaps all calculations of self-interest, all past results of experience, all threatenings of God.

4. This discovers also to us the futility of the ideas of many on a point of much importance. Many will not believe God's testimony concerning *the eternity of punishment*. They trust in the efficacy of penal inflictions on the sinful to restore them to a right mind. "The fire will burn out the dross from the corrupt: the gold will at length appear." This is a false and foolish supposition. It is here negatived by the voice of prophecy. The mighty intellect of Satan knows the unchangeable holiness of God, sees that as long as God shall be holy, and himself sinful, so long God must be against him. He has experienced imprisonment a thousand years: has felt the superior might of the

Most High : has learned by the slow lapse of centuries how vain are all his plans, how uniformly defeat has extinguished them. Surely, then, we should be apt to imagine, he will say to himself—" It is folly to strive with God. This heavy captivity of a thousand years has not indeed destroyed my hatred of God, but it has at least taught me prudence. I will not offend against Him openly. I will keep my enmity locked in my own bosom. I am once again at liberty : I will not do aught rebellious again to forfeit it, and to draw down final and eternal wrath." Is such the result ? Nothing of the kind. He is the tiger ; while enclosed in his dungeon, his love of blood is undiminished by his captivity : and as soon as his prison doors are loosed, he is off to his jungle and his prey once more.

THE MILLENNIUM

4. "And I saw thrones, and (men) sat upon them, and judgment was given unto them : and (I saw) the souls of those that had been beheaded because of the testimony of Jesus, and because of the Word of God : and whosoever worshipped not the Wild Beast, nor his image, nor received his mark on their forehead, or on their hand, both lived and reigned with the Christ a thousand years. 5. And the rest of the dead lived not until the thousand years were fulfilled. This is the first resurrection. 6. Blessed and holy is he that hath part in the first resurrection ; over these the second death hath not authority, but they shall be priests of God and of the Christ, and shall reign with him a thousand years."

We have now arrived at a much controverted portion of the book : may the Holy Spirit enlighten us with true conceptions of the period described !

We inquire first :—

Is the resurrection here spoken of FIGURATIVE or LITERAL ?

This is the great point of controversy on this book. We think that the case is very easily decided.

We ask first—Will the literal interpretation stand here ? It will. Does it produce absurdity to suppose that the resurrection may be of persons really slain ? By no means. Then the literal interpretation is the true one.

Allegorists would have us believe that the resurrection here spoken of is a figurative and corporate one. " The party of Antichrist is put down, the Christian party (or the Church) is exalted and in power."

Now we reply first, That if *this* resurrection may be explained away, so may all others. We answer next, *That if the resurrection be figurative and corporate, the death which precedes it is figurative and corporate also.* We forbid you, then, to assume that Christ's cause is put down by the literal beheading and slaughter of individual believers. That is literal death, and you may not steal our weapon. There may be the figurative and corporate extinction of a party, by the dying out of the principles which created it, in the minds of its partisans. *That* you may take, if you will : and if you are Calvinists, you will find it a live bombshell in the camp.

We proceed, then, to apply our lever. The death which is suffered by the saints is literal and individual; such, therefore, is the resurrection. The first proposition needs no long proof. It will not be denied that Jesus calls His followers literally and individually to die for Him. Matt. x. 21, 28, 30 ; xxiv. 9 ; Rev. i. 13 ; vi. 11 ; xiii. 15 ; Luke xii. 4, 5, etc. It will not be disputed, either, that not a few have, in obedience to our Lord's words, simply and literally given up life for His name. As, then, the life surrendered was literal and individual, literal and individual is the life restored.

We advance. Is the second resurrection literal or figurative?

Hitherto it has been assumed almost universally, that the judgment of the dead (verses 11-15) is a literal resurrection. But if that be literal, then, as the first resurrection is related to the second, as a part to the rest of one great whole, if the second resurrection be literal, so is the first. You cannot have the real root of a figurative tree; or the figurative branch of a literal tree.

The question may be brought to a point briefly thus. On antimillennarian views, the present dispensation is to continue till the end of the world. More and more is the gospel to increase, and to subject at length all nations to its sway, while believers become more and more patterns of everything good and holy. Whence, then, is to come the burning up of the globe for sin? Where is the evil on man's part, and the wrath on God's, which are to be the causes of the world's destruction? On this view, Christ should return, only to welcome His people, and they to receive Him with joy. What say the Scriptures about our Lord's second advent? Joel iii.; Isa. xiii., xxiv.; Matt. xxiv., etc.

"I saw *thrones, and* the *souls* of the beheaded." (Accusative case.) "And *whoever* worshipped not lived." (Nominative case.)

Three classes are named in the verse.

1. The first is indefinite. "Men sat on the thrones."

2. The second consists of early martyrs for God's cause.

3. The third is composed of those who struggle with the last enemy, even Antichrist.

To these three parties resurrection and royalty are assigned.

The thrones of the twenty-four elders on high have

disappeared: they are seen no more. Here are unnumbered thrones set on earth.

What, then, are the conditions of obtaining a seat on one of these thrones?

The occupants of them are here spoken of only indefinitely. They are, I believe, the same parties who descended with Christ as His army. This would appear more clearly, if we read verses 1-3 of this chapter as a parenthesis. The army of warriors who come with Christ reign with Christ. As those who fought with Joshua, with Joshua inherited the land; so those who with Christ war, with Him reign.

"Will all believers, then, reign with Christ?" By no means. The kingdom of the thousand years is never said to belong to those who only believe. There are not a few texts addressed to believers which declare that certain classes of them shall not enter the kingdom.

(1) Those whose (active) righteousness shall not exceed that of the Pharisees. Matt. v. 20.

(2) Those who, while professors of Christ's name, *do not* the will of His Father. Matt. vii. 21.

(3) Those guilty of strife, envy, and contention. Luke ix. 46-50; Mark ix. 33-50; Matt. xviii. 1-3.

(4) Rich disciples. Matt. xix. 23; Luke vi. 24; xviii. 24.

(5) Those who deny the millennium. Luke xviii. 17; Mark x. 15.

(6) The unbaptized. John iii. 5.

(7) See also 1 Cor. vi. 9. 10; Gal. v. 19-21; vi. 7, 8; Matt. x. 32, 39; xvi. 26; xviii. 17, 18; Luke ix. 26.

"But will only the martyrs have part in the millennial kingdom?"

This is making the gate too narrow, as the other makes it too wide. Those who suffer for Christ, even though not unto death, will reign with Christ. Rom. viii. 17; 2 Tim. ii. 11, 12.

The conquerors in Christ generally will have part in it. Rev. ii. 26, 27. Those who "receive the abundance of the grace and of the gift of righteousness will reign in life by the one Jesus Christ" (Rom. v. 17). (See Greek.)

But many other texts describe those who will partake of the first resurrection.

"And judgment was given unto them."

There seems to be a direct reference to Dan. vii. "The judgment was set, and books were opened" (10). "The saints of the heavenlies (Heb.) shall *take the kingdom and possess the kingdom* for ever, even for ever and ever" (18). The False Christ prevailed "Until the ancient of days came, and JUDGMENT WAS GIVEN *unto the saints of the heavenlies:* and the time came that *the saints possessed the kingdom*" (22). (See also ver. 27, and ii. 44.) Thus the latter portion of the verse expounds the former. We learn that the thrones which John saw were no mere pageant of royalty; but that royal power to decide causes, and to pass sentence, and to regulate the nations, accompanied the outward ensigns of sovereignty.

This is the more observable, as contrasted with God's previous injunctions upon His Church. Jesus forbade His disciples to act the civil magistrate, as unsuited to the present dispensation of mercy, and to their own sinful condition now. "Judge not, that ye be not judged" (Matt. vii. 1, 2; v. 40). "Judge nothing before the time, until the Lord come" (1 Cor. iv. 5). And the apostle blames the Corinthian believers who were already full, and rich, and "reigning as kings" while apostles were hungry, thirsty, naked, in danger of death. He desired indeed, that both might reign together. 1 Cor. iv. 8–14. But all reigning now, while our Lord is rejected, is the exercise of judgment "before the time." There is a judging indeed of those within the Church; but, as regards the world, the apostle disclaims it. "What have I to do to judge them that are without? do not ye judge them that are within? But them that are without God will judge"[1] (1 Cor. v. 12, 13).

Jesus Himself, when asked to decide in a civil suit, refused. "Man, who made Me a judge, or a divider over you?" (Luke xii. 14). He refused to judge, because, as He said, He came not to judge, but to save the world. John xii. 47.

But now Jesus is sent forth with power to reign, and to subdue all to His Father.

Hence now is fulfilled the word, "Do ye not know that the saints shall judge the world?" "Know ye not that we shall judge angels? How much more things that pertain unto this life?" (1 Cor. vi. 2, 3).

"And I saw the souls of those who had been beheaded." "How," say some, "can a soul be seen?" Very easily: the soul or ghost resembles the body which it has left, and is perfectly an object of sight, although it cannot be handled. Thus Saul saw the soul or ghost of Samuel.

Why it is noticed so specially, that John saw the souls of "the *beheaded with an axe*," it is not easy to say. It is not meant to exclude those slain by other modes of death. Else the apostle Peter would be shut out, because he was crucified; the apostle James, and John Baptist, for they were slain, not with an axe, but with a sword; and John himself, who was put into a cauldron of boiling oil, but escaped alive. So also the Two Witnesses would be excluded, for they are to be crucified; and those who have endured the more fearful

---

[1] So read the best MSS., and the critical editions.

death by fire. The beheading by axe is probably mentioned, because it was, or because it *will be* the more common mode of death to the saints. The Romans scourged with the lictor's rods, and then beheaded with his axe. This view is confirmed by the word used concerning those under the altar : of them it is only said that they were "*slain*," the mode of death being left undefined.

Here, then, the *martyrs alone* appear. But they are only one of three classes. And the difficulty experienced by Burgh and others with regard to the passage, as though martyrs alone would be partakers of the first resurrection—has arisen from overlooking the previous class, which is not composed exclusively of the slain for Christ. The beatitudes of the Sermon on the Mount, and many other passages, prove that others also shall partake in the joys of that day of glory. "Blessed are the *poor in spirit :* for *theirs is the kingdom of heaven*"; that is, the millennial kingdom. So it is promised to the doers of God's will (Matt. vii. 21), and the vehement seekers after it. (xi. 12.) Also the Saviour promises a recompense at "*the resurrection of the righteous*," for those who make feasts not to receive a return now, but for such as cannot requite them. Luke xiv. 12, 14. Jesus in the Seven Epistles promises chiefly reward to *works* : here consolation is held out chiefly to the *sufferers* for Him.

Why were these servants of God slain ?

"For the witness of Jesus." This marks them as martyrs of the New Testament. John describes himself as thus suffering for his testimony. Rev. i. 2, 9. They "did *well,* and *suffered for it.*" This is our strange calling : quite contrasted with that of men under Moses' law, where obedience was to win honour and present reward. Deut. iv. 6. These were slain not for sin, but for holiness. These bearers of Jesus' flag of truce into the camp of the rebels were assassinated by those whom they came to serve. Thus they resemble Christ, and are by His Father " counted worthy " to reign with Jesus. They lost their lives for Him. A thousand years requites the loss of ten or twenty for Jesus' sake.

Behold the fulfilment here of that favourite word of Jesus, so often recorded by the Holy Ghost. " He that found his life (soul) shall lose it ; and he that lost his life (soul) for My sake shall find it " (Matt. x. 39 (Greek) ; xvi. 25, 26 ; Mark viii. 35-37 ; Luke ix. 24 ; xvii. 33 ; John xii. 25). Those who gave up life for Christ receive the peculiar bliss of the thousand years : those who saved life by refusing to witness for Christ, or by denying Him, lose life—they are not admitted to the glory of the thousand years.

There were others slain " for the word of God."

This distinguishes the saints of the Old Testament. They are described in the same terms at the fifth seal. The kingdom of Christ encircles God's martyrs, both under the Law and under the Gospel. Even so the Saviour's beatitudes include both. " Blessed are *they who have been persecuted* (see Greek) for *righteousness' sake*. Blessed are *ye* when men *shall* revile you and persecute you, and say all manner of evil against you falsely for *My sake*" (Matt v. 10, 11).

The next words point out to us another group.

" And whosoever worshipped not the Wild Beast, nor his image, nor received the mark on their forehead or their hand, both lived and reigned with the Christ a thousand years."

A new class is here presented to us : a new construction ushers it in. The False Christ is the enemy whom Jesus finds in possession of the field at His return. But there are a few, who, upheld by the Spirit of God, and fearing the awful threatenings of this book, refuse to adore him. To such belongs a place in the millennial kingdom, to whatever dispensation they might have been assigned originally, whether believers in Jesus, born under the law of Moses, or dwellers in heathen lands.

While the dragon and his king rule, the mark which carries damnation is set by each on his person. But soon Satan's king is dethroned, and he himself imprisoned, and now the heroic refusers of his image and mark live and reign. We have been introduced to this company before, in the conquerors who stand on the sea of fire. xv. 2. As they have peculiarly suffered for God, they have peculiar glory and bliss.

These three classes, then, "both lived and reigned with the Christ a thousand years." The companies of saints named in chapters v. 9, 10; vi. 9; vii. 9; xii. 11; xv. 2; all meet in this time of reward. All three classes consist (in general) of the dead restored to life. The Hebrew word "lived" includes the idea of a return to life. "The soul of the child comes into him again, *and he returned to life*" (1 Kings xvii. 22). "As they were burying a man ... when the man was let down and touched the bones of Elisha he *revived* (returned to life) and *stood upon his feet*" (2 Kings xiii. 21; xx. 7; Isa. xxxviii. 9). That is the sense of the Greek also, as we find in this book, i. 18, where it is spoken of Jesus' return to life after death.

In the faith of this lies the especial consolation of those called to suffer persecution unto death for Jesus' sake. "If all the saved will be possessors of the same duration of glory, why should so many pass quietly through life, and *I* have to endure suffering, imprisonment, martyrdom ? Why should I not yield for peace' sake, and for the sake of self-preservation (the first law of nature), what is required of me ? "

Here is the answer vividly given. "Because by so

doing, you lose the special glory of the thousand years, and meet Christ's face of displeasure. Surrender life, and a thousand years of joy and glory are provided by God to recompense that small loss endured for His sake." "Faithful is the saying, for if we *died* with Him, we shall also *live* with Him. If we *suffer*, we shall also *reign with* Him, *if we deny Him, He also will deny us*" (2 Tim. ii. 11, 12). The "we" who suffer, are the "we" who reign. Real as the headsman's axe now, so real the throne to the sufferer. Can the martyr be one party, and the reward be given to one *that never suffered, nor is to suffer?* Is that the act of "the righteous Judge?"

They not only lived, "they *reigned* with the Christ."

These favoured ones "reign" with Christ. "Life" and a "kingdom" are by no means necessarily connected. This, then, communicates to us the news of a fresh privilege. They not only live with Christ; with Him they reign. Their reign begins only after resurrection. The Creed of Pope Pius supposes that the saints reign with Christ as naked spirits. "Likewise that *the saints reigning together with Christ* are to be venerated and invoked" (7th Article).

At length they reign awhile: for a thousand years, while the earth lasts. Afterwards, when the earth is destroyed, they reign for ever and ever. xxii. 5. If the reign here be only figurative, so is the reign there.

At this point most of the year-day interpreters are inconsistent. For if a day in prophecy signify a year, then the thousand years of bliss intend a period of 365,000 years! Or if they affirm the thousand years to be only literal years, then we hold them to the inference that the thousand and odd *days* must be literal *days*. This follows, not only from the principle of consistency in computation, but also on the ground of equity. Can it be accordant with justice, that *the*

False Christ should rule two hundred and sixty years longer than the True Christ?

5. "And the rest of the dead lived not[1] until the thousand years were finished.

If this be the revival of a party of holy men, it is not "*the first*," or the twentieth. "But," it is replied, "there was a resurrection also of dead persons before this, as Jairus' daughter, Lazarus, and others" (Matt. xxvii. 52, 53). The Holy Spirit does not reckon those cases as the first resurrection. The resurrection is not the mere act of rising; it includes the glory then possessed. The time of enjoyment and reigning with Christ ensuing on the rising from the dead, is here taken into account. The raptures of the saints occur in different battalions. But all resurrections, beginning to be reckoned from the thousand years, and introducing their partakers into the kingdom of Christ, constitute together the first resurrection.

"This is the first resurrection." Here is a word of explanation, resembling many like passages in the book. That must be taken literally, whatever be symbolic. Then resurrection is not figurative here, but literal. The sacred writer in saying, "the first resurrection," implies that there is a second. He implies, too, that while the resurrections differ in regard of time or order, they are of the same description in regard of their essence as resurrections.

To the overcoming saint Jesus promises a place on *His* throne as distinct from His Father's, a place on that which He now occupies. iii. 21. Where is Christ's throne seen to be distinct from the Father's? Not in chapters iv. and v. There Jesus is between the throne and the elders. Not in the final state of things in the

---

[1] So read the best MSS. and the Critical Editions.

city. There it is " the throne *of God* and *of the Lamb* " (xxii. 1). It must be, then, in this chapter, xx. 4. There the throne *of the Christ* is set up, and favoured ones reign with Him.

The elders, when Christ takes the book, confess His worthiness, because of His death, and acknowledge those whom He has made priests and *kings*, and who *will reign over the earth.* v. 9, 10.

This is nowhere asserted or beheld, if not fulfilled in xx. 4. For after it, the earth is wholly destroyed.

5. When the seventh trumpet sounds, " *The kingdom of the world* becomes that of our Lord and of His Christ " (xi. 15). And the elders describe further the results which ensue. God exerts His *power* and reigns. The nations are wroth, and God's wrath descends. Neither of these is the case now. 'Tis the time of mercy: the nations are indifferent. 'Tis then the time of reward to God's people, and of destruction to the destroyers of earth. Neither of these things is going on now. 'Tis the evil day, as yet, of the combat with Satan. Eph. vi. 10-18. 'Tis not the destruction of the wicked now. But God is " reconciling the world to himself, *not imputing their trespasses to them* " (2 Cor. v. 19).

The kingdom has come to heaven, when favoured saints, awaking from the dead in resurrection-bodies, are caught up to God's throne, and are rapt thither that they may rule the nations with rod of iron. xii. 5-12. They reign, after Satan is cast down, first from heaven, and then into the pit. Neither of these things has yet been effected. Not yet is it " Woe to earth, because Satan has but a short time! " Or else " woe also to the saints : " because the day of the Lord, the great and very terrible, is upon them! Against this the Holy Spirit comforts His watchful ones. The presence of the Lord will gather us to itself ere the falling away from Christianity takes place, and the great apostle of Satan's Lie appears. 2 Thess. ii. 9. Not yet has a king of Rome risen from the dead; not yet is Satan worshipped as the lord of the kings of earth; not yet have the ten kings appeared who reign as long as the Antichrist does. xvii. 12.

Of the resurrection of reward there are several notices.

1. Jesus advises His disciples to make feasts for those who cannot repay them, because they should be " blessed," and be " recompensed at *the resurrection of the just*" (Luke xiv. 14). There are, then, two resurrections: one for the righteous alone.

2. Jesus, in His reply to the Sadducees, says, " They which *shall be accounted worthy* to attain *that age*, and *the resurrection from* among the dead [not, ' from death '], neither marry, nor are given in marriage. Neither can they die any more, for they are equal unto the angels, *and are the children of God, being the children of the resurrection*" (Luke xx. 34–36). That resurrection into which none but persons " accounted worthy " can enter, must be a resurrection of the righteous only. It is identified with a special portion of time— " *that age*." All who partake of it are *God's sons, because they partake of it*. This could not be true, if the wicked and the righteous rise together. It must be, then, the resurrection of Rev. xx., for " Blessed and holy is he that has part in that." The righteous only partake of that.

3. There is a " resurrection of life," for those " who have done good " (John v. 29). After it comes the resurrection of judgment, for those who have done evil. How clearly the two resurrections of Rev. xx. expound this!

4. In Phil. iii. 11, Paul tells us what was " the prize of his calling " towards which he pressed onward. " If by any means I might attain to the *select resurrec-*

tion that is from amongst the dead" (Greek). Here is a resurrection which leaves many in their graves, a select resurrection. 'Tis a resurrection *of privilege, not obtained even by all believers*. For was not Paul a believer, when he wrote those words? Yet he was seeking for it, as a *prize* proposed to believers. He feared lest, " having acted the herald to others, he himself should become rejected " with regard to this prize. 1 Cor. ix. 27. (Greek.)

5. He confirms this in Rom. vi. 5. Speaking of those immersed upon the profession of faith in Christ, and thus buried and risen with Christ in baptism, he adds, " For IF we became planted together in the likeness of His death, yea we shall be also *of the resurrection* " (see Greek). See to it, believer, that that "if" does not impede your entrance into the kingdom!

6. " Blessed and holy is he that hath part in the first resurrection: over these the Second Death hath not authority, but they shall be priests of God, and of the Christ, and shall reign with Him a thousand years."

The general description of the risen as " blessed and holy," is the result of Jesus' previous adjudication of them. The king has called His servants before Him; but some have behaved themselves unworthy of their calling as servants, and have been dismissed as unworthy to partake that reward.

Those that enter the kingdom are " blessed." They are happy in their circumstances: they are " holy," in relation to their state.

" Blessed " is the word continually used by our Lord to describe the lot of those partaking the millennial kingdom. " *Blessed* are the poor in spirit; for theirs is *the kingdom of heaven* " (Matt v. 3–11; Luke vi. 20; xii. 37, 38, 43). " Thou shalt be *blessed:* for thou shalt be recompensed at the *resurrection* of the *just* " (Luke xiv. 14, 15).

Their blessedness seems to have an especial reference to their situation, as kings; their holiness is in closest connection with their priesthood. The world taunted them as hypocrites in their life, despised them as fools and fanatics, that threw away the good things and enjoyments of the world for nought. But they trusted the promises of God and are not deceived. Their holiness is owned, and as pure of heart they have access to God. Their suffering for Christ is confessed, and rewarded with the kingdom of God.

Happiness and holiness are now wedded together, never to be severed. Here holiness is often led into deepest trouble, through the might of Satan, the wickedness of the world, the weakness and struggles of the flesh. This is the resurrection and kingdom of "*the saints*," as foretold by Daniel vii. 18, 22, 27. Those then, who, though believers. have displayed an unsanctified spirit and conduct, will be excluded. 1 Cor. vi. 8–11. " YE are doing wrong and defrauding, and that your brethren. *Know ye not that unrighteous persons shall not inherit the kingdom of God? Be not deceived :* neither fornicators, nor idolaters, nor adulterers, nor effeminate, nor Sodomites, nor thieves, nor covetous, nor drunkards, nor revilers, nor extortioners, shall inherit the kingdom of God. And such were some of you : but ye were washed clean, but ye were justified, but ye were sanctified, in the name of the Lord Jesus, and by the Spirit of our God."[1] The apostle esteemed this so clear a deduction, so well known a principle, that persons unsanctified would not partake the kingdom of the saints, that he wondered how any Christian could be ignorant of it.

And he warned them to let no thought of election or conversion, or of the privileges of believers in Christ,

---

[1] For the corrections, see the Greek.

embolden them to persevere in the way of sin, with the hope that no threats of God could apply to His elect.

Three blessed results attach to their position of trust and honour.

1. " Over these the SECOND DEATH hath no authority."

We have first the negative advantage. No punishment is theirs. There are in the Apocalypse two Deaths, a present and a future. Both are *places*. The first Death, or the bottomless pit, exists now. Jesus holds its keys. i. 18. The Second Death is the lake of fire ; as the chapter teaches. Ver. 14. Exemption from this latter is a promise to the conquerors of the churches.

The promise made to the conquerors of the churches during the time of their previous life is now fulfilled. " He that overcometh shall not be hurt by the second death." These, then, are in great part the overcomers from among Christ's churches.

This statement sounds strangely in our ears : for we are quite accustomed to forget that even those justified by faith will be recompensed according to their works. Matt. xvi. 24-27 ; Rev. xxii. 12. Here it is implied that over some greatly offending believers the Second Death may have authority.

" And his lord was wroth, and delivered him to the tormentors, till he should pay all that was due unto him. *So likewise shall my heavenly Father do also unto you, if ye from your hearts forgive not every one his brother their trespasses* " (Matt. xviii. 34, 35).

" Not in the lust of concupiscence, even as the Gentiles which know not God. That no man go beyond and defraud his brother in the matter : because that the Lord is the avenger of all such, as we also have forewarned you and testified " (1 Thess. iv. 5, 6).

The promise of escaping this was made to the angel of

Smyrna when in danger of death for Christ's sake. But what if a believer through fear of death denied Christ? What seems the manifest implication of Luke xii. 4, 5?

"And I say unto you, *my friends,* Be not afraid of them that kill the body, and after that have no more that they can do. But I will forewarn you whom ye shall fear: *Fear Him, which after He hath killed hath power to cast into hell; yea, I say unto you, Fear Him.*"

The fear of God is to overbalance the fear of man.

"Do you mean, then, to deny, with the Wesleyans, the perseverance of God's elect?" By no means; that is a truth standing on firm grounds. But even John, who in his Gospel so strongly teaches *that,* as strongly asserts in the Saviour's words, the punishment of believers who die in sin unrepented of. What says that memorable passage?

"*If a man abide not in me, he is cast forth as a branch, and is withered; and men gather them, and cast them into the fire, and they are burned*" (John xv. 6).

And the Saviour's promises of the saint's perseverance are made in a way whose force has been missed by our translators. "Verily I say unto you, If any keep my saying, *he shall not for ever see death*" (John viii. 51, 52).

"I give unto them [my sheep] eternal life, and they *shall not perish for ever:* neither shall any pluck them out of my hand." "I am Resurrection and Life: he that believeth in me, though he die yet shall he live, and every one that liveth and believeth on me *shall not die for ever*" (John xi. 25, 26).

"Do you mean, then, that all those who are excluded from the millennial glory taste of death for a thousand years?" By no means. Some will be simply shut out, as unworthy of reward. But some are great offenders: some have been cut off in their sins: witness Ananias and Sapphira.

2. "But they shall be priests of God and of the Christ."

By priests we understand those holier than others, accepted by the God they worship, admitted nearer to Him than others, and bearers of messages to and from Him. All these things belong to the favoured ones of this scene. They are holier than others, clothed in resurrection-bodies, privileged to enter the Holiest of the temple in heaven. They are intercessors for the earth in that day : they bear to God the petitions of men : they receive back from God His replies to men.

At this time there are two temples, and two sets of priests ; the earthly temple and the priests of Aaron's line, who offer sacrifices that *cleanse the flesh*. Heb. ix. 13. There are the risen priests also who minister in the temple of the new covenant. The temple below is but "the outer court" of the temple above. But in the temple below Jesus as the Christ takes His seat.

The life of a believer in Jesus now is intended to be a preparation for that day. He is constituted already a priest to "offer up spiritual sacrifices, acceptable to God through Jesus Christ" (1 Pet. ii. 5, 9 ; Heb. xiii. 15, 16). He is directed to lift up *prayer and praise for all*. 1 Tim. ii. 1, 2. He is learning to discern between the good and evil. Heb. v. 14. He is endeavouring to instruct others, and turn them to God. At length, if obedient to his calling, he is "accounted worthy" to exercise his priesthood in the day of Messiah's kingdom, while yet the earth lasts ; to see with Messiah of the travail of his soul unto death. The nations dispute not their priesthood, as did the Israelites that of the sons of Aaron ; it is sealed, not with the token of resurrection, but *in its reality*.

They are priests of "God and of the Christ."

God and Jesus as *the Christ* are worshipped during the millennial age, in preparation for the final adoration of "God and *the Lamb*." Jesus, therefore, is God : for the priest is a minister of God. The title " the Christ " is only four times used in this book, and on all four occasions it refers to the millennial kingdom.

3. "They shall reign with him a thousand years."

Is the promised kingdom a session with Christ on His throne, while the dead are being judged, at the close of the thousand years ? Nay, the kingly authority is exercised during a thousand years, previous to the judgment of the dead. And what place is there for priesthood, while the dead are judged ?

The subjects of these kings are the Gentiles ; the authority over the twelve tribes of Israel being given by promise to the twelve Jewish apostles.

Here is at length the lawful union of the kingly and priestly offices. Under the Law, the kings might not be priests : and no priest became a king. Under the Gospel, the saints were priests, but were forbidden to be kings. 1 Cor. iv. 8–14. Now the risen are both priests and kings. Here is the perfection of government. For the rulers are the righteous, no longer tempted by sin or Satan. With full knowledge, perfect impartiality, and love of God and man, they rule their subjects. If there be any evil, it springs from the governed, not from the governors.

But this is not the final state. 'Tis only for a thousand years. 'Tis a transition-period between the old earth and the new, partaking of the characteristics of both. Then is fulfilled the word of the elders—" They shall reign over the earth."

THE LAST REBELLION

7-10. "And when the thousand years are finished, Satan shall be loosed out of his prison, and shall go forth to deceive the nations that are in the four quarters of the earth, Gog and Magog, to gather them together to battle ; the number of whom is as the sand of the sea. And they went up on the breadth of the earth, and encompassed the camp of the saints, and the beloved city: and fire came down out of the heaven from God, and devoured them. And the devil that deceived them was cast into the lake of fire and brimstone, where both the Wild Beast and the False Prophet are, and they shall be tormented day and night for ever and ever."

The Jewish prophets have in general no glimpse beyond the millennial period, in which their nation attains its distinct height of supremacy and glory. But this book leads us far beyond into eternity, where the Jew's distinctive position is no longer maintained.

Satan led our first parents to be discontented : he will thus lead the nations. But what mode will he adopt ? I think we may fairly conjecture, that he will stir up the *Gentiles* against the *Jews*. It is natural to man to be jealous of a superior. The Jew during the millennium is made to take a height far above the nations or Gentiles. Isa. lx. 10-12, 14, 16 ; Isa. lxi. 5, 6.

These words fret many Gentile souls now. How will they gall the spirits of the unconverted then ? Here, then, is fuel which he will know how to kindle. "Gentiles ! Are you poor spirited enough to submit any longer to the Jews ? that ill-favoured, money-getting, abject race, whom your fathers despised and loathed ? Whose are the great warriors of whom history speaks ? whose the mighty kings ? the great in arts ? the giant discoverers of science ? Gentiles ! Your fathers ! Will you, then, any longer tamely bow at the feet of these outcasts ? Why should the Jew hold the primacy ? 'The Gentile his inferior ? ' It is a lie against nature and history : the past and the present. Assert your native superiority ! Rise and wrest the sceptre from these oppressors ! Determine that you will be free ! Will it, and liberty is yours ! Go up to Jerusalem once more, not to pay homage there, not to confess *that* the metropolis of earth, but to destroy it, and set up a centre of your own ! "

Thus he deceives them. He makes them imagine it degradation to submit to God's appointment.

All past mercies are forgotten in deep ingratitude. They will not have the holy to reign over them : they refuse Christ Himself, the Perfect King.

Satan does not now attempt to deceive *Israel* or their king, though once he prevailed against David, and drew down God's displeasure on Israel and *Jerusalem*. 1 Chron. xxi. 1.

The promise of God preserves them from any further wile of his. Isa. lix. 21.

The devil goes into the four quarters of the globe on this errand, a new Peter the Hermit, preaching the crusade of many races against one. Great his encouragement. Multitudes unnumbered answer to his call. The nations are in the main still his seed. The seed of Satan must be purged out from among men, that in the new earth there may be a peace never disturbed. The evil generation will not have passed away till the earth itself is destroyed.

But this is a stumbling-block to some. "Whom will he find willing? Only the holy are left on the earth, after the Saviour's sword and His judgment have severed the evil from among the good " (Rev. xix. ; Matt. xxv. 31–46). It is true that, at the commencement of the millennium, only the holy will be found. But are the offspring of the holy holy likewise ? Must not grace step in, or the child of pious parents is only a fallen son of Adam ? This, then, accounts easily for the last fearful hosts of sin. At the close of the millennium there are thousands not renewed.

Amidst the nations, or as inclusive of them, two names are given, "Gog and Magog."

Magog is mentioned as one of the sons of Japheth. Gen. x. 2. Gog is named, if we will trust the Septuagint, in Num. xxiv. 7. "His king shall be higher than Gog." "Magog," if I mistake not, is still found in our days, softened into "Mogul."

Asia, north of the Oxus, was described by the Arabian writers as inhabited by Turks. "Turk with them is a widely-diffused term, applied as that of Scythians by the ancients, to designate all the nomadic tenants of those extensive regions. They seem already to have been viewed with no small portion of dread and horror. Bakoui describes them as living partly in tents and partly in villages; as brave, hardy, and having the air of wild beasts; their face broad, their nose flat : 'they are furious, unjust, and live like beasts.' The Tartars are mentioned as a race of Turks further to the north, and still more savage. 'They resemble beasts, their heart is hard, their character bad, they are without faith or religion'" (*Murray's Discoveries in Asia*, i. 56). Gog and Magog were by the Arabian writers considered to be located about those parts.

The writer observes that from the east of Asia, almost as far as the confines of Germany, is a wide expanse of level plain, resembling the ocean. This was called by the ancients Scythia. The moderns, severing the European part, call the residue Tartary. Fierce and wild were their manners; so that tribes by us considered barbarous, spoke with horror of a Scythian devastation. "The series of invasions, therefore, which have poured down from those regions, have always been numbered among the most dreadful calamities to which the human race is liable ; they have been compared to a scourge, which the Deity holds continually in His hand to chastise the crimes of mankind " (p. 71). Thence came the hordes of Goths, Huns, Turks, and then the Mogul Tartars under Zinghis Khan.

We are to understand, then, that the northern nations, especially the Tartars, Russians, and the adjacent nations, will be conspicuous in this invasion.

We must distinguish it, however, from the invasion of Gog and Magog in Ezek. xxxviii. It is after that, that the millennial times occur. After this later inroad, the earth is burnt up.

" The number of whom is as the sand of the sea."

Satan has now no king with him : all kings are of Christ's appointment : they are the favoured risen. Before the devil sent out evil spirits with miracles to persuade ; and had two supernatural human assistants. Now he is alone. Then he set up a false religion as the basis of the rebellion. Now, his time probably being far shorter than before, he aims only at collecting an army for battle.

At the commencement of the thousand years, but few are left alive on earth, because of the fearful destruction of the ungodly. But now, as the result of peace and plenty for a thousand years, the population of earth is enormous. In their vast numbers they put their trust : forgetful that God in former days has destroyed armies characterized by the same incalculable proportions.

It is worthy of remark, that the point for which these go up to fight against God is granted in the next dispensation, and on the new earth. In the new world, all the nations occupy the same level. Of course the rebels have no place there. But God in mercy there removes this stone of offence. And had they waited but a brief period, they would have attained the object they so unlawfully and ungratefully sought.

Satan's last resource is war. Once he has fought in heaven ; once on earth. He attempts it now for the third and last time.

But some say of this scene,—" It is *incredible*, if all that has preceded be literally true, that ever men should be so frantic as to rush on Jerusalem when defended by the Son of God visibly seated in glory there ! "

Such little know what man and Satan are. Such have little profited by the records of the past. Is it incredible that after ten plagues supernaturally sent, and confessed to be from God, Pharaoh and his hosts should still assail the people of Israel visibly defended by the pillar of cloud ?

Is it incredible, that after the earth had opened and swallowed up the congregation of Dathan and Abiram, and the fire of God had struck dead the two hundred and fifty presumptuous burners of incense, that *the next day* " *all the congregation of Israel murmured against Moses and against Aaron, saying, Ye have killed the people of the Lord* " ? (Num. xvi. 41). Was that a fact ? So will this be.

" They went up on the breadth of the earth."

But what is " the breadth of the earth ? " It is once used of the earth, or globe in general. Job xxxviii. 18. But I am inclined to think that in this place we should translate it, " on the breadth of *the land*," referring the expression to the land of Israel, as it is in Isa. viii. 8.

The expression seems to intend a design on their part to enclose the whole of the land of Israel, so as to cut off all, allowing none to escape.

Zech. xiv. 16–19 teaches us that, in general, the nations will be disinclined for the long yearly pilgrimage to Jerusalem, in order to keep the feast of tabernacles. For God's threats are directed against their not going up. But in this case, there is too great a willingness : they go up, not for worship, but for war. And no doubt, it seems both to Satan and to themselves a master-stroke of policy, to turn against Christ the command hitherto enforced to go up to Jerusalem. "If He will have us go, go we will : not to bend before Him, but to overturn His throne." This enforced pilgrimage is the point in which their subjection to the Jew most strikingly appears.

In the previous war against God, it seemed as if He had been foolish in drying up Euphrates, and the Easterns take advantage of it to fight against Israel. Now the command to go up to Jerusalem seems another weakness on the part of the Most High, of which they will avail themselves. But the foolishness of God is wiser than man. Jehovah sees the heart of these warlike pilgrims : known unto him are their plots. He gathers them, as weeds, for destruction.

In pursuance of their purpose, " they compassed the camp of the saints."

What is meant by " the camp of the saints " ? The expression, rightly understood, is full of interest.

When Israel was moving out of Egypt under God's guidance, into the land of promise, it became the Lord's host. Exod. xii. 17, 41, 51. When its tents were pitched it became the Lord's camp. Exod. xiv. 19 ; xvi. 13.

Now, under the guidance of the greater Joshua, " the *armies* " of heaven have descended from on high. xix. 11. They are the *camp* of heaven on earth now; for the aspect of heaven towards earth is military. Though at rest, they are prepared for war.

I cannot agree with those who believe that the saints who reign with Christ will not be upon the earth. They can, no doubt, ascend to heaven, and to the new Jerusalem—their real centre—when they will; but Christ will be oft on earth, and surely they will be there also.

The millennium is Messiah's "rule" "in the midst among *enemies*" (Ps. cx. 2). The "iron rod" tells of martial law proclaimed. It is destruction to foes. Earth is treated as conquered in battle. Messiah descends to "judge and *make war*" "*in righteousness*." Against this, then, as the chief obstacle to Satan's project, their advance is mainly directed. This body of heavenly kings can be, on occasion, warriors also. So were they at first: so are they seen at last. This confirms our inference, that the armies who come from heaven become the kings enthroned in xx. 4. They watch over Jerusalem and its temple.

That "the camp of the saints" refers to the army of the risen who come with Christ, seems to be corroborated by the immediately precedent occurrences of the word "saints." They are those especially holy before God. "Rejoice over her, thou heaven, and ye *saints*." "The fine linen is the righteous acts of *the saints*" (xviii. 20; xix. 8). "Blessed and *holy* is he that hath part in the first resurrection" (xx. 6).

It is probable that this attack of the nations is made at the time of the feast of Tabernacles, when less suspicion would attend the gathering of such vast multitudes, and when most of Israel would be gone up to the temple. This would be the time, too, at which the Gentiles' subjection to the Jews would be felt most sorely, and when the nations might be most easily collected; that being the time when the autumnal fruits had been gathered in.

Lest any should imagine that the wickedness of earth is owing to a corrupt form of government, and should say (as many might be apt to do, from a view of the forms of wickedness in the last days), "Ah, you see these evils spring from *kings*. Again and again

Scripture traces the latter-day transgressions to *them*. The *people* are always sound-hearted for Christ in the main; but for the influence of corrupted kings they would never have been leagued against the Lord Jesus, as we see, at His coming." Scripture shows us that when there are no kings of earth but the perfect governors of Christ's appointing, the *people* go astray. Satan deceives the nations, even when the weight of government is all against him. No! no! the mischief lies deeper far than any form of government.

They assail also "the beloved city."

Their encompassing at once the camp and the city, and filling the breadth of the land, shows something of their immense multitudes. For the land of Israel near Jerusalem, where it is hemmed in by the Dead Sea, is fifty miles broad. And the distance between the millennial temple and the millennial Jerusalem of Ezekiel is something like forty miles. They assail the two, then, from north, south, and east, perhaps from the west also.

It is not named Jerusalem, it is not called even "the *old* Jerusalem;" a name of greater tenderness distinguishes it. But it is entirely supplanted by the New Jerusalem, as soon as its day is over. "The slave [Ishmael] abideth not in the house for ever: but the son [Isaac] abideth ever" (Greek). John viii. 35.

"Fire came down out of the heaven from God, and devoured them."

For the offence of not coming up to Jerusalem to worship, God threatens the withholding of rain: a slow punishment, which would, at any time, admit of repentance on the nation's part. But, for the crime of coming up in warlike array against His city and king, the stroke of wrath is instant, and there is no room for penitence. Offenders are cut off in their sin in a moment.

Here, as in the former case, the dupes of Satan are first dealt with, then Satan himself. As the incorrigible Deceiver, who loves and makes a lie, his career is finished in woe: fire falls on them, and kills them. But *he* is cast "into the lake of fire and brimstone." That awful abode of the lost was kindled as soon as the millennium began. It now receives him, for whom and for whose angels it is destined. Matt. xxv. 41. For Satan is not consumed by the fire from above, as men are. He is not in flesh, as are the hosts whom he leads. He is to dwell visibly in eternal fire, as before he was shut up in the bottomless pit, away from sight.

In that awful pool of woe the Wild Beast and the False Prophet have lain all the thousand years. These are the two whom Satan for awhile delivered from the bottomless pit, by means of the key granted him. After their increased wickedness displayed during the time they were at liberty, they were consigned to a more fearful place still.

Satan has now sinned after judgment tasted and mercy experienced, even as those two had. He is therefore smitten as they have been, and are. All three are evidently persons. For a thousand years the two sons of men were punished more severely than he, because more mercy had been shown to them. For before both of them had the good news of a Saviour been brought, and rejected. Paul stood before Nero to make his defence (2 Tim. iv. 17), and was at last slain by him, together with unnumbered other Christians.

As the thousand years are a period of peculiar glory to the saints who wrought on behalf of God's kingdom, so is it a time of especial woe to these its most inveterate enemies.

Thus we trace God's general appointment. At death the souls of the lost go into the pit. Out of it they come to be tried; and after being sentenced as risen men, they are cast into hell, or the lake of fire.

In that lake they and the three specially mentioned " shall be tormented day and night for ever and ever." No further exit, for these firebrands, into God's universe ! *Eternally* they shall suffer. It is no marvel, if in our day the awful doctrine of eternal punishment is frequently attacked : but the evidence for it is overwhelming.

Here the difference between temporary and eternal punishment comes directly into view. We are set at the close of the temporary vengeance : and there the Holy Spirit traces for us the line of future wrath. It is not millennial wrath alone that the wicked are to endure. After that period is over, we are instructed that onward, without a break, *torment* is to continue. It is not annihilation, and relative punishment, in consequence of transgressors being blotted out of conscious existence. It is life and conscious life in misery— " TORMENTED FOR EVER AND EVER."

THE FINAL JUDGMENT

11-15. " And I saw a great white throne, and the Sitter on it, from whose face the earth and the heaven fled : and place was not found for them. And I saw the dead, the great and the small, standing before the throne :[1] and books were opened ; and another book was opened which is (the book) of [life : and the dead were judged out of the things written in the books according to their works. And the sea gave up the dead that were in it : and Death and Hades gave up the dead that were in them : and they were judged each according to their works. And Death and Hades were cast into the lake of fire. This is the Second Death, the lake of fire.[1] And if any was not found written in the book of life, he was cast into the lake of fire."

In the Holy Spirit's words we have the scene which is usually called " the Judgment Day." It is also fre-

[1] So Tregelles.

quently called, " the General Judgment." It is supposed to be ushered in by trumpet-sound : whereas the last or seventh trumpet sounded a thousand years previously, and then ushered in Messiah's kingdom, and the resurrection of the righteous. Not then is the time of the rising again, and judgment of all men. The saints have been judged long before, in the presence of Christ seated on THE JUDGMENT SEAT, not on THE THRONE.

"But why dost thou judge thy brother ? or why dost thou set at nought thy brother ? *for we shall all stand before the judgment seat of Christ.*[1] For it is written, ' As I live, saith the Lord, every knee shall bow to me, and every tongue shall confess to God.' So then every one of us shall give account of himself to God " (Rom. xiv. 10–12).

" We must all be manifested before *the judgment seat of the Christ* that each may receive the things done by the body, according to the things he did, whether (the issue) be good or bad " (2 Cor. v. 10).

This throne is a different one from that which appears in the temple. Chap. iv. That was set for judgment on the living, while the earth lasted ; and the rainbow was round it : for there were promises of mercy still encircling Israel and the earth. But now the earth departs for ever : there is no rainbow here. Earth and heaven stood before *that* throne : they pass away from *this*. Both continue under the thrones of Christ, and His favoured ones, during the millennium. They depart now. None but one sits on this throne which judges the dead. So mistaken is that view which imagines the saints to be co-assessors with Christ when He passes sentence on the dead. The rewarded are to sit with Him when He rules and breaks in pieces the refractory living nations. ii. 26, 27 ; iii. 21.

---

[1] For "Christ" the critical editions read "God."

The thousand years being now finished, the dead judged are " the rest of the dead." And as those happy ones of the first resurrection were not in danger of the second death, these on the contrary are. This is " the resurrection of judgment," for those who have done evil.

It is a " great throne." Great is the occasion on which it appears : great the final winding up of the affairs of the earth. 'Tis the supreme throne, self-poised in air. The inferior ones, on which the saints sat who reigned with the Christ, do not appear beside it. But One, the monarch of all, sits thereon.

It is a " white " throne. That is the colour of pure justice. It will judge the earth in righteousness. Alone in its spotless purity, the orbs of the sky removed from before it, it attracts and fixes every eye. It is set to adjudicate the cases of all the dead. The question of eternal life and eternal death is the one it decides.

Most things belonging to Christ in this book are white. His hair, His horse, the clouds on which He sits, are of this colour.

John notices next the person of the Judge who took His seat thereon. He is not described ; but it seems certain that it must be Jesus. For the Father committed all judgment to the Son. John v. 22, 27. He is " appointed of God to be judge of dead and living " (Acts x. 42 ; xvii. 31 ; Rom. ii. 6 ; 1 Pet. iv. 5 ; 2 Tim. iv. 1). It is not the throne of the Father and the Son.

His awful aspect and wondrous power are sublimely described by their effects. Earth and heaven both fled away from before Him. This is doubtless the moment described by Peter. 2 Peter iii. 10, 7, 12. It is the conclusion of the Great Day of God. Those who make the conflagration to take place at the commencement of the day, and before the millennium, are involved in wholly needless difficulties. "The Day of God" is of a thousand years' duration, as Peter, in the same chapter, tells us. v. 8. "But it is more than a thousand years," say objectors. "There is the little time of Satan's last rebellion beside." Be it so. Do any think that such an expression must be construed as strictly as the commercial truth—that "sixteen ounces make a pound?" Probably, too, there is a double beginning of the thousand years ; so that it is possible that, computed from another starting-point, it may be exactly the period.

How is the earth burned up? No doubt by the "fire which came down out of the heaven from God." Of the force of that, the history of Elijah supplies evidence. At the prayer of the prophet, "The fire of the Lord fell, and consumed the burnt sacrifice, and the wood, and the *stones*, and the *dust*, and *licked up the water that was in the trench*" (1 Kings xviii. 38). Then its fierceness wrought no evil to the globe : for the sacrifice drew off its terrors. But now it falls on the earth unbroken by an accepted victim : it sets fire to earth itself. The gases of the sea become combustible, and the earth is one sheet of fire rolling away out of its orbit to destruction.

Men stand self-poised in air before the throne. No longer do bodies of clay fasten them to the soil of earth. Risen from the dead, they await the sentence of the judge.

"But does not this make a third coming of Christ necessary?" Strange, that the objection should ever have been made. The Saviour is already on the earth ; and when the earth speeds away He is seated on the throne which occupies the place of the lost globe.

No word is dropped here of the Saviour's coming from heaven to earth to judge, as the antimillennarian theory supposes. He has come long before (chap.

xix. 11), and now that His reign is past, the earth, the scene of it, departs.

Many will not accept the Scripture doctrine of the utter destruction and disappearance of the old globe. What is the reason is perhaps hard to say. But most will with earnestness contend that the fire will only purge the world, not destroy it. Perhaps this is owing to the felt connection between the entire destruction of man's abode and the eternal suffering of the wicked. With some it arises from fancied scientific reasons. "Matter cannot be annihilated." True, *man* cannot annihilate it; but *cannot God?* Did He not bring it into existence out of nothing? Can He not hurl it again into nothingness? This answer often brings out into view the fact that many do not believe in *creation*. Their God did not make all things out of nought. He only framed them out of pre-existent matter. Such are indeed consistent : but they are opposed to the glory of God, and to the testimony of His word. Gen. i. 1; Heb. xi. 3. Moreover, the apostle argues that the prophecy in Haggai foretells a final shaking of heaven and earth preparatory to their entire removal : in order that the new creation may supersede them. Heb. xii. 26–28.

Such is also the testimony of that type of Moses' day—the leprous house. Lev. xiv. 34. If the leprosy broke out in a house, the priest was to bid them empty it.

Does not this emptying of the suspected house answer to the carrying away of Israel captive? After that, the priest should go in and see the house. This was typified by the Saviour's first coming. He saw tokens enough of leprosy, and denounced them. Then was the priest to leave the house, and cause it to be shut up seven days. The house was to be left to itself to determine its internal state. Even thus has Jesus gone away, and the world has been permitted to run a career unbroken by miracle, or the visitation of the Son of God. But after seven days the priest is to come again and look, and if the streaks of green or red increased, he was to cause the house to be scraped, and to pour away into an unclean place the dust so scraped off. He was also to cause new stones to be inserted in the place of those which were removed, and to plaster the house.

The plague is spread indeed, when the angel from on high descends. Chap. x. Jesus has foretold that it will be. The evil spirit with seven others worse than himself has entered and defiles the house.

Then comes the change and restoration of earth after its fall, which the millennial visit and reign of Christ introduce. The wicked are removed from among the living and cast into Tophet, while those risen from the dead take their place, and earth wears a new face under the new generation of men. "But," it was commanded, "if the leprosy break out anew in spite of this restoration of the house, it should be pronounced unclean." "He shall break down the house, the stones of it, and the timber thereof, and all the mortar of the house: and he shall carry them forth of the city into an unclean place" (Lev. xiv. 45). The house is utterly destroyed then: its unclean stones, timber, and dust are used no more,

See also Ps. cii. 26, 27; Matt. xxiv. 35; Heb. i. 10-12.

But if any further proof were needed, the words of this passage are evidently designed to furnish it. The result of the passing away of the heaven and the earth is, that "PLACE WAS NOT FOUND FOR THEM." How this can consist with their atoms being remoulded, and constituting the place in which the redeemed shall live, would puzzle the acutest to discover. And when next the subject is treated of, the passing away of the heavens and earth is declared to be followed by the appearing of new ones. xxi. 1.

The apostle then " saw the dead, the great and the small, standing before the throne."

" The books " are principally the voluminous records of sins committed. An impartial biography of all the lost bears witness of continual transgressions. But another book of a different character appears, " The Book *of Life*." Those books stand charged with death to offenders. This brings life. The books which speak against men are many, for they record their many evil deeds, and they occupy a large space. But the Book of Life, we may well suppose, contains the names only, and not the deeds, of the saved.

Why is it opened ?

Most reply—that it affects the judgment *negatively* only. It is presented, only to discover that none of the names of the culprits before the throne are found in it. I am persuaded that this is a mistake arising from an error with regard to the millennium—that it embraces all believers—all the saved of every age.

That that is a mistaken view, evidence has been given. If a part in the millennium flow from faith, all believers will have part in it. If it be a " reward " " according to works," a prize of the race set before the Christian, then some will be " accounted worthy " of it ; some will not.

If the deeds of any stand recorded against them, and they have not forgiveness, will not that suffice to condemn ? Need there be any inquiry—" But are they in the Book of Life ? " Can they be in the Book of Life, while their deeds of evil in that hour stand against them uncancelled ? And if written in the Book of Life, can their deeds still be standing against them ? This is the hour of simple justification, or the entrance on eternal life through grace.

The book is opened, therefore, as *positively* affecting the scene before us. Some of God's elect are there. The book decides the lot of some, both of the dead, and of the living. Who are to enter into the city is settled by the Lamb's book of life. xxi. 27. There is proof of its positive employment.

1. Some, then, of the elect are among the *dead*. They were not counted worthy of *reward*. As dealt with according to their own works, they could but be excluded. Many never confessed Christ, but were secret disciples. Such Christ would not confess at His coming. Matt. x. 32, 33 ; vii. 21. Some for sin were excluded from the churches of the saints, died unrepentant, and were never restored to their places. But that binding on earth bound also in heaven. Matt. xviii. 15-18. Jesus reaffirmed the sentence of the Church. Not all accounted worthy of a place in the Church by their fellow-disciples will enter. But all justly accounted unworthy to sit down with the saints on earth will assuredly be shut out from the kingdom of heaven. There are many other classes of the excluded, which the reader would do well to search out for himself.

There will probably also be some of those both during the patriarchal ages, and under the Law, who will be saved, while not enjoying reward.

2. Multitudes of the *living* are in the Book of *Life*. It is with regard to them principally, if I mistake not, that it is presented. The hosts of Satan were consumed by the fire of God. But not all the world joined that impious expedition. There was one nation at least, not one of whom was found in its ranks. Israel is all righteous.

What becomes, then, of the living of mankind when the earth is burnt up ? They do not appear among the dead. We learn only inferentially. They appear on the new earth as "the nations." They are transferred, therefore, alive from the old world to the new. But before they enter that world, it is decided whether they are of the serpent's seed or not. This is the moment at which the great separation takes place : all the non-elect are excluded from the new heavens and new earth wherein righteousness dwells. How is the lot of the children and the females, who never joined the army of the rebels, decided ? By the Book of Life !

If not found there, their lives would be only sinful, and their influence disastrous. The Book of Life, therefore, admits all written in its pages, and excludes all not mentioned there. According to its entries is it determined, whether the individual enter the lake of fire, or is admitted to the new earth and the city of God.

But next we have the award as given against the culprits of the dead. They were "judged out of the things written in the (first-named) books." That evidence alone was sufficient ; no moral testimony, as in our courts, was needed. No erroneous statement was there, no offence overlooked. The memory of each, supernaturally enlarged, and cleared in resurrection, perfectly corresponded with the accusing records of the books of human deeds. By these they "*were judged.*"

They were judged "according to their works." This is the principle of justice : they received their deserts. The principle takes two applications.

1. First as to the *quality* of the works. Were they good or evil ? Evil is requited for evil done.

2. Secondly as to the *quantity*, or the degree. The decent worldly man will not be so heavily doomed as the pirate, the murderer, the blasphemer, the adulterer. The heathen sinner will not be so heavily sentenced as the refuser of Gospel light. The youth cut off at fifteen, will not have so heavy a load to bear as the

aged sinner of fourscore. Here is the doom of the dead in relation to the throne, and the records of its court. All are doomed for evident acts of sin committed. Each is adjudged to the intensity of torment which his deeds deserve.

Of course the saints who have previously reigned with Christ and dispensed judgment, are not now set as foes at the bar, to take their trial for life or death.

We have next a notice given of the places whence the dead come forth. They are three: the sea, Hades, Death. This gives us the disposal of the dead in relation to their places of custody. The subordinate spaces of the globe surrender their dead. At this General Assize all the places of custody deliver up their prisoners.

Why the *sea* is named, I am unable to say.

It is not said, "The earth gave up the *living* on it," or " the sea gave up the dead *under it*."

The other two places keep the *souls* of men. Surely the sea does not. It holds the bodies, and the mouldering bones of the drowned: but must not their souls go into the two places afterward specified? I am not ashamed to confess myself at a loss here.

The sea is not cast into the lake of fire, and it does not appear in the new earth. It flees away, then, with the heavens and earth. The sea is reckoned one of the unclean parts of the earth, as being the abode of the dead.

Death and Hades next give up the souls they detain. Both are names of places. Jesus has the key of both. Where both are mentioned, as distinguished from each other, Hades signifies the place of the righteous dead. "Death," is that of the souls of the lost.

"Death" is put before Hades in this place. Ordinarily the reversed order obtains. Job xxvi. 6; Prov. xv. 11; xxvii. 20. But here the prominent topic is the condemnation of the lost, and therefore the place of lost spirits in both cases occupies the conspicuous position.

The thousand years are over : this is the second resurrection. But it is not said, " Cursed and unholy is he who hath part therein ; over these the Second Death hath power, and they shall dwell with the False Christ, and False Prophet, and Satan, and be tormented for ever and ever."

From this again it follows, that there are some of the saved who stand before the judge. All those whose souls issue from the place of the righteous dead, of course, are saved. At death the souls of the saved and lost are separated, as we learn by our Lord's parable of Dives and Lazarus.

Of those who came up it is again recorded that "they were judged each according to their works." This is the great principle which the Holy Ghost would impress on us. Impartial justice presided. *By* their works, as good or evil fruit, was the character of the tree decided. *According* to their works, in number and heinousness, was the measure of damnation awarded. For every seed of sin sown, appears the answering thistle in the day of reaping. "The wages of sin is death."

There is no word of reward now. It is, Life Eternal, or Eternal Death !—which ?

The next announcement cannot be understood by those who suppose that the " Death " here named is a spiritual thing. But understand both to be spoken of places, and the sentiment is easily intelligible. These old prisons are no longer needed.

Why are they cast away ? Because there is now no intermediate state. They were employed once in detaining the souls of the righteous and of the wicked, till the judgment reunited body and soul. But now they merge into the eternal place of the lost. There are only those risen from the dead : and Hades defiled by the dead belongs not to heaven. It is therefore cast, with the First Death, into the Second, or the lake of fire.

And then follows a notice, that the Second Death is another name for hell, " the lake of fire." The lake of fire is a real place, no less than the others. The fire and brimstone are real, as truly as the resurrection bodies of the condemned.

" And if any was not found written in the Book of Life, he was cast into the lake of fire."

But there was another class, whose places could not be adjusted by their actions. There were infants, cut down in earliest youth, who had not begun to act. There were those living upon the earth when the throne is set. The award to these is given, if I am not mistaken, by the Book of Life. After the effects of the books of human deeds to condemn, comes the agency of the Book of Life in saving. " If any "— it is not added " of *the dead :* " and hence I conclude that it refers in its full sweep to both the living and the dead.

The books stand connected with the prison-delivery of the jails. Their sentence was for death. Here is sovereignty, rejoicing to save without deeds, or against desert.

Its aspect is here stated only negatively, and in reference to the place of punishment, " the lake of fire." If not in that book, the person was cast into the lake. Its positive aspect as introducing into the city of life does not appear, till that city has been shown us. If any are not elect, they are seed of the serpent. If seed of the serpent, they are only evil, and would discover their enmity by deeds of sin, as before. Hence they are excluded from the place of the holy, shut up amidst the children of the Wicked One, their kin. There are finally but two states, heaven and hell. The lake of fire is hell, or " Gehenna of fire."

Thrice the words " the lake of fire " close the adjoining sentence at the conclusion of the chapter. The Holy Spirit would have the awful sound dwell on our ears, and sink into our hearts. It is the consummation of the *altar* and the *laver* in the temple. The laver was the place of water for washing that which was unclean. The altar was the place of fire to consume the victim. The place of the lost, then, unites these points. 'Tis the place of the permanently unclean ; 'tis a lake. 'Tis the place of the victims of divine wrath ; 'tis an altar of everburning fire.

As, then, the places of all the tenants of earth have been decided for ever, and none but the elect enter the new earth, the final state must be stable.

None, then, of these will ever fall. God undertakes their upholding. The new covenant rests entirely on God's power, not on man's.

CHAPTER XXI

THE FINAL STATE

1. "And I saw a new heaven and a new earth: for the first heaven and the first earth passed away: and the sea exists no more."

THERE will be a "new heaven." From this it would appear that a new atmosphere and new stars will surround the new world. The former stars have fallen, the former atmosphere departed.

Here begins another epoch. There is a new creation in honour of the second Adam; just as there was a creation prepared for the first. As a fresh surface of earth greeted Noah after his coming forth out of the ark, so after the last deluge of fire the escaped come forth upon a new world. Its physical and moral standings are altered.

As Hengstenberg observes, the corruption of the creation began with persons, and then it seized on material things; so God restores first the fallen persons, and then the creation.

The earth is new. Two promises of new heavens and earth are found in Isaiah.

1. The first is given just after the Most High discovers to us the last form of evil on the earth, and declares the contrasted portions of His friends and His foes. "For behold I create new heavens and a new earth; and the former shall not be remembered, nor come into mind" (Isa. lxv. 17).

2. Again the Holy Spirit promises them, in the midst of one of the clearest prophecies of millennial bliss : the nation of Israel is to abide, and its names and tribes, as surely " As the new heavens and the new earth which I will make " (Isa. lxvi. 22).

This is a promise reiterated and expanded by Peter. 2 Pet. iii. 5–13. It is a promise common to both the Jew and the Church of God.

In the Jewish prophets the millennial season is the one fully developed and greatly insisted on : of the final state scarce a glimpse is afforded. In this book, on the contrary, which gives the far fuller mind of God, the millennial day appears but as a brief episode ; and the eternal arrangements of the Most High take the prominent place which becomes them. What are a thousand years to eternity ?

" The sea exists no more."

This feature of the new globe would especially strike an eye accustomed to the old, and more particularly that of John, the fisherman accustomed to sail over the sea in quest of subsistence. The sea now occupies about three parts of the globe : but then the whole world will be habitable.

God of old brought the ocean upon the earth to destroy its inhabitants. He uses it to plague the guilty in the latter day. But on the new earth there shall be no waters of barrenness and of *death ;* only waters of life. The new earth is not to be the field of commerce and its deceits, or of war and its strifes. Military and naval greatness depart with Babylon swallowed up because of her sins. In our Lord's day, the fish of the sea were used for the supply of human necessity. But on the new world, it would appear, as we shall see, that animal food will not be used.

The sea occurs frequently in the Old Testament descriptions of the millennial day. The Saviour's dominion is to be from sea to sea. Zech. ix. 10. The abundance of the sea shall be converted to Israel. Isa. lx. 5. The Dead Sea is to be healed, and to be full of fish, which fishermen are to take. Ezek. xlvii.

This forms a great feature of distinction between the covenant with Noah, and the new covenant. The covenant with Noah specially regarded the sea as the instrument of God's wrath, and set bounds to it, " while the earth remained." The inhabitants of the sea were not taken into covenant with God on that occasion. Hence they do not appear among the four " living creatures :" though fish are mentioned as among the animals given up into the hands of the patriarch and his sons. Gen. ix. 2.

THE NEW CITY AND ITS BLESSINGS

2. "And (I saw) the holy city, the New Jerusalem, coming down out of the heaven from God, prepared as a bride adorned for her husband. 3. And I heard a great voice out of the throne saying, ' Behold, the tabernacle of God is with men, and He will tabernacle with them, and they shall be His people, and God himself shall be with them and be their God. 4. And God shall wipe away every tear from their eyes, and death shall be no more, nor mourning, nor scream, neither shall there be any more pain : for the former things passed away.' "

John sees it " descending out of the heaven from God." It is no part of that creation which is to be shaken, and therefore to pass away. It belongs to a new creation, and therefore is to abide for ever. Heb. xii.

In the Hebrews, the apostle speaks not of the new city till after he has spoken of the coming of Christ. In the Apocalypse it was not beheld by John till the heavenly country appears. The New Jerusalem does indeed exist during the millennium (xix. 7, 8), and so does the heavenly temple, and both together exert mighty power for good. But John does not behold it till the *millennium is over*. Not till then does it descend to men and the new earth.

There are two descents of the city. The first from its invisible abode to visibility. This takes place before the millennium. xix. 7–9. During the millennium it appears to be suspended over the earth, the top of the ladder which unites the earth and heaven. The second is its descent to the new earth, there to abide for ever, after the millennium is past.

Even thus there are two descents of our Lord. The first into the air, the second into the earth. Thus, too, He rose first to the level of the earth, remained there forty days, and then ascended on high.

John beholds the city descending at the proper point of time, just as he sees the throne being set, as the new dispensation begins. He beholds its first entrance on the earth, and is taught, in the words which follow, the great results which flow from this new move of God.

"*Behold* the tabernacle of God is with men."

It is not any longer the Most High taking a people from among the rest of mankind to be His, leaving all others at a distance from Himself and unclean: but all men, or all "the nations," constitute the people of God.

Blessings were dispensed to Israel, and judgments averted from them, by virtue of the tabernacle, the presence of God, and the priests who served in it. It is so more fully in this case. The tabernacle of chapter vii. was "the tabernacle *of testimony in the heaven*." This is "the tabernacle of fullness and *realization on the earth*." The priests then were afar from men: now they are within their reach.

The city descends to earth, as I suppose, with all its priests and kings complete; yea, God Himself is there, and finds men on the earth. " The tabernacle of God is with MEN."

But now each individual man is elect, never more to fall. Hence the nations are holy for ever. The standing given to Israel by grace during the millennium is now extended to men in the flesh universally. From the days of Abraham God's plan had been to take a nation for His own out of the midst of mankind. But that was only by way of preparation for this final display of His goodness in making all men His people. The privileges of Israel are no longer distinctive. " But is not that unjust to Israel ? " That is the question which Jesus tries, and decides in the negative in the parable of the Labourers in the Vineyard. Matt. xix. 16–xx. 16.

That which God promises to Israel in Ezek. xxxvii. is carried out at length toward men. God gathers them from the old earth, cleanses them from their defilements, and promises that they shall no more defile themselves. One shall be their king, and His tabernacle shall be in their midst. Because of the abode of that in their land, God would sanctify Israel. Now, because the tabernacle of God's own building is on earth, He sanctifies men in general.

There exists, however, a great distinction between the *priests* and *kings*, the dwellers in the tabernacle, and the *nations* outside it. This obtained in millennial times. Israel had one station, the priests another. " Men " and " the nations " in the flesh are distinguished from God's " servants " risen from the dead. This will appear more fully afterwards.

Why is it called " the *tabernacle* ? " Why not " the *temple* ? " If I mistake not, it is in order to throw back our eye to the time of God's first taking up His abode with His people in the wilderness. Then the tabernacle stood in the midst, the great centre of unity to all the twelve tribes. They were all marshalled in orderly array around the abode of God, who dwelt with them in their camp. Now the city is the tabernacle, and is the nations' great centre. They are gathered around it, as I conclude from the arrangements of the three gates on each of the four sides of the city. The priests were to pitch tent in an inner circle around the tabernacle. The sketch is now filled up by the entire cleansing of the priests of the new covenant. They are able to abide in God's tabernacle, to dwell in His holy hill. The flesh, in its weakness or its sin, interferes no more.

These words teach us that we are not engaged now with any millennial arrangements of the old earth. For during the millennium Israel alone is God's earthly people. There is the distinction of circumcised and uncircumcised, of God's covenant-people, and "the stranger" (Isa. lx. 10 ; lxi. 5 ; lxii. 8 ; Ezek. xliv. 9 ; xlvii. 23 ; Jer. li. 51 ; Joel iii. 17).

It was the surprised observation of Solomon, when he looked at the temple he had built, "But will *God* in very deed dwell with *men* on the earth ? Behold heaven and the heaven of heavens cannot contain thee, how much less this house which I have built!" (2 Chron. vi. 18). Now 'tis fulfilled. Fulfilled far more widely and gloriously than Solomon dreamed of.

The tabernacle of God is no empty pageant, the God of the tabernacle is there. Nor does He enter it to leave it again, there He dwells for ever.

Men "shall be His people, and God Himself shall be with them as their God."

This promise implies that the heart of mankind shall be opened to love and obey God. And in turn it is implied that God's bounties shall flow forth unimpeded to them. This is seen in Jer. xxiv. 7 ; Ezek. xi. 18–20. Mankind in the flesh occupy the place of millennial Israel, with certain great advances even on that standing.

"God shall wipe away every tear from their eyes."

All had shed tears before : now past sorrows shall be healed and forgot. Sorrow, tears, cries, were the consequences of the fall. Gen. iii. 16, 17. Now those consequences are blotted out.

This happy portion was granted long ago to the Great Multitude rapt to the throne of God in resurrection. Rev. vii. 17.

"Death shall be no more, nor mourning, nor scream."

Death occurs during the thousand years (Isa. lxv. 20 ; lx. 7) both on man and beast. The offender is cut off at once in his sin. Jer. xxxi. 30 ; Ezek. xliv. 25-27. Hence it is now said, "Death shall be no more." It has existed till that time.

But, then, as sin and the sinful have passed away for ever, so have death and sorrow no entrance on the new earth. The word translated "*crying*" in the Authorized version appears to mean the loud cry of suffering from any cause, from pain, or oppression, or God's vengeance. Exod. xi 6 ; xii. 30 ; 1 Sam. iv. 14 ; Gen. xxvii. 34 ; Isa. v. 7.

The following passage will vividly illustrate this word.

"As we passed through the streets. *loud screams*, as of a person frantic with rage and grief, drew our attention towards a miserable hovel, whence we perceived a woman issuing hastily with a cradle containing an infant. Having placed the child upon the area before her dwelling she as quickly ran back again : we then perceived her beating something violently, all the while filling the air with *the most piercing shrieks*. Running to see what was the cause of her cries, we observed an enormous serpent, which she had found near her infant, and had completely despatched before our arrival. Never were maternal feelings more strikingly portrayed than in the countenance of this woman. Not satisfied with having killed the animal she continued her blows, until she had reduced it to atoms, unheeding anything that was said to her, and only abstracting her attention from its mangled body to cast occasionally a wild and momentary glance toward her child " (*Dr. E. Clarke's Travels*, ii, 439).

" Neither shall there be any more pain."

The Greek word used may describe both the toil of man inflicted by the fall, and the sorrows laid on the woman. Sin shall not enter, nor any of its black-robed train.

" For the former things passed away."

The old dispensations are passed : the old earth, with its scenes and its materials, is no more. Here are more than Israel's blessings, without the conditions laid on failing men. Evil in its roots, as well as its stem, is cut off for ever for the saved. These woes cleaved to the old heavens and earth, and the old covenant could not remove them : but the new sweeps away both together.

THE JUDGMENT OF THE SAVED AND LOST

5–8. "And the Sitter on the throne said, ' Behold I make all things new.' And he saith, ' Write : for these sayings are faithful and true.' And he said to me, ' They are done. I am the Alpha and the Omega, the beginning and the end. I will give to him that is athirst out of the fountain of the water of life without cost. He that overcometh shall inherit these things,[1] and I will be his God, and he shall be my son. But the cowardly, and unbelieving, and abominable, and murderers, and sorcerers, and idolaters,

---

[1] This is the true reading, as the critical editions agree.

and all the false shall have their portion in the lake which burneth with fire and brimstone, which is the Second Death.'"

This passage refers to the lot of all those to whom "the prophecy of this book" shall come. We have heard of the lot of "the nations" of the new earth. But there is a far higher position, the portion of the citizens of the new city. The citizens are God's "servants" (xxii. 3), who see His face alway. The nations are God's "people" who go up to His house at times as pilgrims. Those outside the city are "men," those within are God's "sons." The citizens are all kings: those outside are the subjects of the dwellers in the Lord's courts. The distinction of the heavenly and the earthly calling, or that of the Church and of Israel, subsists, in substance, for ever.

As our path now is beset with greater difficulty and enlightened with peculiar light, so will our station hereafter be loftier.

All is new. This is in contradistinction from the millennium, for that is the day of the *restoration* of the *old things*. God says not, "I *purge* the *old* materials," but "*I make all things new.*"

However hard to realize, these words express God's will; and His power will assuredly execute them. Therefore they are literally to be taken.

"And He said unto me, They are done."

Those words "It is done" imply that this new creation shall certainly come to pass, and shall abide. God speaks of the things that be not, as though they were. It is to abide. Who shall make it undone ? The end returns to the beginning. God's plan, which often seemed broken by the malice of Satan, and the faults of men, is at length complete. God, who began creation in Genesis, takes not leave of it till Revelation, when it is complete beyond possible overthrow.

"I am the Alpha and the Omega, the beginning and the end."

This, I suppose, is designed to assure us that the whole scheme of things from Genesis to Revelation, in spite of the different phases of things, and many contrasts, really proceeds from one Designer. The Creator of the first world creates also the second.

The present world is the wilderness—the place of drought, as of old. 2 Sam. xvii. 29 ; Deut. viii. 7, 15 ; xi. 11. But the Christian is not to murmur, lest, like the disobedient Israelites, his carcase fall in the wilderness. He is bound to fight, he is clothed with the armour of God, he is called to overcome. To Israel the water was given before the battle. To the Christian the strength of the Holy Ghost and His gracious consolations are given. But he is to enjoy the victory at last, both in body and in soul. And then the desert will be ended ; and blessings, both the spiritual and the natural, will be his for ever. The water to be given is future :—" I *will* give."

This promise of God is addressed to men now alive, in order to affect their conduct. The Sitter on the throne adjudges the place of each who hears. Either his thirst is to be quenched in the fountains of waters in the new city ; or else unquenchably to oppress him in the lake of fire. The thirsty is one who can be reached now by the Spirit's words—" Let him that is athirst come." "*Whosoever wishes, let him take the water of life without price*" (xxii. 17). These words do not belong to the millennial nations in the flesh. They will not be called to fight, or to come off victorious. They walk by sight, not by faith. They need not thirst.

" He that overcometh shall obtain these things."

What is to become of the saints who reigned a thousand years with Christ, after those years are past ?

Where are those saints to be placed, who do not attain to the reward of the kingdom? This passage, I believe, informs us.

Here are unfolded God's principles of judgment in reference to the citizens. The former verses stated the *unconditional* blessings enjoyed by the *dwellers on the new earth*. Now we have the *condition* of the *citizen's* entrance into the new city of God.

The conqueror is to enjoy these things. The reference primarily is to the saints of the Church, as the concluding words of each of the Seven Epistles to the Churches prove. ii., iii. But the reference seems to be not to them solely. There are those who fight against and overcome the Antichrist. There are also the saved under the Law.

And probably there may be two aspects of overcoming: overcoming so as to be rewarded, and then partaking in millennial glory; and overcoming as compared with the total unbelief of the worldly. "This is the victory which overcometh the world—even our faith," and the final entry into eternal life in the city of the risen.

The nations outside are not conquerors. They were never called to wrestle, as we are, with the world and Satan. They lived in millennial joy.

The conqueror shall " inherit " these things.

We mean by " inherit " something different from that which the Hebrew and the Greek of the New Testament intend. It does not mean to have a claim to an estate by virtue of *birth*. It means only " to obtain a lot," or " portion; " as the next verse shows. " The cowardly *shall have their portion* in the lake."

" And I will be his God, and he shall be My son."

This sentiment resembles greatly that expressed above (in verse 3) concerning the men of the new earth in general. But more closely examined, the differences are very great. In the former case, men are dealt with in the mass. "God will be with *them*." "*They* shall be His *people*." Here the application is individual. "*His* God." "*He shall* be my son." And how greatly does the being God's "*son*" exceed the being one of His "people" only!

God's omnipotence is in favour both of "the nations" and the risen: but the one live on God's land, the other in His *house*. What will sonship be, when not the spirit alone is redeemed, but the body also in resurrection?

But what shall be the lot of those overcome in this war? The dread alternative is now presented to us. They are distributed into eight classes. They are described in plain terms; not, as the saved are, in figurative words.

1. The first named are the "cowardly." This does not refer to the timid, doubting believer, but to those who refuse to receive Christ, or who give up their faith in Him through fear of men. These are the first and great contrast to the victors. Luke xiv. 26. These, then, are not afraid of God, but of men; not of sin, but of holiness.

2. "And unbelieving." These fear not God's threats, and do not trust or desire His promises. The two things are closely connected. What can become of those who will not trust God? who declare by their lives that Truth is unworthy of confidence? Men are angry if we will not trust them. How much greater reason has God to smite those who will not put confidence in Him? "This is the victory which overcometh the world, even our faith" (1 John v. 4).

3. "And abominable." This seems to refer to persons guilty of unnatural crime. Lev. xviii. 22, 26, 27; Eph. v. 5. Of such sins Sodom was guilty, and her doom of fire from heaven, and the plain turned into a

lake, was a foretaste of the destiny of those condemned because of such offences.

4. "And murderers." Noah's covenant inflicted death on such persons. The covenant with Israel affirmed the same penalty. But there is another sentence beyond the death of the body, which is here disclosed, to deter all from that treasonable defacement of their Maker's image.

5. "And whoremongers." God's displeasure against this sin was manifested in the wilderness, when Israel fornicated with the daughters of Moab. Solomon has an awful word concerning this offence. Prov. xxii. 14. The Gospel reiterates the warning. Heb. xiii. 4. Antichrist denounces marriage.

6. "And sorcerers." Commerce with evil spirits is a sad reality. It is one of the lusts of the flesh, and to it man has been ever prone. Gal. v. 19, 20. Moses threatened the sin with death temporal: but this shows its final doom. In Antichrist's day Satan's self is worshipped.

The word here used includes the use of drugs for poisoning. These two classes of sin often went together. How greatly in our day is poisoning extending itself!

7. "And idolaters." Strictly taken, idolatry seems to mean the worship of dead images fashioned by man. But the worship of any gods but the one True God, or polytheism, seems to be included. God will grant no dwelling with Himself to those who give His due to others.

8. "And all the false." The article precedes this class. Does it not include more sins then merely those of lying? Satan was the first liar, and his place, as we have seen, is in the lake of fire. The greatest of lies is that of the Antichrist, who denies the Father and the Son. 1 John ii. 22.

All these classes are to find their eternal inheritance in the lake of fire and brimstone. The theory of the final salvation of man and devils finds no place in Scripture. Damnation, as well as salvation, is part of the Gospel message. It says not that the wicked are to suffer a thousand years, and after that to be brought forth purified. The door shuts on a view of their sin and their endless punishment, after the new heavens and earth are presented to us.

The place of final punishment is not a prison, but a lake. This is not according to human ideas. It is the awful contrast to the portion of the blest. Fire stands opposed to water ; a pool to a fountain, life to death. The one quenches the thirst : the other heats it to intolerable fury. The rich man, as a separate spirit, asked a drop of water to cool his tongue. His thirst and anguish will be increased, when his body is resumed at the judgment day.

The Dead Sea, memorial of Sodom's sin and punishment, stood within view of God's chosen city. So the lake of fire seems to form part of the new earth. As, when Sodom was swallowed up, the Dead Sea arose ; so when Babylon is swallowed up, the Lake of Death appears.

It is a place of " brimstone " as well as fire. How suffocating the fumes of sulphur ! Always to be stifled in such an atmosphere, how terrible !

"It is the Second Death." To the saved no more *death :* to the lost no more *life !* Their abode is not the " Shadow of Death," but 'tis now the Second Death in its full reality.

THE GENERAL DESCRIPTION OF THE CITY

9-14. "And there came one of the seven angels that had the seven bowls that were full of the seven last plagues, and talked with me, saying, 'Come hither, I will show thee the Bride, the wife of the Lamb.' And he carried me away in spirit to a mountain great and lofty, and showed me Jerusalem the holy city, coming down out of the heaven from God, having the glory of God. Her luminary was like a very precious stone, like a crystal jasper. It had a wall great and lofty; it had twelve portals, and at the portals twelve angels, and names written thereon, which are the names of the twelve tribes of the children of Israel. On the east three portals; and on the north three portals; and on the south three portals; and on the west three portals. And the wall of the city has twelve foundations, and on them the twelve names of the twelve apostles of the Lamb."

The New Jerusalem is called "the Bride." This is a name probably not to continue for ever. It is a title given to one newly married. The Law recognized this peculiarity. "When a man hath taken *a new wife*, he shall not go out to war, neither shall he be charged with any business: but he shall be free at home *one year*, and shall cheer up his wife which he hath taken" (Deut. xxiv. 5). The Old Jerusalem is compared to a bride, but is not directly called so. Isa. xlix. 18; lxi. 10; lxii. 5; Jer. ii. 32.

By the title "the Lamb's wife," this city is identified with the one which is mentioned before the millennium. xix. 7.

Messiah, like Abraham, has two wives: one the earthly Jerusalem, the other the heavenly. Isaiah was permitted to speak of the heavenly Jerusalem, as the mother long barren, but at length without pain filled with children. John now sees her as the Bride.

That John may see the city, he is taken, not bodily, but "in spirit to a mountain great and lofty." Around Mount Sinai there was no city, only the bleak desert. The better covenant has both mount and city united, if

I mistake not. The mount on which John was set was, I believe, the summit of the twelve foundations of the city. The city is twelve thousand furlongs in height, when the foundations are added to the amount. Suppose the foundations to take up three-fourths of the height; then John would be standing on a great and high mountain, at the best possible point of view to take in the various glories of the city.

Highly illustrative of this is Stanley's notice of the earthly Jerusalem. "The situation of Jerusalem is in several respects singular amongst the cities of Palestine. Its elevation is remarkable: not indeed from its being on the summit of one of the numerous hills of Judea, like most of the towns and villages, but because it is on the edge of one of the highest table-lands of the country. Hebron indeed is higher still by some hundred feet, and from the south, accordingly, the approach to Jerusalem is by a slight descent. But from every other side the ascent is perpetual; and to the traveller approaching Jerusalem from the west or east, it must always have presented the appearance, *beyond any other capital of the known world, we may add, beyond any important city that has ever existed on the earth, of a mountain city;* breathing, as compared with the sultry plains of the Jordan, or of the coast, a mountain air: enthroned, as compared with Jericho or Damascus, Gaza or Tyre, on a mountain fastness" (*Sinai and Palestine*, p. 170).

This its elevation is increased just before the millennium by the great earthquake, while all the adjacent country is made a plain around it. Isa. ii.; Zech. xiv. Thus God gives intimations of His final purpose of making His city to be set on a lofty mountain. The nations and Israel sought for their worship "high places" as the fittest points. The Most High gives effect at last to this tendency of the human mind.

The Church of Christ was to be a city set on a mountain spiritually: now its literal abode is on it, and its luminary is the light of the world.

That it is not a blessed state of the Church mystically described, is clear from many considerations. The Church is swept away, as we have seen, before the prophetic parts can begin. If mystically to be taken, it were no revelation. The state of the Church is described in literal terms in this very book. That is revelation: this were an enigma.

The city is part of the Church's hope. It begins to be exhibited to her while militant (Rev. iii. 12), she enjoys it after the battle is past.

Why should it not be a real city, literally taken?

If all the saved who rise from the dead are to be congregated into one city, must it not be stupendous in its dimensions?

We have seen that two other cities are named in this book—Jerusalem the Old, and Babylon the Great. Are not those literal? They are. So, then, the city which supersedes them both. It must be a real city; for the last trump has sounded, and *mystery has ceased, as was promised.* x. 7. When Babylon the Great was shown to John, it was represented in mystery; and John wondered, and the angel explained. Here John wonders not, nor does the angel interpret, for there is in the description nothing mystical to explain.

Was not the temple realised in wood, and stone, and gold, under God's direction? If magnificence so great and material attended the old covenant, which was to be done away, how much more shall a like glory attend the better covenant!

To those who imagine that at death the believer at once enters heaven, and enjoys, as a "*glorified spirit*" (an idea unknown to Scripture), the bliss of God's presence, it is no wonder if the expectation of a material world and city seems absurd; but that is only because they have so long left out of sight the *resurrection of the body*—that cardinal and peculiar doctrine of Christianity. Philosophers could dispute about the *immortality of the soul;* but Jesus, by His resurrection, brought to light the final incorruptibility of the body.

Another question of much interest may here be noticed.

In the ideas of many, the description of the New Jerusalem which follows is millennial. For myself, I am persuaded that we have in the verses which follow an account of the eternal relations of the city of God. I will therefore briefly consider the question :—

1. That the eternal standing of the city is in question I gather from xxii. 3, " There shall be no more curse." Now at the close of the millennium comes the most fearful sin and wrath of God, with the Second Death.

2. I infer the same conclusion from xxi. 24-26. " The kings [and the nations] bring their glory into it." Accordingly, the gates are allowed to stand open all day to permit their entrance. But none are allowed to go in save those written in the Lamb's book of life. Now entrance into the heavenly city would not be possible during the millennium : for then the city is only suspended over the earth : it does not come down upon it. To meet this difficulty the holders of the opposite view translate verses 24 and 26—" bring their glory *unto* it," not " into it."

To this I make two replies :—

1. Who are the kings of the earth during the millennium ? They are the sons of God risen from the dead. Do they, then, go no further than the gates of

the city? I suppose it will be granted that they go in. So, then, do the nations, of whom the same phrase is used.

2. But secondly, the proposed amendment of the translation is unfounded. Whenever a verb of motion capable of signifying penetration or entrance into a penetrable subject—such as a river, house, etc., is followed by the preposition ($εἰς$) " into "—there entrance is affirmed.

Where it is supposed that the person stops outside of the enclosed or penetrable space, there another expression is employed ($ἐπί$).

Every language must possess and recognize this distinction, which is of the utmost consequence to men in their communications one with the other.

But this is not all the evidence. The context were of itself enough to settle the question. Why are the gates to be left open, but for the entrance of the kings and nations?

But against this view there is one strong objection— one so strong that from it, no doubt, has sprung the idea I am now combating.

"The leaves of the tree were for the *healing* of the nations." "What make you of that? Does not that prove that sin and death are abroad still? And if so what time but the millennial can be the one supposed?"

I do not think that the expression used implies either sin or death. It is certain from xxi. 4, that in the new earth there shall be neither death nor pain. But may there not be infirmity? I mean, in the case of those still in bodies of flesh. I suppose there may. As age creeps on there may be decay of strength, needing the leaves of the tree of life to be applied, in order to the restoration of full vigour. There are other cases of infirmity which may be suggested. The removal of such infirmities would account for and satisfy the expression used.

"Come, I will show thee *the Bride*." Here is the mystic *name*. "And he showed me the holy *city*." Here is the literal reality, described by the previous name, because of its connections with the past actions of God.

At the former notice of its descent, it was spoken of as a "bride prepared for her husband." Here a still higher glory is discovered to us. She descends, being in everlasting possession of "the glory of God."

Ezekiel was privileged to see this glory (often called "the Shekinah") depart from the temple, the city, and the earth. To him, too, it was given to behold the vision of its restoration to the earth and the temple. Ezek. xliii.

But then it was called "the glory of *the Lord;*" the glory of *the God of Israel*." Now it is "the glory of *God*." In the earlier occasions it was attended with a "darkness." The cloud abode on the mount and filled the house. Now cloud has passed away. Ezek. xliii. 2; Isa. lx. 2–7; xl. 5; lx. 1; Hab. ii. 14.

The Jew shall have all his promises, and far more than his deserts; but he shall not enjoy them alone.

The glory before had to tarry till man had completed his workmanship of the tabernacle and the temple. Here the building descends all complete, and the glory is there already. The glory was compelled to leave the temple, because of sin. But now it abides for ever: for sin is put away. This is the *first* time that the glory of God is named in this book. Jehovah has been represented before; but His glory had not yet appeared, because it was the time of indignation. His avenging of blood is not the time of the full display of His glory.

The city occupies the place of the temple of old.

"Her luminary was like a stone most precious, as a crystal jasper."

Is this luminary the same as "the glory of God?" I suppose not. Besides the brightness of God's presence there is a visible orb of light overhanging the city. It is a local luminary like the star of Bethlehem, and hence it is said "*her* light," rendering the city independent of any other, and making the metropolis a means of light to all the nations living around. This duality of the city's illumination seems to be clearly proved by its second occurrence. "The *glory* of the Lord enlightened it, and the Lamb is the *lamp* thereof" (ver. 23).

The tabernacle of old had two centres of light. The sanctuary was lit by the seven lamps of the candlestick. The Holiest was lighted by the glory of God's presence.

So in the temple in heaven—we have (1) seven lamps in the Sanctuary: and (2) seven torches in the Holiest. Chap. iv.

Our luminaries are opaque bodies, diffusing light from a luminous surface: but the luminary at last is crystal.

The New Jerusalem, considered as the temple, has "the glory of God."

Regarded as the city, it has a luminary of its own. It diffuses, not white light, like that of the sun, but coloured rays, like those of some of the stars. Its luminary is like jasper, in respect of its colour: it is superior to jasper, in that *that* is opaque quartz, but this is a transparent crystal. What the colour of the light is cannot be said, from our ignorance of the exact kind of stone designed by the writer.

The city besides has a "wall great and high."

The wall is high, as related to the mansions inside the city; but it is low, in comparison with the vast height of the twelve foundations.

The New Jerusalem has " twelve gates."

Even a casual glance at this wonderful city shows us how completely the number twelve runs through it. The number which has been prominent up to this point is seven ; but henceforth it is discarded. Five is the number of nature : four plus one, or the world and God regarded as one. Seven is the number of dispensational perfection. But every successive dispensation ended in failure. Here is the eternal and unfailing scheme. The two numbers seven and twelve are beautifully related one to the other, so as to be significant of this sentiment. Seven is subdivided, as we have often observed, into four and three. Four indicates the creature; three, the Creator. Seven consists of four and three in juxtaposition, and represents God and the creature in contact. But twelve consists of four *into* three, and represents the Creator and the creature in intimate and perpetual union.

Six, or one less than seven, and but half the sacred twelve, is the number of the False Christ. To the city of man belong *seven* mountains, on which the Harlot reposes. But the New Jerusalem has *twelve* foundations. The Usurper has *ten* kings, who uphold his cause : Jerusalem has *twelve* apostles, and twice 144,000 first-fruits.

Ten is the number which in general characterizes the arrangements of the tabernacle, and still more the temple of Solomon, and the future temple of Ezekiel. The tabernacle was to have *twenty* pillars in its length, *ten* for its breadth ; the length of the tabernacle court was a *hundred* cubits ; its breadth, *fifty*; the height of its pillars, *five* cubits. So also in the future millennial temple of Ezekiel. Ezek. xl. 11, 14, 15, 17, 19, 21, etc. See 1 Kings vi.

Twelve gates will not be too many for entrance into, and exit from, so vast a city. The tabernacle had but one entrance : it was not thrown open to all the world. Access to God was guarded, and granted only to the peculiarly-cleansed officials of the king. In the Jerusalem of the millennium also there are to be twelve gates. Ezek. xlviii. 31–34.

At the gates are "twelve angels." We understand at once the reason of this. They are "ministering spirits," set as sentinels ; for nothing that defiles may enter the city. Angels do not rule then : they serve. It is remarkable that this is the only notice we have of angels' presence near the city. They are no longer enthroned, but doorkeepers ; they answer to the porters, chosen from among the Levites, who kept the entrances into the temple. 1 Chron. ix. 24.

Something more than a mere "gate" is understood by the word. It signifies a porch or a structure enclosing the gate, probably containing chambers.

The evil city was "the Mother of the Harlots of the Earth ; " the Holy City is the centre for the Fathers of the tribes of God. The names of the twelve tribes were engraved both on the stones of the High Priest's breastplate, and on the two onyxes, which rested on his shoulder. Here they occupy their final place.

The city does not now belong to one tribe, nor is it included in the lot of Judah or Benjamin : it is the focus of all the nations. It is a neutral city, like the book before us. It owns all previous dispensations. 'Tis built as the dwelling-place of the men of faith, whether of the Old Testament or of the New. In this light it is exhibited by the apostle in the Hebrews xi. ; xiii. 14. It is mother of all.

The arrangement of the gates is symmetrical. The city is an exact square ; hence the need of access to each quarter is the same. It is not erected, like most of the cities of men, at different times and by various builders ; hence one plan reigns throughout.

The wall has twelve foundations. These are the great peculiarity of the city. In other cities, foundations are slight compared with this. They are covered up from sight. Here they underlie the whole city, elevate it to a wondrous height, and are its chief and most striking adornment. They represent it as the settled city, never to be moved. The Old Jerusalem was shaken by earthquake. The cities of the Gentiles, just before the Saviour appears, are laid in ruins by shocks destroying their foundations. But this abides unshaken.

On the foundations are engraved " the names of the twelve apostles of the Lamb." The God of the city is author both of the Law and of the Gospel. Jehovah is the God of justice, evidenced by the Law and its tribes : and of mercy, as witnessed by the apostles and their testimony.

Apostles are witnesses of grace : on them, as foundations spiritually, the Church rested. Eph. ii. 20. As foundations are more important than gates, to them is assigned the nobler position. They inscribed not their own names thereon, but God glorifies them, when the names of the conquerors and monarchs of earth are forgot.

The names are those of " the twelve apostles of the *Lamb*." There were many other apostles beside the twelve originally chosen. The New Testament notices at least twelve others. Acts xiv. 4, 14, etc. But the twelve original ones were those chosen by Jesus in the flesh.

THE DIMENSIONS OF THE CITY

15–17. "And he that talked with me had a golden measuring reed, that he might measure the city, and its portals, and its wall. And the city lieth foursquare, and its length is as large as its breadth, and he measured the city with the reed for twelve thousand furlongs. The length and the breadth, and the height of it are equal. And he measured its wall a hundred and forty-four cubits, (according to) the measure of a man, that is of an angel.

But two measures are named: first the general measure which runs through the great dimensions of the city, and then the height of the wall. It is remarkable how little of detail is given here, when compared with the accounts of the tabernacle and the temples of Solomon and of Ezekiel.

The city portals are named, but their dimensions are not given. It is not a little remarkable, that while this is the city of our mansions, no individual habitation of the saints is described.

Doubtless the great reason of this want of detail is, that God builds this structure, and man the others. Man needs exact details. In the New Jerusalem we shall enjoy the results of God's completed architecture.

But what a prodigious height! How can this be literally understood? By a consideration of the height to which the foundations rose. That height is not given; save in the very general description, that the city's base was a great and lofty mountain. If we suppose that the height of the foundations was two-thirds of the whole 12,000 furlongs, we shall, I think, get a far more feasible view of the city than on any other conjecture.

The height of the wall above the foundations is only 144 cubits.

But what is the measure of the cubit? In Ezekiel

the cubit was peculiar : it was larger than the ordinary cubit by a hand-breadth. Ezek. xl. 5; xliii. 13.

The cubit used by the angel was an ordinary one. The angel's size was not gigantic : it was a man's ordinary height : and the cubit is a measure taken from a man's stature. Does not this prove the description to be literal ?

The city, as I suppose, towers above the walls on every side, street above street, and terrace above terrace, till its highest point is attained in the great square in which stand the throne of God and the tree of life.

THE CITY'S MATERIALS

18–21. "And the superstructure of the wall of it was jasper; and the city was clear gold, like clear glass. The foundations of the wall of the city were adorned with every precious stone. The first foundation was jasper; the second, sapphire; the third, chalcedony; the fourth, emerald; the fifth, sardonyx; the sixth, sardius; the seventh, chrysolite; the eighth, beryl; the ninth, topaz; the tenth, chrysoprasus; the eleventh, hyacinth; the twelfth, amethyst."

The wall is considered as consisting of two parts— its superstructure and its foundations. The part rising above the lowest level of the city was of jasper; the foundations of the wall in their twelve stages are then given. In Hebrews, the apostle speaks of the foundations of the *city*. The Holy Spirit here speaks of the foundations of the *wall*. The same precious stones were foundations of both. The false city rested on seven mountains : the Holy City on twelve, or on one— according as we notice the foundations separately, or regard the unity of the whole result.

The material of the city in general is gold, the most costly and beautiful metal known to man. The house of Solomon was framed of wood and stone, plated over with gold. This city is built of solid gold. In Jerusalem, while Solomon reigned, silver was despised. No silver is used in this city. In Solomon's time, they became curious in the best sorts of gold; and those of Ophir and of Parvaim were most in request. 2 Chron. iii. 6. Here is a gold beyond that of Ophir; 'tis transparent as glass! yet 'tis used for the least costly parts of the city. The Holiest of Solomon was plated all over with gold—a type of this.

The Harlot-city was "*gilded* with gold, precious stones, and pearls" (xvii. 4). The Bridal-city is built of solid gold, precious stones, and pearls.

Concerning the twelve precious stones, but little that is certain can be said. Little is known by the learned in general with regard to the precious stones now in use. Less still seems to be known concerning the precious stones of old, and what stones of modern times answer to the names of old.

There were twelve stones in the High Priest's breastplate. I give their names as found in the Greek of the Seventy. Exod. xxviii. 15.

   1. Sardius   2. Topaz   3. Emerald
   4. Ruby   5. Sapphire   6. Jasper
   7. Ligure   8. Agate   9. Amethyst
  10. Chrysolite   11. Beryl   12. Onyx.

I will now just make a few remarks on the stones here named.

1. The first is Jasper. This, as known to the moderns, is believed to be a species of quartz, opaque, of various colours: green clouded with yellow, blue, brown and white. Some imagine that a diamond of a blue colour may be meant (*Notes to Pictorial Bible*).

B. Taylor, in his *Travels in Greece*, speaks of "huge blocks of *jasper of all imaginable hues*" (p. 411).

2. Sapphire. By this is meant a precious stone, of a blue deeper than lapis lazuli, with veins of white, or

spots of gold. It is very translucent, azure or sky-blue. The largest known weighs 133 carats of four grains each (*Mawe on Precious Stones*).

3. Chalcedony. This is usually of one uniform colour throughout, usually a light brown, and often nearly white; but other shades of colour are not infrequent—such as grey, yellow, green, and blue (*Kitto's Cyclop.*).

4. The Emerald is a precious stone of a deep green. The largest known of old was sent from Babylon to the King of Egypt: four cubits long by three broad (*Theophrastus*, p. 64). The largest now known is but six inches long by two in diameter (*Mawe*, p. 104).

5. Sardonyx. "A precious stone, exhibiting a milk-white variety of the onyx or chalcedony, intermixed with shades or stripes of the sardian or carnation: hence the compound name of sardonyx" (*Kitto*).

6. Sardius. This is generally believed to be the cornelian, of a flesh colour.

7. Chrysolite. "The prevailing colour is yellowish green and pistachio-green of every variety and degree of shade, but always with a yellow and gold lustre" (*Kitto*). With this Mawe seems to agree. The Greek means "golden stone."

8. Beryl is a stone of a sea-green colour, probably the one now known as aquamarine. In Russia is one weighing six pounds, valued at 30,000 dollars (B. Taylor's *Greece*, p. 411).

9. The Topaz is a precious stone, whose "prevailing colour is a wine-yellow of every degree of shade" (*Kitto*). Some suppose it to be the stone which moderns call chrysolite. "That of the ancients appears to have been pale green" (*Stuart*). "Its colour is pistachio-green, with other shades" (*Pictorial Bible*).

10. Chrysoprasus is "either of an apple or a leek-green colour." From its golden-green, like that of the

leek, its name seems to have been derived. The Greek means "green as a leek."

11. The Jacinth, or Hyacinth. The *Pictorial Bible* describes it as "a violet-coloured gem, probably a variety of amethyst, differing only in colour from that beautiful gem."

12. The Amethyst is "of a colour which seems composed of a strong blue and deep red; and, according as either of these prevails, exhibits different tinges of purple, sometimes approaching to violet, and sometimes declining even to a rose-colour" (*Kitto*). With this Mawe pretty nearly agrees.

Since there are such difficulties in the way of identifying the stones, and of defining their colours, it is hard to speculate on the combined effect of colour presented to the apostle's eye. Here is that stated by M. Stuart: "In looking over these various classes, we find the first four to be of a green or bluish cast; the fifth and sixth, of a red or scarlet; the seventh, yellow; the eighth, ninth, and tenth, of different shades of the lighter green; and the eleventh and twelfth, of a scarlet or splendid red. There is *classification*, therefore, in this arrangement: a mixture not dissimilar to the arrangement in the rainbow, with the exception that it is more complex."

In that word — "the rainbow" — is supplied, as I suppose, the key to this wonderful structure.

In the rainbow science discovers *seven* colours; *three* primary ones, red, yellow, blue: and *four* derived ones, orange, green, indigo, violet.

Now if we compare the colours of the foundation stones with those of the rainbow we shall find, I believe, a designed resemblance, though, from our ignorance in regard of the precious stones, we cannot come to any very close or satisfactory conclusion. The stones, then, with their colours, and the tints of the rainbow, are as follows :—

	1. Jasper, greenish ? yellow ?
	2. Sapphire, azure.
	3. Chalcedony, doubtful, green and blue.
THE RAINBOW.	4. Emerald, green.
1. Red	5. Sardius, red.
2. Orange	6. Sardonyx, red and white.
3. Yellow	7. Chrysolite, yellow.
4. Green	8. Beryl, sea-green.
5. Blue	9. Topaz, yellow.
6. Indigo	10. Chrysoprasus, golden-green.
7. Violet (lake)	11. Jacinth, violet.
	12. Amethyst, rose-red.

If we omit the first four of the stones we may trace a very considerable resemblance between the two series of colours.

It should be observed that each colour in the spectrum does not take up exactly the same space, but some occupy a much larger interval than others. The following statement is taken from Dr. Lardner's work :—

If the spectrum be divided into 360 equal parts, the proportion of each will be as follows :—

Red	56
Orange	27
Yellow	27
Green	46
Blue	48
Indigo	47
Violet	109
	360

Answerably to this we may find in the foundations

one colour occupying a greater space than another, because two foundations may be of similar hues, even though each precious foundation be of the same altitude. It will be noticed that the colours which in the present world are *seven*, as suited to its passing away; in the future world are *twelve*, which is in harmony with the abiding nature of the new world's city.

If we will make choice of a colour for some of these stones which are of various hues, we arrive at a regular arrangement of them in this manner.

{ 1. Green.
  2. Blue
  3. Blue
  4. Green

  { 5. Red
    6. Red

{ 7. Yellow
  8. Sea-green
  9. Yellow
  10. Golden-green

  { 11. Purple
    12. Purple.

But we inquire into the spiritual significance of this. Why should the rainbow be the basis of the new city?

Because of its connection with the history of the covenant with Noah. We saw in chapter iv. how much that covenant was in the mind of God. The covenant in its first aspect has been accomplished. The throne foretold in it has made inquisition for blood; but the ark and the going forth thence was typical of things yet to come.

A deluge of fire has swept the old world, and destroyed it: but some of the inhabitants and of its creatures have been transferred in a new ark to a new world, under the conduct of a greater than Noah. When the patriarch came forth from the ark, he built an altar, and offered sacrifices thereon. " The Lamb " of God is the one sacrifice now ; and if God smelled a " savour of *rest* " (marg.) in Noah's sacrifice, how much more must eternal security be based on the bloodshedding of the Lamb of God ! If God could say that He would no more curse the ground for man's sake, because he was *evil* wholly, how much more shall He send only blessing, because man thenceforth is *good ?* The seasons were then to keep their rounds while earth remained : much more on the new earth in which righteousness alone dwells. If the Lord could pronounce blessing on the creatures and man then, much more now ! Then animals might be slain for food : we do not read of this in the new earth ; but only of the fruits of the tree. Man was then to execute judgment on the murderer ; but at this period God Himself has passed the eternal sentence on the assassin, and he lies in the lake of fire. Then the Most High declared His covenant between Himself and four sets of creatures, that no more should a flood destroy the earth. And of this promise the rainbow was to be a token and memorial.

But the new world is established on better and more solid promises. Hence the rainbow, which was before a passing sight, has become solid. There is no cloud now to be brought in wrath over the earth : the bow abides in perpetual light. But indeed it is no more a bow, a weapon of wrath ; 'tis the city's foundation. In Ezekiel and in Rev. iv. the rainbow is seen as the attendant of the throne : but the bow is of a single colour only. Now, the throne is established on the top of the memorial of the covenant, and the abode of the risen is with God there. That which in Noah's covenant was transient, is now perpetual, and God's better priesthood, fixed in resurrection on the footing of the Great High Priest, abides.

It seems very probable, indeed almost certain, that the general aspect of the city is pyramidical. The lowest foundation would far exceed the topmost one in breadth. I suppose, too, that around the upper surface of each of the foundations runs a broad ledge, on which the pilgrim nations will rest and encamp while travelling into the city. This idea of terrace above terrace in the foundations and in the city itself, seems confirmed not only by the great buildings in Babylon, as described to us, but by the ruined structures in Central America and Yucatan, discovered by Stephens and Catherwood.

The twelve gates are twelve pearls. How precious these gems are is known to most! Job sets the pearl side by side with gold and precious stones. Job xxviii. 15-19. The Saviour speaks of all a merchant's property being sold to purchase one pearl of peculiar value. Pearls form the suitable ornaments of the most wealthy monarchs. But how small the largest! With mortal men they are for ornament, not use. They are to be cautiously handled, because easily broken. In the city of God pearl forms the massive portals.

The pearl is used by our Lord in His parable to signify righteousness. The Jew was sent to seek righteousness by the Law. But as soon as the true Jew found Messiah's precious righteousness, he surrendered his own to obtain it. Phil. iii.

The foundations of the city speak of *mercy:* the gates of *righteousness.* Israel's tribes are the witnesses of God's justice, as the apostles are of His grace. The entrance of all the saved into the city of God is through grace and righteousness. "That as sin reigned by death, even so might *grace* reign *through righteousness* unto eternal life, by Jesus Christ our Lord" (Rom. v.

21). "Open to me the *gates of righteousness*," says the Psalmist, "I will go into them, I will praise the Lord. This is *the gate* of the Lord into which *the righteous* shall enter "• (Ps. cxviii. 19, 20).

It was not possible to engrave names on pearls as found in this world : they are too frail and too thin to bear the tool of steel. Even thus man's righteousness is too frail and imperfect to bear the pressure of God's demands of perfection : but the righteousness of God is capable of every perfection.

As no pearl could be engraved, onyxes, which are precious stones bearing the nearest resemblance to pearl in their colour, were chosen by God to foreshadow the gates of pearl of His future city. There were but two onyxes, each containing six names of the tribes of Israel. They were fastened to the high priest's dress, even as the breastplate was. They were set on the shoulders of the chief priest, above the breastplate ; even as the gates of the city stand above the foundations. They were linked to the breastplate by chains of gold, even as the foundations and the gates are braced together. The onyxes and the breastplate were cased in gold ; even as the foundations and the gates are linked together by the crystal gold of the city. The gates of *righteousness* stand on the foundations of *grace*. The moral emblem and the physical reality coincide in the city of God.

There is no entrance into the heavenly city by our works, but by the righteousness of Messiah.

How to translate the Greek word rendered by the English Version "street" is difficult. There must be many "streets" in so vast a city with twelve gates of entrance. But there is one "square" ($\pi\lambda\alpha\tau\epsilon\hat{\imath}\alpha$) or "broad space." It seems that it must be in the centre of the city, and at its highest point, where the throne of God is set, and the tree of life is planted. To this, as to a common centre, all the streets of the city tend. This is an arrangement much adopted in some parts of the world, as in Mexico, where it is called—from the Greek word here used—*plaza*. Of Polish towns Bayard Taylor observes, " In the centre is usually a spacious square, which serves as a market place " (p. 319).

The streets of the world's cities, however magnificent, are disfigured by mud, which soils the feet and the garments of the passengers and citizens. Ps. xviii. 42 ; Isa. x. 6. The streets of the new city are of solid gold. Kings esteem it a privilege of theirs to have their meals served on vessels of gold. But the meanest believer at last will tread on pavement of crystal gold, unsullied with a stain.

RELATION OF THE CITY TO THE DWELLERS OUTSIDE IT

22-27. "And no temple saw I in it ; for the Lord God of Hosts is its temple, and the Lamb. And the city hath no need of the sun nor of the moon, that they should shine for it : for the glory of God enlightened it, and its lamp was the Lamb. And the nations shall walk by means of its light : and the kings of the earth bring their glory into it. And her portals shall not be shut by day : for the night shall not be there. And they shall bring the glory and the honour of the nations into it. And nothing common shall enter into it, nor any one who makes abomination or a lie : but those (only) who have been written in the Lamb's book of Life."

In the New Jerusalem John saw no temple. This constitutes one of the great differences between it and the Old Jerusalem under the old covenant. The temple of old was the proof of sin's presence. The God of holiness must keep the godless and sinful at a distance. Atonement must be made daily, lest the presence of

Jehovah should destroy the people among whom He dwelt.

But then sin is past away. Atonement the most complete has been made. Man sins no more. Nothing, therefore, now shuts off God from the eye and feet of His saved ones.

There is, therefore, no one fenced spot where alone God is—that being holy, while the rest of the city is profane : it is now " the Holy City " everywhere. The presence of God constitutes the whole of it one temple. A temple is a house in which God dwells : the whole city is now His house.

From this we can be sure that the present passage does not describe millennial times.

There is a *temple*, partly on earth, partly in heaven, distinct from the two *cities*. Sin is not at an end. God still dwells in His heavenly temple : the Christ dwells in the temple below. But when " the outer court " of the heavenly temple passes away with the burning earth, the temple, too (it would appear), is set aside. Thenceforth we see only one city, and that city is also the one temple of God. It has already been described as " God's tabernacle " (xxi. 3).

At first the city is discovered to us as related to Jesus alone : it is His " Bride." Now we have the city as related to both the Father and the Son. It is a point I am not able to account for, that we have no notice of the Holy Spirit's dwelling in the city or the new earth.

" The Lamb " is no name of a passing dispensation merely. Jesus' aspect as the Sacrifice and Priest endures for ever. And if the temple of any god be the place where the Deity resides, then Jesus, in unity with the Father, is the Deity of the New Jerusalem.

Verse 23 answers an important question affecting the city considered as a temple—" How is it lit ? " Its standing is peculiar. The earth is then lit by two great luminaries, as of old—the one ruler of the day, the other of the night. The earth is mainly dependent on them for the supply of light ; but the *city* is independent of both. "The *city* hath no need of the sun, nor of the moon, that they should shine *for it*." It has two sources of illumination—the glory of God, and the Lamb's light.

"And its lamp is the Lamb."

Jesus appears not now as King of kings—such as He was exhibited in chapter xx.—but as the object of worship and giver of light. Jesus, at His appearing on the old earth, was the giver of moral light to the world. John i. 5–9 ; viii. 12 ; ix. 5. Now from His blessed person stream rays of perpetual day to the dwellers in the city. On the top of the Mount of Transfiguration His face shone awhile as the sun ; but now His glory abides.

In the Holiest of the heavenly temple the Holy Spirit was the lamp. "There were seven torches of fire burning before the throne, which are the seven Spirits of God " (iv. 5). This renders the absence of any notice of the Sacred Spirit, in the description of the eternal city, the more remarkable.

Where the *city* is spoken of, Jesus is twice named separately from the Father ; but when *Paradise* is revealed to us, the Father and Son are exhibited in union : the throne is that of " God and the Lamb."

" And the nations shall walk by means of her light."

The reading, " the nations *of them that are saved*," is not genuine. It arose from erroneously regarding all the saved as consisting of but one body—instead of perceiving that the nations are one mass, the citizens another : and these words, once introduced, have kept up the error.

This twofold division of mankind obtains throughout eternity. There are " the nations " still on the new earth. The word intends men in the flesh ; just as it does now, and during the millennium. But the risen from the dead form another and nobler body. They dwell within the city ; the nations outside. The nations have lands appointed to them, as on the old earth. The distinct bodies of different races abide still.

The nations " walk " by means of its light.

This is nearly equivalent to "travel ; " walking being the ordinary mode of travelling in Palestine.

These words teach us that while the city is independent of the earth's sources of light, the nations are not independent of the city : at least when they go up to appear before God. They need no guide to the city, for its luminaries form a constant beacon. Even by day, the nearer they approach the more do the beams of its glory enlighten them. But especially by *night*, and when there is no moonlight, they find the benefit of its beams. Very lofty indeed is the city, and its luminaries being more exalted still, its light is diffused very widely.

The New Jerusalem is the centre of the new earth and its nations, as the Old Jerusalem was the metropolis of the twelve tribes. The number twelve found in Israel's tribes marks the permanency of nations on the new earth. The nations at length have taken the position occupied by Israel of old.

Pilgrimage is a portion of the plans of the Most High for the new earth also. Only the differences are very worthy of notice. No laws are given concerning the frequency of the going up : no penalties are set. The laws of the Creator are now written on the heart, and observed freely : for all are God's elect, and all taught of Him.

Behold in this city's position, too, another reference to Jesus' words concerning His disciples. " YE ARE THE LIGHT OF THE WORLD. A CITY THAT IS SET ON A MOUNTAIN ($ὄρος$) CANNOT BE HID. Neither do men light a lamp and put it under the bushel, but on the lampstand, and it giveth light to all in the house. So let your light shine before men, that they may see your good works, and glorify your Father which is in heaven" (Greek) (Matt. v. 14-16). That which Jesus' disciples were to be to the old world, in a spiritual point of view, they are now, both morally and physically. They are one; one in heart, one in their abode. The world believes that God has sent Jesus.

"The kings of the earth bring their glory into it."

By "the kings of the earth" are meant the kings of the nations. As the nations are now transferred to the new world, so have they kings. Subordination of ranks is a part of God's abiding scheme for eternity. They are called "kings *of the earth*," to distinguish them from the kings *of the city*. For there are two classes of kings: those made kings and priests to God by Jesus' blood, who are risen from the dead and dwell with God; and those who are men in the flesh, and live among the nations outside the metropolis. For the citizens are *kings of kings*, and "they shall reign for ever and ever" (xxii. 5).

The kings of the nations, then, sensible of their inferiority, and desirous to appear before God and His risen servants, bring presents.

By their "glory" seems to be intended whatever is peculiarly precious and beautiful in their countries. Gen. xxxi. 1; Esther i. 4.

Thus the light of the city as internal, or related to the citizens, is presented to us in ver. 23. The external light, or its relation to the dwellers without, is discovered to us in ver. 24. On their journey to or from the city, they are enlightened and guided by it, even as were the Magi of old by the star. For the pilgrimage to it is a long journey. And even when its foundations are reached, a long ascent lies before them.

Is there any connection between the fifteen "Songs of Ascent," and the fifteen hundred miles of the city's height ?

"And her portals shall not be shut at all by day : for there shall be no night there."

I believe that this paragraph gives peculiarly the city's relations to those without. Day and night still exist for the world at large. Five times are " day and night " named in this book.

When the old earth is just about to be burned up, and Satan is cast into the lake of fire, it is said that he and his two coadjutors are to be " tormented *day and night for ever and ever* " (xx. 10). This proves that day and night take their turns for ever.

Night still exists for the nations. This we have inferred from their travelling by the light of the city. Then the word " day " refers to them too. The gates of the city are not shut, while the world's sun is above the horizon. That shines for the nations of the earth and their kings. They need darkness and its attendant sleep still, as men in the flesh.

And this is very interesting, as connected with the twenty-four hours of our day. The two *twelves* of day and night, here also it would seem, are to abide : and to be divided as they are now.

When, then, it is said—" They are not closed *by day* " —it is implied that " they are closed *by night*." And this accounts for the introduction of the next clause, " for there shall be no *night there*." As though John had said—" Against the pilgrim-nations they are shut ; for they have the alternations of day and night. But I do not mean to contradict what I have said of the *city's* independence of earth's sources of light. ' There is no night *there*.' I refer to the world at large." The citizens, I suppose, possess the privilege to enter at all times.

Her inhabitants do not sleep: they need not rest, for they are men of resurrection. Nor is this reason assigned for the shutting of the gates. It seems implied that it is to keep out for awhile the nations who have come on pilgrimage to her. It may be connected with meetings of the citizens among themselves: the day may be the time of receiving the nations who come from a distance. Certainly the pilgrim nations will need sleep; and the night will be the fitting time for them to repose, ere they enter the city.

The power to enter at night would be a superior privilege of the risen. This, too, would give especial force to some passages of the New Testament.

Christians are called " children of light, and of the day," now, in a spiritual sense. " We are not of the night, nor of darkness." When fully redeemed at length, it is true of them literally also. They are children of light, and sons of the day, for they live in one unbroken noon of brightness. 1 Thess. v. 5–8; Luke xvi. 8; John xii. 36; Eph. v. 8–14; 2 Cor. vi. 14, 15.

" And they shall bring the glory and honour of the nations into it."

Why is it not said more simply and naturally— " The nations shall bring their glory into it "? I believe it is implied that the nations are introduced by the citizens. The citizens are the priests of the new temple, the wardens of the new city.

Some examination of the enterers is implied, I believe, in the next verse. It seems supposed, too, in the angels standing as sentinels at each of the gates.

" They shall bring " implies that parties accompany the nations. So in the xlvth Psalm, 14, 15.

As the nations at last take the place of Israel, so the superiority which belonged to Israel, only in a higher degree, passes on to the priests and kings of God.

I read in these words, that the different countries of

the new earth will have different and special products, and that it will be their delight to bring with them presents of whatever is accounted most valuable in their land. The prophecies of millennial times will confirm this. " All they from Sheba shall come. They shall bring gold and incense " (Isa. lx. 6). " I will extend peace to her [Jerusalem] like a river, and *the glory of the Gentiles* like a flowing stream " (Isa. lxvi. 12).

They bring " the nations' " glory. Before, the kings of the nations brought their presents. Now the nations that attend their kings, do so. The nations are never called " dwellers on the earth ; " which seems to show that the phrase was used in the former part by way of blame. The risen are not " nations : " they are not in the flesh, not set in families, they are a selection *out of* all nations.

Notice, also, that the fourfold division of men on the old earth is gone. We read no more of " *tongues* and kindreds, tribes and peoples." But one tongue, I suppose, is now found on earth.

They not only bring their presents to its gates, but they are introduced within its walls. " A man's present," says Solomon, " maketh room for him and bringeth him before great men " (Prov. xviii. 16). This word " bring " shows that they habitually dwell outside it, but are admitted within upon special occasions. Again it proves that the context is speaking of the times after the millennium. During the millennium there is a gulf between the old earth and the new city. And not till the last day of earth is the book of life opened, on which depends the entrance into the city of God.

The harder cases of controversy which their judges and kings cannot decide are brought up to this metropolis to be solved. Advice of similar kind was given to Moses, and accepted by him. Exod. xviii. Thus it was commanded to Israel under the Law. Deut. xvii. 8–13.

But there is no command now, and no threat. The law is written within the heart.

But, perhaps, some may be startled and inquire, "What cases in a redeemed and holy world can there be, which will call for adjudication?" It is true that they will be few comparatively, after the blinding effect of men's evil lusts is removed: yet it is easy, by looking back at the past, to see that many questions may arise concerning the division of heritages, and other things, which will call for no little wisdom. The question of the daughters of Zelophehad was one of that kind. Moses could not solve it; it needed to be referred to God. It did not spring, as far as we can see, from any wrong spirit: and the wisdom of God met it.

They bring to the city of their wealth: in it are the waters of life, and from it they carry away the leaves of the tree of life, which grow there for their healing. Kings and nations now come up not in selfish cupidity, but in love to God and His glorified servants.

If the nations go up into the New Jerusalem, it would seem probable that they will be received into the mansions of the citizens during their stay: unless we assume that they bivouac in the city.

Is it not with a view to the final arrangement of God that we read, as part of the Christian character, the precept, "Be not forgetful to entertain strangers" (Heb. xiii. 2). "Given to hospitality" (Rom. xii. 13). "Use hospitality one to another without grudging" (Peter iv. 9). This virtue is peculiarly enforced on church officers. 1 Tim. iii. 2; Titus i. 8.

"And there shall not enter into it any thing common, nor whoever maketh an abomination, or a lie; but those who have been written in the Book of Life of the Lamb."

Naught "common," only the sacred, splendid, excellent articles of gift, may be borne within the city.

Then it runs on in strict accordance with the former verse : ver. 26 describes the aspect of that which is admissible : this, of that which is not allowed to be carried in.

Or are we to take it in a stronger sense, as including certain ceremonial uncleannesses, which may for a time exclude from the walls of the city ? Mark vii. 20. Either way it proves that we are dealing with the *flesh*. This word applies only to the nations, and their admittance. The risen are not mortals in the flesh. The question of their entrance, and its turning on moral qualities, was already stated. Verses 6–8.

" Nor whosoever maketh an abomination or a lie."

Here the gender changes : it refers evidently to persons. Moral qualities are now in question.

The expression in the Greek, " maketh abomination," · has two senses, both of which, I think, are included here.

1. It signifies—" making an idol." " Shall *I make* the residue thereof *an abomination ?* Shall I fall down to the stock of a tree ? " (Isa. l. 9–18 ; xlv. 16 ; xlvi. 6).

2. It means also the commission of any grievous act of immorality. After speaking of various unlawful lusts, the Lord says to Israel, " Ye shall not *commit* [Hebrew and Greek, ' make '] any of these abominations " (Lev. xviii. 20–30 ; Deut. xii. 31 ; Jer. viii. 12 ; xi. 15 ; Ezek. xxxiii. 26).

Another form of sin is specified—or maketh " a lie."

This would seem to be taken generally and extensively for every form of a lie.

None of these shall enter : God dwells within.

But while the negative aspect has been treated, the positive has yet to be stated—Who may enter ?

" Those written in the Lamb's book of life."

This refers to all, whether citizens, or individuals of

the nations. All who enter, whether as inhabitants or pilgrims, enter as elect. This is the only certain and permanent basis for eternal life. God's decree and power make the final fall of His elect impossible. Here is personal election: not election to the use of means; but to the enjoyment of bliss eternal.

The words are designed to lead us back to the final judgment. Then the book of life was displayed for the first time. xx. 15. It was there used with regard to the escape from wrath: those found in it were not cast into the lake of fire. And they were of two classes.

1. Those who were dead before the Lord's appearing, but not accounted worthy to receive the reward of the thousand years. Those who were accounted worthy to obtain a part in the reign of Christ entered the heavenly city during the millennium. But many will enter the city of grace, as men of faith and saved by God's election, who will not enjoy *reward*. 1 Cor. iii. 15. It is not said that all who are written in the Lamb's book of life enjoy the reign of Messiah. But they do enter the city in its final state. Here lies the distinction between eternal life, God's free gift to every believer, and the kingdom of heaven, the reward to the doers of good. Matt. vii. 21.

And in the words now under consideration appears the positive side of the book of life. It not only delivers from the Second Death: it admits into the eternal city of God.

2. The other class was the men living in the flesh on the earth, who were not guilty of the final rebellion. Were they to be permitted to dwell on the new earth, and to enter as pilgrims, the holy city? That is decided by the sovereignty of God. The *dead* are judged according to their *works*. Of the living the question is—" Are they of the serpent's seed? or of the

Woman's?" That is decided by God's knowledge and election.

It is "the Lamb's" book. The names written therein are those given to Him by the Father. They are redeemed by His blood and righteousness. The city is His bride: the enterers in are her children. The throne belongs to God *and* the Lamb.

CHAPTER XXII

THE CITY AN EDEN

ITS INTERNAL RELATIONS.

1-5. "And he showed me the river[1] of the water of life, bright as crystal, proceeding out of the throne of God and the Lamb. In the midst of its square, and on each side of the river, was the tree of life, bearing twelve (kinds of) fruits, and yielding its fruit every month: and the leaves of the tree are for the healing of the nations. And there shall be no more curse : and the throne of God and of the Lamb shall be in it ; and His servants shall serve Him, and they shall see His face, and His name shall be on their foreheads. And there shall be no more night ; and they shall not have need of the light of lamp, or of the light of the sun, for the Lord God shall shed light on them : and they shall reign for ever and ever."

UNDER the Gospel, and in preparation for the Church of Christ—which is called out of earth to heaven—Jesus spoke of water, and was mistaken ; for He meant spiritual waters, and they took His words literally. John iv. 10-14 ; vii. 38. Now that the time of mystery is over, water is taken by many spiritually, and again the word is mistaken.

The waters of the Harlot City were symbolic. xvii. 15. Hence the angel expounds them to be nations. Without that interpretation, we had not discovered their meaning. But here no interpretation is given, for they are literal. No interpretation is needed : mystery has for ever departed.

[1] See Tregelles.

In the New City we read not of *wine*. The waters of life take its place. There was no wine in Eden. We first read of it after the Flood; and then only to learn Noah's sorrowful fall thereby. Gen. ix. 21. Wine seems to join on fitly to the eating of the flesh of animals then first granted to man.

Wine is owned of God, as used by Melchizedec after the triumph of Abraham's victory. Gen. xiv. 18. Wine is not granted in the desert, but water alone. Deut. xxix. 6. But when the people of God has entered the land, wine is named, together with flour and oil, as one of the necessaries of life. 1 Chron. ix. 29; 2 Chron. ii. 10–15; Ps. civ. 15; and Rev. vi. 6.

Not to drink wine was a strange, unheard-of thing. Luke i. 15; vii. 33. It was used with the sacrifices in the temple of God. Exod. xxix. 40; Lev. xxiv. 13; Num. xv. 5–10; xxviii. 14.

Jesus turned water into wine at the marriage of Cana. He promises disciples that He will drink wine with them at His return in His kingdom. Matt. xxvi. 29; Mark xiv. 25. In the earth's day of millennial glory there is to be a feast to all nations with wines on the lees. Isa. xxv.

But that is not to last. There were indications of the final cessation of it, at least, for the risen. Those peculiarly dedicated to God, as the Nazarites, were to abstain from everything that came of the vine. Num. vi. Jesus, departing from earth, took the Nazarite vow, and has kept it till now. Matt. xxvi. 29.

The *priests* were forbidden to take wine while engaged in their duties. Lev. x. 9. Even in millennial days, they are to abstain. Ezek. xliv. 21. *Kings* should not drink wine, says Solomon. Prov. xxxi. 4. The inmates of the New Jerusalem are both *priests* and *kings*. Wine is to be used as a cordial for the sorrowful, says the wise man. But sorrow has now for ever departed. Wine in the book of Revelation is mainly "wine of wrath," and of sin. xiv. 8–10; xvi. 19; xvii. 2; xviii. 3; xix. 15. But sin and wrath are both past.

The new earth seems to return to the fruits of the tree, and the waters of the earth—the Lord God's first appointment for human sustenance.

Though the surroundings of the throne of God in chapter iv. have departed, the throne of God exists yet. Government must subsist to all eternity. It is the throne "of the *Lamb*," in memory of the Saviour's reconciling God with His offending creatures. We shall ever be reminded of the approach through the Mediator.

In Rev. xi. 15, the rule is described as that of "our Lord and His Christ." The thrones are separate in the millennium. The throne of God is above: the throne of Christ is below. Then comes the judgment-throne. At length appears the joint throne, after judgment is past. Justice and mercy are met together; and life for ever flows from the meeting of the two. God is all in all.

Israel, by asking a king instead of having Jehovah as their sovereign, severed the *house of God* (or the place of worship) from the *throne*. Now the throne of God in the city is the focus alike of worship and of government.

"In the midst of its square" was the tree of life.

Reasons have formerly been given why the word here used should be regarded as something more than a "street." The New Jerusalem must have many streets; there is but one plot as its centre. The word signifies "a broad place." It seems to point out the upper and central portion of the city. It appears to answer to the Holy of Holies; as the city in general corresponds to the sanctuary, and the foundations to the court of the priests. With this central portion all the other streets, I suppose, communicate : towards it, as their natural centre, they tend.

"The Plaza, being the market place, is usually a large open space, giving effect to the view of the church ; and it mostly *contains a fountain of water in its centre, and has a row of trees round it, which also adds to the general effect.*"

The very name "plaza"—in Italian, "piazza"—seems to be derived from the Greek word used here ($\pi\lambda\alpha\tau\epsilon\hat{\iota}\alpha$).

Paradise and Jerusalem are combined. As it is Eden, we have a river and tree. As it is a city, we have a throne and a street, or square. This is its advance upon what we read of old. "The *tree of life* was in the midst of the *garden*" (Gen. ii. 9 ; iii. 3).

How are we to understand "the tree of life ? "

It is quite true, that the expression "tree of life" is used figuratively in Scripture. "Happy is the man that findeth *wisdom*." "She is a *tree of life* to them that lay hold upon her" (Prov. iii. 13, 18). "The fruit of the righteous is a *tree of life*" (xi. 30). But in these cases every one sees that the expression is figurative. There is no description of its fruits every month, and of the uses of them.

What shall we say of the following ? Does it speak of a literal tree ?

"The tree on which the bread-fruit grows, besides *producing two and often three crops in a year*, yields a valuable gum, or resin, which exudes from the bark. It is probable that in no group of the Pacific Islands is there a greater variety in the kinds of this valuable fruit than in the South Sea Islands. *The several varieties ripen at different seasons, and the same kinds also come to perfection at an earlier period in one part of Tahiti than in another ; so that there are but few months in the year in which ripe fruit is not to be found in the several parts of this island.* The missionaries are acquainted with nearly fifty varieties" (*Missionary Records*, p. 11).

How strong the resemblances here! If the one be a literal tree, so is the other.

"But how can one tree stand in three different places? How can it be in the midst of the square, and on both sides of the river?"

Two replies may be given.

1. Its nature is like that of the banyan tree of India, which spreads over an immense space, having, not one stem, as with us, but many: each bough sending down fibres, which after awhile become fresh trunks of the tree.

2. The word used in the original is a singular one. It signifies generally "timber." It probably designates a *kind* of tree, not one individual specimen of it.

The tree of life was of old "in the midst of the Garden" (Gen. ii. 9; iii. 3). That is its place still. The tree is in the midst of the square, and the square is in the midst of the city.

The soul of man not only loves the society of the city, but God has made him also to find delight in the beauty of the country.

The herb, then, will no longer be man's food. The fruit of the tree was originally appointed to supply him. But sin came in, and then, in order to compel toil, the Most High made the herb to be his support. How small the proportion of food that wheat contains, as compared with an apple-tree? The apple-tree needs not ploughing and sowing, harrowing and weeding. Year by year it yields its unlaboured crop. Baron Humboldt found that, from a plot of ground, which, when planted with wheat would support but two, fifty might be fed, if planted with the banana-tree. Now the tree is again destined to supply men. The staff of life is no longer a reed, but a tree. The tree of life is restored to man : the cherubim and sword no longer fence the way. Those guards were not around it at the first. They are now withdrawn : the marks of the fall are no more, the Tempter can tempt no more. The marrings of God's original plan are past : the unbroken design is at length unrolled before us. The Bible is the history of the devil's disturbance of the original plan. That disturbance is for ever removed, and the enemy's power destroyed.

With the herb as his food man was driven from God's presence, compelled to toil and die. But all is reversed now : his food is the fruit of the tree, his dwelling in God's presence, he needs not labour ; he cannot die.

The tree of life of the heavenly tabernacle was typified under the Mosaic economy by the table of shewbread.

The wooden table was covered with *incorruptible* gold, that it might signify the tree of *life*. Man cannot make a living tree : his nearest resemblance to it is a table covered with bread. The table was to be crowned around its border : for death is swallowed up in victory. The hindrances to man's eating of the tree of life are triumphantly removed. There were to be rings of gold in its sides, that it might be borne to and fro by men, according to the journeys of the children of Israel. That which the Law could not make steadfast, the grace of God establishes. The tree is firmly fixed at last by God, to bloom and bear for ever.

The twelve cakes were tokens of the twelve manner of fruits here, and of the eternity of God's provision for His people. They were to be arranged in two rows. Even thus the tree of life grows on this side and on that side of the river of life. They were to be renewed every week ; on the day of rest fresh loaves were to be set in God's presence. Here the fruits are removed once a month. Bread would not keep good so long. But now the true rest is come, and God, not man, supplies and changes the bread of His people. The fruit was to be for the priests the sons of Aaron only: as our Lord also remarks. Even so the fruits of the tree belong to the citizens of the New Jerusalem only. There were in Israel ordinary bread, and "bread of the presence," or "shew-bread." This is the "*bread of the Presence*" of God, in a sense far loftier than was known to Israel. It feeds those who dwell in His house for ever.

How great the superiority of this tree above any on the old earth! Here we have but one kind of fruit on any tree, unless it be grafted. We have ordinarily but one crop of fruit in the year; and two, or at most three, crops of fruit is the extreme limit. But there, fed by the river of life, and enjoying the light not only of the sun amd moon, but of the luminaries of the city, it puts forth twelve kinds of fruit, and bears twelve crops in the year. It is a tree planted by the waters, that fears no summer drought, or winter frost. Jer. xvii. 8; Ps. i. 3; Ezek. xix. 10.

From this we learn that the new earth will possess both a sun and a moon, as now. The year will be divided into "months" by the moon; and the year will consist of twelve of them, determined by the earth's course around the sun, as now. But there is not either autumn or winter in the city. Each month is one of bloom and fruit. On this earth the curse attendant on the Fall has shut up the powers of the soil and of the tree. But there the good pleasure of God makes both put forth a fertility hardly to be imagined by us.

The Lord God at creation gave both herb and tree to man to supply him with food. Gen. i. 29. Here the herb is passed by: the tree alone is named. Moreover, we are dealing with the privileges of the city only; the new earth at large abounds doubtless with both herb and tree. The trees that bear fruit were not to be cut down by the Israelites when they besieged a city : for they were man's life. Deut. xx. 19, 20. They might eat of them, but not cut them down. But now there is no dread of a siege, nor will the axe be heard upon the boughs of the tree of life. Amidst the plenty of the Garden, amidst its trees " pleasant to the sight and good for food," one tree was reserved for God. Now there is no restriction : the fatal tree of the knowledge of good and evil is no longer there. Nor does the soil bear thorns and briers now : for the curse is past.

In the city of God there is constant variety of fruits : month by month the kind is changed. There is no need of storehouses, or of modes of counteracting the tendency of fruit to corruption ; the tree bears for all the citizens, and there is no cessation in its crops.

" The leaves of the tree were for the healing of the nations."

The tree of life was only found in Eden. In the new world, it is not found outside the city.

In every tree there are superior and inferior parts : the leaves are inferior to the fruit. Thus also among mankind as settled in the new earth, there are two great classes : the risen, and those still in the flesh. To the risen sons of men belong the *fruits :* and they give of the *leaves* of the tree to the nations. The holy bread of the Presence might be eaten by priests alone in the Holy Place.

The fruit of the tree is not something spiritual. It is not to be enjoyed now in the time of warfare. It is to be bestowed after the victory is won. " To him that *overcometh will* I give." The manna of the desert is past. The land and its tree and fruit are reached.

The saint accounted worthy to reign possesses it, it would seem, during the thousand years. Afterward it belongs to all the saved and risen from the dead, whether of Israel, or of the Church.

Its leaves are intended " for the healing of the nations."

It must indeed be allowed, that in the eternal state there is no death, nor pain. xxi, 4. But still there may be weakness and the painless decay of the body.

The nations are still in the flesh. It is thought by some that the tree of life, ere Adam fell, was designed to renovate his life from time to time, so as to prevent all necessity of death. It may be so now. The bodies of the nations may be invigorated by the application of the leaves of the tree of life. It may be that they may employ them against mechanical injuries to parts of their frame.

The Scripture distinguishes between "infirmities," or want of strength in various forms, and "diseases." " Himself took our *infirmities*, and bare our *diseases* " (Matt. viii. 17). To Timothy troubled with infirmities Paul recommends the fruit of the vine. 1 Tim. v. 23.

" There shall be no more curse."

This word of promise comes in at this point with much comfort. We have just had the tree of life described. But, by the tree of the former Paradise, sin entered, and death. Will it be so again ? No.

The tree of the knowledge of good and evil has done its work. All the saved have a conscience : but it no longer condemns. The rest of their nature is wrought into harmony with it.

Man is no more to be tried : grace fixes his joy for ever. We read no more of the angels in connection with the city. At xxi. 12, we find them sentinels outside the walls. But no more are they noticed, lest our fears should be excited. By an angel sin entered. We are not told anything of the animal creation of the new globe. For by an animal the devil deceived our first parents. Under the millennium we have the promise that the wild beasts shall be tamed : here they are not named. By the vegetable creation Noah sinned, and a new curse fell upon a portion of men. But now there shall be no more curse, either from God or from men.

"And the throne of God and of the Lamb shall be in it."

Now God Himself takes the throne. There is no more any law or penalty written outside the man. God's Spirit has written all within. The King of kings holds His seat visibly among His obedient subjects. There is no sin or danger.

It is now "the throne of *God* and of the *Lamb*." It must never be forgotten that the saved have fallen, and been rescued by grace.

The Redeemer abides in view of His people as the sacrifice and priest. In each view of the city "the Lamb" is named. Seven times does the word occur in connection with the New Jerusalem. xxi. 9, 14, 22, 23, 27 ; xxii. 1, 3.

By the title "His servants," are characterized those to whom the message of the Apocalypse is sent. Rev. i. 1 ; ii. 20. But it embraces at length all the saved risen from the dead, whether from among the patriarchs, the Law, or the Gospel.

Distinctions between the citizens, as educated by God under the patriarchal, Mosaic, or Christian dispensation, do not appear in this final view of the city. As the differences between Israel and the Gentiles are blotted out, so perhaps will these finally disappear. The city is set before us in the Hebrews as the resting-place of the men of *faith*. Heb. xi. And although the Law was not of faith, but of works, yet those who obtained a good report under it obtained it by faith. In David's day, the differences between his mighty men and the rest of his subjects came into view. In the reign of Solomon they disappear.

It is said "*His* servants" shall serve. Why not "*their* servants"? Because the unity of the Godhead will ever abide. God and the Lamb are one God. "I and the Father are *one*."

They "shall serve Him."

Heaven, or the final state, is not one of idleness, but of service to God. The word used signifies "priestly service:" no servile work is theirs.

"And they shall see His face."

This among earthly sovereigns is the privilege of courtiers and ministers of the palace; not of the king's subjects in general.

God at length discovers Himself to His subject-kings, as the King of kings. He allows Himself to be seen as God, by His worshippers and priests.

At last the "beatific vision" is granted. We are equal unto the angels; even the most favoured of them. For not to all of those servants of God is it given: but of those who act as guardian-angels of the elect, Jesus tells us, "That in heaven these angels do always *behold the face* of my Father which is in heaven" (Matt. xviii. 10).

"And His name shall be on their foreheads."

A hundred and forty-four thousand have the name of God and of the Lamb written on their foreheads *before the millennium begins, and as the sign of a peculiar glory.* xiv. For to them it is given to follow the Lamb in His progress from part to part of His dominions. But now that special mark seems to be imparted to all the dwellers in the city: and we read no more of the Saviour's movings to and fro.

"And there shall be no more night."

The citizens need no sleep, and therefore they have no night. Herein this Paradise of God stands distinguished from the Eden of old. Then man was only a "living soul," possessed of an animal body. Now the risen are immortal tenants of a spiritual body. Herein also it is distinguished from millennial Jerusalem. The inhabitants, as men in the flesh, will need sleep even if there should be no night there.

Glory lit up the Holiest of the temple: but its rays shone not into the sanctuary; much less into the region round it. Here, however, the glory of God enlightens, not the Holiest only, but the whole temple and all the region round. During the Day of the Lord seven torches lit up the Holiest: for it was night without. Now they have passed away; for there are no new acts of wrath.

"And they shall not need light of lamp or light of sun: for the Lord God shall give them light."

Lamplight is one of the proofs of civilization. But now the necessities of the earth are ended to the citizens of the heavenly abode.

They are independent of the presence of the sun by day. Though his rays fall on the celestial city, they do not constitute their day. They can serve by day or by night, within doors or without, without needing the heavenly or earthly light, which the rest of the world require.

The difference between male and female is not noted now.

Information is given us concerning the supply of water and of fruits. But nothing is said of the clothing of the inhabitants. To the disciples of Christ now all care about these things is forbid. Their heavenly Father will bestow all that is needed. They are to lay up no store on earth of food or clothing, for God will feed. They are not to be anxious about clothing, for their heavenly Father will provide. Matt. vi.

19–34. And if this be true of God's sons on earth, how much more of those on high ?

The *nations* walk by the *city's* light ; the *citizens*, by the light of *God's presence*. On this earth God gives light by distant luminaries : there He dwells among His perfected people, and His glory lights them immediately.

" And they shall reign for ever and ever."

Hence it is evident that there must be a distinction of mankind into rulers and ruled. If some are kings, some must be subjects. The kings here spoken of are the servants of God's throne, who wait on Him and His service continually, and see His face. This is true of the citizens, not of the nations. The citizens, then, are the kings ; the nations are their subjects. The victors of the Church are to rule " *the nations* " (ii. 26). The Man-child caught up to God's throne is to rule " all the nations " (xii. 5). To the conqueror is given a special foretaste of this glory during the thousand years. But it is the general destiny of the sons of God risen from the dead. The nations are transferred from the old earth to the new : but they are still to be ruled.

There are two kinds of kings. There are special and local kings, who rule particular tribes or nations. These are called " kings *of the earth* " (xxi. 24). They dwell outside the city, and are men in the flesh, who at the head of their respective nations bring their tribute to the *kings of the city*. The kings of earth are far inferior to those made kings and priests while here below by the blood of the Lamb. Those who wait on the throne of God are kings of kings.

There is a manifest difference in principle between the reign of the risen over the kings of earth and that which prevailed during the thousand years. Then it was a ruling " with rod of iron : " for offenders were to be found, who must be destroyed by the sword of righteousness. There is no such necessity now.

"The nation and kingdom that will not serve thee *shall perish*" (Isa. lx. 12), has been fulfilled mournfully on the old earth, and in reference to the Old Jerusalem. But there is no rebellion against the New Jerusalem.

Nothing is now said directly, as there was in millennial times, of the *priesthood*. The absence of sin has modified some things. Men need not atonement now. During the millennium we read—"They shall be *priests* of God and of His Christ, and shall *reign*." At length the notice of the priesthood is dropped. Priests were used in Israel as judges: they were to discriminate between good and evil. But, as in Israel's happiest day, the *priests* and *prophets* were subordinate to the *king*, so the kingly office is now prominent. It is *eternal*. That expression, "His servants shall *serve Him*," seems the only direct statement concerning the eternal priesthood of the risen. The word used there is one specially applied to priestly service.

This passage throws the clearest light on the eternal employments of the saved of the Church and of Israel. They are not perpetually *worshipping*, and singing praises. They have active engagements: they reign.

Man governed all the other creatures at first, because he was made in God's image. The citizens of the New Jerusalem reign over all others, because in a new and peculiar sense they are made, in resurrection, partakers of God's image and likeness.

The reign of the conquerors with Christ is but for a thousand years; and it comes to an end. This is for ever. That dominion is not enjoyed by all the risen: this is. Then the rulers move up to heaven whenever they will: the ruled are on earth. Now both are on the same earth, and much nearer to God.

The millennial kingdom was bestowed on some as "fellows" or associates of "the Christ" for awhile. Heb. iii. 14 (*Greek*). For Jesus' reign as the Christ is to be given up, after all is subdued to God. 1 Cor. xv. But these rule as servants of the throne of God, after all is subdued to Him.

God's city is superior to any of Rome or Greece. The relics of those fallen cities show us harbours, bridges, *temples*, aqueducts, theatres, stadia, amphitheatres, *tombs*. These are not found in God's city of holiness, and life. There is no workman, no millstone, no voice of bridegroom or bride. Nor is any account given us of any song uttered there: a point which I am unable to account for.

The new earth and the New Jerusalem are manifestly the completion of Jehovah's previous plans. They possess all the perfections of the former earth and city; they are not encumbered with their imperfections.

If we compare this city and its regulations with the millennial ones appointed for Israel and Jerusalem, we shall find both resemblances and differences. Ezek. xl.-xl.viii.

In Ezekiel's temple there are bloody sacrifices still. There are still cherubim and palm-trees in the house: still God's concealment of Himself in the Holiest. There are laws which the priests are to observe: a gate which is to be kept shut. Levites are disgraced: strangers may not enter the sanctuary. There are laws concerning the priests' clothes, food, *marriages*, teaching, judgments, *defilement by the dead*, and concerning the priests' maintenance in general. There is atonement, there is sin; there are feasts, sabbaths, the daily lamb. The title of God is still Israelitish. The sanctuary and the city are separate. xlviii. 8, 15. There are seas still, and some parts of the land unhealed.

The size of the new-built city of earth is *four thousand five hundred cubits*, with suburbs. The city itself is *profane*. 15. In the Apocalypse, the city is *holy*, and is a square of *twelve thousand furlongs*; nor are there any suburbs, so far as we know.

THE EPILOGUE.

6. " And He said unto me, These sayings are faithful and true: and the Lord God of the spirits of the prophets sent His angel to show His servants what must take place speedily. 7. And behold I come quickly: blessed is he that keepeth the sayings of the prophecy of this book. 8. And I, John, heard and saw these things. And when I heard and saw, I fell down to worship before the feet of the angel that showed me these things. 9. And he saith to me, ' See thou do it not: I am fellow-servant of thee, and of thy brethren the prophets, and of those who keep the sayings of this book: worship God.' "

There is a close connection between the opening and the close of the book. The opening of the book testifies that God gave Jesus the Apocalypse to "*show to His servants things which must shortly come to pass.*" The ending declares that "*the Lord God of the spirits of the prophets*" sent his angel to "*show unto His servants things which must shortly come to pass.*" By "the spirits of the prophets," as we suppose, were signified the two different classes of revelation embodied in the Old Testament and in the New. This is confirmed by the parallel expression in i. 2, where we read that John bore witness of the *word of God* (Old Testament) and *of the testimony of Jesus Christ* (New Testament) whatsoever things He saw."

A blessing follows, invoked on the head of the keepers of the book in both of the first divisions.

In both, too, it is stated that "the season is near."

And lastly, Jesus tells us, in the notice to the churches, that He sent His angel: a thing which is mentioned in the first verse of the first chapter.

The title given here to the Most High is singular: so singular that it has been altered by copyists into one more easy of comprehension. Instead of "the Lord God of *the spirits* of the prophets," they would read, "The Lord God of the *holy* prophets." But the more difficult phrase is evidently the true one. The agency of the Holy Ghost upon the Lord's inspired ones is intended. Two passages in some degree resembling this occur in 1 Cor. xiv. "Even so ye, forasmuch as ye are desirous of *spirits* (*Greek*) seek that ye may abound (*Greek*) to the edifying of the Church" (12). "The *spirits of the prophets* are subject to the prophets" (32).

The sacred writer here alludes, we suppose, to the different inspirations of the Old Testament and the New. The Law was given under the spirit of bondage and fear. The Gospel is given with the spirit of adoption. But the God of the Old Testament and of the New is one. The dispensations of mercy and of justice both take their rise from one divine source, and both conduct to one heavenly home. The names of patriarchs and of apostles are borne on the city's front.

"Prophets" mean here, as usually, inspired men foretelling the future.

Jesus is "the Lord God." Compare together what is said of Jesus, and what of the Lord God. "The Revelation of *Jesus Christ*, which God gave unto Him *to show unto His servants things which must shortly come to pass;* and He sent and *represented it by His angel unto His servant John*" (i. 1). "*The Lord God sent His angel to show unto His servants the things which must come to pass shortly.*" "I, *Jesus*, sent *my angel*

to testify these things unto you in the churches"
(xxii. 16).

God's "servants" are to know these things, and to credit them before they come to pass. The difference between the standing of believers in Jesus throughout the Epistles of Paul, and that given in the Apocalypse, is very great. As members of Christ they are "sons of God." Here they are only denominated "servants." The reason of this is, as I suppose, because this book looks at final salvation as it affects both those of the Old Testament and those of the New. Hence it takes necessarily the lowest term which will apply to both classes alike.

The events here foretold "must" come to pass. God has said so: His word cannot be broken. The plagues must descend, because of sin. The joys must be granted, because of God's purpose and promise in Christ. They must be done "shortly." But the hours are calculated by God's clock: and that moves much more slowly than man's.

"Blessed the keeper of the prophecy of this book." God would single out to especial notice and blessing this book: man in his folly, yea, even saints of God, despise it. Let us keep its sayings! Let us retain its truths in our understanding and heart! Where it is practical, let us beware! Babylon and her lures are around us: let us flee them! Let us beware of the Great Antichrist, and be kept from his day of temptation, by praying that we may be accounted worthy to escape it!

This prophecy may be understood, before its words come to pass.

How unlike is God's book to the productions of man! Men's books seek to glorify themselves. But here is John twice confessing his sin. How frail are the best of God's saints! Twice does John worship the angel, within a very short period: twice is he rebuked.

Holy angels refuse such homage. For a being to worship an inferior, is absurd; to adore an equal, scarcely less so. But may we not worship one of an order confessedly superior to us, one connected with us, and able to assist, yea, sent for the very purpose of aiding us? This is the question here decided.

Man is prone to idolatry: only by grace preserved from it. If John, so great and holy an apostle, twice fell, what marvel if the whole nominally Christian Church fell into it for hundreds of years: yea, is now caught in the snare, and Protestants are returning thereto? If we may not worship even an angel, because he is a fellow-servant; much less Peter or Mary: much less pictures and images! John was rebuked for the *posture* of worship which he took before the angel, ere any words of adoration were uttered. "Thou shalt not *bow down* to them" were the words of the Law also.

But whence came it that John a second time offended? The reason, I judge, is that John imagined from the words which just preceded that the angel was Jesus. "Behold I come quickly." He tells us that what "he *heard* and saw" produced this. "When he *heard* and saw," he fell down. No such word as "I come," occurs on the previous occasion. Nor is it easy to understand how an angel should say such words.

Twice this offence is committed: it being designed, as I believe, to teach us that what was once permitted under the Old Testament, is now withdrawn for ever. Jesus, on several occasions under the Law, and before it, appeared as an angel, and received worship; without any blame being laid on the party rendering it. He appears as an angel even in this book: but only before the millennium. We are to learn now, whatever words an angel may use, that Christ will no more take such a form. For there is no further need of His humiliation; all His adversaries and ours are put down, all His chosen are redeemed. Thenceforward the adoration of any angel is unlawful.

When John fell at the feet of the angel, he is twice met by—" See thou do it not." When he falls at our Lord's feet, he is addressed with the words, " Fear not ! " The angel depreciates himself and elevates John to his level. " I am *fellow-servant* of thee, and of thy brethren the prophets." But Jesus takes thereupon the title of superiority which involves Godhead, and justifies worship. " I am First and Last." The angel bids John to direct his worship to the person of God alone. But Jesus, having accepted the worship as His due, gives commands to His servant John—" Write *therefore* the things which thou sawest."

10. " And he saith to me, ' Seal not the sayings of the prophecy of this book: for the season is near.' 11. He that committeth injustice, let him commit injustice still : and the filthy, let him be filthy still : and the just, let him do righteousness still : and the holy, let him be sanctified still. 12. Behold, I come quickly : and my reward is with me, to render to each as his work is. 13. I am the Alpha and the Omega, the first and the last, beginning and end. 14. Blessed are they who wash their robes, that they may have a right to the tree of life, and may enter in at the portals into the city. 15. Outside are dogs, and sorcerers, and fornicators, and murderers, and idolaters, and every one who loveth and maketh a lie.

16. I, Jesus, sent mine angel to testify these things to you in the churches. I am the root and the offspring of David, the bright and morning star. 17. And the Spirit and the Bride say, Come thou ! And let him that heareth say, Come thou ! And let the thirsty one come. Whosoever wishes, let him take the water of life without price. 18. I testify to every one that heareth the sayings of the prophecy of this book, If any add to these things, God shall add to him the plagues that are written in this book. 19. And if any take away from the sayings of the book of this prophecy, God shall take away his portion from the tree of life, and out of the holy city, which are written of in this book. 20. Saith he who testifies these things, Yea, I come quickly. Amen. Come, Lord Jesus ! 21. The grace of the Lord Jesus be with all the saints. Amen."

1. "Seal not the book." The book in general is designed of God, not to remain an impenetrable mystery, but to be understood by His saints. Can we not say, that the book is not beyond our comprehension, if only we sit down to its study on right principles? Interpret it on grounds common to other Scriptures, and its meaning is clear, not only in its main outlines, but deeper still.

2. "Seal not the book." This is in contrast with Dan. xii. 4, 8, 9. Even to one who was a prophet, no light was to be given on the secrets of that book at that time. Not so with the Apocalypse. It is to radiate light to God's servants, whether of the Church or of Israel.

Why this difference? In Daniel's case another dispensation—the Mystery of God—was to intervene, ere the fulfilment of the words was given. But the Church is set in the last of the dispensations before the fulfilment of these things. Christ has come, and His followers are called out to be His fellows in the glory, and He is coming again to introduce Daniel's hopes. There is nothing that must intervene between us and that coming. It is the last time: on us the ends of the ages have met.

"He that committeth injustice, let him commit injustice still."

If I mistake not, in these two pairs of good and evil characters, lies a reference to the two classes of God's servants which run through this book.

By "the just" or "righteous" are meant the holy of the Law. The word is used in the Old Testament and in the New alike to describe such. Matt. x. 41; xiii. 17; xxiii. 28, 29. Compare Rom. v. 7, 8.

By the "holy," as opposed to the foul, are meant the saved of the churches, who wash their robes in the Lamb's blood.

These and the following words seem to be generally regarded as affirming—"that when these events were consummated, everything would be fixed and unchanging: that all who were then found to be righteous would remain so for ever; and that none who were impenitent, impure, and wicked, would ever change their character or condition."

But the words before us are spoken, not of the results of the day of judgment, but of "the book of this prophecy," and of the time when it was first sent forth by the apostle. They seem, therefore, to mean that God had herein openly spoken His mind as to the future, and presented the most tremendous motives to holiness, and dissuasives from sin. But in spite of these awful discoveries, the two great classes of the holy and the wicked will abide still, each ripening for the judgment and final award. Like these are the angel's words to Daniel, when he announced to the prophet the sealing up of the book.

"Many shall be purified, and made white, and tried; but the wicked shall do wickedly: and none of the wicked shall understand; but the wise shall understand" (Dan. xii. 10).

How mistaken, then, are those who imagine that the Gospel, even with its clearest revelations of the terrible results to the godless, and its wondrous joys to the holy, will ever convert the world! Some turn the Apocalypse itself against themselves. Far from being warned, they are only hardened thereby. "Who can understand such mystery?"

"I am the Alpha and the Omega, the First and the Last, beginning and end."

These titles of God belong to Jesus. Thrice are they used in this book: at the beginning once; twice at the close. They are designed, as I judge, to assure us that the various dispensations since the creation of the world are all the arrangement of one God. Diverse as are the principles of some of God's economies, all proceed from one source and tend to the glory of the one true God. The words refer us to Isa. xl. 10, " Behold, the Lord God will come with strong hand, and His arm shall rule for Him : behold, His reward is with Him, and His work before Him " (lxii. 11) ; and assure us that Jesus is the Jehovah of the Old Testament.

" Blessed are they who wash their robes."

This variation from the received text is very startling.

It is read by the Alexandrian and Sinaitic Manuscripts, by the Vulgate, Ethiopic, and some Armenian copies, and by Lachmann, Buttmann, Ewald, Theile, and Tregelles, among the critics. It is also the most difficult reading. It seems as if there must have been intentional corruption on the part of some. Probably some might fear, lest it should be taken literally : as though cleanliness were the whole of godliness. But the seventh chapter and its view of the Great Multitude are quite enough to preserve from mistake all but the wilfully blind. *They* entered into the *temple*, through washing their robes in the Lamb's blood. But the temple was but a transitory condition. The Lamb was to lead them on to the fountains of life in the eternal *city*. This sentiment, then, discovers to us that the same cleansing which admits as priests to the *temple* will finally admit to the *city*, and its everlasting repose.

The difference of the tenses used on the two occasions is instructive. "These are the comers out of the Great Tribulation, and they *washed* their robes." As exalted to the throne of God, their need of cleansing is over. They had ceased to wash : they were beyond defilement then. But this is a word to the living saint. It is to be his *custom to wash*. Here are frequent defilements, and need of frequent cleansings. Blessed are they who frequently apply for forgiveness through their Priest and Sacrifice. Jesus once for all washed from our sins us who believe, when first we came to Him. i. 5, 6. But for offences committed after that, we need special pardon.

One defilement robbed Adam of his part in the tree of life. But this washing restores to us the lost tree, and makes us citizens of the City of God. The Lamb was slain by the sword of fire that guarded the tree. But in Him was its flame quenched: and by that blood we are welcomed there now. Eternal life and its tree are ours.

But wherein consists the blessedness of the washing?

"That they may have right to[1] the tree of life."

"That they may enter into the city at its portals."

The two aspects of the eternal bliss of the risen are here conjoined. Their abode is *Paradise :* and therefore theirs is the *tree of life*. He who began with that discovery of His mercy ends with it. Their abode is the *city of God :* and therefore it is their blessedness to enter *its gates* at their pleasure.

Thus these views of the city are intended of God to act practically on His saints. His promises and threatenings are motives which are to affect our conduct. Faith, mixed with the report of the good and heavenly land and city, will keep us from disobedience.

"Without are dogs."

Of course the reference here is moral. Dogs were unclean in the eye of the law: holy things were not for them. Matt. vii. 6; Phil. iii. 2. By this word seems to be meant those guilty of unnatural crime. Such were found in the holy land of old. 1 Kings xiv. 24; xv. 12; 2 Kings xxiii. 7; Lev. xx. 13. But

---

[1] Literally, "That their power may be over the tree." So in 1 Cor. xi. 10, it should be translated "Power *over* herhead," not "power *on* her head."

into the holy city to come they shall never enter.

By comparing this description of the lost with that previously given in xxi. 8, it seems to be taught that the place of eternal punishment shall be on the new earth. The lost are to lie in the lake of fire and brimstone, and that lake is outside the city. So the lake of Sodom was near Jerusalem: so Tophet is to be nearer still to millennial Jerusalem.

Sorcerers are to be shut out. They prefer unclean spirits to the Holy Spirit: they are necromancers, defiled by the dead. How greatly is this sin on the increase in our day! And it is defended, too, as if Jesus had put the prohibition of Moses aside! It is asserted that the scene on the Mount of Transfiguration is a proof of Jesus' rescinding the old law against this iniquity. Its advocates forget to prove that Elias and Moses were separate spirits.

Fornicators are thrust outside. They were typified of old by those who had issues.

The murderer dares to deface the image of God, borne even by the fallen of mankind. For this high treason, the criminal is for ever banished from the sight of the Holy One.

"Idolaters," too, are put outside the city: they outrage the claims of God. While idolatry is regarded by man as a trifling sin, it is by the Most High accounted the highest treason.

Lastly, "liars" are excluded. These form, in both enumerations of the lost, the last class. God is a God of truth. The false will learn His displeasure in the awfulness of their doom.

How clearly does this passage prove that, as the result of God's redemption, not all are cleansed, not all are saved. The means of cleansing avail for many, but not for all. Not all are within the city. How mischievous is the doctrine of universalism!

Endless punishment is the lot of the lost. It is their sentence upon three grounds.

1. It is *just*, that they should be shut out of the place of the holy; because of their *past acts of evil*.

2. It is *fit* that they should be excluded: because of their *present unholy state of spirit*. They are not fit to associate with the holy and servants of God. They have no sympathy with the renewed. They are the Serpent's seed.

3. It is *wise*, that the two parties should be severed. The lost are burning brands; ever ready to set on fire all that come near them. They are poisonous plants, bearing the seeds of mischief and ready to scatter them all around. They are unhappy themselves, and would destroy, in great measure, the happiness of the saved, if suffered to come among them. Now all these reasons remain eternally; so does their punishment.

"I, Jesus, sent mine angel to testify unto you these things in the churches."

To Jesus belong all the saved, whether fallen or unfallen.

"*My* servants." "*My* two witnesses." "*Mine* angels."

Again the importance of the book is pressed upon our notice from a consideration of the greatness of the person who presents it. It is designed to be the especial study of *the churches*. While it speaks of things which will go on upon earth after the watchful of the churches are removed, it nevertheless is full of light and instruction for us during God's time of patience.

Verses sixteen and seventeen address the churches. We have returned, now that the prophetic part of the book is closed, to the Church's usual standing in this dispensation, as set among the things which *are*. The Person of the Bridegroom is presented to draw out the affections of the spouse after Him. But both Jesus' titles are taken from the Old Testament.

Before (i. 1), this book was spoken of as given to "the servants of God": now, to "the churches." The churches are a far narrower class than "the servants of God." But the book was at first sent only to "the churches": for Israel in that day was only the unbelieving shadow of its former self. Till the churches are removed, there are none but those bodies to listen to God's testimony.

Jesus takes two titles in relation to David. He is "the offspring" of the king of Israel: He was a man of David's race. This is God's testimony against the Gnostic deceit, that the Christ was not born, but a spirit that came on Jesus after His baptism. It is God's witness against the Swedenborgians, who hold that the Saviour after His resurrection has put off all that which He received from His mother Mary. This truth Timothy, who dwelt among Gnostics, was to affirm and to hold fast, "Remember that Jesus *Christ* [not 'Jesus' alone] has been raised up from the dead, *of the seed of David*, according to my Gospel" (2 Tim. ii. 8; Rom. i. 3).

Jesus is "the root of David." Before David came into being, Jesus existed. John viii. 55–59. He is the Son of God, the Creator of David. Thus, and thus only, can we answer the sacred enigma which Jesus set before the unbelievers of Israel. Jews would admit that the Messiah was David's son: but how was He also David's Lord? Matt. xxii. 41–46.

He is "the bright and morning star."

Our Lord takes three titles.

He fulfils the promise uttered by Balaam. "There shall come a *star* out of Jacob, and a sceptre shall rise out of Israel" (Num. xxiv. 17). He is the *ruling* star of the ascendant. He is the *leading* star promised to Abraham ; the herald of the eternal day to come. Abraham's seed was to be as the stars. But that " seed " had among it one in especial. Abraham's individual Seed is also the special star of stars.

The seven stars of the churches were stars of the night, going out as the day drew on. He abides alone : He heralds the blessed day to come. He went down in gloom once, but has risen now out of death in brightness for ever. He shines as morning star for us watchers in the night.

" And the Spirit and the Bride say, Come ! "

This is the last mention of the Holy Ghost.

The Holy Spirit descended at Pentecost as the result of Jesus' petition that He might abide with the Church, and prepare a spiritual body for the Christ. The Holy Ghost then desires the return of Christ—the accomplishment of God's blessed purposes. How surely, therefore, shall His desires be fulfilled! How great His grace in tarrying amidst the sins of the world and the Church !

The Bride re-echoed the Spirit's word. Who is the Bride ?

It is, I think, the Church, as is commonly supposed. These words are specially addressed to " the church*es* " : but together they form at last a unit. The Church of Christ, as peculiarly destined for Christ, desires His coming.

But this is, I believe, the only place in which the saved of this dispensation are presented to us in this book as one. The two former mentions of the Bride related to the *city* only. xix. 7 ; xxi. 9, 10. The reason of this double reference will be seen, if we bear in mind the difference of the dispensations implied in the two different occurrences. In xix. 7 ; xxi. 9, 10, we were engaged with the things which are yet to appear, after the Church, as God's witness, has ceased to be on the earth. But this closing verse, coming after the prophetic part of the book is ended, reverts to our present standing, and so for a moment the Holy Ghost uses an expression taught in Paul's Epistles.

This call "Come!" is not, as many take it, the Holy Spirit's cry to the sinner to come to Christ. It is the appeal of the Spirit and Bride to *Jesus*, that He will come, "bright morning star," and bring the day of joy.

"Let him that heareth say, Come!"

The believer is "he who heareth." "He that hath an ear, let him hear" (xiii. 9). The believer alone desires the Lord's coming. As the Lord addressed to the saints of the churches an individual call at the close of each epistle, so an individual response is required here.

This word to the hearer will remain in full force even after the watchful of the Church or the whole Church are borne away. Jesus' coming is, to Israel as well as to ourselves, the great point of hope on which all their blessings hinge.

Thrice in the Epilogue does Jesus announce His return.

Three answers desirous of the Saviour's coming are called forth.

"And he that thirsteth, let him come!"

Here is an entire change in the reference of the word—"Come." Before, the hearer was to desire another to come: now he is himself to move. But whither? Who is to come? These are the words of Jesus inviting some to come, while He is away. They must mean that the weary sinner is to come to Himself. And his thirst, if so, and the coming, must be spiritual; and the reference must be like those in the Gospel of

Matthew—" *Come unto me,* all ye that labour and are heavy laden, and I will give you rest."

" He that wisheth, let him take the water of life without cost.

These words are especially spoken to those in " the churches," after the descriptions of the prophecy have ended. Thus the gracious invitations of the Gospel to sinners are still in force. The water of life is figurative and spiritual in this section, as the Bride also is.

The hearers and the thirsty are not of the Church : though the coming and drinking of the spiritual water of life in this droughty desert is the preparation for desiring the coming of our Lord. To all others, the Saviour's return is only judgment and destruction. How can they desire it ?

" I testify to every one that heareth the sayings of the prophecy of this book : if any add unto these things, God shall add to him the plagues that are written in this book."

The Saviour is still the speaker. A class of offences and penalties, not noticed elsewhere, is here set up by the Redeemer's authority. As there is special blessing for the readers and hearers of the book ; so to the abusers of it there is especial woe in store. "*Every* hearer " is addressed : whence it appears to stretch beyond the members of the Church of Christ.

Does not this threatening encircle those who in early days wrote forged Apocalypses in the name of Peter and others ?

This discovers to us one of the great subjects of the book. It treats of " plagues," and they are literally to be taken.

But what if the offence be the taking away some of the words of the book ? Then " God shall take away his part out of the tree of life, and out of the holy city."

The offence is an individual one, and so is the penalty. There is doubtless peculiar danger of forgery in a prophetic work : hence Divine wisdom meets it with a special guard. This threat is a test to all Christians, just as the prohibition to Adam and his wife to eat of the tree was a trial of them.

This threatening of the plagues, and of deprivation of the tree and of the city, is a proof that the tree and city are not symbols of the Church, or of Christ. They are something yet to be enjoyed by the believer.

These threats, too, are designed to teach us the deep importance which God attaches to this book. It is not said of the whole volume of Scripture, nor of the New Testament in general, but of this book in particular.

Eden is presumptively restored to every believer. His is the tree of life, unless he forfeit it by his breach of this law. The tree of life, whether in its leaves or fruit, is the presumptive eternal portion of God's servants after the millennium.

His name will, if guilty of this, be removed from the book of citizenship, and permission to enter its walls, and to dwell in its mansions, will be forfeited. The tree and the city go together. The crime is literally taken ; so is the penalty. There is not only possible forfeiture of the millennial glory, but also of the portion of the risen.

Again, the Saviour sounds the key-note of this book, His coming ! We cannot give too much thought to it. With this truth the book opens : with this it appropriately concludes. Jesus' coming shall bring the promised bliss.

To this John responds with holy desire—" Come, Lord Jesus ! "

The grace of Jesus embraces both classes of God's servants. Only the sanctified at last will be found within the city. Grace is the only ground on which any can stand for eternity.

ADDED NOTE [1920]

ON (1) MANUSCRIPTS, (2) VERSIONS, (3) CRITICAL EDITIONS OF TEXT.

As Govett refers (not infrequently) in footnotes to Greek manuscripts of the Apocalypse, as well as to versions and "critical" editions of the text, the following remarks may be added for the benefit of those who do not know Greek.

There are three complete, and two incomplete, "uncial" MSS. of the Apocalypse. These are all very old, and are called uncials because written in capital letters. Of these uncials the most important are ℵ (the Sinai Codex, edited by Tischendorf in 1862), A (the Alexandrine Codex, now in the British Museum). The most famous of all Biblical manuscripts is B (the Vatican Codex), but *this does not contain the Apocalypse*. There are many other manuscripts written not in capitals, but in running script; these are called cursives. These are later in date than the great uncials, but they are often important because, in some cases, they have been copied from manuscripts even older than ℵ and A (these latter of the fourth and fifth century). Of the versions of the original Greek by far the most important is the Vulgate, the Latin translation made by Jerome somewhere about the year 400 ; it is still the official version of the Roman Church.

Of great critical scholars referred to by Govett, a high place must be assigned to Tregelles (1813–1875), whose work on the text of the New Testament is of the greatest importance. Along with Tregelles must be put the German scholar Tischendorf (1815–1874), who discovered the Sinai Codex (deposited at Petrograd).

The Greek text of the Revised Version of the New Testament (1881) was not issued till many years after the publication of Govett's work ; its importance is not very great *in itself*, save in so far that it represents, more or less, the views of the late Bishop Westcott and Dr. F. J. A. Hort, whose famous edition of the Greek Text appeared in the same year. At the present time, Westcott and Hort's text (generally known as W.H.) is the text used by nearly all scholars.

B.

INDEX

Abaddon, Apollyon, 196, 238; cf. 261
Abominations = Idols, 436; cf. 592.
Angels, descending, 204
Angels of Churches = city Bishops, 25
Antichrist, 295, 313
Armageddon, 414
Avatars, 309

Babylon = Rome, 374, 433, 442; the literal, 419, 474
Babylon, second overthrow, 466 sq.
Beheadal, 510
Believers, some excluded from Kingdom, 511, 524
Believers, unfaithful punished, 41 sq., 56; exclusion from communion, 49, note.
Blasphemy, 209, 312
Blood of the Saints, 436
Book, eating of, 213
Bowls (see "Vials"), 402
Bride's marriage robes, 489

Cherubim, 111
Child, the Male, 274 sq.
Churches, not a unit, 34, 67
City of God, literal, 83; the Great City = Jerusalem, 241, 415
— New City, 551, 563, 573
Coming of our Lord, 67
Covenant, the New, 118

Creation, 117
Creation, 541
Crown (as reward), 40, 81
Cup, of Seduction, 431

Dead in Christ, 382
Death and Hades, 20, 21
Degrees of glory, 81
Deification (self-), 304, 319
Diadems, 494
Dispensation, changes of, 100, 266
Dragon, 270

Eagle, 290
Earthquakes, 146, 250
Elders about the Throne, 104 sq.
Elijah, Enoch, 228, 242
Emperors (Roman), worship of, 299, 337
— The Seven, 445
Empires, 300
Eternal Life, 259
— Life v. the Kingdom, 593
— punishment, 507, 536
Euphratean horsemen, 197

False doctrine, our responsibility for, 58, 59
Famine, 134 sq.
Fighting against the Wild Beast, 322
Final state of mankind, 549
Formalism in religion, 63, 64

INDEX

Fornication, spiritual, applied to Church of Rome, 424
Frogs = evil spirits, 410

Gnosticism, 253
God's Name, 315
Gog and Magog, 529

Hades, Gates of, and the Church, 33 ; cf. 73 sq.
Happiness, human pictures of, 77 sq.
Harlot, the Great, 419
Harvest, the, 384
Heaven, opening of, 262
Historicists, 23
Horns, ten, 271
Horses, vision of, 199

Image-worship, 335 sq. ; cf. 378
Infidelity, modern, 318

Jerusalem, 267 ; cf. 277
— the New, 563 sq.
Jezebel, 54 sq.
Judgment of Saved and Lost, 556
— Seat, 537
Justice, 99

Key of David, 72
Kingdom inheritors of, 260
— of the world, 255
Kings, the Ten, 451

Lamb, song of 398
Lamb, the Slain, 122
Lamps, 15, 109 ; Jesus as the Lamp, 585 ; cf. 227
Life v. Soul, 288
Linen = righteous acts of Saints, 489
Living creatures, the Four, 112
Locusts, 185, 193
Lord's Day, 13

Man of Sin, 311
Mark on the person, idolatrous emblem, 341 sq., 403
Marriage supper, 844, 492
Martyrs, why slain, 514
Mercy, the Divine, 167
Michael (= Jesus), 282
Millennium, 509, 511, 533, 257
Milton the poet, 284
Miracles, wrought on behalf of Evil, 332
Mohammed — Antichrist, 324
Months, period expressed in, 223
Mother, the Crowned (=Jerusalem), 277
Multitude, the Great, 157
Multitude, the Great, 276
Mystery, 129, 211

Names, blotted out from the Book of Life, 70
Names of men = celebrated men, 251
Nations, King of the, 216
Nero and the burning of Rome, 461
— redivivus, 353 sq.
Nicolaitans = Gnostics, 33
Number of the Beast, 348 sq.
Numbers, significance of, 6, 7, 223, 237, 251, 281

Oil, sons of, 227, 231

Pergamos, Satan's throne, chap. iii
Persecutions (future), 142 ; Pagan and Papist, 437
Pillar, 82 ; pillars of fire, 206
Plagues, literal, 173
Pope, the, 303 ; Pope Pius, Creed of, 335
Prayers of the Saints, 170

INDEX

Priesthood, 608
Prophet, the False = Judas Iscariot, 329, 501
Ptolemy Philopator, 346
Purple, of Roman Authority, 429

Raptures, 280
Rebellion, the last great, 527
Redemption of Creation, 114
Resurrection of Reward, 520
Rider on white horse, 130
Robes, washed in the blood, 617
Rome, corruption of (Papal), 421
— fall of, 374
Ross = Russia, 498

Sackcloth, 226
Sadducees, 246
Satan bound, 504, cf. 534; his fall, 274; his malignity, 286
Scarlet, colour of Popes and Cardinals, 430
Scorpions, plague of, 190
Sea, Hades, Death, 545
Serpent, 310
Seven Epistles, tenor of, 32
— Kings, 444
Sins, the six, 202
Smoke from the Abyss, 185
Soul versus Spirit, 138
Spirits of the departed, 126, 158
Spiritual coldness, 90
Stars, falling, 144; stars of heaven, 271; Satan as a star, 182; Morning Star, 621
Stone, the Great = the Great City, 481

Stones, precious, 575
Swearing, 210
Sword, 18, 132
Symbolism, 3, 24, 26

Temple of God measured, 217
— rebuilt, 219 sq.
Throne in Revelation, 102 sq., 154, 518
Thrones, the two, 97
Thunders, sevenfold, 208
Tree of Life, 598 sq.
Tribes, order of the, 155 sq.
Tribulation, the Great, 161 sq.

Vengeance, day of God's, 372, 400
Vials, the, 395
Vintage, the, 389
Virgins, the 144,000, 364, 397

Washing, 10
Waters, the mystic, 292, 456
White raiment, 93, 164
Wild Beasts, persons, 296, 301, 307, 324 sq., 428, 439 sq.
—Worship of, 341
Wilderness, flights into, 280 cf. 290
Wine, not in the New City, 596
Winepress, 392
Witnesses, the two, 224
Works, judgment according to, 544
Worldly indulgence, 96
Wormwood, the star, 178

Year-day fallacy, 38, 39

www.ingramcontent.com/pod-product-compliance
Lightning Source LLC
Chambersburg PA
CBHW052040290426
44111CB00011B/1569